KU-023-567

DAVID LLOYD GEORGE

THE GREAT OUTSIDER

ROY HATTERSLEY

**HIGHLAND
LIBRARIES**

100009438

B. LLO

WITHDRAWN

Little, Brown

LITTLE, BROWN

First published in Great Britain in 2010 by Little, Brown

Copyright © Roy Hattersley 2010

The right of Roy Hattersley to be identified
as the author of this work has been asserted by him in accordance
with the Copyright, Designs and Patents Act 1988.

All rights reserved.
No part of this publication may be reproduced, stored in a
retrieval system, or transmitted, in any form or by any means, without
the prior permission in writing of the publisher, nor be otherwise circulated
in any form of binding or cover other than that in which it is published
and without a similar condition including this condition being
imposed on the subsequent purchaser.

Frontispiece picture courtesy of Mrs Jennifer Longford.

A CIP catalogue record for this book
is available from the British Library.

ISBN 978-1-4087-0097-6

Typeset in Bembo by M Rules
Printed and bound in Great Britain by
Clays Ltd, St Ives plc

Papers used by Little, Brown are natural, renewable and
recyclable products sourced from well-managed forests and certified
in accordance with the rules of the Forest Stewardship Council.

Little, Brown
An imprint of
Little, Brown Book Group
100 Victoria Embankment
London EC4Y 0DY

An Hachette UK Company
www.hachette.co.uk

www.littlebrown.co.uk

To Maggie

CONTENTS

ACKNOWLEDGEMENTS

It was Roy Jenkins who, many years ago, suggested that I write a biography of David Lloyd George – a politician he disliked so heartily that he could not contemplate writing the book himself. My first thanks are therefore due to Lord Jenkins for stimulating the unreasonable ambition to compress the story of such a long and eventful life into one volume. It could not have been achieved without the help for which I express my sincere gratitude.

J. Graham Jones, the director of the Welsh Political Archives, and his staff in the National Library of Wales made it possible for me to examine the Lloyd George papers in their collection. Mari Takayangi and her colleagues provided equally invaluable help during the days I spent in the House of Lords working on the collection of documents which passed from Countess Lloyd George, through Lord Beaverbrook to the parliamentary archives. Mr James Illingworth generously allowed me to see the previously unexamined political papers left by his grandfather, Percy Illingworth MP, Chief Whip to Herbert Asquith. Jennifer Longford (née Stevenson) was equally generous in making available the Lloyd George and Frances Stevenson papers which remain in her possession. Neville Masterman lent me copies of articles and essays written by his mother and father when they were close to Lloyd George during the years of his political greatness. Professor Prys Morgan – as well as filling in gaps in my knowledge of nineteenth-century Wales – allowed me to read and quote from his English translation of D. R. Daniel's unpublished Lloyd George memoir. The London Library consistently and swiftly found copies of the many obscure books written by Lloyd George's early associates. The library of the House of Lords produced ancient copies of Hansard with remarkable alacrity.

Cynthia Shepherd, my PA, typed the first draft, compiled the two appendices and provided invaluable assistance in the compilation of the notes and references. My thanks are also due to Richard Beswick – my editor at Little, Brown, my publisher – and to his colleague Iain Hunt who, assisted by an anonymous copy editor, patiently eliminated the 'literals' which I am pathologically unable to avoid.

My greatest gratitude is due to Professors Kenneth O. Morgan and Anthony King. Lord Morgan read the third draft of my manuscript. Thanks to his correction of errors and rectification of omissions, the fourth and subsequent drafts were much improved. Not once did he show the slightest resentment that I had invaded a field which he has dominated for forty years. Tony King – a friend for almost half a century – read the penultimate draft, ruthlessly identified confusions, contradictions and inconsistencies, and made detailed proposals about how each one could be eliminated. Of course, the shortcomings which undoubtedly remain are my responsibility alone.

CHAPTER 1

THE LAND OF MY FATHERS

David Lloyd George – certainly the most famous and perhaps the greatest Welshman of all time – was born in Manchester. But, as he told his son, nationality 'has nothing to do with geography . . . It is a state of mind.'[1] Lloyd George's state of mind was Welsh. Blood and upbringing shaped his character, not the accident of birth which made him officially English. Charm, energy and ruthless determination would have guaranteed success wherever he had spent his youth and early manhood. And he would have been guaranteed an enamoured following by his vitality – the Promethean fire, because of which so much was expected and so much forgiven. But it was Llanystumdwy and Criccieth that created his defining attributes. The rebellious schoolboy and the insubordinate young solicitor became the Great Outsider – a man who felt no obligation to respect the rules of the society in which he lived. His upbringing – both the teaching of his Church and the adoration of his uncle – made him an outsider who felt superior to the establishment which he despised. That confidence combined with ambition, conviction and contempt for convention to make him the authentic radical of British political history.

The Chancellor of the Exchequer who created the welfare state and became the Prime Minister who was credited with winning the First World War was born plain David George. The Georges of Pembrokeshire farmed at Trecoed, near Fishguard – according to family folklore their ancestors' reward for fighting with Henry Tudor on Bosworth Field. They remained farmers for three hundred years, but William George – David's father – 'devoted his energies to improving his mind rather than cultivating the soil'.[2] He wanted to 'bequeath to posterity . . . thoughts that breathe and words that burn'.[3] William's mother had more prosaic plans and apprenticed her son to a local physician. His interest in becoming a doctor waned when William discovered that the practice of medicine involved the tedium of seeing patients. Next he considered becoming a lawyer. Then a draper. Eventually he turned to teaching, but still wrote in his diary, 'I cannot make up my mind to be a school master for life . . . I want to occupy higher ground somehow or other.'[4] His 'ambition above all things was to be a scholar'. His destiny was continual disappointment.[5]

In 1841, William George, just twenty-one, registered as a student at the Battersea Teachers' Training Institute. He was already showing symptoms of the disease which killed him. 'I am getting to feel rather apprehensive about myself. I brought up 2 or 3 specs of blood before I went to London.'[6] However, he completed the course and, for the next fifteen years, moved from school to school – always looking for something better, but never finding it. After nine months at Ealing, he spent a year at Newbald, in the East Riding, and left at short notice, abandoning forty-seven items of personal property and all his books.[7] After an extended holiday – during which he replaced his books and his lost greatcoat – he was appointed head of the Hope Street Unitarian School in Liverpool. It was a broad-minded foundation. William George – a pious and practising Baptist – was acceptable both as head and as teacher in the associated adult Sunday School.

In Liverpool, William George at last made friends who he thought were suitable to his status and intellectual standing. They included Thomas Goffey, a solicitor who was to have an important influence on the careers of both his sons. But Liverpool soon lost its charm. He left the city, a week before Christmas 1852, taking with him a full set of the *Penny Encyclopaedias* and a copy of *Webster's Dictionary*, inscribed: 'Presented to Mr William George by the teachers and conductors of Hope Street Church Sunday School as a token of their esteem.'[8]

In April 1854, William George opened his own 'proprietary' – that is to say private – school in Haverfordwest in Pembrokeshire. Family legend attributed the initiative to his marriage to Selina Huntley, a rich but sick widow who either owned the school building or financed its purchase. The venture did not succeed. The English in the town wanted schools which were owned and governed by the Established Church. The Welsh resented the promise that 'great attention will be paid to the study of the English language, a knowledge of which is indispensable to the successful pursuit of every business and profession in this country'. Selina George, on whom the school depended, died sometime during 1856. At the end of that year, the widower considered becoming second master at Blaenau Ffestiniog in Gwynedd, in one of the 'British Schools' which were being established in Wales.* He decided against and in August 1858 accepted a similar appointment at Troed-yr-Allt in nearby Pwllheli.

Troed-yr-Allt was close by 'The Castle', the home of a Miss Evans, who employed, as her companion, Elizabeth Lloyd of Llanystumdwy. Betsy's father, who had died in 1839 when she was eleven, had been one of the two shoemakers in Penymaes, a village near Criccieth. He had also been the pastor of Capel Ucha. The Lloyds were Children of God – a Baptist sect whose members aspired to follow the simple teaching of the early Christian Church. Children of God believed that it was better to attend an 'orthodox' Baptist service than to miss Sunday worship altogether. So Betsy Lloyd joined the congregation at Capel Berea in Criccieth. There she met William George. They were married on 16 November 1859.

The Georges' first child, a girl, survived for barely a month. The second, Mary Ellen, was born on 8 November 1861. By then William and Betsy George had moved to Newchurch in Lancashire. The new school proved no more acceptable than any of its predecessors. 'The place itself we could do with very well – though cold and damp the place is healthy . . . It was . . . the people connected with it who did not suit me . . . I would rather be the master of workpeople than their servant.'[9] William George was saved from the humiliation of being employed by 'rough working men who had not the means to act liberally, even if disposed to do so' by Doctor John Daniel Morell, a recently appointed school inspector.[10] Thanks to Morell, George became temporary head of a school in Manchester. He rented 5 New York Place, Chorlton-upon-Medlock. There, on 17 January 1863, Betsy gave birth to a son. He was christened David.

The family did not remain in Chorlton-upon-Medlock for long. In the autumn of the same year, William George gave up schoolmastering for ever and bought the lease of Bwlford, a smallholding of thirty acres near Haverfordwest. By then he knew that he was suffering from consumption and hoped that life in the good fresh air of Wales would

---

*National, or English, Schools were Anglican foundations in receipt of government grants. British Schools were the Nonconformist (financially independent) institutions.

improve, if not cure, his condition. Late in May 1864, he caught a chill from which he never recovered. He died, aged forty-four, on 7 June.

Much of what is known of William George is hearsay which cannot easily be distinguished from fable. But his second and posthumous son – the third surviving child – wrote about two qualities which, he claimed, endeared his father to all who knew him. One was 'the spirit of restless ambition' – a characteristic which his elder son inherited in full. The other was an inclination to agonise if he were guilty of even the most harmless deception. 'This particular trait of my father's character', young William George wrote, 'was not transmitted, in its undiluted form, to his son David.'[11]

Betsy George – not strong, widowed at thirty-five and living in a part of Wales where she had no family or friends – was left with two infant children and the knowledge that a third would be born before the end of the year. So she sent the telegram that changed her life, the lives of her children and – because of its consequences for her eldest son – the course of British history. It read 'Tyrd Richard'. And Richard Lloyd, her brother – who had never before spent a night away from home – did not wait to discover the cause of his sister's distress. 'Come Richard' was enough. He walked twenty miles to Caernarvon, and caught the next train to Haverfordwest.[12]

Richard Lloyd was known in Llanystumdwy for his red beard, his upright ways and his patrician demeanour. He had inherited the family bootmaker's business and, because he employed two men in the workshop at the side of Highgate Cottage, he was regarded as the senior of the village's two cobblers. The sign which hung over the gable end, RICHARD LLOYD GWNEUTHWYR, was illustrated with rough pictures of his stock-in-trade – a working boot, as worn by farm labourers, and a more elegant 'top boot' for the senior servants of the local gentry. Men's boots cost ten shillings, women's eight shillings and sixpence.[13]

The boot-making business was only part of Richard Lloyd's inheritance. He had followed his father as joint pastor of Penymaes Church. Neither he nor William Williams – the Criccieth draper with whom he shared the ministry – was paid. The Disciples of Christ did not believe that anyone should receive material reward for spreading the Word of God. Like his father, he was 'called' to the work. But, after June 1864, he acquired a second vocation. 'My uncle', said David Lloyd George, 'never married and set himself the task of educating the children of his sister as a sacred and supreme duty. To that duty he gave all his time, his energy and his money.'[14] He did his duty to all of them. But the most important part of his additional calling was preparing his nephew, David, to fulfil his historic destiny. Thanks to fate, or unusual powers of perception, Richard Lloyd recognised that he was nurturing an extra-ordinary boy. He anointed his prodigy by adding an unhyphenated 'Lloyd' to his name. It was a privilege which the younger brother – obedient, assiduous and intellectual – was denied.

Politicians are sustained through the setbacks which are their inevitable lot by conviction, self-belief and good luck. Lloyd George was fortune's favourite. Conviction was an occasional spur to his intent. His self-belief never wavered. There were times when he feared that he would fail, but he never doubted that he deserved to succeed. He owed his invincible self-confidence to Uncle Lloyd, the first in a long line of men and women who gladly sacrificed themselves, and all around them, for the greater glory of David Lloyd George. He was also one of the few benefactors whose help was acknowledged.

Richard Lloyd was his nephew's philosopher as well as friend. When the 1910 Finance Bill was finally passed and 'The People's Budget' was paying for old-age pensions, he received a bound copy of the act, inscribed 'To the real author of this budget with his pupil's affectionate gratitude.'[15] A second bound copy was sent with an equally appropriate inscription 'To my brother with deep appreciation of his devotion and self-sacrifice which enabled me to give so much of my time to public work.'[16] It was an acknowledgement that the whole family had paid the price for sharing their lives with a man of destiny.

The suggestion that the loss of a father could be a son's good fortune should be made with great caution. But had William George lived, the young David would have either remained on the Haverfordwest farm or moved from town to town as his father searched for the contentment which always eluded him. William George spoke virtually no Welsh. In 1858, when he was teaching in Pwllheli, he apologised for being unable to address a Baptist minister in what he described as his 'mother tongue'.[17] Without Welsh spoken at home, David would have been a different man. It was the culture as well as the politics of Wales – as introduced to him by Richard Lloyd – which convinced him that he was born to storm the fortress of the establishment.

Richard Lloyd stayed at Bwlford Farm until his sister's property, stock and the furniture were sold. The new tenant bought the lease and stand-ing crops for £64 – a bargain for a property which justified a rent of £30 a year. The sale of the furniture raised £34 and the livestock £57.[18] William George had saved £640.[19] So – after outstanding bills were paid – Betsy George inherited £768. Even by the standards of the day, it was not a fortune. But when Betsy moved in with her brother in Llanystumdwy, an investment income of £46 a year made her the wealthiest woman in the village. The annual rent for Highgate Cottage was £7.[20]

The Lloyds and Georges, three adults and three children, shared two bedrooms and an earth midden. David Jones – the local shopkeeper who owned the premises – was not a perfect landlord. There were holes in the brick oven which had to be blocked with paper and dough before the weekly baking could begin.[21] But the character of the cottage gave history a false impression of the family's circumstances. The hard times only really began after Betsy George used her capital to pay for David and William to become articled solicitor's clerks and Uncle Lloyd abandoned his business the better to help his nephews pursue their careers. David and William, the best-dressed boys in the village, wore knee-breeches while their school fellows dressed in the long shorts which were the uniform of working-class childhood.[22] William – as is often the fate of second sons – sometimes wore clothes which no longer fitted his growing elder brother.[23] But his sister attended a private school in Criccieth where a Miss Wheatley's 'main objective was to teach deportment to the girls of the middle class and those of the upper working classes'.[24] That was not the sort of education enjoyed by the daughters of the very poor.

In 1914, the Chancellor of the Exchequer said that 'the need to be careful' had dominated his boyhood. 'It was always – not once or twice or occasionally – a struggle for my mother at the end of the week. The last sixpence of every week was a coin of destiny. My mind was impressed at the time by the terrible importance, every week, of the last sixpence and it is still impressed upon my mind. It is the strongest impression of childhood.'[25] That, as distinct from grinding poverty, was a more or less accurate description of his early life. But sometimes the truth was not enough to sustain the myth of triumph over adversity. In 1898, he 'recalled' that the family 'scarcely ate fresh meat'.[26] The 'greatest luxury was half an egg for each child on a Sunday morning'.[27] In his autobiography of his brother, William George disposes of the suggestion in one dismissive sentence: 'I certainly never remember any such dramatic performance.'[28]

The stories of childhood poverty were augmented with descriptions of cultural deprivation, including the claim that, as a boy, all he had to read were a couple of battered almanacs and dog-eared back numbers of

The Examiner.[29] In fact Highgate Cottage was 'well-stocked with books in both Welsh and English'.[30] When Richard Lloyd and his sister set out on their journey from Bwlford Farm to Llanystumdwy, 'William George's library of books, packed in tea chests, formed the largest item among the luggage with which they were burdened.'[31] In 1880, when David was seventeen, the books moved, with the rest of the family, to Criccieth.[32] Uncle Lloyd, who left his reading until in bed by candle-light so as not to interrupt his working day, took the printed word seriously. So did his nephews, who recorded in a notebook precise details of what they had read.[33] In terms of learning and literature, David Lloyd George had a privileged upbringing which set him aside from the other village children.

The despatch of regular letters – which described in detail life, first at Westminster and then in Whitehall – was one of the few demands that Uncle Lloyd made on his protégé. If, from time to time, he did imagine himself in the young man's place, he never allowed his dreams to deteriorate into envy. The most severe criticism of his part in the forty-year relationship – made by William, his other nephew – was that David 'could do no wrong and woe betide anyone who said anything to the contrary . . . Whether this unrestrained admiration was wholly good for the lad on whom it was lavished, or indeed the man who evolved out of him, is a matter on which opinions may differ. It was certainly a bit trying for anyone in Uncle Lloyd's entourage who did not take such an extreme view of David's perfection.'[34]

William George often criticised his brother – usually privately and to his face. But it was not until ten years after David's death that he allowed his resentment to show through the façade of humble acceptance which normally accompanied his sacrifice. In February 1964, Lord Beaverbrook offered to buy the family letters that William hoped to use in a book of his own. He replied, 'I think I have done my share of honouring Dafydd during his lifetime . . .'[35]

The Children of God – or the Campbellites as they were popularly known – were a small, exclusive and, in some ways, extreme sect. They shared, with the Baptists, Methodists and Congregationalists, a feeling of outrage that they should be regarded by the Welsh establishment as subject to the laws and customs of the Church of England, and they believed that Nonconformists were custodians of the Welsh language and culture. Most of the Llanystumdwy families resented domination by the Church of England. Yet the Campbellites held such a severe view of the religious obligation that they were in a minority even among the oppressed. David Lloyd George grew up an outsider among outsiders.

Sixty years on – with the negotiations which led to the creation of the Irish Free State nearing their dramatic climax – Thomas Jones, the Assistant Cabinet Secretary, visited the Prime Minister in his bedroom to obtain approval of a letter which he had drafted as an ultimatum to Sinn Fein. He noted the 'huge pieces of red mahogany furniture', the 'hotch potch of feeble pictures' and the rows of books – 'chiefly light novels, but also *The Letters of Luther* and Roget's *Thesaurus*'. But the most startling feature of the room was a framed biblical text 'worked in silk thread'. It was not 'God is Love', 'No Cross: No Crown' or any of the other standard Nonconformist rubrics. It was Chapter 28, Verse 7 of the book of Job. 'There is a path which no fowl knoweth and which the eye of the vulture has not seen.' That was the road which, all his life, Lloyd George chose to travel.[36]

Perhaps no other route was open to an instinctive radical. Inevitably, as a result of his humble origins, he was assumed by much of the establishment to be motivated by envy. In 1925, F. W. Brotherton – a Conservative of no distinction – sent Lloyd George his judgement on the Liberal Party's call for more progressive taxation. 'Sir William Harcourt had his faults, but he was a gentleman and a scholar and had some inheritance to tax. You, I believe, inherited nothing except, it may be inferred, a rancour against those more fortunate than yourself.'[37] Lloyd George's pride in his humble beginnings gave him a self-confidence which he would not have possessed had he envied or aped his social 'betters'.

During the second half of the nineteenth century the valleys of South Wales – bustling with their coalmines and steelworks – felt an increasing economic affinity to industrial England. Although the mighty Penrhyn quarry in Caernarvonshire supplied slate to the world, North and Mid-Wales remained predominantly agricultural. Most of the farms were rented. In 1880, 16.1 per cent of English farms were owner-occupied. In Wales the figure was 10.7 per cent. In Caernarvonshire it was 4.2 per cent.[38] Eighty per cent of tenant farmers and their workers were Nonconformists. Yet the large landowners and much of the squirearchy were English by birth, inclination or descent. On Sundays they worshipped in the Church of England.

During David Lloyd George's formative years, a combination of religious resentment and economic grievance combined to ensure profound hostility between English Church and Welsh people.

Agricultural rents included tithes, paid by the local farmer to the vicar or rector of his parish in order to support an alien priesthood. The injustice did not create the sort of revolutionary fervour which swept through rack-rented Ireland. The Welsh religious revival which had begun in the 1850s gave the whole campaign a moral dimension. There was no equivalent of the Fenian movement which maimed cattle, burned barns and assassinated the ascendant aristocracy. But the land – the rent which was levied upon it, the leases by which its use was circumscribed and the tithes which its tenants were required to pay – was a cause waiting for a champion.

David Lloyd George became that man. First he articulated Welsh grievances. Then he mobilised the Welsh Liberal Party to fight for the principality. Finally, as he evolved into first a national and then an international statesman, Wales became the homely association which left no doubt that he was still a man of the people. During the 1910 election campaign – when the bitter battle over financing his new pensions bill was at its height – Lloyd George reminisced about gathering firewood during his Llanystumdwy days. 'It was little use going into the woods after a period of calm and fine weather, as I generally returned empty-handed; but after a great storm, I came back with an armful. We are in for rough weather. We may even be in for a winter of storms which will rock the forest, break many a withered branch and leave many a rotten tree torn up by its roots. But when the weather clears, you may depend on it that there will be something brought within the reach of people that will give warmth and glow to their grey lives.'[39]

Hope and bitterness went hand in hand. In 1911, his third year at the Exchequer, Lloyd George showed visitors from London to the grave of John Parry, land agent to the squire, and told them that after the defeat of the Conservative candidate in the 1868 general election, 'he turned out sixty-eight tenants whom he knew to be Liberals. Some of their children were at school with me.' Wales had made him a class warrior.[40] It also made him a natural performer. His first public appearance was in Llanystumdwy Chapel, singing 'Cofia, blentyn, ddneyd y gwir' ('Remember, child, to speak the truth'). He assured the 1911 Christmas Eisteddfod that it was a rule which he had followed ever since.[41] The audience ignored the implausibility of the assurance and roared its approval.

Throughout his life, David Lloyd George loved – indeed was in love with – the *idea* of Wales. But he was far from enchanted with the reality. During his years in Parliament he visited his constituency, the house

which his wife called home and his family as infrequently as possible –
even to the point of spending Christmas on foreign excursions with
political friends while his children unwrapped presents which he had
sent them through the post, accompanied by letters which reiterated the
undying affection of their absent father. In 1908, the recently appointed
Chancellor of the Exchequer rashly chose to express his real feelings
about home and hearth to D. R. Daniel, whose Welsh-language biography was, fortunately for Lloyd George's reputation, never published.

> Criccieth is just a cold sea to me, always an old and grey, mixed
> and miserable place. In London there is always some interest and
> endless life there: somewhere to go, something to see. You feel
> you are in the stream of life there. The life of a country village is
> deadly and uninteresting. The most unpleasant season of my life,
> by far, was my boyhood spent at Llanystumdwy. I'd never go
> through that again at any price.[42]

As Lloyd George grew older, he grew more frank about the unconge-
niality of his childhood. In 1911, during one of his rare visits to
Criccieth, he was emphatic. 'I would not have my childhood again.'[43]
By 1946, shortly before his death, he regarded his boyhood as 'discontented, cramped and unhappy', the years when he never saw 'the
brighter side of life'.[44] Yet he chose to be buried by the Dwyfor, the
Llanystumdwy river in which he had played as a boy. Sentimentality is
often the weakness of the ruthless and the brave.

In 1898, when he had been in the House of Commons for eight
years, David Lloyd George wrote to his brother with the joyous news
that he had met 'the Diocesan Inspector who examined me at
Llanystumdwy School . . . He remembered me as one of the (two)
pupils who remembered everything.'[45] But although the school and its
master were indispensable to his success, Lloyd George – even as a
boy – found its existence a cause for resentment and rebellion.

The National School at Llanystumdwy recognised neither the Welsh
language nor the existence of any denomination other than the Church
of England. The foundation governors were Sir Hugh Ellis-Nanney,
squire of Llanystumdwy, Miss Catherine Priestley, another local
landowner, and the Anglican Bishop of Bangor. The headmaster was
David Evans – a man who, by the standards of his day, was remarkably
enlightened. Young David entered the school when he was three and a
half and made rapid progress to Standard Seven, the level of attainment

at which most boys left school for work in the fields. But Evans had created another class which he called '7X'. Boys of particular merit sat
round a kitchen table close to his desk in the larger of the two school-
rooms. David Lloyd George – and subsequently his brother William –
took his at the 7X table and learned algebra and geometry.

David did so well that Evans suggested that he become a pupil
teacher, an escape route from the Welsh working classes which often led
to ordination. Pupil teachers were normally expected to be communi-
cants of the Church of England and Betsy Lloyd 'would rather have her
sons break stones at the side of the road than turn their backs on the
little Baptist Church at Penymaes'.[46] But Evans and the Reverend
David Edwards, the rector of Llanystumdwy, were prepared to recommend that David be allowed to enrol as a pupil teacher without formal
admission into the Church of England. David, who already had greater
ambitions than a life spent in front of a class of village children in
North Wales, showed remarkably little gratitude to the men who were
prepared to ignore the demands of their faith in order to give him
what they believed would be his best chance in life. A month after the
offer of a teaching career was made, he led the school in the revolt
which, after he described it to the *Review of Reviews*, became the incident that defined his rebellious nature.[47]

The Nonconformist pupils at Llanystumdwy National School – 80
per cent of the whole register – were expected to observe the rites and
respect the rituals of the Church of England. By the late 1870s dissent
was common. Feast day marches were boycotted. David Lloyd George
stopped William Williams, a classmate 'shining with soap and sharp in
his best suit on his way to confirmation, and persuaded him to turn
back'.[48] And on 6 May 1878 – the day of the year on which the local
gentry visited the school 'to watch the proceedings and express their
approval thereof with benevolent smiles.'[49] – came the protest.

The ceremony began with the Reverend Watts, the chief school
inspector, and his assistant – a Mr Roberts whom William George
remembered for his extravagant moustache – examining the general
governance of the school.[50] They paid Evans the greatest possible compliment by observing that 'the children were neatly dressed, clean and
very well-behaved'.[51] They then moved on to a Scriptural Knowledge
Examination which was, in effect, a competition. Each brother won a
prize. David was presented with the *Treasury of History and Biography for
the Young*. William received an uplifting work entitled *Sunday Evenings
at Northcourt*. Then, 'the schoolmaster stood up in front of the joint class

and, on a signal from him, we all stood up. After glancing round to see that the inspectors and visitors were ready, he called in a quiet voice for the recital of the Creed.'[52] Nothing happened. David – offended by the idea of Nonconformists swearing allegiance to a Church of which they were not members – had persuaded the whole class to remain silent. The rector, 'a white-bearded and venerable-looking old gentleman, stepped forward and gently suggested that, as they all knew the words perfectly well, they should say them in unison. The silence continued for a full minute.'[53] William – seeing the headmaster, 'face ashen and pitiful to behold' – ended Evans's humiliation by shouting from the back of the room, 'I believe.'[54] The rest of the school joined in. The protest was over.

The story of the protest was confirmed by William George, but (like so many accounts of Lloyd George's boyhood) it was embellished by the early biographers. The myth-makers claimed that David gave his brother 'a sound thrashing for breaking the silence'. That, wrote William George, was an invention. 'The protest had been carried far enough to be effective and David was strategist enough even then to realise that victory pressed beyond a certain point was apt to defeat its own purpose.' The younger brother chose his words with care. It was self-interest, not compassion, that made Lloyd George – from time to time – magnanimous in defeat.

David Lloyd George was entitled to insist that he could not, in conscience, affirm his allegiance to the Established Church. On 7 September 1875, three weeks after his twelfth birthday, his uncle had baptised him a Child of God in the little brook which ran alongside the Penymaes Church in Criccieth. But the silent protest was not against the demands of an alien religion. It was the first of the rebellions that revealed a crucial characteristic. He was an enemy of authority in all its forms. And he had a second motive. Even then, he wanted to control events rather than be controlled by others. In youth, as well as age, dominant characters feel a compulsion to dominate.

The idea that he was a defender of his faith is confounded by his own explanations of his religious progress. According to one story, on the night which followed his baptism, 'he meditated on what he had done and confessed, his eyes staring into the darkness, and saw all the heaven of his doctrine and his imagination of yore being shut before him'.[55] Another account claimed that a year before the christening, he described himself as 'in hell. I saw no way out.'[56] The more plausible, though more prosaic, explanation of his disenchantment was that he looked forward to the 'prayer meeting [which was] held every week on a Thursday with loathing – the same prayers, the same phrases . . . the same talk, week after week'.[57] His account of why – in early man-hood – he returned to religion is less convincing. He claimed that it came about as a result of reading Thomas Carlyle's *Sartor Resartus* and that he was prepared for reconversion by one of Charles Spurgeon's famous sermons. If that was so, the epiphany was brought about by an unusual combination of the intellectually unintelligible and the rhetor-ically intolerable.

Whether or not Lloyd George regained his faith, expediency as well as sentiment made a return to religion inevitable. Nonconformity was inextricably linked with the culture and the politics of Wales. He accommodated the need to respect that connection by claiming to follow a creed of his own invention. 'I know I have the religious tem-perament, but if an angel from heaven came to demand it, I could not write down what my convictions are.'[58] His brother insisted that, although there was lack of obedience, there was no lack of belief. Perhaps William was deceived by a characteristic noted by George Riddell – assiduous diarist, Liberal MP and newspaper proprietor who became one of Lloyd George's long-standing friends and patrons. In 1918, as the First World War ended, the Prime Minister reminisced about how 'as a boy [he] admired the great preachers', and he added, 'I never tire of listening to them.'[59] That was evidence, not of faith in the gospels, but of reverence for the spoken word.

Lloyd George was an orator in an age when oratory was admired. The assumption has always been that he possessed a spontaneous genius which allowed him to extemporise brilliant speeches. In fact, the archives contain handwritten drafts which were polished, typed and learned by heart. They were based on careful plans. The notes with which they began still exist.

Small and minor difficulties.
Relations with Foreign powers.
Insistence.
Now reduced to a minimum.
Hectoring.[60]

Wales made him a preacher who condemned the exploitation of a sub-ject people and expressed his anger at the 'unconscious and half-conscious contempt with which the Englishman regards the Welsh people'.[61] But he was not always the champion of the oppressed.

According to William George, his brother's schooldays were characterised by a 'ruthlessness in the pursuit of [his] aims, despite the pain and
humiliation it might cause' and 'the disregard of others' feelings'.[62] A
small boy,

> younger than David, was sitting on the outstretched branch of a
> tree up which he had climbed and on which he was enjoying him-
> self by the gentle up and down motion of the branch. David came
> along and started shaking the branch violently, swaying it to and
> fro and up and down. The little lad was nearly frightened to death
> but David continued to rock the branch until he had had enough
> of the game himself.[63]

Sometimes the game had political overtones – as witness the 'boycott
organised shortly before he left school of an English boy who had
become a pupil'.[64] Yet despite his antagonism towards the English, he
was a British patriot. During the Franco-Prussian War, he organised a
defence force of other boys to protect Llanystumdwy against attack
from the French, the Germans or both. His courage was not limited to
childish fantasies. He fearlessly offered to fight four boys who roughly
handled his younger brother but, in general, he regarded loyalty as a
virtue which should be employed only sparingly. When an orchard
owner decided that the boys of the village were stealing fruit, he
employed David to act as 'steward' on the understanding that, while he
kept his friends at bay, he would take as many apples and pears as he
wanted for himself.[65]

David Lloyd George was more admired by his teacher than liked by
his peers. David Evans – the schoolmaster who promoted him to class
7X – takes second place only to Richard Lloyd in the list of men who
made possible the escape from Llanystumdwy. He was, however,
responsible for only part of what was undoubtedly an eclectic education. When Lloyd George returned to the village in 1909 to speak to his
old schoolfellows he told them, 'Yonder smithy was my first Parliament
where, night after night, we discussed and decided all the abstruse questions relating to this world and the next, in politics, in theology, in
philosophy, in science.' [66] Discussion of the affairs of the day also often
interrupted the work of the Highgate bootmakers – even though good
Campbellites felt detached from the discontent and disillusion of the
world beyond their chapels. Argument – or at least theological disputation – ran in the Lloyds' blood. Uncle Lloyd's father – founder of the

bootmaker's business and pastor of Capel Ucha – had helped to form Cymreigyddion, a society devoted to the discussion of religious and morally improving topics. It debated 'Who is the greatest enemy of the state, the Drunkard or the Deceiver?' and 'Whose lust is the greater – the Drunkard's for strong drink or the Miser's for wealth?'[67]

It was, however, less elevated considerations which determined David Lloyd George's future. He was attracted by the law. Bob Jones, the son of the village tailor, visited Pwllheli on market days to do business for his father. When his work was done, he found amusement in watching the proceedings of the Petty Sessions in the County Court. Usually he witnessed nothing more exciting than paternity and attachment cases. But Jones returned to Llanystumdwy with tales of forensic triumphs – particularly as performed by a Denbighshire solicitor called Louis. David, always susceptible to the charms of oratory, wanted to follow Louis's footsteps and Betsy aspired for her son to be like Thomas Goffey – her late husband's friend from Liverpool, who enjoyed the family's unrequited esteem. Regular preparations were made for his visits to Highgate Cottage. Sometimes his arrival was thought to be so imminent that the children were told to wear their best clothes. He never came. Each Christmas a prize turkey was bought from a neighbouring farmer and sent to Mr Goffey with the family's love and admiration. Mr Goffey, it was said, earned three hundred pounds a year and, in addition, was paid three and sixpence for every letter which he wrote on a client's behalf.[68] Young David no doubt determined that one day he would become an elusive celebrity rather than a member of the disappointed family who waited for him in vain.

Three obstacles barred David Lloyd George's path to becoming an articled clerk – the first rung on the professional ladder. He had to find a solicitor who would employ him, his family had to pay a hundred-pound 'articles fee' to his employer and eighty pounds in stamp duty to the Excise, and he had to pass the Preliminary Examination of the Law Society – which required him to demonstrate at least a rudimentary knowledge of French and Latin.

David Evans helped him with the Latin.[69] But he prepared himself to translate the set text (a passage from Julius Caesar's *The Conquest of Gaul*) by committing to memory Latin roots which he found listed in an appendix to an old English grammar. The French he learned not from, but with, Uncle Lloyd. Together, the forty-year-old man and the fourteen-year-old boy worked their way through an old French-language edition of *Aesop's Fables* with the aid of a French dictionary.

The 'hard study' was accomplished 'in the little parlour at Highgate which was also a home library where a formidable array of books was stored'.[70] And it was successful. On 3 November 1877 – a month after David Lloyd George sat the Preliminary Examination in Saint George's Hall, Liverpool – the news that he had passed reached Llanystumdwy. The £180 to secure his articles would be found from his mother's savings. All that was needed for the great leap ahead was a solicitor looking for an articled clerk.

Myrddin Fardd ('The Bard Merlin' as the Llanystumdwy blacksmith was known) catalogued gravestones and, in consequence, thought himself an antiquarian. He was a friend of both Richard Lloyd and Edward Breese, senior partner of Breese, Jones and Casson, solicitors of Portmadoc, and a Fellow of the Royal Antiquarian Society. Breese, at Myrddin Fardd's suggestion, accepted David Lloyd George into his office for a six-month trial with the promise that, if he proved industrious and enthusiastic, he would be articled to Randall Casson, a junior partner in the firm.

The arrangement was an early example of Lloyd George's natural ability combining with his good fortune. Breese, Jones and Casson were the solicitors for the Tremadog Estate – the owners of the reclaimed land on which Portmadoc had been built. Land law was their speciality and land became the issue which propelled Lloyd George into Parliament and beyond. Edward Breese was also the Liberal Party's agent for Merioneth and South Caernarvonshire. Fate had conspired to send Lloyd George on his way into history.

CHAPTER 2

THE FEVER OF RENOWN

Breese, Jones and Casson had been founded by David Williams, the uncle of Edward Breese and a friend of W. A. Maddocks, who had reclaimed the land on which Portmadoc was built by damming the mouth of the river Glaslyn and draining the tidal estuary. The houses, built on the reclaimed land, were known as the Tremadog Estate. The tenants were required to insure their property against fire with Breese, Jones and Casson and the company's youngest employee had the duty of collecting rents and premiums. The firm's accounts for 12 November 1878 show that Lloyd George received fifteen shillings from the company's cashier for delivering leases, engrossing mortgages, examining rate appeals and attending (so that he could subsequently report upon) court hearings.[1] His studies were concentrated on land law. They provided his introduction – through the medium of Williams's *Real Property* – to the subject which was to become the fiery chariot on which he rode to parliamentary glory.

Throughout his life Lloyd George made a distinction between two classes of landowners – those who improved their property and therefore deserved higher rents and those who merely exploited changes in value which they had done nothing to earn. When – with Breese, Jones and Casson thirty years behind him – the price of land in the Thames Basin's 'golden triangle' was increased from three pounds to three thousand pounds an acre – simply as a result of the Port of London's decision to expand its docks and harbours – Lloyd George compared the beneficiaries with William Maddocks. He had reclaimed Portmadoc from the sea, but still charged reasonable rents and sold the houses to sitting tenants at affordable prices.

The young articled clerk became the weekday lodger of Mr and Mrs Owen on Portmadoc High Street and travelled back home to Llanystumdwy every Saturday. His zeal to 'get on' prompted improving activities which ranged from shorthand lessons to attempts to change his public persona.

> J G Jones, clerk of the County Council, said that I was regarded as independent and reserved. I'm not acquainted with the great majority of people in Portmadoc and therefore cannot make myself familiar with them. However, I feel I cannot continue independent and reserved towards unacquainted people if I really do mean to be a success as a lawyer.[2]

Despite the shortcomings of character and ability – real or imagined – David Lloyd George was articled to Randall Casson, the junior of the three partners. On 24 January 1879, Uncle Lloyd travelled to Portmadoc and paid the hundred pounds which the Law Society required, and the stamp duty which was demanded by Customs and Excise.

Casson – after a few months friend as well as mentor – introduced Lloyd George to the anxieties and jubilations of elections. Epiphanies – moments when the pendulum swings and the world changes – are rare events. Early biographers attempted to identify a moment when the hand of fate first rested on Lloyd George's shoulder. In fact, his passion for politics grew in the usual way. In the years between 1880 and 1885 he gradually found great causes in which to believe and he discovered that he enjoyed the risks, the excitement and the elation of success that politics provides.

On 25 March 1880, he 'went up to Llanfrothen with Mr Casson with the intention of canvassing'.[3] It was the year of William Gladstone's Midlothian Campaign – a triumph for sustained oratory in what, to a young romantic, must have seemed the cause of oppressed minorities. Casson and Breese were Gladstonian Liberals. So was Lloyd George, until the Grand Old Man showed more interest in Ireland than in Wales. But it was John Roberts – Deacon of the Children of Christ's Chapel in Portmadoc, candlemaker and radical – who encouraged him to air his youthful views. Roberts had been charged by Uncle Lloyd with keeping his nephew on the path of virtue. It was not an easy task.

What Lloyd George himself described at the time as 'flirtations' were later assumed to be early manifestations of his abnormal sexual appetite. Perhaps they were, but there is not much evidence to suggest that he chased girls with any more enthusiasm than is usual in young men. Richard Lloyd certainly disapproved of his nephew's behaviour. One Saturday, after his weekend return to Llanystumdwy, David wrote in his diary, 'Uncle gave it me when I came back and told me I was becoming the talk of the town, that I must mend my ways in this matter at least.'[4] The young miscreant was particularly determined to overcome temptations to indolence. 'I must stick to my reading or my time will be wasted and I shall be no better than the clerks I am determined to supersede.'[5]

Political disputation almost certainly occupied more of his time than girls. His first public speech was a denunciation of Disraeli's answer to the 'Eastern Question' – the collapse of the Ottoman Empire and Russia's ambition to dominate the Balkan States which emerged. Disraeli was pro-Turkey. Lloyd George was not. His speech at the Portmadoc Debating Society was adjudged a failure. He spoke in English and his address was said to suffer from 'defects of style common in those . . . embarking upon the partially known regions of an alien tongue'.[6] Lloyd George had become a Welshman. He had also become a man of strong opinions. Sitting in the audience at a Portmadoc debate on women's rights, he thought that Breese – an opponent of female suffrage – was 'very good' and that his adversary, a Miss Becker, 'did not touch on some of his arguments'. But he did 'not see why single women and widows managing property should not have a vote in the adjustment etc of the taxes'.[7] It would fall to him, in 1917, to take the first steps towards righting the wrong.

Uncle Lloyd, handicapped by failing eyesight, gave up bootmaking. William aspired to follow his brother into the law. So it was convenient – and apparently financially prudent – for the whole family to lease Morvin House in Criccieth where, it was hoped, both young men would be articled and David could be encouraged to concentrate on his studies. He had already decided to behave more respectably. On 26 March 1880, when he 'Went to see proposed new house',[8] he 'saw the girls afterwards', but he 'was reserved with Jennie' – a young lady of whom nothing is known except that Lloyd George regarded her as a liability. 'I want to get rid of her – we are being talked about.'[9] It was a bad week for poor Jennie Evans. Next day, he 'took scarcely any notice of her' and, two days later, he 'avoided her' and wrote in his diary, 'It costs me some trouble to get rid of that girl.'[10] The unavoidable loss of liberty that followed the move to Criccieth was unwelcome, but he had no regrets about leaving Highgate Cottage. His diary entry for 9 May

1880 states only the bare fact. 'Llanystumdwy: slept there for the last
time – perhaps for ever.' The following day he was more frank. 'Left
Llanystumdwy without a feeling of regret, remorse or longing.' He
was thinking about the future, not the past.

In Criccieth the family was, in William George's words, 'on the
verge of respectable poverty'.[11] David did not concern himself with
such matters. He had found politics and become a journalist. In
October, under the pseudonym 'Brutus', he sent, without invitation, a
Liberal polemic to the *North Wales Express*. He did 'not relish the idea
of that refusal which Editor, overwhelmed with a redundance of such
trash, will have to accord to some of them'. The article was published
on 5 November. His attack on Lord Salisbury, Disraeli's successor as
leader of the Tory Party, anticipated the speaking style which was to
make him so loved by his friends and hated by his enemies. It
denounced an idea by denigrating the man who held it.

> He is a relic of what he has been; the ruins of a character which,
> if not noble, at least seemed to be stable. Office proved to be too
> much for him. It has shattered his reputation. The prejudice and
> rancour of his unalloyed Toryism he still retains, but the consis-
> tency and integrity of character which once graced these
> propensities have departed.

By the end of the year, politics had become such an overwhelming pre-
occupation that even the terrors of the Law Society's Intermediate
Examination could not completely dampen his spirits. He arrived in
London on 11 November and was met at the station by a relation who
occupied his interest before examination day by visits to Madame
Tussaud's ('horror of horrors. I shall never go again'), Charing Cross
Station ('saw electric lighting for the first time') and the British
Museum ('interesting but too much of a good thing').[12]

At home in Wales, Richard Lloyd's anxiety about his nephew was
increased by guilt. Because of his elevated ideas about learning, he had
encouraged David to 'study every book, chapter and note, foot and
footnote' rather than 'cramming to pass only'. As the examination
approached, he began to fear that his advice had produced an expert in
the law who could not answer any of the set questions. In London,
David was equally apprehensive. 'It seemed ages waiting for the papers.
When they came . . . I found I could answer them pretty fairly – all of
them.'[13] His confidence did not survive the evening. 'If the verdict be

adverse, I scarcely know what to do – to face friends and others who are so sanguine and seem to have no doubt about the result . . .'[14] But next day his first visit to the Palace of Westminster revived his spirits – not because he was impressed but because he felt the stirring of ambition.

> Went to the Houses of Parliament – very much disappointed with them. Grand buildings outside, but inside they are crabbed, small and suffocating, especially House of Commons. I will not say but that I eyed the assembly in a spirit similar to that in which William the Conqueror eyed England on his visit to Edward the Confessor, the region of his future domain.[15]

He had the grace to add, 'Oh, vanity.'

Despite his apprehension Lloyd George wrote to Randall Casson on the evening of the examination assuring him that he had passed. Casson replied that he 'never had the least doubt of the outcome' and made a generous offer which was accompanied by the postal order which made acceptance possible. 'By all means stay a week longer if you like. There is plenty to do and see on one's first visit to London.'[16]

On his return to Criccieth, perhaps out of gratitude, the putative solicitor joined the Portmadoc Volunteers under Casson's command. He was a most unsatisfactory soldier. 'At first I had intended to drill with the recruits but somehow by mistake I joined the battalion. A very awkward predicament. My braces broke just before the drill and my trousers were continually coming down.'[17] But whatever the embarrassment of service in the ranks, the weekend recruit drill brought him even closer to Casson – though it required him to live several lies. Uncle Lloyd was not told his nephew bore arms on a Saturday afternoon and, even worse, that he drank beer with his patron and sometimes worked with him in his garden on a Sunday. The relationship between solicitor and clerk was marked by 'the growth of a dining, gossiping, present-giving friendship' which William George – who had been accepted as an articled clerk only because of his brother's influence – came close to envying. William's 'dealings with the same gentleman was [sic] that of shy country lad towards a standoffish headmaster in a posh private school'.[18]

It seemed that William would always be in his brother's shadow. David, who accompanied him north to Beaumaris for his first law examination, had 'some doubt whether Willie will pass'. With typical absence of modesty, he attributed the potential failure to his own inability to 'prepare him myself'.[19] William passed with ease – a practice he followed until his finals in which he (unlike his brother) was awarded first-class honours. Another hundred pounds and the Excise fee were withdrawn from Elizabeth George's family savings and there were two articled clerks in the family.

Uncle Lloyd judged his nephews against exacting standards. During the summer of 1882, he was initially delighted by their participation in the Criccieth Castle Festival essay competition. Their joint entry, entitled 'Cash and Credit', won the first prize of two guineas, but Uncle Lloyd's pride and pleasure evaporated when he realised that they had competed for money. At Christmas that year, David rose in his uncle's estimation by agreeing to give a series of sermons on the evils of drink. He joined the United Kingdom Alliance, took the Blue Ribbon Pledge of total abstinence and added a speech on the evils of drink to his repertoire. His first address on the subject – in Llanystumdwy during December 1882 – began with 'stammering and stuttering' but he warmed to his subject with such fervour that, in a much applauded climax, he called for an Act of Parliament to prohibit the sale of alcohol.[20] But it was in the Portmadoc Debating Society that he made his name. Between November 1881, when he was elected a member, and January 1884, when he was due to sit his final law examination, he spoke almost every week – sometimes contributing from the 'back benches' but most often as one of the principal advocates. He opposed the proposition that Irish landlords should be compensated for losses under the Irish Land Act, supported the extension of the County Franchise, denounced the 'late war in Egypt' as 'indefensible' and contributed to parochial discussion with equal fervour. He spoke with passion in favour of the motion that 'ladies be admitted to membership of this society without payment of an annual subscription'.[21]

From the start, Uncle Lloyd was worried about his nephew taking part in weekly debates. 'My honest opinion is that he would be better employed preparing himself for his final examination.'[22] But the law books did not offer the prospect of local fame. The *North Wales Express* reported that he 'denounced the war in Egypt' in 'a most eloquent harangue' and the *Caernarvon and Denbigh Herald* was of the opinion that 'the speech delivered by Mr George. . . would probably have gained praise had it been delivered in the House of Commons'.[23] On 2 June 1883, the *Herald* bestowed the ultimate accolade – a paragraph in a gossip column. Local notables were paired with literary quotations which were said to represent their achievements and character. David Lloyd George qualified for a verse by Doctor Johnson.

When first the college rolls receive his name
The young enthusiast quits his ease for fame,
Restless burns the fever of renown
Caught from the strong contagion of the gown.

He was beginning to exhibit the dash and daring which, over the years, was to encourage the forgiveness of his many failings.

Lloyd George's response to the mention, confided in his notebook, was admirably restrained and recognised that audacity was not enough. 'June 2 – titbit poetry – referring to my thirst for renown etc. Perhaps (?) it will be gratified. I believe it depends entirely upon what forces of pluck and industry I can muster.'[24]

Uncle Lloyd's forebodings proved justified. David Lloyd George was meant to sit his Final Examination in January 1884, within weeks of his twenty-first birthday. But he was not ready and was withdrawn because of the fear that he would fail. A four-month postponement left little time for revision, but enough to allow apprehensions to grow. The candidate left for London in April 1884 with no great hope of success, claiming that he felt physically sick and announcing that his ill health would prevent him from sitting the extra papers which were required of 'honours students'. The cousin and family benefactor, with whom he stayed in London, wrote home to Wales to warn Uncle Lloyd that his nephew had been kept awake all night 'with bad headache and neuralgia'.[25]

Before he left his lodgings for the Law Society Hall in Chancery Lane, his spirits were much improved by the receipt of a supportive letter from Uncle Lloyd and a 'most comic' note from his brother William.[26] He was so encouraged by the way in which he answered the questions that he decided to remain another week in London and attempt the honours papers. He passed the time with a visit to the Metropolitan Tabernacle in the Elephant and Castle in which he heard Doctor Charles Haddon Spurgeon preach the sermon which contributed to the restoration of his faith. He also visited the House of Commons, where he felt mild guilt at 'thoroughly enjoying' a speech in which Lord Randolph Churchill ridiculed Gladstone.[27]

David Lloyd George passed the examination with third-class honours (and thereby qualified as a solicitor) six months after his articles had expired. His intention, which it took some years for him to achieve, was to shake the dust of Wales from his feet and find both fame and fortune in London – 'a fellow may make a successful lawyer down here and

amass a tidy, though not a large fortune; but as for any higher object –
fame – London is the place for that'.[28]

During Lloyd George's youth in Criccieth and Portmadoc, women
were always a damaging distraction – despite his habit of giving himself
good advice through the medium of his notebook. 'This I know – that
the realization of my prospects, my dreams, my longings for success are
very scant indeed unless I am determined to give up what without mistake are the germs of a "fast life" . . . What is life good for unless some
success, some reputable notoriety be attained.'[29] The danger could be
contained as long as his feelings amounted to no more than youthful
infatuation. But he developed the unfortunate habit of falling in love.

Religion was the first matchmaker. John Roberts, the radical preacher
and candlemaker, took David with him to visit an evangelical mission at
Penmachno, near Betws-y-Coed in Snowdonia. At the Sunday evening
service he met Miss Jones of Glasgwm and after the hymns were finished
they walked together in the hills. David was 'awfully afraid of it becoming known by all the sisterhood and through them to other persons from
Portmadoc and Criccieth who may go there to preach'.[30] But he still
made regular visits to Penmachno to meet the girl who, he understood,
had told a friend, 'I prefer him to anyone I have ever been with.'[31] The
relationship ended when Miss Jones heard that Lloyd George was seeing
other girls in his home town. Fidelity was beyond him.

By early 1883, he was in love with Liza Jones, a well-known local
singer whose engagements in the county made meeting difficult. The
relationship was further complicated by Miss Jones's attachment to a
local schoolmaster, whom she eventually married. Lloyd George was
inconsolable in his desolation.

> A miserable Sunday in all respects for me . . . L. went to
> Beddgelert on Friday to sing in an Entertainment there and in
> spite of my earnest requests that she would not go, but the little
> Jezebel has stayed there over Sunday which has given me unutter-
> able pain throughout the day. In earnest I do not know what to do
> with the girl. I wish to God I had never meddled with her, but I
> am afraid it is too late now. She has acquired a wonderful mastery
> over my idiot heart.[32]

The popular image of Lloyd George – old, overweight and in urgent
need of a haircut and remedial work on his shaggy moustache – suggests

that, despite the attraction of his ardour, there was nothing surprising about his rejection. But photographs of the young lawyer leave no doubt that, although it might have been the allure of power and fame which enabled him to make so many later conquests, in the Criccieth years he cut a dashing figure. Twenty years after they first met, D. R. Daniel – journalist, Nationalist and friend from Lloyd George's youth – recalled how, back in 1887, he had been struck by 'the incomparable brilliance of his lively blue eyes'.[33] Miss Jones was not equally impressed.

Discontent was added to anguish. At Beddgelert David Lloyd George's 'feet were wet all day owing to leaky shoes'[34] – the consequence of the poverty into which the family had descended as a result of maintaining two articled clerks. Throughout 1884, Richard Lloyd struggled to pay his way and was forced to accept the shame of borrowing from friends. On 4 February he 'received £1 from W W for family needs. I felt it to the quick as it was not convenient for him.'[35] William Williams, a chapel deacon, provided the money 'to give to D L G for his journey to London to sit for his finals'.[36]

Lloyd George's failure to find work in London – to which he aspired, his brother believed, in order to forget Liza Jones – was another example of the good fortune which followed him. It was Welsh politics and a Welsh constituency which propelled him into the House of Commons at a speed that London Liberals would not have contemplated. But the ambitious twenty-one-year-old – dissatisfied with provincial life and still imagining that he suffered from a broken heart – was bitter about his inability to break out of rural Wales. He accepted, with reluctance and bad grace, Randall Casson's offer of a place in his firm as assistant solicitor – salary one pound a week – after it was agreed that he should also be paid commission on any new work he brought to the partnership. The scheme was doomed from the start. Casson resented paying the commission and regretted having accepted the idea. Lloyd George thought that his talents were undervalued by Casson and wasted in Portmadoc. Poor William – moving towards the end of his articles – was caught in the crossfire of an increasingly bitter battle. When the conflict was at its height, he often carried messages between the warring solicitors – neither of whom was prepared to speak to the other directly. Casson showed more concern for William's embarrassment than the unfortunate young man's brother. As the Law Society Finals approached, he suggested that William work at home, free from the tensions of the office, and he offered to pay for a short holiday in London – just as he had done for David – when the examination was over. William sat the honours papers in January 1885. When he returned home, to rejoice at having been awarded a first, he discovered – much to his surprise – that David had left Breese, Jones and Casson to set up on his own account.

It was a reckless decision, for the family was still in desperate financial straits. For some months, Richard Lloyd was unable to pay the rent on the Criccieth house and David Lloyd George could meet his day-to-day expenses only by accepting a loan from Thomas Jones, another Portmadoc solicitor. But he still obstructed his uncle's attempts to avoid the indignity of further debt by taking in lodgers. William was exasperated. On 4 July 1884

> Lady called to see the house – wants a bedroom and sitting room. We offered her accommodation for 25/- but she says she won't take them because D.Ll.G says, if she comes, he'll go away. What can we do in the face of this situation now? . . . Uncle hasn't anything to lend for the time being.[37]

David Lloyd George was persuaded to change his mind and, 'having given his gracious consent', the family began 'cleaning the place for lodgers'.[38] From then on 'paying guests' – particularly in the summer season – were a regular part of the household. They included Rider Haggard, the author of *King Solomon's Mines*.

David Lloyd George became a figure of importance in Wales through his membership of three societies for which he tirelessly campaigned – the Anti-Tithe League, the Welsh Farmers Union and the Liberation Society. They had related aims, for land reform was, in Wales, irrevocably linked to the tithes and glebe rents which farmers paid to the Church of England and its clergy. The largest and most influential of the reform movements was the Liberation Society, dedicated to disestablishment of the Church in both England and Wales. In Wales its most effective supporter was Thomas Gee, the Denbigh publisher of the *Banner and Times of Wales*, a Calvinistic Methodist minister and an active supporter of the Liberal Party. By the end of the 1870s, Liberalism, disestablishment and Welsh Home Rule were all driven onward by more compelling forces than radical journalism. The agricultural depression had hit Welsh farming particularly hard. By the early 1880s, farmers – living from hand to mouth – regarded the tithe as proof that Wales should be run by the Welsh.

In the autumn of 1884 – when David Lloyd George was working as a dissatisfied assistant solicitor and William was beginning to worry about his Final Examination – Gee invited Joseph Chamberlain, President of the Board of Trade, to visit Wales. Chamberlain was the personification of radical nonconformity and had been the leader of the Birmingham radical caucus which, while it controlled the corporation, had bought the local gas company and used its profits to improve the town's drains and water supply. He was no more in favour of Home Rule for Ireland than for Wales – though he favoured something called 'Home Rule All Round'. But, as a Unitarian, he was in complete sympathy with the Welsh Nonconformists' demands for disestablishment. The rising star of Gladstone's second administration was booked to speak in Newtown on 18 October and in Denbigh on 25 October. A week before his arrival, Brutus welcomed his visit in an article which was composed in a style which was to become Lloyd George's polemical trade mark. Chamberlain, he wrote,

> is a radical and does not care who knows it as long as the people do. He is convinced that the aristocracy stands in the way of the development of the rights of man and he says so unflinchingly though he may be howled at as an ill-mannered demagogue by the whole kennelry of gorged aristocracy and their fawning minions.[39]

The new hero retained Lloyd George's admiration long after he deserted the Liberal Party. His unforgivable offence was not his forming a Unionist alliance with the Conservatives but, by precipitating war against the Boers, becoming the champion of great nations against small. Even then, the vehemence with which he attacked his fallen idol created the suspicion that – in his political youth – Chamberlain was the man he wanted to be.

Lloyd George was certainly sympathetic to Chamberlain's radical imperialism. But his first campaigns concerned neither the empire nor social reform. Instead he became the farmers' champion. When J. A. Davies of Cae Tyddyn wanted legal advice about his lease, Myrddin Fardd (the Llanystumdwy blacksmith) suggested that he employed 'a young chap at the point of starting as a lawyer in Criccieth'. Davies – who later claimed that he was Lloyd George's first client – was so impressed with 'the fine-looking young fellow' that he asked him to speak at a farmers' meeting in Pwllheli Town Hall. The speech at Pwllheli was a triumph – although the hero of the night claimed that he was 'too shy to make his way to the Town Hall alone'. If so, he quickly overcame his reticence. According to Davies, 'he gave the most suitable and telling speech . . . We all marvelled and were ready to say "nobody ever spoke like this boy. Here is a born orator to take up the poor farmers' grievances."'[40]

In the following autumn, there was a further slump in agricultural prices and most Welsh landlords agreed to lower their rents. But the Church Commissioners and Christ Church, Oxford (also a major landowner in Wales), refused to follow suit. Nor would the Church reduce its tithes. The farmers' response was the Anti-Tithe League, formed with Thomas Gee as its president. Lloyd George became the secretary of the South Caernarvonshire branch and toured the northern Welsh counties, denouncing the tithe and defying League policy by promoting a rent strike. He remained unrepentant, and miraculously free from blame, when the inevitable violence began – refusal to pay rates leading to distraint of property and distraint leading to assaults on bailiffs. His outrage was genuine. But he also recognised the issue's potential as a vehicle – both for him and for the Liberal Party to which he felt increasingly committed. This tithe issue, he wrote in 1887, 'is an excellent lever wherewith to raise the spirits of the people'.[41]

His success as a popular orator was a shaft of sunlight in an otherwise bleak year. His rivalry with Randall Casson grew increasingly bitter after he set up his own practice in the back room of Morvin House. Yet despite the difficulty of earning a decent living, there was no question of concentrating on the law to the exclusion of politics. There were several speeches to be made every week – debating society, tithe campaign and, with decreasing frequency, temperance. A career in Liberal politics had increased its appeal with the defeat of Gladstone in 1885. Lloyd George had enjoyed the election campaign – speaking at Liberal meetings, heckling the Conservatives and acting as a poll 'watcher' on election day. He was, he had decided, a firm Liberal but not a Gladstonian.

The Grand Old Man had been the architect of his own destruction. British sovereignty over Egypt had been confirmed by the defeat of Arabi Pasha at Tel-el-Kebir – a victory which caused Lloyd George to express his pleasure at the imagined sound of imperial gunfire. But the Grand Old Man had felt a Christian duty to extend the rule of civilised law south into the Sudan. When he realised that subduing the Mahdi was beyond the power of the available forces, General Charles Gordon was sent to organise and command the withdrawal. Gordon believed it was his duty to disobey orders and stay. He died with the garrison in Khartoum and became an instant saint and martyr. Gladstone, held responsible for his death, was doomed. Lloyd George was by instinct an imperialist – though in that, as in much else, more flexible than consistent. There is no record of him criticising the Sudanese adventure before it went wrong. It was Gladstone's Irish policy which offended him.

Lloyd George was opposed to Home Rule, not because he thought it wrong in principle, but because Gladstone pursued it without concern for either the Liberal Party's success or the fate of other, more desirable, policies. Worse still, Ireland enjoyed a concern that was not shown to Wales. In 1881, the Irish Land Act had guaranteed security of tenure and fair rents for tenant farmers. But there was no suggestion of similar legislation for the Welsh. Lloyd George drew a political moral from the way in which his countrymen had been treated.

The Irish, under the leadership of Charles Stewart Parnell, acted together in the interests of Ireland and when the balance of power at Westminster was held by the Home Rule Party, Irish Members were able to make demands upon the government – including for freedoms to which the Welsh had never even aspired. Although majorities had been reduced, in 1885 the Liberals won all but four seats in Wales. If the Irish could achieve so much by making their first allegiance a nation rather than a party, the Welsh should do the same. The obsession with Ireland was not the only reason why Gladstone had to go. 'He had no programme that would draw at all. The people do not understand what entail etc means.'[42] And 'Humdrum Liberalism won't win elections.'[43]

Lloyd George became – albeit temporarily – Chamberlain's man, even though only part of his hero's 1885 'Unauthorised Programme' appealed to him. The policy of 'three acres and a cow' for every agricultural worker was in conflict with his wish to encourage 'good' landowners. He had read Henry George's *Progress and Poverty* – bought with money he should have used to take out a subscription to the Law Lending Library – and come to the conclusion that 'the appropriation of rent is nothing but aimless plunder. The great object is to get control of the land itself into the hands of those whose interests are so vitally affected by it.'[44] Chamberlain's bravura style appealed to him – particularly since the alternative to official government policy had been brazenly published while its author was still a member of the Cabinet. Party solidarity was never a virtue which David Lloyd George admired. What loyalty he possessed was to ideas. And Chamberlain was the one successful politician in Britain who shared Lloyd George's ideas on the iniquity of unearned wealth and was prepared to articulate them.

> I want you not to accept as final or as perfect arrangements under which hundreds of thousands, many millions of your fellow countrymen are subject to untold misery with the evidence all around them of accumulated wealth and undoubted luxury . . . I believe the great evil with which we have to deal is the excessive inequality in the distribution of riches.[45]

It was those opinions, far more than Chamberlain's views on Ireland, that attracted Lloyd George. But when the Home Rule schism came, he expressed such open sympathy for preserving the union that his uncle was warned, 'D Ll G must be careful or he would be accused of being against the Party'.[46] By then, he had certainly developed parliamentary ambition — and begun to work assiduously towards its achievement. Had he fought the 1886 general election he might well have declared himself to be a 'Liberal-Unionist', even though he despised the Irish 'ascendancy' who were the backbone of the Unionist cause. His Irish heroes were less concerned with creating a Dublin Parliament than with changing the pattern of land ownership.

On 12 February 1886, Michael Davitt — who had founded the Irish Land League seven years earlier — addressed a meeting in Blaenau Ffestiniog. One of the meeting's sponsors invited David Lloyd George to join the audience. It was a daring meeting to organise and a dangerous meeting to attend. Twenty years earlier, Davitt had declared himself a supporter of the Fenian movement and his association with the violence within it had resulted in two terms of imprisonment. The men who brought Davitt to Wales wanted to create a peaceful equivalent to the Irish campaign for tenants' rights. The idea came to very little. But the meeting was another stepping stone along Lloyd George's path to power and fame.

Lloyd George, speaking at a Liberal Club in Criccieth a few days before Davitt's arrival, had advocated the creation of a Welsh Land League — and, in consequence, had been described by the chairman as 'pretty extreme'.[47] Perhaps that is why, just before Davitt's meeting at Blaenau Ffestiniog began, he was invited to repeat his Criccieth performance. At first he felt too nervous to agree — or so he said to the organisers. But he was persuaded to change his mind. There is some doubt about whether he moved a vote of thanks or made one of the supporting speeches. Whichever part he played, his role attracted great acclaim. Never shy at recording his triumphs, he wrote in his note-book – immediately after applauding Davitt's earnest sincerity – 'He highly complimented me, told me that I aroused by far the most enthu-siasm, that it was quite evident I touched the heart of the audience. [Because the speech was in Welsh] He could not understand me [but] he knew very well I was eloquent . . . My speech has gone like wildfire through Ffestiniog. They're going to make me an MP.'[48] From then on there was no turning back from the great ambition.

CHAPTER 3

NOT A GENTLEMAN . . .

David Lloyd George's experience with the two Miss Joneses taught him a bitter lesson. His heart had not been broken, but he had discovered that anything approaching a permanent commitment caused great pain and therefore, unless the object of his affection was steady and reliable, distracted him from the pursuit of success. The 'germs of a fast life', which had infected him in 1880, had been suppressed rather than eradicated by the time that his political ambition took hold. But he knew that his need of the moment was a woman who could provide the stability of indomitable domesticity. Although it would be wrong to say that he looked for a housekeeper, he certainly looked for a wife who would keep house without unduly troubling him. When he found a suitable candidate he pursued her with remorseless determination.

Margaret Owen – his junior by almost four years – met David Lloyd George in June 1884. It was love at first sight for neither of them. He thought her 'a sensible girl without fuss or affectation' which may be one reason why he did not see her again for almost a year.[1] The next reference in his notebook records the *grand soirée* of the Criccieth Debating Society. 'Took Maggie Owen home a short way – her mother waiting for her in some house.'[2] He was soon to discover that her mother usually was.

The Owens of Mynydd Ednyfed – a farm on the brow of a hill at the north of Criccieth – met all the requirements of North Welsh respectability. They were both prosperous and pious. Richard Owen, Margaret's father, was a deacon of the Calvinistic Methodist Church at Capel Mawr and was so well respected – for both his judgement and his probity – that he was often asked to arbitrate between buyers and sellers of stock. Margaret, the Owens' only child, had been educated privately at Doctor Williams's School for Girls in Dolgellau. Most favoured among her many suitors, at least by her parents, was the Reverend John Owen MA, minister at Capel Mawr.

It was two years before Lloyd George was sure that he wanted to marry Margaret Owen. At the end of 1884 he cut out and kept an advertisement from a local newspaper. 'Matrimony. A lady aged 21, medium height, fair, blue eyes, golden hair, considered very prepossessing and of a very affectionate nature with private income of £800 pa would like to hear from a nice gentleman wanting a loving wife.'[3] We do not know if he approached Miss Tempsford of Lamb's Conduit, London, or why a young woman with so many charms and virtues chose to advertise for a husband. By the beginning of 1886, his mind, perhaps even his heart, was set on Margaret Owen.

Throughout the winter and spring his diary entries grew more enthusiastic. 'I am getting very fond of this girl. There is a combination of good nature, humour and affection about her . . . Never felt more acutely than tonight that I am really in deep love with girl . . . First time I used a term of endearment towards her. Feel I am becoming very fond of her.'[4] The relationship progressed slowly. On 31 December 1885, he sent Margaret a visitor's ticket to the debating society with the message that she had 'no need to arrange for an escort home'.[5] On 22 May 1886, he invited her again and renewed his offer of a 'reliable escort after the meeting'.[6] In November that year they kissed for the first time.[7] They had been discussing marriage since August.

David's sister, Mary Ellen – relieved by news of a respectable liaison – was 'well pleased' and said she 'thought a lot' of Margaret, but when David spoke to William of his 'predicament in regard to love', his brother said he 'did not approve' of what he assumed to be another amorous adventure. The secret was kept from Richard Lloyd, who had grown so anxious about his nephew's not very late-night excursions that he began to walk the streets of Criccieth as a deterrent to what he regarded as disreputable behaviour. Gossip had it that on one evening, anxious to preserve his privacy, David hid his uncle's boots – a story only credible on the assumption that a master cobbler owned only one pair. It is certainly true that on Sunday, 18 July 1886, David Lloyd George – aged twenty-three and a qualified solicitor – 'jumped over wall and hid behind Turnpike cottage' rather than allow his uncle to see that he had spent the sabbath with a girl. Not surprisingly, Margaret's

parents had no doubt that their daughter could do better than marry a
suitor who was 'not a gentleman but a Welsh country lawyer'.

The Owens were particularly worried about what they called 'sceptical vagaries' – their prospective son-in-law's habit of vacillating wildly
between devout belief and agnosticism. Margaret herself was more concerned by his reputation as a 'ladies' man'. Their early relationship was
notable for letters in which he justified his failure to keep assignations
or complained that he had waited for her, as arranged, but in vain.[8] She
was often kept at home by her parents – forcing the couple to make
secret rendezvous which Lloyd George found a humiliation. 'I somehow feel that it is deeply unattractive to take by stealth [that] which I
am honestly entitled to.'[9] He was frequently prevented from honouring
an appointment by the demands of his work. His notes of explanation
were always more reproof than apology. 'I do not think you would have
encouraged me to desert my post until I had satisfactorily discharged my
duties – would you?'[10] At one moment of revealing anger and regret, he
set out the basis of their relationship.

> Now once and ever let us have an end to this long-standing wran-
> gle. It comes to this. My supreme idea is to get on. To this idea I
> shall sacrifice everything – except, I trust, honesty. I am prepared
> to thrust even love itself under the wheels of my Juggernaut if it
> obstructs the way – that is if love is so much trumpery child's play
> as your mother deems courtship to be . . . My love for you is sin-
> cere and strong. In this I never waver. But I must not forget that I
> have a purpose in life. And however painful the sacrifice I may
> have to make to attain my ambition, I must not flinch.★[11]

In August 1886, Lloyd George 'pressed M to come to a point as to what
I had been speaking about [proposal of marriage]' and wrote, 'She had,
at last, admitted that her hesitation was entirely due to her not being
able to trust me.' He swore 'by God in Heaven' that she could and she
assured him 'if you will be as true and faithful to me as I am to you, it
will be all right'.[12] She was to prove a great deal more true and faithful
to him than he was to her – as well as more shrewd than is sometimes
supposed. Margaret's doubts illustrate the truth of Harold Nicolson's

---

★Lord Morgan – who edited and translated the Welsh passages in the *Family Letters* –
dates the ultimatum as 'probably 1885'. W. R. P. George suggests 'the end of January
1887'.

assessment of Lloyd George's character. 'The good fairies gave him everything at his Christening, but the bad fairy said "people won't trust you".'[13]

On 6 December 1886, Lloyd George told Margaret, 'I trust you will have something to report to me tomorrow as the result of the interview with your mother. As I have already intimated to you, it is of trivial consequence to me what your mother's views of me might be – so long, of course, as they do not affect yours. All I wish for is a clear understanding so that we may, afterwards, see for ourselves where we stand.'[14] There is little doubt that, by then, Margaret *wanted* to marry him and he *expected* to marry her. But in the early months of 1887, Lloyd George's fidelity was again put in doubt.

Yet another Miss Jones – Annie, the sister of Liza who had earlier caused such heartache – sued John Jones of Caerdyni for breach of promise and asked David Lloyd George to represent her. John Jones was Lloyd George's cousin. That in itself was enough to cause some surprise that the brief was accepted. But Lloyd George insisted that his relationship with Annie Jones was purely professional. In the hope of convincing Margaret of his innocence, he broke the rules of professional conduct by sending her the letters which would be used as evidence that Annie had received an offer of marriage. However, Margaret's parents possessed information which they regarded as conclusive proof that he had a personal attachment to one of the sisters. They discovered that a visit to the plaintiff's house – allegedly to discuss the progress of the case – had concluded with Lloyd George joining Annie and Liza in choruses of several popular songs.

Lloyd George insisted in his own defence that he was there at the invitation of Lloyd Williams, the schoolmaster whom Liza had preferred to him and who, despite that, had become his friend. His letter of explanation to Margaret was returned with a covering letter which began 'My Dear Mr George'. It left no doubt about either her determination that he should withdraw from the case or the reason why she was so desperate for him to do so. Thanks to his reputation, everyone would suspect the worst. 'All the old stories will be renewed again. I know there are relatives of mine at Criccieth and other people as well who will be glad to have anything more to say to my people about you, to set them against you and that will put me in an awkward position.'[15] Lloyd George's reply was robust to the point of brutality. It began with the, possibly justified, assertion that the Owens objected to his association with the Jones girls because their mother sold fish. 'My God never decreed that farmers and their race should be esteemed beyond the progeny of a fishmonger and, strange to say, Christ, the founder of our creed, selected the missionaries of his noble teaching from among fishmongers.' Her request for him to abandon the case was rejected out of hand. He would not 'give up a fee of £50 to £100 because of gossipy, dried-up and desiccated old maids'. The final paragraph began, 'You ask me to choose. I have made my choice, deliberately and solemnly. I must now ask you to make yours.'[16]

Margaret Owen was always going to choose David Lloyd George. Indeed, had it not been for parental pressure she would have chosen him earlier and with few, if any, reservations. It says much for her devotion – and her strength of character – that she withstood that pressure and remained constant, despite what the correspondence revealed about her future husband's character. Throughout fifty years of turbulent marriage – during which the interests of Lloyd George's career always took precedence over the needs of his family – she rarely complained. And she accepted the other women in his life – one permanent and many other casual affairs – with stoic resignation. In consequence, she represented certainty and stability in her husband's unsettled life. When his political career seemed near to collapse or his private life was in turmoil, she was unchangeable – the recipient of the regular letters that described his triumphs and demanded that she write to him more often. She met neither his physical nor intellectual needs. But she was indispensable. Perhaps the secret of their relationship is revealed in letters written many years apart. His routine letters to his 'good old mother'[17] and his 'round little wife'[18] were written in the same affectionately patronising style.

After a few more months of mutual recrimination – during which he bought a ring which she rejected – Margaret Owen accepted him as he was. Her letters began 'Dear David' and ended 'with much love'. For a time the Owens' attention was diverted from their daughter's future by a dispute in their chapel. Evangelistically inclined members wanted services in English to attract the attendance of immigrants from beyond Offa's Dyke. Traditionalists combined with Nationalists to insist that Welsh chapels had a duty to protect and preserve the language. The Owens' future son-in-law – never in favour of pandering to the English – was in sympathy with the traditionalists and suggested that the Owens transfer allegiance to the steadfastly Welsh Disciples of Christ. Perhaps common cause softened the Owens' attitude. Sometime during 1887, Margaret began to argue with her parents, not about whether or not she should marry David Lloyd George, but about what the date of the wedding should be and where it should be held. The Owens claimed that their only concern was their daughter's happiness and urged delay so that, after stock was sold in the following autumn, they could give the young couple enough to buy a house. Lloyd George, who questioned their motives, insisted that he wanted nothing, but could see advantages in a brief delay. By January 1888, he felt sufficiently confident that the wedding would go ahead to tell Richard Lloyd of his intentions. 'Told Uncle my reasons for not telling him before – he took it very well. Mam had been breaking the news to him. He said that everyone told him my little girl was a charming and sensible lassie. He told me to learn steadiness, domesticity and unselfishness etc.'[19]

There was one more battle to be fought before the wedding could go ahead. Richard Owen insisted that it be held in a Calvinistic Methodist chapel. Lloyd George agreed – as long as his uncle presided. Neither the bridegroom's mother nor his brother attended the ceremony, either because of the chapel's denomination or because, as William George wrote in old age, the plan was always for a quiet wedding. Uncle Lloyd, in his diary, reflected the subdued spirit of the day. 'January 24th 1888. WG to Portmadoc early. DLlG and myself to Pencaenewydd, self-ministering. John Owen read chapter and prayed, back per coach to Criccieth and home. May Heaven make it to Dei and his Maggie, a very bright red-letter day.'[20]

After a London honeymoon – Doctor Spurgeon again at the Metropolitan Tabernacle and a performance of *Hamlet* at the Globe – they returned to Criccieth on 8 February and, for the next three years, lived with the Owens at Mynydd Ednyfed. So began a marriage of improbable stability – David Lloyd George obdurate in his determination to achieve his ambition and Margaret almost equally stubborn in her insistence on bringing up their family in the way she chose, irrespective of her husband's convenience. One of the least reliable biographies described the night of his first election to Parliament. When David Lloyd George returned home, elated and triumphant, on the shoulders of his cheering supporters, Margaret sent the maid to lean out of the bedroom window to tell him, 'Hush, you'll wake the baby.'[21] The story has no provenance. But the invention reflects, or at least caricatures, the true nature of a relationship which, because it provided a perverse version of stability, became another example of David Lloyd George's good fortune.

By the time of his marriage, Lloyd George was a solicitor with his own practice – a status which he had acquired with considerable difficulty and,

to a substantial degree, because of the help of his brother. He was in competition with Breese, Jones and Casson, and Randall Casson, in particular,
felt bitter about what he regarded as gross disloyalty. William George –
who returned to the Portmadoc law firm after his post-Intermediate
Examination in January 1885 – feared that he would 'have many delicate
and difficult passes to go through' before he completed his articles with
a firm which his brother was said to have betrayed and would, in consequence, 'be afraid to entrust [him] with confidential matters in case [he]
might . . . use that knowledge against them'.[22] David – either unaware of
or untroubled by his brother's dilemma – increased William's anxiety by
insisting that, in his spare time, he acted as his unpaid assistant. One
entry in William's diary plaintively notes, 'David gave me a job which
lasted till 2am.'[23]

Lloyd George's solution to the unreasonable demands on his brother's
time was the transfer of William's articles from Breese, Jones and Casson
to himself. He represented the transfer as beneficial to both parties. 'Am
trying to induce William to come over to me – he'll gain something in
cash – a good deal in practice (he can conduct matters himself) and he
would gain incomparably more in fact, knowledge of men's self-reliance
whilst, at the same time, he would help materially to build up the business, as he has a much better system than I have with working.'[24] In
February 1886, he was still 'pressing William' to join him and claiming
that he had 'more points of law to decide in a week than Breese, Jones
and Casson had in a year'.[25]

Casson refused to sanction the transfer. So, until he qualified, William
continued the unpaid work for his brother. Then, on 10 May 1887 – ten
days after he was awarded first-class honours in his Final Examination
and admitted to the ranks of solicitor – he joined David, who had
moved out of the back room of Morvin House into offices in Criccieth
High Street. The firm of Lloyd George and George which was thus
created remained in business for fifty years and, until Lloyd George
entered the Cabinet in 1905, supported him with a salary which was out
of all proportion to the work he did on its behalf.

Lloyd George had made his first appearance in court – 13 January
1885 – on behalf of the County Court bailiff in Portmadoc. His
second – defending an obviously guilty party in an assault prosecution –
ended in victory because a witness gave false evidence. Work came
slowly. But on 24 January, believing that if 'he was patient things would
come round' and that 'reasonable charging is the best way to success',
he opened a second office in Blaenau Ffestiniog.[26] On the first day 'not

a soul called to see if [he] was alive or dead'.[27] Gradually the work – usually humdrum – increased. Then, in 1889, fortune presented him with the opportunity to set Welsh Liberal politics on fire.

At first it seemed to be just another poaching case – four quarrymen in front of the Caernarvon County magistrates accused of unlawful net fishing in the lower lake in Nantlle Valley. The facts of the case were not in dispute. But Lloyd George argued that the act under which they had been prosecuted related only to poaching in rivers and, since the Nantlle lower lake could not be thus defined, the magistrates had no locus in the matter. When the chairman of the bench ruled that the question of jurisdiction would have to be decided by a higher court, Lloyd George replied, 'Yes sir, and in a perfectly just and unbiased court too.' It was a technique which he developed as a lawyer and perfected as a politician – the personal assault upon his opponent to enliven the battle of ideas. Naturally, the chairman of the bench took offence. 'If that remark of Mr Lloyd George's is meant as a reflection upon any magistrate sitting on this bench, I hope he will name him. A more insulting and ungentlemanly remark to the bench I never heard during my whole experience as a magistrate.'[28]

Lloyd George replied that 'a more true remark was never made in a court of law', provoking the chairman to demand, 'Tell me to whom you are referring?' So Lloyd George told him. 'I refer to you in particular.' A pantomime then took place. First the chairman withdrew in protest. A second magistrate asked Lloyd George to apologise and, on receiving no reply, also withdrew. So did a third. A fourth magistrate was then called from another part of the court. He made the same request and was similarly rebuffed – as was a fifth magistrate whose demand for an apology was answered by a statement to the bench.

> I say this. At least two or three magistrates of this Court are bent upon securing a conviction whether there is a fair case or not. I am sorry that the Chairman has left the Court because I am in a position to prove what I have said. I shall not withdraw anything because every word I have spoken is true.[29]

Four magistrates then returned and, ignoring the calculated assault on the integrity of the bench, announced that 'under the circumstances it is better if the case continues'. Lloyd George subsequently received a letter asking him to account for himself – which he certainly did. His reply asserted that the magistrates 'were more intent on protecting the fish in the Nantlle lakes against the inroads of the quarrymen than in doing justice'.[30] The men were convicted. It seemed of little consequence – except to the men themselves. A great blow had been struck against established authority. Impertinence had triumphed over pomposity.

From then on much, if not most, of David Lloyd George's time was spent defending tenants' rights. The work coincided with his view that landowners often enjoyed an income to which they were not morally entitled. The poor – without necessarily endorsing his political theory – often tried to redress the balance by poaching and theft. Many of those who were caught were defended by Lloyd George with skill and enthusiasm. Using his oratorical powers to defend the people against privilege solidified his reputation as a radical. It was confirmed by a second act of benevolent fate – the request to defend the Roberts family of Llanfrothen against the charge of trespass and wilful damage with the claim that they had done no more than exercise their rights under the Osborne Morgan Act of 1880.

The act – named after Gladstone's Attorney General and forming part of the liberalisation of Church law – allowed Nonconformists to be buried, according to the rites of their own denominations, in ground consecrated by the Church of England. However, Richard Jones, the Rector of Llanfrothen, believed that he had discovered a way to circumvent a reform which he deplored. In 1864, a Mr and Mrs Owen had given the church a piece of land to supplement its overflowing cemetery. No deeds had been exchanged, though in 1869 a new wall was built (at the cost of the parishioners) to encompass both the old churchyard and its extension within the same boundary. The year after the Osborne Morgan Act was passed, the Reverend Mr Jones suggested to Mrs Owen (by then a widow) that, since the land was legally still hers, it should be officially transferred to the ownership of the church with a deed of covenant which required all burial services performed within its curtilage to follow the form of service laid down by the Church of England prayer book and to be conducted by a priest of that denomination. Local Nonconformists protested but with no effect until, in 1888, the family of Robert Roberts, an old quarryman, decided to take direct action.

Robert Roberts's daughter had been buried in Mrs Owen's gift of land and her father's last wish was to be buried by her side. Preparations for the funeral had begun when the Reverend Mr Jones received the official notice required under the Osborne Morgan Act. Quoting the covenant, he required the grave which had been prepared to be filled in. Instead he offered the family what Lloyd George called 'a spot bleak and sinister in which were buried the bodies of the unknown drowned that were washed up from the sea in this region of shipwrecks or of suicides or of the few Jews who die in this district'.[31] The Roberts family pleaded with the rector, but he was immovable. When they consulted David Lloyd George, he told them that right was on their side. If there were no other way, they should take the law into their own hands.

On 27 April 1888, the family's formal request for the keys to the locked churchyard was refused. That night they broke open the gate, dug a grave next to where Robert Roberts's daughter lay and buried the old quarryman there according to the rites of his Church. The following day, the rector took out a summons in the Portmadoc County Court alleging trespass by Roberts's son and seven other defendants. It claimed damages for the offence of 'wrongfully entering the plaintiff's land, digging a grave therein, burying a corpse and conducting a funeral service'.

The case was perfectly suited to Lloyd George's temperament and reputation. The alien Church was attempting to impose its dogma on the pious Welsh people. And the dispute was over the use of land – Lloyd George's preoccupation for much of his life. Wisely he asked for a trial by jury. It found that Mrs Owen's land had, in effect, become part of the churchyard in 1864 and that, since the Osborne Morgan Act applied to it, the defendants were entitled to insist that Robert Roberts be buried within it according to denominational rites of his family's choosing. Judgement was reserved for two months. When the hearing was resumed, the judge ruled – out of incompetence rather than malice – that damages and costs had been awarded against the defendant. Lloyd George – with admirable and unusual restraint – produced written evidence, including the foreman's note, to prove that the jury had dismissed the plaintiff's case. But the best that the judge would agree to was that the case went to appeal.

Lloyd George regarded the barrister who represented the Roberts family in the Divisional Court as 'Very weak'. His not altogether objective letter home complained, 'I thought he failed to put some of our most forcible points.'[32] It continued, 'Coleridge [the Lord Chief Justice] . . . insisted on knowing something more about the contention which had arisen between Mr George and the judge as to what the verdict actually was . . . The paper is not in court, I suppose.' It was then that the usually unsung hero of Lloyd George's climb to fame had his moment of glory. 'The affidavit, prepared by our Will, was handed in with the identical scrap thereto attached.'

The case was won, though Lloyd George (privately) cast doubts on his reputation as the champion of the people by confessing that he did 'not care a button about the result'. What mattered was, 'So far as the County Court Judge is concerned, I have triumphed.'[33] By happy co-incidence, on 1 January 1889 – two weeks after the victorious appeal and the public acclaim that the successful defence of the Roberts family provoked – the Caernarvon District Liberal Association met to choose a candidate to fight the next general election.

During the six years between his admission as a solicitor and his election to Parliament in 1890, it was never easy to distinguish between Lloyd George the politician and Lloyd George the lawyer. In both roles he spoke in the same flamboyant style. At a public meeting called to protest about tithes and glebe money, a curate asked the crowd, 'Why do you listen to this little attorney? If you go to his office you'll pay six and eightpence for him to speak a word to you.' Lloyd George admitted to being 'A lawyer – a little lawyer who tries to make a living with an occasional six and eightpence.' But he added, just to remind the audience about the subject of the meeting, 'If you don't come to me, I shan't ask you to pay me anything. But as for this man, whether you go to hear his sermons or not, you have to pay him just the same.'[34] Initially, he believed that his political convictions would help him make his way as a lawyer. Then he realised that his work as a solicitor would assist in making him a Welsh (and therefore by necessity Liberal) Member of Parliament.

Perhaps it was Michael Davitt's commendation that strengthened his resolve to enter the House of Commons, though, long before that date, he had thought of a political career. After he met Davitt, there were increasing attempts to make the hope a reality. By 1886, he was working hard to secure a parliamentary nomination both in the Caernarvon Boroughs, of which Criccieth was part, and in Merioneth, where friends in Harlech, supported by some of the Blaenau Ffestiniog quarrymen whose interests he had represented, pressed his claim.

The Merioneth constituency was all but spoken for by Thomas Ellis – a man who, but for his premature death, would have become a major figure in Liberal politics. Ellis – the son of a tenant farmer – spoke Welsh and could boast three uncles who had been evicted from their property in 1859 after the land reform protests. He was, however, in many ways a metropolitan figure who, after the University College in

Aberystwyth and New College, Oxford, had become secretary to the Member of Parliament for Norwich. Lloyd George had first met him at the beginning of June 1886,★ and although he might have been expected to resent an 'Anglicised' rival for parliamentary honours, he seems to have taken an immediate liking to a man with whom he had little except Liberalism in common.[35]

When he discovered that Ellis hoped to contest Merioneth, he announced that he would allow his name to go forward only if, as some rumours suggested, Ellis were forced to withdraw because he could not raise enough funds to fight an election. It may be that he had heard that the Blaenau Ffestiniog quarrymen had – despite the views of the radicals in their midst – decided to support Ellis. Whatever his reason, Lloyd George not only stepped aside but supported Ellis against Morgan Lloyd, an opponent of Irish Home Rule who asked for his endorsement.

In Caernarvon, Thomas Love Jones Parry – the sitting Member on whose behalf Uncle Lloyd had persuaded his young nephew to carry a banner twenty years earlier and co-founder of the Welsh settlement in Patagonia – proposed to stand again. David Lloyd George, who was thus unlikely to fight the 1886 general election, began to convince himself that the inevitable was also desirable.

> I would not be in nearly as good a position as regards pecuniary, oratorical or intellectual quality to go to Parliament now as, say, five years hence. Now I would put myself in endless pecuniary difficulties – an object of contempt in a House of Snobs. Besides, I am not yet as thoroughly established in judgement as I ought to be.[36]

The reference to the 'House of Snobs' is one of the few examples of genuine class consciousness matching Lloyd George's class antagonism. But, although he never felt handicapped by lowly birth and breeding, he often drew attention to his origins in order to win arguments – and to assuage his disappointment in 1886.

The Tory Party and its anti-Home Rule associates won the 1886 general election with a majority of 108 over all other parties. In Wales the swing to the Conservatives was 1.9 per cent as compared with 5.7 per cent in the whole of Great Britain. It marked a reinvigoration of

---

★The usual claim that they met after the Michael Davitt meeting is – like the idea that Davitt set Lloyd George on his political career – wrong.

Liberalism in the principality. The North Wales Liberal Federation was founded in Rhyl on 14 December 1886 and its conference adopted a programme which was certainly more radical than Whig. It included the disestablishment of the Church in Wales with the distribution of endowments among Welsh good causes, fair rents determined by land courts, long leases and recompense for tenants when they improved their rented property. A resolution calling for 'the principle of . . . National self-government to be applied to Wales . . . for the sake of the efficiency of the Imperial parliament' was proposed and debated, but the proceedings closed before a vote could be taken. There were mumblings about Irish Home Rule but no serious thought of rebellion against Gladstone's policy. Affection and respect were still strong enough to maintain acquiescence for the Grand Old Man's passion. But there were doubts about prejudicing an entire legislative programme in order to achieve one policy. Why – if so much time and moral capital could be employed meeting the demands of one Celtic race – did no one speak of meeting the needs of Cymru? Lloyd George – in half-hearted support of Home Rule All Round – wondered why Wales was so supine in defence of its own interests.

With the next general election most of a full Parliament away, and the Conservative Party enjoying a majority over the Gladstonian Liberals and the Irish Nationalists combined, Lloyd George returned to the practice of law and the promotion of Welsh causes. Both subjects were calculated to improve his political prospects. In September 1887, he was approached about putting his name forward as prospective candidate for Caernarvon District – as the Caernarvon Boroughs were properly called. His diary entry for 4 September 1887 suggests that once he felt he had a foothold in the constituency party, he took to the pursuit of the candidature with a determination which was solemn as well as serious.

> Got an invitation this morning, I mean to cultivate Boroughs as, if the Unionist Government holds together another three years, I may stand a good chance of nomination as Liberal candidate. There are two or three impressions I must be careful to make in the meantime. 1st and foremost that I am a good speaker. 2ndly that I am a sound and thorough politician. 3rd that I can afford to attend to my parliamentary duties.[37]

William George would have been relieved to know that he proposed to attain his third objective by working at his 'business well, so as to build up a good practice'. In the event – glamorous cases aside – securing his financial base was left to his most faithful friend.

Perhaps it was the prospect of marriage – the wedding was then six months away – as well as a real hope of the Liberal nomination, which made Lloyd George work methodically to secure the Caernarvon candidature. Whatever the reason, he concentrated his public speaking on the two issues which most exercised Welsh Liberals – temperance and tithes. He edged away from public association with the Welsh Land League, which was still treated with suspicion by respectable Liberals, but kept a close association with Gee by helping to draft the new constitution for the Libertarian Society and by inviting him to speak in Criccieth in May 1888.[38]

He began to widen his circle of political friends. It was Tom Ellis, for whom he had 'stood aside' at Harlech, who introduced him to David R. Daniel, a journalist who, for a while, became a devoted acolyte. Daniel found Lloyd George a 'very pleasant young man, clever at his work as a solicitor and becoming fast a power among the radicals of Lleyn. Just the man to fight the beefy parsons in these parts.'*[39] In January 1888, Daniel joined with Lloyd George in the foundation of a Welsh-language newspaper, *Udgorn Rhyddid* ('Trumpet of Freedom') – which, both surprisingly and dangerously, was described in letters soliciting support as 'altogether socialist and nationalist'.[40] It came to very little and Lloyd George's enthusiasm soon cooled.

Daniel's importance was his ability to portray Lloyd George as more than a young firebrand with unreliable views on Home Rule for Ireland. To obtain the Caernarvon nomination he had to secure the support of the 'more English' northern towns – Caernarvon itself, Bangor and Conway – as well as the boroughs of Criccieth, Pwllheli, Portmadoc and Nevin in the 'entirely Welsh' south of the district. A letter to Daniel, dated 5 July 1888, came straight to the point. 'You have heard that the Caernarvon Boroughs have taken up my candidature . . . spontaneous combustion at a meeting of the Pwllheli Liberal Association . . . Now you have done your part in helping me into this . . . are you prepared to help me in the drag . . .?'[41] He needed a spirited letter to the *Caernarvon and Denbigh Herald* describing him as 'a Welsh nationalist of the Ellis type'. Daniel duly obliged.

The *Liverpool Mercury*, examining the state of Liberal politics, judged

---

*In a debate, a curate from the Lleyn District had claimed that a reduction in tithes would impoverish the clergy. Lloyd George had demolished him.

that 'no Welsh constituency seems to have greater difficulty in finding a suitable candidate than Caernarvon Boroughs', a constituency which was 'apathetic in the faces of difficulty'. The solution to both problems was, in the opinion of the papers, the nomination of David Lloyd George, 'a sound politician and able speaker and popular in the south of the parliamentary division'.[42] The Bangor Liberals accepted the *Mercury's* advice – in Lloyd George's absence on an excursion to Glasgow with his new wife. Told of his success by telegram, he wrote to Uncle Lloyd in triumph. 'Despite all the machinations of my enemies, I shall succeed. I am now sailing with the wind and they against it.'[43]

Caernarvon itself and Conway had still to choose and when, in October, Caernarvon postponed its consideration of the candidates, there was a moment of depression. The delay was the work of Liberals who wanted more time to rally their forces against Lloyd George. He spent the intervening weeks wooing the undecided. William Jones, a Bangor pork butcher, received a particularly obsequious letter congratulating him on a speech that he had made at a temperance rally.[44]

By the date of the selection meeting – 3 January 1889 – the Llanfrothen burial case had made his candidature virtually irresistible. Clement Higgins QC withdrew from consideration leaving Professor Johnson of Trinity College, Dublin, and the Reverend Lloyd Jones of Rhyl as Lloyd George's only competition on the day. Immediately on his arrival at the Caernarvon hall where the decision was to be made, he revealed his anxiety by complaining that a speech limited to fifteen minutes would not allow him fully to express his views. He won easily, but victory did not dim the memory of earlier anxieties. 'Selection last thing on programme so I had to wait upstairs for 2 hours.' However, he had an 'excellent reception. Felt position keenly. Could not speak with much verve.'[45]

The next general election was still three years away. So, wisely, he wrote for advice on campaigning to Francis Scharnhorst – the organiser of the all-conquering Birmingham Liberal caucus – who, despite his close association with Joseph Chamberlain, had remained true to Gladstone and Home Rule. Scharnhorst told him to work on the register of electors by adding the names of eligible Liberals who were not included and making himself known to those who were. His legal practice was used to increase both his fame and notoriety. On 15 February 1889, the birth of his son, Richard, provided the respectability of parenthood.

February 1889 was also the month in which county council

elections – conducted under the provisions of C.T. Richie's reforming Local Government Act – were held. Lloyd George was sufficiently well known, admired and popular to be invited to stand. He declined nomination – an indication of the lack of interest in local government which distinguished him from many Welsh radicals. But he campaigned throughout Caernarvonshire – in particular for candidates who had supported his parliamentary nomination. The result of his efforts was widespread popularity throughout the Liberal Party in the county and appointment to the Aldermanic Bench. H. C. Raikes, a Conservative Member of Parliament, said that 'the election of a boy alderman was only paralleled by the mediaeval scandal of child cardinals'.[46] The title 'boy alderman' stuck – much to Lloyd George's advantage.

There was no question of his deferring to elected members of the council. At his first meeting he moved a resolution which committed the authority to petition Parliament in support of leasehold enfranchisement. It was carried by thirty-six votes to seven. He was, however, less successful in his attempts at political reorganisation. There were, in effect, two Liberal Parties in Wales. The North and the South supported different policies and were often more critical of each other than they were of the Tories. In October 1889, at a meeting of the North Wales Liberal Federation in Caernarvon, he supported a resolution – which he had inspired, but chosen not to propose – that a Welsh National League should be established. It was defeated, with Thomas Gee voting against. His brash self-confidence survived. At the Cardiff meeting of the South Wales Federation the following February, he moved a resolution supporting Home Rule for Wales.

There were Welsh constituencies – including the Caernarvon Boroughs – in which the policy would have lost votes. And Lloyd George certainly had no enthusiasm for Home Rule. But the general election was two years away and it seemed the best issue with which to unite all Welsh Liberals. Perhaps he would have continued his approach march – courting publicity by supporting controversial causes and attempting to improve the party's organisation – into 1890. But on 19 March 1890, Edmund Swetenham QC, the Tory Member of Parliament for the Caernarvon Boroughs, collapsed and died. Margaret Lloyd George broke the news of a by-election to her husband with a deadening lack of enthusiasm.

We had planned to go to Caernarvon for the day. My husband had gone to his office in Portmadoc and I was to join him on the train in Criccieth. It was a fine day, I remember, and I thought that we should have a really enjoyable time. When I got to the station I was handed a telegram addressed to Lloyd George and, thinking it might be for me, I opened it. All it said was 'Swetenham died last night.'[47]

Her description of what followed confirms that she was certainly reluctant, probably unwilling and possibly temperamentally unable to join in her husband's great adventure. 'I knew what it meant. The sunshine seemed to have gone from the day . . . We decided to go to Caernarvon but we had a miserable day. The shadow of the coming election spoilt everything.'[48]

Lloyd George's first task was to write an election address. His brother helped with the work – including the suggestion that it should include a call to arms which, although it embodied the candidate's fighting spirit, would, in a modern election, be regarded as more likely to lose votes than to win them. 'You have the opportunity of blotting out the stain which has, for the last four years, tarnished your parliamentary record.'[49]

The county, he then declared, was 'sick and tired of Mr Balfour's baton and bayonet rule in Ireland' and longed for 'Mr Gladstone's noble alternative'. It promised 'the Disestablishment and Disendowment of the English Church in Wales . . . improvement in the condition of Tenant Farmers and labourers . . . the Enfranchisement of leaseholders . . . the removal in our midst of the disastrous temptations to strong drink . . . One Man, One Vote. A Free Breakfast Table' (which meant no import duties on wheat) and 'Graduated Taxation'.[50] A local Methodist paid Lloyd George's election expenses, thus sparing him the indignity of asking the local party to raise the money.

The Welsh Conservative Party wrote to Gladstone asking if he endorsed so ambitious a programme and received an elegantly dismissive reply. He was not at all surprised by the candidate's 'sanguine anticipations' but he would be astonished if the constituency were to return to Westminster 'a gentleman who, whether Tory or Dissentient, would vote against the claim that Wales is now justly making'.[51]

According to his elder son – writing years later – the local Liberal leadership was less horrified by Lloyd George's uninhibited radicalism than by the discovery that he had 'fathered a child on [sic] a very charming widow in Caernarvon', first known as 'Mrs J' and then identified as yet another Jones.[52] Had her pregnancy become public knowledge the result would have been guaranteed defeat for their chosen candidate and anyone who replaced him. Richard Lloyd George regarded his constantly betrayed mother as a saint and martyr and described his father's infidelities with malevolent delight. But it is unlikely that he invented the whole story. Indeed one consequence of the indiscretion probably contributed to his anger. Richard was always short of money and received so much help in Lloyd George's lifetime that he was disinherited. Yet because of the 'annuity obtained for the [wronged] lady at a considerable cost' as the guarantee of her silence, the man he called his 'half brother . . . had most of the burdens of the world cared for even before he entered into it'.[53] No other evidence supports the claim that Lloyd George fathered Mrs Jones's baby. But many other witnesses confirm that to have done so was wholly consistent with his behaviour. Lloyd George's daughter, Lady Olwen Carey Evans, wrote that her father 'started having affairs with other women very soon after my parents were married'.[54] Whenever they began, they were a feature of his life for the next forty years. The possibilities, though not the certainty, of other illegitimate children are documented in work from less prejudiced sources than Richard Lloyd George. Yet – barely believably – none of the affairs significantly impeded the irresistible rise to glory which began in 1890.

Like all candidates, Lloyd George had to reconcile conflicting demands from his own supporters. Cymru Fydd ('Wales to Be') denounced 'screamers in Welsh politics' who 'scream about land laws, tithes, education and especially Welsh Home Rule'. Clearly the editor had Lloyd George in mind when he condemned 'men of little knowledge and shallow convictions who sought principally to draw attention to themselves'. The paper's hero was Tom Ellis – Lloyd George's new friend. It supported many of the reforms which the 'screamers' demanded but believed that such 'blessings would be attained by constant and steady effort, not screaming'. Yet the Reverend Evan Jones, pastor of the Calvinistic Methodist chapel in Caernarvon, complained that the Liberals' standard-bearer did not shout loudly enough. He interrupted a by-election meeting with the demand that Lloyd George promise not to support Irish Home Rule until he had received a firm promise from Gladstone himself that the Welsh Church would be disestablished.

Fortunately for Lloyd George, the Conservative candidate was Squire Ellis-Nanney of Llanystumdwy, one of the distinguished guests at the church school open day who had witnessed the protest against the

imposition of Anglican observances on Nonconformist boys. He had
accepted the nomination with reluctance and left most of the campaigning to visiting speakers. It was one of them, Sir John Puleston MP,
who attempted to damage Lloyd George with what became a famous
reference to his humble origins. 'The intelligence, the magnificent
intellect of Mr George does not confine him within the narrow limits
of the small Principality of which we are so proud. His ideas are as
boundless as the Empire itself.'[55] The reply which it evoked was contained in the first of David Lloyd George's great political speeches.

> I see that one qualification Mr Nanney possesses . . . is that he is a
> man of wealth, and that the great disqualification in my case is that
> I am possessed of none . . . I once heard a man wildly declaiming
> against Mr Tom Ellis as a Parliamentary representative but, accord-
> ing to that man, Mr Ellis' disqualification was that he had been
> brought up in a cottage. The Tories have not yet realised that the
> day of the cottage-bred man has at last dawned.[56]

Three days before the votes were cast, Lloyd George feared that 'the
Bangor people are not working half as systematically as they ought . . .
I am', he told his wife, 'half inclined to go fishing in the Seiont whilst
the count is on.'[57] But on 11 April – like innumerable other candidates
in marginal seats before and since – he put on a calm, as well as brave,
face as he watched the ballot spread out in apparently equal numbers for
him and his opponent. After a recount he won with a majority of
eighteen votes. He remained the Member of Parliament for the
Caernarvon Boroughs for the next fifty-five years.

A telegram to Uncle Lloyd announced that he had 'triumphed
against enormous influences', would be 'home by six' and that his supporters must not hire a band 'as rumoured to be illegal'. And he added,
'Ask Maggie down.'[58] She came, weeping 'tears of regret for ending her
hopes of a quiet untroubled life in the country'.[59] In old age she
claimed that in 1888, she had 'thought [she] was marrying a
Caernarvonshire lawyer' rather than a politician.[60] But by the time
they met, he had no doubt where his future lay. Indeed he had warned
her that her husband's political ambition must transcend all other considerations. And so it did for the rest of his life.

CHAPTER 4

A FAILURE IN THE HOUSE

David Lloyd George arrived at the House of Commons surrounded by all the partisan rejoicing that is afforded to by-election winners and closely followed by the denigration which Parliament heaps on young men in a hurry. He was met at Euston Station by a 'small landau' which belonged to Alfred Davies, a wealthy London Welshman and himself a Liberal parliamentary candidate. J. T. Roberts, Lloyd George's election agent, travelled to London 'for the express purpose of seeing the reception' and, to Lloyd George's chagrin, 'seemed to feel that he came in, somehow, for a portion of the cheer'.[1] The new Member was introduced to the Speaker by Arthur Acland (the radical MP for Rotherham) and Stuart Rendel, the Leader of the Welsh Liberals. The support of both his sponsors was to prove invaluable during the turbulent days which lay ahead, and it established the pattern of personal relationships which was to characterise his whole political life — instant and boundless devotion from some, matched by immediate and limitless hatred from others.

Wisely, he chose not to make an early maiden speech. On 16 May 1890, a month after he took his seat, he wrote to Uncle Lloyd to explain his continued reticence. 'I shan't speak in the House this side Whitsuntide holidays. Better not to appear too eager. Get a good opportunity and make the best of it — that's the point.'[2] He asked a question on leasehold reform on 24 April, but the good opportunity for a speech did not arise until 13 June. But, although he remained virtually silent in the Commons chamber, he was remarkably vocal outside it and — because his reputation as an orator had preceded him — was more in demand than a new and young Member had a right to expect.

Yet he was not content. His early letters to his wife in Wales were a strange mixture of self-congratulation and self-pity. An account of a meeting on 16 May at Norwood in south London complained that the journalist who reported his speech for the *Banner and Times of Wales* 'knew in his heart of hearts that it was a success from an oratorical point of view, [but] he hasn't the grace to say so'. Then came the defiant reassurance. 'Your David will get on despite them.'[3] The self-congratulation was the expression of genuine belief. Lloyd George knew that, most often, his speeches outside the House of Commons were received with rapture, and he described each triumph in order to rejoice in his own success, not to reassure himself that he had succeeded. But he felt neither awe nor affection for what, four years earlier, he had called the 'House of Snobs', and the metropolitan Members of Parliament who had heard that Lloyd George 'had the gift of the hwyl' felt no affection for him. They had expected 'to see something resembling a Druid appear on the floor of the House of Commons' and were surprised 'to behold a slim, well-groomed young lawyer in a frock coat and with side-whiskers'[4] who, far from behaving with provincial deference, openly expressed his antagonism to men whose rank and status depended on blood and birth. David Lloyd George wore his humble beginnings like a badge of honour.

It is easy to understand why the older and more respectable Liberal MPs wanted to 'snub and sit upon' Lloyd George.[5] He had arrived at the House of Commons with a reputation for dubious loyalty and irresponsible opinions as well as fiery speeches. He had openly sympathised with Joseph Chamberlain's opposition to Gladstone's Irish policy and criticised the organisation of the Welsh Liberal Party in the same language in which he denounced the payment of tithes to the Established Church. The existence of two Welsh Liberal Federations – one from the North, the other from the South – had made the party 'a kind of Punch and Judy exhibition . . . the butt of our old foe's ridicule and not the object of his terror'.[6] In any circumstances the Liberal establishment would have been offended by the provocative expression of those contentious opinions. When they were articulated by a twenty-seven-year-old solicitor who had just fought his first parliamentary election, they became intolerable. His offence was compounded by his conscious decision to be semi-detached from the Liberal leadership. The biographical note which he sent to Dodd's *Parliamentary Companion* for 1890–1 was gratuitously selective. 'Welsh Nationalist, supporting Home Rule, temperance, disestablishment and other items in the programme of the advanced Liberals.'

It was on those subjects that he spoke in the country. On 7 May, Lloyd George addressed a meeting of the Liberation Society in the Metropolitan Tabernacle. Henry Campbell-Bannerman – already a Liberal grandee and destined to lead the first Cabinet in which Lloyd George served – was in the chair. Lloyd George, to his disgust, was the last in a long list of speakers but, by his own account, he overcame that handicap. 'I started very nervous and not intending to hold out more than 10 or 15 minutes but I must have spoken for ¾ of an hour. I roused the audience to such a pitch of enthusiasm that they would hardly allow me to proceed and when I left they rose to their feet and flourished their hats . . . The most profuse compliments were lavished upon my eloquence.'[7] His attack on the Established Church provoked an angry letter of complaint from A. G. Edwards, Bishop of St Asaph (the episcopal seat of which was in North Wales). An even greater triumph was less than a month away.

In the Free Trade Hall in Manchester on 4 June he denounced the proposal – included in the Budget presented to Parliament on the day he took his seat – to compensate publicans when their premises were closed down for reasons of public policy. His own account of the response to his speech can be described only as ecstatic. 'When I sat down, there came a sight which I shall never forget – the whole dense and immense audience seemed for a moment stunned but, recovering, they sprang up as one man and flung hats, handkerchiefs, sticks, hands – anything they could get hold of . . . I was overwhelmed with congratulation.'[8] The *Cambrian News* shared the rapture. The waving of hats and hands was described as 'very much akin to madness' and he was 'overwhelmed by cries of "go on" and a voice from the gallery "we will stop with thee all night my boy . . ." It is to be regretted that Wales does not send more of these young men to represent her in Parliament.'[9]

Neither Lloyd George's mellifluous voice nor his aggressive speaking style changed significantly during the twenty years in which he rose from backbencher to Prime Minister. The contents of his speeches were almost entirely destructive. Demolition of his opponents' arguments was rarely followed by the construction of something to put in their place. There was never a suggestion of an underlying ideology or philosophical principle – both of which were alien to his nature. Because he understood the excitement that personalised assaults caused, he rarely failed to name the men he held responsible for the scandals which he exposed. Ridicule and righteous indignation came hard upon each other's heels. But he was never the law-giver, handing down the tablets from on high. Lloyd George and his audience were one – outsiders to a man. 'Caernarvon District', wrote *The Times* – referring not to the constituency but to its Member of Parliament – 'has the misdeeds of the establishment much more at heart than the misdeeds of Mr Balfour.'[10]

Although his technique was far less effective in the House of Commons, his maiden speech, made during a debate on the Local Taxation Bill on 13 June 1890, was well received. Arthur Acland had moved the amendment which would deny publicans compensation for the closure of their premises. The new Member for the Caernarvon Boroughs revisited the subject of his Manchester triumph. Despite the convention that maiden speeches avoid controversy, he mounted an assault on the licensed trade in general and attacked Lord Randolph Churchill and Joseph Chamberlain by name. Lord Randolph had a vicarious interest in the debate. He had introduced the original bill in what his son, Winston Churchill, was to call 'the last great speech which he made in the House of Commons'.[11] The slighting reference to Chamberlain was entirely gratuitous. Lloyd George had decided that he would be David to the two Goliaths. The tactic, like the words he used, had been carefully thought out. According to his brother William, even at school he had to fight 'the enemy when [he] was at his strongest, thus ensuring that victory, if secured, would be complete and final'.[12]

Randolph Churchill was described as supporting 'at best a kind of mushroom teetotalism which grew, no-one knows why or where, and has disappeared, where no-one exactly knows', and Chamberlain – the hope and hero of Nonconformity – was said to have 'recently entertained a company of brewers and so strong apparently was [his] view in favour of compensation that he expressed great surprise that it should have been thought necessary to approach him on the subject'. It all led up to a carefully prepared climax. 'The noble lord and the right honourable gentleman are political contortionists who can perform the great trick of planting their feet in one direction and setting their faces in another.'[13]

The following day he wrote to tell his wife that he had been 'overwhelmed with congratulations' and there was 'hardly a London Liberal paper or even a provincial paper which does not say something commendatory about it'.[14] On the morning of his maiden speech, he had written a letter home which did not even mention that he was about to make his parliamentary debut. While he was waiting – and, if he were like any other House of Commons virgin, worrying – he defended himself against his wife's complaint that a Sunday visit to Kew Gardens confirmed that he put pleasures before prayers. It leaves no doubt about why he was reluctant to go home to Wales.

> There is a great deal of difference between the temptation to leave your work for the pleasure of being cramped up in a suffocating malodorous chapel listening to some superstitions I have heard a thousand times before and, on the other hand, the temptation to have a pleasant ride on the river in the fresh air with a terminus at one of the loveliest gardens in Europe.[15]

According to House of Commons folklore, a good maiden speech is usually followed by a flop. Lloyd George defied precedent. When he spoke a second time – on a motion to reduce Miscellaneous Advances – he was destructive, offensive to authority and totally in command. He was also determined to appeal to an audience outside Westminster. The 'advances' which he chose to oppose were a grant of £439 towards the cost of the installation of Prince Henry of Hanover as a Knight of the Garter and £2769 'equipage money' to repay expenses incurred by the Lord Lieutenant of Ireland. The speech included characteristic insults. 'What service', he asked, 'has Prince Henry of Prussia ever rendered this country? He has not yet rendered any service to his own.' The Lord Lieutenant was dismissed as 'a man in buttons who wears silk stockings and has a coat of arms on his carriage'. The knockabout was followed by passages of substance about the plight of the poor.[16] They were the mark of the class warrior, which was so clear that Queen Victoria sent Gladstone a message of complaint.

Lloyd George's class antagonism was not a political pose. Nor was it the result of very profound views about the nature of society. It was a reflection of what he thought about himself. When he was Chancellor of the Exchequer – and might have been thought to be reconciled to membership of the establishment – he told D. R. Daniel, 'I never had a hand stretched to me from above – but I've had hundreds of zealous and faithful friends, pushing me from behind.'[17] He came from, and was the champion of, the deserving poor. His second House of Commons speech was made on behalf of the 'thousands of hard-working, thrifty people [who] are living a life of hopeless, ceaseless toil'. It was because of them that he rejected the proposal 'to spend hundreds decorating a foreign Prince and thousands in adorning a mere supernumerary'. He spoke as a reformer, not a revolutionary. 'I do not believe that this gorgeousness and ostentation of wealth is necessary to maintain the Constitution. On the contrary, I think it does far more to repress than to promote sentiments of loyalty.'[18]

On the night before his second House of Commons speech, Lloyd George – anticipating that he would be accused, at best, of discourtesy to the throne and court – wrote in his diary, 'I may lose much influence. These MPs are so frightfully decorous and respectful. My audience is the country.'[19] At the time, he almost certainly meant Wales. But his horizons were beginning to expand. The reference, in his second speech, to the government's report on the conditions of employment in sweated industries was the first indication that he was becoming less concerned with Welsh nationhood than with the continued division of Great Britain into two nations.

Despite the success of his first two speeches, the 'Welsh Notes' in the *Manchester Guardian*, described the Member for Caernarvon Boroughs as a 'failure in the House and completely eclipsed by Sam Evans', another young Welsh MP.[20] L. A. Atherley-Jones (a Liberal of an older generation who sat for North West Durham) wrote in his memoirs that Lloyd George's 'early speeches were, with a thin thread of argument, incoherent declamations: so much so . . . that, according to what a press gallery reporter told me, they required dressing-up before they were fit for publication'.[21] The criticism – some of it the expression of resentment towards a young and 'unclubable' upstart – hurt. A month after his election, Lloyd George asked his wife to send him a copy of the *Banner and Times of Wales*, the leading Welsh-language weekly. He understood that Vincent Evans, one of its columnists, had been critical 'in his superior fashion'. The offender had already been chastised. 'I told him last night to his face [that] he assiduously cracked up Tom Ellis and Ellis Griffith [two other Welsh MPs] and ran down everyone else in their way.'[22] That was not the way to win friends in the press gallery, but Lloyd George was too offended to care.

During the autumn of 1890, Lloyd George spoke 'in the country' on ten occasions. On 20 September, having travelled north to St Helens, he shared a platform with John Morley. He had become enough of a 'figure' to act as supporting speaker to a Liberal grandee. His speech began with a conventional attack on Arthur Balfour's repression of Ireland. But, after condemning the English and Scottish landowners in the province, he went on to denounce 'the same miserable minority in Wales who, because of a certain class and a certain religion, think that they have the right to monopolize the resources of the soil and think that they have the right to monopolize the education of the country'. Carried away by his own eloquence, he ended with a peroration which was absolute gibberish. Landlords were, as a class, corrupt. 'And more than that to set their lords and baronets to defame and revile my country in the ears of Royalty.'[23] Nevertheless the audience rose to their feet and cheered.

Even if he could have enjoyed the comforts of home and family, Lloyd George would have spent his evenings addressing enraptured public meetings. But, with his wife in Wales, the delights of domesticity were not available to him. After his arrival in London he had lived in a succession of unsatisfactory lodgings and flats, beginning with rooms in Acton in west London which were lent or rented to him by Alfred Davies. After a month or two, and an experiment with life at the National Liberal Club, he leased a set of rooms in Verulam Buildings, Gray's Inn, and wrote to Margaret what, for him, was a letter of unusual sympathy and understanding.* 'With a porter at the gate and two housekeepers on the premises and your own chambers double-doored and windows iron bolted, you surely ought to feel secure until your husband comes home.'[24] Margaret responded with a visit two weeks later. But circumstances conspired to increase her determination to remain in Wales. In August 1890, after a difficult pregnancy, she gave birth to a daughter, Mair Eluned. Throughout the summer Lloyd George's letters home referred, time after time, to his *need* for Margaret to be in London. In June, he told her, 'I can't stand this solitude much longer.'[25] In July – after asserting that 'next year you must be up with me altogether' – he claimed that he 'never felt satisfied about going to any big meeting' until he had 'submitted his speech for her approval'.[26] That was nonsense, but the bogus confession of insecurity was intended to reinforce his plea for her to join him. It was an unreasonable demand to make on a woman in the last weeks of pregnancy. And what hope there was of her making her home in London after the birth was extinguished when her father, at last able to keep the promise which he had made before her wedding, built a pair of semi-detached houses on the Portmadoc Road in Criccieth – Llys Owen for him and his wife and Bryn Awel for his daughter and son-in-law. To Margaret, the attraction of a house of her own in Wales was irresistible. So, after the summer of

---

*A full list of properties – rented, bought or received as gifts during a nomadic life – appears in Appendix I.

1890, the relationship changed. He would never again write of 'Maggie ... lying on the hearth waiting for me'.[27] Margaret Lloyd George became an occasional wife and a constant, if often distant, friend while her husband took his pleasures where he could.

Rich Welshmen living in the capital were more than willing to offer hospitality to a young and amusing compatriot whose name regularly appeared in the national papers. Lloyd George accepted their invitations but retained a healthy contempt for their lifestyle. He described them to Margaret in language which cannot have persuaded her that she was missing very much by living in Criccieth. 'A young Welshman who [kept] a drapery establishment in Oxford Street' was, together with his wife, one of the first men of substance to entertain Lloyd George. He was D. H. Evans, 'a light-headed feather-brained fellow with some good nature and much practical shrewdness. She is purse proud and consequently contemptible. We [MPs] are fit company for a beautified draper's wife but I despised her from the moment she talked about the Welsh Society in London being led by drapers' assistants.'[28] That was typical of the way in which Lloyd George happily bit the hand that fed him dinner. He accepted the favours, but his views remained his own.

Lloyd George's complaint that Gladstone would never give Wales the Home Rule which he was offering to Ireland was half-hearted. He did not want a separate parliament in Cardiff or Caernarvon. His real objection to Gladstone's obsession was the obstacle which it provided to moving forward on any of the issues which he held dear – temperance, tithes and disestablishment. He was flattered by the lobby rumours that the Grand Old Man had expressed admiration of his maiden speech and, during his early months in Parliament, awestruck by the Prime Minister's patrician eloquence.[29] But Gladstone was not a radical and Lloyd George was.

It was not Lloyd George's habit to counterfeit respect for authority. But he was some years into his ministerial career before his true opinion of Gladstone was recorded. By then he was categoric. 'Gladstone was always a Tory at heart. He belonged to the worst section of the middle classes – that section which thinks itself aristocratic.'[30] When his friend George (by then Lord) Riddell asked him to be frank about the old hero, he replied, 'I did not like him very much.'[31] The dislike was more political than personal. But the first meeting did nothing to improve an inevitably distant relationship.

On 29 April 1890 – a little less than three weeks after the Caernarvon by-election – members of the Calvinistic Methodists of Criccieth set out on a day excursion to Hawarden, Gladstone's home on the Welsh–English border. Their new Member of Parliament went with them. After a tour of the gardens, a favoured few of the pilgrims – including Lloyd George – were invited into the house for conversation with the Grand Old Man himself. The new Member of Parliament (aged twenty-seven) took the opportunity to tell the Prime Minister (aged eighty-one) that he must advocate Welsh disestablishment with more vigour. Gladstone replied that the North Wales Liberal Federation would be unwise to demand that their MPs threaten to vote against Irish Home Rule until Welsh grievances were remedied. He added that many factors – including the presence of Welsh bishops in the House of Lords – complicated the position. Lloyd George, resenting the implication that – unlike Scotland – Wales was a natural and historic member of the Anglican Communion, disputed the notion with a force which annoyed his host. So Gladstone crushed his guest by asking – with no clear relevance – if he knew how many Nonconformist chapels there were in Wales in 1742. Of course, Lloyd George did not. Gladstone did. It was 162. There the argument ended.[32]

Throughout the summer of 1890, Lloyd George's speeches invariably referred, in passing, to the necessity of pressing ahead with Home Rule – not because the cause was just, but in order to remove the 'road block' which was an obstacle to other legislation. He would not have chosen to mount 'the fiery chariot' in the first place and he regretted that the Liberals who remained true to Gladstone, after Joseph Chamberlain's defection in 1886, had not tried to prevent the 'old man in a hurry' from riding helter-skelter to disaster. 'While the action of the Welsh people then was noble and generous, it would have been far better for them if they had declined to support him in a course which would lead to the disruption of the party and the consequent loss of disestablishment for a long time.'[33]

On 17 November 1890, the cause of Irish Home Rule was dealt a crippling, some believed fatal, blow. Captain William O'Shea was granted a divorce on the grounds of his wife's adultery with Charles Stewart Parnell, the leader of the Irish Party. Less than two years before, a Special Commission had absolved Parnell of the charge that he supported the Fenians who had murdered Lord Frederick Cavendish, the Chief Secretary for Ireland, in Phoenix Park, Dublin – a charge based on letters which were published by *The Times*, although that paper knew, or should have known, that they were forgeries. The vindication had added to Parnell's hero status in Ireland. His supporters gloried in his refusal, during the divorce hearings, to contradict even the most lurid inventions about his conduct. The allegations were made during a trial in open court which was held while the Liberal Party was meeting in Sheffield – surrounded by North of England Nonconformists, some of the most censorious people in the Victorian world.

On 25 November, while the Union of the Hearts – the alliance of assorted Irish Nationalists – was being slowly dissolved in Committee Room 15 of the House of Commons, Lloyd George felt only admiration for the soon-to-be deposed Irish leader's composure. 'The Irish Party is now upstairs discussing Parnell's future. I saw him just now in the tea-room looking calm and self-possessed.'[34] As Parnell lost Irish support, he also lost Lloyd George's sympathy. Two days later his judgement was, at least by implication, censorious. 'Everyone is preoccupied with Parnell. Well it appears that the fellow is brazening it out.'[35] On 28 November, he had lost all respect for a 'base selfish fellow' even though, on 3 December – while the Irish Party was still agonising about its future – he was again impressed by a demeanour which was as 'cool and defiant as ever'.[36] By then, he had no doubt that the Irish leader was 'a bad lot' – not because he had broken the seventh commandment, but because his self-indulgence had undermined the cause which he championed.[37] 'If Parnell sticks and his party stick to him, it is generally conceded that Home Rule is done for.'[38] Gladstone – the most upright of politicians, who *Punch* believed would 'have been a better politician had he been a worse man' – required Parnell's resignation for the same reason. Twenty years later, Lloyd George told Frances Stevenson – at the beginning of their lifelong relationship – that 'no man has the right to imperil his party and its objectives for the sake of a woman'.[39] And – in an act of breathtaking insensitivity – gave her a biography of Kathleen O'Shea to prove his point.

The fall of Parnell was assumed by both Gladstone's friends and foes to mark the end of his attempts to impose Irish Home Rule on a reluctant party and recalcitrant Parliament. That judgement underestimated the messianic determination of the octogenarian Prime Minister. But a group of young Welsh Liberals – led in fact if not form by Lloyd George – sought to fill what they believed to be the political vacuum with policies which had been overlooked for years. They would fight for Wales as the Irish Party fought for Ireland – obstructing government business until ministers met their demands. By the time the Irish Party split over the Parnell divorce, Lloyd George had already tasted the heady fruit of highly publicised rebellion. There is every indication that he enjoyed the notoriety.

The Tithe (Rent Charge Recovery) Bill had been presented to the House of Commons in 1889 and withdrawn because of lack of both time and support. It was reintroduced in February 1890 in exactly the same form. Tithes were to be made a direct charge on landlords, leaving them with the choice to collect reimbursement from tenants or meet the full cost themselves. A bill that made tithes easier to collect also increased the income which they generated. Radical Nonconformists urged Liberals to vote against it. Lloyd George could not agree. He wanted the tithe not abolished but redirected from Church incumbencies to educational and social projects.

On 5 June 1890, F. S. Stevenson, Member of Parliament for Eye, moved an official Liberal 'instruction' to the standing committee which was to consider the bill. Had it been carried, the committee would have been required to 'provide for the equitable provision of tithes in accordance with the altered conditions of agriculture'. Its effect would have been a reduction in the level of tithes. But the instruction was defeated with Lloyd George and D. A. Thomas (the Member for Merthyr Tydfil) voting against its acceptance. There was a predicable howl of outrage from the Welsh Nonconformist press.

Lloyd George wrote, explaining his attitude, to the chairman of the Caernarvon District Liberal Association. He was committed 'to a policy of nationalising the tithe [and] strongly objected to any suggestion which will result in the frittering away of this valuable national endowment. The notion that any part of the savings would be passed along to the tenants is fanciful.'[40] When the complaints continued, he insisted that his policy would 'add twenty-five percent to the value of the tithe – no mean thing by the time it is nationalised'.[41] In fact, he had no idea of the reduction in revenue which the instruction would have brought about. But by voting against the party whip and justifying his rebellion with a coherent argument, he had made an early declaration of independence. When the Welsh Liberals thought of harassing their own leadership, Lloyd George was happy to set the pace.

The Tithe Bill was given a second reading in a single day of parliamentary time. It was then that Lloyd George and three other Welsh Members – Sam Evans, Tom Ellis and Wynford Philips – took over the role of the Irish Party and began the campaign of obstruction and harassment. The best and easiest way of wasting time – what guerrilla tactics in Parliament usually amount to – was to move numerous amendments when bills were discussed 'in committee of the whole House' and to debate them at great length. The four insurgents had no hope, or intention, of 'improving' the bills, the normal purpose of amendments. Lloyd George wrote to Thomas Gee on 2 February 1891, 'Of course we shall be defeated, but by these discussions we manage to keep the pot boiling and the Liberal Party is thereby awakened to the fact that Welsh questions are very useful – quite as useful as Irish ones – to hurl at the government.'[42]

The amendments usually reflected the honest convictions of the men who moved them. Lloyd George proposed that appeals against tithe valuations should be heard in the county courts – not by the Land Commissioners, whose objectivity he doubted – and that defendants in criminal proceedings which arose from the eventual act should have the right to trial by jury. Both proposals were defeated. But the voice of Wales was heard in the land, even though Liberals (no less than Tories) were infuriated by the hours of speeches which examined every issue from the perspective of the principality.

The Education Bill, introduced in June, provided the perfect opportunity for a protracted display of both Nonconformist principles and political prejudices. The Salisbury government proposed to abolish fees in both church and board schools and, at the same time, end the payment-by-results calculation of teachers' salaries. The bill's ostensible purpose, and its undoubted result, was the extension of free elementary education. But Liberals suspected that the real motive was the preemption of their party's plan to abolish fees in board schools, reduce state aid to church schools and watch while denominational education became increasingly beyond the means of most families. A change of government seemed likely. In six years, twenty seats, previously held by Salisbury's Tories, had been lost to Liberals in by-elections.

Lloyd George instinctively accepted the unworthy interpretation of the government's motives. The entrenchment of denominational education – perhaps in schools less broad-minded than the one which he attended – would allow the Church of England to continue imposing its sectarian views on Methodist and Baptist children through teachers whose salaries would be paid by Nonconformist taxpayers. In the second reading debate he 'urged the government to take the opportunity to give free education in a generous form, free from denominational trammels and worthy of its name'.[43] His plea being ignored, he moved on to amendments which would achieve his objective. One aimed at preventing school managers from limiting the appointment of teachers to applicants of a specified denomination. Another, if passed, would have required government grants to be used for the extension of technical education rather than the eventual reduction of fees. Both were lost.

While the guerrilla war was being waged in the House of Commons, Lloyd George continued to make speeches in the country which reflected the convictions which became the bedrock of his politics. He believed that religious instruction should be provided only outside normal school hours and he was equally convinced of the injustice of tithes to pay for the upkeep of the Church of England and its clergy. But it was poverty and the land which increasingly concerned him. He told a meeting at Bangor on 21 May 1891, 'One out of every twenty of the population is on parish relief.' Yet there were 'noblemen and squires enjoying riches which they are at their wits' end to know how to squander and commanding such amplitude of resources that they are running to waste for want of use'.[44] And often – sin worse than all other sins – their wealth was unearned.

> As the law stands at present, a landlord may let his land for building purposes, charge a ground rent ten times the agricultural value of that land and at the end of sixty years take possession of land, buildings and all. Yet although the local rates are being used to improve his property by drainage, gas, street improvements and in other ways, he does not contribute a penny towards the expenditure. The whole of the expenditure, so far as the land is concerned, falls on the poor householder who, after paying heavy rates and extortionate ground rents, has to surrender all the fruits of his labour to a landlord who does nothing.[45]

Before the end of the year, taxation of land values was to become official Liberal Party policy – one of the ragbag of promises included in what came to be called the Newcastle Programme. John Morley was one of the architects of what amounted to a manifesto. He was careful not to overstate either its intrinsic merits or the party leader's enthusiasm for what it proposed. All he claimed was that Gladstone 'gave his blessing to the various measures'. Loyalty prevented him from adding 'without enthusiasm and only because the first item on the long agenda was Irish Home Rule'. The Newcastle Programme is sometimes described as the Liberal Party's formal acceptance of a radical social programme – a switch in direction which it was said was made possible by the departure of the Marquis of Hartington and the other Whig grandees. Morley offers a more pragmatic explanation – a view which

Lloyd George endorsed and supported. 'After five years of a pretty exclusive devotion to the Irish case, to pass by the British case and its various demands for an indefinite time longer would have been absurd.'[46] The list of Newcastle Programme objectives began with Irish Home Rule. But the disestablishment of the Church in both Wales and Scotland came second. Only slightly lower in order of priority were the taxation of land values, local options for licensing laws and the abolition of 'entails' which restricted the terms of bequests. The catalogue continued with calls for manhood suffrage, triennial Parliaments, house-building in rural areas, the encouragement of smallholdings, the creation of district and parish councils, the payment of MPs and the introduction of an employers' liability law. Fears that the package was insufficiently comprehensive were allayed by hints that there was more to come, possibly including a legal limitation of working hours in heavy industry and mining.

In the week which followed the National Liberal Federation meeting at Newcastle (and the adoption of the programme which took the city's name) the Church of England's Annual Congress convened in Rhyl. David Lloyd George regarded the choice of venue as deliberate provocation and said so. His speech was couched in the uninhibited language of class war.

> The priests of this church arrogantly claim to be the spiritual successors of Peter, the plain, bluff, honest old fisherman. Why, if he could have turned up at the Church Congress held in this town the other day there is not a prelate or prebendary or dean amongst them who would not have shunned him . . . But can you, by any stretch of the imagination, picture Peter coming down to attend the Church Congress in a special train, with a man in buttons dancing about him, carrying a jewelled crosier and marching in an elaborate procession to attend the Congress?

The speech ended with the ultimate reproof. 'The Congress ran two beer booths in its grounds.'[47] A. G. Edwards, the Bishop of St Asaph, defended the Church in a speech which was more reproof than rebuttal. Lloyd George responded to the response – thus ensuring weeks of acrimonious debate.

At the height of the controversy Lloyd George became a father for the second time. Before the birth of Mair Eluned, the Criccieth law firm of Lloyd George and George had supported Betsy George, Polly

George and Richard Lloyd as well as the two brothers, Margaret Lloyd George and her infant son. After August 1890, there was another mouth to feed from the same limited earnings. Six months earlier, as he had rejoiced at his brother's by-election victory, William Lloyd had asked himself 'two practical questions. A. How is D to live there? B. How am I to live down here?'[48] The answer was from hand to mouth. At the end of one of Margaret's rare visits to London she had telegraphed William. 'Dei wishes me to ask you to send him £5 by return please. He has been using some of my money. If he doesn't get it your dear sister cannot return home on Saturday without leaving her husband quite penniless in this great city.'[49] Of course, William responded. He accepted that he was 'the breadwinner for two families'.[50] But he received scant gratitude. 'You are quite right about the practice,' Lloyd George told his wife. 'Will would never have worked it up. He keeps it together very well, but my name helps him materially to do so.'[51] Perhaps so. But without Will there would have been no practice. Fortunately, William George was prepared to make any sacrifice to ensure his brother's success

As William was struggling to balance the family books, his brother was trying to change the ownership of a number of Welsh newspapers. As we have seen, in 1888 he had attempted to alter the political balance of the Welsh press by founding, with D. R. Daniel, *Udgorn Rhyddid*. The paper survived for just a year and then went out of business. His second attempt at ownership was more securely based. The plan was to acquire control of established newspapers. And he recruited as advisers and investors men of influence and considerable wealth. Chief among them were two confusing Thomases. Both were South Wales Liberal MPs. Alfred Thomas, a man of forty and the Member for Glamorganshire East, was the president of the Baptist Union of Wales and enjoyed a private income. D. A. Thomas (also Alfred), who represented Merthyr, was a mine-owner and coal-broker. Both men were to become – for better and for worse – inextricably linked with Lloyd George's political and financial fortunes for the next twenty years.

They were joined in the enterprise by Major Evan Rowland Jones, Liberal candidate for Carmarthen District, proprietor of *Shipping World*, United States Consul for South Wales and a generally dubious character whose attraction included a vicarious association with Abraham Lincoln, Lloyd George's boyhood hero, whose portrait had hung on the Llanystumdwy cottage wall. Jones had fought with the Union Army at Gettysburg. Three of Lloyd George's political friends – Thomas Ellis,

Sam Evans and Herbert Lewis – were asked and agreed to show their support by subscribing small sums of capital. William Abraham – the miners' MP from the Rhondda who was known as 'Mabon', his Druid name – did the same. The result was the acquisition of *Y Genedl Cymreig* (the most popular Welsh-language newspaper) and the creation of the Welsh National Press. The company then bought the *North Wales Observer and Express* (for which the young Lloyd George had written his attack on Lord Salisbury) and *Y Werin*. The two papers joined with Thomas Gee's *Banner and Times of Wales* in the demand that the Liberal leadership – in government or opposition – must pay a price for Welsh support.

For another year, Lloyd George and his friends demonstrated their determination to strike a hard parliamentary bargain. The Clergy Discipline Bill, which received a second reading on 29 April 1891, provided an ideal opportunity to illustrate the power of a destructive minority. Lloyd George's opposition was based on what he must have known was a total misinterpretation of the bill's purpose. It is not, he said, 'the function of the state to attend to matters of spiritual discipline'. The bill was meant to deal with temporal indiscretions and, as such, was heartily welcomed by Gladstone, who intervened in the debate gently to correct his young Honourable friend and lead him back to the path of virtue. Lloyd George was not willing to be led.

Gladstone was so determined to see the bill through that he accepted membership of the standing committee which considered it clause by clause. Undeterred, Lloyd George and three Welsh colleagues battled on – always returning to the point that the real solution to the problem was disestablishment. The committee stage was completed only after its chairman, Henry Campbell-Bannerman (then aspiring to be no more than Speaker of the House of Commons) imposed an arbitrary limitation on the number of speeches each Member could make on individual amendments. Gladstone's mood changed from benevolence to fury. He spoke in every debate until he realised that he was helping to prolong the proceedings. Then, according to Lloyd George, 'He would just sit and shake his head at us when we moved an amendment and glare at us with his fierce eye.'[52] Stuart Rendel, the Welsh Liberals' leader, was near to despair as he saw his fragile coalition 'tumbling down like a pack of cards'.[53] John Morley reacted more robustly. He hoped that Lloyd George would lose his seat in the impending general election.[54]

The new Tory candidate for the Caernarvon Boroughs – Sir John

Puleston, or 'Pleasant Puleston' as he was known – was a far more formidable candidate than Ellis-Nanney had been. He was Welsh by birth, owned a house in Pwllheli and had, for years, been a patron of the National Eisteddfod. A touch of romance was added to an otherwise bland character by the fact that, like Major Jones, he had served in the Union Army during the American Civil War. Soon after his selection as Tory candidate for the Boroughs he had been appointed Constable of Caernarvon Castle, a role which provided great opportunities to entertain the local squirearchy and be reported in local newspapers. It had been Puleston who, during the by-election campaign, had made comments about Lloyd George's pretensions and thereby prepared the way for the speech which heralded the dawn of 'the cottage-bred men'. In preparation for the general election of 1892, Puleston put his soubriquet aside and tried to incriminate his opponent with exaggerated stories about an incident at a Mansion House dinner. Sam Ellis had refused to rise for the loyal toast. Lloyd George – a not very passionate republican – had risen but not drunk. It was enough to allow Puleston to claim that the Queen had been insulted. Lloyd George was physically attacked as he left a rally in the Penrhyn Hall in Bangor and a fireball, made out of wool and paraffin, set light to Margaret's dress.[55] At least – thanks to Gladstone's linguistic agility – Conservative attempts to exploit his dispute with the Liberal Party's candidate for the Caernarvon Boroughs failed. Asked to repudiate Lloyd George's extremism, Gladstone replied that he had 'no opinion of the conduct of Mr Lloyd George and no title to give one' and added that had he been 'an elector of Caernarvon Boroughs I should vote against Sir J Puleston'.[56]

The general election of 1892 was held on 8 July. Lloyd George (who polled 2154 votes) had a majority of 196 – a respectable but not spectacular result. But the result was a disappointment for the Liberals everywhere except in Wales. The party won 273 seats to the Conservatives' 269. But it had the support of eighty-one Irish Members who were elected (almost) solely for the purpose of securing Home Rule while the Conservatives were reinforced by only forty-six Liberal-Unionists. Salisbury chose not to resign until he was defeated in the House of Commons. But the parliamentary arithmetic ensured that it was only a matter of time before Gladstone formed his fourth administration. The vote of confidence was won by the Liberals on 11 August. Lord Rosebery, after some persuasion, became Foreign Secretary and Herbert Henry Asquith moved straight from the backbenches to the Home Office – an appointment which caused Lloyd George to make

one of the character misjudgements which, from time to time, led him
into error. Asquith, he wrote, is 'the hope of the rising generation of
Radicalism . . . It is considered that, on the whole, he fills the same
position in the Parliament of 1892 as Mr Chamberlain did in that of
1885.'[57] In Wales, the Liberals won all but three seats. Tom Ellis –
despite the doubts of all the Welsh Liberals except Lloyd George –
agreed to become an assistant whip. It was the only recognition that
Wales received.

Rosebery and Asquith were the rising stars of Gladstone's last
administration. Rosebery, the reluctant politician, 'sought the palms
without the dust'[58] and compared democracy to 'holding a wolf by the
ears'.[59] Asquith – the child of the mercantile middle classes who became
the personification of Balliol 'effortless superiority' – never, when
Prime Minister, wholly trusted Lloyd George, his Chancellor of the
Exchequer. When it was to his advantage, Lloyd George happily co-
operated with both the Scottish aristocrat and the Oxford intellectual.
But he was never their supporter or their friend. From the very beginning, Lloyd George chose to travel alone.

CHAPTER 5

A WELSH PARNELL

In the new Parliament the government's majority over the official opposition was only four, but the combined votes of the Liberal and Irish
parties would guarantee the passage of a Home Rule Bill. Progress on
every other measure – bills and budgets – depended on the construction
of temporary alliances. The promise of disestablishment had been
included in the Newcastle Programme. To honour that undertaking the
ministers would have to battle long and hard in an unsympathetic House
of Commons. Lloyd George decided that the time had come ruthlessly
to exploit the minority government's dependence on the support of
Welsh Members. At a victory rally in Conway, in a speech of astounding presumption, he set out the terms on which it was available.

> It is very important that Liberal statesmen should understand
> clearly why Wales is so overwhelmingly Liberal at the present
> moment. It is not to install one statesman in power. It is not to
> deprive one party of power in order to put another in power. It
> has been done because Wales has . . . demonstrated its determina-
> tion to secure its own progress.[1]

At first, it seemed that the aspiration would be realised. In August,
Lloyd George wrote to his uncle with the glad tidings that 'Gladstone
has given us better pledges on Disestablishment than even we dared to
anticipate'.[2] The news that the Prime Minster was to visit Snowdonia
to open a footpath raised high hopes that the optimism was justified.
On the night before the great event, Lloyd George chaired a meeting in

Caernarvon. Gladstone said a few words. None of them was about Wales. The following day's speech on the Snowdon foothills was vague about everything – even land reform, on which, it had been assumed, he would be resolute. At the private dinner which followed the opening, Lloyd George was more circumspect than he had been during his visit to Hawarden. He listened quietly while the Prime Minister talked about corrugated-iron roofing sheets and reminisced about a drunken drover he had known when young.[3]

William George took his mother by coach from Criccieth to 'see and hear the GOM whom most of the Welsh people regarded with adoration'. His account of the day described Gladstone's 'deep sonorous voice which carried magnificently as he stood there . . . on the granite plateau . . . his silvery locks waving in the breeze'.[4] It makes no mention of Mrs George meeting her prodigious (and overtly devoted) son. Carried away by the romance of the occasion, William George believed that Gladstone had announced the appointment of a Royal Commission to investigate and report on the land question in Wales.[5] In fact he had equivocated on the subject and he agreed to a Royal Commission only after much pressure from Welsh Members of Parliament. His fervent supporters pinned their hopes on one less than precise sentence in the Snowdonia speech. Gladstone 'ventured to say that, whatever the pressure of Irish demands may be, even one session of parliament will not be allowed to pass without being able to give some earnest [commitment] to the people of Wales of our desire to deal with, and as far as we can push forward, their just demands'.[6]

So began 1893, a year of Liberal turmoil. At its heart was the real resentment felt in Wales against both exploitation by the English and the failure of a predominantly English Parliament to rectify Welsh grievances. But the fire of rebellion was fuelled by personal animosities and rivalry between different sorts of Liberals and different Nonconformist denominations. Lloyd George was in the thick of the fight because he chose to lead the battle and because he possessed qualities which older colleagues found insufferable. He was presumptuous, bellicose, brash and ambitious. Worst of all, he was clearly more able than any of them – and he knew it.

The long summer and autumn recess was a time to deal with domestic matters – few of which required Lloyd George to return to Wales. Olwen, his second daughter, had been born in April 1892 and since that meant that his wife was even less likely to visit London, he gave up the Verulam Buildings and lodged again with the Davieses in Acton. It was the beginning of two nomadic years. He moved from Acton back to the National Liberal Club. Then he leased Tom Ellis's rooms at Essex Court in the Temple for £25 a year. In 1893, he moved again and at last found in Palace Mansions, Addison Road, Kensington, something like a permanent London home. He stayed there for six years.

Addison Road was as inconvenient as Acton – which he had left because it was so far from the House of Commons – and, at an annual rent of £90, almost four times as expensive as the Temple. But he told his wife that it was 'very charming . . . with a good view . . . The children would see cabs, omnibuses etc rolling along.'[7] His wish – as distinct from a realistic hope – that Margaret would spend more time in London was, at least at the time, genuine. Throughout his many extra-marital relationships – the attachments growing more frequent the longer he was separated from his family – the strange version of love which bound them together survived. It was reinforced by his inability to perform the simplest of domestic tasks – a handicap which prompted constant complaints of neglect and occasional rebukes from the wife who was accused in turn of neglecting him. 'I had the letter and the scolding. Your clean change are all at Palace Mansions in the top drawer of the dresser in our bedroom. Kate put them there as I told you and she told you where they are.'[8]

The Queen's Speech, read to Parliament on the last day of January 1893, was emphatic about only one thing. It promised 'on the earliest available occasion to amend the provision for the government of Ireland . . . [so as] to afford contentment to the Irish people, important relief to Parliament and additional securities for the strength and union of the Empire'. There was no promise of priority for the disestablishment of the Church in Wales. The Welsh Liberals had prepared themselves for the worst. They had met a month before Christmas, anticipating 'something of a rumpus' with Gladstone. 'He is', Lloyd George wrote to his uncle, 'a frightened old fool in some respects . . . I moved that we should listen to no compromise and we agreed.'[9] Even Tom Ellis, although a government whip, urged his colleagues to 'press' the Prime Minister, and at a February meeting the Welsh Liberals repeated their demands.[10] They were not met. Gladstone proposed a compromise. 'Disestablishment is at present impossible. A Suspensory Bill is an essential preliminary.'[11] Publicly, Lloyd George espoused the radical view that 'suspension' – which amounted to the freezing of ecclesiastical revenues – was a diversion rather than a concession.

Privately, he took a more moderate view. He would be 'quite satisfied if we get Disestablishment next year'.[12] At another of the endless meetings of Welsh MPs he persuaded his colleagues to remind Gladstone of the prominence given to the policy in the Newcastle Programme. The Prime Minister's reply referred his critics to the contents of the Queen's Speech and added that the government had not 'announced any plan with regard to the order of business beyond the express declarations'. That sounded ominously like Home Rule first and everything else nowhere.[13] In a letter drafted by Lloyd George, the Welsh MPs asked for clarification. It contained a veiled threat in the form of the hope that nothing would happen which had 'the effect of imperilling Wales' devotion'.[14] Gladstone's reply – that the devotion had not gone unnoticed – encouraged Welsh optimists to believe that their cause was making progress.

The South Wales Liberal Federation, meeting at Aberdare on 14 August, took a sterner view. There was unanimous agreement that unless disestablishment was the first priority in 1894, Welsh Liberals should form themselves into an independent party. The Welsh Liberal MPs – initially reluctant to cut themselves loose – considered the suggestion at a long and acrimonious meeting and eventually decided on a form of words that sounded very like capitulation to the secessionist demands. Unless disestablishment was given priority in the 1894 business programmes they would 'reconsider their position'.

The debate on Irish Home Rule dragged on for almost four months. Despite his impatience, Lloyd George – always impressed by oratory – was full of praise for Gladstone's last *tour de force*. The Prime Minister's introduction of the bill was 'a marvellous performance'.[15] During the long committee stage, 'the shrunken figure, huddled up and torpid' would suddenly be rejuvenated by an opponent's error, allegation or criticism and become 'an erect athletic gladiator, fit for the contest of any arena'.[16] On 1 October 1893 the bill was given a third reading with a majority of thirty-four. Exactly a week later it was rejected in the House of Lords by 419 votes to 43. Gladstone remained Prime Minister for a little more than four months. Then – at odds with his own Cabinet over parliamentary tactics and naval expenditure – he resigned office for the last time.

There were two contenders for the succession: Sir William Harcourt, the Chancellor of the Exchequer, and Lord Rosebery, the Foreign Secretary. No one doubted that Harcourt was the more able as well as the more eager. He was also the more disliked. His conduct, after the

Queen asked Rosebery to form an administration, revealed the character defects which his colleagues deplored. Knowing that a refusal to serve would bring the government down, he insisted on being Leader of the House of Commons as well as Chancellor, possessing the right to call Cabinet meetings on his own initiative and enjoying as much patronage as the Prime Minister. It was not a situation with which Rosebery was equipped to deal. The government was doomed from the start. Lloyd George and his Welsh friends were accused of hastening its end.

The Welsh MPs wrote to the new Prime Minister with a request for a meeting. It was rejected in a manner that, thanks to the recipients' reaction at the time, historians have described as curt to the point of offensive. In fact, though hardly effusive, it was perfectly polite. 'I am much obliged for your letter. I should have no time this week to receive a deputation on any subject and on Monday there is a Party meeting. Wouldn't it be time enough after that to decide whether a meeting would be needed?'[17] The bruised Welsh egos were, in part, soothed by the Queen's Speech – written before Gladstone's retirement – which promised 'measures to deal with the Ecclesiastical Establishments in Wales and Scotland'. And they should have found some consolation in Tom Ellis's promotion to Chief Whip. But Lloyd George had never trusted Rosebery. Two years earlier he had greeted his appointment as Foreign Secretary with the question 'Does he mean mischief?'[18] So specific assurances were sought and Lloyd George prompted the *Caernarvon and Denbigh Herald* to publish a story which was both evidence of his assiduity and a warning to the government.

> Mr Lloyd George and Mr Frank Edwards [the Member for Tadnorshire] . . . had private interviews . . . with Mr Thomas Ellis, Chief Whip, with a view to obtaining some definite Assurances on the intentions of the government to carry a Welsh Disestablishment Bill through the Commons before the end of the coming session . . . Ten or a dozen of the younger . . . representatives of the Principality will not hesitate, if necessary, on some early and critical occasions to withhold their support from the Ministry.[19]

Two weeks later, the *North Wales Observer and Express* reported success. A deputation to Sir William Harcourt had 'obtained a promise that the government intends to carry a bill through the Commons' and that a 'mere second reading' was only the beginning. The best he could offer was the completion of all stages in the Lower House.[20] Everybody knew that the bill would never become law. The House of Lords would kill it off.

Harcourt's intentions were honourable, but his promise could not be kept. Rosebery, despite his personal scepticism about Home Rule, believed that 'every tie of honour' required the policy to continue unchanged and assumed that, in consequence, the Irish Members would continue to support the government. But when Gladstone went the Irish Members lost heart and, for some of them, the daily grind of normal House of Commons business became intolerable. The continual absence of the men who made up the government's majority destroyed what little chance there was of a Disestablishment Bill, or any contentious legislation, making progress. Then Rosebery, most charitably described as 'mercurial' – guaranteed Irish disaffection by telling the Lords – without consulting his colleagues – that Home Rule would be possible only if and when England 'as the predominant partner in the three Kingdoms [was] convinced of its justice and equity'.[21] It sounded as if he accepted that the peers – protecting the people from the prejudice of politicians – had the right to reject a new bill. During the debate on the Queen's Speech, Henry Labouchere – a Liberal radical with a good deal of mischief to his credit – had moved an amendment which promised to curtail the Lords' power. To everybody's surprise, it was carried by two votes. The government had to defeat its own statement on future legislation and reintroduce it in its original form. With the Commons in chaos, the government looked again to Ireland for salvation. The Eviction of Tenants Bill – arbitrators to fix rents and restore tenures – was moved up the legislative programme.

The Times, after announcing that the Disestablishment Bill was doomed, added that 'Lloyd George and his friends' – discussing the Welsh Members as if they were independent of the Liberal Party – 'are quite prepared to stretch a point in favour of the government.' The newspaper understated their depth of anger. Lloyd George, Frank Edwards and D. A. Thomas were described by the *British Weekly* (still Gladstonian despite Gladstone's resignation) as 'Taffys . . . in a state of constant revolt'. Consoling its readers with the reminder that 'they have been overruled on several previous occasions by their clear-headed colleague', it predicted (with a Shakespearean flourish) that 'Taffy will have to eat leek.'[22] 'Taffy', in the form of Lloyd George, responded by resigning the Liberal whip and rejecting the Church (Wales) Bill – which proposed disendowment under a more acceptable name –

because it provided pensions for current holders of Church of England livings. Better to defeat the government than pass a bill which, even briefly, subsidised the alien Church.

The bill was introduced into the House of Commons on 26 April 1894. In the debate which followed, Lloyd George's speech was not a success. He made the mistake of proclaiming his passionate support for the idea of disendowment before he denounced the way in which it was to be brought about. He rejected the protection of existing endowments 'extending exceptional indulgence to an establishment . . . which, during their whole career, had simply had one record – the betrayal of higher interests' and claimed the decision was 'a direct indictment to disturbances to get rid of the clergy'. As always he was quick to pick up errors in his opponents' argument. He ended a sterile argument about the relative strength of the Church of England in Wales and Nonconformist denominations by following the logic of the Attorney General's claim that both communions attracted similar numbers of worshippers. Thousands of Anglicans must have voted for disestablishment candidates in the general election. Such conceits were, he knew, mere self-indulgence. His supporters wanted fire and brimstone.

Arthur Balfour, who spoke immediately after Lloyd George, dismissed 'the historical fantasy' which suggested that a Welsh nation had existed during the Middle Ages and announced that he 'did not intend to follow the honourable gentleman through the embittered controversy which he initiated' and was 'certainly not going to use towards the Nonconformist bodies in Wales epithets which he [Lloyd George] was not ashamed – though he should have been ashamed – to use towards members of that great Communion which he was attacking'. Lloyd George was delighted to have received so much attention. His own assessment of the speech differed substantially from the judgement of Parliament and press. He wrote home to say that he had 'succeeded wonderfully well' in the debate and 'held the House far better than Balfour'.[23]

By the end of May it became clear that not even a Disendowment Bill would receive the approval of a House of Commons third reading. The parliamentary timetable was in head-on collision with Harcourt's hopes of even getting halfway towards keeping his disestablishment promise, and, inevitably, the parliamentary timetable came off best. Much to the relief of Asquith, who had enjoyed his constant meetings with Welsh deputations even less than the twelve late nights of the committee stage, the bill was withdrawn at the end of July with the promise that it would be reintroduced during the 1895 session – leaving Lloyd George to spend another year fighting on the narrow ground of disestablishment when he wanted to campaign on a broader front.[24]

The failure of the Disestablishment and Disendowment bills made the demand for an independent Welsh Liberal Party irresistible in Wales if not in Westminster. On 4 May 1894, during an interview with the *Liverpool Daily Post* – widely read in Wales – Herbert Lewis (the Member for Flint) and Lloyd George were explicit about their intentions. Lewis spoke of raising and stimulating the spirit of nationality. Lloyd George was more practical and less metaphysical.

> There are many who deny our national existence and one can hardly be surprised at that because our support has been so entirely given to one party that our separate identity has become merged into one political party. The ultimate object of this independent action will be to form a Welsh national party.[25]

The call for Welsh MPs to fight for Wales – if necessary at the expense of other causes – offered Lloyd George the chance to establish an impregnable power base. He sincerely believed that the Established Church was an indignity which Wales should not tolerate and a scandalous exploitation of the poor by the rich. But he also recognised it as a vehicle for his own ambition. When his association with disestablishment blurred his image as a defender of less exclusively Welsh causes, he edged away from the campaign as fast as he decently could. But in 1894 it seemed to offer him the chance of forming and leading a Welsh Liberal Party which could struggle for Wales as the Irish Nationalists had struggled for Ireland.

The rebellion gathered force. D. A. Thomas formally repudiated the party leadership. Herbert Lewis announced that he would 'never again fight a constituency as an official Liberal candidate'.[26] Frank Edwards (the Member for Radnorshire) said that, like Lloyd George, he no longer accepted the party whip. What came to be called the Revolt of Four had begun and with it the complicated relationship between D. A. Thomas and Lloyd George – first comrades in the Welsh cause and then bitter rivals for the Welsh leadership. The animosity endured for twenty years, until Thomas – ennobled as Viscount Rhondda and a successful industrialist – was recruited by Lloyd George to help the war effort.

The Revolt of Four was not the coordinated campaign which the name – more used by historians when it was over than by politicians while it was happening – suggests. But the Four toured Wales, arguing in favour of an independent Welsh Liberal Party. On 5 May, a meeting of the North Wales Liberal Party passed a resolution in support of their proposals with only one vote against. The Liberal leadership could ignore them no longer. Lord Rosebery, speaking in Birmingham, began by ridiculing 'some young men and daring natives of the Principality [who] have taken it into their heads to turn the government's majority into a minority in order to obtain disestablishment'.[27] Then he stood on his aristocratic dignity. He had promised to carry a bill through all its stages in the Commons before the end of the session. If the dissidents doubted either his word or his honour they should have the courage to bring down the government.

Rosebery's speech was designed to encourage a counter-revolution and it succeeded. When the Welsh Liberal MPs met on the following day, their agenda included a resolution proposing to censure the rebels. It had been drafted by loyalists on the previous evening. Fortunately for the Four, Major Jones – who had been deputed to second the critical motion – was absent without leave, recovering from a hangover. So the Four escaped unscathed. The fiasco only increased Lloyd George's contempt for his enemies, whom he dismissed as 'more afraid of us [the Four] than of the ministry'.[28]

Three days after the abortive vote of censure, Lloyd George attended the Annual Meeting of the Baptist Association for Monmouthshire. His 'private invitation' had been accompanied by a warning that 'three leading men intended to move a resolution calling upon us to return to our allegiance'.[29] So he was ready for the fight. When he spoke in favour of a resolution supporting the creation of an independent Welsh party, he used the technique which had become his trade mark. He attacked and his attack was personal. 'The Premier . . . stated in Edinburgh that he was a believer in a State Church and did not see why they should not run a State Church as they ran a State Army. The only reason that he has for conceding the Welsh demand was political expediency . . . Lord Rosebery had referred to [Welshmen] as natives of the Principality as if he were referring to a tribe in Central Africa.'[30] At the end of the debate, there was only one vote against the proposition that Wales, like Ireland, should have its own political party. It was cast by an Englishman.

The Welsh Parliamentary Liberal Party responded with renewed attempts to restore trust in the government but, noting the popularity which the Four enjoyed in Wales, wisely flinched from combining statements of support for Rosebery with censure of his critics. At a special meeting on 30 May, 'only four of those present voted against a resolution which declared Members satisfied that the government will do its best to pass the Welsh Disestablishment Bill'. The rest declared that it was the 'duty of the Welsh Party . . . to give the government honourable and consistent support'. The original motion called on Members to 'abstain from endeavouring to create mistrust' but the chairman deleted the offensive words before the resolution was put to the meeting.[31] The pusillanimity confirmed Lloyd George's belief that, with rare exceptions, Welsh Liberal MPs were a 'wretched crowd'.

Intrigue is a demanding occupation. By the end of 1894, Lloyd George – despite, after the birth of Gwilym on 12 December, having four children to support – virtually abandoned his legal practice. He had become the undisputed leader of the campaign for a Welsh political party and he spent his time building what he hoped would be its local organisation and his power base. When Tom Ellis had been promoted to Chief Whip, Lloyd George had replaced him as the guiding spirit of Cymru Fydd ('Young Wales') – originally a cultural movement largely run by expatriate Welshmen who lived in London. Ellis had harboured romantic ideas about replicating Young England and Young Germany. Lloyd George was, by nature, more practical. He gave Cymru Fydd a political dimension. It was his idea that a Cymru Fydd League should be created with branches throughout Wales.

In August 1894 the nascent League had held an inaugural meeting in Llandrindod Wells. Its new constitution set out its cultural aims, including the preservation of the Welsh language. But its main objective was the promotion of a movement which could achieve national self-government for Wales and, in the meantime, would represent the interests of the Welsh working class. The branches were to campaign in local elections for the League's objectives, and in pursuit of that end an amalgamation was arranged with the North Wales Liberal Federation. Alfred Thomas, the Member for East Glamorgan, was elected League President as a gesture of friendship to the South. But it was general knowledge that the Baptist builder from Cardiff was really a surrogate and that the League was another device for improving Lloyd George's prospect of leading the whole nation. It was an ambition which D. A. Thomas, who ran the South Wales Liberal Federation, was determined to frustrate.

In Cardiff on 11 October 1894, Lloyd George made what he believed to be the conclusive case for Welsh political unity. During the previous quarter of a century, there had been fourteen years of Liberal government – and not one bill dealing with Wales's national interests. But Ireland 'had drilled and organised the whole of her progressive forces' and, in consequence, had secured the passage of acts designed to meet its needs. Home Rule had been frustrated by the House of Lords, but two Land Acts had done something to alleviate the hardship of Irish tenant farmers. A powerful Welsh faction, under his leadership, would fight to protect Wales's interests.

It took four months for the government to respond with an attempt to redeem Harcourt's promise and Rosebery's good name. Another Established Church (Wales) Bill was introduced on 25 February 1895. The new bill was, in many particulars, superior to its predecessor. It excluded Welsh bishops from the House of Lords, created a new archdiocese, made tithes payable to county councils, which would be given the duty of distributing them to worthy institutions, and placed burial grounds in the care of local authorities. It also required that the distribution of income from tithes should, as far as possible, relate to the areas in which they had been raised. So Glamorgan, Carmarthenshire and Monmouthshire – together, home to more than half of Wales's inhabitants but with fewer country parishes – would receive less than the more sparsely populated rural counties. In an attempt to make progress, Asquith, the Home Secretary, offered to amend Clause 9 to provide for the creation of a Welsh National Council with powers to decide how tithe income should be distributed. Lloyd George – in an early example of what was to become a habit – made the concession public before it was officially announced. A sizable minority of Welsh MPs, offended as much by Lloyd George's secret negotiations as by the proposal itself, warned Asquith that they were opposed to the idea and feared that it was intended as a stepping-stone to Welsh Home Rule – a fear that Queen Victoria had expressed to Rosebery during the consideration of the 1893 bill.[32] The concession was withdrawn, and Lloyd George – who was enjoying the mayhem as he competed with D. A. Thomas for the effective leadership of Welsh Liberalism – announced that if the amendment was not put down in the Home Secretary's name, he would table it himself. Asquith, exasperated by Welsh determination to spend hours debating a bill which the House of Lords was bound to reject, denounced what he called willingness to 'plough the sand' and added that he would 'rather wreck the bill than accept the amendment'.[33] His anger is easily understood. Few things are so frustrating to serious politicians than long hours spent in Parliament to no purpose, and the futility of the disestablishment debate had become increasingly obvious.

The Church of England knew that some sort of disestablishment was inevitable, the Welsh Nonconformists realised that the tithe system was not as corrupt as they claimed, and Lloyd George wanted to move on to championing less parochial causes. But although he worked privately in search of a compromise – to the point of discussing amendments with Joseph Chamberlain – he had to maintain the reputation for militancy which he had acquired in January 1894, when he urged the electors in the Horncastle by-election not to vote for an anti-disestablishment Liberal candidate.

The stage was set for a belligerent meeting of the Welsh Liberal Federation at Aberystwyth on 17 April 1895. The *Manchester Guardian* judged that the 'real business before the convention will be the re-organisation of Liberalism on more truly representative and national lines'.[34] The pursuit of that lofty objective turned into wrangles about which faction would best serve Wales's interests, what parliamentary tactics were most likely to achieve the results that Wales desired, and who should lead Wales into the new era of national unity.

The conference got off to a bad start with the announcement that, at the suggestion of D. A. Thomas, the South Wales Executive would not attend. At three o'clock – the appointed time for the first day to begin – only Thomas Gee (the nominated chairman) and Beriah Evans (a journalist who was to become secretary) were in the hall. The second day was better attended but more acrimonious. J. Bryn Roberts – Member for the South Division of Caernarvonshire – questioned the motives of the conference organisers and then attempted to end all doubt by asserting that Lloyd George wanted a vehicle for his Welsh leadership. A couple of hours of discursive debate followed before Gee concluded the meeting by announcing, without evidence and on dubious authority, that the South Wales Liberal Federation had ceased to exist.

In the House of Commons, debates which could be claimed to have the slightest Welsh dimension became occasions for demonstrations of national loyalty. On 25 April, Lloyd George was reproved by the Speaker for arguing against the London and North Western Railway Bill 'on the grounds that the railway company has adopted a certain policy as regards the non-employment [of] monoglot Welsh plate-layers'.[35] On 9 May, he wrote to his brother to say, 'We divided three times today against the (railway) bill. Of course, we were beaten but we made a pertinacious protest.'[36] Nothing so irritates government whips than rebellions that stretch on through days and nights with the rebels indifferent to whether they win or lose. Rumours swirl around the tea-rooms. In May 1895 ministers heard the dreaded news that Gladstone – who defended the Church of England in all its manifestations – had cancelled his pair with Charles Villiers. He had not appeared in the House since he resigned the premiership, but it was immediately assumed that he was about to make a dramatic return and denounce the Established Church (Wales) Bill.

The thunderbolts were never let loose. Nor did Lloyd George move his threatened amendment to Clause 9 because it was never reached. On 20 June, the government survived a committee stage vote with a majority cut to seven. The next day the House of Commons carried a resolution which censured the Secretary of State for War for his failure to ensure that the army possessed sufficient supplies of cordite – the explosive used in the production of rifle ammunition. It was a snap vote on a Private Member's motion in an almost empty House. There was no truth in the allegation and the vote – which the official opposition supported with great reluctance – could have easily been reversed. But Rosebery – ignoring majority opinion within the Cabinet – resigned. The recriminations which followed the subsequent election and the Liberal Party's crushing defeat attributed his reluctance to carry on, at least in part, to the debilitating effect of the Welsh rebellion.

Salisbury, the new Prime Minister, dissolved Parliament sixteen days after he took office. Polling in the general election began on 13 July. A hundred Liberals – including Sir William Harcourt and John Morley, then Chief Secretary for Ireland – lost their seats and the Conservative–Liberal-Unionist coalition returned to office with a majority of 152 over all other parties. Lloyd George fought the campaign in the knowledge that many of his Welsh colleagues would be happy to see him lose. Bryn Roberts – unopposed in his own constituency – replied to an invitation to speak at a Caernarvon election meeting with an unapologetic refusal to support a 'Welsh Parnell'.[37] Depressed by Roberts's snub, the candidate wrote home with the news that the *Chronicle* 'says that I shall be out by 30'. In 1895, polling took place over several days and Lloyd George's depression was increased by the 'staggering blow' of losing 'Harcourt who', he told Margaret, 'got 2000 last time and is now out by 300'.[38] The letter ended, 'I shall want collars and cuffs for Tuesday.'[39]

The Conservative Party had once more chosen Ellis-Nanney as its candidate, thus allowing the Liberals to fight the sort of campaign which Lloyd George most enjoyed. His only excursion into policy – though significant in itself since it was his first mention of the subject – was a reference to Joseph Chamberlain's estimate that a national old-age pension would cost half a million pounds a year. The money, he told a meeting in the Caernarvon Guildhall, should be raised by making land-lords pay tax on ground rents.[40] But his stock in trade was personal attacks. At Bangor on 4 July, Chamberlain's honour was called into question in a preview of what was going to become a constant theme during Lloyd George's opposition to the Boer War. 'Mr Chamberlain is anxious to know whether the government has given sufficient orders to a firm called Kynoch and Co of Birmingham. The chairman of that company is Mr Chamberlain's brother. There are four Chamberlains who have large holdings in that firm.' Squire Nanney was the constant target of Lloyd George's invective. 'The Tory candidate belongs to that favoured class of men that thinks that things as they are, are exactly as they ought to be . . . He is a squire and so the constitution guarantees him a heavy rent roll.'[41]

The result in the Caernarvon Boroughs was declared on 20 July. Lloyd George was elected with a majority of 194 votes – only two fewer than in 1892. Next day he had the supreme satisfaction of receiving a plea for help from Osborne Morgan, the candidate in East Denbighshire and a bitter opponent who had become the titular leader of the Welsh parliamentary Liberals.★ 'At the commencement of this struggle,' Lloyd George wrote, he 'gave me a nasty jab in the ribs which, had he any strength at all, would have finished me off.' The response to the request for help was less magnanimous than malicious. 'Now I am having my revenge in rushing to the rescue of the man who tried to drown me.'[42] Morgan more than doubled his majority.

Not everyone reacted to Lloyd George's success in the manner of Osborne Morgan. Bryn Roberts kept the old wounds open by explain-ing in Gee's *Banner and Times of Wales* why he had refused to support the Caernarvon Boroughs' Liberal. The candidate had, he said, 'allied him-self with the Tories and Parnellites to overthrow the government. I and many others believe that his work, and that of Mr D. A. Thomas, were the principal means of upsetting the Ministry. They would not have resigned on so trivial a matter as the cartridges had they not seen that they had lost control over their followers when their majority was so small.'[43]

★Lloyd George also owed Morgan a debt of gratitude. He had originated the act which made possible the defence of the Roberts family in the Llanfrothen burial case.

Lloyd George – who believed that a government so easily disheart-
ened barely deserved to survive – made no response. He defended his
record by asserting that his desire to amend parts of the Disestablishment
Bill had been endorsed by the government. Tom Ellis, friend and Chief
Whip, confirmed his claim with partisan enthusiasm. If backbench
revolts had contributed to the government's loss of nerve, the crucial
vote had, he said, been on an amendment moved by D. A. Thomas in
an attempt to secure extra tithe income for South Wales. Asquith
denied Ellis's interpretation of the events. Quietus on the episode was
pronounced by a backhanded compliment from the *Manchester
Guardian*, which judged, magisterially, that 'it is not on such points as
these that some of us are disposed to criticise Mr Lloyd George. He has
done work in the House of Commons which needed to be done and
which demanded a good deal of courage and resolution.'[44] It might
have added that the demeaning wrangle typified the behaviour of most
defeated and demoralised governments.

Back from Scotland, Lloyd George returned to the work of forming
a Welsh political party. His letters home were full of the usual bombast.
'I made the best speech I ever made in my life.'[45] However, he knew
that the Tory victory had made an effective Welsh rebellion far less
likely. So he decided on a last desperate attempt to settle the issue once
and for all. The obstructive South Wales Liberal Federation would be
superseded and engulfed by the Rhondda Liberal Association which
would then amalgamate with the North. At first, the plan seemed to be
working. A demonstration in the valley was 'simply immense . . .
Nothing like it . . . in the memory of the oldest inhabitants . . . The
Rhondda has been captured.'[46] A specially rewarding feature of the
rally was the obvious discomfiture which it caused to William
Abraham – the MP for Rhondda who, despite being universally known
as Mabon, was an implacable opponent of Welsh Nationalism.

A meeting of the South Wales Liberal Federation was planned to be
held in Newport on 16 January 1896. Lloyd George determined to take
no chances and spent days canvassing the delegates. On the eve of the
meeting, all the Rhondda delegates agreed to support the crucial
motion, calling for the Federation to amalgamate with Cymru Fyddites
as a first step along the path to unity. 'That', wrote Lloyd George,
'cripples Mabon's mischievousness.'[47] There was a suspicion that the
mischief included encouraging the rumour that the desire to unify the
Welsh Liberal Party had, as its motive, the hope of representing a Cardiff
constituency. At a meeting in Caernarvon in June 1895, Lloyd George

'contradicted in the most unqualified terms' the suggestion 'that it was his intention to desert the Boroughs to seek a seat in South Wales'.[48]

The optimism was misplaced. D. A. Thomas had outsmarted Lloyd George. About fifty Englishmen, members of the Newport delegation, were allocated seats in front of the platform. Districts which favoured Lloyd George were disenfranchised. East Caernarvon and West Monmouthshire were refused admission. Pembroke and Cardiganshire received the credentials which would have granted them a place at the conference two days after the meeting was held. When Lloyd George spoke, he had to endure the novel experience of being shouted down. The crucial motion was lost.

Lloyd George's letter home, sent from Neath two days later, announced his intention to 'fight it out'. But the 'bellicose mood' which he described was no more than a show of defiance and did not last for long.[49] He knew that the battle for an exclusively Welsh political party could not be won. He had failed because he did not realise that the adulation which followed an oratorical triumph did not last long enough to translate emotion into action, unless the audience had been inspired to fight for something in which they already believed.[50] In 1896, as eighty-three years later, Wales did not want Home Rule.

Fighting for lost causes was not Lloyd George's way. His friends did not accuse him of abandoning the cause. They accused the cause of abandoning him. 'Wales', wrote the journalist Harold Spender, 'practically gave him to England.'[51] In fact, with a resilience which was one of his greatest strengths, he looked about him for another vehicle to carry his ambitions forward. He moved on, leaving Cymru Fydd to become 'a term of derision'.

CHAPTER 6

ALL THAT GLISTERS

Whether Wales abandoned Lloyd George or Lloyd George abandoned Wales, after the Newport meeting his political persona changed. Notoriety had made him feel a national politician. And his nation was Great Britain. In one of the pieces of good fortune which were essential ingredients of his success, he was presented with an opportunity to debate a measure which was a perfect bridging passage between the two stages of his career. The Agricultural Rating Bill applied to both England and Wales, but it raised most antagonistic passion in the Welsh rural counties. It was a passion which Lloyd George was happy to articulate. The bill could plausibly be represented as further proof that British landowners exploited a privilege to which they did not possess a moral right.

The Agricultural Rating Bill was business left over from Gladstone's last administration – though that did not inhibit Lloyd George's assault. It was intended to provide desperately needed support for an industry in distress. In 1877 the price of wheat averaged 56/9 a quarter. By 1886 it had fallen to 31/- and in 1889 to 29/9. The hopes of a permanent increase, encouraged by higher prices in the next two years, were not realised. The officially calculated price for 1894 was 23/-.[1] And as prices fell, agricultural wages – influenced by both the new militancy of farm workers and the drift from the land – rose. In response to the decline which was becoming a depression, Gladstone had set up a Royal Commission. Its 1896 report proposed that rates on land under cultivation should be reduced by 50 per cent and that the loss of revenue to the local authorities should be made up by Treasury grants. Rate

relief was a modest proposal which Salisbury implemented, as his predecessor would have done. But it provided another opportunity for
Lloyd George to demonstrate the qualities on which his early success
was built – independence of mind, quickness of wit, willingness to
take on the big battalions and a disregard for political consistency.

Welsh tenant farmers and their workers were antagonistic to their landlords for reasons which did not prejudice the parallel relationships in
England. In Wales the landlords were, or were thought to be, an alien
race – English in origin and Church of England by religion. And Welsh
resentment against the 'English Ascendancy' was increased by the government's rejection of the Royal Commission's additional recommendation
that farm rents in Wales should be determined not by negotiations
between the unequal partners but by county courts. Gladstone – with two
Irish Land Bills as precedents – would certainly have implemented all of
the Commission's findings. Salisbury was more selective.

In the second reading debate on the Rating Bill, Lloyd George set
out the principle which informed his entire philosophy of landownership and use. Owners should not receive added income from increases
in land values for which they were not responsible. It was a precept
which he was to repeat, time after time, during the great Budget
debates in 1909 and 1910. True to what, by 1896, was his established
style, he spiced his argument with personal attacks on the landowners
who received the profit which they did not deserve. The objects of his
invective were the Tory Cabinet ministers whose rates would be
reduced when the Rating Bill became law.

The total rate reduction – which the bill provided throughout
England and Wales – was £1,550,000. Lloyd George had calculated that
members of the government would benefit by £67,000 a year and that
the capital value of their estates would increase by £2,250,000.[2] He
named the ministers, one by one, and announced – with dubious legitimacy – the size of the personal saving which they would enjoy. The
Prime Minister's annual rate bill would be reduced by £2000. Balfour,
the Leader of the House of Commons, would be better off by £1450 a
year, and the Duke of Devonshire (Lord President of the Council) by
£10,000. Henry Chaplin's rates would fall by only £700 a year, but he
was attacked with particular bitterness. As President of the Local
Government Board, he had introduced the bill.

None of the ministers whom Lloyd George vilified could have
regarded the rate reductions as much more than petty cash. But to
tenant farmers the savings seemed like a fortune. And Lloyd George fed

the class antagonism of the wider Welsh public with the complaint that, while ministers chose to subsidise their own class, the Welsh tin-plate industry, also in desperate decline, had been refused government help.[3]

The committee stage of the bill – taken on the floor of the House of Commons – dragged on into July, with Lloyd George moving amendment after amendment. On 19 May he caused outrage on the Tory benches when – during the discussion of a proposal that the reduction should not apply to the proportion of rates which was used to alleviate poverty – he questioned ministers' motives for introducing the bill. Their object, he claimed, was not the relief of agricultural distress but the enhancement of land values. Three days later, he contrived – as all rebels must from time to time – to be excluded and suspended from the House of Commons.

The occasion of his expulsion was – like most colourful incidents in the Commons – principally a matter of concern only to those who take parliamentary procedures seriously. At 3.40 p.m. on 22 May, the chairman of the Committee of the Whole House allowed the government to move 'That Clause 4 Stand Part' – thus ending the debate on that section of the bill. Lloyd George, together with Herbert Lewis, John Brunner (Member for Northwich and Lewis's friend and patron) and three Irish Members, refused to 'proceed to the division'. The chairman of the committee lacked the authority to discipline the recalcitrants, so, after an initial skirmish, the Speaker was called into the chamber. He gave the six Members another opportunity to leave their places and vote. Lloyd George, Lewis and two of the Irish Members persisted in their disobedience. They were 'named' and, in consequence, Arthur Balfour moved that they should be suspended for a week.* Lloyd George's jubilation was so intense that he could not wait for the post to carry the good news home to his family. 'I wired you this morning informing you of our suspension. You will have had full particulars in the evening papers. All the radicals are delighted beyond measure. Say it is the best thing yet that has happened for the cause.'[4]

The people of Caernarvon agreed. At a public meeting on 28 May there was unanimous support for a resolution which gave full support to the Boroughs' Member of Parliament 'in making an effective protest on

---

*The rules have changed. MPs can now remain in the chamber while votes are taken. Punishment was not so unwelcome in 1896 as it became after 1911. MPs, not being paid, had no salary to lose.

behalf of ratepayers generally against class legislation, having for its object the passing of measures of legalised robbery'.[5] The hope of an independent Welsh Liberal Party may have faded. But Welsh Liberals were clearly different from their English counterparts – few of whom would have defended a dissident MP in the language of the class war.

A month later, Elizabeth George died. On 23 June 1896, Lloyd George returned to Criccieth for his mother's funeral. It was one of the many occasions on which his family sought to shelter him from a grief which they assumed was more unbearable than their own – and from which, since he was destiny's child, he must be protected. He spent less than a day in Criccieth. In his diary that evening William George wrote, 'All of us agreeing, DLLG had better return to London for his own sake; feeling keenly and affecting his health. His going we felt would help by absorbing him in public business.'[6] Back in London, the sorrowing son agreed. 'The best way of casting off a sense of loss is to throw oneself into one's duties.' The letter ended with a tribute to his mother. But it began with what was really on his mind: 'Harcourt accepted one of my amendments.'[7]

The Agricultural Rating Bill was not his only distraction from grief. An Education Bill (which increased the grant to church schools), a Franchise Bill (which extended the operational area of the London and North Western Railway Company) and a Military Manoeuvres Bill (which empowered the War Office to acquire and requisition land) were before the House. Lloyd George opposed them all. He also objected to the cost of the Royal Parks and Gardens being borne by the nation as a whole when only London enjoyed the amenity which they provided, spoke against the motion that committees should not meet on the morning of Ascension Day, and protested against the proposal to finance a railway system in Uganda. He had made his mark on Parliament by becoming a constant irritant to the government and, in the self-loving chamber of the House of Commons, had won golden opinions by using its rules and traditions to harry and chasten his enemies. He became a 'House of Commons man' when that status was necessary for his progress. Later, when there was serious work to do, he abandoned the trivial role that had helped to establish his reputation as a national politician.

The 'From the Cross Benches' column in the *Observer* reflected the improvement in his reputation. 'Early in his career he suffered from the indiscretions of an enthusiastic countryman who hailed him as "the Welsh Parnell". In endeavouring to live up to the mark Mr Lloyd

George succeeded in obscuring what the House has recognised this session as sterling qualities in debate.'[8] Those qualities included 'a perfect
mastery of the subject'. The *Daily Chronicle* was less measured and even
more complimentary. He was 'at first looked at rather suspiciously, but
at the end of the session [he was] appreciated by all. Of all the young
men on the Liberal side, I should certainly say that Mr Lloyd George
has made the greatest mark this session.'[9]

Letters of self-congratulation were written both to William and to his
wife, but not to Uncle Lloyd, who had caused offence by urging him
to work even harder.* 'Harcourt said the whole House recognised the
eminent services I had rendered in connection with the bill . . . This is
a most unusual thing for a leader to single out one of the men who has
fought against him for special praise.'[10] Not even the confused syntax
can obscure his pride in being publicly congratulated by one of the men
whose policy – when the Liberals were in government – he had
obstructed with unwavering determination. Life was good. It would
have been better had his money worries been resolved.

In September 1894, he had told the Caernarvon District Liberal
Association that 'the heavy expenses incurred in frequently undertaken
general elections would make it impossible for him to stand at the next
general election'.[11] He did not mean it. The warning was meant either
to stimulate local supporters into raising more funds or to reconcile
William George to bearing the financial burden of his brother's political career. Although David was no more than a sleeping partner in
Lloyd George and George, 'his drawings for the first quarter of 1892
amounted to the sum of £276:12:1 and included his household
expenses in Criccieth; a sum of £40 paid to Mr Richard Owen, his
father-in-law, and two quarters' rent of Palace Mansions, the London
residence, which amounted to £28 a quarter'.[12] He earned a little from
journalism. In 1892, the *Star* had asked him to write 'a weekly article . . .
of about a column and a half' and in the following year he had begun
his long association with the *Manchester Guardian*.[13] His total earnings
from that paper during 1893 were £57/12.[14] William was his brother's
keeper.

When William George published his memoirs in 1958, he did not
hesitate to describe the extent of the 'willing sacrifice' that he had
made on his brother's behalf. He had known from the beginnings of the

---

*One, to Margaret, asked, 'Would he have me kill myself?' Another threatened, 'If
I hear he fumes again, I shall apply for the Chiltern Hundreds.'

partnership that 'politics were then, and were likely to be, David's main interest'. But, at the age of twenty, when it began, he 'did not realise how soon the responsibility of building up the practice and carrying it on would devolve almost entirely' on him, or how great his brother's calls upon it would be. One consequence of those demands was the grave indignity of 'a sharp letter from the bank manager, drawing my attention to the fact that the firm's account was overdrawn to the extent of £1,583'.[15] Much to his credit, despite the urgent need for funds and the humiliation of debt, William George was deeply reluctant to become involved in what became the first of his brother's dubious commercial ventures – but he was persuaded to agree.

On 21 August 1896, the *Caernarvon and Denbigh Herald* reported that 'Mr Lloyd George and Mr Herbert Lewis sailed for Buenos Aires. It is not impossible that if a sailing of steamships is found convenient, they may extend their visit to Patagonia in order to visit the Welsh colony there.'[16] No doubt Uncle Lloyd thought it a deplorable way for a busy and impecunious backbencher – with a wife and family in Wales – to spend nine weeks. But a letter Lloyd George sent to his brother just before he sailed for Argentina suggested that the excursion had a serious purpose.

> Heard from Patagonia. Von Heyking has returned leaving an engineer on the ground. He says 'the gold deposits are no doubt exceedingly rich'. He says the reefs were never thoroughly tested. In fact he says that the syndicate's money might as well have been thrown out of the window . . . The creditors are threatening bankruptcy proceedings against the syndicate out there. Their claims aggregate £700. Von Heyking thinks he might be able to settle with them on reasonable terms on behalf of the Liquidator . . . That is the sort of thing I might settle if I took a voyage there. Ellis would come with me.[17]

The 'syndicate' was a group of speculators on whose behalf a David Richards from Harlech had acquired the mining concession on land in the Welsh colony at Chubut in Patagonia. Von Heyking was a mining engineer who had been employed to save what he could of the company. The Welsh Patagonian Gold Fields Syndicate – as it was called in its articles of incorporation – had, he said, failed because it lacked capital and competent management. The fact that it had found no gold was not, apparently, included in his litany of problems. Lloyd George –

made a partner during late 1892 in the belief that he could raise the funds necessary to finance the actual mining operation – had recruited Major Jones and Doctor G. B. Clark (the Liberal Member for Caithness) to assist him in that endeavour and to share the eventual spoils. Doctor Clark was as dangerous an associate as 'the Major' – though his weakness was for unorthodox politics rather than women and drink. At medical school he had been enough of a committed Marxist to become a member of the First International and he had been elected to Parliament from Caithness as 'the Crofters' Candidate'. He became an enthusiastic Gladstonian only after he had defeated the official Liberal nominee.

William George's diary makes clear that his brother had involved him in the dubious enterprise without his consent. 'October 7 1892. DLlG per 11.6 train. Met him at station with a stranger, he said next to nothing what he was about. Rather peculiar character he seemed to me.'*[18] Ten days later, he must have realised that whatever was happening had a South American dimension. 'Mr Richards (Harlech) and Williams (Montevideo) here with DLlG.'[19] Five days later, his brother's role had been made clear. Lloyd George was 'off to Bethesda, then London, National Liberal Club', with the object of raising funds for the mining syndicate.[20]

The plan to exploit the mining concessions in the Corcovada Mica and Teca goldfields was revealed to William George long after it had been decided that he would play a crucial part in its governance. The syndicate had been established with an initial share capital of £1000 – half of which was the assumed value of the 'land and machinery'. Lloyd George had arranged for its registered office to be 'at least theoretically' located at Effingham House, Arundel Street, the home of Major Jones's *Shipping World*. He had also agreed – without telling the working partner – that Lloyd George and George should be the company solicitors and remunerated for their services by the grant of five hundred shares from Richards's five thousand.

William George – told of his new responsibilities – was properly pessimistic. 'What if the gold mine turns out to be a mere illusion of the Patagonian desert?' But instead of urging his brother to face reality, he bemoaned the fate which would befall him when his apprehension proved justified. 'It simply remains for me to drudge along in the old

---

*The stranger was almost certainly one Hoefer, a mining engineer/consultant about whom little else is known.

way until God knows when. That is all.'[21] The attempts to raise capital had mixed results. A trip to Paris failed to secure any investment, but a visit to Bethesda was more rewarding. J. T. Hughes, described as 'a moneyed chemist', bought £1800 worth of shares.[22] W. J. Parry – a journalist, spokesman for the North Wales quarrymen and sometime chairman of Caernarvonshire County Council – subscribed enough to give a radical respectability to the enterprise. By December 1892, the whole £5000 issue had been taken up. A board of directors was appointed. Thomas Lewis, a prosperous flour merchant who was Member of Parliament for Anglesey and famous within Nonconformity for his lectures on visits to the Holy Land, was made chairman. Lloyd George knew that the enterprise could not stand much public scrutiny. He told his wife that Lewis was given the job 'at my special request. He is a good blind to the public.'[23] The organisation in place, the directors decided to do what they should have done before they risked their own and their gullible friends' money. They decided to find out if there was any gold in the three holdings and if, supposing there were, it could be mined at an acceptable cost.

In March 1893, it was agreed that Parry should become the agent and general manager and sail to Argentina 'forthwith'. David Richards, who had owned the Argentine concession and initiated the plan to exploit it, was sent to Patagonia. He was to work, exclusively, on the syndicate's behalf for eighteen months, beginning with a fortnight in Buenos Aires 'for the purpose of attending to matters relating to the titles' and then another fortnight in Chubut Province 'to purchase various items necessary for the exploration'. When he arrived at the goldfields, he was to 'investigate and examine' the tract of country and report to the board of directors. He was to keep a diary which showed 'the disposition of his time' and a 'statement of account'. He was to receive a payment of £450 and two hundred shares in the company. Failure to carry out his duties would result in the immediate cancellation of his contract.

A contract which is drawn up in such precise terms, includes the obligation to account for details of time and ends with a note on how it can be terminated does not suggest that the employers have great faith in their employee. But Lloyd George, who went to Liverpool to see Parry off, assured his wife that the whole board was confident that the venture would succeed. 'Parry looked as happy as an April morning and the others were almost as elevated. High hopes seemed to possess them all.'[24] However, he did take the precaution of recruiting Hoefer – who was already in Argentina – to make an independent assessment of the prospect of striking and mining gold and, no doubt, also to report on Parry and Richards.

It would be wrong to say that thoughts of a Patagonian fortune distracted Lloyd George from the business of the House of Commons. But a letter to his wife, sent as early as 8 August 1893, reveals an unusual detachment from public affairs.

> The old man announced this afternoon that there would be an autumn session. I have a good mind to pair if all is well about disestablishment and run over to Buenos Aires to see our title complete . . . The sea voyage will set me up for years and I will be doing good work and somebody must go . . . What do you say. Don't mention it to uncle.[25]

Richard Lloyd would certainly have been unyielding in his opposition to an enterprise so clearly based on self-delusion and so near to being a fraud perpetrated on gullible investors. On 16 August, a second letter – unusually marked 'confidential' – announced that the plan to visit Argentina was cancelled.

> Patagonia is, I fear, a failure . . . Hoefer wires that the property falls short of representations . . . Will and I may be able to save ourselves to a great extent by a stiff lawyer's bill; but we must of course lose a lot of money. Not a word to anyone, remember, but to Will.[26]

Hoefer was back in Britain in September with the news that, in his opinion, Richards 'is more of a fool than a rogue. [He] simply assayed the surface. There is a chance that the stuff may improve as you go deeper . . . There is gold there but he [i.e. Hoefer] did not think that it would pay to work it unless the quality of the quartz improved.'[27] The doubts did not prevent Lloyd George from looking for new investors. Indeed in a damagingly frank letter he makes clear that he has no scruples about overstating the syndicate's prospects. 'We have just been discussing a scheme to sell all our shares in Buenos Aires. The Spaniards there are getting up an excitement about the business and it would be easy to feed that excitement and dispose of the whole thing to them.'[28]

The Spaniards lost interest. But Lloyd George's appetite for throwing good money after bad was insatiable – as long as the money was not his own. The Andes Exploring Company was set up in Bangor. It offered 'to take a 100 shares at 10/-' and Lloyd George had hopes of 'raising another £1,000 ourselves'. He told Margaret, 'You may rely upon it that I am not going to risk another penny piece.'[29] The time had come to give his uncle similar reassurances. 'Will must have told you what I am engaged in now as to the Patagonian business. If we raise the money we are bound to find something good out there . . . Whatever is done, I am entering into no personal liability or responsibility myself.'[30] The new financial arrangements were sanctioned at an Extraordinary General Meeting of the company which Hughes, the Bethesda chemist, complained was improperly convened.[31]

On Boxing Day 1893 – separated as usual, by his own choice, from his family at Christmas – Lloyd George called in at the National Liberal Club to collect any letters which might have been left for him there. He had no reason to expect a message of any importance. Only his restless spirit induced him to persuade R. O. Davies to drive him into central London. The journey was justified. A telegram from Patrick A. Chance, a Dublin solicitor and MP, had been delivered to the club five days earlier and a letter from him had followed it forty-eight hours later. Chance represented a client who would invest £5000 in the Patagonian goldfield and wished to serve as a director of the company.

Lloyd George was understandably jubilant. After the debts were cleared the company accounts would still show a surplus of £3700. 'This means restored credit which is a great fact. Besides, the big expense has already been incurred: buying machinery, taking to the ground, taking your men out there etc.'[32] But the news was not all good. Richards was 'blundering around destroying horses' and 'No telegram yet from Chance as to payment.'[33]

Anxiety about Chance's unreliability was overtaken by humiliation – personal for David Lloyd George and professional for his brother. Charles Breese – once the young men's mentor and then Lloyd George's competitor and scourge – 'sent two or three letters' demanding payment of the monies owed to J. W. Jones, a Portmadoc worker who had been shipped to Argentina but received no wages. Lloyd George's immediate response was clear and confident. 'Tell Charlie Breese that Richards had no authority whatsoever to run into debt but that if we can get some evidence that what J W J did pay was expended for our benefit we will pay notwithstanding.'[34] Within twenty-four hours, Lloyd George's mood changed. A second letter countermanded his previous instruction. 'As to J W Jones we had no money and we simply had to put him off – until we get a report on the case from W J

Parry. We must keep that up even if a writ is issued.'[35]

Parry was in Patagonia. It was his second voyage of exploration. The first had ended when, according to Lloyd George, he had 'played the fool' and 'run away in panic'.[36] Willingness to re-employ him confirms the quality of the syndicate's management – especially since his mandate was to remedy the errors made by Richards, who was judged to have 'blundered wholesale'.[37] Work had been suspended without realising the legal consequences of leaving the 'gold field' unattended. 'Sixty lots marked and allocated to the syndicate have been claimed by some German people. The mining laws of this country throw open abandoned claims.'[38] Whether or not Parry performed more competently on his second mission than on his first, he returned to London without gold. On 24 November 1894 the syndicate was effectively, though not legally, wound up.

For two years, Lloyd George assumed that Patagonia offered only fool's gold. Then, in the summer of 1896, Von Heyking revived his hopes of the syndicate making him an illusive fortune, and Lloyd George decided that if the first step was to find somebody who could persuade the creditors 'to settle . . . on reasonable terms', it would be prudent to do the job himself.[39] So on 21 August 1896 Richard George noted, without comment, 'DLlG sails today via Southampton to Buenos Aires in RMS Packet Clyde.'[40]

There is no doubt that Lloyd George intended that trip – for which he expected the liquidator to pay – should be as much concerned with pleasure as with work.[41] Henry Dalziel (later the proprietor of *Reynolds News*) accompanied Lloyd George and Herbert Lewis. Neither Dalziel nor Lewis was a major shareholder in the syndicate. But Lewis had become, and was to remain, Lloyd George's faithful friend and ally in all his great endeavours. Although wildly different in background and character, the two men enjoyed each other's company. Letters home during the journey mentioned business in passing, but mostly read like holiday postcards. 'Tell Dick I see shoals of flying fish . . . I am steaming round the bay with a party in a little tender . . . Bananas hanging in clusters on their stems.'[42] Inevitably – allowing for Lloyd George's temperament – once he arrived in Buenos Aires, he began to discuss with Von Heyking the prospect of creating a bigger and better goldmine.

The first scheme – about which the local manager of Baring Brothers was consulted – involved the amalgamation of several mines. The hope – necessarily unspoken – was that the barren field at Chubut would combine with more rewarding claims. Lloyd George's opinion of

Von Heyking changed radically several times during the three weeks in Argentina – an early indication of his lifelong mistake of making snap judgements about prospective allies and subordinates. The discussions on the goldmine's future were little more than interruptions in a programme of dinners and excursions. The three MPs (Dalziel was the Member for Kirkcaldn Burghs) visited Quilmer and Cordova, but not Patagonia. They never even saw Chubut – according to Lloyd George's letter to his brother, the urgent reason for his visit to the South Atlantic. On 24 October they set sail for home. Nothing had been decided. No bills had been paid. There had been no meeting with the outstanding creditors. And the talks about amalgamation with other mines had, like so much of the adventure, been wishful thinking. The syndicate was wound up at a formal meeting on 6 December 1900.

In terms of business, the trip to Argentina had been a failure. But business had always been only one of its objects. Lloyd George wanted, and believed that he deserved, a holiday. And he had enjoyed himself. Richard Lloyd George – his son, but not a totally reliable witness to his father's life – suggests that he enjoyed himself too much. 'There was a Spanish lady, married to a successful businessman . . . Father found her Latin ways and personality exotic . . . The affair almost finished in tragedy. The outraged husband issued a challenge – a duel, either swords or pistols.'[43]

The postscript to that unlikely story describes Lloyd George being smuggled out of Buenos Aires after shaving off his moustache in the hope that the enraged husband would not recognise him.* Richard Lloyd George also suggests that his mother – the saint and martyr of his biography – guessed why her husband had returned clean shaven and that, in consequence, 'there was another quarrel, this one more violent than I had ever known'.[44] If so, it was, for both husband and wife, entirely out of character. However, on his return to London, Lloyd George did face the first of the sexual scandals which threatened to destroy his career. Margaret supported him and believed in his innocence, from first to last.

On 9 October 1896, while Lloyd George was still in Argentina, William George received a letter from G. O. Roberts, a Caernarvon solicitor and Liberal agent for the constituency.

---

*In *The Young Lloyd George*, John Grigg suggests that Richard Lloyd George confused visits to Argentina and Canada, where his father, for reasons unknown, certainly *did* shave off his moustache.

J T R* informed you on Wednesday last of certain reports being circulated about DLlG . . . My own opinion is that a stop will have to be put to these reports at once by some means or other . . . It is the one matter talked about in the pubs . . . and is being spread broadcast by the Tories.[45]

William George, who had already heard the story, 'thought it was mere gossip which was best ignored altogether' and had 'honestly come to the conclusion that the story cannot be true'. He had no doubt that 'when D returns . . . he will be able to deal with the affair effectively'. In the meantime he hoped 'to God that neither uncle nor Maggie will hear anything of this slander'.[46]

The 'slander' was precise. On 10 August 1896, a Catherine Edwards − cousin to Margaret Lloyd George and the wife of David Edwards, a general practitioner in Cemmaes, Powys − had signed a statement which her husband claimed to have written at her dictation. The Edwardses had not 'lived as man and wife for some years' and David Edwards had long suspected that Catherine was committing adultery. On 8 August 1896, after a medical examination on which he had insisted, she was found to be six or seven months pregnant. When confronted with the fact of her condition she had made 'a full admission'.

I, Catherine Edwards, do hereby solemnly confess that I have on February 4 1896 committed adultery with Lloyd George MP and that the said Lloyd George is the father of the child and that I have on previous occasions committed adultery with the said Lloyd George.

The child was born − prematurely, according to Mrs Edwards − on 19 August.

There was no doubt that Lloyd George had stayed with the Edwardses on 4 February, the night on which the alleged adultery took place. The Edwardses were strong Liberals, good company and distant relations. Their house was a convenient staging post between Criccieth and the world beyond Wales. Doctor Edwards's daybook recorded the visit and his nightbook confirmed his wife's claim that he had been

---

*J. T. Roberts was Lloyd George's first election agent.

called out in the early evening to attend a patient and not returned until early morning.

G. O. Roberts told William George, 'If it is true, then D's days are numbered.'[47] But since he hoped it was the 'most devilish trick to blacken a man's name', he set about proving that the story was false.[48] He visited the proprietors of the temperance hotel in which Mrs Edwards had given birth and was told that no mention had been made of the child's paternity and that – as far as the proprietor knew – mother and child had returned to the family home. Doctor Owen, who had delivered the child, believed – though he could not be categoric – that the pregnancy had run its full term. If that was so, the child could not have been conceived on 4 February.

Lloyd George arrived home in Criccieth on 27 October and – no doubt reinforced by the evidence which Roberts had unearthed – wrote at once to Doctor Edwards about 'the strange rumour' for which, he had heard, the betrayed husband was responsible. The letter was a challenge as well as an outraged denial. 'I ask you with confidence that you should either accept my assurance that I have never perpetuated so gross an outrage upon the hospitality and friendship you extended to me, or that you should at once institute proceedings which would enable me to reply to so monstrous a calumny.'[49] Edwards replied by return of post. He denied that he had broadcast 'the statement to me from her [which] was quite unsolicited'. However, what followed was less than an absolute acceptance of Lloyd George's innocence. 'I *should* not have the least suspicion of such an improper act on your part.' The contingent verb suggested that, until more was known, Edwards was not prepared to absolve Lloyd George of responsibility.

The ambiguity did not go unnoticed. In his next letter to the doctor Lloyd George wrote that he *gathered* that the doctor did not accept Mrs Edwards's allegations. Any suspicion that the doubts could be left unresolved was removed by the next sentence. 'Would you mind telling me whether she or anyone else to your knowledge had made any written statement on the point?'[50] Lloyd George was making clear that he was looking for evidence to support a prosecution for defamation of character. Eight days later, Edwards sent a formal message. 'I have placed my case in the hands of Mr William Woosnam, Solicitor, Newtown.'[51]

Edwards was cooperative. He was prepared to show his wife's confession to Lloyd George – though the correspondence between husband and wife was not admissible evidence in a libel action. In March 1897, Mrs Edwards applied for a judicial separation. Doctor Edwards then sued for divorce on the grounds of adultery, citing as co-respondent Edward Wilson, the station master at Cemmaes Road railway station. Mrs Edwards responded with the claim that her husband was the father of the child and that he had written the confession and forced her to sign it with threats of violence. Doctor Edwards refuted the allegation and added that he had never believed the accusations against Lloyd George.

While Arthur Rhys Roberts – a Newport solicitor with whom, that summer, Lloyd George had set up a legal practice at 13, Walbrook, EC1 – dealt with the fall-out from the Edwards case in London, William was still required to devil in Wales. The preliminary hearing of Edwards versus Edwards began on 19 July 1897. Lloyd George's letter, denying adultery, had been supported by Doctor Edwards's absolution, so it was generally agreed that Lloyd George was not a party to the action. But the judge – Sir Francis Jeune, President of the Probate, Divorce and Admiralty Division – thought it necessary to refer to two strange aspects of the case. The first proved nothing but the judge's faulty grasp of logic – or his lofty view of medical ethics. It amounted to the unjustified assertion that if Doctor Edwards had, as his wife claimed, dictated the confession, he must – at least at the time – have believed it to be true. His second comment was more logical, and considerably more damaging to Lloyd George. He had been offered an opportunity to appear in court and clear his name on oath and it had been rejected.

The main hearing began on 18 November 1897. William George's complaint about the amount of time that he had spent preparing his brother's submission probably owed more to his distaste for the nature of the case than his aversion to long hours of work. 'I got up at 6.10am. Went to Aberystwyth. Took Mrs E's evidence. A very trying business.'[52] His notes on the meeting include Doctor Edwards's statement that he did not 'believe Mr Lloyd George to be the father of the Respondent's illegitimate child'.[53] His submission took on a particular importance when Mrs Edwards's barrister announced that his client could provide no evidence to support the allegation of cruelty by her husband. Moreover, if the charge were changed to adultery with person unknown rather than with Edward Wilson, his client would offer no defence. Wilson's counsel added that he had a great deal of evidence which he was happy to introduce as proof of his client's innocence. Bargrave Deane QC, for Doctor Edwards, amended the charge and listed the events which led up to Edwards's petition. The jury and the world was left to wonder, 'If not Wilson, who?'

The list of events submitted to the court included Mrs Edwards's 'confession'. In the preliminary hearing, Lloyd George's name had been carefully concealed. The man against whom the accusation of paternity had been made was referred to as 'AB'. Deane chose to reveal that AB was, in fact, the Member of Parliament for the Caernarvon Boroughs. He then made clear that he regarded the allegations as certainly unfounded and probably malicious. Lloyd George was, therefore, left with a dilemma. Should he go into the witness box and swear under oath that he had not committed adultery with the unfortunate Kitty Edwards? The position was complicated by Edward Wilson's formal declaration of his innocence.

At first William George recommended that his brother should do the same, although Margaret Lloyd George argued with great passion that it would be wise to avoid the publicity of a formal statement, no matter how convincing the exculpation might be. Lloyd George's instincts were in favour of silence. So the ever faithful and compliant William came rapidly to a new conclusion. 'The circumstances have changed to a considerable extent. In the first place, the charge itself has been withdrawn and in the second place the vigorous measures you took at the time with a view of bringing your slanderers to justice has scotched the scandal.'[54] And so it turned out, though the affair was laid to rest only after a story in the *Caernarvon and Denbigh Herald* – claiming that he had chosen not to assert his innocence – was confounded by a bogus statement, published in the name of William George. It suggested that Lloyd George had been on his way to court to give evidence when he heard that the case was settled and a personal démarche impossible. Lloyd George himself – always quick to turn adversity into advantage – wrote to *The Times* to complain that the law did not allow him to cite Mrs Edwards's 'confession' as evidence in a libel prosecution. He represented himself as the innocent casualty of a war between husband and wife.

The true nature of Lloyd George's relationship with Mrs Edwards is made clear by a note she wrote – for some reason on black-edged mourning paper – and posted from Cemmaes on 15 February 1894. One passage raises questions. 'You must come to spend either Easter or Whitsuntide with us. I have been told that Carno people are going to ask you to speak there. In that case it can be managed.' Another leaves little room for doubt. 'I am addressing this to the Club and the minute you have read it please commit it to the fire.'[55]

Although Lloyd George was not the father of Mrs Edwards's child, the likelihood must be that, nevertheless, he had an adulterous relationship with the mother. That explains his reluctance to be cross-examined on oath. And it was also consistent with his character. What remains is the difficulty of reconciling his all-consuming ambition with the reckless willingness to risk everything for little more than a casual relationship. All his life Lloyd George believed that – as long as he was willing to sacrifice the lady of the moment when danger threatened – he would avoid exposure. In his autobiography, Richard offered another reason for his father's dangerous conduct: apart from the occasional round of golf, women were his only relaxation.[56]

Local supporters never doubted their Member of Parliament's innocence. J. G. Griffin, outfitter and draper, sent him a copy of a resolution passed unanimously by the Conway Liberal Association which typified sentiment in the Boroughs. It 'sincerely complimented Mr Lloyd George on his complete vindication from the foul and baseless accusations and sympathises with him in the cruel position in which he was unjustly placed'.[57] But Lloyd George did not always succeed in deceiving his family. News of the Edwards affair was kept from Uncle Lloyd until it was clear that accounts of the trial would soon appear in the newspapers. Then William George had the duty of breaking the news. His account of the way in which the old man reacted does not suggest that he had absolute faith in his nephew's probity. William George told 'him the truth as painlessly as [he] could, but it was a great shock to him and he had several bursts of crying before he managed to control himself'.[58] However, Margaret Lloyd George seemed to have no doubt that her husband had never been involved with Mrs Edwards. After she 'discovered everything about the scandal', her brother-in-law wrote, 'She bears it like a true girl. Of course, she doesn't incline to believe it.'[59]

Faith in her husband's innocence had been reinforced by his ability – a feature of his whole life – to remain calm in the face of destruction. Although a thoroughly bad husband, David Lloyd George was, by the standards of the day, a good father. And at the height of the Edwards crisis, his demonstrations of genuine paternal affection must have provided reassuring evidence that he was a family man. On 1 July 1897 – as part of Queen Victoria's jubilee celebrations, Members of Parliament and their families were invited to Windsor. Mary Lloyd was staying with the Lloyd Georges and her letter to her brother Richard reported that Dick, then aged eight, had announced that he would rather go to the zoo. '"You would prefer to see the monkeys than the Queen?" David asked. "Yes" said Dick with great emphasis,' to his father's clear delight.[60] He was less enthusiastic about Gwilym's inadequate grasp of English – a clear sign that he was spending more time in the Land of his Fathers than with his father in London.[61] But it all created the illusion of a stable family. Six months later Margaret's confidence in her husband's fidelity was shattered by the discovery of his liaison with Mrs Timothy Davies – Mrs Tim, as she was known to Lloyd George and his friends.

CHAPTER 7

AN END TO HIRAETH

Timothy Davies was the son of a prosperous Carmarthenshire miller. At the age of fourteen he was apprenticed to a Liverpool draper and in 1885, after ten years as a journeyman, he opened his own shop in Waltham Green in west London. It was the beginning of what became a retail empire. The financial stability enabled him to build a career first in local and then in national Liberal politics. He facilitated the transition by cultivating prominent members of the party. Twice, while he was looking for a more permanent London home, Lloyd George was the Davieses' guest. In September 1895, the Lloyd Georges and the Davieses went on holiday together to Scotland. Davies paid the bill.

All that is known about the fortnight spent in Oban is that both families were almost drowned when their sailing boat was caught in a storm in Oban Bay and that Lloyd George acquired a taste for golf. We do not know how the relationship between Lloyd George and Mrs Davies ended. But it is clear why it began. Even Richard, Lloyd George's son – who was bitterly antagonistic towards all the women in his father's life – described her as 'a lively, attractive creature, rather loquacious, very stylish, perhaps a little flamboyant'.[1] In fact she was all that Margaret Lloyd George was not, could never have been and did not want to be. She was also there. After the holiday, Lloyd George and the Davieses were in London. Margaret Lloyd George was too often in Criccieth.

The Lloyd Georges blamed each other for the long periods spent apart. In February 1896, Margaret had received a sharp rejoinder to the complaint that her husband no longer minded that two hundred and fifty miles divided them. 'It is quite true what you say about one getting accustomed even to these periodic separations from one's family – but all the same I get spasms of homesickness. You know very well that the pressure to bring us together invariably comes from me.'[2]

That was true. Before the turn of the century, Lloyd George wanted his wife to be with him in London. That was one of the reasons why he had moved to Palace Mansions. But Margaret remained stubbornly attached to Criccieth. When pregnancy and miscarriage made travel difficult for her, he proposed that they should share a permanent home in the capital. A wife had a duty to meet her husband's needs. And two houses was an extravagance which they could not afford – despite his plans to set up a London law practice.

> You must bear in mind that we are spending more than we earn. I draw far more than my share of the profits though I don't attend to 1/10th of the work. This is neither fair nor honourable . . . Unless I retire from politics altogether and content myself with the position of a country attorney, we must give up the comforts of Criccieth for life in London.

There was, he went on to explain in an unusually sympathetic letter, no need to assume that the change meant moving into the hurly-burly of one of the central boroughs.

> If you prefer we can take a home in the suburbs – say Ealing or Acton – Ealing for choice. The air is as good as anything you can get in Wales as it is free from the smoke of the great city. Or, if you prefer, we could go still further out and live, say, in Brighton.[3]

His wife was not persuaded, and by August 1896 the character of the correspondence had been transformed by one of those chance events which change lives and destinies. Somehow – improbable though it must seem, taking account of her constant absence from London – Margaret heard from a Palace Mansions servant that there had been 'a very early visitor to Lloyd George's flat'. Her response combined anger and anguish in almost equal measure and made clear that she had known 'or suspected' for some time that her husband was having an affair with Mrs Timothy Davies.

> This business I tell you comes between you and me more so than you imagine and is growing, and you know it and yet you cannot

shake it off. It pains me to the quick and I am very unhappy. If you must go on as at present, I don't know where it will end . . . Beware, don't give place for any scandal for the sake of your own personal self and your bright career.[4]

Nothing in Margaret Lloyd George's character – or in her behaviour during the forty years of married life which followed – suggests that the mention of a possible scandal was a threat rather than a warning. But Lloyd George and his apologists (including some biographers) have chosen to interpret her concern as blackmail. That enabled him to reply with unrestrained, and deeply unattractive, fury.

You threaten me with a public scandal. Alright – expose me if that suits you. One scandal the more will but kill me the earlier. But you will not alter my resolution to have neither correspondence nor communication of any sort with you until it is more clearly understood how you propose to guide your course for the future. I have borne it for years and have suffered in health and character. I'll stand it no longer, come what may.[5]

Letters must have crossed in the post. For when he wrote home again two days later, in even more abrasive language, he began, 'Your letter this morning made me wild.' He described, in corrosive detail, why. 'There was the same self-complacent, self-satisfied Phariseeism about it.' He then went on to list her failings.

Be candid with yourself . . . drop that infernal Methodism which is the curse of your better nature and reflect whether you have not rather neglected your husband. I have more than once gone without breakfast. I have scores of times come home in the dead of night to a cold, dark and comfortless flat without a soul to greet me . . . I am not the nature, either physically or morally, that I ought to have been left like thus . . . You have been a good mother. You have not – and I say this now not in anger – always been a good wife.

Margaret can have had no doubt to whom her husband referred when he told her, 'I can point you, even among those whom you affect to look down upon, much better wives.'

The most unpleasant aspect of the letter is its opening sentence.

'That telegram just saved you.'[6] After she wrote in anger for a second time, Margaret Lloyd George had lost her nerve and wired an apology. Yet Lloyd George still chose to recriminate in the most brutal language. He was employing the tactics which helped to propel him into the premiership. Margaret's telegram was an act of submission. Defeated adversaries – a wife no less than a political rival – were never treated with magnanimity. He exploited her capitulation by making clear that she was responsible for the infidelities – and that she should not expect him completely to abandon the pleasures and comforts which she denied him.

There is no doubt that Margaret Lloyd George did neglect her husband – scandalously by the standards of the male-dominated society in which they lived. Whether or not her detachment was the cause or justification of his conduct is open to debate. But one sentence in the second brutal letter goes a long way towards explaining his relationship with 'Mrs Tim' and many other ladies. 'In many respects,' he wrote, 'I am as helpless as a child.' He needed to be looked after – fed, amused, flattered, encouraged. It was not a role to which Margaret was suited. So he constantly looked elsewhere.

Lloyd George's relationship with Mrs Timothy Davies survived for another ten years and continued – probably in a more sentimental than carnal form – even after Frances Stevenson came into his life. Margaret was spared nothing. After she complained that he preferred Mrs Tim's company to hers, he replied, 'So would anybody. Mrs T with all her defects – and to these I am not blind – is at least fairly interesting.'[7] Perhaps it was Lloyd George's brutality which made Margaret so submissive. Her complaints about Mrs Tim continued but were expressed in the language of a wife who feared that her husband's good nature was being abused rather than one who knew she was being deceived. Lloyd George, for his part, added unconvincing reassurances to his letters home. 'Returning from Lewes where I have been having a game of golf with Tim . . . No Mrs Tim. She has gone to Llandrindod with the kids.'[8]

Margaret – perhaps at last realising that her husband's philandering could be reduced, though not eliminated, by giving him more attention – began to spend time in London when, in 1899, the Lloyd Georges acquired what she regarded as a suitable house in Trinity Road, Wandsworth. Proximity did not ensure fidelity. In time Mrs Tim would become part of the family. When David Lloyd George and his austere brother set off on an Italian holiday, she was on the quayside to wave them goodbye. She was accepted but never forgiven by Margaret.

However, had it not been for Mrs Tim, the Lloyd George story would have come to a sudden end in 1905. Between two speaking tours of Scotland, during the run-up to the anticipated general election, he had a reoccurrence of the throat infection which had become a regular feature of his campaigns. His tonsils were removed but Margaret stayed in Wales rather than supervise his convalescence. A couple of days after he returned home, he suffered a severe throat haemorrhage which, had there been no one with him, would have been fatal. Happily, Mrs Tim was in attendance. She called for an ambulance and saved his life.

Whether or not Margaret's disinclination to come to London made her a bad wife, her husband's reluctance to go home to Wales made him, by modern standards, a thoroughly unsatisfactory constituency MP. Indeed in terms of the championing of parochial issues he was for long periods not a constituency MP at all. His role was to lead his people, not to succour them. When he visited the Caernarvon Boroughs he made speeches or, very occasionally, appeared in court. At his rallies his subjects were the emotive issues which roused Wales in general and Welsh Nonconformity in particular. In court he acted for defendants who attracted popular sympathy. Local issues attracted him when they related to the handful of disparate ideas which made up his political philosophy.

Lloyd George was in Argentina in September 1896 when the dispute at the Penrhyn slate quarry in Bethesda began. The quarrymen had demanded a minimum wage of 4/6 an hour, an end to the employment of unskilled, low-paid, contract labour and the recognition of the committee which negotiated on their behalf. All the demands were rejected by the owner, Lord Penrhyn. When seventy-one men were sacked, the rest of the workers came out on strike in sympathy. On his return from South America, Lloyd George immediately became their champion.

The quarry was not in Lloyd George's constituency, though many of the quarrymen's cottages were. But it was neither the duty to defend his voters nor solidarity with the workers which made him rally to their cause. Trade unions and trade unionism never appealed to him. Perhaps he was moved by the plight of the locked-out quarrymen and their families, for he endorsed the appeal which raised £20,000 to alleviate their suffering. But what really motivated him was a chance not to defend the poor, but to attack the rich. Lord Penrhyn had offended against one of the few principles that consistently influenced Lloyd George's politics. He had made a fortune from land which he owned but did nothing to improve.

Between September and Christmas 1896, a list of Lord Penrhyn's numerous iniquities was included in every speech that Lloyd George made. When the House reassembled in the New Year, he added his name to a motion condemning the quarry-owner's conduct. After a Welsh choir gave a fund-raising concert in a London Methodist chapel, he 'took them to the club and gave them tea' and 'spoke at the overflow meeting'.[9] The dispute dragged on into 1897, giving Lloyd George the chance to support the quarrymen in the way he did best and most enjoyed. A great rally was organised in the Caernarvon Pavilion. The guest speaker was John Burns, a trade unionist who was the Independent Labour Party afterwards Liberal Member for Battersea and would, eight years later, serve alongside Lloyd George in the Campbell-Bannerman Cabinet. Eight thousand quarrymen and their wives filled the hall and cheered Lloyd George's assertion that, although 'a principle of labour was involved', the dispute raised 'a principle of far greater importance . . . namely the right of the people to the land, to the mountains and to the resources of the earth'.[10] Lord Penrhyn, because of his morally dubious inheritance, was able to choose between locking up the resources of the earth or stealing £200,000 a year from the quarrymen's wages. It was the speech of a class warrior outraged at the theft of what Karl Marx called surplus value. Lloyd George was not guided by book-learned philosophy. His principles were built on his experience. And such as they were, they endured. In his 1909 Budget, Lloyd George proposed a tax on mining and quarrying royalties.

The dispute was suspended when W. J. Parry (who had failed to rescue the Argentine venture) brokered a deal. But Lloyd George neither forgave nor forgot – even though by 1897 he had himself become the part owner of a quarry. He had invested in the Dorothea slate mine in Caernarvonshire's Nantlle Valley. The enterprise, like the Patagonian gold syndicate, failed. No doubt that made it easier to attack quarry-owners who made money from their workmen's labours. During the second reading of the Voluntary Schools Bill – an emasculated version of an Education Bill which had been introduced and abandoned in the previous year – he chose Lord Penrhyn as an example of how, in some parishes, wealthy landlords were spared high rate demands because Nonconformist parents made voluntary contributions towards the upkeep of the schools. The poor made sacrifices for their children's education while the rich exploited their devotion.

The Education Bill of 1896 had been the occasion, though not the cause, of the radicals' temporary, but overt, rejection of Home Rule.

On the fifth day of the debate, John Dillon – leader of the largest group of Irish Members – had announced 'with a great deal of pain' that he felt obliged to abandon the Nonconformist allies who had supported Irish causes, and vote for a bill which proposed to increase the public subsidy of sectarian education. The main beneficiary would be the Church of England, but Catholic schools – educating the children of two million Irish immigrants – would also benefit. The *Methodist Times* announced that 'when Mister Dillon . . . sat down after giving his official support to the Second Reading of the Education Bill, Gladstonian Home Rule gave its last sigh and died'.[11] The *British Weekly* judged that the 'Irish had severed the last links which bound them to the Liberal Party'.[12] John Redmond, the leader of the smaller Irish faction, called Dillon 'the man who killed Home Rule'.

Lloyd George played a surprisingly small part in the 1896 Education Bill debates. But when, in the next session of Parliament, the Voluntary Schools Bill was presented to the House, he made up for lost time and opportunity. His most destructive invective was directed at the Irish MPs who had supported sectarian education and, more significantly, Ireland in general.

When Dillon proposed an amendment which redistributed the subsidy – more to poor areas and less to rich – Lloyd George said that the Irish leader typified the attitude of a nation which expected to live at Great Britain's expense. Dillon's only interest, he claimed, was getting more for Catholic schools. Why should the House assume that the Irish living in England were poorer than the Methodists and Nonconformists who ran a substantial number of schools but, because they were provident, paid for them themselves? 'The Honourable Member for Mayo proposes not merely robbing another area but robbing another creed.'[13]

If Lloyd George possessed any strong views on the future of Ireland they were encompassed in the colloquial phrase Home Rule All Round – a euphemism for a federal state. The idea, originally taken up by Joseph Chamberlain and then lost in the bitter battles over the first Home Rule Bill, had been revived in the autumn of 1895 by Cymru Fydd. During that October, an article on the subject appeared in *Young Wales*. Lloyd George had espoused the idea, briefly and half-heartedly. But when it was discussed in the Radical Manifesto Committee – a caucus which he had created – he had agreed that other constitutional reforms, most notably the abolition of the House of Lords, were more important and deserved greater priority. At Thomas Gee's funeral in

1898 he told J. H. Lewis that 'it would have been better, back in 1886, if the Welsh had declined to support Gladstone but followed Chamberlain into Home Rule All Round'.[14] But that was all in the past. Lloyd George always looked to the future.

Gee – propagandist of land reform and an early patron of its most dynamic advocate – was one of the few men towards whom Lloyd George felt genuine gratitude. 'He treated me always as a father would a child – affectionately.' His letter home, which told Margaret of Gee's death, reveals real human emotions in his expression of regret that he had failed to reply to Gee's last letter. When Tom Ellis died seven months later – still only forty – Lloyd George's reaction was very different. The best he was able to do by way of expressing his grief was to rejoice that 'the last thing that Ellis ever read was a letter from me . . . and he laughed outright at the joke in it'.[15] In death as in life, Ellis existed for Lloyd George only as a reflection of his own ambition and personality.

Gee's death broke another of Lloyd George's links with Wales. It came six months after he had made his last half-hearted attempt to mobilise Welsh Liberalism behind the national interests of the principality. In late 1896, the Liberals of Flint and Denbighshire had called for a conference to examine the future of a demoralised and divided party. It was held, under Gee's sponsorship, in January 1897. The delegates did no more than demand another meeting, an alternative to action that became the pattern of progress. But the eventual creation of a Welsh Liberal Council provided the first opportunity for Lloyd George to step back from Welsh politics. Sir George Osborne Morgan, the latest in the line of leaders elected by Welsh Liberal MPs, died on 25 August 1897. The Member for North Monmouthshire, Reginald McKenna – who was to become an implacable enemy – proposed that Lloyd George should fill the vacancy. The offer was declined with thanks on the pretext that another candidate might more easily achieve the unity which the Liberals of Wales so desperately needed.

The Liberal Party remained deeply divided over the future of Home Rule. One faction supported it in principle, and believed that, right or wrong, Mr Gladstone's inheritance must be respected. A second rejected it in principle while a third – itself unable to agree about the principle – opposed it because it was an electoral liability. On 11 February 1898, Lloyd George became the physical manifestation of radical disenchantment when he walked out of the House of

Commons. He did so while John Redmond was moving an amendment to the address which called for 'national self-government for Ireland' to be implemented by an independent Parliament and executive 'with authority over all affairs distinctly Irish'. It was a modest proposal by Irish Nationalist standards. The areas of policy for which the Dublin government was to be responsible certainly did not include defence and foreign policy and might be argued to have excluded trade and some items of taxation. Redmond made clear that his amendment was no more than symbolic – a reaffirmation of Irish nationhood on the centenary of the ill-fated uprising which had ended with the defeat of the invading French forces and the capture (and subsequent execution) of Wolfe Tone. Some of the Liberals who joined in Lloyd George's theatrical exit had been offended by Redmond's attack on the ark of their covenant. Redmond had claimed that their commitment to electoral reform was designed to reduce Irish representation at Westminster. Lloyd George had particular cause to feel outraged at the questioning of his motives.

At the Leicester meeting of the National Liberal Federation, at the beginning of 1898, he had set out the classic case for ending plural voting and abolishing the House of Lords – in typically polemical terms.

> We give one vote, or probably no vote at all, to the man who handles the plough and ten to the man who handles the hunting whip . . . One vote to the busy bee and ten to the devouring locust. It is not the soil of the country but the soul which we want represented in the House of Commons. After all, they have got a House all to themselves which they guard as jealously as if it were a pheasant reserve.[16]

Lloyd George had a more complicated motive than the wish to reassert that Home Rule could not be allowed to stand in the way of reform. By abandoning Redmond he was making plain that Irish Nationalists could no longer regard Liberals as their constant and unquestioning allies. And by taking that responsibility upon himself, he was edging towards a dominant role in the party.

Lloyd George went on to emphasise his determination to break with the Irish Nationalists by voting against John Dillon's motion which called for the creation of a Catholic university in Dublin. He justified his opposition with a brazen volte face. The Conservatives, he claimed, were attempting to kill Home Rule by kindness. The offer to the

Catholic hierarchy was a squalid bribe, intended to persuade the Irish parties to abandon Ireland's destiny. A few days earlier he had supported the idea himself.

The Irish had committed what Lloyd George regarded as the ultimate act of political folly. Unlike many of his colleagues, he had come to terms with – indeed positively welcomed – the new politics. The age of the extended suffrage – brought in with the Reform Bill of 1867 – required Members of Parliament to pay attention to, if not respect, the opinion of the people on whose votes they depended. But the Irish

> had managed to alienate the sympathies of a large mass of the electors throughout the country, men who were as eager, as earnest in favour of conceding Home Rule as any Irishmen among them . . . All these people have been dampened in their ardour and killed in their enthusiasm and that was to a large extent attributable to a series of follies perpetrated by the Irish leaders themselves . . . The preposterous resolution moved by Mr Redmond, insisting upon an independent parliament for Ireland . . . had made it impossible for them to continue the alliance.

The speech was, by implication, a redefinition of Home Rule – at least as it might apply to Wales. The Welsh wanted only 'to manage their little local affairs', which he defined as education, disestablishment and land reform. They were certainly 'not going to be cut off from their interests in the Empire. Welsh blood was in the very fabric. It was the cement which held the Empire together.'[17]

Lloyd George's unremitting hostility had what was almost certainly its intended effect. On 17 August, he was able to quote to Margaret a comment from the *Newcastle Daily* editorial which – unlike many of the compliments which he gleefully reported – represented the view of most of his colleagues.

> Mr Lloyd George had distanced all competition. He delivered some of the more daring speeches of the session and his attacks on some of the clauses in the Irish Local Government Bill were admirably sustained. The Member for Caernarvon has strenuously repudiated the idea that the Liberal Party is bound to support any Irish legislation which may appear good to the Nationalists. He has earned himself enemies but he has made the foundation of a big Parliamentary reputation.[18]

Criticism of his elders, and supposed betters, was an established feature of Lloyd George's technique for getting noticed. In 1898, it was extended to a new and dangerous area of policy – foreign affairs. The risk was increased by his inconsistency. His imperialism ebbed and flowed with unpredictable tides. In a speech of undisputed audacity he sailed into open conflict with Henry Campbell-Bannerman, the new leader of the Liberal Party.

General Kitchener, flushed with the slaughter of twenty thousand Dervishes at Omdurman in September 1898, had advanced up the Nile and laid claim to the territory on behalf of the Khedive of Egypt. At Fashoda he had met a small contingent of French soldiers who impertinently refused to withdraw. Prime Minister Salisbury hoped for peace with honour but Chamberlain insisted that the French must beat a humiliating retreat or risk war. Rosebery – a genuine imperialist but, after his resignation as Liberal leader, an ever more enthusiastic mischief-maker – announced that the Unionists' unyielding attitude towards the French was 'the policy of the last [Liberal] government, deliberately adopted and sustained'.[19] He had led that government, so he spoke with some authority. To much astonishment, his successor, Campbell-Bannerman – who had been his Secretary of State for War, though never an imperialist – endorsed his judgement. Lloyd George, though younger, was wiser. Speaking at Haworth in Yorkshire, he called for moderation while, at the same time, rejoicing in Britain's naval strength, in a compliment which was designed to appeal to the jingoists who were clamouring for France to be put in its place.

> If we go to war, what will be the outcome? I know enough about the condition of our Navy to say with perfect confidence that France will be defeated. But that is not all. If we defeat France we shall be defeating the only power on the Continent with a democratic Constitution. Emperors, Kings and aristocratic rulers will mock at the whole thing – two great democratic Powers at each others' throats, the only countries where you have perfect civil and religious liberty in Europe quarrelling with each other to make sport for the titled and throned Philistines of Europe.[20]

It was a speech of remarkable power and prescience. But parliamentary reputations are rarely built on speeches alone. Politicians have to grind their way up the greasy poll. In May 1899 Lloyd George accepted

membership of the House of Commons Select Committee on the
Aged and Deserving Poor.

Joseph Chamberlain had believed in, and advocated, some form of
'old-age pension' ever since being leader of the radical caucus on the
Birmingham Town Council, and he had twice succeeded in persuading
the government to set up an inquiry into its cost and feasibility. Both
investigations had been handicapped by terms of reference which
required them only to consider schemes financed by contributions
raised from the beneficiaries. On each occasion the Friendly Societies
had lobbied against the introduction of what – as distinct from dole to
the destitute – they regarded as a threat to their existence. As a result,
neither the Abadare Commission (1895) nor Lord Rothschild's Treasury
Committee (1898) had been willing to recommend the introduction of
a national pension. Chamberlain was a genuine believer. When he tried
a third time, the pressure of political necessity was on his side. Unionist
MPs combined to demand that some progress be made towards the
establishment of a national pension and one of them, Lionel Holland,
the Conservative Member for Bow and Bromley, announced his intention of sponsoring a Private Member's bill which reflected their views.
The government's response was a third committee of enquiry – chaired,
for safety's sake, by Henry Chaplin, the Conservative Member for
Sleaford and President of the Local Government Board. His terms of
reference allowed consideration of a pension scheme which would be
subsidised by taxation.

It was Lloyd George's first chance to build rather than to demolish –
to offer solutions instead of criticism. He proved himself capable of creating as well as destroying. As always he sounded as enthusiastic about
penalising the rich as he did about benefiting the poor. But he produced
a memorandum of positive proposals which combined some of the traditional prejudices about the undeserving poor with a more modern
view – that those who yielded to the working-class temptations of dishonesty and indolence should be given the chance to redeem
themselves and qualify for the state's largesse.

The Lloyd George scheme offered a pension of 5/- a week to all citizens over sixty-five years of age whose annual income was not more
than £26, had not been convicted of an indictable offence and had not
benefited from parish relief. The disqualification was not, however, permanent. The stigma of both conviction and pauperism could be washed
away by behaviour which proved that, despite earlier lapses, the prospective recipient had become a responsible citizen. Rehabilitation could be

demonstrated by membership of a trade union or Friendly Society for twenty years. A Friendly Society or Post Office annuity of 2/- a week, of ten years' duration, would also be taken as proof that a working-class sinner had come to middle-class repentance.

The scheme was to be administered not by the parish councils – always an object of Lloyd George's enmity – but by the county councils. They would pay for the pension from their rates and then receive a grant or aid from the government which, crucially, would vary according to the size of the county's population. Councils would be permitted to pay more than the basic 5/- a week but would be expected to meet the extra expenditure from their own resources. And, in one important respect, the Lloyd George scheme broke new ground. Everyone whose annual income was below £26 qualified for payment on the principle that 'if proof of destitution is demanded as a condition precedent to receiving a pension, there is no essential difference between pensions and outdoor relief [the Poor Law's minimal payment to paupers]'.[21] Lloyd George was still undecided about the merits of an insurance-based scheme and he privately regarded provision for unemployment as more important than protection in old age. But he was edging towards the idea of a pension *by right*.

Chaplin accepted Lloyd George's amendment to his own proposal and agreed that 5/- should be the *minimum* weekly pension and that an increase of up to 7/- should be allowed if the addition was locally financed. The Boards of Guardians were to administer the scheme and the Treasury grant would reflect the differences in size of population from area to area. Lloyd George was at least as gratified by the discomfiture of his enemies as he was by the acceptance of his ideas.

> Old Age Pensions is through . . . I have added some millions onto the bill for them. I am sure I put on 2 or 3 millions yesterday and a similar sum today. Never mind it all goes to the poor who really need it. It has the additional advantage of putting those bandits who are now in power in a nice fix. They can neither carry out these recommendations nor drop them – not without discredit . . . Chaplin told me today that the Chancellor of the Exchequer is already swearing at him.[22]

It was just as well that Lloyd George thought of the Chaplin Report as primarily an opportunity to discomfit his political enemies. For, as he must have known, there was no real prospect of it being accepted by the government or of Chamberlain – the original advocate of a national pension – arguing for its acceptance. But ministers – no less conscious than Lloyd George of the odium they would attract by outright rejection – set up a departmental committee to determine the cost of adoption and implementation.

Lionel Holland – whose threatened Private Member's bill had frightened the government into setting up the Chaplin Committee – resigned his seat and stood against Chamberlain in Birmingham as a Liberal and an advocate of the reform which he claimed had been betrayed by its original champion. Lloyd George – outraged by the failure of his old hero to live up to expectation and conscious of the need to find a new villain to replace the Church of England establishment – turned on Chamberlain with renewed fury. But the old enemy, in the form of the Tithe Rent Bill, still had to be confronted.

The government's revised proposals included the offer to exclude tithe income from the assessment of rateable value of rectories and vicarages – at a cost of £87,000 to the Exchequer. During the second reading of the bill Lloyd George claimed that the needs 'of the shopkeeper and the quarryman . . . are forgotten. Only the case of one section of the community is to be considered . . . The squire and the parson have broken into the poor box and divided its contents between them . . . The men who were promised some provision for old age are still left out in the cold.'[23] His pleas were ignored and the old had to wait until he became Chancellor of the Exchequer ten years later. The Budget that provided the first pension was drafted by Asquith and introduced by him in the House of Commons days after he became Prime Minister in 1908. But Lloyd George, although he inherited the legislation, can lay claim to parentage of the idea. Only Joe Chamberlain – the other great radical of British history – has an equal claim.

Lloyd George, in the great tradition of social reformers, felt no obligation to share the hardships which the poor endured. But a variety of deprivations were forced upon him. He never spared himself in the execution of his political duties and, because of his obsession with remaining in London at the heart of politics – as well as his preference for making speeches rather than keeping house – he often lived in considerably less than comfort. On 27 May 1892 he had written home with the admission, 'I haven't changed my drawers for whole fortnight' and the request 'Please send me a pair per parcel post.'[24] References to stale food and cold lodgings were a feature of the letters which he wrote home almost every day and which provide an insight into his complicated character. The main purpose of the correspondence – to his brother and uncle as well as his wife – was to record, perhaps for posterity, his triumphs and the congratulations which followed. That innocent pleasure was often accompanied – when writing to Margaret – by a less attractive weakness. Letters to her were peppered with accounts of his conduct which, although superficially reassuring, were clearly intended to demonstrate how much he was in demand. Sometimes there was a playful rebuke. 'You are a jealous little creature! Miss May is not there. As a matter of fact, I have not seen her for months.'[25]

Women were his major weakness. His minor self-indulgence was foreign travel.* Usually it was undertaken with London friends rather than with his wife, and the time was spent neither in admiring antiquities nor exploring unknown territory but in talking about politics. Usually he thought it necessary – as in the case of Argentina – to claim that a serious purpose justified the cost of the ticket. Often his holidays were a week or two added to a parliamentary delegation's official visit to a conveniently exotic location. His first experience of foreign travel had been to the 1892 Conference of the Inter-Parliamentary Union. The House of Commons bought him a ticket to Berne and he broke his journey in Paris where, according to his letter to Margaret, he found the Eiffel Tower smaller than he had hoped. In 1898 and 1899, he was in Rome. The ticket – overland to Marseille, then by sea to Tangier, Algiers, Tunis, Malta and Naples before turning north – was bought by Lloyd George and George. When, during the summer of 1899, he felt the urge to travel again, he was fortunate to be included in a House of Commons delegation to Canada. He sailed on 19 August 1899.

On 7 September, he wrote to his wife from Winnipeg with a complaint. 'One can't get an idea from the telegraphic news in the Canadian papers as to how things are going about in the Transvaal.'[26] Eleven days later, in Vancouver, he had gained a better impression of the situation in South Africa. His letter to his brother was read to a meeting at the Caernarvon Guildhall on 6 October. 'The news from the Transvaal threatens to alter my arrangements. War means the summoning of

---

*A complete list of his numerous foreign excursions appears in Appendix II.

Parliament and the former seems now inevitable. The prospect oppresses me with a deep sense of horror. If I have the courage I shall protest with all the vehemence at my command against the outrage which is perpetrated in the name of freedom.'[27]

CHAPTER 8

GO FOR JOE

In 1895, Doctor Leander Starr Jameson had led a raid into the Transvaal which he, and his backers, foolishly believed would ignite an explosion of rebellion among the Uitlanders – 'foreigners' to the country, including settlers from Britain and the white dominions. After five days – defeated and surrounded by the Boers – he surrendered on the promise that the raiders' lives would be spared. Joseph Chamberlain, then Colonial Secretary, who was almost certainly a party to the raid, escaped censure – largely because he was a member of the House of Commons Select Committee which enquired into its origins. Lord Rosebery described it as an 'Elizabethan adventure',[1] and the Poet Laureate published verses in praise of Jameson's gallantry. While many radicals expressed their passionate opposition to what was undoubtedly an illegal act, Lloyd George preferred to ridicule both the abortive coup and the British politician whom he blamed for what he represented as a national humiliation. At Penarth on 28 November 1896, he had got near to rejoicing that 'South Africa, a small republic, with an army the size of an ordinary German principality, has been able to defy Great Britain'.[2]

His greatest scorn was heaped on Chamberlain. In February 1896, he rejoiced that 'the Government have had a snub from old Kruger the Boer and Chamberlain has met his first reverse as Minister'.[3] Two years later, he was still attacking both the government's South African policy and its undoubted progenitor. He employed a series of inspired, if slightly mixed, metaphors.

Some people talk as if they have the British Empire in their backyard. They put up a notice, 'No admittance except on business',
and set up Chamberlain there and say 'Beware of the dog'. Well,
let him bark! . . . If there is one thing that the Liberals want it is a
man on the Front Bench to unmask the pretensions of this electro-
plated Rome, its pedalling imperialism and its tin Caesar.[4]

The history of South Africa confirms the link between trade and the
flag which Lloyd George suggested was personified by Chamberlain.
When the Afrikaners, who had founded the Transvaal, defeated the
'soldiers of the queen' at Majuba Hill in 1881 and achieved virtual
independence, Britain's sense of national humiliation had been assuaged
by the belief that its South African power and prosperity could be concentrated in the imperially secure Cape Colony. Then gold was
discovered in the 'Boer Republic' at Witwatersrand and within five
years the annual income of the Transvaal rose from £196,000 to
£4,000,000.[5] Little of the new wealth was enjoyed by the Boers themselves. By 1896 two-thirds of the Transvaal population was made up of
Uitlanders, aliens within the state who – according to Johannes Paulus
Kruger, the devout Dutch Reform Church Prime Minister – stood for
'luxury without order, sensual enjoyment without art, riches without
refinement and display without dignity'.[6] The Boers decided that the
best way to protect their territory, cultural integrity and faith was to
deny citizenship to the Uitlanders – many of them British by birth.
Safeguarding their rights within the country of their adoption became
Britain's pretext for subduing the Afrikaners. In reality, Britain fought
the Boer War for diamonds, gold and what a song of the time called
'world-wide glory'. The relationship between the British South Africa
Company and the British government was so close that, during the
siege of Kimberley, Cecil Rhodes – who 'owned' the town – was
allowed to dictate how it should be defended.

   Great powers need excuses for imposing their will on small nations.
So the campaign against the Afrikaners began with the charade of
negotiations. Sir Alfred Milner, Britain's High Commissioner in South
Africa, met Kruger twice.★ At the second meeting Kruger offered
eventual full civil rights to the Uitlanders in return for Britain's formally

★Milner had a radical past. When he was chairman of the Board of Inland
Revenue – at thirty-six the youngest in history – he had persuaded Sir William
Harcourt to introduce death duties.

abandoning its claim to sovereignty over the Transvaal. Milner made the classic civil service error of pandering to his minister's prejudices – in the case of Chamberlain, the passion to protect Britain's imperial reputation. He telegraphed London, 'The spectacle of British subjects kept permanently in the position of Helots . . . does steadily undermine the influence of, and the respect for, the British Government within the Queen's dominions.'[7] According to Lord Salisbury, before the telegram arrived 'the country, as well as the Cabinet – excepting perhaps Mr Chamberlain – [was] against war'.[8] But the mood changed. Britons never, never shall be (Greek) slaves.

At the end of a debate initiated by Liberal backbenchers to express 'strong disapproval of the conduct of the negotiations', Campbell-Bannerman abstained. Asquith and Edward Grey – the heir to the Liberal throne and the party's foreign policy specialist – voted with the government. One hundred and thirty-five of the one hundred and eighty-six Liberal MPs – Lloyd George among them – voted for the motion. He did not speak in the debate. He had decided to 'reflect on the situation for a month'.[9]

Milner wrongly believed that the Boers would capitulate without a fight if the British government made an early show of strength. In the late summer of 1899, he chose to 'precipitate the crisis . . . before it was too late' to intimidate the Afrikaners into submission.[10] When it became clear that he had misjudged their mood, he insisted that, when the fighting began, Britain 'must be seen to be forced into it'.[11] The Boers were provoked into firing the first shots. Officially the war began on 11 October 1899. Publicly, Lloyd George – an instinctive if somewhat selective imperialist – shared the generally accepted view. 'The Boers have invaded our territories and until they are driven back the Government is entitled to money to equip forces to defend our possessions.' But it was not a judgement that Lloyd George happily embraced. South Africa was one of the few moral issues over which he agonised. 'I wish this war was over. I cannot, without the greatest difficulty, get my mind on anything else.'[12]

In June, Chamberlain – accepting Milner's judgement that 'the fellows won't fight' – had asked Campbell-Bannerman to support him in 'a game of bluff' by endorsing the despatch of ten thousand troops to South Africa. Campbell-Bannerman had refused with the comment that such a contrivance was 'unworthy of the country' and 'dangerous when [the government] did not know what it might lead to'. In October, he became convinced that 'The Boers committed an act of aggression which it is our duty to resist,' so he voted for increased military expenditure.[13] By then, Lloyd George had made up his mind which side he was on. 'The way these poor hunted burghers have been driven in self-defence to forestall us aggravates our crime. There is something diabolical in its malignity.'[14] He felt genuine sympathy for the Afrikaners – a small race and religion with whom he identified. But he also realised that fate – and Joseph Chamberlain – had presented him with another opportunity to display both his courage and his independence. When Campbell-Bannerman called the South African conflict 'Joe's War', Lloyd George took Henry Labouchere's advice to 'Go for Joe'.[15]

The first blow was struck during the debate on the third reading of the Consolidated Fund Bill. Lloyd George attacked the government on carefully chosen territory. The British government had claimed that it was bringing democracy to the Transvaal. Lloyd George reminded the House that Kruger had agreed to give the Uitlanders the vote in elections to both Transvaal chambers within seven years. Yet in Britain 'a man, although he may be a permanent resident, cannot get a vote for one chamber; while, for the other, if he lives forever he will never get a vote'.[16] It was a typical Lloyd George debating point, and it was augmented by an attack on Chamberlain for misrepresenting the causes of the war. The speech ended with the ingenious assault on agricultural rate relief. Tory politicians had benefited by three million pounds from a bill which they had driven through Parliament. They were not in a strong position to talk about corruption in Witwatersrand. It was an entertaining parliamentary performance but not a considered statement on the merits of the war. Indeed the attacks on the House of Lords and other favourite targets were intended to enable him to attack the government without condemning resistance to the Boer 'invasion'.

On 27 November 1899, the equivocation ended when he announced 'there are no circumstances which would justify us fighting'. For a war to be 'just there must be an overwhelming good cause' for its prosecution. That, he told a Carmarthen rally, was not the case in South Africa. While pretending to negotiate, Britain was 'sending thousands of soldiers to South Africa'. There were dangers in swimming against the tide of jingoism, but he proposed to set out his objections despite the dangers. 'I would be recreant before God and man if, in addressing my fellow countrymen, I did not offer a protest against what I consider an infamy. I will do it tonight if I leave Carmarthen tomorrow without a friend to bid me good-bye.'[17]

Even though he called himself an imperialist, Lloyd George's Welsh upbringing had made him the genuine champion of small countries oppressed by great nations. But an appeal to principle was less likely to excite opposition to the war than a calculation of how much it would cost the taxpayers.

> The war, I am told, has already cost £16,000,000 and I ask you to compare that sum with what it would cost to fund the old age pension schemes . . . Not a lyddite shell exploded but it carried away an old age pension and the only satisfaction was that it killed 200 Boers – fathers of families, sons of mothers. Are you satisfied to give up your old age pension for that?[18]

Pensions were never far from his mind, but concern for the casualties of the war was usually selective. The virtues of the Boers were constantly compared with what he claimed were the vices of the Uitlanders. The Boers were a small nation – a country with a smaller population than Carmarthenshire. 'Fancy the British Empire against Carmarthenshire. The Transvaal is not unlike Carmarthenshire.' Milner had no doubt that the Boers meant to build a white republic serviced by slave labour.[19] But Lloyd George regarded them as like 'the old Welsh Puritans of this country. They are fine men, more godly men than those for whom we are fighting.'[20] The Uitlanders, on the other hand, were degenerates – 'German Jews, 15,000–20,000 of them.'[21] It is a comment which, even after making allowances for the standards of another age, does Lloyd George no credit. But he was not alone in his anti-Semitic prejudice. Keir Hardie – the first Labour Member of Parliament – joined with John Burns to promote a House of Commons early day motion which attributed the war largely to Jews and foreigners. Even John Morley, the disciple of John Stuart Mill, claimed that 'a ring of financiers and Jews are really responsible for the war'.

For some weeks after the Carmarthen meeting Lloyd George rarely mentioned South Africa. Even when he did, the references were confined to the conclusion of a speech which largely dealt with the tried and trusted subjects of disestablishment and the threat of more Church of England schools. He was trying to reconcile principle and politics. His instinct prompted him to belabour the government, but he could not risk appearing to attack British troops under fire – especially at a time when, contrary to expectation, they were being driven back by Boer irregulars.

During 'Black Week' in December 1899, 719 men were lost at

Stormberg, 950 men at Magersfontein and 1100 men at Colenso. On 27 December, Lloyd George spoke in Oxford to the Palmerston Club. He dared not appear to rejoice at British defeat and British deaths. So he began with an elegiac tribute to the fallen. 'We shall miss many gallant men from the roll call of our warriors.' But, recklessly – and perhaps insensitively – he added, 'There is something infinitely more precious that we shall miss and that is the distinction of being the hope and the shield of the weak and oppressed in all lands.' Then, in a passage of breathtaking hypocrisy, he posed as a friend of the native African – revealing a staggering truth about the South Africa Company's employment practices.

> There might be something magnanimous in a great Empire like ours imperilling its prestige and squandering its resources to defend the poor helpless black. Unhappily, here again is a fiction. The Kaffir workmen of the Rand are better treated and have better wages and more freedom under the dominion of the 'tyrant' Kruger than they enjoy in Kimberley or Matabeleland, where the British pay wages under the benign patronage of Mr Cecil Rhodes.[22]

The speech contained the usual leavening of barbed jokes. Chamberlain had referred to the Transvaal as 'the country we created'. In consequence, Lloyd George claimed, 'the new imperialists will have to procure a revised version of the scriptures – a Birmingham edition commencing, "In the beginning Joseph Chamberlain created heaven and earth"'. Then came an appeal to pure principle. 'Lord Rosebery would sharpen England's sword to make it more deadly. Let him rather purge the Empire's conscience so as to make its statesmen more upright.' The peroration was built around his obsession with rate relief, which he described in highly contentious language. The Transvaal was in open revolt, 'but it can be said of the Boer farmer who lined the trenches that the hand that grasped a Mauser was never soiled with a bribe. He fought for the freedom of his native land and there is no more sacred cause for which a man may die.'[23]

Two days after his Palmerston Club speech, Lloyd George – perhaps apprehensive about accusations that he lacked patriotism – gave an interview to the *Morning Post* which, in modern political jargon, 'clarified' his position. 'We cannot go cap in hand to the Boers and say "we have sinned against heaven and thee", but there are many ways of stopping the war.' The one which he favoured was an appeal to President McKinley of the United States, who – he believed – was ready and willing to arbitrate. The role which he assigned to the Liberal Party was less than heroic. Instead of urging the all-out opposition which he had once seemed to favour, he advised the leadership 'to stand clear of the whole business. The government have made their bed, let them lie on it.'[24]

At Criccieth on New Year's Day 1900, Lloyd George chose to celebrate the new century with an historic analogy which – while its implications were obvious enough – was certainly not a head-on assault against the government. 'I was at Carthage a short time ago and saw the place where it had been. No trace was left, no sign. The people had been great in their day and afterwards went forth, as they thought, to conquer the world.'[25] By then news of another disaster had arrived in Britain. The Boer irregulars, though badly outnumbered, had defeated the British Army at Spion Kop. Queen Victoria told Balfour, 'We are not interested in the possibilities of defeat. They do not exist.'[26] But much of Britain feared that the Empire was going the way of Carthage. Prudent politicians were careful not to offend the patriotic instinct. In February, the Liberal Party attempted to put on a show of unity by moving an amendment to the Loyal Address around which all its Members of Parliament could rally. It criticised the government's 'lack of foresight and judgement' in its 'preparation for the war now proceeding' but it did not condemn the war itself.

Lloyd George, speaking from the backbenches, aimed to attract the support of the Welsh Nonconformists. He condemned Chamberlain for provoking the war. But his bitterest scorn was heaped on the Uitlanders. Their crime was not playing a sufficiently active part in the war which he condemned.

> I should have thought that [their] greatest pride . . . would have been to take part in this conflict and fight for their supposed rights. But how many have availed themselves of the privilege? They prefer to lounge about the hotels of Cape Town while English homes are being made desolate on their behalf. Seven thousand of the Uitlanders are fighting for their intolerable oppressors. How many are fighting for their rights? Barely a battalion out of the whole 80,000 and the remainder are living in security, grumbling about their losses, and without turning a thought for those who are suffering in the war . . . such men and their grievances are not worth a drop of British blood.[27]

A month later, in the House of Commons Lloyd George asked, rhetorically, how widely it was known that the miners of the Transvaal were paid four times as much as British colliers and that the eight-hour day was enforced by law in the factories of Johannesburg.[28] But he also paid a fulsome tribute to the British soldiers – with special praise for the Welsh among them. Private soldiers, he complained, were paid 1/3 a day, colonial volunteers 5/-. Lloyd George had resumed his role as parliamentary guerrilla.

After opposing the adoption of the Annual Estimates – a statement of the government's proposed expenditure – he moved the adjournment of the House rather than 'vote supply' for the army. Finally – in the company of Sir Wilfrid Lawson, Liberal Member for Cockermouth and the war's most passionate opponent, and the Irish Members – he voted against the second reading of the Finance Bill. Some members of his constituency party reacted strongly against his conduct, but it was too late to turn back. 'They can kick me out next time, if they will. I have no doubt that they will, but I won't recant a syllable, no not even moderate my views even a shade.'[29] Instead he decided to hold a meeting in Bangor and meet his critics head-on.

A meeting in Glasgow on 6 March 1900 had encouraged him to continue his bold approach. Despite having endured 'the worst public meeting row [he] had ever witnessed – 10,000 people outside, trying to break into the meeting – surging, struggling, fighting, yelling like savages and a small Armageddon going on inside',[30] he had managed to deliver his prepared address. He had begun by expressing his sympathy for soldiers who had been wounded and the families of soldiers who had been killed in action that day. Then, taking advantage of the respectful silence which followed, he said what he had always planned to say. The war was morally wrong.

Two days later he read in the *Labour Leader* ('the organ of the [recently formed] Labour Party throughout the country') that 'the triumph of the Glasgow evening . . . was the oratorical speech of Mr Lloyd George – fact, arguments, apt quotations and impassioned appeal followed each other in quick succession, completely captivating the audience and betimes rousing it to bursts of wild enthusiasm'.[31] After that, attempts to persuade him to abandon the Bangor rally were doomed to failure, even though on 20 March he discovered that the trustees of the Penrhyn Hall would not allow the meeting to go ahead unless they received substantial guarantees of compensation in the event of their premises being damaged by riot. The requirement allowed

Lloyd George to claim that he was fighting for free speech in Wales as well as self-determination in South Africa. His real reason for going ahead with the meeting was set out in a letter to his brother.

> There may be a general election. You may rely on Chamberlain forcing dissolution at the height of war fever. If the policy of abstaining from meetings to instruct the people is adhered to, judgement will go by default against us and we will be hopelessly beaten – and we will deserve to be. If the [Liberal] Association still deprecates meetings, I will resign my candidature as I cannot hope to succeed if I am shut up.[32]

The Bangor rally went ahead and, inside the Penrhyn Hall, there was no more disturbance and distraction than was to be expected at a normal hustings. A few 'Imperialists' had gained admission and heckled throughout Lloyd George's speech. But the real threat to the speaker's safety came from the crowd outside. Police were called to guard the doors and at one point a nervous chairman thought aloud that the din and disruption might make it necessary to abandon the meeting. He was publicly corrected by Lloyd George, who told him, 'We can get on with it right enough.'[33] A resolution denouncing any settlement which would involve the suppression of the existing Boer Republics was carried by an overwhelming majority.

Lloyd George had insisted on entering the hall by the front door rather than by the 'artists' entrance' which speakers normally used. He chose to leave by the same route. The crowd outside, unlike that which had greeted him on his arrival, was obviously hostile. But he ignored the waiting cab and began to walk – without any clear destination – down the High Street. He had gone only a few yards when he was hit over the head with a heavy stick. Stunned but not injured, he was ushered by the police into a café where he remained, under police protection, for the rest of the evening. When the crowd dispersed, he was smuggled out of the back door and, after accepting the offer of a cab at the second time of asking, was driven home.

South Africa was becoming an obsession and, like all obsessions, its pursuit carried great dangers. There was no risk of his becoming a House of Commons bore – the fatal destiny of most Members who pursue a single issue to destruction. Fortunately, his language was always sufficiently violent to entertain even his most bitter enemies. What might have destroyed him was a determination to return to the subject even if it meant fighting his opponents on the most unfavourable ground – the conduct of troops under fire and the generals who directed them. On 29 June 1900, during a debate on the provision of medical services to the army in the Transvaal, he crossed the most perilous of Rubicons by calmly asserting that 'nobody in the House doubts that the lives of our troops in Natal and elsewhere have been sacrificed to serve political exigencies'.[34] Balfour's predictable response – preceded by the dubious assertion that he had 'never heard a more disreputable speech' – was that Lloyd George had accused 'the Generals in the field of engaging in military operations not otherwise justifiable, but prompted solely for political ends'. Lloyd George insisted that he 'had never made any charge against our Generals, the charge was against politicians', and he added, 'I adhere to it.'[35] But from then on he was constantly driven to make the defensive claim that he had nothing but admiration for the private soldier.

It was not an assurance which the Imperialists of Liskeard in Cornwall were prepared to accept. On 5 July a meeting planned to be held under the chairmanship of Arthur Quiller-Couch, writer and Liberal activist, had to be abandoned when '100 or 150 hobble hoys . . . stormed the platform'.[36] That was to be the pattern of Lloyd George's public appearances for the duration of the war. But it was the March meeting at Penrhyn Hall that influenced his conduct during the spring and summer of 1900. A year earlier, William George had warned his brother that, if he continued to attack the government while not condemning the war, he might be caught in the crossfire of two extremes. At moments of great emotion Lloyd George spoke as if he would willingly abandon his candidature and his constituency for ever. But politics was his life and rejection by the Caernarvon Boroughs was unlikely to be followed by the swift invitation to contest another constituency. Fences had to be mended.

Ever since his first election, Lloyd George's absences from Wales had been accepted with resignation by both his wife and Caernarvon Liberals. His local party had remained content (as is the way of local parties) because he continued the passionate articulation of their strongest prejudices. But there were both radicals and Liberal Imperialists in his local constituency who – objecting to his ambivalence over the war – would exploit his apparent detachment from the boroughs he represented. So, during 1900, Lloyd George became a good constituency MP. Within the space of three months he obtained (or took credit for) a Board of Trade grant of £20,000 towards the cost of a breakwater in Pwllheli harbour, saved (or claimed to have saved) Caernarvon ratepayers £18,000 by persuading the Local Government Board to pay most of the bill for a new waterworks, arranged (or said he had arranged) a £5000 loan from the Caernarvonshire County Council which enabled a local engineering firm to buy the plant necessary to build the Nevin light railway, and announced that he had frustrated a plan to reduce police numbers in Conway in order to increase the establishment in Llandudno. This burst of local activity did not prevent him from being burned in effigy in Criccieth.

A change of fortune in South Africa had added to Lloyd George's problems. For a year he had attacked an increasingly unpopular war. But after Sir Redvers Buller was replaced as Commander-in-Chief by Lord Roberts and victory seemed near, the tide of popular opinion turned. In May 1900, Mafeking – besieged by the Boers for 217 days – had been relieved to general rejoicing. In the office of Lloyd George and George, the clerks celebrated with red, white and blue bunting and paper Union Jacks.[37] The Liberal Party – visibly split over the war – began, as divided parties often do, to reopen old wounds. Rosebery proposed the formal rejection of Home Rule.

According to the *North Wales Observer and Express*, 'what [was] true of the Liberal Party as a whole [was] true, only more so, of the Liberal Party in the Caernarvon Boroughs'.

> Its leaders are openly at variance on the Transvaal issue. Nothing is being done or attempted to keep the party up to its fighting strength. There has been no public meeting for a long time past. If he will pardon our saying so, even Mr Lloyd George might have rendered his party more efficient service by holding a series of meetings in his own constituency since his return from Canada rather than addressing London Welshmen and Flintshire Liberals.[38]

By then Lloyd George was consumed by righteous anger – carried away by his own rhetoric as well as temperamentally sympathetic to the plight of small nations. Nothing could deflect him from pursuing his campaign against the war and the man he held responsible for its continuation. On 25 July Sir Wilfrid Lawson moved to reduce the salary of the Colonial Secretary by £100 – a symbolic gesture of disapproval. During the debate, Lloyd George declared, 'A war of annexation . . . against a proud people must be a war of extermination and that seems to be what we are committing ourselves to – burning homesteads and

turning women and children out of their homes.' The monocled Joseph
Chamberlain had given an 'electioneering performance . . . I venture to
say that there is no worse eyeglass than the ballot box, and it was
through that eyeglass that the Right Honourable Gentleman has been
looking.'[39] The debate was another triumph for Lloyd George and
went some way – but by no means all the distance – towards justifying
William's claim that his brother 'practically led the opposition to the war
both inside and outside parliament'.[40] But it was a humiliation for the
Liberal Party. When the vote was taken, it split three ways.

A month later, the battle between Chamberlain and Lloyd George
became personal. The British forces had captured Bloemfontein and
confiscated the official archives of the independent Orange Free State
Government. Among the impounded papers, there were letters to
President Steyn from several Liberal Members of Parliament. The
Colonial Office made the discovery public but refused to reveal the letters' contents. Inevitably, it was assumed that 'pro-Boer' MPs had
given aid and comfort to the enemy, and it was taken for granted that
Lloyd George was one of the miscreants. Safe in the knowledge that
none of the letters was from him, Lloyd George waited for the opportunity to turn the incident into an indictment of Chamberlain's
conduct. It came on 8 August after the Colonial Secretary – asked why
he had not published the letters or at least revealed their contents –
replied that he had first to confirm their authenticity and then obtain
permission from the signatories. In the meantime, he could say only
that they were 'not proper letters to have [been] written' by Members
of Parliament.

Speaking immediately after Chamberlain, Lloyd George said what
every Member – Unionists no less than Liberals – knew to be true. 'If
giving the actual words used would have been more damaging to the
reputation of Honourable Gentlemen on this side of the House, I venture to say that the Right Honourable Gentleman would have done it.'
Foolishly, Chamberlain chose to reply at once. He could at least say that
the rumours had 'greatly exaggerated the purport of the letters'. The
admission that they were neither treasonable nor subversive was a gift to
Lloyd George. 'If they were exaggerated, who did the exaggeration? It
must be someone in the Colonial Office.' Chamberlain had sent his
request for permission to publish 'at a time when no reply could possibly be given before the rising of the House'. He then asked, 'Was this
the course of a gentleman?' and answered his own question in a way
which was calculated to wound the screw manufacturer in a Cabinet of

dukes and earls. 'I venture to think that no other Member on that side of the House would have done such a thing.'[41]

The suggestion that Chamberlain had behaved dishonourably was no more than a prelude to a more savage – but less justified – attack on the Colonial Secretary's integrity. Harold Spender – journalist and then a Lloyd George acolyte – had noticed that a report of the War Office Contracts Committee revealed that 'the government cultivated certain munitions firms'.[42] In the House of Commons, Lloyd George elaborated on the discovery. 'A certain firm which had sent in the highest tender was told that if they reduced their tender a large order would be given them . . . Nominally it has . . . been in business for 20 years but everybody is aware that until certain gentlemen from Birmingham who have influence with a member of the government . . .' There was no need to say any more. It was clear enough who and what he meant. The firm was Kynoch's and its chairman was Arthur Chamberlain, the Colonial Secretary's younger brother.* Displaying a bogus public spirit, Lloyd George demanded that the report's recommendation on improved contract procedures should be 'ruthlessly' implemented. The alternative, he implied, was continued corruption. In his eagerness to root out wrongdoing, he employed a strange word to describe the provenance of the information on which the House was being asked to make a judgement. Members, he said, had to rely on 'innuendo'. Chamberlain, thinking that he could regain the initiative, offered ironic agreement. 'Hear hear! By innuendo.' Lloyd George had stumbled but he quickly regained his balance with a reference to the Steyn affair. He was taking his lead 'from the Right Honourable Gentleman who insinuated treason, insinuated impropriety of language and, above all, insinuated that he had treated Honourable Members in a gentlemanly manner by offering them an opportunity of which they could not avail themselves'.

Chamberlain had little choice but to answer the allegations. He had 'no interest, direct or indirect, in Kynoch's or in any other firm manufacturing ammunition or war materials'. He never discussed business with his brother. 'I have nothing whatsoever to do with his private concerns, any more than he has anything to do with my public concerns.' Then he stood on his dignity – always a sign of defeat in the House of Commons: 'It is a gross abuse to attack a public man through his relatives for whom he is not responsible.'[43]

---

*Arthur Chamberlain, unlike his brother, was a Gladstonian Liberal who supported free trade.

Joseph Chamberlain was innocent and Lloyd George knew it. His justification for making the false accusation was that he was trading smear for smear. But the allegation was not a sudden response to Chamberlain's misuse of the Steyn letters. During the 1895 general election he had made similar claims (without the evidence of the White Paper to provide spurious justification) in reply to a question about the claim that a cordite shortage had brought down the Rosebery government and he had mentioned Chamberlain's supposed conflicting interest during a speech in Bangor the previous April. It was a line of attack which he employed with malice aforethought. And he was to return to the subject – with even greater venom – as the war went on. The 'innuendo' served its purpose. Richard Lloyd read the newspaper reports of the fracas and wrote in his diary, 'Nothing like it in the House for years. Chamberlain hardly ever fared so badly in his public career.'[44]

Parliament was dissolved on 25 September 1900. Two days later, speaking at Tunstall in Staffordshire, Chamberlain set the tone of the campaign by announcing, 'A seat lost to the government is a seat gained by the Boers.'[45] Lloyd George faced the general election in the knowledge that he had ended the session by further enhancing his reputation as a political privateer and solidifying his position in his constituency. T. P. O'Connor, newspaper columnist and Irish Nationalist MP, wrote that 'to get between' the candidate for Caernarvon Boroughs and his countrymen would 'be like getting between a tree and its bark'.[46] The candidate himself had sufficient confidence to spend the first week after dissolution negotiating about the purchase of the *Daily News* and the next ten days on holiday in France. Margaret was not invited to join him but William George was offered the prospect of cycling along 'the magnificent roads' of Picardy.[47] William was too busy to accept. Perhaps, after their return, Lloyd George came to believe that choosing work rather than pleasure would have been the wiser course for – as was usually the case sometime during an election campaign – he began to worry about his prospects. On 26 September, a week after his adoption meeting, he told Herbert Lewis, 'I am by no means safe yet. There are 15 important defections in Pwllheli alone.'[48]

Lloyd George's adoption meeting speech began on safe ground – Church, land and an attack on Tory jingoism. 'The man who tries to make the flag an object of a single party is a greater traitor to that flag than the man who fires upon it.' It was followed by the concession that if he had originally been wrong about the war, 'it was an honest mistake'. The government was attacked as always, but he was careful not to sound like 'a friend of the enemy'. Imperialists were pleased – and the real pro-Boers astonished – to hear him suggest that the Transvaal should accept Home Rule within the Empire. His peroration conceded the possibility of his career ending in honourable defeat.

> Five years ago you handed me a strip of blue paper to hand to the Speaker as your accredited representative. If I never again represent these boroughs in the House of Commons I shall have the satisfaction of handing it back to you without a single stain of human blood upon it.[49]

Lloyd George's Unionist opponent was Henry Platt, a Bangor banker who had been mayor of the town and high sheriff of the county. He was a colonel of militia and used his rank as proof of his patriotism, a qualification which he claimed was lacked by his opponent, who had 'been on the enemy's side throughout the war and insulted generals and soldiers of the Queen'. Colonel Platt was challenged to defend his allegations of disloyalty at a face-to-face meeting. Wisely, he declined the invitation. However, his agent – another colonel – repeated the allegations. 'Mr Lloyd George did, as a matter of fact, stigmatise our soldiers as "hired troops" and he made a discreditable attack upon our generals whom he denounced in the House of Commons as "having sacrificed the lives of our troops in Natal for political exigencies".'[50] It was nearly true. Lloyd George had said that the government had pressed for visible progress in Natal against military advice.

Lloyd George met the allegation of disloyalty head-on in a fifteen-page election address. It provided twenty paragraphs of evidence to prove that 'Mr Lloyd George has proved himself to be the soldiers' friend.' Then it went into what – in a modern campaign – would be regarded as unreadable detail about the speeches which he had made in Parliament (including twenty-four 'on railways and light railways'), his efforts on behalf of 'Wales and the Welsh language' (including his opposition to 'Wales having to contribute to the upkeep of London Parks') and the high esteem in which he was held by both friend and foe.

Lloyd George was re-elected with a majority of 296 – 100 votes more than in the by-election victory of 1890. According to Spender – whose report on the result for the *Manchester Guardian* was not wholly objective – 'with silver tongue he had won back their hearts and his people were with him again'. Political prose had never been so purple. When the crowd, at Lloyd George's bidding, sang 'that great anthem of Wales "Land Of My Fathers", the darkness above us gave the whole scene a ghostly majesty . . . The sea of resolute faces gave a sense of vast indefinable strength.'[51]

The *Caernarvon and Denbigh Herald* reported that, on the Liberal Club balcony, the victorious candidate 'clasped his faithful partner in his arms and gave her an affectionate and impassioned kiss in the sight of the cheering multitudes'. He then told the newspaper, 'I am more proud of my countrymen than ever before. While England and Scotland are drunk with blood Wales is marching with steady step on the road to liberty and progress.'[52] The public rejoicing and the good night's sleep which followed being over, he set out for Montgomeryshire, where polling day was a week later. A. C. Humphreys-Owen, the Liberal candidate, was in danger of losing his seat. For a second time, Lloyd George went to the aid of his critics within the Liberal Party. Again he relished making sure that Humphreys-Owen's victory was barely less painful than defeat.

If Lloyd George honestly believed that the Welsh election results had been significantly different from those in the rest of the United Kingdom, he was wrong. Candidates who had accepted the label of pro-Boer without any of Lloyd George's caveats were elected from Battersea (John Burns) to Northampton (Henry Labouchere). The Liberals won 177 seats (1,572,323 votes) to the Unionists' 411 seats (1,767,958 votes). The difference in votes cast for the two parties would have been far larger if 163 Unionists (compared with 22 Liberals) had not been returned unopposed. The government gained only six seats, two of them in Wales. The idea of a 'Khaki landslide', which Lloyd George chose to encourage, was – unlike in 1918 – a convenient election stunt. The government won because it was trusted and the opposition was not. Divided parties do not win elections – as the Unionists were soon to learn.

When the new House assembled it must have seemed that the election had changed nothing. The war went on and the first controversial debate – formally the discussion of another amendment to another Loyal Address – was a Lloyd George-initiated attack on Chamberlain. 'Ministers of the Crown and Members of either House of Parliament holding subordinate office in any public Department ought to have no interest, direct or indirect, in any firm competing for contracts with the Crown' unless there were procedures in place which 'prevent any suspicion of influence or favouritism in the allocation of such contracts'.

Lloyd George's speech listed all the companies which could possibly have benefited from their association with the Colonial Secretary. He even suggested that captured Boers had been imprisoned in Ceylon so that the Colombo Commercial Company, in which the Chamberlains had a small interest, could be employed to build their compound. He could offer no proof of wrongdoing because no wrong had been done. Yet, with the exception of a typically oblique rebuttal by Arthur Balfour – 'wanted a man to serve Her Majesty with no money, no relations and inspiring no general confidence' – nobody chose to defend Chamberlain. Campbell-Bannerman, a man of conspicuous honour, actually spoke in support of the amendment. So did Richard Haldane (the Liberal Member for Haddingtonshire and Future Secretary of State for War), McKenna and even Asquith. Lloyd George, who had, without compunction, sold shares in a goldfield which he knew had no gold, succeeded in uniting the Liberal Party behind a demand for politicians to be, like Caesar's wife, beyond reproach.

The campaign against the war had been suspended in December 1899 while Lloyd George made one of the excursions into commerce which regularly interrupted, and sometimes imperilled, his career. A week before Christmas, William George received a letter which told him that he had become the secretary of an insurance company. The intention was to use its financial strength to acquire a Liberal – and pro-Lloyd George – newspaper.

The paper which he hoped to acquire was the *London Daily News*. Rumours that the 'Lloyd George syndicate' had bought the paper circulated in London during the early weeks of the new century. But at the end of January 1900, the syndicate was still £200,000 short of the necessary £250,000.[53] Negotiations continued throughout the year and were still dragging on when Parliament was prorogued on 8 August and dissolution was announced on 25 September. Between those two events he considered diverting his attention towards the purchase of the *North Wales Echo*. On 31 August, he told his wife that he had 'just arranged for the purchase of the *Echo* – very favourable they are . . . As I have told you all along, it is well worth £300 a year to our office and it brings us into contact with people who can put a lot of money in our way.' But hopes of acquiring a national daily newspaper were not extinguished. 'If we are fairly successful in getting our capital we may be able to come to terms with the *Daily News*. That would be a tremendous deal.'[54]

Only one national newspaper, the *Manchester Guardian*, opposed the war. Although the *Daily News* was a Liberal paper, it supported Milner and therefore argued that the war was necessary and just. H. W. Massingham, the editor of the *Daily Chronicle*, was personally opposed, but his proprietor insisted that the paper reflected his views and Massingham resigned and joined the *Manchester Guardian* – which was drowned out by the *Telegraph*, *The Times*, *Morning Post* and *Daily Mail*. Fortunately for Lloyd George and those who thought like him, the *Daily News* was in severe financial difficulties. The acquisition of the *Echo* lost its charm. The work of raising the necessary capital began.

It was unreasonable to suppose that George Cadbury – Quaker, Birmingham chocolate-maker and passionate opponent of financial profligacy – would invest in an ailing newspaper. But Lloyd George, who had never met him, asked for his help in a letter which said that Cadbury had a moral obligation to make the *Daily News* a force for good – a duty which it could immediately perform by opposing the Boer War. Cadbury provided £20,000 and curtly refused to meet Lloyd George in a letter that confirmed that he regarded the venture as more than philanthropy. 'All you want is the money I have promised and I fear I could not help you to get any more . . . We do not want any cranks as shareholders. The venture is not likely to pay unless commonsense and business capacity are combined.'[55] J. P. Thomason, the former Liberal Member for Durham who had left politics for business and possessed both of the attributes which Cadbury demanded, subscribed the same amount. By 8 January 1901 – although he was still searching for £30,000 of working capital – Lloyd George felt able to refer in a letter home to 'my *Daily News*'.[56] 'Wouldn't you like a fortnight on the Riviera?' he asked William – the idea being that his brother should accompany him on a rest cure. 'I want to be fit for the fight when the session opens. It is clear to me that the radical section in England are looking more and more to me for a fighting lead.'[57] He might have added that he had proved that he was a politician of substance by raising the capital necessary to buy a national daily newspaper. Campbell-Bannerman described the acquisition as a 'happy change. Now we shall have something besides the *Westminster Gazette* that we can read.'[58]

Britain was winning the war in South Africa, but the Boers were being beaten slowly and at considerable cost of money and men. Lord Roberts, the Commander-in-Chief, responded by toughening up the British tactics – not simply burning homesteads which were known to have harboured commandos, but demolishing every property near to the scene of a Boer raid. The British High Command announced the introduction of its new punitive policy in the mistaken belief that the prospect of a devastated veldt would act as a deterrent. At Bangor, Lloyd George greeted the announcement with righteous contempt. 'Lord Roberts has written to General Botha to say that where the rail-way line near a Boer farmhouse is damaged, the farmhouse will be destroyed and all the cattle and supplies will be removed within an area of ten miles around it. Is it civilised warfare to starve women and chil-dren? The remedy is to abandon the call for absolute surrender.'[59] Three weeks later in Liverpool, he asked his audience to imagine the invasion and occupation of Lancashire. If the local stretch of the London, Midland and Scottish Railway line was cut, 'a German Lord Roberts would burn every house in Liverpool, Warrington and Saint Helens'.[60]

In the 1901 King's Speech debate – Queen Victoria had died on 22 January – Lloyd George, consciously moderate again, suggested that the Boers should be offered 'full autonomy . . . subject to the overlordship of the British crown'. Campbell-Bannerman – fearing that the promise of what amounted to immediate autonomy would split the party – asked the Liberal Chief Whip to persuade Lloyd George not to press his amendment to a division. He agreed and his speech reflected not his disagreement with government policy but horror at the humanitarian consequences of continued conflict. He quoted a letter written home by Lieutenant Morrison – 'mentioned for gallantry in despatches' – during Major-General Smith-Dorrien's advance into the Transvaal. 'The country is very like Scotland and we move from valley to valley, lifting cattle and sheep, burning and looting and turning out women and children to weep in despair beside the ruins of once beautiful homesteads. It was the first touch of Kitchener's iron hand.' Winston Churchill, a new Member of Parliament who spoke next, ignored the convention which requires maiden speeches to be uncontroversial and suggested that Lloyd George would have done better to have moved his moderate amendment and abandoned his extreme speech rather than vice versa.[61]

General Herbert Kitchener – promoted, on Lord Roberts's retire-ment, from Chief of Staff to Commander-in-Chief – was 'clearing the veldt' with unrestrained savagery. At the same time he was attempting to negotiate an honourable peace. At a meeting with President Botha at Middleburg in the Transvaal on 19 February 1901 – in itself a remarkable event – he had agreed to an amnesty for rebels who were not accused of specific crimes and agreed immediately to lay down their arms. The tentative deal was repudiated by Milner with the full backing of

Chamberlain. So Kitchener reverted from diplomat to soldier and renewed the 'blockhouse and wire policy' with increased severity. As the Boer commandos were gradually driven out of the Transvaal and their farmhouses burned, women and children were taken to what, without any initial pejorative intention, were called 'concentration camps' – with terrible consequences.

On 24 May 1901, Sir Alfred Milner arrived back in England for rest and recuperation. He was greeted like a hero by, among others, Asquith, his old Balliol friend. Among the less exalted passengers on his boat was Emily Hobhouse, who had been sent to South Africa by the Distress Fund for South African Women and Children. She toured Britain describing the conditions in the camps and denouncing the brutality. Alfred Harmsworth – the proprietor of the *Daily Mail* and soon to become Lord Northcliffe – was not impressed. She was 'not impartial' and had 'no balance in her judgement'.[62] Challenged about his attacks on her integrity, Harmsworth produced figures to show that, during his campaign of excoriation, the paper's circulation had increased. 'You see,' he said, 'we were right.'[63] Campbell-Bannerman – according to some accounts, introduced to Emily Hobhouse by Lloyd George – took a different view.

Also on 24 May, Lloyd George asked St John Broderick, the Secretary of State for War, how he could justify the mortality rates in the camps – 261 of the 1100 children detained in February and March had died. The answer was both callous and dismissive. He 'could not be expected to remember all the statistics'. Luxury being inappropriate, no doubt there were hardships but 'War is war.'[64] Campbell-Bannerman took up the subject three weeks later, during questions to the Leader of the House. Balfour was unable or unwilling to provide authoritative information on the death rates in the camps. Next evening, at a dinner given in his honour at the Holborn Restaurant, the Liberal leader described the reply he had received, after his 'request was refused', as a disquisition on the nature of war. Then, in reference to the reply which Lloyd George had received from Broderick, he asked, 'When is war not a war?' and then provided his own answer, 'When it is carried on by methods of Barbarism in South Africa.' The newspapers – which always seize on 'splits' as an easy source of a headline – reported only a speech by Morley at the same dinner, which, they claimed, was more evidence that the Liberal Party was divided. Three days later, Campbell-Bannerman used the same phrase again and was engulfed in outrage.

Lloyd George, seizing on the mood of the moment, moved the adjournment of the House of Commons in order to discuss 'the treatment of non-combatants in South Africa'. He had no intention of offending Honourable Friends who disagreed with him about the general propriety of the war but merely wished to protest against the treatment of Boer women and children. By referring a second time to 'methods of barbarism', Campbell-Bannerman had driven Liberal Imperialists into paroxysms of anger and fear. Were they being marginalised within – or even driven out from – the party? Campbell-Bannerman increased their apprehensions by voting for Lloyd George's motion. Fifty other Liberal MPs (including Asquith and Haldane, who publicly rebuked his leader during the debate) abstained. The sociologist and economist Beatrice Webb – then an enthusiastic Liberal Imperialist – complained about the indolence of her friends. 'They suddenly woke up to find the Liberal Party in the House of Commons under the leadership of Lloyd George . . . Campbell-Bannerman had been captured.'[65]

The divisions within the Liberal Party were profound. Imperialists, who believed in Britain's moral duty to civilise and police the world, were in conflict with the increasingly influential advocates of detachment from overseas adventures, who were pejoratively identified as 'Little Englanders'. New Liberals, radicals who believed in the state's duty to protect and improve the welfare of its citizens, competed with what was left of the Whig tradition of free trade and government detachment from the life of the citizen. The conflicting groups were split among and within themselves over Home Rule for Ireland. Asquith had no qualms about asserting the view of one faction. 'We held and still hold that the war was neither intended nor desired by the Government and people of Great Britain, but that it was forced on us, without adequate reason entirely against our will.'[66] The Liberal Imperialists hoped that Lord Rosebery – despite his manifest character defects and the failure of his brief ministry – would return and replace Campbell-Bannerman.

Lloyd George continued to calculate the cost of the war. On 12 December 1901, he told a meeting in Wrexham that their share of the war was £120,000 added to the town debt and 'per contra six little graves in Africa'.[67] Four days later, Rosebery made a much heralded speech in Chesterfield which, although it contained little of substance, was significant as a sign that he was back in the political arena. It described traditional Liberal policy – the implication being Home

Rule – as 'fly-blown phylacteries' – a strange choice of metaphor meant to indicate that he wanted a change of direction.★ Despite its obscurity the speech appealed to Lloyd George, for he planned to give it an almost immediate – if qualified – welcome during a speech which he intended to make in the Birmingham Town Hall on 18 January.

During the first two weeks of the New Year, the *Birmingham Daily Mail* had regularly predicted that 'the most violent anti-British Member of Parliament' would never be allowed to pedal his sedition in Joseph Chamberlain's home town. Once again, faint hearts suggested that the meeting should be cancelled. Once again Lloyd George refused. The nearest he would go to making a concession was in the selection of a chairman. A well-known Liberal Imperialist was invited to preside with the assurance that the speaker was an Imperialist too – but an Imperialist who opposed the Boer War. Two days before the meeting the chief constable of Birmingham made an official request that the meeting be cancelled and the elderly Imperialist chairman accepted his doctor's advice to stay in bed. Lloyd George was obdurate. The meeting must go ahead. Warned that a mob awaited him in Birmingham, he travelled by the slow train rather than the express and was smuggled out of New Street Station by Mrs William Evans (the wife of the leader of Birmingham's Welsh community) and her teenage niece. Another plea from the chief constable was rejected and the platform party – complete with another Liberal Imperialist to act as chairman – moved off to the Town Hall. They entered, without being noticed, through a crowd estimated to be thirty thousand. There were 350 policemen in the town square.

About fifteen minutes after Lloyd George's arrival at the Town Hall the doors were opened 'to admit ticket holders'. The mob pushed the stewards aside and stormed in, monopolising the seats and aisles. 'A tempest of noise and a sea of waving Union Jacks filled the scene'. Both the chairman and Lloyd George made a token effort to speak but

> Suddenly and, as it seemed, at a signal, the crowd in the body of the hall made a rush for the platform and were confronted by a body of policemen who had been stationed beneath it. There was a very ugly struggle and, according to those who witnessed it from the platform, many of the attacking force were armed with

---

★Phylacteries are the leather wallets in which Orthodox Jews keep copies of holy texts.

such weapons as sticks, hammers and knives . . . The crowd then attacked those on the platform with stones, barbed bricks, bottles, cans and the like.[68]

The platform party – reluctant to admit victory to the mob – asked the chief constable to clear the hall. The attempt failed and the speakers retreated to a room behind the platform while the police did what they could to prevent the destruction of the building. At last convinced that lives, including his own, were at risk, Lloyd George agreed to leave the building disguised as a policeman – though it is hard to imagine that he made a convincing constable. As soon as he was on his way back to the Evanses' house, the mob were told that he was no longer in the building but their blood was up and they began to break the windows in the nearby Council House – the headquarters of the mighty corporation which Joseph Chamberlain himself had built. The building was saved by a baton charge during which a man of twenty-seven was killed – 'struck down' by an unidentified policeman, according to the coroner.

At home in Highbury, in the west Birmingham suburbs, Joseph Chamberlain received a late-night telegram. 'Lloyd George, the traitor, was not allowed to say a word. Two thousand citizens and others passed a unanimous vote of confidence in the Government and admiration for your unique and fearless service to King and Country.'[69] A week later in the Members' Lobby of the House of Commons, Chamberlain was subjected to the sort of banter which some MPs still believe is proof of the sophisticated relationship between government and opposition. 'What's the matter with Birmingham?' W. S. Caine, Liberal Member for Camborne and a friend of Lloyd George, asked him. 'Everyone expected you to kill Lloyd George. Why did you let him escape?' Chamberlain's reply made Rosebery's reference to phylacteries seem like a model of clarity: 'What is everybody's business is nobody's business.'[70]

Perhaps Lloyd George was acquiring a taste for danger or it may have been no more than braggadocio which prompted him to prepare the way for a meeting in the West Country by telling the *Daily Express*, 'If the Bristol people want a fight, they can have it.'[71] To the general astonishment of police and public the evening passed off without major incident – or much attention to Lloyd George's speech, apart from surprise that he was allowed to make it. The comments about Rosebery – which were originally intended for Birmingham – were overlooked but later published in the *New Liberal Review*.

The great need of Britain is a statesman who has the courage first to find out the truth about South Africa, then to believe the truth, in the next place to tell the truth and finally to act upon the truth. The immediate future will prove whether the Empire has at last discovered such a statesman.[72]

Lloyd George was keeping a foot in both Liberal camps.

On 20 January, the House of Commons debated a Liberal amendment to the motion to endorse that year's King's Speech. It was constructed in a way which, it was hoped, would attract the support of the whole parliamentary party.

That this House, while prepared to support all proper measures for the effective prosecution of the war in South Africa, is of the opinion that the course pursued by Your Majesty's Ministers and their attitude towards a settlement have not conduced to an early termination of the war and the establishment of a durable peace.[73]

The second half of the amendment was almost identical to Lloyd George's unofficial motion, which he had prepared for the King's Speech debate a year before. But that was not enough to persuade him to support what was intended as a unifying initiative. He announced that he would support an amendment to the amendment which asserted that the methods by which the war was carried on were 'barbarous and have aroused the indignation of the whole civilised world'.[74] The language with which he dismissed the attempt at compromise shocked even the pro-Boers.

The official Liberal amendment was, he said, a double deceit – 'one set of gentlemen asked to support what they regard as a criminal enterprise as an inducement for another set of gentlemen to believe in a proposition which they did not believe to be true'.[75] The Liberal leader was a hostage of the Imperialists and 'he had been treated by his captors as the Boers treat their prisoners. He has been stripped of his principles and left out on the veldt to find his way back as best he could.'[76]

Campbell-Bannerman described himself as 'content . . . because Lloyd George's outburst has greatly angered the party generally and forced some of that [anti-war] wing . . . to vote for us.'[77] Only nine Imperialists (including Asquith, Grey and Haldane) abstained. But while Campbell-Bannerman 'saw nothing to regret in the whole thing', some of his friends were neither so calculating nor so forgiving.[78] H. J. Wilson, the Liberal Member for Holmfirth, spoke for many of his colleagues when he told Lloyd George 'C-B . . . deserved our confidence and thanks. That being so, I was pained and shocked at your language more than I should like just now to describe . . . It seems to me impossible that you should, in your calmer moments, approve of it yourself.'[79]

Herbert Lewis – a fellow MP who spoke with the frankness of a friend whose devotion survived for almost fifty years – had no doubt that Lloyd George was 'for the time being, the most unpopular man in England' and suggested that 'he feels his position very keenly'.[80] The popular image was, and remains, that of a man who took adversity in his stride, the happy warrior who captivated an antagonistic meeting by dismissing a heckler who sang the national anthem with the rebuke: 'That is an insult to the King. It is an insult to sing so badly.'[81] The strain of unpopularity was beginning to show. Looking back, in 1910, he confessed, 'Nothing I could ever go through again would be as bad as that. My business was going to rack and ruin. I dare not venture on the golf course. I should have been stoned.'[82] To add to his woe, money was scarce. He thought of economising by leaving the house in Wandsworth and moving into what Spender called 'a worker's flat', with Margaret letting the house in Criccieth and moving in next door with her parents.[83] His wife refused. Richard, their twelve-year-old son, was bullied so badly at Dulwich College that he was sent to live with Uncle Lloyd and enrolled in a school at Portmadoc. There was some comfort to be found in reunion with his old friends.

On 14 February 1902, Rosebery spoke in Liverpool with, he said, the intention of clarifying his Chesterfield speech. The new chosen image was a clean slate – 'clean of Home Rule in Ireland until some form of imperial federation should allow a local and subordinate legislation as part of that scheme'. But it seemed that having wiped the slate clean, he had nothing new to write upon it. That was enough to allow Lloyd George to adjust his position again. The nation would never accept Liberalism from 'a man who handed it to them with a pair of tongs'.[84]

For once, Lloyd George was wholly in tune with the Liberal leadership. Campbell-Bannerman – his patience exhausted – issued a clear public challenge to Rosebery. Was or was he not still a Liberal? Rosebery replied, 'I remain outside the tabernacle but not, I think, in solitude.'[85] Lloyd George interpreted the complicated metaphor as a threat to set up a rival organisation. He told the *North Wales Observer and Express* that Rosebery's conduct 'will compel practically the whole of the Party to rally to CB . . . there is no room for a third party'.[86] Rosebery's chances of again leading the Liberal Party had been destroyed and Lloyd George knew it. He was not a man to hitch his wagon to a falling star.

The war and the parliamentary battle against it raged on with increasing bitterness. Chamberlain called John Dillon a 'good judge of traitors', and John Dillon called Chamberlain a 'damned liar' – for which insult he was suspended from the House of Commons. Lloyd George was accused of rejoicing at British defeats and received an apology for the implication that he was 'exalting over the death and mutilation of his countryman'. Looking back, almost a decade later, he spoke about the hard years of the war with righteous satisfaction, 'On the Day of Judgement when I have to answer for my sins – and God knows I have enough to answer for – I shall say only one thing, "Sir, I was a pro Boer". And he will let me in.'[87] The Almighty, being omniscient, would have known that Lloyd George's attitude to the war was more complicated than he made out. But, politically, it did the trick. After his last speech on the subject, he sent his wife, back in Criccieth, the usual account of his triumph which described his feelings in less uplifting language. 'Your sweetheart made a job of it last night. Several have told me that it was the best I ever delivered in the House . . . Dilke [Sir Charles Dilke, Liberal Member for Forest of Dean] tells me that this morning he thought I was like Shelley's Adonais. I had at last, through toil and trouble, got to fame.'[88]

It was a strangely inappropriate comparison. Lloyd George was Prometheus. The Boer War had enabled him to soar to the heady heights of national notoriety. It had not made him universally popular. But it had made him noticed – the first requirement of an ambitious young MP. It remained to be seen if he would use his Promethean fire – like Prometheus himself – to benefit the world.

CHAPTER 9

NONCONFORMITY'S CHAMPION

The Unionist Party which won the 1900 general election was destroyed by the hubris which often confounds a government with a three-figure majority – the belief that it needs to accommodate no other policies or prejudices than its own. Normally such governments are killed by one lethal, self-inflicted wound. The Unionists died from multiple injuries sustained over two full years. The final blow was the civil war over free trade, precipitated by Chamberlain's demand for 'Imperial Preference'. But the government was already crippled by its support for measures which Nonconformists regarded as an assault on their faith and an affront to their high moral standards.

An Education Bill reorganised the management of elementary schools, initiated new investment in previously neglected Church of England schools and was therefore said to discriminate against Nonconformity. A Licensing Bill provided compensation to publicans who lost their licences. The South African goldmines were allowed, indeed encouraged, to recruit 'Chinese indentured labour' – men who worked for below-subsistence wages and lived in closed compounds which, it was claimed, were sinks of vice.

Although Lloyd George's campaign against the changes in school governance made a major contribution to the Liberals' subsequent victory, the Unionist schism over free trade – which Lloyd George played a crucial part in widening and deepening – has always dominated the history-book accounts of how the election was won. That is because it was a civil war in a political party. In the battles over the Education Bill, Lloyd George led an army of ordinary people. The newly enfranchised lower middle classes – many of them Nonconformist in sympathy if not conviction – were saying, 'Listen to me.'

The Education Bill was presented to the House of Commons by Arthur Balfour on 24 March 1902, the day after the Boers sued for what became a lasting peace. Its principal (and admirable) purpose was the extension of technical and 'higher grade instruction'. Its inspiration was the report of the 1895 Royal Commission which Balfour was attempting to implement for a second time. An earlier bill had been rejected by a coalition of opposites. Tory backwoodsmen feared that Church of England schools would be controlled by the government. Liberal Nonconformists suspected that denominational schools would be entrenched rather than left in an uneasy compromise between sectarian demands and a state-imposed education system which, as the Education Act of 1870 intended, allowed public provision only when the Churches – usually the Church of England – failed to provide what are now called 'faith schools'.

No doubt the Cabinet, with other things on its mind, would have let the matter rest had not the London Technical Education Board – acting on behalf of the Camden School of Art – complained that the London School Board had acted *ultra vires* by subsidising 'higher grade instruction'. When the courts upheld the complaint, the government was faced with a choice between legislation and abandonment of all improvements in education which the Royal Commission and Balfour wanted to implement. Bills borne out of sudden necessity usually run into trouble.

Local school boards were to be abolished everywhere except in London, where the pattern of local government was far too diffuse to make a single authority possible. County boroughs, counties and the larger boroughs were to become local education authorities and were to administer voluntary (that is to say, church) schools as well as the old board schools, which, from then on, were described as 'maintained'. For the first time church schools were to receive public funds – a vital necessity if the quality of their teaching, teachers and buildings was to rise to the standard needed in a modern nation.

At the time when the 1902 bill was introduced into Parliament, more than half the elementary pupils in England and Wales were being taught in church schools – like the one in which David Lloyd George had refused to recite the Anglican creed. In more than eight thousand parishes they provided the only education which was available. The Nonconformists – happy with the Cowper-Temple clause which, in practice, meant teaching from the Bible rather than a prayer book – looked forward to the day when the church schools, which hovered permanently on the brink of financial disaster, were absorbed into the state system. Balfour, despite his genuine desire to improve the standard of national education, regarded the bill as an opportunity to provide church schools with the funds which guaranteed their future.

At first Lloyd George's enthusiasm for better schools transcended the demands of sectarian loyalty and personal ambition. On 24 March 1902 a letter to Margaret – at home in Criccieth awaiting the birth of Megan – contained only one criticism of Balfour's proposals. It amounted to the regret that, in one particular, they did not go far enough. Implementing the reforms was to be 'left entirely to the discretion of each county council'. Apart from that, he 'rather liked the bill', which he thought was 'quite as much as one would expect from a Tory Government, in fact more than anyone could anticipate'. He was absolutely right to add, 'Llanystumdwy School will be under the County Council and a very great improvement that is.'[1]

He then added a note on family matters. It was an example of his unattractive habit of reassuring his wife about his fidelity and, at the same time, reminding her that he was not entirely to be trusted. 'Mrs Tim' had been looking after the children during the final stages of Margaret's pregnancy and he had visited the Davieses' to bring his daughter, Mair, back home. 'Don't tell me off, old Maggie. I was a very good boy, I can assure you. I have no fear of cross-examination. I know how, with those sly eyes of yours, you watch every move and twitch of my telltale face.'[2]

Apologists have suggested that Lloyd George, at first sight, misunderstood the consequences of the Education Bill. In fact, his initial enthusiasm is not in doubt. On the day after the letter home was written, the *Western Mail* reported that, during an interview, he had described himself as 'not unfavourably impressed . . . judging it from a purely Welsh point of view' – though he went on to say that there might be problems in England because 'the county councils are not as interested in education as the Welsh counties are'.* He 'reserved further judgement . . . until he had seen it in print'.[3] Before he was able to

---

*On page 124 of Frank Owen's *Tempestuous Journey* the quotation appears as 'not favourably impressed'. There is no way of knowing if the 'un' was lost through a printer's error or omitted in order to protect Lloyd George against the charge of opportunism.

make that careful study of the text, the bill was engulfed in an avalanche of Nonconformist criticism which also swept away what real inclination he ever possessed to judge the details of the bill on their merits.

The *Daily News* – the paper in which Lloyd George had persuaded Cadbury to invest and make the voice of radical Nonconformity heard – had expressed its opinion of the bill on the same morning that the *Western Mail* reported the 'not unfavourable' opinion of Lloyd George: 'The School boards are to be destroyed because they stand for enlightenment and progress.'[4] During the following week its editorials continued the campaign against what it called 'The Bishop's Bill'. The attitude of England's free churchmen was established the moment that Arthur Balfour⋆ sat down after moving the acceptance of the bill by the House of Commons. Doctor John Clifford, the minister of the West London Baptist Chapel, was in the Distinguished Strangers' Gallery to hear the statement and announced, as soon as the Prime Minister had finished, that he opposed the bill in principle. Doctor Clifford was the moral and spiritual – though not the intellectual – leader of English Baptists. During the following week, it became clear that Balfour's proposal had excited the unanimous antagonism of the Nonconformist establishment. Lloyd George trimmed his sails. By 8 May, less than six weeks after he had given the Education Bill a cautious welcome, he had so adjusted his position that Massingham could write in the *Daily News*:

> Until Mr Lloyd George spoke tonight, Nonconformity – its intellectual attitude to education, its historic associations with the settlement of 1870 [i.e. the Education Act], now being torn up, and its contribution to the religious problem – has gone without a recorder and a champion. Mr Lloyd George took the vacant place tonight.[5]

Lloyd George had found another cause to champion. Like his campaign to unite the Welsh Liberal Party, the battle against Balfour's Education Bill ended in defeat. For Lloyd George, the result was less important than the contest. He had taken a giant step towards the status of national political leader.

Self-promotion was not Lloyd George's only reason for opposing the bill. He had several genuine objections, albeit most of them only

---

⋆Although Balfour succeeded Salisbury as Prime Minister in July 1902, he continued to pilot the bill through the House of Commons.

obliquely concerned with the bill's intrinsic merits. The bill was the creation of the Unionist Party – for which his loathing had been increased by the Boer War. He believed it his duty, as well as his delight, to frustrate all its ambitions. And by becoming the political spokesman of English Nonconformity, he could pursue what was becoming his obsessive assault on the character and conduct of Joseph Chamberlain. In his time, Chamberlain had also claimed to speak for radical Nonconformity. Lloyd George was able to represent him as an apostate.

The real surprise was not that Lloyd George came to denounce the bill but that, for an unthinking moment, he greeted it with a qualified show of sympathy. Resentment of the privileges which were enjoyed by the Church of England was in his blood. He was passionately in favour of disestablishment and fervently against Nonconformist farmers contributing to the upkeep of Anglican rectories through the payment of tithes. A public subsidy to Church of England schools must have seemed to be an extension of the religious hegemony which he was born to overthrow. Support for the bill – based on the improvement which it might make to the education system – would have been entirely intellectual. Opposition was visceral. And he had another reason to oppose the bill – which he admitted with reckless honesty: 'The Education Act of 1902 has presented Wales with its greatest political opportunity' to assert its nationhood.[6]

Immediately after he changed from pro to anti, the worst that Lloyd George could say about the bill was that it 'tended to pander to priest-craft'.[7] For the next month – suffering for part of the time from the laryngitis which was a chronic, if periodic, affliction – he chose to speak on less controversial subjects. Two days after the bill was formally introduced, his address to a public meeting in Conway amounted to a lecture on the procedures of the House of Commons. At Pwllheli on 27 March he did allow himself a word on 'the proposed revolution in education'. Initially he was moderately constructive. His ambition was to see England and Wales follow the Swiss model – 'the child of the artisan would then have the same chance as the child of the noblest house'. The speech included a little polemic. Again it was the obscure accusation that 'Priestcraft is the root of evil in this country and, if the new bill becomes law, priestcraft will have gained its desire.'[8] But for another month he showed remarkable restraint – even to the point, on 15 April, of attending a Free Churches Conference on the subject but declining an invitation to speak.

On 21 April, he was 'In the Library getting up a *solid* speech – full of statistics' for a meeting at Swansea. He told his wife, 'they will expect brimstone' but he planned 'to give them bread'.[9] His speech contained more facts than usual. An audience, three thousand strong, heard another exposition of the complementary objections – principle and cost – which he had deployed so successfully against the Boer War. 'Two million pounds a year is to be added to the rates to further increase the propagation of sectarian education.'[10] The peroration came near to predicting – if not threatening – revolution.

> There was a time when the people of this country had mastered the Bible and at the same time there arose in this country a monarch who taxed the people without their consent for purposes to which they objected. There also arose a state priesthood who wanted to exalt over their extravagant pretensions. There was a famous scripture reader, with Welsh blood in his veins, of the name of Oliver Cromwell. He had mastered all the revolutionary and explosive texts in that Book and the result was destructive to the state priesthood. The bench of bishops was blown up, the House of Lords disappeared, and the aristocracy of this land rocked as though an earthquake had shaken them.[11]

Between the preparation of the speech and its delivery, Megan, the Lloyd Georges' fifth child, was born. Her father wrote home to say that he 'could not put into words the thrill of joy and affection' which he felt after receiving the telegram 'announcing that all had passed off well'.[12] However, he did not hurry home to Wales to see his new daughter. The campaign against the Education Bill demanded his attention. The opening debate – spread over four parliamentary days – was about to take place.

Lloyd George waited 'to catch the Speaker's eye' with an impatience which was reflected in his low opinion of the Liberal Members who preceded him. In his letter home – composed in the present tense and presumably written in the chamber – he told his wife, 'Haldane is now speaking in support of the Bill. It will help, as far as it goes, to damage the Liberal Imperialists.'[13] Then it was Ellis Griffith, the Member for Anglesey, who failed to live up to expectations. 'He told me before he got up that he had a good speech – but it turned out to be a dismal failure.'[14] Lloyd George was called at the beginning of the fourth and last day – by which time there were claims to refute and concessions to reject. He began with a recital of the statistics which he had gathered in preparation for his Swansea speech. Then with the unerring instinct which – until his last year as Prime Minister – enabled him to identify the chinks in his opponents' armour, he turned to the aspect of the bill which perpetuated what was clearly discrimination against the Nonconformist Churches.

> You cannot base any good system of education on an injustice to a large section of the community. In Wales, at any rate, the vast majority of children are Nonconformists, yet they are not allowed to enter the teaching profession except on condition of their becoming members or attending the services of the Church of England.[15]

The exclusion was not quite so absolute as he made out. The church school in Llanystumdwy had been willing to make an exception for him and for his brother. But it was near enough to the truth to prick progressive consciences on both sides of the House. And thanks to the incompetence of Sir William Anson, the Parliamentary Secretary to the Board of Education, he was able to drive the point home. On the previous day, Sir William had, in Lloyd George's words, offered to remedy what he conceded was a grievance by 'supporting an amendment by which Nonconformist children would be allowed to enter the lower grades of the teaching profession'.

> There are one million of these children, containing among them probably the best suited for the teaching profession. But however well-behaved, able and bright they may be all you will say to them is 'we will allow you to become a lower grade official in this school, but nothing beyond that'.[16]

The speech ended with an appeal to Irish Members. Lloyd George 'believed in the sacred cause of small nationalities of which [the Irish] had been the guardians in the House of Commons'. This was not the time for them to 'join in oppressing Nonconformists, who had been their friends, at the behest of enemies of their faith'.[17] The Parnellites had already sacrificed his respect and support. In 1897, they had 'thought fit in the interest of their own schools ... to support the system which forces Nonconformist children to go to Anglican schools where they are excluded from teachership'.[18] Surely they would not betray their friends again. But they did. On the advice of Cardinal

Vaughan, Archbishop of Westminster, they put the interests of the Catholic Church – the hope of public investment in its schools – above all other considerations. From then on Vaughan became second only to Chamberlain on Lloyd George's list of villains and the Catholic Church a profoundly sinister institution. On 5 June, he told a Liberal League rally at the Queen's Hall that the whole bill was originated by Cardinal Vaughan and supported by the Anglican convocation for the benefit of 'that section of the clergy that is taking Protestant pay for teaching Catholic doctrine' – a stupendous aphorism which suffered only from the defect of being pure invention.[19]

Rosebery and Asquith both spoke at the Queen's Hall rally. The invitation to Lloyd George to share the platform with such illustrious figures was a certain indication of the growing esteem in which he was held within the Liberal Party. He was not a man to be overawed by seniority or authority. But the meeting marked – if it did not cause – another brief change of attitude towards Rosebery. Six months earlier, Lloyd George had condemned him after he had demanded that 'the slate should be wiped clean' of Home Rule. But – perhaps because of the second desertion by the Irish Nationalists – he had begun, even before the Queen's Hall meeting, to make public his private reservations about the policy for which, according to his perverse interpretation of history, the Liberal Party 'threw over [its] most cherished leaders . . . even the Right Honourable Member for West Birmingham', Joseph Chamberlain.[20] He had always held the view that, whatever its intrinsic merits, Irish Home Rule was worth neither the destruction of the Liberal government nor the postponement of other legislation. Rosebery had become the principal exponent of that view. But there was also an element of self-interest in his surprise announcement – made to the *Caernarvon and Denbigh Herald* – that he would welcome Rosebery's return as Liberal leader.[21] There was a real risk (or chance) of Henry Campbell-Bannerman's being deposed. Lloyd George was determined to be a member of whomsoever's Cabinet followed a Unionist defeat. He had been flattered by an invitation to Berkeley Square to discuss Rosebery's speech in the House of Lords debate on the Education Bill and he wanted to keep the relationship in good repair.

The committee stage of the Education Bill occupied forty-nine days of parliamentary time between June and December 1902. Lloyd George made 104 speeches, asked 25 questions, moved 13 amendments and intervened – with brief comments, refutations and corrections – 155 times.[22] But it was Sir Alfred Thomas, by then the chairman of the

Welsh Liberal MPs, who moved the amendment to Clause 12 which –
by abolishing the committee set up by the Welsh Intermediate
Education Act of 1896 to administer school policy in the principality
and replacing it with local education authorities of the sort that the bill
proposed for England – made last-ditch resistance possible. Balfour
accepted it as a sop to Welsh opinion. Lloyd George used it to mobilise
Welsh opposition.

The idea of making the change may have come from Lloyd George.★
When the Welsh Liberal MPs expressed reluctance to abolish a system
which had the supreme advantage of being different from the English
model, he displayed 'tremendous determination and driving force' in
persuading them to support the Thomas amendment.[23] Giving power
to the county councils would, he argued, improve the prospects of
administering the new act in a way which respected the legitimate
demands of Nonconformists. Balfour – anxious to make some sort of
concession to the troublesome Welsh – convinced himself that the
change did no more than bring consistency to the administration of
education in the two countries. The government accepted the amendment and the battle against the bill moved out of Parliament and into
the county halls.

It was not the only amendment which Balfour accepted. He agreed
to the complete deletion of Clause 5 and the replacement of school
boards by local education authorities became obligatory rather than at
the discretion of the county councils. So the one aspect of the policy
which Lloyd George had initially criticised was removed. But, by then,
he was looking for trouble, not improvement. The proposal to drop
Clause 5 was carried 286 to 134, with Lloyd George voting against.
Originally he had regarded the local option as evidence of 'what a
miserable weak thing this Government is'.[24] By the time the clause was
debated he had fallen in line with Nonconformist opinion and claimed
that it was necessary to allow local councils the choice of not subsidising church schools from the rates.

The Birmingham Unionists shared Lloyd George's revised view of
the bill. At a specially convened private meeting they demanded an end
to religious tests for teachers in church schools and an increased role for
local authorities in the appointment of school managers. Chamberlain
subdued the revolt by threatening to resign from the local leadership. In

---

★W. R. P. George, his nephew, described the amendment as being 'instigated' by his
uncle but provides no evidence to substantiate his claim.

the House of Commons Lloyd George made great sport at the Colonial
Secretary's expense.

> Even in Birmingham they could not hold a public meeting in sup-
> port of the Bill even when the Colonial Secretary addressed it
> himself . . . The argument used by the Colonial Secretary with
> regard to the Bill showed that he clearly recognised that his sup-
> porters were against it. He did not say 'the Bill is a good one' but
> 'if you do not carry this Bill, I shall resign and then mark the con-
> sequences'. There shall be neither dew nor rain on the British
> Empire for seven long years.[25]

Chamberlain, who spoke immediately after Lloyd George, ignored the
references to his Birmingham troubles and chose instead to take issue
with the allegation that the government had made the 1902 election a
referendum on the justice and conduct of the Boer War and that, in
consequence, it had no popular mandate for any other of its policies –
including education reform. He claimed that, despite having a special
responsibility for affairs in South Africa, he had only once ever suggested that it was the crucial issue of the campaign. Two days later, a
letter from Lloyd George was published in *The Times*. It listed twelve
occasions on which Chamberlain had been categoric that voters were
making a choice between the Unionist government and the Boers.

As the bill's committee stage dragged on, Lloyd George opposed all
attempts to make it more acceptable to Nonconformists. He wanted
their outrage to remain unabated but had to find more acceptable reasons for opposing ameliorative amendments. The Conservative
Member for Greenwich, Lord Hugh Cecil – not normally a reasonable
man – proposed that parents be allowed to withdraw their children from
religious instruction based on denominational theology with which
they did not agree. Managers of church schools would be required to
arrange alternative instruction for pupils whose religious affiliation was
different from that of the foundation. When the idea was first discussed, Lloyd George had supported it as an affirmation of the
Nonconformist right to be different. But the amendment was not called
during the summer committee stage and by November – when it was
debated at the report stage – all he wanted was conflict and confrontation. His objection was transparently spurious. There would, he said, be
hundreds of disputes about which child received which form of religious instruction, 'one theological sect saying "this boy belongs to us"

and another saying "he belongs to us". At one time the child would belong to one sect and in a week or fortnight there would be a successful Jameson Raid.'[26] He was not alone in rejecting the idea. The Tory High Churchmen – who could not contemplate the prospect of Nonconformity gaining a foothold in Anglican schools – voted down the amendment. And Lloyd George, having demonstrated the weakness of his case by defending his position with pure mumbo-jumbo, voted with them. Balfour, who recognised the proposal's healing qualities, abstained.

The House adjourned for the long autumn recess before the third reading debate – allowing Lloyd George to spend three weeks in Zermatt with Frank Edwards while Maggie stayed in Wales nursing baby Megan. Back in London in early September – where he addressed the Trades Union Congress on behalf of the Penrhyn quarrymen, who were again on strike – he recklessly announced the tactics which he would employ if the Education Bill became law. The parliamentary fight would go on right up to royal assent. But 'reckoning up its chances', he judged them to be 'slightly in favour of safe passage.' But the Welsh county councils – which, thanks to the Thomas amendment, would have the task of implementing the act – could still resist applying its provisions to schools within their areas. Caernarvonshire had already announced that it would not administer the new system of grants. The rest must follow suit. 'Our purpose', Lloyd George said, 'is not merely to render the Bill, if it is carried, a nullity but to use it as a weapon to tear down the present education system.'[27]

The third reading – which marked the Education Bill's acceptance by the House of Commons – was completed on 3 December. Balfour's final speech included a generous tribute to Lloyd George, 'who, throughout these debates [had] played . . . a most distinguished part . . . I believe that in the opinion of both sides of the House and of the country, the Honourable Gentleman has shown himself to be a most distinguished parliamentarian.'[28] Asquith was equally complimentary. In his letter home, the hero of the hour could not resist embellishing his triumph. He claimed that after Balfour's encomium, 'the general cheering in the House was very remarkable; the Tories being nearly so hearty as our own men'.*[29]

Lloyd George – still not quite forty and no more than a back-

---

*To fill his cup of happiness to overflowing, it was also the day on which Rosebery invited Lloyd George to his house in Berkeley Square.

bencher – had led the whole opposition battle against the 1902 Education Bill. Campbell-Bannerman had been slow to recognise its political significance. As late as 24 September he wondered, 'Is it not time and urgent that we should do more regarding the Education question? . . . Evidently the Non Cons are worked up to a heat they have never been before.'[30] Apparently unaware of Lloyd George's guerrilla campaign, the Liberal leader failed to take his own advice and remained so detached that Herbert Gladstone, the Liberal Chief Whip, thought it necessary to warn him that party members had noticed that he had played virtually no part in the education debates. 'They are anxious to hear your voice,' Gladstone wrote. 'The Education movement has gathered great force and we may be on the eve of a crisis.'[31] Lloyd George seized the opportunity to fill the vacuum which 'C-B' had left and to improve the reputation which he had won by his opposition to the Boer War. 'Mr Lloyd George,' wrote *The Times*, 'ardent Welshman though he is, has won a place not as spokesman for Welsh causes but of militant English Nonconformity.'[32]

The battle against the Education Bill, which Lloyd George fought and lost in the House of Commons, had been conducted according to the conventional rules of party conflict. Continuing the fight in the country required a strategic daring and tactical ingenuity which Lloyd George feared some of his allies did not possess. In July 1902, he expressed his doubts to William Robertson Nicoll, editor of the *British Weekly*, the semi-official journal of Nonconformity. 'The House of Commons has yet to be convinced that Nonconformity in any part of the country but Wales means business.'[33] When Nicoll tried to reassure him that his fears were groundless, he revised his opinion only to the point of assuming that England's resistance would be misconceived and therefore simultaneously unpopular and ineffective.

He was right. In November 1902, an anti-bill rally in Alexandra Palace had attracted a crowd of almost twenty thousand men and women – fifteen thousand in the hall and over four thousand on the grass outside. They were addressed at length by Doctor Clifford, who advocated passive resistance. Nonconformists should refuse to pay at least that portion of the rate which was to be spent in or on church schools. Like all such appeals to the emotions of mass meetings, the idea was accepted by the audience with thoughtless acclamation. But when, in a calmer atmosphere a month later, the National Committee of Free Churches met in Birmingham, a substantial minority – largely made up of Wesleyan Methodists – was strongly opposed to breaking the law. A

Passive Resistance Committee was set up with the motto 'No Say. No Pay'. But within weeks the Anti-Martyrdom League was formed to pay the rates that the passive resisters withheld. Lloyd George was determined that the Welsh should not follow the English along either path – capitulation or pointless militancy.

> There is no greater tactical mistake possible than to prosecute an agitation against an injustice in such a way as to alienate a large number of men who, while they resent their injustice as keenly as anyone, either – from tradition or timidity – decline to be associated with anything savouring of revolutionary action.[34]

That was the preamble to his 'Address to the People of Wales' – a manifesto for the campaign against the bill which was published on 17 January 1903. It proposed an aggressive, but in his view more practical, way of denying church schools the public subsidy which the new act would provide. The plan of action was described in one of the military metaphors so beloved of politicians. 'Let us capture the enemy's artillery and turn his guns against him.'[35] The responsibility for defying the law was to be removed from individual ratepayers and assumed by the county councils. The tactic was just as illegal as withholding rates, but Lloyd George claimed that it had been endorsed during a 'conversation with one of the highest legal authorities in the Kingdom'. The anonymous expert had been categoric. 'In his opinion,' Lloyd George said, 'no council can be compelled' to operate the Education Act. 'And if a County or Town Council do not put the law into operation, no-one will have the opportunity of refusing to pay rates because rates will not be demanded.'[36] He wanted both to preserve his reputation as a doughty fighter for good causes and, at the same time, behave in a way which was appropriate to a budding statesman and future Cabinet minister. So he asserted that he would 'not go a step beyond the strict limits of the law' and invented a legal fiction on which he could base his claim to political respectability.

The law required church schools to maintain themselves in an adequate state of repair. Many of them – chronically short of funds – were unable to fulfil that obligation. Lloyd George's plan was to deny the government subsidy to all schools which, when 'inspected by architects and engineers', fell short of Board of Trade standards. The 1902 Education Act did not provide local education authorities with the power to punish defaulters. And Lloyd George knew it. What was more, Clause 1 of the act made clear that the government had the power to instruct reluctant councils to pay and that 'any such order may be enforced by *mandamus*' – the power to make a court order which offered the choice between compliance and prosecution. Lloyd George had written 'Imprisonment?' against Clause 1 in his copy of the bill. But – gambling on the government's flinching from indicting all of Welsh local government – he added, 'Will the Government *mandamus* the county councils? I hope they will try it.'

The belief that Balfour had no stomach for the fight was reinforced by the decision to postpone the full operation of the act until February 1904. The postponement was more of a trap than a concession. Nonconformists, hot with righteous anger, would have to keep up the temperature of opposition for a full year, and the Prime Minister rightly suspected that Lloyd George did not look forward to spending all of 1903 leading the campaign. It had served its personal purpose and the time had come to move on. Concessions leading to a compromise were growing increasingly attractive when, by happy coincidence, during a train journey from Chester to London on 3 February 1903, Lloyd George shared a compartment with A. G. Edwards, Bishop of St Asaph – that vocal opponent of Lloyd George's campaigns against the Established Church. The conversation began cautiously. But, as it progressed, each man was pleasantly surprised by the other's moderation.[37] Edwards was on his way to meet Robert Morant – the inspiration of the school reforms who was about to be confirmed as permanent secretary at the Board of Education. The bishop told Morant that he had found Lloyd George 'conciliatory'.

Edwards judged, from the Morant meeting, that ministers expected the dispute between government and councils to end in deadlock – a stalemate which he attempted to avoid by bringing churchmen and the councillors together at a meeting in the Saint Asaph Bishop's Palace. It set the agenda for more discussions at Llandrindod Wells in which Lloyd George took part. He was in an emollient mood. An archdeacon, who had complained about the bellicose language used in the 'Address to the People of Wales', was assured that the public and private Lloyd George did not always hold identical opinions. The address was not to be taken as a statement of real principle: 'It was a fighting speech. I had my war paint on then.'[38]

The fear, felt and expressed on both sides, was that although the generals might come to an agreement on armistice terms, their troops would want to carry on the war. But bishops, no less than politicians, believe in the healing force of discussion. So yet another meeting was arranged. At the Palace Hotel in Westminster attempts would be made to resolve the two most contentious issues – the appointment of teachers and the form which religious instruction should take in rate-supported schools.

However, there could be no compromise on the appointment of teachers. Even if the formal religious test were abandoned, boards of management – appointed by the Anglican bishops – would still discriminate against Nonconformist applicants for teaching posts. Teachers, Lloyd George said, were 'civil servants'. Why should they be appointed by a clergyman? It was the build up to a typical joke. 'With equal fitness he might appoint the excise man. Really the parson has more in common with the excise man. They both deal with spirits and bondage.'[37]

His 'Address to the People of Wales', although generally destructive, had offered a constructive suggestion about how religious education should be conducted in Welsh schools. His suggestion (which he called 'the colonial promise') was basically the scheme which he had rejected – with the claim that there would be 'Jameson Raids' by Nonconformists on Anglican elementary schools – when Lord Hugh Cecil had attempted to include it in the original bill. If it were agreed that school managers must appoint teachers without reference to their religious affiliation, he would, when the time was right, 'advocate the extension to such managers ample facilities for teaching to their own denomination the doctrine of the Church to which they belonged'.[40]

Much work had to be done on the implementation of the 'colonial' principle. Long hours were to be spent arguing about whether the religious instruction should be in 'school hours' or during a thirty-minute period before the school formally met – with classes starting half an hour later on that day to enable pupils to arrive at the usual time! But the offer of compromise was enough to persuade Bishop Edwards that there was the basis for a 'concordat' which might be acceptable to all the warring factions. He should have known better.

Although the Catholic hierarchy had attended in force, no other Church of England bishop had taken part in the Westminster Palace Hotel meeting and John Owen, the Bishop of St Davids, had expressed his open hostility to continuing discussions. On 18 February, Lloyd George told his brother, 'The fat is already fizzling in the fire.' Morant had warned the Archbishop of Canterbury that 'the bishops are furious with Asaph for giving away the churches' case' and had gone on to explain his fears that the reforms would be sacrificed to party interests.[41] Balfour would not consider compromise, insisting that 'The Opposition front bench do not want to see anything like a settlement arrived at because the education cry is likely to be useful in a general election.'[42] He misjudged the religious fervour but was right about the political zest for battle. Tory Brecknockshire and Radnorshire agreed to implement the act as soon as it came into force, but Welsh Liberals – reinforced by massive gains in the local elections – could not wait to start the fight which Lloyd George had told them they could win. At a rally in the Albert Hall – said to have been attended inside and out by seventeen thousand supporters – he had been treated like a hero. And in Newport on 30 November, Campbell-Bannerman had called him 'your foremost champion – yes the champion of us all against clerical pretensions and political injustice'. But among the militants there were a few radicals who had grown suspicious of Lloyd George. Hs inclination to protect his flank encouraged sniping from two directions. Some Nonconformists wondered why, when he was leading them into battle, he was also discussing peace terms with the enemy. And – since political success breeds envy – more and more of his colleagues resented the adulation he was being accorded by the growing army of Liberals who, ignoring his negotiations with the bishops, trusted him to lead them to outright victory.

Despite its political potential – the Nonconformist vote was crucial to a Liberal victory – there were Liberal MPs who, during the spring and early summer of 1903, regarded the continuing debate over denominational education as a diversion from an issue of far greater importance. The Unionist coalition was beginning to break up. During May, Chamberlain – who had left the government in order to enjoy the freedom to campaign – spoke with increasing passion in favour of Imperial Preference. Even after his resignation, he remained a major influence on Balfour and the Tory Party. Asquith had confirmed his status as heir apparent to the Liberal leadership by his powerful defence of free trade, and Lloyd George, by denouncing what he claimed was the Unionists' enthusiasm for a 'bread tax', had become a major figure in the battle which was to end with the resignation of the government. But the Education Bill remained – whether he liked it or not – the issue with which he was identified.

In the end, Bishop Edwards's proposed concordat foundered on a single disagreement. The St Asaph Diocesan Conference insisted that boards of church school management must be composed of church and lay nominees in equal numbers and the councils would not agree to teachers being appointed by boards which did not have a majority of lay members. Lloyd George, fearing that Nonconformists would be held responsible for the breakdown and he would share the blame, published an article in *The Pilot*. It attributed the collapse of compromise to the Church of England's refusal to 'lose the power of patronage'.[43] In April, he had told the Conference of Welsh Local Authorities in Llandrindod Wells, 'If we are now compelled to face the disagreeable necessity of fighting this Act it is not because we did not, in the first instance, seek the ways of peace.' His speech ended with a tribute to the Bishop of St Asaph, among the Welsh clergy 'the best fighting man of the lot'. That was the excuse for a little homely philosophy which he silently hoped the delegates would accept as a comment on his own conduct. 'The best fighters are not always the worst men in coming to terms.'[44]

According to the *Illustrated Mirror*, it was 'Mr Lloyd George's personality' and 'the prominent and sensational role which this well-known MP has taken on the political stage' – rather than the more recently acquired reputation for compromise and coalition – which 'made His Majesty [the King] desirous of having dinner with him'.[45] It was arranged at Lord Tweedmouth's house in Park Lane. Harold Spender reported that Lloyd George spoke only one word to his sovereign. Asked if he played bridge, he replied 'No' and was told, 'That is a pity. It's a very good game.'[46] But in a letter home Lloyd George offered a rather different account of the evening. He quoted John Morley.

'I dined with the King Saturday night and he said to me – "Well I met your friend Mr Lloyd George last night"'. JM replied 'I hope he made a favourable impression on Your Majesty'. He answered with emphasis, 'a *very* favourable impression'. That is what Tweedmouth also says.[47]

During the week of Lloyd George's royal triumph, the Liberals made fifty gains in the Welsh local government elections – a remarkable result for a party which already held more than two-thirds of the county council seats. Every 'progressive' candidate – both Liberal and Independent – had signed a statement, drafted by Lloyd George, which promised to refuse rate aid to church schools with buildings which were in need of repair. T. P. O'Connor described the building standards contrivance as 'Driving a coach and horses through an Act of Parliament.'[48] When both Brecknockshire and Radnorshire changed hands in the Liberal landslide, the *South Wales Daily News* concluded that the results were 'the knell of the government's education policy in Wales'.[49] Nobody believed that Balfour would accept Lloyd George's challenge to *mandamus* all of Wales.

Neither the Bishop of St Asaph nor Lloyd George was quite ready to abandon the hope of agreement. The bishop proposed to introduce a private bill – incorporating the principles of the concordat – in the House of Lords. In the House of Commons, Lloyd George made a last plea for compromise which, despite claiming that the government should accept the judgement of the Welsh people, carefully avoided 'the usual pyrotechnics'.[50] Balfour was not impressed. On the day which followed the call for moderation, the Cabinet gave its approval to the Prime Minister's plan for regaining the initiative. On 26 April 1904, the Education (Local Authorities Default) Bill was published. It allowed the Treasury to make direct payments to schools which had been denied local authority subsidies and delete equivalent amounts from the government's grant to the offending county councils.

During the weeks between the bill's presentation and its receipt of royal assent, the government took direct action against Carmarthenshire, which had, much against Lloyd George's advice, refused to implement any aspect of the Education Bill. The inquiry, under A. T. Lawrence QC – a future Lord Chief Justice – concluded that the council was behaving unlawfully in refusing to recognise or administer any of the forty-eight church schools within the county. So, contrary to Lloyd George's prediction, *mandamus* proceedings were instigated against a Welsh county. A new battle had to be fought.

The 'closure', ending debate on Clause 4 of the Default Bill, was moved after four hours of debate. Lloyd George first announced his refusal to vote and then, amid cries of 'Dishonesty!' – an entirely 'unparliamentary expression' – he and fifteen other Members were 'named', the quaint Westminster expression for being expelled from the chamber. Asquith, technically in charge of the Liberal Party's response to the bill, led the whole opposition out of the chamber in a show of support and sympathy for the censured Members. It was not the sort of theatrical gesture which came naturally to him, but Lloyd George was setting the tone and the pace – and thereby proving that he had become a major politician.

Lloyd George was uncertain about how to respond to the new situation, except to rename the proposals the 'Welsh Coercion Bill'. He wished to move on. The government was planning to introduce its new Licensing Bill. It was a natural target for Nonconformist indignation and he wanted nothing to divert him from the task of articulating it. On

23 June 1904, he was able to write home with the glorious news that he had been 'busy with Asquith and [Herbert] Gladstone . . . planning the great battle'.[51] The next day, after announcing 'The Asaph Bill going well', he made a frank admission. 'I want Education out of the way to fight the publicans. You cannot fight on two fronts successfully.'[52] His optimism about its progress proved unjustified. After weary days in the House of Lords it was abandoned, much to the delight of John Owen, Bishop of St Davids, who had advised the government, back in April 1903, to 'nip in the bud . . . the St Asaph terms'.[53]

The Welsh Members of Parliament met in August 1904 to decide what their new tactics should be. They accepted, without much discussion or any dissent, Lloyd George's plan of action. He had become the acknowledged leader of Welsh Liberalism and, in the opinion of Herbert Lewis, Wales had become 'a one man show'. So, although 'there were many doubts about the wisdom of his policy' – which amounted to asking Nonconformist parents to withdraw their children from church schools – they agreed to support what came to be called the Welsh Revolt.[54] A 'well-informed correspondent' of *The Times* gave a full account of what was supposed to be a private meeting. The parents' boycott was to be reinforced by the resignation of school managers so that, in the example which Lloyd George chose, 'the whole administration of Education in Caernarvonshire will rest with Mr Morant'.[55] In a necessary concession to the traditional Welsh passion to put education ahead of all other considerations, he later clarified his plans to the *Review of Reviews*.[56] Independent schools would be set up to make sure that the pupils were not denied teaching.

The Times devoted an editorial to the Welsh Members' meeting – a considerable accolade in itself and, in part, a flattering acknowledgement of Lloyd George's arrival in politics' front rank. It was also, like so many *Times* leaders, loftily censorious.

Five or six years ago in his callow Parliamentary youth, these schemes might have been regarded as the promising methods of self-advertisement [employed] by a young politician who must at any cost attract attention. But that time has long gone . . . He has become a serious politician and a serious claimant to high office . . . He is to be, they say, President of the Board of Trade.

Yet he had 'condescended to become the cheerleader of a rebellion' which could only 'destroy all respect for parliament'.[57]

Unbeknown to both *The Times* and 'the fanatical countrymen' who were marching behind his banner, Lloyd George still hoped and worked for a compromise. There were more meetings with the Bishop of St Asaph and attempts to revise and resurrect the concordat. The idea of the two men meeting Morant was modified and Edwards saw him alone. Morant feared that Lloyd George had 'now roused a mob he cannot quell'.[58] Lloyd George himself announced that 'they are shaking in their shoes'.[59]

The campaign against the 1902 Education Act had all the trappings of democracy. Meeting followed meeting and even the largest rallies ended with the assembled multitude endorsing, on a show of hands, the plan of campaign. The same rule was observed at the National Convention of Wales, held in Park Hall, Cardiff, on 6 November 1904. Lloyd George's speech was punctuated with cheers at the end of every sentence, and resolutions demanding closures, resignations and boycotts were carried with unanimous acclamation. But Balfour's report to the Cabinet reflected the truth about the Cardiff convention. 'There had been a great deal of make-believe in the meeting.'[60]

There were fourteen Members of Parliament on the platform. D. A. Thomas and Bryn Roberts – opposed both to the policy and the emergence of Lloyd George as the de facto leader of Welsh Liberalism – were said to be in America. No further details of their absence were known. Some county councils were showing signs of wanting to plan their own destinies rather than take instruction from the Member for Caernarvon Boroughs. Merioneth had been in open revolt against his leadership. Teachers were growing anxious about how they would live if their schools closed. The Free Church Council promised £100,000 to fill the gap left by the Treasury grant.[61] As so often happens, doubts were raised by what was meant to be reassurance. Lloyd George's guarantee that funds would not run out before the general election, when the Balfour government would be beaten, raised questions about what would happen if the Unionists survived. *The Schoolmaster*, reflecting the views of the National Union of Teachers, began to question the wisdom of the whole strategy.

It was then that Tom John, the president-elect of the National Union of Teachers, met John Owen, the Bishop of St Davids, and told him that, if both sides in the dispute refused to yield, many teachers would face great personal hardship and the whole Welsh school system would be in danger of collapse. The Campaign Committee of the Welsh Liberal Party – fearful of some sort of compromise – met in death-or-glory mood. Lloyd George did not attend. He knew that the committee would pass a resolution which would require him either to give up the leadership of the Welsh education campaign or advocate a policy which he regarded as folly. He was an extremist no more.

All that was left was a war of attrition which the Welsh county councils could not win. The Default Act took effect in January 1905 – postponed not because of Lloyd George's rearguard action but because it was, rightly, assumed that Welsh nerves would crack while councils waited for the final assault. Barry was threatened with the withdrawal of its total grant after it failed to pay the salaries of teachers in Roman Catholic schools. It immediately changed its policy. To make clear that the government would not tolerate the slightest default, Merioneth was warned that it was in default because it had underpaid its church schools by £364 during the period September 1903 to November 1904. Montgomeryshire proposed to withhold teachers' salaries until the church schools brought their buildings up to an acceptable standard. When the wages were paid directly by the Board of Education, the Liberal councillors resigned their seats and the Unionists who remained took control and implemented the 1902 act in full. Then the Liberal majority in Carmarthenshire – with the encouragement of Lloyd Morgan, the local Member of Parliament – decided that the struggle would achieve nothing and accepted their duty to manage and finance church schools. The battle was lost.

Lloyd George's reputation remained intact. Almost from the start, he had favoured and worked for a compromise. Yet he retained the heroic aura of the man who had led the last-ditch resistance. Indeed his esteem was so great that, when even the diehards had accepted that justice would only follow the election of a Liberal government, he felt confident enough to give them a warning.

> We shall not get all we want. We shall have to make concessions and we shall be wise to do so . . . We must try to effect a settlement which the Tories, when they are in power again, have no chance of upsetting. And if we are to do that we must concede something – must sacrifice some of our ideals.[62]

The campaign against the Education Bill had guaranteed him a place in the next Liberal Cabinet. A year before it was formed, he had begun to think like a Cabinet minister.

CHAPTER 10

PROTECTION, PROPERTY
AND PUBLICANS

In the spring of 1904, Lloyd George told his brother that he was determined to move on from his campaign against the government's education policy and open a second front.[1] The attack was to be directed towards the Licensing Bill which had been published on 2 May 1904, six days before the publication of legislation to enforce the Unionists' education reforms. What Lloyd George called the Brewers' Endowment Bill provided compensation for dispossessed landlords. It was meant to accelerate the reduction in the number of licensed premises and therefore might have been expected to win the support of a good Welsh Baptist. But Lloyd George announced his opposition to the idea as soon as it was mooted. Once again, he was less interested in the merits of the measure than in the opportunity which it provided to harass the government, and again he was dissatisfied with the way in which some Liberal colleagues supported him in the battle. '[Ellis-]Griffith made a mess of it. Moved an amendment at the wrong point.'[2] In July, a protest against the amount of time allocated to the debate ended in victory for three Members of Parliament whose destinies were to become inextricably entwined. 'We kept them up all night – even then they could not get their bill through without trenching on today's sitting. This has consequently to be dropped. The Licensing Bill cannot now be taken this week. It was a great fight and we beat them – McKenna, Churchill and I.'[3]

Reginald McKenna had fought alongside Lloyd George in the battle against the Education Bill. Winston Churchill was a new recruit to the

Liberal cause who had crossed the floor of the House a couple of months earlier. His friendship with Lloyd George – which had begun that spring – lasted, despite some turbulent passages, for the next forty years. It was borne – like Churchill's apostasy itself – out of the biggest shift in Conservative policy since the Tories 'found the Whigs bathing and ran away with their clothes'. Sir Robert Peel had repealed the Corn Laws in 1846. Joseph Chamberlain demanded what amounted to their reintroduction. Churchill, knowing that Balfour would eventually capitulate, crossed the floor in protest and became, for a full decade, one of the heroes of radical England.

During his five years as President of the Board of Trade in Gladstone's second administration, Chamberlain had made no great show of disagreement with the orthodox Liberal doctrine of free trade. The great conversion was based as much on his judgement of what was most likely to safeguard the strength inherited from Britain's past as his estimate of what was best for Britain's economic future. As the debate raged on, he advanced all sorts of supplementary arguments in favour of 'protection'. But the real purpose of the scheme was made clear enough by its name – Imperial Preference.

The idea had been discussed and the name used during the Conference of Dominion Prime Ministers which was held in the summer of 1902. Canada discriminated in favour of imported British goods and Wilfred Laurier, the dominion's premier, suggested that Britain should reciprocate. To Chamberlain, an Imperialist anxious to strengthen the ties of blood and birth, it seemed the right moment not just to accept but to extend the idea. Michael Hicks-Beach – Chancellor of the Exchequer during the campaign in South Africa – had imposed an import duty on corn and flour to meet the escalating military bills. Lloyd George – a free-trader by inclination – endorsed the decision in a way which was not intended to be helpful. The poor would suffer. But, he said, 'the sacrifice is worth it if it helps to bring home what war means' – especially to the jingoistic working classes.[4] Charles Ritchie, Hicks-Beach's successor at the Treasury, and a devout free-trader, took a more high-minded view. It was only a matter of time before the government split.

On 16 May 1902, Chamberlain told the Birmingham Liberal Unionist Association:

The Empire is being attacked on all sides . . . If, by adherence to economic pedantry, to old shibboleths, we are to lose opportunities of closer union which are offered us by our colonies and if we do not take every chance in our power to keep British trade in our hands, I am certain that we shall deserve the disasters which will infallibly come upon us.[5]

At three Cabinet meetings in March 1903, the argument for a degree of protection was supported by a majority of the ministers who were present. But when the Chancellor threatened to resign, they lost their nerve and agreed to abolish the Boer War tariff. The general question of protection would be considered at a later date. Balfour believed that the whole issue could be resolved in a way which maintained at least the appearance of party unity. He would not have held that view had he heard the Messianic language with which Chamberlain (in South Africa to discuss the dominion's future governance) described his support for

a policy of Imperial Preference and Empire development by means of which . . . the essentials of life, industry and trade within the Empire should be available for the Empire, assured as to quality and regularity of supply and gradually reduced in cost . . . under a defensive tariff against the outside world and a preferential abatement in favour of all parts of the Empire.[6]

The Cabinet returned to the subject on 15 May. It was agreed that two eventualities – 'the necessity to retaliate against foreign countries or the expediency of a closer union with our colonies' – might justify the abandonment of free trade.[7] Balfour announced that he would use the collective decision as the basis of his response to a delegation of protectionists who were due to meet him later in the week. Chamberlain added that, at a meeting in Birmingham on 16 May, he 'proposed to say much the same but in a much less definite manner'.[8] His speech ended, 'I leave the matter in your hands. I desire that a discussion on the subject should now be opened' – the formula employed by politicians who want to disagree with their party's policy but not be blamed for doing so. Little else he said was consistent with the assurance that he had given to Balfour and the Cabinet.

I say it is the business of British statesmen to do everything they can, even at some present sacrifice, to keep the trade of the colonies with Great Britain, to increase that trade, to promote it, even if in doing so we lessen our trade somewhat with foreign competitors . . . You want an Empire. Do you think it better to cultivate trade with your own people or to let that go in order that you can keep the trade of those who are your competitors?[9]

The Annual Register was right to judge that 'No political event in recent years has produced such a startling effect as the pronouncement on fiscal policy made by Mr Chamberlain in Birmingham.'[10] Within a week, Lloyd George was to provoke him into making an even more startling announcement.

It came about almost by accident. In April 1903, in a speech in the Palace Theatre, Newcastle – inspired by the industrialist and social reformer Seebohm Rowntree's revelation that 30 per cent of the citizens of York lived below the poverty line and Charles Booth's description of the London poor – Lloyd George barely mentioned the split in the Unionist ranks. The army's admission that three out of every five potential Boer War recruits were medically unfit for military service had, he said, confirmed his diagnosis that the land, its cost and its availability, lay at the heart of all the country's social problems. 'The land in London is worth about £500,000,000. It is worth more than all the municipal debt throughout the kingdom – the money which has been sunk in great municipal enterprises, in waterworks, sanitation, lighting, tramways and roads . . . Who created the wealth? It is not the landlords.'[11]

That was the nearest Lloyd George ever came to a definitive statement of his political philosophy – revealed, in typical Lloyd George style, not by the exposition of a theory but by an illustrative anecdote.

London was a swamp and the landlords did not even create that. All the wealth has been created by the industry, energy and enterprise of the people who dwelt in London. Every year the value of the land is improving in London by the capital sum of £10,000,000. The improved value is due to the energy of the people, not to the landlords into whose coffers the enormous sum of money pours. Whilst the landlords are going to their racecourses, the property is increasing by this enormous sum. Out of this sum of money, what do they contribute to public expenditure? If these great communities had not expended money upon sanitation and lighting and roads this value would never have been created . . . It would hardly be believed by anyone outside this country that the landlords had not contributed a penny towards that great local expenditure.[12]

The consequences of the land monopoly – and the exorbitant rents which the monopolists were able to charge – had been made plain during the deliberations of the Select Committee on Old Age Pensions. If entitlement to benefit began only at sixty-five, most workmen would die before they qualified for a payment. 'Why? The explanation is to be found in the terrible habitations to which a large proportion of our workmen in large towns are driven at the end of the day's work.'[13]

The Newcastle speech wandered from subject to subject, as Lloyd George's speeches usually did.* There was a reference to the iniquities of the Education Bill, the scandal of compensating miscreant publicans and Lord Penrhyn's continued persecution of his quarrymen. The hated landowners were accused of a new crime. They had 'so manipulated parliament that it is all in the hands of one class . . . It does not matter up to the present which party is in power, you have practically the same people governing the country.'[14] There spoke Lloyd George the class warrior – a man who did not feel an unquestioning tribal loyalty to his Liberal allies.

The attack on the social structure of Parliament which followed sounded like a defence of democracy, but the assertion that working men had a right to play a part in determining the destiny of nations made the second deviation from the central Newcastle theme all the more strange. Thousands of men and women had 'cried out for war' and then complained about its cost. They were 'inconstant because they gave neither time nor any serious thought to the study of politics'. He concluded that there was 'too great a disposition to play up to the whims and caprices of what is known as the man in the street'.[15] Most politicians have felt the same from time to time. Few have dared to make their feelings public.

A week after Chamberlain had made clear his support for Imperial Preference, the House of Commons debated a Private Member's bill which proposed the introduction of an old-age pension. Lloyd George took the opportunity to repeat what he had said in Newcastle about the scandal of poverty. His speeches – whatever their main subject – usually excoriated his numerous enemies in a single paragraph of multiple condemnation. So in typical form he claimed – with considerable justification – that, had not £250 million been squandered on the war in South Africa, the government could easily have afforded to find the

---

*The speech is reproduced in full as an appendix to du Parcq's semi-official biography.

cost of the old-age pension. That led – naturally and inevitably – to a denunciation of Chamberlain, the fallen idol who had abandoned his concern for the British poor in favour of imperial grandeur.

> The Right Honourable Gentleman had an old age pension scheme. He was a man of many schemes and this was one of them. He was like the man who was fond of quack medicine . . . He went through the country recommending it – travelling for it – and a very good living he made out of it but the profits were not distributed among the deserving poor. The Right Honourable Gentleman pocketed the votes of the working class and forgot all about old age pensions.

There was then much play on a reference which Chamberlain had made to his meditations on policy while 'contemplating the illimitable veldt'. It was the kind of cheap point that the House of Commons loved then and loves now.

> The Right Honourable Gentleman has seen the beauties of the illimitable veldt and forgotten all about temperance, finance, education and old age pensions . . . In 1894 the Right Honourable Gentleman had said that the deserving poor were impatient for this reform. Had the plan become less important? Or was it that they were less poor or less impatient? 'What,' says the Right Honourable Gentleman, 'are you clamouring for your pension still? Turn your thoughts away from these worldly, insignificant affairs and contemplate the illimitable veldt.'[16]

Chamberlain had, at Balfour's insistence, agreed not to speak on Imperial Preference in the House of Commons. But Lloyd George's scorn was too much to bear unanswered. Chamberlain emerged, dramatically, from behind the Speaker's chair and fell into a trap baited by his own arrogance. Replying – without preparation – to an intentionally provocative challenge is always dangerous no matter how adroit a minister may be. Had Chamberlain done no more than assert his continued support for the introduction of an old-age pension, he would have got away with nothing more damaging than the demand to know where the money would be found. But he chose to answer the damning question before it was asked. Because he had come into the Commons chamber 'accidentally', he was unprepared and could not give exact figures. But he understood the annual cost of a national pension to be £10 million.

> Before any government can consider a scheme of that kind, it must know where it is going to get the funds. I do not think that old age pensions is a dead question and I think it may not be impossible to find the funds, but that no doubt will involve a review of the fiscal system which I have indicated as necessary and desirable at an early date.[17]

A 'review of the fiscal system' could mean only the reimposition of import duties. Lloyd George, almost unintentionally, had provoked Chamberlain into breaking his promise not to speak in the Commons on the subject and exposing the deep division within the government – as well as offending the Unionist old guard who regarded old-age pensions as the height of fiscal irresponsibility. In Cambridge, on the day after Chamberlain's statement, Lloyd George exposed the full the horror of what the Colonial Secretary proposed.

> In order to protect the Colonies, we must put a tariff upon food and raw material. Protecting manufactured goods doesn't help the Colonies. We must tax corn, wool cotton, raw material which is used for manufacturers. It is all very well to talk about our Colonies. Our first duty is to the people at home.[18]

Only a moment of hubris-induced madness can account for the second mistake – even more disastrous than the first – which Chamberlain made within a week. On 28 May, Charles Dilke joined with Lloyd George in initiating a debate on the way to finance a national old-age pension. When Lloyd George suggested that Chamberlain's only plan was to pay the bill by reintroducing the import duty on corn – amounting to the introduction of a permanent 'bread tax' – Chamberlain intervened again. Imperial Preference would both pay for the pension and increase wages. But he could not leave it there. As a sign of his contempt for the lack of courage displayed by his adversaries, he added, 'If you are to give a preference to the Colonies – I do not say that you are – you must put a tax on food. I make the Honourable Gentleman opposite a present of that.'[19] Thanks to Lloyd George, Chamberlain had admitted that Imperial Preference meant more expensive food.

The new campaign – Lloyd George versus the 'bread tax' – was enlivened by what had become the expected rhetorical sallies. After the Colonial Secretary spoke in Glasgow, supported by several pillars of the Scottish aristocracy, the occasion was celebrated with the explanation that 'when a statesman of Chamberlain's position comes forward and proposes a return to the Corn Laws, lords and dukes and earls and squires and baronets are found running and clucking like a flock of fowls when they hear corn shaken in a tin'. And Lloyd George ended his speech with a passage of breathtaking effrontery. Free trade was a confident assertion of Britain's ability to compete with the rest of the world. Chamberlain took the unpatriotic view that the rubric 'Made in Britain' was not a guarantee of commercial success. 'I can't stand these people who are always running down their own country.'[20]

Lloyd George was ideally suited to exploit the political capital that could be made from the threat of a bread tax. But he realised that Chamberlain's complete policy – when honestly described – had undoubted attractions. On 1 January 1904, Winston Churchill – at the time still accepting the Unionist whip in the House of Commons but already willing to join any alliance against Imperial Preference – had written to Lord Hugh Cecil about a conversation with Lloyd George which had taken place over lunch on 31 January 1903.

> He said, unless we have something to promise as against Mr Chamberlain's promises, where are we with the working men? He wants to promise three things which are arranged to deal with three different classes, namely fixture of tenure to tenant farmers subject to payments of rents and good husbandry: taxation of site values to reduce rates in towns: and something of the nature of Shackleton's Trade Disputes Bill for the Trades Unions.* Of course, with regard to the brewers, he would write 'no compensation from public funds'.[21]

Churchill, five months away from crossing the floor, was 'very careful not to commit [himself] to any of these points' but he was clearly attracted by the idea of reform.[22] It is not clear when he became equally

---

*In July 1901, the House of Lords – considering the Taff Vale Railway Company versus the Amalgamated Society of Railway Servants – had ruled that trade unions were financially responsible for the actions of their members. The unions were pressing for a review of law.

attracted by David Lloyd George. They first met at the bar of the House of Commons after Churchill's maiden speech on 18 February 1901. They exchanged jovial, if slightly Delphic, criticisms. Lloyd George accused Churchill of 'standing against the Light', and Churchill retorted that Lloyd George took 'a singularly detached view of the British Empire'.[23] By that autumn, Lloyd George felt so well disposed towards Churchill that he told a meeting at Llanelli, 'We do not always agree but at the same time we do not black each other's eyes' – a strange, if guarded, compliment to be paid to a Tory MP. Churchill was not so quickly enamoured. On 23 December, he wrote, in a letter to a Birmingham Conservative, 'I think Lloyd George a vulgar, chattering little cad.'[24]

Relations improved – encouraged no doubt by Churchill's increasing disenchantment with the Unionist coalition. In a letter to William George, dated 31 December 1903, Lloyd George told his brother, 'Met Churchill by appointment today. He is willing to come over to our side and thinks that thirty other Unionists will accompany him.'[25] Churchill's estimate of likely desertions proved optimistic. But his own defection was already taken for granted by others, if not yet admitted by him. On 1 January 1904, J. L. Wanklyn MP – one of Lloyd George's Liberal colleagues – sent him a New Year's greeting which included the question, 'How do you like your new stable companion, Winston Churchill? You will make a perfect match-pair but I should be devilish sorry to try and drive you.'[26]

Churchill was ready to become not just a Liberal but a 'New Liberal'. He had written to Balfour, after Chamberlain's declaration, to warn the Prime Minister that he was 'utterly opposed to measures which will alter the Free Trade character of this country and I consider such an issue superior in importance to any other before us'.[27] He was almost as critical of attempts to reduce the flow of 'mostly Jewish' immigration from Europe. More important, in terms of the role he was to occupy during the next decade, he too had been horrified to discover the extent of poverty in turn-of-the-century Britain. He told a meeting in Blackpool that Seebohm Rowntree's account of conditions in York had 'made his hair stand on end'.[28]

Perhaps his disillusionment with the government had been accelerated by the Oldham Unionist Association announcing that it would not support his candidature at the next election and the decision of his own front bench to lead the whole parliamentary party out of the Commons chamber in the middle of his speech on the motion for the 1904 Easter recess.* But it was support for free trade which began his helter-skelter progress to becoming, by the standards of the time, a libertarian Home Secretary. Churchill crossed the floor of the House on 31 May 1904.

> He entered the Chamber . . . stood for a moment at the Bar [of the House], looked briefly at both the Government and the Opposition benches and strode swiftly up the aisle. He bowed to the Speaker and turned sharply to the right to the Liberal benches.[29]

Much has been wrongly made of the fact that he chose to sit next to Lloyd George. In fact he had wanted sit in the place his father had always occupied. But Henry Labouchere was in Lord Randolph's old seat and young Winston got as near to it as he could in an act of filial piety. All doubt about his choice should be removed by his expression of gratitude for the generous tributes which followed his maiden speech. He attributed them to 'a certain splendid memory which many Honourable Members still preserve'.[30]

On 4 June, Churchill and Lloyd George both addressed a Liberal rally at the Alexandra Palace, after which Churchill was persuaded, with some difficulty, to visit Wales. He was invited to make a constituency tour – Caernarvon, Rhyl and Llandudno – but feared that 'three meetings will be a great exertion. I am working away at my father's life and it is hard to divert one's attention suddenly onto current political questions when one is immersed in the politics of the past.'[31] But on 18 October he spoke in Caernarvon and called Lloyd George 'the best fighting general in the Liberal army'.[32] The friendship was sealed by the cottage man's visit to Blenheim on 17 July 1906, by which date the Liberals were in office and Lloyd George was a member of the Cabinet. But, although the relationship was slow to develop, it was eroded by neither time nor rivalry. It was generally assumed that their unbridled ambition 'must come between them in the future, when, if not before, they "meet face to face . . . on that narrow path which leads to the highest pinnacle of honour"'.[33] But, although there were some near misses, the ultimate collision never occurred. In 1917, Lloyd George rescued Churchill from political oblivion and in 1940

---

*Churchill had only himself to blame. Balfour left the chamber as he rose to speak. Senior Members have never felt obliged to listen to young backbenchers. But Churchill accused him of 'lack of respect and deference' before belatedly adding 'to the House'.

Churchill offered Lloyd George a place in the Cabinet of his wartime coalition.

In his life of Winston Churchill, Roy Jenkins suggests that their friendship – far from being undermined by their rivalry – was built upon it. 'They were the two British politicians of genius . . . in the first half of the twentieth century' and they recognised, valued and benefited from each other's brilliance.[34] Both men were sufficiently self-confident to believe that they could withstand competition from even the most talented friend and rival, and they shared a common view of politics. Few fixed principles. No abiding loyalties. Love of the battle itself which was almost as great as the determination to win. For the lifetimes of the Campbell-Bannerman and Asquith Liberal governments they both believed in exalting the humble and meek, but only Lloyd George wanted to put down the mighty from their seats.

Both men believed in taking the fight to the enemy with a cavalier disregard for facts and figures which did not suit their convenience. On 29 March 1904, Lloyd George, in what he claimed to be his considered judgement on the introduction of Chinese indentured labour into the South African goldmines, told the House of Commons that the Boer War had been fought and British lives lost 'not so much so as to secure the emancipation of white labour as to introduce slave yellow labour'.[35] Outrage at exploitation swiftly gave place to an appeal to self-interest. 'Do you know that we have an Act of Parliament in South Africa . . . that prevents British workmen from landing unless they have £25 in their pockets? How many British workmen have £25 to spare? But the Chinamen are pouring in in shiploads without a single cent in their pockets.' Then, in the space of a single sentence, prejudice turned into an affirmation of the brotherhood of man. 'After all, the black man is the native of the country and he has as good a right – a better right – than either Dutchmen or British.'[36]

In 1904, both Chinese indentured labour and Imperial Preference were, to Lloyd George, side-shows. The big event was the Licensing Bill but, for a time, he ran his campaign against the 'Brewers' Endowment Bill' in parallel with the continuing battle to frustrate the 'Welsh Coercion Act'. As late as August 1904, he still had the confidence to predict that the education reforms could be frustrated: 'We shall beat them. Feel sure of it.'[37] But win or lose – and he effectively lost – he needed a new cause to champion and a new enemy to demonise. The government provided him with both. The cause was temperance and the enemy was the brewing industry. As always he chose to denounce the accompanying disadvantages rather than applaud the central benefits. The intention to reduce the number of licensed premises was overlooked and great emphasis was placed on the likelihood that the public houses whose licences were renewed would be given virtual security for life. And he was able to add a Welsh dimension to his criticism. Alcohol licences should be subject to a local veto. Wales must have the right to close its public houses on a Sunday.

During the first reading debate on 20 April 1904, he claimed that the system of closure and compensation would result in a 'value being created for the worst type of house and a corresponding burden being placed on the better type. The well-conducted and better class houses are to be taxed for the sake of a class of property which ought to be destroyed.' The prospect of compensation would increase the value of the most disreputable licensed premises. 'The Prime Minister is creating a new business, a new Stock Exchange gamble – that of speculating in bad, rotten public houses.'[38]

Lloyd George never underestimated the value of personalising the political battle and, knowing the importance of naming enemies, he made an extraordinary attack on Balfour. Publicans in the Prime Minister's Manchester constituency had, he claimed, been bribing the police to allow them to flout the licensing laws. After a new and crusading chief constable had purged the force of corruption, the publicans had – according to Lloyd George's story – approached their Member of Parliament and demanded compensation, which was duly provided in the form of the Licensing Bill. When Balfour repudiated the whole story – adding that he knew nothing of police corruption in Manchester – the charge against the Prime Minister was amended to the accusation that he neither knew nor cared what was going on in his own backyard. In the country Lloyd George spoke with such uninhibited excess that it is difficult to believe that even the audience at a London temperance rally took him seriously.

The cry of the orphan has risen against it. The wild plea of the poor is against it. The moans of the myriads to whom it has brought sorrow and shame have ascended to the Throne against it. The arm of the Most High is lifted against it and woe to the party, woe to the statesman and woe to the government that intervenes between the recreant and his doom.[39]

By May 1904 the government was near to death. Lloyd George thought of himself – and was generally regarded – as certain to be offered a place in the Liberal administration which, it was generally assumed, would soon be formed. From time to time he thought it necessary to sound like a statesman as well as a tribune of the people – employing his talents to deal with the same subject in several distinct ways, according to the demands of his audience. A week before he tugged at the heartstrings of the London teetotallers, he had addressed the House of Commons in quite different tones. His speech on the second reading of the Licensing Bill conceded 'Everybody admits that a reduction of licences is desirable, that as to drinking habits we compare badly with other civilised nations in the world and that great evils are produced by intemperance.' The effect was slightly reduced by the assertion – diametrically opposed to the truth – that the Prime Minister had declared, 'nothing can be done and . . . the only reform possible is a further protection of the drink trade'.[40] But it was clear that he was determined to evolve from guerrilla to staff officer.

The Balfour government struggled on until the end of 1905, for much of the time without Chamberlain. He had resigned in September 1903 after assuring Balfour that he would support the government on every issue except free trade. The Duke of Devonshire – the personification of *noblesse oblige*, who had three times declined the premiership – followed suit with great reluctance and only after he had been accused of betraying his free trade colleagues. The Chamberlain dynasty's place in the government of the nation was preserved by the promotion of Austen to the Treasury – a far more senior position than anything his father, who was infinitely more able, had ever occupied. The political world was changing. Lloyd George was more aware of the need to accommodate the new order than most of his colleagues.

In the 1900 general election, the Labour Representation Committee had won only two seats. During 1903, Herbert Gladstone, the Liberal Chief Whip, and Ramsay MacDonald, the Labour Party's General Secretary, negotiated a secret pact which provided for each party to give the other a free run in constituencies which, if the anti-Conservative vote were not split, could be wrestled from the Unionists. It was a natural enough partnership – forged, in part, by a mutual antipathy to protection and hardened by the Liberal belief that there was nothing to fear from a ragged army of trade unionists, Fabian intellectuals and Marxists who had never read Marx. In the spring of 1904, Lloyd George – speaking in South Glamorgan – felt that he could afford to patronise one of Labour's candidates. 'I have known Mr Brace for many years. He is the kind of representative of Labour we want in the House of Commons . . . There is no better type in the House than the Labour representative – sturdy and honest. No-one casts a breath of suspicion on their integrity.'[41] But, by November, the complacency had been replaced by open anxiety.

> We have a great Labour Party sprung up. Unless we can prove, as I think we can, that there is no necessity for a separate party to press forward the legitimate claims of Labour, you will find that . . . the Liberal Party will be practically wiped out and that, in its place, you will get a more extreme and revolutionary party.[42]

Lloyd George feared, and was right to fear, the Liberal decline which would follow the absorption of the party's radicals by a new class-based party. That Liberal decline was inevitable. But, between the wars, it was to be accelerated by Lloyd George's conduct. Campbell-Bannerman – who was to lead the Liberal Party into victory in the 1906 general election – 'always thought more of his policy, and making it prevail, than he did of himself'.[43] When Lloyd George became Prime Minister, he ensured the death of the Liberal Party by reversing that order of priorities.

During the heady months of late 1905 – when the collapse of the government was eagerly anticipated by the Liberal Party – many of Campbell-Bannerman's colleagues hoped to replace him with a more dynamic leader. He had been appointed as a stopgap after Rosebery had resigned in 1896 and Harcourt had followed suit barely a year later, and Asquith had declined to assume the burden of leading the Opposition on the grounds that he had a young family to support and could not forgo his earnings at the bar. Campbell-Bannerman had never been considered more than a competent Cabinet minister – and, by some of his colleagues, not even that. The Conservatives claimed that he had left the army short of cordite and he had performed badly in the subsequent censure debate which ended with the resignation of the Rosebery government in 1895. For a time he had talked openly of abandoning party politics in favour of the Speaker's chair. He had also offended the Liberal Imperialists by his uncompromising opposition to the Boer War. The fears that he did not have the talent or the tact to be a successful Prime Minister were compounded by doubts that his health would stand up to the job. As the election and the prospect of government grew closer, the plots against Campbell-Bannerman thickened.

In September 1905, Richard Haldane – staying with Asquith at Glenrothes on the north-east coast of Scotland – suggested that they visit Edward Grey at his shooting lodge, fifteen miles away at Relugas, in order to discuss the party leadership. There is, as is usually the case with conspiracies, some disagreement about what was decided.[44] But whether or not they divided up the great offices of state, they certainly agreed that 'CB' should go to the House of Lords – possibly as Prime Minister – leaving Asquith to lead the Commons, as well as becoming Chancellor of the Exchequer.

Although the 'Compact of Relugas' is now regarded as the moment when the Liberal high command launched its failed *coup d'état*, there had been conspiracies of one sort or another for at least a year. Lloyd George – cultivated by Rosebery during the debates on the 1902 Education Bill – clearly enjoyed being at the centre of the intrigue. On 11 January 1904, he wrote to Margaret from Grey's country house at Fallodon in Northumberland.

> Grey met me at his private station. I had a very long walk with him in the morning and we had a very frank chat about the prospective Liberal ministry – if it comes off. He says I am certain to have a seat in the Cabinet. Told him I must bargain for Wales. His ideas are dangerous. Rosebery Premier and Asquith Leader of the House. The former is possible, but the latter I fear impossible as it means shelving CB and Morley. I told him that it could not be done. He is more bent on an Asquith Leadership in the Commons than a Rosebery Premiership. He would prefer a Spencer Premiership with an Asquith Leadership.[45]

Over the years, Lloyd George had spoken of almost every member of the Liberal leadership in highly complimentary terms and denounced each one in calculatedly offensive language. In March 1903, he had been so open in his support of Rosebery's return that Keir Hardie warned him against seduction by the attentions of a man 'who loves neither you nor your tenets but has taken to flattering you'.[46] The flattery about which Hardie spoke was Rosebery's suggestion to Wilfrid Scawen Blunt that Lloyd George was 'the most able of the radicals' and the danger against which he cautioned was the 'Whigs game of gagging their dangerous rivals'.[47] It was not only flattery that attracted Lloyd George to Rosebery. He wanted to rally round what, at the time, he thought would be the victorious standard. On the day that he arrived at

Fallodon, an article by him was published in the *Sunday Sun*. It pro-claimed that he was 'far from irreconcilable to the wider Liberalism of which Lord Rosebery is the representative and leader'.[48]

On 1 December 1904, Lloyd George told Herbert Lewis about a conversation with Lady Leconfield, Rosebery's sister. Despite his natural iconoclasm, he was clearly proud to boast of such intimacy. Hubris may account for his decision to refer to himself in the third person.

> G put it to her plainly that in relying on the Liberal League to secure the Premiership for him he [i.e. Rosebery] was leaning on a broken reed. Grey expects the Foreign Office, Asquith the Chancellor of the Exchequer and Haldane the Lord Chancellorship. But, said G, is it not obvious that, if those three men secure those great offices you must give the Premiership to the other section? If they can secure those offices they will leave Rosebery in the lurch.[49]

To the Rosebery family, he was an enthusiastic Imperialist, warning against the desertion of his allies. To radicals, he spoke just as strongly in favour of Rosebery's candidature, but argued that he offered the best prospect of a progressive administration. Lewis's diary records that Lloyd George 'urged [Morley] to make Lord R Premier. "If you do that", he said, "he will of necessity be bound to give far greater consideration to the other section of the party than they would otherwise receive".' According to Lloyd George, Morley 'could not see it'.[50] Perhaps he did not like what he saw.

By February 1905, Lloyd George – according to Henry Labouchere, not an invariably reliable witness – was campaigning for changes which seem remarkably like the outcome favoured by the Relugas conspirators seven months later. Labouchere told Campbell-Bannerman, 'our very opportunistic friend Lloyd George was explaining to me a plan for you to go to the Lords. I said to him that as his object was to be in the Cabinet, he would do well to stick with you as I gathered from an observation which fell from you that you were all for this.' The story about Campbell-Bannerman's intention of putting Lloyd George in his Cabinet was an invention. Labouchere judged that an appeal to self-interest was 'the best plan to deal with these sort of cadgers'.[51]

Naturally enough, Lloyd George's detractors echo Labouchere's view that his machinations were intended to guarantee him the patronage of whoever eventually led the Liberal Party. His most supportive biogra-phers – much to the credit of their intellectual ingenuity – suggested that his intrigues had more honourable motives. Despite their differences over individual policies, Rosebery and Lloyd George shared a theory of politics and government. Both men, the explanation goes, held the view that statesmen must rise above party loyalty. Men of talent and goodwill should come together and do their best for the nation, untrammelled by old alliances and ideological prejudices. It is a view of Lloyd George's motives which could be held only by someone with no experience of practical politics.

On the other hand, the allegation that he was motivated solely by ruthless self-interest is barely more credible. He was assured, on every side, that he would have a place in the next Liberal Cabinet. It was very nearly taken for granted that the great offices of state were already spoken for – Herbert Gladstone at the Home Office, Asquith at the Treasury and Grey at the Foreign Office. So it seems unlikely that he intrigued in the hope of being offered one middle-ranking job rather than another – unless, as some historians have suggested, he hoped to supersede Asquith as Leader of the House.

The idea was canvassed by the radical journalist W. T. Stead. Examining Lloyd George's prospects in the *Review of Reviews*, he wrote, 'Is it possible that he may be the Leader of the House of Commons in the next Parliament? If Sir Henry Campbell-Bannerman should go to the House of Peers and personal feuds render Mr Asquith impossible we might go further than Lloyd George and fare considerably worse.'[52] To achieve that result, the feuds would have had to reach the proportions of a bloody civil war – and reduce the chances of the Liberals even forming a government. No doubt Lloyd George dreamed of a dramatic elevation. But in his waking moments he could not have expected to overtake Asquith – his senior in years and parliamentary service as well as a former Home Secretary – in 1905. And, if Rosebery did return, Asquith – as one of the Relugas conspirators – would certainly expect to benefit from the restored leader's gratitude.

The explanation for intrigues and conspiracies lies in the strange psychology of politicians. When power and place are about to change hands, they feel a need to be part of the process – if only vicariously. If leaders are threatened and changed without their playing even an oblique part in the machinations, their egos are damaged. Taking sides is a way of proving to themselves, as well as to others, that their opinions count. Involvement in the machinations confirms that their opinions and support are valued. Lloyd George conspired because he was a politician. And he conspired on behalf of Rosebery because that was the only conspiracy open to him.

During the summer recess of 1905, Lloyd George divided his time between holidays and campaigning in the country. A cruise with John Morley in Stuart Rendel's yacht was followed, typically in a life of contrasts, by an August visit (with his son Richard) to the Haverfordwest cottage in which his father had died. He told his brother that it was a very nice place with a real touch of style about it. But it was 'most untidily kept'. He saw the gate which he and his sister Mary had barricaded with stones in the hope of preventing the removal of their furniture after the cottage was sold in anticipation of the move to Llanystumdwy. 'Not the old gate. That has been taken down and put up elsewhere.' His speeches followed the usual pattern. Asquith, who was a candidate for the rectorship of Glasgow University, received his support and endorsement in the form of an address which ignored the candidate's qualifications and character but promised a revision of the pattern of landownership which was more of a burden to the nation than the national debt.

In Glasgow he was struck again by the constriction of the throat which had troubled him for years. His tonsils were removed but, during what he believed to be his convalescence, he suffered the severe haemorrhage which, but for Mrs Timothy Davies's swift action, would have ended his life. The doctor she summoned ordered a complete rest of at least three months. Lloyd George could not afford the cost of a holiday, so he wrote to his brother asking for the money. The usually selfless William George replied that he was tired too and suggested that they should go on a cruise together. Lloyd George, instinctively in command, advised his brother of what was essential for a comfortable sea voyage – heavy flannels, thick socks, substantial overcoat, a trilby hat and fifty pounds for contingencies. They set out from Southampton for Genoa on 13 November. The Italian tour which they planned moved on from Florence to Rapallo when they met a tourist who had arrived direct from England. When he told them that the London newspapers were predicting that the government was about to fall, William – who had tired of the holiday and pined for work – offered to return home at once and telegraph his own assessment of the situation to his brother. He landed back in Britain on 1 December and within hours sent a coded message to Rapallo. Lloyd George was back in London two days later.

Henry Campbell-Bannerman had survived as Liberal leader by ignoring his colleagues' dissatisfaction, which – in the case of Haldane – had gone as far as to suggest that, in the event of a Liberal election victory, the King should send for Asquith or Rosebery rather than the victorious party leader. On 13 November 1905, only a couple of months after the

Relugas Compact, Campbell-Bannerman had called on Asquith. Mrs Asquith was having her hair washed by her maid, but as soon as the visitor left, she tied a shawl round her head and rushed into the library to hear her husband's account of the historic conversation:

> CB thought that things looked like coming to a head politically and that any day after Parliament met we might expect a General Election. He gathered that he would probably be the man the King sent for. CB then looked at me and said 'I do not think that we have ever spoken of a future Liberal Government. What would you like, the Treasury I suppose.'

He ended the inconclusive conversation by adding that he knew of 'the suggestion by that ingenious person Richard Burdon Haldane' that he should go to the House of Lords – a suggestion to which 'nothing under heaven and earth' would make him agree.[53]

Balfour resigned on Monday, 4 December 1905. Lloyd George's epitaph on the government – memorable but meaningless – was 'they died with their drawn salaries in their hands'.[54] Some Liberals – hoping for time in which to secure a change in leadership – urged Campbell-Bannerman to refuse to take office and, instead, insist on an immediate dissolution of Parliament and an election. He refused and on 5 December Edward VII – after suggesting that, for his health's sake, he might be wise to accept a peerage – invited him to form a government. The advice was rejected and the King's commission accepted. The work of constructing a new Cabinet began. Newspapers predicted that he would fail because the Relugas conspirators would refuse to serve. Asquith made a 'personal appeal' for 'my dear CB to . . . solve this difficulty' by going to the Lords. The suggestion was dismissed and Asquith accepted the Treasury. Grey proved more difficult to accommodate. Lord Cromer was offered the Foreign Office but replied that he 'did not have the health and strength to undertake the work'.[55] Sir Alfred Milner was then considered. In the end Grey agreed.

While the press and many politicians made increasingly certain predictions that the Liberal grandees would soon bring him down, Campbell-Bannerman calmly got on with the job of making less exalted appointments than the great offices of state which his critics wished to hold. Lloyd George became President of the Board of Trade with a salary of two thousand pounds a year. He remained a member of the Cabinet – in one capacity or another – for the next sixteen years.

CHAPTER 11

THE POODLE BARKS

It took Henry Campbell-Bannerman some time to form a government. So there were days of speculation about who would receive, and accept, an invitation to serve – a constant feature of political life which still causes both gratification and anxiety to the ambitious young men and women whose names appear in newspaper prophecies. Lloyd George displayed both emotions – and his remarkable capacity for self-congratulation – when, having reported to his brother that he had nothing to report, he went on to describe a 'plebiscite' conducted by the *Pall Mall Gazette*. 'I was the only new man elected to the Liberal Cabinet as President of the Local Government Board. I came second for Home Secretary, second for Board of Trade and Postmaster General.'[1]

Lloyd George's anxiety was prolonged by his own carelessness. When he moved house from Trinity Road to Routh Road (also in Wandsworth), he had forgotten to give the Liberal leader's office his new address. So the letter which invited him 'to call on CB on Friday' languished in the House of Commons for a day. He explained its significance to his anxious family. 'It means Cabinet, I think, for that is the first thing they settle.'[2] And he added a gloating reference to the plight of his less fortunate friends – a usual, if unattractive, emotion on such occasions. 'Winston and McKenna not yet heard, which shows that they have not been reached even as names.'[3] On 8 December, the triumph was confirmed.

Board of Trade with a seat in the Cabinet. They want me there as that is the Department most directly associated with the great fight to defend Free Trade in the House and in the country against Joe's attacks. I am delighted. I shall have the Labour Department – Supervision of Railways – Harbours – Bankruptcy – Foreshore and above all that grand new building by the House of Commons. Winston and McKenna think that I have the most important post in the Ministry at this juncture . . . I have asked for pledges about Education and the extension of self-government for Wales – and got both.[4]

If Churchill and McKenna valued the Board of Trade so highly, their judgement was not shared by the new incumbent, whose letter home expressed a joy he did not feel. Lloyd George told D. R. Daniel that he was reluctant to lead the Board of Trade because it had proved incapable of forcing Lord Penrhyn to accept arbitration during his protracted dispute with his quarrymen. He revealed his true feelings with the claim, not meant to be ironic, that the new office building was the department's greatest attraction. He would have much preferred the Local Government Board, the destination for which he was initially intended. However, the King – reluctant to have repairs to the royal palaces supervised by John Burns, a man who, in the royal estimation, was a republican – persuaded Campbell-Bannerman not to appoint him First Commissioner of Works, but give him Local Government instead.* It is at least possible that Campbell-Bannerman told Lloyd George that he had been chosen to match and master Chamberlain. Putative Prime Ministers – particularly those who are finding difficulty in forming an administration – are inclined to flatter on such occasions. But if any assurances were given about Welsh self-government, they were probably not meant and certainly not kept. Perhaps the compliment was meant to help reconcile Lloyd George to a junior Cabinet post and a salary that was £3000 less than he would have received as a full Secretary of State.

Lloyd George had made his name – in the country and in Parliament – by condemning, root and branch, both the Boer War and the 1902 Education Act. But at forty-three, with no ministerial experience behind him, he could not have reasonably expected one of the great offices of state. Yet it seems that he did.[5] Newspapers had suggested that he might become Home Secretary. However unlikely the

---

*Burns accepted the offer with the words, 'Congratulations Sir 'Enery. This is the most popular thing you 'ave ever done.'

prospect of greater things, it is clear – from the obviously bogus protestations of pleasure – that joy of entry to the Cabinet was initially moderated by disappointment about the seat he would occupy. But his letters home leave no doubt that the disenchantment did not last for long. Indeed it did not survive the initiation into Cabinet government.

On 11 December, he was made a member of the Privy Council. 'The Ceremony passed off admirably ... King very gracious ... I drove away with Lord Elgin and Morley in Lord Harcourt's brougham.'[6] The next day he saw his office for the first time – 'a room large enough to contain the whole of no. 3 Routh Road'.[7] Two days later he was 'gradually getting into my work and liking it' and attended his first Cabinet meeting.[8] His description of the proceedings – 'very interesting' – does not suggest that he was carried away by the wonder of it all. But by then he had better things to do than listen to the views of his colleagues. He 'had to decide questions arising over Portmadoc Railway and Criccieth Foreshore ... It is within my power absolutely to stop the proceedings or let it proceed.'[9] The new President of the Board of Trade had discovered that action is more enjoyable than words.

According to the letter in which Lloyd George set out the joys of office, he particularly welcomed the prospect of working with 'a first rate chief of the Permanent Staff – Sir Francis Hopwood, a very able man and an excellent Radical'.[10] If the admiration which he described was genuine, it does not seem to have been reciprocated. Hopwood told Almeric Fitzroy, the Cabinet Secretary, that his new master refused to read written submissions but required his civil servants to precede crucial meetings with oral briefings.[11] At least the Permanent Secretary gave his new master credit for swallowing and digesting – with impressive speed – all the information with which he was fed. That is why Hopwood called him 'The Goat' – a nickname that stuck for the rest of Lloyd George's life and came to be associated with other aspects of his character. Only wishful thinking caused Chamberlain gleefully to record in his diary, 'Lloyd George has lost his fire and I am told is a bad administrator.'[12] Chamberlain was wrong on both counts. Hudson Kearley MP – a businessman four years older than the President, who became Parliamentary Secretary to the Board of Trade – described Lloyd George's technique more sympathetically and more accurately.

He had no wide knowledge of affairs. He had no knowledge at all of business. He had, as I soon found, a marked dislike of office

routine. But he had genius and, having that, a man can afford to
dispense with a great deal of the equipment that most of us find
necessary for a prosperous journey through life . . . In Lloyd
George's case it has manifested itself as an extraordinarily quick
and subtle understanding of human nature combined with
unbounded courage.[13]

Sir Francis Hopwood quickly moved on to the Colonial Office and his
place was effectively taken by Hubert Llewellyn Smith, who remained
acting Permanent Secretary during Lloyd George's two years at the
Board of Trade. Llewellyn Smith, a friend of the devoted Harold
Spender, was to remain in Lloyd George's service for the next ten
years – in the Treasury, the Ministry of Munitions and at the Paris
Peace Conference.

Despite some dubious associations – as the Board of Trade's
Commissioner for Labour, he had shown some sympathy for Ben
Tillett, the dockers' leader – Llewellyn Smith's promotion was a comparatively orthodox appointment.* The same cannot be said of the
employment of Lloyd George's second private secretary. John Rowland
was recruited from Wales where he had been a schoolteacher and the
secretary of the Cardiff Cymreigyddion Society. He was the first of the
men Lloyd George brought into the civil service from the great world
outside Whitehall and Westminster – a practice which, at its height,
gave businessmen key positions in the Ministry of Munitions and, in
consequence, changed the course of the First World War. The 'imports'
were a testimony to two attitudes which he developed at the Board of
Trade – admiration for the self-made commercial class and near-
contempt for most of the public-school- and Oxbridge-educated
permanent civil service. The special advisers who haunt ministries
today were a Lloyd George invention.

Recently appointed Cabinet ministers are impatient to get on with
the work of their departments. But Lloyd George had to wait until the
general election had been fought and won. Campbell-Bannerman
opened the national campaign at a rally in the Albert Hall on 21
December with a speech which was universally regarded as depress-
ingly bland. Lloyd George, who by accident or design had arranged to

---

*Hudson Kearley was ennobled as the Viscount Devonport and became chairman
of the London Port Authority. During the 1908 dock strike, Tillett offered up a
public prayer, 'O God, strike Lord Devonport dead.'[14]

speak in Caernarvon on the same night, was dutifully cautious about the policies with which he was associated – land, old-age pensions and disestablishment of the Church of England. He explained his reticence with an admission. 'It comes to me as a shock that I am not allowed to speak as I like. Up to now, I have done so without much regard for the consequences, but from the present moment my loyalty to eighteen colleagues will prevent me from discussing a variety of subjects with the freedom I should like to exercise.'[15] He did, however, feel able to promise new education and licensing bills, which would be more acceptable to the Nonconformist conscience than their Tory predecessors, and an amendment to the law which would overrule the Taff Vale judgement which had made trade unions liable to pay damages for losses caused by their striking members. There was a ritual condemnation of tariff reform and a righteous denunciation of 'Chinese slavery'. Despite the inhibitions imposed by office, the speech received the rapturous reception which he had come to expect in Wales.

Lloyd George spent most of the campaign in other Liberal candidates' constituencies, leaving the local effort largely to Margaret and his son Richard, by then a young man of sixteen. He anticipated that the Liberal landslide, which everyone took for granted, would make his seat safe for the first time, and his confidence increased when the Caernarvon Boroughs Unionist Association chose as its candidate a man who seemed to possess neither the capacity nor the inclination to become a Member of Parliament.

R. A. Naylor was a Warrington timber merchant who spoke no Welsh and was a stranger to Wales. He was a hymn writer, an attribute which was thought to appeal to a predominantly Nonconformist constituency. But he was an ardent supporter of Imperial Preference, which antagonised some of the most influential Unionists in the area. His only initiative during the whole campaign – inviting all the children of Criccieth to an afternoon at the circus – attracted only ridicule. Gwilym, Lloyd George's younger son, was one of the beneficiaries. The grateful father wrote Naylor a fulsome letter of thanks which was printed in the local newspapers.

Manchester was among the first boroughs to go to the polls. Every Unionist candidate, including Arthur Balfour, was defeated. A Liberal victory in Caernarvon Boroughs – where polling day was a week later – now seemed certain. Naylor did not even wait in the Town Hall for the declaration of the result. Lloyd George won with a majority of 1224 out of a total of 5218 votes cast.* The Caernarvon Boroughs had indeed become safe for the Liberal Party for the first time. The national result was an unprecedented Liberal landslide. The party won 377 seats – a majority of 220 over the Unionists and 84 over all other parties. However, the other parties – 83 Irish Nationalists, 24 'Lib-Labs' and 29 nominees of the Labour Representation Committee – were all committed to support the major issues in the Liberals' election programme. The government had an effective majority of 356 over the Opposition. Huge majorities always encourage inflated expectation.

Two-thirds of all Liberal candidates had offered themselves for election with the explicit promise of supporting the introduction of a national old-age pension. It was a less contentious proposition than disestablishment or the end of the religious tests which preceded the appointment of teachers in church schools. But, unlike those proposals, it was expensive. Lloyd George – who had said so much on the subject in opposition – had been questioned about the prospects of early action on the eve of polling and had given a studiously cautious reply. His response was a model of ministerial responsibility. What had seemed possible before the Boer War had drained the nation's coffers was no longer within the nation's grasp. Progress would be made 'gradually' until the national finances were 'spick and span'.[16] His first formal speech from the government despatch box – as well as properly concentrating on his own responsibilities – included a general warning about the modest rate of possible change.

> This government . . . is in its infancy and the moneybox is not very full at this moment. We have not the money to spend on all those schemes on which we would like to spend money. The Government have decided to have an inquiry, in the form of a Royal Commission, which will extend not merely to coast defence but to other kindred subjects – such as waste land and probably afforestation . . . I do not think that anything is to be gained by very hasty action. After all, the sea has been at work for a good many centuries.[17]

It was a prudent, not to say prosaic, beginning to a ministerial career which had been preceded by years of backbench pyrotechnics. The Opposition front bench responded with surprised approval. Andrew

---

*Lloyd George 3221; R. A. Naylor 1997.

Bonar Law, the Conservative Member for Glasgow Blackfiars and Hutchesontown, did not think he 'could complain about the tone which has been taken by the President of the Board of Trade'.★ Lloyd George had begun as he meant to go on. For a while emollience was to replace aggression. He even claimed to enjoy being shaded from the heat of battle. Years later, with the Board of Trade long behind him, he told a Law Society dinner how much he had enjoyed freedom from controversy.

> There was a repose about it to which I had been quite unaccustomed. After years of strife politically, I found myself at peace with all my neighbours . . . and it was quite a delightful experience to be able, for two or three years, to work in a department where there was really no political feeling, no political bias and no political prejudice.[18]

It was certainly in that spirit that he approached his first major task – the drafting and presentation of a Merchant Shipping Bill.

Two days before Christmas 1905, Lloyd George had promised to 'put a stop to the overloading by foreign ships'. He proposed that vessels 'registered abroad but [doing] business in British ports should be governed by the same regulations as British ships'.[19] The rules which he had in mind governed safety provisions and the quality of seamen's accommodation. Whatever his motives, the anticipated result of his proposals was the 'protection' of British merchantmen and shipping companies against 'unfair competition' from foreign owners who cared little for the welfare of their crews – often composed of Indians who were known by the slightly derogatory name of 'Lascars'. Management and men were content with the proposed new regulations, which disadvantaged foreign competition. But their enforcement was not as easy as the Board of Trade originally supposed.

No ship was to be allowed into a British port so heavily loaded that the Plimsoll Line was submerged. But merchantmen rose in the water as they burned off coal. So a ship could sail the Atlantic dangerously low

---

★John Grigg, in *The People's Champion*, writes that Lloyd George endeared himself to the House during the subsequent debate by calling an opponent his 'honourable friend'. In the unlikely event of that being so, the House of Commons has changed its style. A hundred years later such a 'slip of the tongue' would be greeted with derision.

in the water and still arrive at London or Glasgow apparently con-
forming to British regulations. It seems that when Lloyd George
promised a bill he did not understand the difficulty – indeed the impossibility – of making foreign ships conform to existing British law. When
it was explained to him, he applied the only remedy possible. The
Merchant Shipping Bill would lower the Plimsoll Line for both British
and foreign shipping. Conscious that his plan might be opposed by both
masters and men, he decided to adopt a new legislative technique – and
anticipate, by seventy years, the pre-legislative scrutiny of draft bills. He
invited the shipowners to comment on a draft bill in the hope that,
having thus demonstrated his goodwill, they would be more easily
convinced of its merits before it reached the House of Commons.

According to Hudson Kearley, the 'shipowners could hardly believe
their ears'.[20] No doubt they were gratified both by Lloyd George's
courtesy and the confirmation that most of the bill's provisions – by
making their foreign rivals conform to British standards – would
improve their competitive position in the freight market. Whatever the
reason, their support – more willingly given than the qualified agreement of the Seamen's Union – enabled the President of the Board of
Trade to claim that 'Ship Owners and Sailors bless the bill' and that its
universal welcome justified a non-partisan examination by Parliament.[21]
It would be discussed in the House of Commons Committee on Trade
and he would be sorry 'if the Whips were used'.[22]

The Times regarded 'the dismissal of responsibility as a little odd and
scarcely complimentary to the nursling'.[23] But the Commons accepted
the suggestion in the undoubtedly sincere spirit in which it was made –
even though Lloyd George, in his second reading speech, followed his
usual habit of diagnosing the disease rather than prescribing the remedy,
and was, as a result, less conciliatory in tone than the shipowners had
been encouraged to expect. Nevertheless, the bill was given an unopposed second reading.

During the committee stage the bill expanded from forty-three to
eighty-five clauses. Most of the additions were the result of suggestions
made to Lloyd George during constant consultations with interested parties which influenced the contents of the eventual act as much as, if not
more than, the parliamentary debates. Joseph Havelock Wilson – the
founder of the National Union of Seamen and the Liberal Member for
Middlesbrough, who sat on the committee – complained, with some justification, that the government's amendments were more likely to favour
the owners than the sailors. He was particularly critical of Lloyd George's

refusal to increase the amount of sleeping space which the law required to be available to each seaman. Lloyd George knew that the proposed change was related less to a desire to improve the living conditions of British crews than to the hope of reducing the number of Lascars who could be signed on at cheap rates. Knowing how important their recruitment was to employers who struggled to compete with cost-cutting rivals, he excluded them from the regulation which required all seamen to have a working knowledge of the English language – and justified the exclusion with an irresistible appeal to Imperial sentiment. 'The Lascar is a Britisher. You cannot make a Britisher of him simply for the sake of bragging about the extent of your dominions and then the moment he asks for a share of your privileges say, "You are a foreigner".'[24]

Only two of the twelve bills promised in the 1906 King's Speech became law – the Trades Dispute Act (overturning the Taff Vale judgement and absolving trade unions from responsibility for damage done during and by strikes) and the Merchant Shipping Act. Lloyd George was fêted by the shipowners and congratulated by *The Times* for displaying 'his more sober and statesmanlike qualities'.[25] It was assumed, by those who did not know him well, that he had suppressed his natural prejudices and inclinations in the interest of both improving shipping law and securing a personal parliamentary triumph. In fact, despite the fiery speeches and the occasional espousal of extreme causes, Lloyd George was, at heart, a consensual politician if and when agreement achieved more or less the result he wanted. His instinct – when he had responsibility for great affairs – was to seek agreement. Sometimes he pursued what he saw as the national interest. On other occasions he either promoted his own cause or snatched at a quick solution. But his technique was to work towards a mutually acceptable outcome. He was willing to combine with anyone and everyone who shared his objectives. The morality of his methods and the character of his allies were always less important than achieving the ends which he thought right for himself and the country. The essentially pragmatic approach to the Merchant Shipping Bill was just one more milepost on a long journey. It had begun when, as a hopeful Liberal candidate, he considered endorsing Chamberlain's rejection of Home Rule and continued during his attempts, together with the Bishop of St Asaph, to define a role for the Established Church in Wales which satisfied the radicals and was acceptable to the hierarchy. It changed the course of history when, after two flirtations with the idea of all-party government, he led the predominantly Tory coalition which won the First World War.

The pragmatist in Lloyd George made him an ideal President of the Board of Trade. He introduced, under the ten-minute rule – a device normally employed by backbenchers – a Census of Production Bill. It was warmly welcomed by Chamberlain. And even while the government was being accused of backsliding over its promise to disestablish the Church in Wales, he was able to turn from refuting the claim that he was chief apostate to the solid merits of the Patents and Design Bill – a measure intended to prevent foreign companies from taking out British patents for the sole purpose of inhibiting rival research and development. This was welcomed by Andrew Bonar Law, on behalf of the Unionist Party, as the first sign of the government's conversion to protectionism. A second act extended the life of patents beyond fourteen years, leaving Bonar Law with nothing to say except that he 'played the very interesting role of supporting the measure'.[26] A Companies Amendment Bill – which required information on financial standing to be supplied to shareholders and creditors – was based on the report of a committee of experts which had been set up by the Balfour government. It was passed without dissent. Lloyd George celebrated his legislative success with an ironic complaint about the institution which, when 'he had his war paint on', he excoriated. 'I have a personal grievance against the House of Lords. They have treated me rather well. I have had a rather large number of bills . . . and they have blessed them all.' He could not resist spoiling the joke by adding, 'I think it was because they could not understand them.'[27] The truce, perhaps better described as armed neutrality, did not last for long.

After the Colonial Conference of 1907, trade commissioners were added to the staff of the High Commissions in Canada, Australia, New Zealand and South Africa. The new appointments were part of Lloyd George's campaign to boost British exports. He attempted to improve British salesmanship by exhortation. Again, he was ahead of his time.

> Go anywhere and the first man you meet is a German commercial traveller. That is one reason our trade is going. They take the trouble to learn the language of the people with whom they are dealing . . . Go to any part of the world and the Englishman pushes his goods in Scotch.[28]

But while Lloyd George, the good administrator, was spending his time on the sober issues of responsible government, the storms on which he had ridden to national fame were blowing up again. In opposition, the

Liberals had promised to right the wrongs of the 1902 Education Act and to change the terms of compensation to dispossessed publicans. In office, repeal and reform were proving more difficult than they had anticipated. Yet the Nonconformist lobby would not wait.

There were 177 Free Churchmen on the government benches in the House of Commons – more than had sat in any Parliament since the Commonwealth and larger in number than the whole Conservative and Unionist Opposition. R. L. Morant, who recognised that changes in the governance of schools were inevitable, prepared a draft bill which he thought was acceptable to Nonconformist opinion. Asquith described its purpose with admirable clarity. It was designed

> to put an end to the dual system created by the Act of 1902; to secure that every school maintained out of rates and taxes should be under the exclusive management and control of the representative local Authority; to abolish religious tests and the obligation to give denominational teaching, in the case of all teachers appointed by the Authority and paid out of public funds; to permit Cowper-Temple teaching in the 'provided' [state] schools as well as the 'transferred' [ex-church] schools; to give facilities for denominational instruction, but not by the regular teachers.*[29]

Such a bill would never have won even the reluctant acquiescence of the House of Lords. Neither Nonconformists nor Anglicans regarded the provisions as adequate. Schools in boroughs or urban districts with a population of more than five thousand would be allowed, at the instigation of four-fifths of parents, to offer denominational education provided by regular staff at public expense. Since most Catholics lived in towns and cities, 90 per cent of their children could receive acceptable religious instruction 'on the rates'. On the other hand, because the villages of England and Wales were predominantly Protestant, 75 per cent of Church of England children could not. Nonconformists – who had always been satisfied with the Cowper-Temple Clause on religious instruction – objected to the provision on more complicated grounds. If managers appointed teachers who were active members of the Church of England, religious teaching in church (and ex-church)

---

*The Cowper-Temple Clause was an amendment to the 1870 Education Act which required religious teaching in schools to be based on biblical text and therefore undenominational.

schools would still have a bias. However, the Lords were expected to amend the bill so as to allow religious tests before appointment and other contentious amendments were expected. One of them came from Lloyd George. With great reluctance and under great pressure, the Cabinet agreed to add New Clause 37 – the mandatory establishment of a national Welsh Council composed of members from the Welsh county authorities. Nobody was quite sure what its powers would be. The case in favour had been argued entirely in terms of the obligation to show respect to Wales. As a result Lloyd George was able to describe it in different ways to different audiences. A message sent to a Liberal Conference on Education, held in Colwyn Bay on 9 March, suggested that it would do little more than supervise teacher training and the same impression was given to a conference of church leaders which was held in Cardiff on 23 March.[30] The assembly of bishops (Anglican and Catholic) and Nonconformist ministers gave the proposal their unanimous support only to discover later that a Cabinet paper, circulated after the agreement in principle, had suggested that the council should 'have the power to supply, or aid in the supply of, education of all kinds in Wales'.

There was some surprise that Lloyd George remained so strongly committed to the idea of concentrating Welsh political power. By 1906 he was a national, not a regional, politician, and his determination to preserve and enhance that status was demonstrated by his unwillingness to throw his whole weight behind the essentially Welsh issue of disestablishment. But the creation of an all-Wales authority of some sort seems to have become a question of honour – the redemption of past failures. It was an issue which he could not let go. So great was his zeal that, in the House of Commons on 17 July, he announced that a Minister of the Crown would be responsible for the Welsh Council's operation. The reaction was entirely predictable. The Opposition was affronted that the machinery of government had been modified without consultation, and the King told the Prime Minister that the appointment of a 'Minister for Wales' without the sovereign's sanction was intolerable. Campbell-Bannerman, who was barely better informed than the King, asked the President of the Board of Trade to explain himself. Lloyd George replied, in schoolboy fashion, that he had attempted to obtain the Prime Minister's agreement but had been unable to find him. He had, however, told Asquith and Augustine Birrell (the President of the Board of Education) what he intended to say. He had not meant to propose the creation of a new ministry or the appointment of a new minister. Faced with the Commons' concern that the new Welsh Council would not be accountable to Parliament, he had merely said that an existing member of the government would answer for it in the House – carrying out his additional duties without any additional salary. The day after he gave his explanation he felt sufficiently confident of his position to write to the Prime Minister a second time. A junior Treasury minister should be made responsible for the Welsh Council. His hope was that his friend, Herbert Lewis, would get the job.

The Education Bill was given a third reading in the House of Commons on 30 July.* Balfour, back in the Commons after a by-election, in his closing speech, shattered the Liberal illusion that the Conservative peers would never defy the wishes of so large a Commons majority.

> The real discussion of this question is not now in this House and has not been for some time; the real discussion must be elsewhere, and everybody is perfectly reconciled to the fact that another place is going to deal with large tracts of the Bill which we have not left time even to touch upon . . . It is in the highest degree improbable that the Bill will come back in the shape in which it leaves us. The honourable gentleman who has just sat down controverted a prophecy of mine that the Bill would never pass. Does he think the Bill will ever pass? I do not think that he or anybody else does.[31]

After that, it was hard to argue that Lloyd George – or anybody else – was unjustified in complaining that the Lords was being explicitly employed to frustrate the will of the elected Commons. During the recess the Unionist Party came to a formal decision to accept the strategy proposed by Lord Lansdowne, the leader of the Opposition peers. 'The Opposition is lamentably weak in the House of Commons and enormously strong in the House of Lords. It is essential that the two wings of the army should work together.'[32] Balfour replied that it was important not to behave in a way which enabled the Cabinet to 'accumulate a case against the Upper House . . . and appeal, at the next election, for a mandate to modify the constitution'.[33] But he nevertheless expected the peers to fulfil the prophecy which he had

---

*Even the Catholic Church was not entirely satisfied with the benefits of the bill. It wanted the sectarian teaching option to be available in all schools. In consequence, the Irish Nationalists voted against the third reading.

made at the end of the third reading debate. The scene was set for a bitter autumn battle.

Lloyd George, with a regular salary to spend for the first time in his life, took his entire family – Margaret, brother William and the children – on a summer voyage to Lisbon. His ticket was upgraded to 'upper deck', courtesy of Owen Philips, the Liberal MP for Pembroke and Haverfordwest and the director of the steamship company. The Eisteddfod was never missed. So Lloyd George was back in Britain by late September, just in time to address a public meeting in Llanelli. Recalling Balfour's prediction, he anticipated that the Education Bill would be emasculated in the Lords. Never mind, he said, it will be passed one day 'very probably when the House of Lords is sleeping as it frequently does'.[34] Unfortunately, in his rhetorical enthusiasm, he suggested that the peers had already vetoed the Education Bill. Lansdowne wrote to *The Times* with a correction and contradiction. The King, who had not been aware of the Llanelli speech until he read the Lansdowne letter, took exception to a member of 'his' Cabinet attacking the Upper House of Parliament. Another complaint was sent to the Prime Minister.

Campbell-Bannerman's reply combined the admission that Lloyd George had behaved improperly with an explanation of his conduct which exhibited understanding and a degree of affection.

> Lloyd George is essentially a fighting man and has not yet learned that once he gets inside an office his sword and spear should only be used on extreme occasions and with the consent of his colleagues. In all business connected with his department and in House of Commons work he is most conciliatory, but the combative spirit seems to get the better of him when he is talking about other subjects. I greatly regret his outburst and hope it will not be repeated.[35]

He wrote to Lloyd George in the same avuncular spirit and received a reply which was a model of gratitude and penitence. 'I am greatly obliged to you for the kind way in which you convey to me the King's rebuke. If you wish me to make no further reference at present to the House of Lords question, of course I shall take care to avoid it.'[36] Whatever he believed at the time of writing, it was a promise which he was, by nature, unable to keep.

A fortnight after the King's rebuke he spoke in Spalding. No doubt

with his promise to the Prime Minister in mind, he began his passage
on the progress of the Education Bill with what sounded like meek
acceptance of the limitations which had been placed upon him: 'I wish
I could say all I thought about the House of Lords. If you ask my opinion three weeks hence I might be able to tell you.' It is not clear why he
expected the interdict to be lifted before Christmas. In any event he
went on to give his opinion there and then. Lansdowne had spoken of
'revising' the bill. 'Bowdlerising' would be a more appropriate word. He
went on, with heavy sarcasm, to look forward to the eventual production
of a 'nice and proper measure' which would be acceptable to the clergy.
The 'new addition' was being edited by the Archbishop of Canterbury
with the assistance of Lord Halifax and the Duke of Norfolk. He ended
with a veiled threat. The whole episode would conclude with an outcome which was 'far from agreeable' to the House of Lords.[37]

The King responded with a very unregal threat, conveyed by his private secretary, Francis Knollys, to the Prime Minister.

> HM desires me to say that, notwithstanding your remonstrance,
> Lloyd George has made another indecent attack on the House of
> Lords. Mr Lloyd George is very anxious that the King and Queen
> should go to Cardiff next summer to open some new docks there
> and they have half consented to do so, but the King says that
> nothing would induce him to visit Cardiff unless Mr Lloyd
> George learns to behave with the propriety of a Cabinet
> Minister.[38]

It was too late for propriety. The Education Bill, sent up to the Lords
on 30 July, had imposed severe limitations on sectarian religious instruction. The Education Bill to which the Lords gave a third reading on 6
December provided for sectarian education in all schools in England
and Wales. Speaking at the Palmerston Club in Oxford on the same day,
Lloyd George described the transformation which had taken place
during the committee stage in the Upper House.

> The poor Bill left the House of Commons with a good majority
> to speed it on its way. It has been stripped and wounded and left
> half dead. I am sorry to say that the priests and Levites did not
> even pass by. They joined the freebooters . . . I am told that there
> are other bills which, when they go up to the Lords, will be sim-
> ilarly dealt with . . . The road from the people to the throne must

be cleared. It is intolerable that every petition that comes from the people to their sovereign should be waylaid and mutilated in this fashion . . . If the House of Lords persists in its present policy, it will be a much larger question than the Education Bill that will come up for consideration. It will be the issue of whether the country is to be governed by the King and the peers or by the King and the people.[39]

Knollys wrote to the Prime Minister as soon as the speech was reported in the London newspapers. 'His Majesty feels he has the right, and it is one on which he will insist, that Mr Lloyd George should not introduce the sovereign's name into those violent tirades of his.'[40] Campbell-Bannerman's response was admirably robust. Lloyd George was understandably angry that the 'bill had been turned upside down' and the sovereign had been mentioned as a respectful indication that it was the 'King's Government' which the House of Lords was undermining. The note of impatience in his reply was understandable. He had to decide how to deal with what amounted to a new education bill. Lloyd George wanted the peers to be challenged and faced down – if necessary by calling a general election. But the government's courage was tested by events in the West Riding of Yorkshire – tested and found to be wanting.

In October 1906, the Court of Appeal had overturned the decision of the County Court and ruled that the West Riding Local Education Authority was within its rights to withhold from four denominational schools an amount of rate subsidy which was equivalent to the salaries paid to teachers who gave denominational religious instruction. That meant that local councils were no longer subject to the penal sanctions to which the Liberal Party in opposition had objected. Morant took the view that the policy of the Board of Education was unchanged and that it should appeal to the House of Lords in the hope that its powers over LEAs would be restored. Augustine Birrell, the President of the Board, was convinced that, since the act was still in force, it was his constitutional duty to defend it and, after two months of wrangling, the Cabinet – despite loud protests from Lloyd George – agreed that an appeal against a decision which supported its policy was the 'proper' course.

Without any hope of making progress, the government sent the Education Bill back to the House of Lords with all the peers' amendments deleted. The Lords reinstated their changes. Lloyd George –

surprisingly supported by Edward Grey, the Foreign Secretary – thought that the government should go to the country at once and campaign on the question which was going to dominate politics four years later, 'Who shall rule, peers or people?' But the Cabinet consensus was that enthusiasm for the Education Bill – even among prominent Nonconformists – was not sufficient to sustain a campaign. So the choice lay between accepting the Lords' version, with an extension of denominational education, or dropping the bill completely.

John Burns – who, as well as being the only 'working man' in the Cabinet was its least progressive member – argued for acceptance. Lloyd George, at least according to his own account, advanced the argument against. He recalled the action of the Cabinet in 1870 'when, by accepting amendments to the Foster Education Bill . . . it aroused much anger among Nonconformists [whose] defection chiefly caused its ruin at the polls'. Nonconformists, he said, 'were not merely interested in education from a Nonconformist point of view'. They were 'Liberals, keenly anxious that the government should live'. Lloyd George never underestimated the effect of his eloquence. But perhaps he was right to say, 'If I had not made that speech, they would have given way, all along the line, on the question of teachers.'[41] So the Education Bill was abandoned and Augustine Birrell moved to the Irish Office. Before he left, he agreed to the setting up of a Welsh Department with its own permanent secretary within the Board of Education. A small step had been taken towards distinguishing Wales from the rest of the United Kingdom. Reginald McKenna, the new President, represented a Welsh constituency, but the patronage which flowed from the new arrangement was distributed by Lloyd George.

It was clear that the House of Lords, having tasted blood, would savage other Liberal bills. Campbell-Bannerman – in a speech that echoed Gladstone's warning to the Fenians – described as 'intolerable' that the second chamber should be 'the willing servant' of one party but 'neutralise, thwart and distort' another and reminded the peers that 'the resources of the British constitution are not wholly exhausted'.[42] Something had to be done. But nobody was clear what it should be. So a committee was set up to consider constitutional reform. Lloyd George was made a member but – doubting that much practical progress would be made – spent little time in its deliberations. The work was done by Asquith and Lord Crewe, Lord President of the Council, who proposed and gained the committee's support for a scheme which was more ingenuous than practical. Disputes between the two Houses should be resolved by a joint meeting composed of one hundred peers and the whole House of Commons debating and voting upon the disputed issue. Campbell-Bannerman was far too serious a politician to support anything so unworkable. His alternative, which was accepted by the Cabinet, was the 'suspensory veto' – the principle which was adopted in 1911 and which still, in an extended form, applies today. If the House of Lords rejected a bill twice, the third time it was passed by the Commons it would automatically become law. The proposed reform was announced to the Commons on 23 March 1908, together with the decision to reduce the life of Parliaments from seven to five years. Lloyd George spoke on the third day of a four-day debate and, as usual, spent most of his time attacking his adversaries rather than defining and defending his own position. His speech – deriding the claim that the House of Lords was the 'watchdog of the constitution' – contained one of the most memorable phrases in modern rhetoric. 'Watchdog! The House of Lords is Mr Balfour's poodle. It fetches and carries for him and barks at and bites anybody he sets it on to.' The government motion was carried by 423 votes to 127. No attempt was made to translate the proposals into law.

So the first two years of Liberal government were punctuated by bills which were withdrawn, bills which were emasculated and, in the case of the Licensing Bill, a proposal which – although promised during the election – was not even introduced. One consequence was a display of Lloyd George's split personality. One editorial noted that he 'continues to present the curious dual phenomenon of a fiery Hotspur on the platform and a shrewd administrator in the office and legislative chamber. Not many men of Mr Lloyd George's age have made a political reputation. He has made two and is sustaining them both.'[43]

In fact the House of Lords was of immense value to Lloyd George. He genuinely hated it as an institution and despised most of its members. But when he wanted to express his impatience with the government's timing, he could camouflage his criticism behind a barrage of recrimination. He was particularly critical of the proposed strategy known as 'filling the cup' – continually sending the Upper House radical bills in the hope that their Lordships would be shamed into letting some of them through. He told a meeting at Pontypridd that 'the ruffian has to be turned out of the premises'.[44] A speech in Manchester – billed as a demand that the Lords did not hinder the passage of the Licensing Bill – turned into an admission of anxiety about the whole progress of the government, lightly disguised as a claim for the supremacy of the House of Commons.

If, at the end of an average term of office, it is found that Parliament has done nothing seriously to cope with the social conditions of the people, to remove the national degradation of slums and widespread destitution in a land glittering with wealth: if they do not arrest the waste of national wealth on armaments: if they do not save up so as to be able to provide honourable sustenance for deserving old age: if they tamely allow the House of Lords to extract all the virtue out of their bills so that when the Liberal statute book is produced it is simply a bundle of sapless legislative faggots fit only for the fire, then a cry will arise in this land for a new party. And many of us in this room will join the cry.[45]

A year earlier, speaking to the Welsh National Liberal Council, he had dismissed the idea of a new party posing any sort of threat. 'Frankly I don't believe there is the slightest cause for alarm. Liberalism will never be ousted from its supremacy in the realm of political progress until it thoroughly deserves to be deposed because of its neglect or betrayal of the principles it professes.'[46] But twelve months of legislative failure had reminded him of what he and Churchill had agreed back in 1904. The Liberal Party needed to offer the working man an attractive alternative to Chamberlainism. In the new political age, governments had to respect the will of the people.

The House of Lords offered a convenient excuse for abandoning at least one of the distractions which, like Irish Home Rule in Gladstone's day, diverted the Liberal Party from what really mattered. Lloyd George – despite his strong objection to tithes and enforced denominational education – had never been as great an enthusiast for full-scale disestablishment as his speeches (made 'when he had his war paint on') suggested. The time had come to lay the argument to rest. He was a serious national politician and he proposed to spend his time on serious national issues.

CHAPTER 12

THE TWO IMPOSTORS

L loyd George had denounced the presumption of the Church of England to a point at which he felt that he was entitled to dispose of disestablishment by suggesting a compromise. There was no hope of legislation passing into law and he was not prepared to allow a lost cause to stand in the way of more important policies or create the impression that he could not escape from the politics of Wales. Other Welsh MPs regarded the promotion of a bill as necessary proof of the government's respect for the principality. Among them were D. A. Thomas, Sam Ellis and Ellis Griffith. They argued – without much logic to support their case – that the likelihood of a House of Lords veto made it essential for disestablishment proposals to be presented to the House of Commons during the first two years of the Parliament. Lloyd George appealed to the Bishop of St Asaph, who, by then, had become a friend. How would the Church in Wales respond to a 'very mild and kindly Disestablishment Bill'?[1] He was willing to make concessions – albeit on behalf of colleagues who had not been consulted about his initiative and who, had they been asked, would have rejected his proposals out of hand.

Bishop Edwards reported to Randall Davidson, the Archbishop of Canterbury. The proposed scheme required only one material sacrifice, the loss of tithes. Property and glebe land would remain in the Church's possession. 'Mr Lloyd George would rather like to get disestablishment carried out with a minimum of friction.'[2] In fact, Lloyd George wanted to seize the initiative from the hands of those Welsh MP who – in his opinion – overrated the importance of the issue and underrated him.

When he met Edwards and Davidson in the Bishops' Robing Room in the House of Lords – and it was clear that there could be no immediate agreement – he suggested what could have been little more than a diversionary tactic, a Royal Commission. The bishops agreed and the Cabinet approved the proposal three weeks later. Sir Roland Vaughan Williams, a Lord Justice of Appeal, was appointed chairman with instructions to 'consider the origin, the character and the value of provision for spiritual needs in Wales showing what has been done and what needs to be done in each parish both by the Church and by Nonconformity'.[3] The combination of chairman and terms of reference turned out to be a disaster.

The Royal Commission began its work in October 1906. The chairman ruled that the terms of reference made much of the Nonconformists' evidence inadmissible. The Church's domination of Welsh education was, he believed, none of his business. In consequence, the object – the relief of feelings – was not achieved and, as the weeks dragged on, the Nonconformists began to grow impatient. Lloyd George thought the best way to combat the growing unrest was to return to the attack. His chosen targets were the House of Lords and those Nonconformists who were urging the government to publish a bill at once. The assault – made at a Caernarvon dinner arranged to celebrate his forty-fourth birthday – encompassed both the peers (who were accused of 'spiteful vandalism') and the doubters who questioned the government's commitment to a policy which he was trying to abandon. Like all inflammatory speeches it received far more coverage than would have been afforded to a calm examination of the same subject.

> The fact is that Wales would not get a dog's chance of fair play from the Lords. They hated its Radicalism, they despised its Nonconformity and they could engage their scorn freely because Wales was so small. And he would say this to his fellow countrymen. If they found the government manoeuvring their artillery into position for an attack on the Lords, the Welshmen who worried them into attending to anything else until the citadel has been stormed, ought to be put in the guardroom.[4]

The speech was not well received even in Lloyd George's own constituency. The Nonconformist Association of North Caernarvonshire passed a resolution which repudiated any suggestion that disestablishment should be postponed until the House of Lords was reformed.

The campaign for immediate action was led by the *British Weekly*. In April it broke the news that three of the four Nonconformist members of the Royal Commission had resigned, reminded the government that 99 per cent of Nonconformists voted Liberal and called upon them to 'revolt' without suggesting what form the insurrection should take. Campbell-Bannerman's admission that the Licensing Bill had been withdrawn because of the threat of a Lords veto increased concern. He announced that a new education bill – designed to restore the policy the Lords had destroyed – would be introduced in the next session, but no mention was made of disestablishment. The champion of the cause, who was expected to lead the charge, was held personally responsible for the reluctance to advance. 'Mr Lloyd George', wrote the *British Weekly*, 'is a supremely clever man with a quite ecclesiastical turn for manoeuvre. He has done brilliantly in his department, but what has he done for Wales? . . . He is detained by mysterious providences from appearing at Nonconformist gatherings nowadays, but he will have to explain himself to the nation that has trusted him.'[5] The work of fence-mending had to begin at once.

The Reverend H. Elvet Lewis – independent minister, poet and hymn writer – wrote Lloyd George an open letter asking for assurances that a disestablishment bill would be introduced in the lifetime of the Parliament. Whether or not the enquiry was solicited, the answer was ready and gladly given. Lloyd George was filling the role occupied by Lord Rosebery ten years earlier and giving the same meaningless assurances as those which he had received from the then Liberal leadership. His reply to Lewis – sent, the letter said, with the agreement of the Prime Minister – was that a bill would certainly complete its passage through the Commons before the next general election. The promise was reinforced by the renewed acceptance of speaking engagements in Wales. And Lloyd George began to cultivate William Robertson Nicoll, the editor of the *British Weekly*, who had previously been denied attention because of his support for the Boer War. The friendship formed with Nicoll was to prove invaluable in the years ahead. The *British Weekly* sold twice as many copies as the *Daily News* and four times more than the *Westminster Gazette*.

Lloyd George was on holiday with his family for most of September 1907. When he returned home he discovered that the *British Weekly* had published a letter from the president of the Calvinistic Methodist Assembly announcing that a Welsh National Convention would be held in Cardiff during the following month. There were rumours of attempts to draft resolutions which, while not sufficiently extreme to prejudice their success, were deeply critical of the government in general and Lloyd George in particular. An article by Robertson Nicoll – which was based on an interview with Lloyd George – reminded readers of the assurances given to Elvet Lewis, and the adjacent 'Notes of the Week' column predicted that a disestablishment bill would not be long delayed. Lloyd George's friends told him that he would be unwise to attend the Cardiff convention. Confident of his powers to persuade, Lloyd George ignored their advice. His hope was that he would go to Cardiff armed with a strong statement from the Prime Minister, promising a disestablishment bill at no fixed date. Campbell-Bannerman was not a man to hedge or temporise. Lloyd George was told, 'You may repeat what I said to the deputation last session.'[6] That was no more than an expression of sympathy and the admission that progress was unlikely while the two Houses of Parliament were in conflict with each other.

Undaunted, Lloyd George met the convention leaders and promised them, without justification or authority, that a disestablishment bill would be introduced no later than 1909. As a result, the official resolution – put to the convention on the following day – expressed more pain than anger. But an amendment was moved from the floor by the Reverend Evan Jones. The convention agreed that no candidate who did not put disestablishment at 'the forefront of his programme should be adopted for a constituency in Wales'.[7]

At the beginning of Lloyd George's speech – essentially a reply to the charges which had been made against him and the government – Evan Jones interrupted to ask if he believed that the question of disestablishment should have been put before the country in the general election. Lloyd George replied with one word. 'Certainly.' After that the personal battle was won, but he increased the magnitude of victory with a speech which – although it barely mentioned the central issue – made him again the hero of Welsh Nonconformity.

> Who said that I was going to sell Wales? Seven years ago there was a little country which I had never seen fighting for freedom, fighting for fair play. I had never been within a thousand miles of it, never knew any of its inhabitants. Pardon me for reminding you – I risked my seat. I risked my livelihood [a voice from the audience added, 'You risked your life']. Yes I risked my life. Am I going to sell the land I love? God knows how dear Wales is to me.[8]

The *British Weekly*, totally converted to Lloyd George's cause, judged that he 'left the platform more than ever the people's leader'.[9] But he had become, during the previous two years, the leader of more than the people of Wales. When rightly warned that the disestablishment question would rumble on, he felt able to dismiss the suggestion that the dissidents might still damage him with the assertion that Wales was 'a new nation and new questions have come to the surface'.[10] After he had written to the Prime Minister to tell him that the Cardiff meeting 'went very well. You will not be troubled by Welsh disestablishment any more this session', he was able to move on to what office had convinced him were more important matters.[11] Responsibility had taken the place of romance. The President of the Board of Trade had to safeguard the nation from the disruption of a railway strike.

The railway system in Britain, which fifty years earlier had been the envy of the world, had begun its long-term decline. Most of the track had been laid before 1860 and the proliferation of independent companies made it difficult to raise capital to modernise the whole system. Wages had risen by only 5 per cent in twenty years and industrial relations – always prejudiced by the management's refusal to recognise the unions – were complicated by the existence of two competing organisations. The Associated Society of Locomotive Engineers and Firemen aimed to organise the craftsmen. The Associated Society of Railway Servants claimed to represent all grades of employee. The railway companies refused to raise wages and most of them would not recognise the unions which sought to negotiate on the men's behalf.

Lloyd George had told the Cabinet in April 1907 that

the action of the companies is so keenly resented by many Members of the House that, unless something is done to ensure that it will not continue, there is some real danger that private bills containing valuable proposals for providing new facilities for public and for trade, affording employment for labour, may be postponed or wrecked.[12]

The ASRS had sent a list of 'demands' to the various managements in January. They included higher wages, shorter working hours and, most important of all, recognition. The union had been recognised by the North Eastern Railway (where Edward Grey had been managing director) since 1897. None of the other companies replied. But, at the end of July, Lord Claud Hamilton – the chairman of the Great Eastern

Company – told his shareholders that recognition was out of the question. The ASRS, he said, represented only a small minority of railwaymen. Richard Bell, the Labour Member for Derby and ASRS's general secretary, decided to meet the criticism by organising a recruitment drive. His tour of the country, making new members, was a spectacular success. In Manchester on 13 September, three thousand men attended his meeting and as many were shut out of the hall. Encouraged by the extent of his support, he decided to increase the pressure on the railway companies by arranging a strike ballot. It confirmed, by a majority of nine to one, that the men were willing to withdraw their labour. Hamilton told his shareholders that the real purpose of the proposed action was neither terms of employment nor recognition but the overthrow of existing society.

Lloyd George's civil servants advised him not to intervene. Hudson Kearley, the Parliamentary Secretary – relying more on his experience as a businessman rather than a politician – was, on the other hand, sure that intervention was essential. So was Noel Buxton, the Postmaster General, who had just recognised the Post Office Clerks' Union. Lloyd George's reaction was based less on a careful appraisal of the conflicting advice than on his instinct. He was, by nature, an interventionist – a man who 'put things right'. He felt no affection for the unions. His letter to the Prime Minister, which started with a passage which described his success at the Cardiff convention, ended with the announcement that he proposed to call the railway company directors to the Board of Trade.

> It is too early to put the Conciliation Act into operation but there is a real danger of a strike being rushed owing to the ill-advised insolence of the directors – witness their dismissal of union officials . . .* Before I meet them I want your sanction as to the general line of action which I suggest should be pursued . . . in the event of my being met with a blank refusal to negotiate.[13]

If the companies remained obdurate, the Conciliation Act would be invoked. But the procedures which it involved could not be allowed to drag on. Procrastination by the companies would inevitably lead to a

---

*The 1896 Conciliation Act empowered the Board of Trade to appoint arbitrators to enquire into the causes of an abuse. It was generally regarded as ineffective.

profoundly damaging national railway strike. Unless agreement was quickly achieved, Parliament must be asked to approve legislation for compulsory arbitration. Bell – who was asking for no more than a meeting – must be assured that the 'government would take a strong line, if he is to hold his men'.

Lloyd George was not, by instinct, sympathetic towards organised labour, though his scepticism about the value of the Conciliation Act was clearly influenced by his experience of the Penrhyn quarrymen's dispute, when he had been unequivocally on the side of the workers. But the merits of the railwaymen's case, about which his letter to the Prime Minister left little doubt, were not his concern. He approached the possible railway strike with only one object in mind – preventing it. In Otober 1907, it seemed to him that the best way to achieve that aim was to put pressure on the companies rather than on the trade unions.

The first meeting with the companies was held on 25 October. Hudson Kearley, who was present, saw the hostility of the seventeen company chairmen evaporate in the face of Lloyd George's charm. 'When he began they were frigid, indifferent, barely attentive. I could see the little smiles and nudges with which they punctuated his opening sentences. Then came a change. Within a few minutes every man in the audience was following the speaker with rapt attention.'[14] Lloyd George's report to the Prime Minister was, by his standards, remarkably lacking in self-congratulation.

> I submitted to them a carefully thought out plan for settling the dispute with their men – based on schemes actually in operation in the iron and steel and coal trades. I asked them to consider and, if they thought they constituted even a basis for negotiation, we could later on discuss details. They left in a conciliatory frame of mind. What they will do next weekend when they meet in secret conclave, I cannot tell. But I am very hopeful of a settlement after today's meeting.[15]

A letter to his brother William, describing the same event, was written in the more familiar language. 'An excellent beginning. They almost fell on my neck including Lord Claud Hamilton. Old Stalbridge was also very nice. I have won their confidence and that is almost everything. You never saw anything like the change in their demeanour.'[16]

For once, Lloyd George did not exaggerate the extent of his success. All the railway company chairmen were impressed by his performance and one or two of them became so sympathetic to his point of view that they offered him encouragement. Sir Herbert Maxwell (a former Unionist MP and a director of the Glasgow and South Western Railway) wrote to him immediately the meeting was over to thank him for the 'tactful and considerate manner' in which the business had been conducted. Colonel Mark Lockwood (a sitting Unionist Member and director of the London and North Western Railway) sent him a confidential account of the chairmen's lunch which followed the meeting. 'Without being optimistic I can say that the tone of our conversation was hopeful.'[17] But more pressure was, in Lloyd George's view, essential. On 29 October he 'got the *Daily Mail* to write an article demanding compulsory arbitration in Railway Strikes. That fixed them,' he told his brother.[18]

It did not fix them as firmly as Lloyd George believed. When, on 31 October, he met the chairmen again he had to 'threaten them' with compulsory arbitration before they would agree to prepare a scheme which satisfied the unions' demand for 'a satisfactory method of dealing with grievances . . . and more opportunities for the men to deal with the conditions of their lives'.[19] The union leadership had decided that, if their primary demand was met, they would not insist on formal recognition, and Lloyd George almost certainly knew that they contemplated a tactical retreat. But he felt no obligation to pass on the good news to the company chairmen. The 31 October meeting ended with their agreement to search for a compromise.

The union – whose members did not know that their leaders were ready to offer a major concession – had organised a rally in the Albert Hall for 3 November. On the evening of 2 November, Lloyd George sent Richard Bell an invitation to meet him on 6 November. The message carried the clear implication – though no assurance – that a settlement of some sort was possible. The rally went ahead, with predictably bellicose speeches, but the strike was postponed until after the meeting at the Board of Trade. Three days later the company chairmen showed Lloyd George a plan which they believed their companies would endorse. They were told that if they confirmed their support for the scheme before the end of the day, he would insist on the union's accepting it there and then.

The chairmen were reluctant to agree before the shareholders of their companies had endorsed their scheme. Lloyd George would not wait. Haste was part of his negotiating technique. Delay, he warned, would be fatal. If the owners insisted on consultations, the union would do the same. Indeed it would insist on balloting its members and a ballot would be disastrous. The railwaymen had already voted in favour of a strike and would almost certainly reject the terms of the proposed agreement. The owners capitulated and signed the agreement at half past eleven on the morning of 7 November 1907. The unions signed at half past three in the afternoon. The strike had been averted without the disputing parties ever meeting. Tough talking had won the day. But it had been augmented by charm – a quality brilliantly illustrated by Nigel Nicolson in a comparison of radical Liberalism's two heroes. 'When you talk to Winston Churchill, you think that he is the most important man in the world. When you talk to Lloyd George, you think that you are the most important man in the world.'[20]

The agreement was not between the parties – each of whom signed identical individual compacts with the government. So the management was spared the indignity of even an implied recognition of the union. All the scheme involved was the creation of a joint conciliation and arbitration committee composed of members nominated by the employers and 'representatives of the workers' who would be 'employees of the company' and not, therefore, full-time trade union officials. What little chance Bell had of claiming a victory was destroyed by an editorial in *The Times* which pronounced that the new arrangement had removed all need for trade unions in the railway companies.[21]

In fact, the agreement had changed nothing. It was sabotaged, manipulated and eventually completely bypassed by the railway companies' management. The railway unions became a casualty of Lloyd George's negotiating style – determination to make a quick bargain rather than find a permanent solution to the underlying problem. Throughout the years of reconciling warring factions which lay ahead, the merits of the rival positions and the legitimate interests of the opposing parties rarely concerned him. All he aimed to do was bully or bribe, charm or cheat his way to the announcement of a settlement. Hamilton, the most bellicose of the railway directors, boasted that Bell had failed to discharge his mandate and rejoiced that he would pay a heavy price for his failure. 'Once he signed the agreement his doom was sealed.'[22] He was right. Bell was replaced both as general secretary of the ASRS and as Member of Parliament for the railway town of Derby because he was thought to have settled for far too little.

Lloyd George became an instant national hero. He was the man who had saved Great Britain from a potentially ruinous national railway strike. The Prime Minister, announcing the good news to the King, said that the nation 'was largely indebted' for its deliverance to 'the knowledge, skill, astuteness and tact of the President of the Board of Trade and those around him in his department'.[23] The newspapers, the man of the hour told his brother, were 'without distinction of party wild with enthusiastic and amazed satisfaction. The King has written expressing his delight.'[24] *The Times* described Lloyd George as 'the greatest asset of the government with the commercial classes' and at a state banquet at Windsor Castle, held in honour of Kaiser Wilhelm II of Germany, the personal congratulations of the royal family were heaped upon him.[25] The Kaiser, Lloyd George wrote home, 'spent three times as long with me as he spent with Campbell-Bannerman and talked for so long that the King came and fetched him away'. The Queen added a homely touch to the regal encomia by remarking that she had seen 'a nice photograph' of Lloyd George 'with his little girl'. The proud father's radical instinct survived the fêting and the flattery. He told his brother, with unaccountable surprise, that 'The King was against the working man in the matter of the railway strike . . . He is a Tory at heart. God help the people with such overlords. The Kaiser is just as bad. I came away hating all kings.'[26]

D. R. Daniel saw Lloyd George in Criccieth 'shortly after the nego-tiated settlement with the railwaymen'. His praise was prophetic. 'I said to him . . . You have succeeded extraordinarily in politics, but I always feel that you would have made [the] greatest name for yourself and mark upon history in a warlike period of the world's history.'[27]

Lloyd George's approach to negotiation was pragmatic to the point of cynicism, but the result was often at least a temporary agreement that a mediator, with less fluid views, could not have achieved. 'Nothing could have been more skilful than his handling of diverse elements. He had an almost uncanny way of persuading men in opposite camps that they really meant the same thing – which was the thing he wanted them to mean.'[28] The technique enjoyed its greatest success when directed at, or perhaps against, interests which were not represented by his natural friends and allies. It was because he felt coldly detached that he was able to succeed, where Balfour's government had failed, in persuading the disparate elements which controlled Thames shipping to come together to form a Port of London Authority.

A Royal Commission, which reported in 1902, had recommended that the powers possessed by Thames Conservancy, the Watermen's Company and Trinity House be concentrated in a single body. The new public authority, it went on to say, should own and manage the assets of the India, Surrey Commercial and Millwall dock companies. Agreement to what amounted to nationalisation was not easily achieved. Lloyd George achieved it by more than the application of a sophisticated negotiation technique. He had the sense to accept expert advice. Kearley, parliamentary secretary at the Board of Trade, persuaded him to negotiate a price rather than acquire the docks by compulsory purchase and to assure the employers that he approached the need to improve the port's investment and efficiency without any preconceived ideas.

> I cannot see my way to recommend any scheme yet to Parliament and I must take at least another year to make up my mind. I quite realise that it is a problem which has to be dealt with but it is far better that I should take another twelve months . . . to arrive at some sort of understanding than that I should hurriedly plant on the table of the House of Commons an ill-considered scheme.[29]

The radical demagogue had become the great conciliator.

Within two weeks, Disaster, the second of Kipling's 'two impostors', had followed Triumph into Lloyd George's life. Preventing the rail strike had elevated him to the heights of public esteem and he was still enjoying the nation's plaudits when he was suddenly plunged into the depths of private grief and despair.

At the turn of the century, Margaret had moved, with surprisingly little resistance, to Wandsworth in London – first to Trinity Road and then to Routh Road. On 25 November 1907, while chairing a routine meeting at the Board of Trade, a civil servant handed him a note. 'Mrs Lloyd George tells me that she is not able to come up to town because Miss Mair Lloyd George came home from school this afternoon not feeling well.'[30] Mair Eluned was seventeen, Lloyd George's eldest daughter and her father's favourite. Frances Stevenson – a fellow pupil at Clapham High School – wrote that she possessed 'a certain sadness in her face and a thoughtfulness beyond her years'.[31] Early biographers described her beauty and talent in extravagant language and told poignant stories of Lloyd George singing Welsh hymns with Mair accompanying him on the piano. All that is certain is that her father's devotion was genuine and his immediate concern over the news of her ill health real.

Mair had complained of a pain in her side for several days, but it was not until the morning of 29 November that a specialist was called in to examine her. He diagnosed a burst appendix and recommended an immediate operation. In conformity with the precedent set by Edward VII in 1901, it was performed at home. The location – whatever its consequences for the success of the surgery – added to the burden, both emotional and physical, on the family. Just before noon, William George – in court at Criccieth – received a telegram from his brother. It asked him to travel to London at once. He abandoned court and client and left Criccieth on the next train east. Had Polly, their sister, not been unwell, she would have travelled with him and become Mair's nurse. In her absence, Margaret – who employed only Welsh staff in her London home – engaged Anita Williams, a nursing sister at London's Royal Northern Hospital.*

Mair Eluned died during the afternoon. Her last words were a tribute to her Baptist upbringing: 'He is just and merciful.' Lloyd George's reaction was described by D. R. Daniel as 'tortured almost to the edge of madness . . . He got no grain of comfort from the usual springs. Some hand of darkness had taken his beloved from his heart . . . He got no joy from following her on the wings of imagination.' Great though his grief undoubtedly was, Lloyd George saw his daughter's death as a tragedy for himself as much as for her. 'It has come at a time when I have had such a curious success in my career . . . when I have been put on a sort of pinnacle, just so that I should become the target for the cruel blow. It is sure to leave a cruel mark upon me . . . I am sure to be much better a man than I was.'[32]

William George decided that his brother's grief was so unbearable that he 'should be kept clear of the house while certain necessary preparations for the funeral went on'. So Lloyd George was taken to the Board of Trade where 'high officers tried to divert [his] thoughts from his sorrow by relating humorous stories and Lobby gossip about famous politicians past and present'.[33] Meanwhile Margaret Lloyd George bore the burden of making the arrangements for the burial of their daughter, which, naturally enough, she decided should be 'at home' in Criccieth.

Lloyd George travelled to Wales in the Royal Saloon coach which the Great Western Railway put at his disposal as a mark of sympathy and respect. He was accompanied by his brother and Herbert Lewis, a devoted and selfless friend who, for a quarter of a century, was at Lloyd George's side through most of his public and private crises. Mair was

---

*Ms Williams, Pembrokeshire born and bred, fitted in to the family so well that she was retained to look after Polly during her fatal illness – and married William George.

buried next to the vault which the Owens – her maternal grand-parents – had purchased for their own burial. Her mother was not at the graveside, for convention did not allow women to witness the last rites.[34] So the mourners were led by her father – 'a pathetic figure, lean-ing on the arm of his Uncle'.[35] Lloyd George was dissatisfied with the funeral arrangements which he had played no part in planning. It looked, he said, as if his daughter had been buried in a pauper's grave. At his insistence, her body was exhumed some weeks later and re-interred in the Owen vault, on which was placed a statue of Mair engraved with her last words.

On the afternoon of the funeral, Lloyd George and Herbert Lewis went on a six-mile walk

and the change of atmosphere seemed to do Ll-G good. Spent the evening at Garthcelyn [the home of William George] in conver-sation that sought to divert the current of Ll-G's thought. Laughter and tears were very near to one another and in the midst he had to leave us for a while. He returned and kept us all amused and interested with a brilliant flow of literary, historical and reminis-cent talk.[36]

The flow of post-mortem conversation was interrupted by the receipt of a message from the Board of Trade. Lloyd George's healing gifts were needed in Manchester, where the cotton 'fine spinners' were contem-plating a strike which would close down the whole industry. So for a time all thought of Mair – lost, missed and mourned – was put out of his head. Work, the great healer, diverted his attention and revived his spirits. The strike was averted and he returned south. The news that his wife was to meet him at the National Liberal Club was greeted with joy and gratitude. 'I am so pleased that you are joining me up in London tomorrow night darling. Your placid and brave spirit has a soothing effect on my turbulent and emotional nature.'[37]

He did not need her brave and soothing spirit for long. The Bishop of St Asaph, himself in mourning, advised a continental holiday but, because of urgent ecclesiastical commitments, was unable to join Lloyd George in a brief escape from harsh reality. So Kearley was recruited to drive Lloyd George and his sons to the South of France, where he planned to spend Christmas at Lady Nunburnholme's villa in Nice. He invited his wife to join him. But when she chose to stay in Wales he decided that solace, comfort and consolation would nonetheless be most easily found on the Riviera. Yet he still wrote to Margaret, 'No-one can cure me except you and your darling children and I think I alone can cure you. There will always be a scar . . . Still I do not even now despair of life. We have four sweet children and we have each other.'[38] Writing thirty years later, Frances Stevenson – by then Lloyd George's second wife and widow – suggested that he did not mean a word of it. 'They each had their poignant grief but could not go to each other for sympathy and understanding . . . The gap of incompatibility, which had always been there, became more emphasised and difficult to bridge.'[39]

It is impossible to know if the emotions – expressed in Lloyd George's letters home – were genuine. Perhaps he did not know himself. A man with normal feelings would have recognised how incompatible his words and actions were. But he believed that the people around him had an obligation to support and succour his genius. Usually they agreed. Before he left for France, he told Herbert Lewis, 'I need you badly. I am depressed, tortured with grief.'[40] Lewis immediately agreed to join him. And the family and friends he left behind occupied their time assuaging his grief rather than their own. He had told his wife and brother that he could never face Routh Road again. So while he was on holiday they reorganised his life. Brynawelon, the house in Criccieth, was sold and Margaret, together with the girls, moved into Llys Owen, her parents' house next door. A new London house was rented in Chelsea's Cheyne Row.

Sometimes it seemed that Lloyd George expressed extravagant concern to convince himself that he cared. 'What about servants? Have you thought that out? Do you mean to have a nurse housemaid who can attend to Megan? Your housekeeping allowance must be increased to ensure regular meals for the young ones.'[41] It would not have been easy to provide. Lloyd George was thought to be so short of money that at the end of 1907 – partly as a tribute to his success in ending the railway dispute – some of his colleagues had suggested that he receive an allowance from private party funds to augment his salary. Herbert Lewis promoted the idea but Lloyd George – although resentful that he was paid less than half the salary of a Secretary of State – turned down the idea out of hand. 'I am not going to accept the charity of the party come what may.' Pride was not accompanied by gratitude. 'This is an offer made to me because they find jealousies and rivalries so great that they cannot raise the status of my office . . . But I won't have it. I'll take my chance.'[42] He did not have long to wait.

CHAPTER 13

THE GREAT WORK BEGINS

S ir Henry Campbell-Bannerman resigned the office of Prime Minister on 4 April 1908. His resignation had been expected since November the previous year when – after addressing the annual Colston Banquet in Bristol – he had suffered a severe stroke. He had returned to work in the following January, following two months' rest and recuperation in Downing Street, but the resumption of his duties had been accepted as no more than a postponement of the inevitable. There had been neither intrigue nor speculation about who would replace him. Everyone knew that it would be Herbert Henry Asquith. By the end of February, the change seemed so imminent and the succession so certain that the King thought it right to discuss the composition of the new Cabinet with the Prime Minister in waiting. Asquith promised to do no more than fill the vacancies created by his elevation.

Asquith was undecided about the future of the Treasury. He had been a prudent Chancellor. Between 1906 and 1908 the national debt had been reduced by £45 million and the budget had been kept in permanent surplus. The caution must, he believed, continue. At first he thought about keeping the job himself. Gladstone – as he told the King – had set the precedent. Then he decided that, in the world of 1908, the Exchequer would demand a minister's full-time attention. There was also the politics of balance to be considered. An 'Imperialist' had to replace a 'radical' in Number 10 Downing Street. It was necessary for a radical to take over from an Imperialist next door.

David Lloyd George made such an indelible mark upon the Treasury that, a century after his appointment, it is easy to forget that he was not the only candidate to succeed Asquith. During the last week in February 1908, he discussed with Herbert Lewis the merits of threatening to resign – not, it should be noted, actually resigning – from the government if he was not made Chancellor.[1] John Morley was the choice of the more venerable Liberals, but had disqualified himself with an elegantly oblique reference to his age. 'I suppose . . . I have a claim from seniority of service for your place at the Exchequer but I don't know that I have any special aptitude for it.'[2] A more threatening candidate was Reginald McKenna, an ally in the struggle against the Education Bill. Financial Secretary when Asquith was Chancellor, he had won the new Prime Minister's admiration and been promoted to First Lord of the Admiralty. He was Asquith's sort of man – Trinity Hall to his Balliol – and therefore a dangerous rival. Lloyd George regarded rivals as enemies.

In retrospect, it seems that Lloyd George's claim to the Treasury was irresistible. He had, by general consent, been a spectacularly successful President of the Board of Trade and, although a radical, he was also an 'economist' – a description which, in the Edwardian Liberal Party, meant that he wanted to 'economise' on public expenditure. Although there was no real risk of his leaving the government – either to found a Welsh Party or lead a Welsh Liberal revolt – a disgruntled Lloyd George would have been almost as much of a problem inside the government as out. Asquith had no choice but to make him Chancellor.

When at the end of March 1908, Edward VII was told that Campbell-Bannerman was sinking fast, he asked that the Prime Minister's resignation be delayed until the royal winter holiday was over. The doctors decreed otherwise. So the Seals of Office were returned on 4 April and two days later – the King having declined to return home – Asquith caught the nine o'clock boat-train to Paris. On 8 April, in the Hotel de Palais, Biarritz, he became the only British Prime Minister to 'kiss hands' on foreign soil. That night he wrote to Lloyd George.

It gives me great pleasure, with His Majesty's approval, to ask you to accept the office of Chancellor of the Exchequer.

The offer which I make is a well-deserved tribute to your long and eminent service to our party and to the splendid capacity which you have shown in your administration of the Board of Trade . . .

The only stipulation that I make is that, following a precedent

twice set by Sir Robert Peel, you should leave me with the introduction of the Budget for the present year. The change of
government has come at a time when it would not be fair, or even
possible, either for you or for me to follow the ordinary course.[3]

The message reached Lloyd George on 10 April. He tried and failed to
telephone his brother. So the glorious news had to be put in the post.
'I am Chancellor of the Exchequer and consequently second-in-
command of the Liberal host.'[4] After details of proposed meetings
with the Prime Minister and the arrangements for the Budget statement, there was the announcement that 'the world says that it is a
much more dazzling promotion than Asquith's'. The letter ended with
a poignant reference to Mair. 'There is a great sadness for me in the
promotion. It is hard that my poor little girl should have been taken
away before these events which would have given her such great joy.'[5]
The letter included the usual protestations of affection for the family
which he neglected.

The announcement had been preceded by several days of speculation, much of it correct. So it was at least possible that the *Daily
Chronicle*'s announcement of Lloyd George's promotion on 8 April –
the day on which Asquith wrote with the offer of the Exchequer and
two days before the letter was received – was merely the anticipation
of what all well-informed communicators expected to happen. But
there is another explanation which some biographies accept without
providing much supporting evidence. Lloyd George, they claim, told
the *Daily Chronicle* that the job was his three days before he received
the formal offer. There was certainly a plausible reason for his doing
so. On 3 April – while Campbell-Bannerman was still Prime
Minister – Asquith had told Lloyd George that he was minded to offer
him the Treasury. Only one thing could then have prevented the
promise being kept. That was an objection from the King – who had
twice thought it necessary to complain about Lloyd George's conduct.
Lloyd George may have thought that pre-emptive publication would
prevent a royal veto. Whether or not Lloyd George was the culprit, his
detractors took it for granted that the *Daily Chronicle* stories were just
another example of his devious behaviour, and it seems that, for at
least a time, Asquith – affronted by the leak – accepted the same
explanation.

The new Prime Minister arrived home from Biarritz on 10 April –
the day on which Lloyd George received the formal offer of the

Treasury. On the same night Margot, Asquith's wife, wrote to Winston Churchill (about to succeed Lloyd George at the Board of Trade) in the sort of language which hides the hope of causing trouble under the pretence of providing a friendly warning.

> I am told that Lloyd George dines with you tonight. I wish you would speak to him and tell him quite plainly that the staff of the *Daily Chronicle* have given him away to 3 independent people . . . Lloyd George's best chance if he is a good fellow, which I take your word for, is not to lie about it when H speaks heavily to him.

The rest of the letter was not entirely coherent. But it did make clear that the King was furious, that Lloyd George would be 'done like a dog' unless he gave up 'his whole Press campaign', and that Churchill could 'save him and the whole Cabinet' if he behaved 'courageously'.[6] It is not clear whether Churchill endorsed, or even understood, Margot Asquith's predictions of catastrophe. Perhaps his decision to report his dinner conversation to her husband rather than reply to her letter is some indication of his reaction to the hysteria of her complaint. 'I broached the matter to Lloyd George. He denies it utterly. I told him that you had learned that several colleagues thought he was responsible, but that you had of course no knowledge yourself. He intends to speak to you tomorrow on the subject.'[7]

Lloyd George wrote rather than spoke. His letter began, 'I thank you for the flattering proposal contained in your letter and even more for the flattering terms in which it is conveyed to me . . . I shall be proud to serve under your Premiership and no member of the Government will render more loyal service and support to his chief.' It ended with a categoric denial of responsibility for the leak which was a rebuke as well as a rebuttal. He was amazed to discover that the Prime Minister could think him 'capable of what is not merely a gross indiscretion but a downright and disreputable breach of trust'. Then – in a paragraph which was much corrected in the preparatory draft – came what makes the letter a crucial testament of Lloyd George's character.

> Men whose promotion is not sustained by birth or other favouring conditions are always liable to be assailed with suspicions of this sort. I would ask therefore, as a favour, if you would not entertain them without satisfying yourself that they have some basis in truth.[8]

He was doing more than arming himself against future assaults. Lloyd George was asserting that, despite his new eminence, he was, and would always remain, an outsider. The pride which he took in that status did not make him the most gracious of companions. D. R. Daniel commented on the way in which he accepted the favours of rich patrons. 'Always the best hotels, the best food, the most comfortable seats – whatever the cost that was his motto always and his weakness was that he never had a sense of delicacy in accepting favours.'[9] Nor did he ever feel any obligation to reciprocate by using his influence on behalf of his benefactors. His company was payment enough. Arrogance and a sense of not belonging to the world which he exploited kept him, in that particular, honest.

Asquith accepted Lloyd George's 'disclaimer . . . without reservation'. He 'confessed' to being 'a good deal annoyed to find . . . a substantially accurate forecast of the proposed changes' in the *Daily Chronicle*. The suggestion that he, or his wife, had been anxious that 'Winston . . . should inform you of what was being said' implied that he was seeking to protect rather than to accuse.[10] Lloyd George suspected that McKenna was his accuser. But both men, knowing that they had important work to do together, moved on.

On 4 May, the government turned again to the 'Brewers' Endowment Bill'. The reform of licensing laws was unpopular even among men who were not habitual drinkers, but the second reading of the bill provided the new Chancellor of the Exchequer with the opportunity to make one of the destructive speeches at which he excelled. By suggesting that small investors would suffer, the Opposition had once more 'dressed up widows and orphans for the occasion' – two categories of the deserving poor who were always said to be harmed by the introduction of policies which penalised the rich. 'The widows and orphans seem to have picked out all the worst mines in South Africa, all the mines which could not exist without Coolie labour and invested in them. I thought that they had lost all their money there. But it seems that the money they have lost they have reinvested in Meux's brewery.'[11] The Liberal backbenchers cheered. But it was a brief interlude of high spirits in a despondent spring and summer. The government was unpopular. The Unionists had won by-elections in marginal Ashburton and Ross and overturned a substantial Liberal majority in Peckham. The country had tired of 'Old Liberalism' – the politics of temperance, disestablishment and fiscal rectitude. The election of 1906, as is often the case, had been more a rejection of the defeated party than an endorsement of the victors.

The Budget of 1908 – presented to the House on 7 May – is now regarded as a turning point, the crossroads at which the government chose to follow the 'New Liberal' route. An attempt to follow a similar path had been made in November 1906. W. H. Lever – the soap millionaire and Liberal Member for Wirral – had introduced a bill to introduce a non-contributory old-age pension. It came to nothing – even though Campbell-Bannerman had promised, earlier in the year, that the government would support such a proposal. The progress of reform often needs political necessity to be reinforced by moral conviction. During 1907, the force which Lloyd George had warned might crush the Liberal Party had shown that it was waiting to fill the radical vacuum. A Labour candidate won the Jarrow by-election. Then the Liberal–Nonconformist citadel of Colne Valley was captured by Victor Grayson, a mysterious, if unaligned, socialist. In a letter to his brother, Lloyd George expressed the view of many Liberal MPs: 'It is time we did something that appealed straight to the people. It will, I think, help to stop this electoral rot and that is most necessary.'[12]

At the Trades Union Congress's annual conference in Bath, a resolution demanding the introduction of an old-age pension had been carried unanimously. The government's response was set out by Asquith in his Budget statement. A bill, which was about to be presented to the House of Commons, would establish a national old-age pension – available from 1 January 1909, the date stipulated in the TUC's resolution. The government's scheme was less generous than the one which the unions demanded. The Bath resolution had proposed a non-contributory pension of five shillings a week for every man aged sixty-five or more. The Budget statement proposed five shillings a week at seventy (seven and sixpence for a couple) with the proviso that it would be withheld from vagrants, criminals, lunatics and anyone with an income of more than ten shillings a week. The Finance Bill made provision for financing the scheme only during the first three months of its operation. The 1909 Budget would raise the revenue to cover the longer-term costs.

Nobody knew what the long- or short-term costs would be. The government announced its intention to introduce the scheme before it had the benefit of actuarial advice. Asquith, in his Budget statement, reminded the House of what he seemed to think was a cause for self-congratulation. The Liberal Party had gone into the 'last election, entirely unpledged in regard to this matter'. In short, it knew neither how much money was needed nor where the necessary money would come from. Ministers lived in the hope that the Treasury was more or less right when it estimated the total annual cost at £6 million.

Lloyd George, who would take the Finance Bill through the House of Commons, realised that the debates would provide him with regular opportunities to shine as well as make him the man who gave an essential boost to the Liberal Party's standing in the country. His belief in the need for a national old-age pension was not in doubt – though he had pursued his passion with remarkable fiscal irresponsibility. Chamberlain became his early hero because he was the first senior politician to take up the cause of the ageing poor. But, although he ignored the arithmetic, Lloyd George genuinely believed in the need for reform. Interest in other aspects of social policy developed slowly. It was largely the result of his association with the group of young Liberals who had successfully campaigned for school meals in 1900 and school medical inspections in 1907. Winston Churchill, who was far more progressive on social questions in general, had encouraged the new Chancellor to meet them and take their ideas seriously. Consideration of wider social issues made him realise the limitations of the bill which was to be the centrepiece of the new government's legislative programme. He made clear, privately, on the day after his promotion to the Treasury was announced, that he wanted to go further.

> In my opinion, old age is not the hardest burden . . . Lonely and sad though old age may be, the way to carry it is not far and the old has only his own burden to carry. The tragedy which appeals most to me is seeing the worker whose strength is ebbing away and yet, because of his family burdens, has to go every day to the quarry or the factory.[13]

It was not only what he regarded as mistaken priorities that worried him about the bill. In the first paper he put to the Cabinet as Chancellor he warned that the 'cost may turn out to be nearer 7 millions' than the six that had been estimated.

Much to his credit, and no doubt to the surprise of the House of Commons, the speech with which he opened the second reading debate on the Old Age Pensions Bill on 15 June 1908 reflected his reservations. He described the proposals as 'purely a first step . . . a necessary experiment' and went on to express his true convictions.

> We do not say that it deals with all the unmerited destitution in this country. We do not even contend that it deals with the worst part of the problem . . . It might be held that many an old man,

dependent upon charity, was better off than a young man broken down in health or who cannot find a market for his labour.[14]

The assertion that the government had an obligation to heal the wounds inflicted by a heartless economic system was the acceptance of duties far wider than the provision of an old-age pension. It was a statement of New Liberal philosophy – the community's responsibility for the well-being of its members. 'These problems of the sick, the infirm, of the men who cannot find a means of earning a livelihood . . . are problems with which it is the business of the state to deal. They are problems which the state has neglected for too long.'[15]

Some Victorian prejudices remained. The bill distinguished between the deserving and the undeserving poor. Scoundrels and loafers could 'not be treated on the same basis as men who have given the best of their lives in the service of the state'. Guiltless paupers might eventually be included in the scheme. On that point he waited for the report of the Royal Commission on the Poor Law due to report in the following year. It provided little help. The minority report which proposed that separate government departments should seek to alleviate different forms of economic distress – including paying unemployment benefit in times of industrial depression – was rejected. The majority report, which, in effect, wanted a more compassionate Poor Law, was quietly ignored. John Burns – President of the Local Government Board, to whom the Royal Commission reported – held fast to the view that poverty should be punished as the 1834 Poor Law Act required. Despite that, Lloyd George made a calculated move towards a more comprehensive system of what had yet to be called 'social security', based on need alone. Germany – the nation which, as an example and an enemy, constantly intruded into Edwardian political thinking – possessed 'a prosperous scheme for old age, for infirmity, for sickness and for unemployment'.[16] The whole range of benefits was – Lloyd George said – paid for by the compulsory contributions of the beneficiaries. In fact there was no unemployment insurance in Germany. But the error was less important than the implication that there was more to come and that he, at least, was prepared to argue for 'insurance' schemes in which the payments were 'funded' by contributions.

The Unionist Opposition, with much justification, accused the government of not knowing where the money to finance the scheme would be raised, and Balfour was particularly concerned about bogus claimants in Ireland who could not be checked because, until 1865, there had been no registration of births there. The bill survived the committee stage with only two significant amendments. One changed the basis of payment from a flat rate to a sliding scale. The proposed 5/- a week payment for all pensioners with annual incomes of less than £26 was replaced by payments which ranged from 5/- for incomes of under £21 a year, to 1/- for incomes of £31. The other amendment abolished the married couples' joint payment of 7/6, leaving husband and wife with 5/- each. Lloyd George had proposed both changes to the Cabinet but they had been opposed by Asquith on the grounds that they would add to the cost. Lloyd George, who loyally defended official government policy during the Finance Bill's committee stage, was vindicated. The graduated payment – although it included more potential recipients than the flat-rate scheme – saved money. Few pensioners who earned £31 a year bothered to claim a shilling a week.★

Shrewdly, Lloyd George played the role of prudent Chancellor and represented his critics as profligate. The Unionists moved 'wild, illogical, irrational amendments without any sense of responsibility or regard to their cost to the revenue, in order to be able to say to every class in turn "We voted for you and those wicked radicals voted against you"'.[17] Labour's Philip Snowden spoke with 'arid ferocity' and 'made the great mistake' of reacting to the 'single step' by insisting on the government's 'either not taking it at all or leaping the whole flight of stairs at once. We would rather begin with an incomplete scheme and do something for the 572,000 persons outside the Poor Law.'[18] The significant words in the passage were 'begin' and 'incomplete'.

Doing more – the clear hope of Lloyd George's response to Philip Snowden – was an aspiration which had to yield priority to more immediate demands. Asquith had underestimated the cost of the pension. In the letter to the King in which he reported the Cabinet's conclusions on the subject, he had been precise. The scheme would cost no more than £6.5 million and that there would be, at most, half a million recipients. Even Lloyd George's rival estimate of a minimum of £7 million had proved over-optimistic.[19] By the end of its first year of operation the pension was being paid to 699,353 recipients and the total cost had risen to £8.5 million. It was soon to rise to £10 million a year – coincidentally about the same amount as the cost of new naval construction, the second burden that the Exchequer had to bear.

★The married couples' 'concession' cost £400,000 a year. Lloyd George estimated that including paupers would add another £400,000 to the annual bill.

In February 1906, the Royal Navy had launched the *Dreadnought*. It was faster as well as more heavily armed and armoured than any ship afloat. From then on jingoism and the obsession to maintain naval superiority over Germany made building more battleships of the same class irresistible. The Board of Admiralty suggested that eighteen should be laid down. The *Dreadnought* – designed for the Italian Navy but rejected by the government in Rome as too expensive – cost £2 million, twice as much as the cost of a conventional battleship. If Lloyd George met the navy's demands, the people who, according to his second reading speech on the Old Age Pensions Bill, had waited too long – the sick and the unemployed – would have to wait still longer.

In the first flush of 'economist's' enthusiasm, Lloyd George told his brother that he was 'not going to increase taxation to pay for Old Age Pensions until [he had] exhausted all means of reducing expenditure'. His determination had been increased by conversations over dinner with 'Sir Guy Fleetwood Wilson, one of the chief War Office men' – though not, apparently, an apologist for War Office extravagance. 'I mean to cut down on Army expenditure,' Lloyd George wrote, 'and he is helping me.'[20] However, six weeks later, during the committee stage debate – and no doubt stimulated by the adrenalin of confrontation – he spoke of tax increases with uninhibited exuberance.

I have no nest egg . . . I have got to rob somebody's roost next year. I am on the look-out for which will be the easiest to get, where I shall be least punished, where I shall get most eggs, and not only that, but where they can be most easily spared which is another question.[21]

Whether or not the Chancellor, at that stage, seriously contemplated a tax raid on the rich, he certainly remained committed to reductions in naval and military expenditure. That, naturally enough, alienated the navy and army ministers. McKenna, the First Lord of the Admiralty – at sea on the Admiralty Board yacht – received a telegram which he mistakenly and unaccountably thought proposed an increase in the Dreadnought programme. It did no more than suggest that some naval shipbuilding might be brought forward into the current year – an idea proposed by Winston Churchill as a way of reducing unemployment in the North of England and on Clydeside. The misunderstanding embittered the battle to hold down naval expenditure and increased the antagonism between McKenna and Lloyd George. The Secretary of

State for War, Haldane – who, although a fellow radical, had never liked the Chancellor – reacted almost as strongly to proposals to make savings in the War Office. Indeed, he was so infuriated by Lloyd George's plans to economise that he made the bizarre suggestion that he, rather than the Chancellor, should chair the Public Expenditure Committee.[22] Asquith equivocated. Lloyd George was making more enemies than friends.

There was a growing suspicion among colleagues that – for all his dash and daring and his record of success at the Board of Trade – Lloyd George was not a competent or industrious minister and that he covered his incompetence by making flamboyant speeches and forging close links with friendly journalists. Charles Hobhouse, the Liberal Member for Bristol East and Financial Secretary to the Treasury, admired his chief's capacity to 'pick up the essential details of a question by conversation' but deplored his 'absolute contempt for detail and ignorance of common facts of life [which] make him a bad official'. It was a strange noun by which to describe a Chancellor of the Exchequer and Hobhouse, a 'gentleman Whig' of the old school, was not a reliable witness. But at the end of June 1908, Asquith, who was beginning to have his own doubts about Lloyd George's competence, instructed Hobhouse to 'see him weekly on the financial position and let him know how things stood'.[23] Junior ministers spying on the heads of their department on the Prime Minister's instructions are a feature of Cabinet government. By comparison with more recent practitioners, Hobhouse had a simple task. It was easy enough to discover Lloyd George's intentions. He proclaimed them. There was a sovereign remedy to all financial ills which he proposed to prescribe and to administer – an urban land tax. The idea was supported by an argument of dubious merit. 'If there is to be an extension of the pension system on contributory lines, the property which is improved by the labour of the community should contribute its share.'[24] The non-sequitur confirmed that Lloyd George – forced, by office, to face reality – expected the new benefits to be partly, but not entirely, funded by the insurance principle. It was still essential to reduce overall expenditure.

In July 1908 – having carried the burden of both the Finance Bill and the Old Age Pensions Bill into the summer – he came to the rational, but hardly practical, conclusion that the best way to reduce the pressure for an increased naval budget was to improve relations with Germany. He therefore decided to embark on a mission of personal diplomacy which he hoped would make the arms race redundant. The precedents did not suggest that the démarche would yield much success. Lord Tweedmouth – McKenna's predecessor at the Admiralty – had tried to demonstrate Britain's friendly intentions by sending the Kaiser a copy of the Naval Estimates for 1908–9 before they were presented to the House of Commons. The Germans had accelerated their warship building programme and Tweedmouth had been sacked.

Bismarck's welfare programme provided Lloyd George with a legitimate reason to visit Berlin. But until his attempts to forge a rapprochement offended both capitals, he made little attempt to hide the real purpose of his visit. He had met the German Ambassador, Count Paul Metternich, at Edward Grey's house and – despite telling him that, if necessary, Britain would spend £100 million to frustrate Germany's plans to achieve naval supremacy – the two men had enjoyed what Lloyd George regarded as a successful discussion about a mutual agreement to slow down the arms race.[25] His own position was made clear when he spoke in the Queen's Hall on the same night. 'My principle is, as Chancellor of the Exchequer, less money for the production of suffering, more money for the reduction of suffering.'[26] Britain had an overwhelming naval supremacy. 'Yet the cry went up "Let there be Dreadnoughts".' Britain, he claimed, 'did not require them . . . Do not forget that when you wonder why Germany is frightened at alliances and understandings.'[27] Two days later, after reading a *Times* editorial which called the speech 'Singularly reckless and inopportune', he left for Germany in the company of Harold Spender and Sir Charles and Lady Henry. Despite Lady Henry's open infatuation with Lloyd George, Sir Charles – a wealthy Liberal MP – was so attracted by the chance of basking in the Chancellor's reflected glory that he paid the cost of the trip.

As an exercise in diplomacy, the visit was a failure from the start. The Imperial Chancellor, Bernard von Bülow, rejected the request for a meeting and persuaded the Kaiser not to offer the unwelcome visitor an audience. Lloyd George did, however, meet the Vice-Chancellor of the Interior and discussed the German pension plan, an event which helped to clear his mind on the best way to finance welfare schemes and was to prove invaluable when the King and the Prime Minister – alerted by an interview in the *Frankfurter Zeitung* and reports that Spender had invited the *Berliner Tageblatt* to meet Lloyd George – realised the real purpose of the visit. Asquith telegraphed a categoric instruction: Lloyd George must not discuss shipbuilding or naval rivalry with the Kaiser or any of his ministers. The reply was equally unambiguous. 'I do not propose approaching anyone on the international question. I am confining my investigations to invalid and other pensions.'[28] Twenty years later, when he wrote his memoirs, Spender was more frank. 'A deeper scheme was afoot which was nothing less than persuading the Germans to come to a compromise with England over the bitter competition for armaments.'[29]

However, when Lloyd George returned to Britain on 26 August he behaved with perfect fiscal circumspection. He confined his conversations with the waiting press to the subjects which had been the nominal purpose of his visit. He had 'never realised on what a gigantic scale the [German] pension was constructed . . . Old age pensions form but a comparatively small part of the system. Does the worker fall ill? State insurance comes to his aid.'★[30]

Lloyd George had been thinking of fiscal innovations ever since he arrived at the Treasury in May. By the summer he felt able to discuss with Sir Robert Chalmers, the chairman of the Inland Revenue, the prospect of putting into force what, during his political youth, had been his main preoccupation – a tax on land which encouraged improved husbandry and fell most heavily on landowners whose income from sale or rent increased because of added value which they had done nothing to bring about. But although he knew that his hope of extending 'workman's insurance' would not be realised that year, the idea still preoccupied him. Amateur diplomacy aside, his visit to Germany had allowed an examination of the contributory system – a subject which raised violent actuarial passions. The expedition had been preceded by a meeting with the parliamentary agents of the National Conference of Friendly Societies – men who had so much influence in Parliament that they could prevent the passage of a bill which harmed their interests. Lloyd George had assured them that nothing would be done to undermine the private (contributory) insurance schemes.

Lloyd George knew that his plans to extend social security were a political as well as a moral necessity. In March 1908, a letter from Winston Churchill published in the *Nation* had warned that the Liberal Party must begin to address social issues or die.[31] It was a variation on a theme which readers of the *Westminster Gazette* knew well. The

---

★In Germany there had been sickness insurance since 1883, accident insurance since 1884 and old-age pensions since 1889. On the other side of Bismarck's coin were the Exceptional Laws, introduced in 1878. They prohibited the propagation of socialism.

month before, in an article entitled 'Liberalism without Ideas', the newspaper had warned that the Unionists – boasting about the policies which could be financed by the income provided by Imperial Preference – were beginning to adopt the language of social reform.[32] Perhaps the conversion was not genuine. But it made it all the more urgent that someone in the Liberal Party 'pick up the torch' which 'was held so bravely in the old days' by Joseph Chamberlain. Lloyd George believed himself to be that man. Ideas buzzed about his head all summer. By September, he was ready with at least tentative suggestions about what the next step forward should be. He hoped to introduce a scheme of compulsory unemployment insurance which would provide a benefit of ten shillings a week. On the assumption that the rate of unemployment was 3–4 per cent, it would cost £7 million in a full year – £5 million would be raised from the participants in the scheme and £2 million from the state.[33]

A month later, in Swansea, he ran up the flag of 'New Liberalism'. By then the prospect of the Lords rejecting every item of progressive legislation was overshadowing all that the government did. So he was able to begin with a plausible excuse for so little having been achieved. 'We would have done more but for the malignant destructiveness of the House of Lords. Three of the greatest measures the government laboriously carried through the Commons have been slaughtered in the charnel house across the road and they are now menacing the life of a fourth.'* The ritual denunciation finished, he turned to the need for the Liberal Party to change.

> The old Liberals in this country used the national discontent of the people with poverty and precariousness of the means of subsistence as motive to win them a better, more influential, more honourable status in the citizenship of their native land. The new Liberalism, while pursuing this great political ideal with unflinching energy, devotes part of its endeavour also to the removing of the immediate cause of discontent. It is true that man cannot live by bread alone. It is equally true that man cannot live without bread. Let Liberalism proceed with its glorious work of building up Liberalism in this country. But let it also bear in mind that the worshippers at that shrine have to live.
>
> It is a recognition of that elemental fact that has prompted

---

*The Education, Valuation and Plural Voting, and the Licensing Bills.

legislation like the Old Age Pension Act. But it is just a beginning of things. We are still confronted with the more gigantic task of dealing with the rest – the sick, the infirm, the unemployed, the widows, the orphans.[34]

In fact, evidence collected and analysed twenty years later suggests that eradicating destitution in old age was, as well as only 'the beginning of things', an assault on the most emotive, though only the third most frequent, cause of urban poverty. Data from five representative towns confirms that 'primary poverty (insufficient income to meet the needs of physical efficiency)' was most commonly the result of the starvation wages earned by the breadwinners in working families. Second came the death of the chief wage earner. Only in Stanley, a mining town where working lives ended early, did the blame lie with 'chief wage earner ill or old'. In those days, families that could afford it looked after the old.[35] '[R]eciprocity between the generations, mutual support in times of need, was as notable as the dependency of aged parents'.[36]

The speech, like all major Liberal speeches of the time, ended with a warning to the House of Lords. Some Liberals believed that a Lords veto on the taxes which were needed to finance the government's contribution to unemployment benefit was too reckless for the peers to contemplate. Lloyd George thought it an increasing probability. If the will of the people, as represented by the decisions of the House of Commons, were to be frustrated by an hereditary and unrepresentative second chamber, 'then we shall invite the electorate of this country to arm us with the authority to use the most effective means of removing this senseless barrier from the path of progress'.[37] New Liberalism was ready for battle.

CHAPTER 14

WOMEN TROUBLE

Lloyd George's brief trespass on Foreign Office territory had antagonised not only Edward Grey. The excursion to Germany had damaged his reputation with many more colleagues because of the company he kept. There were deep suspicions that he had committed the unforgivable sin of entering into a relationship with the wife of another Member. While Lloyd George was in Germany, Asquith had talked to J. A. Pease, a junior whip, about his Chancellor's involvement with Lady Henry. The Prime Minister had been assured that the scandalous rumour was 'founded on a platonic relationship due to a pushing American heiress' – an absolution which, because Pease was known to dislike Lloyd George, carried special weight.[1] The evidence suggests that Pease was wrong. Letters, sent the following year from Lady Henry to Lloyd George, complain of his neglect in terms which suggest that in 1908 he had been far from negligent.[2] Halfway through the German tour he wrote home to Margaret to say that Lady Henry had left the party.[3] Gratuitous assurances of fidelity were often a sign that he was engaged in an amorous escapade. Whatever the truth about his friendship with Lady Henry, rumours about a scandalous relationship with someone had reached the newspapers. The first hint of impropriety had been published in the 29th July edition of the *Bystander*, a small-circulation weekly magazine. It was first on sale while Lloyd George was in Germany.

It began – as such stories often do – with a legitimate and wholly accurate revelation of real political news. Lloyd George had failed in his attempt to reduce the Army Estimates. Then it asserted that:

Not only is he having a most uncomfortable time of it politically . . .
but it is rumoured that he is now anxious as to the existence of
embarrassment of another kind, which is even less likely to prove of
assistance to his career. Mr George has, of course, been over-loaded
with flattery of late, especially from the fair sex which it is difficult
for a man of 'temperament' to resist. The matter may, of course, be
kept quiet. Also it may not. 'Nous verrons'.

By chance, Lloyd George had agreed to sit for a portrait to be painted
by Sir Luke Fildes, a director of the Graphic Company, which published
the *Bystander*. His first instinct was to write privately to Sir Luke in the
hope of attaining a swift retraction. Several letters were drafted, but
none was sent. Instead he instituted libel proceedings. The *Bystander*
apologised, published a complete retraction and paid three hundred
guineas to the Caernarvon Cottage Hospital. The first episode in a year
of potential scandal had ended happily.

Six months later the *People* printed an even more serious allegation.[4]
It did not name Lloyd George but it was clear that he was the 'prominent politician' who was about to be cited as the co-respondent in a
divorce case when his friends found an 'alternative' way of satisfying the
aggrieved husband. No politician could have survived an uncontested
allegation that he had bought his way out of exposure for what was then
a 'matrimonial offence'. Again his first instinct was to seek redress outside the courts and George Riddell approached W. T. Madge, the
People's managing director, with a request for an apology. It was
rejected. The case came to court on 12 March, less than a week before
Lloyd George presented to the Cabinet the most contentious clauses of
the 1909 Budget.

Richard Lloyd George – a far more prejudiced witness against his
father than J. A. Pease – repeats what he claims to be a verbatim account
of his parents' conversation on the day of the trial. 'You must help me
Maggie. If I get over this, I give my oath you shall never have to suffer
this ordeal again.'[5] If the story is true, only her husband's pleadings persuaded Margaret Lloyd George to accompany him to court, where he
was represented by Rufus Isaacs (destined later to become Lord Chief
Justice of England), supported by F. E. Smith (a future Lord Chancellor)
and Raymond Asquith (the Prime Minister's son). The *People* had
retained Edward Carson, the most formidable advocate of his day. But,
despite the star qualities of the cast, the performance was undramatic.
Lloyd George swore that there was no truth in the allegations and

Carson, without cross-examination, accepted his word and announced that the *People* was prepared to pay £1000 in damages. When next the Chancellor appeared in the House of Commons, there were cheers from both government and Opposition benches.

The Honourable Members did not know that, after the *People* story was published, Pease had told the Prime Minister that it was generally believed that Lloyd George was a victim of blackmail.[6] Perhaps Pease knew the author of letters which the Chancellor received first on 22 March, less than two weeks after the *People* libel hearing had been reported in the newspapers. They came from a Mrs M. Griffith and reveal some of the most disturbing, as well as possibly the most discreditable, details of Lloyd George's private life. The first referred to previously unacknowledged messages and requested the return of 'the two photos of my little son'. The second asked if he imagined that the writer 'would appeal for help if [she] did not need it in the first place'. It added, 'I am able to see the specialist free, but instruments and such like, I must pay for.' The whole episode – especially in light of the letter's detailed description of the child's painful treatment – might be dismissed as an attempt to touch a famous man's conscience, had the letter not been written in language which suggests that Lloyd George knew Mrs Griffith well. It referred to 'the time you asked me down to Wandsworth', and ended with the hope – half plea and half threat – that it would not be necessary to consult a solicitor.[7] All in all, the evidence – as well Lloyd George's reputation – leads to the conclusion that Mrs Griffith was another conquest.

Lloyd George always insisted that both the *Bystander* and the *People* stories were based on memories of the Edwards affair in 1897, when it was alleged that he had fathered an illegitimate child. But there are letters in the Lloyd George family collection which suggest that even when he was Chancellor of the Exchequer he chose to live dangerously. They are so incriminating that it is hard to understand why Lloyd George chose to keep them.

Between 11 and 13 April, a Gladys Gardner sent him at least six letters – each of them written on paper which was decorated with flowers that spelled the name 'Gladys'. Their contents showed signs of both an immature passion and hope – absurd, whether or not based on false promises from the Chancellor – that she and Lloyd George might enjoy a lasting relationship. During one of the frequent references to her conventional marriage prospects, she wrote that she proposed to remain single because otherwise 'we would find it impossible to continue our

friendship on the purely platonic grounds they are on now'. But the
desire for a different outcome was made obvious in letter after letter. 'If
anything untoward happens – to enable me to be with you – we would
bust a fair amount of the Chancellor's screw on a gorgeous tiara.' Gladys
Gardner was clearly a very silly woman. But as one letter makes clear –
'We have managed so well up to date and nobody has heard a whis-
per' – she was encouraged in her silliness by Lloyd George.[8] Perhaps he
subscribed to her theory of public esteem – a view which has gained
currency with the years. 'Winston would become a million times more
popular if it could be thought that he cared enough for some one
woman to risk even a little discomfort for her sake.'[9] Whatever the
nature of the relationship, it was managed – like so many others – in a
way which protected Lloyd George's career. His technique for escaping
scandal was to enter into relationships entirely on his own terms – conducted in humiliating secrecy and ended without concern for the
women's feelings. He was also lucky. His sexual compulsion was so great
that, in the twenty-first century, it would have been diagnosed as a
psychotic condition. He took the risk because it was beyond his power
to resist.

The rumours of damaging personal revelations and discussions on the
possibility of providing benefit payments to the sick began in the
autumn of 1908, a season during which the business of Parliament and
government was constantly interrupted by the increasingly militant
behaviour of the suffragists.* Campbell-Bannerman had given them his
personal support, though he had warned Emmeline and Christabel
Pankhurst that he could not persuade his colleagues to support the
legislation that would make their aspiration a reality. Lloyd George,
although in favour, took a more political view. To give votes to women
on the limited franchise of 1908 would simply increase the Unionist
vote.

The suffragists reacted to rejection by staging a series of demonstrations to exhibit the strength of their support. A procession of thirty
thousand men and women marched through London. The Pankhursts,
claiming that the streets were lined with half a million sympathisers,
made a formal request to meet the Prime Minister. It was refused.
Months of sporadic violence followed, climaxing in the autumn of 1908

---

*The word 'suffragette' was invented by the *Daily Mail* as a term of abuse, taken up
by the *Daily Mirror* because it sounded young and irrepressible and then accepted by
the women themselves. History made it the noun which denoted violent intentions.

with an invitation to 'Help the Suffragettes to Rush the House of Commons on October 13'. On Sunday 11 October, six thousand women assembled in Trafalgar Square to be briefed on the plan of attack. Emmeline and Christabel were arrested and charged with conduct likely to cause a breach of the peace. Christabel, who had just graduated from London University with a first-class law degree, defended herself. When she heard that Lloyd George had been in the Trafalgar Square crowd with the Home Secretary, she called him as a witness for the defence.

CP: You were not alone, I think.
DLG: No, I had my little girl with me.
CP: How old is she?
DLG: She is six.
CP: Did you think it safe to bring her out?
DLG: Certainly. She was amused, not frightened.

Max Beerbohm, who was in the gallery, marvelled at the 'contrast between the elation of the girl and the depression of statesman', who had been trapped by her question into either admitting that he had exposed his daughter to danger or agreeing that the peace had not been seriously broken.[10] Despite the unusual, and unwelcome, experience of being beaten in debate, Lloyd George continued to give friendly evidence.

CP: I want to ask you if, whether in your opinion, the whole of the agitation which these women carried on, very much against the grain, would be immediately stopped if women got their constitutional rights?
DLG: I should think that is very likely.
CP: I want to ask you whether, in your opinion, the women who are in the dock here today are women who are ordinary lawbreakers or would have occasion to come into this court for any other than political reasons.
DLG: No, of course not.

But the cross-examination changed nothing. Christabel Pankhurst was convicted and Lloyd George continued to support 'Votes for Women' if and when suffrage were extended to all adults. On 6 December, he was advertised as the main speaker at a rally organised in the Albert Hall by the Women's Liberal Federation.

After he was warned of the likelihood of the rally being interrupted – perhaps even broken up – by the more militant suffragists, the veteran of the Birmingham Town Hall wrote a note to the Home Secretary. 'As to this Pankhurst business, I agree with you. Let them break up the meeting – a meeting specially convened to support the suffrage movement. That would be the pinnacle of their folly. I have no desire to speak by gracious permission of Queen Christabel.'[11]

Lloyd George spoke in front of a backdrop made up of the wives and daughters of Cabinet ministers, but he did not speak for long before sections of the nine-thousand-strong audience began to heckle him with the interruption which was invariably employed against politicians who supported the suffragist cause: 'Deeds not words. Deeds not words.' Sixty protesters were removed from the hall. On several occasions Lloyd George sat down and silently waited for order to be restored. After two hours, the manager suggested that the rally be abandoned. Lloyd George could not agree. He had an important announcement to make. The hall fell silent, waiting for the momentous news. The government, Lloyd George solemnly announced, would introduce a new Reform Bill before Parliament was dissolved. An amendment would be moved which extended the franchise to women and – since it was supported by most Liberal MPs, including members of the Cabinet – it would certainly be carried into law. The news was greeted with rapturous applause even though it had been common knowledge for some months. The Albert Hall rally ended in harmony.

CHAPTER 15

THE PEOPLE'S DAVID

O n 21 April 1909, Lloyd George – speaking in Manchester a week before Budget Day – told his audience that he was 'a man of the people, bred among them. It has been the greatest joy of my life to have some part in fighting the battles of the class from whom I am proud to have sprung.'[1] The People's Chancellor was about to launch the People's Budget. Measured by what it provided for the following year, the 1908 Budget – which announced that an old-age pension would be in place by the end of the year – was more entitled to that emotive description. But in 1909 – as well as promising extensions to the welfare programme in years to come – Lloyd George more than justified the name he gave his Budget by the income side of his fiscal equation. For the first time taxes – required to finance the old-age pension – had a greater purpose than raising enough revenue to match the expenditure side of the national balance sheet and, as a subsidiary object, discouraging undesirable activities like the consumption of gin and the importation of corn. Taxes became the engine of social policy – the sinews of the war against poverty and the modest beginning of investment in employment. And, just as important, the necessary money was to be raised by tax changes which were expressly designed to take from the rich in order to give to the poor. It could be argued that Lloyd George led a timid revolution. The proposals affected only twelve thousand individuals and only eighty thousand men and women were required to pay estate duties. But new principles had been established. New Liberalism had evolved from theory into practice.

Winston Churchill – the most radical member of Asquith's peacetime

Cabinet – was the first politician of note to speak up for New Liberalism. But it was Lloyd George who gave meaning to the party's new idea. At the time, some of the intellectuals who hoped for a radical dawn regarded Churchill as more likely than Lloyd George to provide the impetus for which they hoped. Beatrice Webb was typical. After meeting Lloyd George at Churchill's suggestion 'to discuss the insurance schemes', she compared the new Chancellor to his successor as President of the Board of Trade and concluded that 'he is a clever fellow but has less intellect and not such an attractive personality – more of the preacher, less of the statesman'.[2] She was certainly wrong about the intellect and probably wrong about the attraction, as Churchill would have certainly conceded. He accepted that he was the junior member of the partnership for reasons which went far beyond Lloyd George's seniority in years and length of parliamentary service. In 1928, Churchill, completing the last volume of *The World Crisis*, met Lloyd George to check some of the facts. When it was over, he told Robert Boothby – his parliamentary private secretary and devoted apostle – that the meeting had gone well but 'Within five minutes the old relationship between us was completely re-established. The relationship between master and servant. And I was the servant.'[3]

That description of the partnership – which so infuriated other members of the Cabinet – was, of course, an example of Churchillian exaggeration. But there is no doubt that Lloyd George was the senior partner in a political alliance which became a genuine, if unlikely, friendship. Lloyd George, despite his dislike of dukes, visited Blenheim but preserved his independence by deserting his host on Sunday morning in order to search for a Nonconformist service – which he found, in a slightly unusual form, at a revivalist meeting in the bracing fresh air of Blenheim Park. Because of him, the Bishop of St Asaph officiated at Churchill's wedding to Clementine Hozier in St Margaret's Church, Westminster, and he was the only witness not a member of either the bride's or the groom's family to sign the marriage register. In 1914, Churchill claimed that they were so close that, for ten years, barely a day passed without their talking together for an hour.[4] Whatever Beatrice Webb may have chosen to believe, Lloyd George was the greater pioneering spirit. But it is doubtful if he could have chartered the new territory of social policy without Churchill's support.

Despite the flamboyancy of their self-promotion – and the claims of envious colleagues – both men worked assiduously at the less spectacular duties which a departmental minister is required to perform.* Lloyd George, on his return from Germany, began the tedious necessity of reconciling the leaders of the Friendly Societies – representing four million members, most of whom had a strong connection with the Liberal Party – to an extension of state-sponsored insurance. David Shackleton, the president of the Trades Union Congress, had told his annual conference that the Home Secretary was about to set up a Royal Commission to examine the possibility of the government moving on from pensions to sickness and unemployment benefits. That had been enough to convince the Friendly Societies that, despite Lloyd George's earlier assurances, the government was about to compete with them on terms – lower payments for tax-subsidised higher benefits – they could not match. They demanded a meeting to discuss the Royal Commission's membership and the terms of reference. Lloyd George responded with an invitation to breakfast at the Treasury during which they were assured that there would be no Royal Commission and that nothing was closer to the Chancellor's heart than the future of the Friendly Societies. He gave no assurance that the state would not advance into their territory, but they left satisfied that the future of their movement was secure.

It was at a larger breakfast in Downing Street, three days later, when Beatrice Webb – working away on the Royal Commission on the Poor Law – first met Lloyd George and came to the almost instant conclusion about his character and capabilities. She and Sidney Webb, her husband, were there – together with Churchill, Haldane and Harold Cox, a Liberal backbench pension expert – to discuss how protection against sickness and unemployment could best be organised. The Webbs were passionate opponents of contributory schemes, which they thought amounted to the levying of a flat-rate tax. Lloyd George supported the insurance principle, and not only because it reduced the tax liability. A man who paid into a scheme would receive its benefits by right. As a result payment could not be made contingent on good behaviour. The disagreement typified the gulf – temperamental as well as intellectual – which separated Lloyd George and the Webbs. Lloyd George was neither egalitarian nor, in this particular, judgemental. The Webbs were both. It was three years after the first encounter before he asked for their

---

*Roy Jenkins judged that Churchill's twenty-four months at the Board of Trade yielded better results than Lloyd George's twenty-six. But Jenkins was writing a biography of Churchill.

advice again. During the intervening years their ideas were transmitted to the Cabinet and its committees by Haldane.

Lloyd George met the Friendly Society officers four times more before the end of 1908. At the third meeting he described his plan for invalidity and disability insurance. It had been devised with the express purpose of both providing universal protection and safeguarding the interests of the insurance societies by the simple expedient of making them the providers of the state system. Men not already in a society would be required to join one and subscribe to its scheme. Their contributions, together with the state subsidy, would finance a five-shilling weekly sickness, disability and widow benefit. An additional one and sixpence a week would be paid for every dependent child. The payments were substantially smaller than those provided by the societies' schemes – in many cases, barely half. That was, in itself, an assurance that the Friendly Societies could retain the membership of most of their existing subscribers. But Lloyd George offered an even greater incentive to acceptance and cooperation. Men who had already invested in private policies would not be required to contribute to the state system. But the society by which they were insured would receive, on their behalf, the state subsidy. 'Profit-making societies' – which distributed the occasional end-of-year surplus between their subscribers – would be excluded. So the benefit club to which Uncle Lloyd had belonged in Llanystumdwy was disqualified on the grounds that, at the end of the year, funds not paid out in benefits were spent on a members' supper.

The Friendly Societies – being cautious by nature and necessity – would not give even their approval in principle until they had made their own costings and concluded their own feasibility study. That, they said, would take at least a year. So, on 15 December 1908, Lloyd George accepted with good grace that, although he would speculate about the scheme in his 1909 Budget statement, there would be no sickness and disability insurance before 1910. It was a reluctant concession but, until they were sure they were safe, the Friendly Societies would not give their approval. Without it, the bill would meet the fate which had destroyed Joseph Chamberlain's bill in 1890.

Lloyd George's willingness to wait was undoubtedly influenced by the decision of the Unionist peers – taken ten days after his second meeting with the Friendly Societies – to reject the Licensing Bill. It had been debated for thirty-two and a half parliamentary days in the House of Commons and was voted down in one afternoon by the House of Lords – despite the government's having made the concession that compensation for lost licences would continue until 1929 rather than 1922. The Unionists' decision was a declaration of war.

The more belligerent backbenchers called for an immediate dissolution so that the nation could condemn the peers' behaviour. Wisely most MPs realised that temperance – a pillar of Old Liberal policy – was not the emotive issue among the Edwardian public that it had been in Victorian England. Asquith told the King that the Cabinet was not sure what to do next.[5] But it was clear that he had a plan – or that he had accepted one which had been devised by the Chancellor of the Exchequer. On the same day that the confession of indecision was sent to Windsor Castle, Lloyd George wrote to his brother. 'No dissolution at least until the Budget is over. The Prime Minister has approved my plans as they are.'[6] Asquith himself, on the same evening, made a speech to the National Liberal Club which contained a hint of his intentions. The election date could not be decided by Lord Lansdowne and his Unionist friends.

> I invite the Liberal Party . . . to treat the veto of the House of Lords as the dominating issue in politics . . . The Budget of next year will stand at the very centre of our work. Finance is an instrument of great potency and also of great flexibility . . . It may be found to be, in some directions at any rate, a partial solvent of what, under our existing constitutional conditions, would otherwise be insoluble problems.[7]

The government proposed to test the Lords' resolve by carrying through the Commons a Finance Bill which was anathema to most members of the Upper House. 'Supply' had been the sole prerogative of the elected chamber since 1678. The peers would, in consequence, be faced with the choice of either endorsing a fiscal programme which they abhorred or ignoring one of the conventions which made up Britain's unwritten constitution.

There is no doubt that ministers relished the thought of confronting the Lords with such unpalatable alternatives. Winston Churchill told Lucy Masterman, wife of Charles Masterman, by then an up-and-coming junior minister, 'We shall send them up such a Budget in June as shall terrify them. They have started a class war. They had better be careful.'[8] And Lloyd George, a week before Christmas 1908, heightened the tension with the claim that a defeat for the Finance Bill would be a victory for tariff reform and the hated bread tax.

We mean to raise the taxes of the – now, I am not going to tell any secrets. Yes I will. I will take you into my confidence. I mean to raise taxes in a way that will not interfere with any productive industry in this country . . . If [the Unionists] want to put the alternative of taxing bread, by all means let them do it.

The speech ended with what was to become familiar vituperation, not so much against the House of Lords as against the peers themselves. They were described as 'stuff bottled in the Dark Ages . . . not fit to drink, cobwebby, dusty, muddy, sour'.[9] The personal attacks continued and grew in ferocity during the long controversy about the Budget and its contents. The violence of Lloyd George's language was a major contribution to the suspicion that he wanted the House of Lords to reject the Finance Bill and meant to provoke them into doing so.

That was certainly the view of some of those who were closest to the Chancellor. 'Those who knew Lloyd George's mind in those days knew also that he foresaw and planned a first rejection by the Lords and endorsement by the country following an attack on the veto to which the Peers, whatever their tactics, were bound to succumb'[10] and, twenty-five years later, in *The Strange Death of Liberal England*, George Dangerfield wrote of 'a Budget crying out to be vetoed. It was like a kid which sportsmen tie to a tree to persuade a tiger to its death.'[11] In old age – reminiscing with Randolph Churchill about the Budget battle – Lloyd George endorsed the view that he had always hoped that the Lords would encompass their own destruction by rejecting the Finance Bill. The evidence of how he behaved and what he said at the time suggests that his judgement about tactics changed as the constitutional debate raged on.

At first Lloyd George regarded a Lords veto as inconceivable. According to Lord Riddell, his friend and mentor, he 'ridiculed the rumour that the Peers would or could interfere with or reject the Budget'.[12] And he rejoiced at his 'exquisite plan of outwitting [them] over licensing' by including the provisions of the defeated Licensing Bill in a Finance Bill which they were constitutionally bound to approve.[13] As late as 1 May 1909 – after the Budget statement had been made – he wrote to his brother in jubilation. He not only wanted but expected the Finance Bill to become law. 'Prime Minister delighted at [the Budget's] reception. The most extraordinary thing is the way the City have taken it. F. E. Smith told me the Lords are not such fools as to throw it out. "Do you think they are mad?" he said to me.'[14]

A year later, when the constitutional crisis was at its height, Lloyd George actually canvassed the possibility of creating a coalition in order to avoid a head-on collision between Commons and Lords. His record – before and after 1909 – confirmed that death or glory was not his style. He was a man who did deals – often hiding his willingness to compromise behind aggressive language, as his complicated manoeuvring on the 1902 Education Bill had demonstrated. There is little doubt that, at first, he wanted to see the Budget proposals become law. They had been his publicly declared aims since his Newcastle speech in April 1908, and in December *The Times* – clearly inspired by him – had announced that the Cabinet was about to approve proposals for graduated income tax, land valuation, increased licence duties, labour exchanges and invalidity and unemployment insurance. The discovery that insurance would have to wait for the approval of the Friendly Societies was not enough to make him feel that the Budget was expendable. The 'plan' which he had agreed with the Prime Minister was meant to end with the peers humbling themselves by accepting a radical Budget into which were incorporated bills which they had previously rejected. The plan worked, although it took two rather than one year to accomplish.

Lloyd George's preparations were complicated by continual demands for increases in the Naval Estimates. The Admiralty, with Reginald McKenna arguing robustly on its behalf, was indefatigable in its demand for Dreadnoughts. The First Sea Lord, John Arbuthnot Fisher, had produced estimates of the German fleet which suggested that, for the Royal Navy to retain its superiority, it would be necessary to build six to eight Dreadnoughts in 1909–10 and six more in 1910–11. Lloyd George complained to the Prime Minister about the 'crude and ill-considered Admiralty demands. I will not dwell,' the letter continued, 'on the emphatic pledges given by us before and during the general election campaign to reduce the gigantic expenditure on armaments built up by our predecessors . . . But if Tory extravagance on armaments is seen to be exceeded, Liberals . . . will hardly think it worth their while to make any effort to keep in office a Liberal ministry.' The Admiralty's proposals were, he wrote, 'a poor compromise between two scares – fear of the German navy abroad and fear of the Radical majority at home . . . You alone can save us from the prospect of squalid and sterile destruction.'[15]

Asquith – sympathetic but angered by accounts of Lloyd George's complaints about the Admiralty, which had been published in the *Daily*

News and *Daily Chronicle* – brokered an agreement which barely saved his Chancellor's face. The Navy League's campaign – 'We Want Eight and We Won't Wait' – was accommodated by plans for four Dreadnoughts to be built in 1909–10 with the possibility of four more to be laid down during the following year. Lloyd George let it be known that he regarded the decision as a betrayal of the party. 'Ll-G's remarks were, I believe,' the Prime Minister told the Foreign Secretary, 'resented by the whole Cabinet with the doubtful exception of Winston.'[16] The behaviour of both men in tirelessly arguing for cuts in the Army and Navy estimates was certainly resented by Asquith. 'Winston and LlG, by their combined machinations, have got the bulk of the Liberal Party into the same camp . . . They go about darkly hinting at resignation (which is their bluff) but there are moments when I am inclined summarily to cashier them both.'[17]

Churchill – in his radical phase – was Lloyd George's adjutant throughout the battle for the 1909 Budget. But occasionally, as was his nature, he assumed temporary command. On 29 December 1908, he had sent the Prime Minister what amounted to a whole legislative pro-gramme which included 'national infirmity insurance', even though he accepted that it could not come into force until the Friendly Societies were reconciled to their new role. The President of the Board of Trade had begun his submission with a call to arms.

> The need is urgent and the moment ripe. Germany with a harder climate and far less accumulated wealth has managed to establish tolerable basic conditions for her people. She is organised not only for war, but for peace. We are organised for nothing except party politics . . . I say thrust a big slice of Bismarckism over the whole underside of our industrial system.[18]

Bismarckism was, paradoxically, to become the political philosophy which, after Germany's defeat in 1918, Lloyd George attempted to 'thrust' on Great Britain. Churchill's early instalment was a programme of 'the class of legislation which the Lords will not oppose'. It included 'Labour exchanges and unemployment insurance, special expansive state industries, Afforestation, Roads. Modernised Poor Law. Railway Amalgamation with State Control Guarantee and Education Compulsory till seventeen'. For the next two years, Churchill and Lloyd George were to be locked in not always friendly rivalry for the title of Radical-in-Chief.

Richard Lloyd – no sacrifice was too great.

David Lloyd George at sixteen – the object of his admiration.

Getty Images

FOUR LIBERAL PRIME MINISTERS

William Ewart Gladstone – 'A worse
man would have been a better politician.'

PA Archive/Press Association Images

Lord Rosebery – 'Sought the palms
without the dust.'

Getty Images

Henry Campbell-Bannerman, who
rebuked A. J. Balfour in the early days
of the Liberal government – 'Enough
of this tomfoolery.'

Illustrated London News/MEPL

Herbert Henry Asquith – 'The last of
the Romans.'

MEPL

A STUDY IN CONTRASTS

David Lloyd George during the
early years of his marriage.
Hulton Deutsch Collection/Corbis

Margaret Lloyd George at
about the same time.
MEPL

1910 – The promise of 'insurance against unemployment and invalidity'.
Illustrated London News/MEPL

1914 – 'The parliamentary draftsmen let me down.'
Getty Images

Lloyd George with his daughter Megan – a passionate
defender of her mother's dignity.

Getty Images

'Apart from the occasional game of golf, women were his only relaxation.'

Getty Images

AN AGREEMENT TO DISAGREE

G.R.

That this House, ~~having heard~~ *accepts* *after hearing* the statements of
the Attorney General and Chancellor of the Exchequer,
in reference to their purchase of Shares in the Marconi
Company of America, ~~accepts and approves those statements~~,
and, ~~while~~ deeming it ~~to be a duty~~ to record its
reprobation of the false charges of the gravest description
brought against ~~those~~ Ministers, without the ~~slightest~~
foundation, ~~desires further to put on record the undisputed
fact that there is no ground whatever for any imputation
of corruption,~~ undue influence, or ~~want of~~ good faith.

accepts
More
Statements

devoid of

in satisfied they acted with honestly & in

good faith

Draft of Resolution submitted June to the

Prime Minister & corrected in his own

hand.

18: vi: 13.

The Cabinet attempted, without success, to express its collective judgement
on the 'Marconi scandal'.

James Illingworth

'Pussy' – Frances Stevenson at
the time she met Lloyd George.

Mrs Jennifer Longford

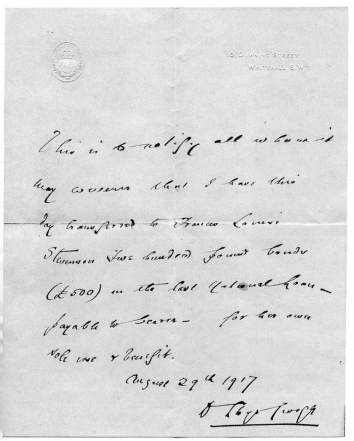

'This is to notify all
whom it may concern
that I have this day
transferred to Frances
Louise Stevenson five
hundred pound bonds
(£500) in the last
notional loan –
payable to bearer – for
her own sole use &
benefit. August 29th
1917' – letter from
Prime Minister Lloyd
George to Frances
Stevenson.

Mrs Jennifer Longford

THE MEN WHO MADE LLOYD GEORGE PRIME MINISTER

Andrew Bonar Law – 'Greater cordiality than is usual between political adversaries.'

Getty Images

George Nathaniel Curzon – 'Bombastic commonplaces … his stock-in-trade'.

Getty Images

Arthur Balfour – 'He saw much of life from afar.'

Getty Images

Austen Chamberlain – 'Always played the game and always lost it.'

Popperfoto/Getty Images

The creation of labour exchanges was already agreed, but before Lloyd George could think about finding finance for new programmes – Churchill's or his own – he had to decide how to raise the revenue which was needed to cover the cost of the first full year of old-age pension and the naval building programme – together estimated to total £15,762,000. It was an opportunity to return to what he had always believed to be a foolishly (or corruptly) neglected source of revenue – land taxes. Not all of his proposals survived. He told Herbert Lewis that he had won the grudging agreement of the Cabinet's Economic Committee by bullying its members. The Attorney General was accused of 'concern for the slum owners' and the Lord Chancellor of being more protective of his 'friends the Dukes' than of the national interest.[19] In the case of the Lord Chancellor, the charge was unjustified, although many Old Liberals in the country were certainly opposed to land taxes in principle, as were the lawyers in the party who believed that some of Lloyd George's proposals offended the sacred law of contract.

The Cabinet accepted three of Lloyd George's five proposals – a 20 per cent tax on increased land values which were not attributable to the owners' improvement or development, a halfpenny in the pound tax on the capital value of undeveloped land, and 10 per cent duty on the profit made by lessors on the termination of a lease. Together they contributed barely £500,000 towards liquidating the total deficit of nearly £16 million. But they were a demonstration of Lloyd George's determination to rob the roosts of the most prosperous hens – as well as a reflection of his profound belief in the injustice of vast wealth accruing to landowners as a result of industrial expansion in which they had played no part. They could not be levied without national land valuation. So the Finance Bill could legitimately include the clauses of the Land Valuation Bill which the House of Lords had rejected. And land valuation was necessary for the further assault on landowners which Lloyd George intended.★

Fifteen and a half million pounds had to be raised to finance Dreadnoughts, old-age pensions, Churchill's labour exchanges, a small 'Development Fund' to stimulate employment and the improvement of national highways through the work of a National Road Fund. Abandoning his predecessor's rule of prudence, Lloyd George reduced repayment of the national debt from £28 million to £25 million. The

★In May 1912 he told Lord Riddell, 'I only put [land taxes] in the Budget because I could not get a valuation without them.'[20]

rest was found from a combination of increases in old taxes and the invention of new. Petrol was taxed at 3d a gallon and motor vehicle licences were graduated according to the horsepower of the car. Asquith, in his second Budget, had imposed different rates of tax on earned and unearned income and ignored the previously sacrosanct principle that income tax should be levied at a flat rate. Lloyd George built on those progressive foundations. Income tax was increased from 1/- to 1/2 in the pound on unearned income and on earned income of over £3000 a year – introducing, for the first time, what came to be called 'supertax'. There were increases in stamp, estate and spirit duties – requiring a revival of the Licensing Laws which the Lords had rejected. The eventual tax package was what survived from fourteen Cabinet meetings at which the various proposals were discussed in groups – land taxes in mid-March, excise duties at the end of the month, income tax and estate duties in early April and the overall pattern of the Budget after Easter.

The First Commissioner of Works, Lewis Harcourt (the son of William, the former Chancellor of the Exchequer, and a man who seemed happy to accept the clearly pejorative sobriquet 'Loulou') was 'the most inveterate in obstructing the proposals while posing all the time as an ardent radical'.[21] Harcourt warned that 'the Budget will ensure the triumph of tariff reform' by guaranteeing the Unionists' re-election.[22] He wrote to Asquith to complain that the 'Cabinet have not realised the savagery of the scale [of income tax increases] on men of moderate means'.[23] The Marquess of Crewe, Leader of the House of Lords, and Walter Runciman, President of the Board of Education, theoretical radicals themselves, demonstrated their doubts by remaining silent. Churchill was steadfast throughout and the Prime Minister – 'who had real sympathy for the poor'[24] – backed Lloyd George 'through thick and thin and with splendid loyalty'.[25]

The Budget statement, made on 29 April 1909, lasted for four and a half hours – not including the half-hour adjournment which was proposed by Arthur Balfour, the leader of the Opposition, in order to revive what was left of the Chancellor's voice. Hilaire Belloc, a Liberal Member of Parliament at the time, believed it to be the worst speech in the history of the House of Commons.[26] More sympathetic observers thought it only the worst in living memory. It began, unpropitiously, with a justification for the extended naval building programme in which Lloyd George did not believe. He then moved on to what he thought important.

All we have to do to put ourselves on a level with Germany – I hope our competition with Germany will not be in armaments alone – is to make some further provision for the sick, for the invalided, for widows and orphans. In a well-thought-out scheme, involving contributions from the classes directly concerned, the proportion borne by the state need not, in my judgement, be a heavy one and is well within the compass of our financial capacity ... The Government are also pledged to deal on a comprehensive scale with the problems of unemployment.

Putting aside the creation of labour exchanges and the £50,000 allocated to promoting basic industries, that passage of the Budget statement dealt with future hopes rather than immediate proposals. The peroration – though magnificent – was equally a statement of aspiration rather than of policy.

This is a war Budget. It is for raising money to wage implacable warfare against poverty and squalidness. I cannot help hoping and believing that before this generation has passed away we shall have advanced a great step towards that good time when poverty and human degradation (which always follows in its camp) will be as remote to the people of this country as the wolves which once infested its forests.[27]

Lloyd George was not disturbed by the poor reception which his speech received. 'He had determined from the start that he would not aim at hwyl and oratory. He had another aim – to set down a manifesto.' Austen Chamberlain – replying for the Opposition and no doubt recalling that his father made his radical reputation by arguing for an old-age pension – was surprisingly sympathetic. 'With a great deal of what he said and with a number of the objects he had set out before the House, I for one heartily agree.'[28] But the ecumenical spirit did not last for long. During the days between the Budget statement and the debate the mood changed. Balfour, having anticipated the invention of the 'trickle-down effect' by emphasising the importance of rich men to the community, went on to denounce the Budget in language that more recent Opposition leaders have copied. Not only was it 'arbitrary and unjust'. It had given 'a shock to confidence and credit from which it will take a long time to recover'.[29] More ominous, Viscount Ridley offered the Conservative peers a justification for breaking with precedent. 'The

Lords should not interfere with the Budget while the country's finances were in the hands of sane men, but now there was a House of Commons controlled by a pack of madmen, they had to take different measures.'[30]

Increasingly both the government and Opposition saw the Budget as offering the economic alternative to tariff reform. In many ways the battle was merely symbolic, but Joseph Chamberlain, still deeply influential among Unionists though absent from active politics because of a stroke, had no doubt that if Lloyd George's programme was accepted and implemented, Imperial Preference would be denied the argument that commended it to the working class – only the income from import duties could finance old-age pensions and disability insurance. The notion that passing the Budget would guarantee the survival of free trade widened and deepened the argument. But in truth the real dispute was a class struggle – haves versus have-nots.

In the country, opposition to the Budget built up slowly. A fortnight after Budget Day, Martin's Bank announced that copies of a petition condemning the tax increases were available for signature in all of its branches.[31] Two weeks later, a Budget Protest League was formed. One of its meetings, held under the chairmanship of Lord Rothschild in the Cannon Street Hotel, attracted a thousand supporters – most of them from the City. That afternoon a Budget League was formed – with Winston Churchill as its president – to defend the Chancellor's proposals. On the same day in Glasgow, Lord Rosebery – a Whig rather than a radical and, by nature, perverse – issued a statement which, in terms of propaganda, was to prove far more important than anything that happened in the capital. The Budget, he said, 'was not a Budget but a revolution'. The anti-Budget campaign had acquired both a justification and a slogan.

For some weeks Lloyd George responded to the criticism with a moderation of language which sometimes bordered on the jovial. 'The inevitable Lord Rothschild' had, he said, claimed that

the Budget was Socialism and Collectivism.* Now I wonder if he knows what Socialism means. I am sure he does not. I suppose it would be too much to ask a financier ruined by the Budget to spend any money on political literature, but I think it would be

---

*It was not the first time that the Budget had been so described. Ben Tillett, the dockers' trade union leader, had already written to *The Times* (24 May 1909) to complain that the comparison was 'a libel on Socialism'.

money very well spent . . . if someone should present him with a
sixpenny handbook on Socialism.[32]

When Lord Lansdowne told the National Union of Conservative
Associations that the House of Lords 'was likely to proclaim that it has
no responsibility for the Bill' it was Churchill who thought it his duty
to reply. 'No amendments, no excision, no modifying or mutilating will
be agreed by us.' If the Lords committed any of those crimes,
'Parliament will be dissolved and we shall come to you on a matter of
high consequence for every cause for which Liberalism has ever
fought.'[33]

At the next Cabinet meeting, Asquith formally rebuked Churchill for
taking upon himself the responsibility of setting out government policy
on so crucial a subject as the dissolution of Parliament – particularly
since the agreed strategy was to dismiss the possibility of the Lords
rejecting the Budget as inconceivable. Influential voices within the
Cabinet – led by Haldane – were arguing for the bill to be amended in
the hope that a tactical retreat would outflank the Unionist peers. Lloyd
George had no doubt they were wrong. 'To drop that part of the Bill
which excites most enthusiasm among our friends would be so
deplorably weak that it must, inevitably, lead to disaster.' Still haunted by
the spectre of a developing Labour Party, he warned, 'there are hundreds of thousands of Liberals who will say that the Party in its present
form is perfectly hopeless as an effective machine for progress and that
it is high time to form or federate with another'.[34] The time was to
come when he at least contemplated an accommodation with Labour.
But that was after it became what would have been the senior partner
in the radical alliance. While the Liberals were in the ascendancy, he
wanted to destroy the party's rivals.

The more he considered the political effects of the bill, the more
confident Lloyd George felt that its radical contents had played a crucial
part in reviving party morale, which was essential. 'I cannot agree . . .
that we ought never to have introduced The Land Clauses . . . The
Party had lost heart. I was told that enthusiasm had almost disappeared
at meetings and we wanted something to rouse the fighting spirit of our
forces. This the land proposals have undoubtedly succeeded in doing.'[35]
Writing to his brother, he was bitter about some Cabinet ministers'
reluctance to guillotine debates on the Finance Bill but confident that
Asquith would give his support to a 'timetable resolution' and that the
party was wholeheartedly behind the clauses which it would hurry

through the House of Commons' committee stage. 'The Prime Minister is for it, but I shall have trouble with the rest of my colleagues who hate the Budget and would very much like to see it killed by time, but they won't as the party is behind me.'[36]

Lloyd George had become convinced – or, perhaps more accurately, had convinced himself – that the People's Budget was a vote-winner. Because of that, he began to consider the benefits of the Finance Bill's defeat. 'I am not sure we ought to pray for it to go through. I am not so sure we ought not to hope for its rejection. It would give us such a chance as we shall never have again.'[36] After July, when he first considered the advantages of the Lords rejecting what he believed to be a popular Budget, he began to defend his proposals and attack its enemies with absolute abandon. An election campaign would pit people against peers and free trade against a bread tax. Whatever the Lords did, Lloyd George and New Liberalism would be the winners. So he heightened the conflict with intentional provocation. On 30 July, in front of an audience of four thousand men and women in the Edinburgh Castle, a public house in Limehouse which had been converted into a temperance hall, he made the speech which confirmed his status as both radical and class warrior.*

He began with an ingenious combination of patriotism and polemic. Because national security was 'paramount in the minds of us all', the Cabinet had agreed to the extended Dreadnought programme. 'We started building. We wanted money to pay for the building. So we sent the hat round. We sent it round amongst workmen . . . They all dropped in their coppers. We went round Belgravia and there has been such a howl ever since that it has well nigh deafened us.' Then he extended the comparison between the response of rich and poor to the Budget as a whole.

> Provision for the aged and the deserving poor. Is it not time something was done? It is rather a shame that a rich country like ours . . . should allow those who have toiled all their days to end in penury and possibly starvation. It is rather hard that an old workman should have to find his way to the gates of the tomb, bleeding and footsore, through the brambles and thorns of poverty. We cut a new path for him – an easier one, a pleasanter one through fields

---

*Mary Soames's edited Churchill letters reveal that her mother, Clementine Churchill, was in the audience, cheering Lloyd George on.

of waving corn . . . There are many in the country blessed by
Providence with great wealth and if there are amongst them men
who grudge out of their riches a fair contribution towards the less
fortunate then they are very shabby rich men.[38]

In a flight of fancy, he claimed credit for having already done what he
hoped to do. 'We are raising money to provide against the evils and the
suffering that follow from unemployment. We are raising money to
assist our great Friendly Societies to provide for the sick, the widows,
the orphans.' Yet these essentially human proposals were being attacked
with 'concentrated and sustained ferocity'. Then, using exactly those
weapons himself, he turned to the land taxes. 'Not merely abstract
principle' but 'a number of concrete cases'. Lloyd George knew the
importance of identifying his enemies.

His first example – the fortunes made by landowners when 'the Port
of London became overcrowded and the population overflowed' – did
not name the guilty men. The figures spoke for themselves. 'Not many
years ago, between the [river] Lea and the Thames . . . the land was
sodden marsh.' But it became 'valuable building land and land which
used to be rented at £2 or £3 an acre' sold 'within the last few years for
£2,000 or £3,000 an acre . . . Who made that golden swamp? Was it
the landlord? Was it his brains? Was it his energy? . . . It was purely the
combined effort of all in the trade of the Port of London – everybody
except the landlord.' The proposed land tax, he implied, was too reasonable to require any justification. Describing it was enough. 'If the
land goes up in the future by hundreds and thousands an acre through
the efforts of the community, the community will get 20% of that
increment.'

It was the passages which followed that caused the gravest offence.
The first identified the Duke of Northumberland, who had sold a small
plot of land to his county council 'as a site for a school to train children
who, in due course, would become men labouring on his land . . . His
contribution to the rates was, I think, on the basis of 30/- an acre. What
did he demand for the school? £900 an acre. All we say is this – if it is
worth £900 let him pay taxes on £900.' Next in line was the Duke of
Westminster, excoriated for increasing ground rent when a lease was
renewed because his tenant had improved the property.

Mr Gorringe had got a lease of the premises at a few hundred
pounds a year ground rent. He built a great business. When the

end of the lease came he went to the Duke of Westminster and said 'Will you renew my lease?' . . . The reply was 'Yes, I will, but only on the condition that the few hundreds a year you pay for ground rent shall in future be £4,000 a year'.

The coal-owners of South Wales were denounced collectively rather than duke by duke.

Have you been down a coal mine? I went down one the other day . . . You could see the pit props bent and twisted and sundered . . . Sometimes they give way and there is mutilation and death . . . Yet when the Prime Minister and I knock on the doors of these great landlords and say to them, 'Here, you know these poor fellows who have been digging up royalties at the risk of their lives, some of them are old and have survived the perils of their trade and are broken and can earn no more. Won't you give something towards keeping them out of the workhouse?' They scowl at us . . . They retort 'You thieves!' . . . If this is an indication of the view taken by these great landlords of their responsibility to the people who, at the risk of life, create their wealth then I say the day of reckoning is at hand.

The Lords' threats were dismissed with contempt. 'They have threatened like this before but in good time they have seen it is not in their interests to carry out their futile menaces.' The speech ended on the high ground of renewed principle.

We are placing the burdens on the broadest shoulders. Why should I put burdens on the people? I am one of the children of the people. I was brought up amongst them. I know their trials and God forbid that I should add one grain of trouble to the anxieties which they bear with fortitude. When the Prime Minister did me the honour of asking me to take charge of the Exchequer at a time of great difficulty, I made up my mind in framing the Budget . . . that at any rate no cupboard could be barer, no lot should be harder. By that test I challenge you to judge the Budget.

The speech inside the Edinburgh Castle would – without any additions or adornments – have caused a sensation. But when it was done and the ovation had died down, Lloyd George addressed an overflow meeting in

a nearby hall. His intention was to emphasise the government's determination to see the Finance Bill onto the statute book without
amendment. And, as was his habit at the height of his rhetorical exuberance, he personalised his argument in a way which added emotion
to what might otherwise have been a musty constitutional argument.
But one line of his peroration – whether or not premeditated – heightened the drama of an already passionate debate.

> Lord Curzon has threatened to amputate the Budget. Well, I don't
> mind Lord Curzon as long as he keeps to those bombastic com-
> monplaces which have been his stock-in-trade through life. But if
> he is going to try here that arrogance which was too much even for
> the gentle Hindu, we will have to tell him that we will have none
> of his Oriental manners* . . . I say to you, without you we can do
> nothing. With you we can brush the Lords like chaff before us.[39]

Four days later, on 3 August, the Prime Minister, at Cowes aboard the
Enchantress, the Board of Admiralty yacht, wrote to Lloyd George. 'On
my arrival here, I found the King in a state of great agitation and
annoyance in consequence of your Limehouse speech . . . He sees the
general tone, and especially the concluding parts of your speech, as a
menace to property and Socialist [in] spirit . . . I have communications
in the same sense from others – very good Liberals some of them.' The
rest of Asquith's letter was a heartfelt appeal to what he saw as reason.

> I have, as you know, heartily and loyally backed the Budget from
> the first and at every stage and I have done, and shall continue to
> do, all I can to commend it to the country. But I feel very strongly
> that, at this moment, what is needed is reasoned appeal to moder-
> ate and reasonable men. There is a great and growing popular
> enthusiasm, but this will not carry us through if we rouse the sus-
> picions and the fears of the middle class, and particularly if we give
> countenance to the notion that the Budget is conceived in any
> spirit of vindictiveness.[40]

In a demonstration of his self-confidence – which others certainly
interpreted as impudence – Lloyd George replied not to the Prime
Minister but to the King. It began with something approaching a

---

*Lord Curzon had been Viceroy of India.

reproof. 'It is no doubt within Your Majesty's recollection that when your Chancellor of the Exchequer laid the financial proposals before you . . . Your Majesty was good enough to listen with consideration and even, on some points, with sympathy for his statement.' However, 'the Chancellor of the Exchequer has found himself subjected in connection with these same proposals to a storm of hostile criticism, the virulence of which he ventures to think is without parallel in the history of financial legislation in this country'. Lloyd George 'ventured to submit . . . that in his recent speech, the first public speech which he has made since the introduction of the Budget, he was justified in retorting upon his opponents in language which fell short of much which had been said and repeated on the other side'.[41] The King signed his reply 'Edward'. But it was written in the detached third-person singular which was thought appropriate for correspondence between sovereign and subject.

> The King readily admits that the Chancellor has been attacked by some members of the Opposition with much violence and regrets it, but he must remind him that though those gentlemen may have passed the fair limits of attack, they are private members and do not hold a high office in the Government, as is the case with Mr Lloyd George.[42]

The whole government had begun to accept that a House of Lords veto was a real possibility, but it was still necessary to dismiss the idea as unthinkable in public. In Birmingham, Asquith described both amendment and rejection as 'out of the question. That way', he warned, 'revolution lies.'[43] On 8 September, the Cabinet, for the first time, discussed the possibility of the Finance Bill being defeated by the peers and the Prime Minister reported to the King at Balmoral that 'such an action . . . ought to be followed by the acceleration of the Register [of electors] so as to secure, at the earliest possible moment, an appeal to the country'.[44] The Cabinet resumed its discussion on 15 September but agreed that it would be premature to decide upon any definite course of action.[45] The next day Asquith met the King at the start of the Prime Minister's ritual autumn visit and discussed the possibility of a royal intervention to persuade the Unionist peers against defying the conventions of the constitution. The King saw Balfour and Lansdowne on 3 October. They told him – out of courtesy as much as cunning – that no decision had been taken. Perhaps the King believed them. On

7 October, the day after the Finance Bill completed its committee stage, Asquith wrote a warning note to Lloyd George.

> The King is making, and will continue to make, every effort that is constitutionally open to him to secure the acceptance of the Budget Bill by the Lords. He is fairly sanguine of success. In the circumstances, as you are (I see) speaking in the country on Saturday, I venture to suggest that you should proceed throughout on the assumption that the Lords will pass the Bill and that such a contingency as their rejecting it is, from both a constitutional and an administrative point of view, well nigh unthinkable.[46]

There is no way of knowing if Asquith really believed that the King's intervention might save the Budget, or if the message which he sent to Lloyd George was no more than tactical advice. Nor can we be sure that the Chancellor of the Exchequer received the Prime Minister's note before he left London for Newcastle on 9 October. If he did, he ignored the advice which it contained. The Newcastle speech, delivered to 5200 Liberals in the Palace Theatre, was a combination of ridicule and scorn which, he must have anticipated, would cause even more offence than Limehouse.

The economy, he asserted, was strong. Even brewery shares had increased in value.

> Only one stock has gone down badly – there has been a great slump in dukes. They used to stand rather high in the market, especially the Tory market, but the Tory Press has discovered that they are of no value ... One especially expensive duke made a speech recently and all the Tory Press said, 'Well now, really, is that the sort of thing we are spending £250,000 a year on?'

The expensive duke he had in mind was the Duke of Northumberland who, having just told the House of Lords that improving working-class houses was less important than safeguarding the rights of property, had been ordered to close and demolish twenty-two of his cottages because they were unfit for human habitation. No one in the audience doubted which duke Lloyd George had in mind when he continued, 'A fully-equipped duke costs as much to keep up as two Dreadnoughts – and they are just as great a terror – and they last longer.' After the jokes came the menace.

Let them realise what they are doing. They are forcing a revolution and they will get it. The Lords may decree a revolution but the People will direct it. If they begin, issues will be raised that they little dream of. Questions will be asked which are now whispered in humble voices and answers will be demanded with authority. The question will be asked whether five hundred men, ordinary men chosen accidentally from among the unemployed, should override the judgement – the deliberate judgement – of millions of people who are engaged in the industry which makes the wealth of the country.[47]

He spoke at the Palace Theatre for an hour and thirty-five minutes. Then he addressed an overflow meeting.

If it does not get through, it will come to you and then you will have two questions to settle. One is the Budget and the other will be the House of Lords. They will be on the same ballot paper. It will be the last time probably that the question will be asked. It is an old question and it is time it should be answered. Who is to govern this country – the people or the peers?[48]

The long day finished with a dinner at the Newcastle Liberal Club. There Lloyd George behaved as Asquith would have wished. The Lords, he said, would not reject the Budget. But he must have known that the Limehouse speech had made rejection more likely – and the speeches in Newcastle had made it certain.

CHAPTER 16

AFTER A STORM

Lloyd George was a public, not a private, man who never allowed himself to be weighed down by the burden of family responsibilities. His affection for Uncle Lloyd and his brother William was increased and preserved by gratitude for the way in which they had supported and sustained him in times of difficulty – particularly when it was feared that one of his peccadilloes, of which they heartily disapproved, seemed likely to be exposed. His relationship with his wife was profoundly ambivalent and, with his daughters, highly sentimental. For Mair Eluned he had felt indulgent love. After she died, Megan – born in April 1902 – became the centre of similar attention. Mair Eluned had been named after her maternal aunt, Mary Ellen – the one member of his family who, in his youth, had openly disapproved of his louche ways. In middle age he found her overt purity irritating, even when her disapproval was directed not at him but at others. When she died of cancer on 8 August 1909, the message from his brother which carried the news illustrated the awe in which he was held by even his closest relative. 'Do not think of us. Do not let this private grief make you pause in the great work you are doing for the poor.'[1] The news moved him to tears. Later in the day – sitting on the front bench during the committee stage debate of the Finance Bill – he told Charles Masterman, 'Death alters things. All this seems to me like the chattering of apes.'[2] It did not alter them for long. After a brief visit to Criccieth for the funeral he was driven off to spend a weekend with the Mastermans in Brighton.

Some family obligations, onerous or not, had to be discharged. One of them, completed during the House of Commons debates on the

Finance Bill, was the building of what became his – or, perhaps more accurately, his wife's – permanent home in Wales. It was built on the hills above Criccieth with a view looking over Cardigan Bay and was generally regarded as a house which lacked style in design and taste in decoration. But Margaret gave it a romantic name. It was called Brynawelon (Hill of Breezes). Frances Stevenson, normally scrupulously careful not to be critical of Margaret Lloyd George, provided the definitive description of the family's domestic arrangements. 'She was effectively a visitor in her husband's house – except in Criccieth where he was a visitor in hers.'[3] Visitor or not, after her husband became Chancellor in 1908, she increased the time she spent in London, as she had following his appointment as President of the Board of Trade.* She discharged her duties 'with natural dignity'. Metropolitan visitors who 'expected to meet a simple peasant woman were surprised to meet a personality of common sense who, although she would have preferred to meet them in Wales, was perfectly able to make them feel at home in an official residence'.[4] No doubt her composure owed something to what she and her husband had made of their new surroundings. 'Number 11 looked as if a small suburban household were picnicking in Downing Street – the same little domestic servant, the same mixture of tea and dinner' as in Wales.[5]

During the weeks which followed the second reading of the Finance Bill, Lloyd George could not have spent many evenings at home. There were 554 divisions during the committee stage and the Chancellor of the Exchequer voted in 462 of them. Most of even the most contentious clauses were agreed, although the tax on undeveloped minerals was replaced by a tax on royalties. The Irish, unhappy about increased excise duties – as always, incited to opposing the government by the overtly partisan Archbishop Vaughan – voted against the Budget more often than they voted in its favour.

On 4 August, Lloyd George was able to report to his brother what he regarded as proof that his enemies would face defeat. 'Lord Northcliffe came to see me last night. He is, as you know, the proprietor of the *Daily Mail* and the *Times*. He told me that the Budget has completely destroyed the Tariff Reform propaganda in this country. He said that they had all miscalculated the popularity of the land clauses. He wants to trim.'[6] Northcliffe was suing for peace. Contrary to popular belief,

---

*Margaret Lloyd George preferred Number 11 (which was a house) to Number 10 (which was a flat over an office).

newspaper proprietors are more likely to support what their readers already believe than attempt to impose their own views on them. But many Unionists were made of stouter stuff than Northcliffe. One of them was his employee, J. L. Garvin, editor of the *Observer*, which the peer had acquired in 1905. He too believed that the Budget was popular in the country. But he reacted to that startling news with more courage than the newspaper's proprietor. The Unionists, he told Northcliffe, would be doomed if they let the Budget pass.

> The Government is, of course, less unpopular than last year. If they pass the Budget substantially as it stands, they will have secured a parliamentary triumph as brilliant as any in our recollection . . . Men like Lloyd George and Churchill will do anything to win. Upon the lines of the Budget, they will keep on winning if we submit now. Our Dukes should be warned to keep off the grass. The strongest and most audacious policy possible should be adopted . . . In short, my belief is now that the Budget ought to be rejected.[7]

Ironically, at the time that the Unionists were beginning to conclude that they would be severely damaged if the Budget were passed, the more adventurous Liberals were gradually coming to believe that they would benefit from its being defeated. By August, Lloyd George was near to euphoric about the prospect of a 'mighty running wind sweeping before it all opposition'. In Newcastle he claimed to have heard

> from all parts of the country, startling accounts of the changes effected by the Budget on public opinion. There is undoubtedly a popular rising which has not been witnessed over a generation. What will happen if they throw it out I can conjecture and I rejoice at the prospect. Many a rotten institution, system and law will be submerged by the deluge. I wonder whether they will be such fools. I am almost wishing that they could be stricken by blindness.[8]

He had convinced himself that the crash would harm the Unionist Party and leave the Liberals unscathed. By the time he made the Newcastle speech, he had decided that, whatever happened, he had won. A letter to his brother began with the usual paragraph of self-congratulation about the reception he had received. 'Nothing like it has been witnessed since the good Gladstone days.' Then he set out his personal and political strategy. 'They must fight now or eat humble pie, and that will be very difficult for a proud tho posillinous [*sic*] aristocracy. I deliberately provoked them. I fear that they will run away in spite of all my pains.'[9] In his estimation, the argument in favour of a fight to the finish had become conclusive. He knew that he was 'far more likely to go down to posterity' as the author of a successful financial scheme 'than as a Chancellor who had changed very little' but 'might be remembered even better as one who had upset the hereditary House of Lords'.[10]

On 4 November, the third reading of the Finance Bill was passed in the Commons by 379 votes to 149. The Irish Members, still unhappy about excise duties, abstained. After two weeks of deliberation and five days of debate, the House of Lords carried, by 350 votes to 75, a motion in the name of Lord Lansdowne – 'That this House is not justified in giving consent to this Bill until it has been submitted to the judgement of the people'. Lloyd George, who had listened to the Lords debate on his Board of Trade bills from the steps of the throne, ignored their deliberations on the Budget as a sign of contempt. When the result of the division was announced, he was having dinner at Frascati's on the Strand.

During the two weeks before the Lords debate began, while the bill was in limbo, the Cabinet had considered securing 'supply' by rushing through a Finance (No. 2) Bill which authorised the collection of those taxes which it was assumed that the peers would accept. The idea was vehemently opposed by Lloyd George on the grounds that it would imply that ministers accepted the right of the Upper House to pick and choose between taxes which the Commons had approved. The only alternative to accepting the then unlimited Lords veto was a general election which determined the will of the people. On 2 December, the House of Commons carried, by 349 votes to 134, a motion which described the Lords' behaviour as a 'breach of the constitution and a usurpation of the rights' of elected Members of Parliament. No doubt, Liberals believed that support for that view on polling day would break the Lords' resolve. Prorogation followed twenty-four days later with polling day set for 15 January 1910. Lloyd George set out on the election campaign with the complacent thought that 'Liberty owes as much to the foolishness of its foes as it does to the confidence of its friends.'[11]

The Chancellor of the Exchequer's confidence in a Liberal victory was not shared by all his colleagues. John Burns predicted that the

Unionists would 'sweep London' and Churchill, optimistic by nature, predicted no more than that 'the parties would be evenly divided' in the capital.[12] While the Finance Bill was making its slow way through the Commons, the Liberal Party had fought and lost a by-election in Bermondsey. The anti-Unionist vote had been split by the intervention of a Labour candidate. The pact between Herbert Gladstone, when he was Liberal Chief Whip, and Ramsay MacDonald, then the secretary of the Labour Party – designed to avoid the two parties slitting each other's throat – had run out. But the Trades Disputes Act had been passed – if not at the behest of the Trades Union Congress, then certainly with its demands in mind – and MacDonald had publicly supported both the Old Age Pensions Bill and the Budget which paid for it. It was, therefore, reasonable to assume that, when the general election came, Labour would not 'let the Tories in'. Most important of all, what in those days were called the 'terms of trade' were improving. The Liberals believed that they could fight the election as the party of prosperity as well as champions of the people.

It was clear from the start that Lloyd George himself would be a campaign issue. The plaudits which he had received after he averted the national railway strike had been magnified by surprise at his conversion from rebel to statesman. After Limehouse, Swansea and Newcastle, there were anguished cries of disappointment – some of them genuine – at what was regarded as a return to his bad old ways. *The Times* feared that the speeches were 'entirely in that early manner which the more hopeful observers of his career [were] now driven to doubt his capacity to outgrow'.[13] The *Daily Mail* believed that he had 'overdone it. His violent and bitter speech at Newcastle will be read with sorrow and indignation by all right-thinking men.'[14] The *Daily Telegraph* claimed that he had 'definitely left the Girondins to join the Jacobins' in a Reign of Terror.[15] By coincidence, on the same day, Lloyd George spoke of the French Revolution to the Welsh Baptist Union. In an original interpretation of its progress, he assured his highly religious audience, 'If France had been a pagan nation, and Louis XVI a Roman Emperor, the Bastille would not have been taken, the Tuileries would not have fallen and France would not have been free.'[16]

The image of Citizen Lloyd George speeding the tumbrel on its way to the guillotine should have been at least partially blurred by the speeches he made on the highly respectable subjects of trade and unemployment. But his platform style did not encourage the impression that he appreciated the solemn role of Chancellor of the Exchequer with bipartisan objectivity. He saw the election campaign as more than a fight for the Budget and a battle with the House of Lords. To him, it was a conflict between two systems – Imperial Preference, which financed social legislation out of the pockets of the poor, and free trade, which required a progressive government to raise taxes from the incomes of the rich. All his speeches on the economy had that theme.

In West Newington he announced that unemployment was down, year on year, by 25 per cent – adding that men who were out of work should feel a particular inclination to vote Liberal. 'If you are going to get unemployed, you had better have it with cheap bread than with dear bread.'[17] In the Queen's Hall he claimed that free trade was such a success that the Tories had been forced to press for an early election because they knew that, by the end of 1910, there would be 'no unemployment and no bad trade'.[18] In Plymouth he assured his audience that Sir Francis Drake would have made sure that freeborn (and free-trade) Englishmen ate beef, not horsemeat like the protectionist peasantry of the German Zollverein.[19] It did not sound like the carefully weighed judgement of a responsible statesman.

The peerage was attacked in almost every speech. But the assaults were almost always targeted on the conduct and character of the House of Lords rather than its lack of democratic legitimacy. Lords kept land prices high and wages low. They thought that the aged poor should be grateful for accommodation in workhouses rather than agitate for an old-age pension and they used their power to enable the Church of England to impose its doctrine on Nonconformist children. Peers were the main beneficiaries of the Rate Relief Act. He had discovered 'a little tailor's shop next door' to Lord Bute's castle in Caernarvon which was more highly rated (for tax purposes) than the castle itself.*[20] He 'would not remain a member of the Liberal Cabinet one hour unless [he] knew that the Cabinet had determined . . . to place on the statute book . . . measures that would ensure that the House of Commons, in future, can carry not merely Tory Bills but Liberal and progressive measures in a single parliament'.[21]

The Liberal Party had still to decide whether to 'reform' the House of Lords by changing its composition or (as Campell-Bannerman had once briefly persuaded his colleagues) by limiting its powers. Whichever option was eventually chosen, the essential legislation had to be passed by the Lords themselves, and Asquith knew that the peers would not

---

*The shop was substantial and located some distance from the castle.

easily be persuaded to vote for change. The remedy for their obduracy was the creation (or the threatened creation) of enough new members to change the balance of the Upper House. But peers are created by the sovereign, not his Prime Minister. And in November, the King's private secretary had told Asquith that 'to create 570 new Peers, which I am told is the number required, would practically be almost an impossibility'.[22]

After the campaign had begun, the position was confirmed during a conversation between Francis Knollys and Vaughan Nash, private secretaries respectively to the King and the Prime Minister. The view from Windsor was that 'the policy of the government [is] tantamount to the destruction of the House of Lords' and that, in consequence, co-operating in its implementation 'would not be justified . . . until after a second general election'.[23] No doubt Asquith welcomed the request to treat the sovereign's decision as secret until the election was over. The truth could be withheld, not as a tactical necessity, but as an obligation of honour. However, because of the Prime Minister's discretion, the whole Liberal Party, with the exception of its leader, fought the first 1910 election campaign in the mistaken belief that victory would – one way or another – solve all the government's constitutional problems.

Knowledge of the rocks and shoals which lay ahead did not prevent Asquith from making speeches which suggested that he was steering a straight course towards a victory for parliamentary democracy. On 10 December – between notification and confirmation of the King's intentions – he told a rally at the Albert Hall:

> Neither I nor any other Liberal Minister supported by a majority in the House of Commons is going to submit again to the rebuffs and humiliations of the last four years . . . The will of the people, as deliberately expressed by their elected representatives, must, within the lifetime of a single parliament, be made effective.

The statement of his intentions was so categoric that the rest of his speech attracted less attention than it deserved – even though, at one point, the Prime Minister reinstated Irish Home Rule as a crucial objective of Liberal policy. It had been Asquith who, at the turn of the century, had reminded Liberals that Gladstone's 'magnificent courage, unrivalled authority and unquenchable enthusiasm' had failed to convince the British people of the need for a Dublin parliament. Having then asked 'the practical question' of whether a Liberal government would seek to succeed where Gladstone had failed, he replied: 'The answer in my judgement is No.'[24] Nine years later, and apparently on his own initiative, he recanted. Clearly the King's message – and the uncertainty of the election's outcome – was on his mind. He was going to need the support of the Irish Nationalists.

Lloyd George – having done his duty by sitting behind Asquith on the Albert Hall platform – left to tour the country. As had become his habit, he spent little of the campaign in his own constituency, though because of its demands he was, unusually, at home in Criccieth for Christmas. The festivities being finished, he travelled to locations as far apart as Falmouth and York, Stockport and Peckham, Birmingham and Brighton. In Grimsby he was mobbed in the ice rink by the supporters of the Tory candidate (who, much to Lloyd George's amusement, had warned of an imminent German invasion) and had to be smuggled out of the back door.[25] In Reading he was shouted down by suffragettes, but in North Kensington, five days later, he said that he would be 'glad to see women get their rights', and he urged his audience not to be prejudiced against a worthy cause by the 'wild hysterical' behaviour of some of its supporters.[26] He paid special attention to South Wales and, as a result, caused some disquiet in his own constituency. At a meeting of his local party he was again asked to dispel rumours that he had been invited to contest Cardiff. He replied with what must have been a spontaneous *coup de théâtre*. The invitation had been issued and had been seriously considered – 'but after all I would rather remain here'. When the applause had died down, he added very quietly, 'I have an attachment for the Boroughs', and then, after a long pause, 'It is greater than I can say.'[27] He sat down to sustained applause – far more popular than he would have been had Cardiff never courted him. That evening, at a public meeting, he dismissed claims that he was becoming Anglicised by completing his speech in Welsh. The final paragraph became one of the most famous passages in all his flowing oratory.

> Yesterday I visited the old village where I was brought up. I wandered through the woods familiar to my boyhood. There I saw a child gathering sticks for firewood and I thought of the hours which I spent in the same pleasant and profitable occupation, for I also had been something of a 'backwoodsman'. And there was one experience, taught me then, which is of some profit to me today. I learned as a child that it was little use going into the woods after a period of calm and fine weather for I usually

returned empty-handed; but after a great storm I always came back with an armful. We are in for rough weather. We may even be in for a winter of storms which will rock the forest, break many a withered branch and leave many a rotten tree torn up by the roots. But when the weather clears you may depend upon it that there will be something brought within the reach of the people that will give warmth and glow to their grey lives, something that will help to dispel the hunger, the despair, the oppression and the wrong which now chill so many of their hearths.[28]

Lloyd George was re-elected Member of Parliament for the Caernarvon Boroughs with a majority of 1078, a slight reduction on the 1906 result. His opponent, H. C. Vincent – Mayor of Bangor and local solicitor – was a far better candidate than his predecessor, R. A. Naylor (a 'stranger to Wales') had been. In most of Wales, Liberal candidates had bigger majorities than ever before, but in two border constituencies – where the farmers were worried about land taxes – the Unionists gained the seats and contributed to what amounted to far less than a vote of confidence in the government. The Liberals won 274 seats – only two more than the Unionists, who made 116 net gains. The Irish Nationalists of one sort or another won 82 and Labour 40. So the government was secure. A determination to break the power of the House of Lords and hope of fulfilling the long-held dream of Irish Home Rule united Liberals, Nationalists and Labour into a loose alliance that, on crucial issues, could cobble together a majority of 124. But the hopes of a never-ending Liberal domination of British politics – excited by the landslide victory of 1906 – were dashed for ever.

There is no easy explanation for why in 1910 the nation held the Liberal Party at arm's length. The January result may do no more than confirm the indisputable, though often overlooked, fact that a government cannot choose the subject on which it fights a general election. Or it may reflect the unique circumstances which brought about the 1906 Liberal landslide. That Liberal triumph had been, if not an aberration, at least a sudden deviation from the normal course of British politics. The size of Henry Campbell-Bannerman's victory had been increased by the strength of Nonconformist feeling against the 1902 Education Act and the deep divisions that reduced the electorate's confidence in an obviously weary Unionist administration. In 1910, the Liberal Party had to rely on its own record rather than the reputation of a deeply unpopular government. But there were other reasons for the disappointing results. In rural areas tenants, no less than landlords, felt under threat from the new land taxes. Many observers of the election, and some participants, believed that another factor had reduced the Liberal vote – the violent, sometimes abusive and rarely constructive speeches of David Lloyd George and Winston Churchill.

Lewis Harcourt – soon to be promoted to Colonial Secretary – told the Prime Minister, 'I was surprised to find how little anger there was about the House of Lords. All my people wanted to know was that we "meant business" and were not in for a compromise or sham fight. They have no conception of the constitutional question.' That seems to suggest that Lloyd George's robust assault on the peers – which certainly dispelled all thought of compromise – was an electoral asset. But Harcourt added that aggressive speeches 'did much harm even with advanced men of the *lower* middle class'.[29]

Lloyd George himself remained publicly indomitable. 'I don't know', he told Masterman, 'what possesses people to go about talking as if we were beaten. We won the election.'[30] It would have been more accurate to say, 'We remained in office.' And Lloyd George's star had paused in its inexorable ascent through the galaxy of British politics.

CHAPTER 17

A REASONABLE WAY OUT

Lloyd George's complacent optimism was unjustified. The Irish Nationalists were pledged to support both the Finance Bill and a Parliament Bill, which would emasculate the House of Lords and open the way to Home Rule. But they were determined not to have one without the other. Initially they had opposed the Budget – specifically because of the increase it proposed in excise duty on spirits and, more generally, because of a feeling of unease about the insurance proposals at its heart. And despite Asquith's Albert Hall speech, they were not wholly convinced that Home Rule still excited Liberal enthusiasm. In Newcastle Lloyd George had claimed that two issues 'were on the ballot paper – the Budget and the House of Lords'.[1] The omission of Ireland from the mandate had seemed to vindicate William O'Brien and eleven independent MPs who had broken with John Redmond because, in their view, the Nationalists gave more to the government than they received in return. If Lloyd George left for his New Year holiday in Nice believing that the Finance Bill would sail through Parliament on his return, a message from the Irish Nationalist MP T. P. O'Connor – which awaited him in London – dispelled the illusion.

> I have grave news to give you. I have seen all the friends here and they are unanimous in saying that we must oppose the Budget unless it is preceded by the announcement of measures limiting the legislative and financial veto of the House of Lords. This to be passed into law the same year.[2]

O'Connor sent an almost identical letter to Edward Grey, which the Foreign Secretary read to the Cabinet. The following day, speaking in Dublin's Gresham Hotel, Redmond made the Nationalists' position public.[3] Cooperation with the government depended upon Asquith's preparing the way for Home Rule by giving firm assurances that the Lords' veto would be extinguished.

Troubles assail faltering governments not singly but in battalions. They attacked the Asquith administration before the new Parliament had even met. George Barnes, the chairman of the Labour Party – learning of the Irish demands and fearing that the Labour Members of Parliament were being treated as 'a mere drifting appendage' – issued a statement asserting that government policy, over both national insurance or Lords reform, was not clear and was therefore 'unacceptable'.[4] He was repudiated by a series of Labour Party figures with less formal standing but more genuine authority. Sensing that the government was in a mood to make concessions, Ramsay MacDonald, Philip Snowden and Arthur Henderson all added requests that sounded like demands to their assurances of sympathy and support. Chief among them was the payment of MPs and legislation to reverse the Osborne judgement of 1909, which had declared that trade unions could not lawfully spend their members' subscriptions on the promotion of political candidates or parties.

Meeting the Labour Party's terms was well within the government's power. But it was impossible to provide the Irish Nationalists with the assurances which they demanded. Asquith had not formally asked the King to create new peers and the Prime Minister assumed that, when the request was made, Edward would refuse. Lloyd George – despite the suspicion in which he was held by the Irish because of their belief that he had broken his promise to drop the 'whisky tax' back in 1908 – was given the task of explaining to Redmond the best that the government could do and asking for support in that endeavour. His démarche was set out by Redmond in a letter to John Dillon. Lloyd George had asked the leader of the major Irish party to support a detailed parliamentary timetable – endorsement of the King's Speech and Budget before Easter and afterwards legislation to reduce the power of the peers discussed, side by side, with the Finance Bill. When the Lords rejected the proposals to end their veto, the King would be asked to create new peers. If he declined, which was almost as certain, Parliament would be dissolved and a summer election would follow. For good measure, Lloyd George threw in the offer to make reductions in, or perhaps even abandon, the increase in the 'whisky tax'. Despite the added inducement, Redmond was unable to guarantee the Nationalists' support.[5]

The Cabinet met two days after Redmond's reply. It was incapacitated by indecision. Ministers were unsure how a limit on the House of Lords' powers was to be achieved and they could not agree what that limitation should be. Grey, Haldane, Crewe and Herbert Samuel (at the beginning of his long Cabinet career) all wanted to abandon Campbell-Bannerman's policy – the abolition of the veto – in favour of changing the composition of the Upper House. Harcourt argued that the election had provided a mandate for abolishing the veto but not for a more radical revision. The Prime Minister was in favour of anything which would avert a constitutional crisis. He told the Cabinet, 'As the elections have turned out, it is obviously quite impossible for us to press the King over guarantees.'[6]

Lloyd George and Churchill, who had led the call for 'something to be done', were less united about what it should be. Churchill wanted an elected Upper House and severe limitations on its powers. Lloyd George was clear that he was 'a single chamber man, but nobody wants a single chamber now . . . It might be accepted if the plan were daring enough to attract Labour and the Irishmen.'[7] For the short term he suggested a referendum. The Cabinet agreed to the preparation of the bill a few days before he lost interest in his own idea.

The Cabinet, which met three days before the state opening of Parliament, was, if Lloyd George is to be believed, near to despair. The usually ebullient Churchill told colleagues, 'I think we are all through', and Edward Grey – equally despondent but more magisterial – feared that he was witnessing the 'final passing of Mr Gladstone's noble dream'. We are, Lloyd George warned, 'blundering into a great catastrophe through lack of nerve'.[8] The language in which the King's Speech dealt with the need for constitutional reform reflected the uncertainty. 'Proposals will be laid before you with convenient speed to define the relations between the Houses of Parliament so as to secure the undivided authority of the House of Commons over finance and its predominance in legislation.' Spirits were depressed still further when Asquith, in what was universally regarded as a disastrous speech during the debate on the Loyal Address, dispelled a misapprehension for which he was (intentionally or not) responsible. There was no immediate hope of the King's rescuing the government by the creation of new peers. On 21 February, Asquith made a statement in the Commons. 'I have to tell the House quite frankly that I have received no such guarantee and that I have asked for no such guarantee.'[9] Alexander Murray, soon to become Chief Whip, thought it 'the worst speech [he] had ever heard him make'.[10] Redmond, who spoke later on the same day, was brutally explicit. The Irish had supported the government during the election because of the Albert Hall promise 'not to hold or assume office' until the Lords' powers were curtailed. There could be only one response to that promise. 'No veto. No Budget.' The Lords – the bastion of the Union – was encouraged in its opposition to the Budget by the hope that, thanks to the Irish Nationalists, the government was not even master of the Commons.

All governments which contemplate defeat are rent with suspicions of betrayal and apostasy. Lloyd George and Churchill – not trusted even in less anxious times – were regarded as the most likely defectors. Unwisely Lloyd George had speculated about an idea which had been in his mind for some time – a government 'composed of businessmen ... which would carry enormous weight in the country', and credence of a sort was given to the idea by the discovery that the Budget League, run by Churchill, was amassing funds for no clearly defined purpose.[11] Arthur Pease confronted Lloyd George, without gaining a satisfactory explanation, about £14,000 which had been received from a businessman in return for the promise of a peerage.[12] Masterman was right to assure colleagues that Lloyd George was doing no more than playing with ideas. It was six years before the idea of businessmen in government became a reality, and twenty before privately raised cash was used to finance a political party which was meant to be Lloyd George's personal fiefdom.

The Cabinet stumbled on towards Easter. Grey – typifying the loss of morale in beleaguered governments – thought of resigning for no better reason than to show concern at the poor quality of Asquith's speech on the Loyal Address. John Morley, whose threats to resign were devalued by their frequency, said he would not tolerate coercion of the Lords. With the Finance Bill in limbo, the Cabinet bought time by gaining parliamentary approval for borrowing as much as it needed to see the country through the next six weeks. On 29 March, Asquith attempted to calm speculation by moving three resolutions which set out the way in which the government proposed to reform the relationship between the two Houses. The Cabinet had, after some agony, agreed to the model of reform proposed by Campbell-Bannerman – not a change in the membership of the Upper House but a limitation on its powers. The Commons was to enjoy exclusive authority over money bills, the House of Lords to possess the power to delay, but not to defeat, other legislation and the life of a Parliament to be reduced from seven to five years. Radical opinion was mollified, if not satisfied, by a preamble to the proposals for immediate action. The government's long-term aim was 'to substitute for the House of Lords in its present form a second chamber constituted on a popular rather than a hereditary basis'.[13]

At least the previously critical Chief Whip was satisfied by what he regarded as 'a grand Parliamentary triumph for the Prime Minister' which restored 'all his lost prestige'.[14] Much of the Liberal Party was less contented. It still seemed that there was no House of Commons majority for the Budget, and a government which loses a Budget in the Commons cannot survive. According to Lloyd George's account of events, the Cabinet had again been on the point of resignation but he – supported initially only by Churchill – persuaded the faint hearts to battle on.[15] Some ministers argued for buying-off Redmond's Nationalists – or the eleven Irish independents – with the promise to abandon the increase in excise duty, not a great fiscal sacrifice since the consumption of spirits was falling. An informal offer was met with a formal refusal. Lloyd George decided that the time had come to end the indecision. On 12 April, he announced that there was no question of varying his original Budget proposals. The next day he asked Alexander Murray to tell the Prime Minister that, unless there was a swift announcement about the appointment of peers, he and his friends would leave the Cabinet. In his view, 'The Irish could not be put off any longer. The Irish would not put the government out on the whisky tax. They would put it out for refusing to ask for guarantees and for not carrying out its own policy.'[16] Asquith rejected the call for immediate action. But Lloyd George's demands assisted him in obtaining royal support. According to a rumour, current at the time, Asquith encouraged the King's sympathy by using the threat of resignations as evidence that, if there were a change of Prime Minister, Lloyd George would take his place.[17]

On 12 April, the Cabinet considered how it should react if, before any constitutional change occurred, the House of Lords again frustrated the will of the Commons. King Edward was in Biarritz. So, an audience being impossible, Asquith set out the government's intentions in a letter. Two days later, the Prime Minister made a statement to the House. If the peers defied the decision of elected Members, 'a crisis of an unexampled and most embarrassing kind would arise'. Only one response was possible.

> The Cabinet have determined that if resolutions carried by the Commons are rejected or laid aside by the Lords it will be their duty at once to tender advice to the Crown as to the necessary steps – whether by exercise of the Prerogative or by referendum ad hoc or otherwise – to be taken to ensure that the policy approved by the House of Commons by a large majority should be given statutory effect in this Parliament.

If the government were forced to resign, 'dissolution would be accompanied by such conditions as would secure in the new Parliament that the judgement of the people, expressed in the election, was carried into law'.[18] Despite the circumlocution no one doubted Asquith's intention. Balfour, in one of the little acts of pomposity which remain a feature of parliamentary procedure, had persuaded the Speaker that the Prime Minister should not make his statement until the conclusion of normal business. But the announcement was still made in time to be reported in the following day's newspapers. So the King received the Prime Minister's letter at the same time as his subjects read accounts of its contents. The royal fury at what he regarded as a gross discourtesy was reflected, perhaps even magnified, in the reaction of Knollys, his private secretary. He told Lord Esher (one of nature's courtiers who had served Queen Victoria) that, were he King, he would rather abdicate than yield to the pressure to create new peers.[19]

The King had more respect for constitutional propriety and, despite his fury, he realised that Asquith's statement meant that the government was determined to have its way. O'Brien announced that the Irishmen he led still regarded persistence with the whisky tax as a betrayal. But Redmond realised that his demands had been met – or as nearly met as reality allowed. He still insisted that he must consult his party before he could promise to back the Budget, but the consultation ended with agreement to support the Finance Bill. When the House of Commons voted on the guillotine resolution – which guaranteed the adoption of the Budget within five days – Redmond's Irish Nationalists voted with the government and O'Brien's independent Irishmen voted against. The bill was carried by a majority of ninety-three. The government was again in command of the Commons and able to make credible demands on both the peers and, if the peers persisted in their obduracy, the

King. Faced at last by a determined Cabinet, the Lords not so much capitulated as made a strategic withdrawal in order to regroup and prepare for the bigger struggle ahead. On 29 April 1910, the Finance Bill of 1909 was given a third reading by 324 votes to 231. The People's Budget was approved a year to the day after its introduction, and the Chancellor celebrated its passing by taking friends to dinner at the Savoy Hotel.

The fiscal battle had been won but the constitutional war had still to be fought. Redmond's Irish Nationalists had been temporarily satisfied with Asquith's assurance that the King would be asked – if the Lords refused to yield – to create new peers. It would not be long before they demanded to know how he had replied. The King's advisers, and their associates in the establishment, recognised that a constitutional crisis had been postponed rather than averted. They began to consider how to respond without accepting the changes which the government demanded.

Edward VII had returned from Biarritz on 27 April. On the same day, Arthur Balfour – at Lambeth Palace with Knollys – offered the Archbishop of Canterbury what he represented as a way of avoiding both crisis and capitulation. The King, he said, would be wholly justified in both refusing to create new peers and rejecting Asquith's request for the dissolution of Parliament. If such a situation were to arise, he would be prepared to accept the King's commission to form an administration. He did not say how the Unionists – with a hundred seats fewer than the combined total of the Liberals, Irish Nationalists and Labour – would carry on the government, but his ability to maintain a minority in office was never tested. Knollys – no longer an advocate of royal resistance – wisely decided that it was his duty to withhold the leader of the opposition's offer from the King. To hand the Unionists the Seals of Office would be to guarantee that the sovereign and his Parliament were in open conflict. So he protected his master from the temptation to stretch the constitution to breaking point. He did not have to keep his secret for long. A week after his return to London, Edward VII died in his sleep.

Lloyd George 'got on excellently' with George V, with whom, soon after the accession, he had an 'exceedingly frank and satisfactory talk about the political crisis'. He told Margaret, 'There's not much in his head.' So when the King 'expressed the desire to try his hand at conciliation', he politely agreed while privately believing that 'whether he will succeed is somewhat doubtful'.[20] Edward's death required the government to re-examine its plans for the House of Lords. 'It had not entered our calculations. What insolent creatures we all are. We reckoned without taking the great ruler into account.'[21]

Although the great ruler did nothing to help the government decide how to proceed, the old King did – thanks to the initiative of a newspaper – offer what was represented as his advice from the grave. His posthumous message was invented and conveyed to his grieving people through the leader columns of the *Observer*. The editorial called for 'A Truce of God'.

> If King Edward upon his death bed could have sent a last message to his people he would have asked us to lay party passion aside, to sign a truce of God over his grave, to seek . . . some fair means of making a common effort for our common country . . . Let conference take place before conflict is irrevocably joined.[22]

J. L. Garvin, the author of the editorial, attempted to convince the Unionist leadership of the wisdom, and expediency, of following his recommendation. 'What I hate,' he told Balfour, 'is the thought of having to drag the new King into the fiercest of political battles. We might win – I think we would – but the ultimate results would not be a good outcome for us . . . Anything worse than a small majority for a Unionist party, compelled to tackle Lords reform and tariff reform, cannot be conceived.'[23] It is not clear why Garvin believed that Balfour, in office, would accept the need to change either the powers or the membership of the House of Lords. Northcliffe, Garvin's employer, was persuaded to support the idea of a truce by the news that the old and frail, but still influential, Joseph Chamberlain had returned from the South of France 'flatly against the idea' but had then been 'largely converted'.[24] A newspaper stunt had been turned into a policy.

Whether or not Garvin correctly reported the dead King's views, there is no doubt that the idea of an all-party conference had been in his mind before he died. It had been put there by Alexander Murray, who became the advocate of the idea inside the government. Lloyd George was sympathetic but – in light of the antagonism of both the *Morning Post* and *Daily News* – thought it expedient to remain silent. The Prime Minister, who recognised both tactical and intrinsic merit in the idea, agreed to call what he described as a 'constitutional conference'. It met on 16 June. Asquith, Lloyd George, Augustine Birrell (the Irish

Secretary) and Lord Crewe represented the government; Balfour, Austen Chamberlain, Lord Lansdowne and Lord Cawdor the opposition.* Although the future of Ireland was one of the subjects on the conference agenda, the Irish Nationalists were not invited to attend.

According to his biographer, Bonar Law accepted membership of the conference with the sincere intention of arguing for a mutually acceptable solution, built around a revival of the proposal that disputes between the two Houses of Parliament should be resolved by joint sessions.[25] But he must have known that the government was highly unlikely to accept the idea. And his second proposition – that finance bills should be the undisputed property of the Commons only when they 'had no social or political consequences' – was clearly anathema to New Liberals who saw the Budget as an instrument of policy as well as a national balance sheet. It was also an absurdity. Some nineteenth-century Budgets had no social intentions. All had social consequences. The idea of a Budget without political content could have been imagined only by a man who believed his own prejudices to be above politics.

There were twenty-one meetings of the constitutional conference before its members acknowledged the futility of continuing. Many of the discussions examined what Lloyd George regarded as theoretical concepts, far removed from the real business of government. The attempt to distinguish between 'ordinary' legislation (which the House of Lords could only delay) and 'organic' or 'constitutional' proposals (over which it might, or might not, have greater powers) illustrated for him the detachment from reality which made the whole proceedings a waste of time. Unless the conference could find a way of making progress towards Irish Home Rule, the legislative logjam would stand in the way of all that he wanted to achieve. Resolving the Irish impasse was not within its power. As the summer wore on, he grew increasingly impatient with the political stalemate. The ideal remedy was an election victory which swept away the opposition. But if that were possible at all, it was a long-term solution. And Lloyd George was always in a hurry.

Outside the conference Lloyd George continued to manage the nation's financial affairs and, unusually for him, devoted some time to

---

*The Unionist delegation's claim to represent the whole nation was undermined by their adolescent relationship. At Eton, Balfour had fagged for Lansdowne, and Cawdor had fagged for Balfour.

his family. Uncle Lloyd visited Downing Street. He had become a well-known, perhaps even famous, figure far outside the principality as a result of newspaper profiles of his nephew which rightly described him as the man who had provided for the Chancellor of the Exchequer in his fatherless boyhood and had, as Lloyd George grew up, become his 'mentor, tutor and comforter in times of trouble'. In his Welsh language biography D. R. Daniel, who met the old man during his visit to London, rejoiced at the thought of 'this famous, honest craftsman from the little countryside of distant Eifionydd, the most Nonconformist preacher in Wales [sitting] in the rooms of his old hero, Gladstone, the highest of churchmen'.[26] Uncle Lloyd's reputation for 'never speaking ill of any man' was slightly tarnished by an expression of regret that Herbert Gladstone, who was born in the house, 'had allowed the title of Lord to be attached to that noble name'.[27] Without malicious intent, he described his nephew as 'heavier now' – attributing the fattening frame not to high living in London and on continental holidays but to a 'tendency on our side of the family to fatten'.[28] He might have added that Lloyd George's hair was longer, his moustache less precisely trimmed and that he occasionally wore a cloak which he had brought home from Austria. He was evolving into the figure immortalised by a thousand photographs and a statue of dubious merit in Parliament Square.

During the last week in June, Lloyd George introduced the second Budget which he could call his own. In the same month he voted against the Conciliation Bill, a measure which – as its name implied – was meant to soothe the savage breasts of suffragists by extending to women the limited voting rights which men possessed. He again argued that justice and political necessity argued against enfranchising women of property but denying the vote to the working classes.★ However, this Budget's proposals, unlike those of 1909, were not designed to benefit the poor at the expense of the rich. It neither introduced new nor increased old taxes – despite an anticipated reduction in revenue which the Chancellor described as cause for rejoicing. The previous year's increase in excise duty had resulted in a fall in the consumption of spirits and, according to Lloyd George, was also responsible for the decrease in the number of convictions for drunkenness. For a second year in succession the Budget statement anticipated the shape of social legislation to come – 'a great national scheme of insurance against unemployment

---

★The TUC and much of the Labour Party opposed the bill for the same reason.

and invalidity'. He also described some of the achievements of the first
stage of the social revolution – something approaching 900,000 men
and women were receiving old-age pensions and on 1 January 1911
another 240,000 recipients would be added to the list when the scheme
was extended to cover paupers. More than 100,000 men had been
found work by the newly created labour exchanges. The opposition had
dismissed as 'reckless promises' all the achievements which he had
described. Yet they had been achieved at the same time as the national
debt had been reduced, ensuring that 'the old country is still the sound-
est investment going'.[29]

Speaking to the City and to the world at the annual Mansion House
banquet, Lloyd George echoed the complaint that many of his predecessors had made – and many more of his successors would repeat. The
Chancellor of the Exchequer was assailed, on one hand, for taxing too
heavily and, on the other, for spending too little. His attack on what
would now be called 'the arms race' – '£450 million spent worldwide
on the machinery of destruction, an increase of £200 million in twenty
years' – confirmed that his defeat by McKenna and the Dreadnought
lobby still rankled. Before the summer was over, an irritant – which
more recent Chancellors have also had to endure – interrupted the consideration of more serious matters. The government, as represented by
the Treasury, was accused of intruding into the private lives of innocent
citizens. The land census was under way. Form Four required landlords
to provide information which had previously been supplied to the
Revenue by tenants. Rosebery – never a devotee of understatement –
led the charge.

> There's a cry of anguish throughout the land and with all con-
> nected with the land . . . Every one of those suffering, fellow
> countrymen is at this moment exposed to an inquisition unknown
> since the Middle Ages but it has tortured them almost to extinc-
> tion. The boot and the thumbscrew have not yet come but the
> Inquisition in every other form is complete.[30]

A parenthesis in Lloyd George's lecture to the Liberal Christian League
at the City Temple was designed to put 'the press hooters, sounding in
the stillness of a dull season' into perspective. Objective witnesses confirmed that 'it took about ten minutes' to answer the census questions.[31]
His defence of Form Four was a prosaic diversion from a highly emotional assault on a system which allowed 'a large mass of the population

in this, the richest country in the world' to live 'well within the area of
poverty and bordering on the frontiers of destitution and despair'.[32] The
attack on 'the idle rich . . . in London clubs or in the country, walking
about with guns on their shoulders' was not unexpected. 'The profligate extravagance with which land by the square mile is thrown away
upon stags, pheasants and partridges as compared with the miserly greed
with which it was doled out for the habitation of men, women and
children' was vintage Lloyd George. So was his denunciation of the
'shallow but common fallacy that, in so much as these rich find employment for, and pay good wages to, those who minister to their comfort,
they are rendering a service to the community'. But the brief comment
on Imperial Preference was as unexpected as it was extraordinary.

> I am not a Tariff Reformer. All the same, I recognise that Mr
> Chamberlain's historic agitation has rendered one outstanding ser-
> vice to the cause of the masses. It has helped to call attention to a
> number of real crying evils festering amongst us, the existence of
> which the governing classes of this country were ignorant of or
> had overlooked.[33]

Some of Lloyd George's legislation at the Board of Trade – the protection of patents and the revision of maritime safety regulations – had been
interpreted as disguised protection by both his critics and the hopeful
devotes of Imperial Preference. However, the City Temple speech was
the first time that Lloyd George had said anything directly in favour of
the tariff reform campaign and it was in sharp contrast to his exposé of
Chamberlain's old-age pensions proposals as being dependent on revenue
raised by 'taxing the bread of the poor'. He was mending fences. The
new and uncharacteristic emollience was related to twenty-nine pages of
typescript which he had composed during the later spring and early
summer and dated 17 August. The Memorandum, as he called it, set out
the case for a coalition government. In the past, it argued, party conflict
may have helped to entrench democracy. But now it was essential to
unite 'the resources of the two parties into joint stock'. Britain faced
'imminent impoverishment if not insolvency'. The catastrophe could be
avoided if men of goodwill came together after 'party rivalries were
eliminated' to work together with 'intelligence and impartiality'.★

★The entire memorandum is published in Kenneth Morgan's *The Age of Lloyd
George*. It is not even mentioned in Henry du Parcq's authorised 1912 biography.

In his *War Memoirs* Lloyd George claimed that the examination of 'compulsory training' – a question which 'should not be shirked' – and the conclusion that 'the Swiss militia system might be considered' were the central themes of the whole manifesto. Reading the Memorandum in full suggests that the idea of education or industrial conscription was no more than a contribution to the paragraphs which examined 'directions in which money can be saved'. The Memorandum's passages on the land, unemployment, insurance and what he called 'national re-organisation' are much longer and carry much more conviction. It was in order to implement policies on those subjects that the coalition was to be created. To Lloyd George, constitutional reform and a solution – any solution – to the Irish question were no more than practical necessities. The object of government – Liberal government or coalition government – was to meet the needs of the 'multitude of industrious men, women and children for whom the earning of a comfortable living, and often a bare subsistence, is difficult and precarious'. The City Temple speech had identified them as his main concern and had proclaimed that 'the time has come for seeking a remedy, not in voluntary effort but in bold and comprehensive effort on behalf of the state'. The Memorandum set out how maximum support for that effort could be mobilised – a task which he could not begin until he had been reinvigorated by one of the continental holidays which were such a regular feature of his years in office.

A week after he had finished dictating the Memorandum, Lloyd George left London (accompanied by the Mastermans) for Austria and Italy. The Oberammergau Passion Play offended his Baptist belief in uncomplicated religion. It was denounced (on dubious authority) as representing 'the Christ of the theologians'. In Venice, typically, he 'refused to see any pictures and remained ten minutes in St Mark's'.[34] Throughout the visit, he was disconcerted by the absence of letters from home. One of the strange paradoxes of his relationship with Margaret was his need to maintain a regular correspondence with the wife he betrayed and neglected.

The holiday was cut short by royal command. Lloyd George was bidden to act as Minister in Attendance on the King at Balmoral – an arrangement engineered by Lord Crewe in the hope of creating a happy relationship between the monarch and his Chancellor. For a time, the trick worked. Lloyd George's first experience of royal hospitality was wholly enjoyable, 'entirely owing to the unaffected and simple kindness of the two principal persons'.[35] Margaret was sent a detailed account of the lunch at which her husband sat between the Prince of Wales – 'quite a nice little fellow' – and the Queen, who 'when the cigars came on . . . remained to smoke a cigarette'.[36] Lloyd George felt sufficiently at home to show the King a copy of his Memorandum and tell him that he proposed to send a copy to Balfour and Alexander Murray. Asquith – Prime Minister and Liberal Party leader – did not yet know of its existence.

The royal duties completed, Lloyd George made his way to Criccieth, where he was immediately joined by Winston and Clementine Churchill. The existence of the Memorandum and its purpose were revealed to them during a game of golf. The alternatives, according to Lloyd George, were a Liberal battle for land reform and national insurance (which might be lost) or the near certainty of pursuing a moderately radical programme under a coalition of progressives from both major parties. 'The real danger was that the government would drift along without any definite policy.'[37] Clementine was in favour of risking everything on a great leap forward. But her husband was more cautious, even though he thought that a coalition was the best hope for providing the 'slice of Bismarckism' for which he yearned.

According to the *War Memoirs*, Asquith saw the Memorandum (which was eventually addressed to him) before it was shown to any politician outside the Chancellor's immediate and intimate circle. But alternative accounts – most notably the biographies of F. E. Smith and Balfour as well as Balfour's *Times* obituary – claim that Asquith, if not the last to know, was not told until after consultations had begun with other political notables who were thought to be sympathetic to the idea.[38] Part of the plan was to elevate him to the House of Lords, where he would have been Prime Minister only in name. So it seems likely that he was never made privy to all of the strategy. However, he was certainly aware of the manifesto's existence by early October, when he told Lord Crewe, with weary detachment, 'LlG has been extending his missionary activities' towards Grey, 'apparently not without producing an impression'.[39]

Lloyd George, frustrated by the failure of informal conversations with the Unionist leadership, asked Churchill to make a direct approach to Balfour and Bonar Law. By then both Grey and Murray had given their approval to the idea of a coalition but not – since the proposition had never been put to them – to the Prime Minister's exile to the House of Lords. On 11 October, Lloyd George sent a note to Balfour which was so amiable that it bordered on the ingratiating.

If you would agree, it would give me great pleasure if you would dine with me tomorrow evening or, failing that, lunch with me after the [constitutional] Conference. The servants are Welsh and could not follow our conversation. The only other person present will be my little daughter of eight summers.[40]

They met over lunch and Balfour reported their conversation to Austen Chamberlain in language which was very near to being dismissive. If his account was accurate, Lloyd George barely mentioned the issues which really concerned him. Defence, the licensing laws and the end of the subsidy to denominational education 'were the things on which he laid stress . . . Something would have to be done for Ireland, probably as part of a general scheme of devolution.' Balfour's letter concluded with the explanation that 'we touched on so many questions and the initial difficulty of forming a coalition seemed so great that I did not think it worth coming to close quarters as to the exact nature and limitations of a programme that a coalition would carry out'.[41] Lloyd George was more hopeful. He told Lord Crewe that a compromise solution to the Irish Question seemed possible. Balfour, he wrote, was 'quite ready to consider any proposal for a federal arrangement'.[42] True or not, the claim made clear that he was prepared to sacrifice the ark of the Liberal covenant on the altar of coalition. A federal arrangement was Home Rule All Round – the policy proposed by Joseph Chamberlain before he split the Liberal Party and destroyed William Gladstone's government.

A willingness to support 'a federal arrangement' – if it were the price of party cooperation – had been a feature of the Memorandum. On 29 October, after consultation with Murray, a Second Memorandum confirmed Lloyd George's willingness to abandon ancient beliefs.*

A settlement of the Irish Question and of the difficulties of congestion in the House of Commons could be attempted on some such lines as were sketched by Mr Chamberlain in his speech on the First Home Rule Bill of 1886 . . . Such a settlement being one which might form a nucleus for the Federation of the Empire at some future date.

---

*The Second Memorandum is published in full as an annexe to chapter eight of Peter Rowland's *David Lloyd George*.

Not only was Lloyd George applauding the work of the Great Satan. He was also commending the disobedience which brought the woe of defeat to Gladstone and his Liberal governments, first in Parliament and then in the country. And that was only the beginning of his heresy. The Second Memorandum offered 'a full enquiry into the working of the fiscal system and the systems of our trade rivals'. It was to precede 'all action on the tariff question'. But, even while a permanent policy was being established, 'A preference was to be given to the Colonies on existing duties.' Lloyd George was offering to create the party which Joseph Chamberlain had hoped to lead.

On 9 October, Balfour had suggested to Lord Esher – with the clear intention that his message should be passed on to the King – that the best way to end the constitutional deadlock was for the Prime Minister to be summarily dismissed and replaced by an elder statesman who was above the party battle. The King had the good sense to ignore the suggestion. The constitutional conference dragged on for another month, but the Truce of God was effectively over. On 10 November, Asquith reported to the Cabinet that the conference would not meet again. Murray proposed an immediate dissolution. The Prime Minister agreed and the second general election which the King – like his father – required before he created new peers would be held before Christmas. The renewal of the party battle meant the end of Lloyd George's plans for a political realignment.

Perhaps they had been doomed from the start. That was certainly Asquith's opinion. 'I was sure it would come to nothing at all. I just laughed at it.'[43] Lloyd George's claim that 'Lord Lansdowne, Lord Cawdor, Lord Curzon, Mr Walter Long [the voice of the Tory squirearchy] and Mr Austen Chamberlain all favoured the plan' is hard to accept.[44] Balfour confessed to being fearful of becoming 'another Robert Peel* in my party'.[45] Even if the party leadership had been attracted by the idea, Lord Chileston – a former Conservative Chief Whip who had retired into House of Lords obscurity – was surely right to say that the party rank and file would never tolerate a coalition with the Liberals. Ireland was, and would remain, at the heart of their objection. The Union was an issue of principle which Lloyd George could not understand. Ten years later, his conduct was to confirm that any agreement that got Ireland out of Westminster politics was good enough for him.

Balfour's epitaph on the episode, as told to his niece and biographer,

---

*Peel split the Tory Party by abolishing the Corn Laws.

was a condemnation of Lloyd George's political integrity. 'Principles mean nothing to him – never have. His mind doesn't work that way. It's both his strength and his weakness. He says to himself at a given moment "Come on now – we've been squabbling for too long. Let's find a reasonable way out of the difficulties".'[46] The truth was more complex. Certainly Lloyd George felt no loyalty to either institutions or individuals. But there were two or three ideas – which could be elevated to the level of principle – to which he remained true all his life and for which he was prepared to sacrifice other political objectives which seemed to him less important. In the Second Memorandum, free trade and Home Rule were expendable. But paragraph 8 was unyielding and explicit.

> A National Scheme for Insurance, Sickness and Invalidity, and to make provision for Widows and Orphans, to be passed this year. Contributions to be levied from both Employers and workmen with a liberal state subsidy. Friendly Societies to be employed as agents where possible.

The proposed coalition was intended to ensure the safe passage of Lloyd George's social programme. Most of it was adopted, on the initiative of the Liberal Party alone, as the result of what he should have recognised as the necessary preliminary to social reform – the reduction of the powers of the House of Lords.

On 29 November, Lloyd George – preparing for battle – received a letter from Margot Asquith. It contained what she described as

> a political appeal . . . Don't when you speak on platforms arouse what is low, sordid and violent in the audience. It hurts those who are fighting these elections with the noblest desire to see fair play. If your speech only alienated Lords, it would not perhaps so much matter. But they hurt not only the king and men of high estate but good poor men. They lose votes.[47]

Lloyd George's response to that extraordinary combination of condescension and presumption is not recorded, though we know that the Chief Whip commented, 'As if we have not enough to do!' and assured Lloyd George that the Prime Minister knew nothing of his wife's initiative. It was no doubt Murray's intervention which prompted Mrs Asquith to write the next day: 'I am sorry if I have vexed you. My motives were of the highest and best.'[48] The apology was spoiled by renewed criticism of some of Lloyd George's more belligerent speeches.

The general election of December 1910 produced a House of Commons which was almost identical to the one that had been elected in January. The Liberals won 272 seats and the Unionists 271, but the Labour Party (42 Members) and the Irish (a combined total of 84) ensured the government's survival as long as it proceeded with constitutional reform and Home Rule. The King remained fearful that the Lords would remain obdurate in defiance of the popular will and that the government would insist that he appoint new peers.

The Parliament Bill, which removed the peers' right to amend or defeat finance bills and reduced their powers from the defeat to the delay of other legislation, was introduced into the House of Commons on 21 February 1911. It completed its passage though the Commons on 15 May. The Lords, after giving it a second reading without a division, adjourned for the Whitsun recess. On the peers' return, they spent six days in committee amending the bill out of all recognition. It seemed that the King would have to intervene. How he was protected from that constitutional embarrassment is still open to dispute. According to Lucy Masterman – wife of the Chancellor's lieutenant and herself a close, though platonic, friend – Lloyd George bluffed Balfour into believing that the King had agreed to appoint new peers on the day before a request for him to do so was sent by 10 Downing Street. Mrs Masterman kept a diary in which the basic facts are usually right, though the details are often woefully wrong. It recorded that Lloyd George and Balfour 'shared a hymn book' at the investiture of the Prince of Wales and, after Lloyd George had accused the Unionists of 'committing suicide', the two men agreed 'to talk things over'. Some of the ground was cleared in preparation for a meeting the next day. 'Well, look here,' said Lloyd George, 'I'll be frank with you. You know we have got the guarantees.' Balfour replied, 'I came to that conclusion lately. But, you know, a lot of our people don't believe it. Lansdowne does not believe it.'[49] The Masterman diary suggests that Balfour had experienced some difficulty in convincing Lansdowne that new peers would be created, but that the next day Balfour visited the Chancellor in his office to say 'they had decided that they must give way'.[50]

The investiture was on 13 July. So, if Lucy Masterman's account is correct, the conversation took place and the concession was made during the day before the Cabinet was shown the request for peers which the Prime Minister proposed to send to the King and a month before the House of Lords passed the Parliament Bill. The temptation is to assume that Lloyd George invented the whole story to convince a handsome woman that he was central to the defeat of the Lords. There is, however, one item in the account of his conversations with Balfour which sounds entirely authentic. He told Balfour, or claimed to have told Balfour, 'I think that, fundamentally, our wishes are the same in this matter. Neither you nor I want to create peers. You because of Home Rule, I because, looking into the future, I know our glorified grocers will be more hostile to reform than your Backwoodsmen.'[51] Reform mattered to Lloyd George. Ireland did not.

The formal account of how the Lords were confounded – consistent with the Masterman diary only if Lord Lansdowne and Balfour were intriguing against their own party – is more prosaic. On 20 July, Lansdowne wrote to the Prime Minister to ask for a statement of the government's intentions which he could read to a meeting of Unionist peers on the following day. Asquith replied that, 'should the necessity arise, the Government will advise the King to exercise his prerogative to secure the passing into Law of the Bill in substantially the same form in which it left the Commons'.* On 24 July, Unionist MPs left no doubt that they understood exactly what the message meant and gave no indication that their leaders were willing to capitulate. The Prime Minister was shouted down in the House of Commons with cries of 'Traitor', 'Who killed the King?' and (although it is not reported in the Asquith biographies) a reference to Asquith's known weakness, 'Why don't you get a drink?'[53]

Some peers still wanted to die gloriously. The Unionists divided into two factions, each of which was given a schoolboy nickname – suitably related to the agricultural labours with whose employment the peers were familiar. The Hedgers were prepared to surrender. The Ditchers wanted to fight on. The Prime Minister, uncertain of the eventual outcome, drew up a list of 249 candidates for ennoblement. It included Gilbert Murray, J. M. Barrie, Thomas Hardy and Bertrand Russell.

On 10 August 1911, the Parliament Bill – sent by the Commons to

---

*The King wrote in his diary, 'I agreed most reluctantly to give the Cabinet a secret undertaking that, in the event of the Government being returned with a majority in the General Election, I should use my prerogative to make peers, if asked to do so. I did dislike doing this very much but agreed that was the only alternative to the whole Cabinet resigning.'[52]

the Lords for a second time – was carried by 131 votes to 114. Thirteen bishops and thirty-seven Unionist peers – under the unexpected leadership of Lord Curzon – supported the government. Balfour, denounced by the *National Review* in an article signed 'BMG' – 'Balfour Must Go' – accepted responsibility for the Unionist humiliation and resigned the party leadership. He remained in the wilderness until the necessities of war called him back to his country's service. Seven years later – with Andrew Bonar Law (his Unionist successor), F. E. Smith (who had led the parliamentary riot of 24 July) and Lord Curzon (the Hedger-in-Chief) – he served in a coalition government under David Lloyd George.

CHAPTER 18

NINEPENCE FOR FOURPENCE

Although the election result had been a disappointment and the House of Lords had yet to be tamed, as Christmas 1910 approached Lloyd George could have had no doubt that his personal star was again in the ascendant. M. E. J. Dillon, the distinguished Russian correspondent of the *Daily Telegraph*, told him that he was the British citizen whose name most continental Europeans knew, and his fame at home (which had been increased by the exuberance of the speeches he had made during the election campaign) seemed likely to grow with the passage of an Insurance Bill which he assumed would be universally popular. The one cause for worry was his health. The pain in his throat had returned. It was necessary, his doctor told him, 'to stop smoking and talking for some weeks'. On 20 December, he left for France with Margaret, Megan and a private secretary. They were joined after Christmas by the Mastermans. Smoking was reduced. Talking continued unabated.

The holiday began badly. As the party travelled across France, *L'Humanite* published an article that was based on an interview which Lloyd George had given to the paper a couple of weeks previously. It concluded that the Chancellor of the Exchequer was a socialist. The *Daily Telegraph* cabled a request for confirmation. A comprehensive answer was provided by an interview with *Le Matin* in which Lloyd George commended the French Prime Minister for the wage settlement he had imposed on railwaymen and promised to maintain the Royal Navy's mastery of the seas. He was to return to that subject, with disastrous results, six months later.

Lloyd George did not enjoy the two weeks which he spent at the Cap Martin Hotel. He was a 'country cousin who liked to be in places where there are bands and functions and a general sense of gala'.[1] He particularly enjoyed Monte Carlo although he never visited the casino. In the New Year, he was lent a car by Joseph Pulitzer, the proprietor of the *New York World*, and the whole party drove on to Nice. At the Hotel Anglais they were joined by Sir John Bradbury, principal clerk at the Treasury, and John Braithwaite, the assistant secretary of the Board of Inland Revenue. A few days later Sir Rufus Isaacs, the new Solicitor General, arrived to advise on the way in which Friendly Societies could play a role in the extension of national insurance but – either because of Lloyd George's impatience with legal niceties or his failure to resolve some of the dilemmas about the bill's contents – the discussions took a more general form. The briefing began on the pier. Bradbury, against the background of brass-band music, reported on his examination of the German system.

One crucial decision had already been taken. Legislation for both invalidity and unemployment benefits would be brought before Parliament in a single bill. Part I would deal with the health insurance. Part II would set out the scheme which Churchill had prepared at the Board of Trade before he was promoted to Home Secretary. Alexander Murray – a Lloyd George ally – had persuaded Asquith that amalgamation was the best way both to manage the parliamentary programme and to acknowledge that Lloyd George was the true begetter of the unemployment insurance proposals which he had revealed to Churchill 'in a weak moment'. The claim that Churchill had stolen Lloyd George's idea was an invention.[2] Initially Churchill fought a losing battle against what was clearly an encroachment on his territory. 'My agreement with you was quite clear . . . It would be for me to decide when I should bring the subject forward. I did not think you would reserve to yourself freedom to oppose me on tactics in cabinet. I should greatly resent it.'[3] But he put up surprisingly little resistance when the day came. He told his wife, 'Lloyd George has practically taken over unemployment insurance to his own bosom and I am, I think, effectively bowed out of this large field in which I consumed thought and effort.'[4] Lloyd George was the boss.

For over a year, discussions on the future of national insurance had been complicated, rather than clarified, by the majority and minority reports of the Royal Commission on the Poor Law. The majority proposed the creation of a single institution with responsibility for

destitution in all its forms. The minority, under the leadership of
Beatrice Webb, wanted a number of departments (including a new
Ministry of Labour) coordinated by a Registrar of Public Assistance.
The politicians (particularly John Burns at the Local Government
Board) worried most about the distribution of responsibility and prestige, but both reports raised questions about the philosophy of poor
relief – particularly the causes of poverty and, in consequence, who
should be eligible for help and on what terms. The majority report was
explicit. 'The causes of distress are not only economic and industrial; in
their origins and character they are largely moral.' The condition of the
poor resulted 'possibly from their own failure and faults'. The discussion
about financing health and unemployment schemes was therefore
extended beyond considerations of public expenditure and the effects
on Friendly Societies. The question 'Who should pay?' became inextricably linked to 'Who is eligible to receive payments?' John
Braithwaite, who became the architect of the 1911 Insurance Act, had
no doubt what the answers should be. 'Working people ought to pay
something. It gives them a feeling of self respect and what costs nothing is not valued.'[5] Contributions also created a class of eligible
beneficiaries who received payment as a right – whatever the causes of
distress. Churchill's dictum sounded harsh. 'The qualification for insurance must be actual. You qualify, we pay. If you do not qualify, it is no
good coming to us.'[6] But it amounted to the decision that 'guilt' – the
sin of self-inflicted destitution – would be no bar. Lloyd George made
the same point more agreeably. 'Medical treatment shall be given without regard to cause or nature of the disease.'[7]

It was agreed, after some argument, that the scheme would be
financed, at least in part, by contributions. It was also decided, in a bid
to avoid antagonising the private insurance companies, that the scheme
should not include 'death benefits', a major source of their business.
But, towards the end of 1910, an article in *Insurance Mail* had announced
'on exceptional authority that the government intended to introduce a
state-aided scheme which was practically industrial insurance'. The
'Industrial Societies' – the Prudential, the Royal Liverpool and the
Liverpool Victoria – specialised in benefits payable after the contributor's death. They included funeral costs, lump sums, widows' and
orphans' pensions. They had already been unnerved by a passage in a
speech which Lloyd George had made at a meeting in London at Mile
End Road during the general election campaign. He had promised to
legislate against 'the anxiety and distress that comes to families when the

breadwinner's health breaks down'. At the time that he made the commitment he had no clear idea how it could be fulfilled or even what, in
practice, it implied. It was not his way to fight on two fronts at once. So
he turned the imprecision of Limehouse from problem to advantage by
'clarifying' his intentions in a way which he believed would turn some
of his enemies into friends. 'The proposed benefits do not include the
provision of a funeral benefit or any immediate money payment on the
death of a contributor or his relative.'[8] The wording, carefully chosen,
amounted to an announcement that, although death benefits had been
abandoned, widows' pensions might still be included in the scheme.

A respectable burial – the 'good send-off' with the ham tea – was so
important to working families that 'sums from 6d a week to 1/6d or
even 2/- go out from incomes which are so small that these sums represent perhaps from 2 to 10 per cent of the whole household allowance'.
Credit was rare, usually 'ready money must be found'. So proud and
prudent women made savings 'which were not of the slightest benefit
to the families concerned' or borrowed from local money-lenders.
Then, 'for months afterwards the mother and children [ate] less in
order to pay back the money borrowed'.[9] Dropping death benefit from
the scheme was more injurious to the poor than later, and less respectful, generations have realised.

The Industrial Societies – run by the great insurance companies –
remained apprehensive. In an attempt to allay their fears that a state
scheme would undercut their subscriptions and exceed their rates of
benefit, Lloyd George – faith in his own powers undiminished –
arranged a meeting with the 'Combine', the association of the twelve
largest companies. Before it took place, his throat became so painful that
he abandoned London for Criccieth and left Isaacs, Masterman,
Bradbury and Braithwaite to deal with the societies' spokesman,
Howard Kingsley Wood, a future Chancellor of the Exchequer.

Wood's negotiating technique relied more on ultimatum than on
persuasion. The Industrial Societies had already mustered enough support in the House of Commons to defeat any attempt to introduce a
state system of widows' and orphans' benefits. So the government
would be wise to abandon the scheme at once. What was more, the
Combine expected its members to be allowed, on a par with the
Friendly Societies, to become agents for the distribution of invalidity
benefit. At a final meeting at the Hotel Albion in Brighton on 19
February, Lloyd George, largely restored to health, agreed to their
demand. The Friendly Societies had lost their favoured status but, as

always, Lloyd George was able to offer private reassurance. The rules of the scheme would require its agencies to be democratically controlled by the beneficiaries and, in consequence, the Industrial Societies would choose not to take part. The private assurance was not honoured. Ten years later – applying the same negotiating technique – he privately told Sinn Fein that, although Ireland would be partitioned, the boundary revision he proposed would guarantee that the Six Counties eventually chose to join the Irish Free State.

The change that most damaged the Friendly Societies was the abandonment of widows' pensions – which accounted for half of the cost of the original scheme. The saving made by its abandonment allowed other benefits to be doubled. With the payment set at its original figure of 5/- a week, state insurance was a poor relation of the Friendly Society policies. When it was increased to 10/-, the Friendly Societies – required to finance their payments from the limited contributions of working men – could not compete. The eventual agreement that the Combine's members could become 'approved societies' was no more than a dance on the Friendly Societies' coffin. The Antediluvian Order of Rakebites and the Ancient Order of Oddfellows ceased to be powers in the land.

Both Lloyd George's health and his temperament prolonged discussion on the actual contents of the bill. He frequently changed his mind about the big issues and regularly refused to spend time on the small. And, because of a recurrence of the still undiagnosed throat condition, he took a prolonged holiday at his fellow Liberal MP Sir Arthur Markham's house in Beachborough, Kent.* While he was there he made notes on the speech with which he proposed to introduce the bill. They included the not directly relevant comment that the 'man who receives rent and ground rent of houses reeking with contamination that kills little children . . . receives stolen property'.[10] Miss Hicks, a voice restorer, made regular visits. But Lloyd George was distracted from the work of his department by his growing, but happily mistaken, conviction that he was suffering from cancer. He did, however, concentrate on one vital issue – whether health insurance should, like Friendly Society schemes, 'divide out' surpluses at the end of each year, if necessary by reducing contributions; or if, like the members of the Combine, it should accumulate reserves against a sudden run on its resources.

---

*Braithwaite was surprised to learn that the recuperating Chancellor had joined the local squirearchy in a badger hunt and at the boisterous party which followed.

At first, Lloyd George believed that the accumulation of a 'fund' of undistributed reserves was neither necessary nor politically possible. He insisted that the contributors – being simple working people – would demand the distribution of accumulated surplus in higher levels of benefit. The Friendly Society scheme to which Uncle Lloyd had contributed worked in that way. Lloyd George also had ideological objections to a fund. 'The State could not manage property or invest with wisdom. It would be very bad for politics if the State owned a huge fund. The proper course for the Chancellor of the Exchequer was to let money fructify in the pockets of the people and take it only when he wanted it.'[11] That echo of the young (and Tory) Gladstone was followed by a burst of New Liberal optimism. 'At no distant date, I hope State will acknowledge a full responsibility in the matter of making provision for sickness, breakdown and unemployment . . . Insurance will then be unnecessary and a great accumulated fund would tempt to extravagant and futile progress of expenditure.'[12]

Braithwaite argued against 'dividing out' on grounds of both equity and financial orthodoxy. A 'fund' would provide stability and if young contributors carried the financial burden at the beginning of the scheme, at the end of their lives the accrued interest would 'make up to them . . . contributions taken off and used by older people'.[13] He travelled down to Beachborough to argue his case and, after some lively discussion, was relieved to hear the Chancellor announce, 'I am inclined, after all, to be virtuous.'* It was neither the demands of equity nor the claims of orthodoxy which had converted Lloyd George. He had responded, like a good Chancellor, to the need to maintain confidence in his prudence and ensure that the financial institutions realised that national insurance respected the rules of sound finance.

The proposals which Lloyd George put before the Cabinet on 5 April 1911 were substantially different from the half-thought-out scheme which had been implied by the Mile End promise. State insurance – administered by 'approved societies', widely defined – was to cover all working people between the ages of sixteen and sixty-five who were earning less than £165 a year, the starting rate for income tax. The weekly contribution was to be 9d for men and 8d for women. It would be financed by three separate payments – 4d from the wages of the

---

*He was also persuaded to call the scheme 'health insurance' rather than 'invalidity benefit'. The latter name, which was thought archaic in 1911, was revived ninety years later.

insured man (3d for women), 3d from the employer and 2d from the government. The slogan which promoted the scheme was '9d for 4d'. In return for a payment which covered less than half the cost, contributors were entitled to unlimited care from an approved society doctor, 10/- a week (7/6 for women) for thirteen weeks of sickness and 5/- a week indefinitely for the chronically sick.★ Each approved society was required to assist in the cost of building and running new tuberculosis sanatoria. Collection of the contributions was to become the responsibility of employers, who deducted their employees' payments from their wages and then bought, on their behalf, an insurance stamp from the local post office. The 'stamp' became – for both supporters and opponents – the symbol of national insurance, derided by opponents of the scheme and exalted by its adherents as the guarantee of security in ill health.

When it was introduced into the House of Commons on 4 May, it seemed that there was universal agreement with the judgement on the proposals made by ministers and reported to the King.

> After searching examination, the Cabinet expressed warm and unanimous approval of the main and governing principles of the scheme which they believed to be more comprehensive in its scope and more provident and statesmanlike in its machinery than anything that had hitherto been attempted or proposed . . . The two measures taken together with the Old Age Pension Act will . . . form the largest and most significant measure of social reform yet achieved in this country.[14]

Lloyd George was confident that the scheme commanded widespread public support. 'I believe there is a general agreement as to its urgency and I think I can go beyond that and say that there is general agreement as to the main proposals.' Its purpose was to 'relieve untold misery in myriads of homes – misery which is undeserved'.[15] Austen Chamberlain – replying on behalf of the opposition – felt unable to speak in favour of untold misery. So he promised that if the Chancellor 'turned to constructive work . . . he [would] not appeal in vain to any section of the House'.[16] His private reaction was less measured.

★The period of benefit was subsequently increased from thirteen to twenty-six weeks, a maternity benefit of 30/- was added for wives of insured men, and manual workers were included in the scheme if they earned more than £160 a year.

'Confound Lloyd George. He has strengthened the government again. His sickness scheme is a good one and on the right lines.'[17]

Next day, the newspapers were ecstatic in their praise. *The Times* described the bill's intention as 'an object all would wish to see realised'. The *Daily Mail*, which had previously called health insurance a 'leap in the dark', made a minor adjustment to its metaphor and welcomed 'a great step forward in social reform'. Two days later, the *Observer* welcomed 'by far the largest and best project of social reform ever yet proposed by a nation. It is magnificent in temper and design.' Even the *British Medical Journal* was unequivocally complimentary. The bill was 'one of the greatest attempts at social legislation which the present generation has known'. It seemed 'destined to have a profound influence on social welfare'.[18]

The support of the *British Medical Journal* lasted for one issue. In the days which followed, the periodical was inundated with critical letters. Many of them expressed anxiety about the status of doctors employed, or apparently employed, by the approved societies. Many more had read reports of the debate which quoted Lloyd George as saying that the 'capitation fee' paid to doctors for each patient in their care would be 'up to 4/-'. The reports were accurate but the Chancellor's statement was wrong. He had meant to say 'above 4/-'. At a special meeting of the British Medical Association Council, Lloyd George corrected his error and offered to move the management of the scheme from the approved societies to statutory local health committees. 'I am entirely with you if you can persuade the House of Commons to consent to the transfer of the whole medical attendance, including maternity . . . you will find me an enthusiastic supporter of that proposal'.[19] The implication that he had always been in favour was as false as the suggestion that Parliament might be opposed. The six other changes which the BMA demanded could not be made. But after the change of employment status, the remaining reservations were not strong enough to make the doctors oppose the bill outright. Once again Lloyd George's negotiating technique – conceding whatever was necessary to achieve the bare bones of his central objective – had worked.

Health insurance was, however, far less popular with the general public – who thought more about the certainty of paying 4d now than the possibility of receiving the fruits of 9d in the distant future – than the Cabinet had anticipated. And the opposition parties in the House of Commons thought it their democratic duty to reflect the popular sentiment. Although Ramsay MacDonald had promised that he and 'his friends' would give their general support to the bill, George Lansbury (always the *soi-disant* conscience of the Labour Party and its future leader) joined with Philip Snowden (ironically, in view of his future conduct) in opposing the contributory system, which they denounced as a poll tax on the poor. Keir Hardie caricatured the government's attitude as the assurance 'we shall not uproot the cause of poverty, but we will give you a porous plaster to cover the disease that poverty causes'.[20] Hardie – like the Webbs, with whom he had little else in common – wanted free sickness and unemployment benefit to be paid for by progressive taxation. And there were the usual objections – often heard in the twentieth century – to the state usurping the role of the trade unions. The state had no right to supply services to working men which their unions provided inadequately or not at all. Their objections actually stimulated Lloyd George into defending the bill in a way which might have encouraged the belief that he approved of trade unions and wanted to see them prosper.

> In Germany, the trade union movement was a poor, miserable, wretched thing some years ago. Insurance has done more to teach the working class the virtue of organisation than any single thing. You cannot get a Socialist leader in Germany today to do anything to get rid of that Bill . . . Many Socialist leaders in Germany will say that they would rather have our Bill than their own . . .
>
> If Honourable Members reject the Bill it will be a very serious responsibility. I do not think it will be one for which the labouring classes would thank them. I would remind them that the Bill benefits the poorer classes.[21]

The objections of the Irish Nationalists were even more bizarre than the Labour Party's reservations. O'Brien said that free medical care was already available in Ireland through the agency of either the Poor Law or the charity hospitals. If the government was determined to increase spending on health, Ireland should be treated separately. The peasantry should be relieved of the burden of making a contribution, and the government's 3d subsidy should be paid directly to the eligible workers – to spend on medicine in whatever way they chose. O'Brien argued that unemployment – not health – was the curse of Ireland. Despite the irrationality of his argument, the Redmondites felt it necessary to echo his populist demands. The Irish workers' contribution was reduced from 4d to 3d, the employer's from 3d to 2½d, and the clauses in the bill which authorised medical cover were amended to exclude Ireland.

On 16 May 1911, Lloyd George, as part of his Budget statement, made an announcement which helped to solidify the often fluid relationship between the government and the minority parties. Members of Parliament were to be paid for the first time. The Unionists denounced the proposal as a straight bribe offered to secure Labour's continued allegiance. In fact, payment for MPs had been part of party policy since the Newcastle Programme of 1891 and Lloyd George had first-hand knowledge of what life was like for a Member without a private income. The Labour Party was not united in gratitude. Its leaders had hoped for a reversal of the 1909 Osborne judgement★ – the House of Lords ruling that meant a trade union could not, legally, contribute to the funds of a political party – and Keir Hardie – whose sanctity, although questionable, was far greater than his intellect – argued that a salary was incompatible with political independence. But by the autumn MacDonald had agreed 'to support a time limit' on the National Insurance Bill. That, Lloyd George wrote home to say, 'means an enormous lightening of my labours'.[22]

Even with a guillotine resolution in place, the National Insurance Bill spent twenty-nine days in committee and grew in length and complexity from 87 to 115 clauses with nine new schedules. Much of the time was spent dealing with technical points raised by a group of Unionist accountants and lawyers under the leadership of Laming Worthington-Evans. They were not points to which Lloyd George found it easy to reply. The President of the Board of Trade who had been reluctant to read his briefs and was impatient with detail had not changed his character when he was promoted to the Treasury. Discipline had to triumph over inclination and he possessed an invaluable power, when he concentrated his attention, to assimilate facts at speed. Even civil servants were impressed by the sight of 'Lloyd George rising to reply, knowing practically nothing when he rose about the particular facts, briefed as he went along by little pieces of paper passed along the bench from the officials' box and yet leaving the impression that the man had a more complete mastery of the subject than his critics'.[23]

The bill was amended in committee – as it had been amended before it reached the House of Commons – because of more pressure from industrial insurance, the Friendly Societies and the doctors as well as the

---

★The Osborne judgement would be reversed by the Trades Dispute Act of 1913.

trade unions, which insisted on becoming 'approved' administers of the scheme. But the Chancellor pronounced his own valediction on the bill which completed its passage through the House of Commons on 6 December and – having been passed without amendment in the Lords – received royal assent on 16 December 1911.

> I have been beaten sometimes but I have sometimes beaten off the attack . . . Members are entitled to say that they have wrung considerable concessions out of an obstinate, stubborn, hard-hearted Treasury . . . Let them be satisfied with what they have got . . . This is not a perfect Bill, but then this is not a perfect world.[24]

While the battle for the bill was being fought in the House of Commons and round the negotiating tables of the Treasury, the campaign in the country was dominated by the opponents of national insurance. Lloyd George naturally rejoiced when, six weeks before royal assent, the *Insurance Mail* wrote, 'The Chancellor has made a good bargain with our insurance institutions and this has support of 100,000 practical insurance men. He need fear no threats.'[25] It was wrong. During the next two months, the Liberal Party lost by-elections in Oldham, South Somerset and North Ayrshire. The rich were implacable in their reluctance to help the poor.

Between the introduction and second reading of the bill, Lloyd George campaigned in the country for its acceptance. He told the people of Birmingham that it had a practical as well as a moral purpose.* 'Money which is spent on maintaining the health, the vigour, the efficiency of mind and body in our workers is the best investment in the market.' That was not the sort of argument which appealed to the bill's pathological opponents. They were too rich plausibly to complain that they were being pauperised by the employers' levy. So they denounced the requirement to 'buy a stamp' for their domestic servants as an infringement of their employees' liberty. The *Daily Mail* – originally supportive of the bill – had changed sides in response to the opposition of its readers. It reflected their opinions by publishing letters from distressed servants under risible headlines – 'The Housemaid's Decision', 'Protest from the Rectory', 'Women Should Show the Way'.[26] The climax of the campaign was a rally in the Albert Hall on 29 November. The Dowager Countess Desart sat on the platform next

---

*The speech appears in full in Volume IV of du Parcq's *Lloyd George*.

to her maid whose objections to the National Insurance Bill were expressed by her employer. The Countess ended her impassioned address with the immortal lines from Shakespeare's *King John*: 'England never did, nor ever shall, lie at the proud foot of the Conqueror.'[27] The campaign left Lloyd George unmoved – even when Rita Humphreys, a romantic novelist, called for the mistresses of pro-bill politicians to go on strike.[28]

The Albert Hall rally, fatuous though in many ways it was, caused Asquith great concern.

> The Daily Mail has been engineering a particularly unscrupulous campaign on behalf of mistresses and maids and one hears from all constituencies of defections from our party of the small class of employers. There can be no doubt that the Insurance Bill is (to say the least) not an electioneering asset.[29]

His concern had been shared by ministers. Edwin Montagu, the Liberal Member for Chesterton, and a political bell-wether, had the temerity to express his concern to Lloyd George. His doubts were dismissed out of hand and, after he had left, the Chancellor exhibited the anti-Semitism which was a usually submerged feature of his character.★ 'Dirty coward. Men of that race usually are.'[30]

Members of the audience at the Albert Hall rally had complained that the Unionist Party had not opposed national insurance root and branch. Wiser Conservatives realised that the government, left to itself, was – in the words of a letter to Bonar Law, sent on New Year's Eve 1911 – 'doing all they can to help us'.[31] Optimism about the Unionist Party's future was increased by 'Labour unrest at home and affairs abroad in so many parts of the world'. As the insurance scheme was being initiated, Harold Spender had offered a view of the proposals which had done nothing to abate Labour's anxiety. 'English progressives [have decided] to take a leaf out of the book of Bismarck who dealt the heaviest blow against German socialism not by laws of oppression . . . but by that great system of state insurance which now safeguards the German workman at almost every point of his industrial career.'[32]

★He grew less prejudiced with age. In April 1937 the *Strand Magazine* contained an article – between short stories by James Hilton and P. G. Wodehouse – in which he denounced discrimination against 'the most remarkable race which ever dwelt on this earth'.

CHAPTER 19

THE DOVE BECOMES A HAWK

Harold Spender – discussing with Lloyd George the way ahead – was right to relate New Liberalism to what he described as 'Bismarckism' – the state's involvement in economic management and the welfare of the citizen. But although British progressives admired and envied Germany's domestic policy, they feared and resented its international presumption. In consequence the government stood ready to meet and match every attempt to extend the influence of Berlin.

On the morning of 1 July 1911, a German gunboat, the SMS *Panther*, tied up in Agadir harbour – ostensibly to protect German interests in Morocco but, in fact, to convince the French, who had troops stationed in Fez, that Paris did not have exclusive rights to influence in North Africa. The Admiralty was understandably anxious about the German Navy acquiring a permanent base on a major British trade route. But there was an even more compelling – and equally embarrassing – reason for imperial intervention in the incipient dispute. In 1904, France and Britain had signed a secret treaty. In return for the acceptance of British suzerainty in Egypt, the United Kingdom would support Morocco becoming a French protectorate. London expressed its concern to Berlin on 4 July. After waiting more than two weeks for a reply, Edward Grey told the Prime Minister that, unless he received a response by 21 July, he proposed to inform the German Ambassador that Britain 'must become party to any discussion' about the future of Morocco and that to make clear the seriousness of that demand, a warship of the Royal Navy would be sent to Agadir.

There are several different versions of what happened on the afternoon of the ultimatum. According to Lloyd George's *War Memoirs*, he was preparing the speech he was to make that evening at the Mansion House when he decided that it was his duty to 'warn Germany of the perils into which her Ministers were hurrying her so needlessly'. He had no independent right 'to intervene in a matter which was in the sphere of the Foreign Office'. So he 'submitted the terms' of his proposed warning to the Prime Minister, who 'fully approved and sent immediately to the Foreign Office to ask Sir Edward Grey to come to the Cabinet Room in order to obtain his views and procure his sanction . . . He cordially assented to every word.' Other accounts suggest that Asquith was ignored and that Grey proposed some changes to the text which Lloyd George accepted. Certainly the Foreign Secretary approved the final draft. A hundred years on it seems astonishing that he agreed to such a provocative declaration.

Most of Lloyd George's banquet speech – assurances about the stability of the economy and praise for the bankers of the City of London – was, as usual, delivered without notes. He then read from a sheet of paper.

> I believe it essential in the highest interests of not merely this country, but of the world, that Britain should at all hazards maintain her place and her prestige amongst the Great Powers of the world. Her potent influence has been, many a time in the past and may yet be in the future, invaluable to the cause of human liberty. It has more than once in the past redeemed continental nations who are sometimes too apt to forget that service from overwhelming disaster and even from national extinction. I would make great sacrifices to preserve peace. I conceive that nothing could justify a disturbance of international goodwill except questions of the gravest international moment. But if a situation were to be forced on us in which peace could only be preserved by the surrender of the great and beneficent position Britain has won by centuries of heroism and achievement, by allowing Britain to be treated where her interests were vitally affected, as if she were of no account in the Cabinet of Nations then I say, I say emphatically, that peace at that price would be a humiliation intolerable for a great country like ours to endure. National honour is no party question. The security of our great international trade is no party question. The peace of the world is much more likely to be secured if all nations realise fully what the conditions of peace must be.[1]

Metternich, the German Ambassador to London, told Grey that 'if the British Government had intended to embroil the political situation and lead towards a violent explosion they could not have chosen a better method than the speech of the Chancellor of the Exchequer'.[2] In Berlin, the British Ambassador was 'abused like a pick-pocket'[3] by the Kaiser, who, a week later, announced an increase in German naval construction 'so that nobody can dispute our rightful place in the sun'.[4] Lloyd George's Mansion House speech, far from securing the peace of the world, brought world war a stage closer.

Lloyd George's detractors assumed – and said – that the crisis in Anglo-German relations had been intentionally provoked to enhance the Chancellor's career or to damage his enemies and rivals. Calculating politicians are assumed to calculate everything. Often they have sudden spontaneous outbursts of genuine feeling. It is at least possible that Lloyd George simply wanted to express his selectively imperialist opinions on the subject and, at the same time, clear his name of pacifism. 'People', he told the Mastermans, 'think that because I am pro-Boer I am anti-war in general and that I should faint at the mention of a cannon! I am not against war a bit. I like Germans but I hate the Junker caste.'[5]

In the high summer of 1911, an undated letter assured Margaret that, although Ambassador Metternich had attempted to persuade the government to disown both the Mansion House speech and its author, 'Germany is climbing down.'[6] Even so, Asquith thought it right to call a meeting of the Committee of Imperial Defence for 23 August. The committee had no fixed membership. Three 'doves' who usually attended – Loreburn, who was Lord Chancellor, Harcourt and Crewe – were not invited. Lloyd George, whose credentials as a 'hawk' had been established in the Mansion House, and Churchill were included in the membership list for the first time. The committee took evidence on preparedness from the First Sea Lord, Sir Arthur K. Wilson, and from Brigadier Henry Wilson, the Director of Military Intelligence. Brigadier Wilson had revised his plans. Previously he had judged that the troops which Britain could send to Belgium, to frustrate a German attack on France from the north-west, would not halt the invasion. In August 1911 he recanted. Six British divisions would 'make the difference' between victory and defeat. The fate of Belgium, and perhaps France, was in Britain's hands.

Admiral Wilson took the traditional sailor's view. Europe was none of Britain's business. The Royal Navy could prevent invasion of Britain.

The army's role was the protection of India from Russian incursion through Afghanistan and the suppression of dissident tribesmen within the Raj. It should keep well clear of continental entanglements. His plan, in the event of war, was first to neutralise the German fleet and then attack the port of Wilhelmshaven and the Kiel Canal to make sure that it could not be brought back into effective use. He had made no plans to transport six British divisions to Belgium. Indeed neither he nor Reginald McKenna, the First Lord of the Admiralty, seemed to know that the General Staff proposed to reinforce the Belgian Army immediately war broke out.

The War Office was as much to blame as the Admiralty for the lack of coordination. But Brigadier Wilson made a more convincing presentation than his naval namesake. Haldane suggested that the two defence departments should be amalgamated – with him in charge of the new ministry. Although his idea was rejected, there was majority agreement that if Britain was not prepared, the blame lay with the Board of Admiralty. Perhaps it was the implied criticism of McKenna that made Lloyd George initially take an interest in military and naval matters which developed to the point of his becoming an amateur strategist. A letter sent to Churchill speculated about ways in which the German High Command could be forced to detach 'at least 500,000 men [from their main force] in order to protect their lines of communication'. It ended, 'I think that the chances of war are multiplying.'[7]

The preparations for war were interrupted by the investiture of the Prince of Wales in Caernarvon Castle – the occasion on which, according to Lucy Masterman, Lloyd George had convinced Arthur Balfour that the Lords would be forced to bow to the Commons' will. As a rule, Lloyd George did not enjoy the company of royalty. But he welcomed the diversion from more serious business as an opportunity to reassert his affection for Wales. The Bishop of St Asaph had suggested a formal, not to say spectacular, investiture and Lloyd George – now the constable of Caernarvon Castle – had taken up the idea with enthusiasm. The bishop, by then a close friend, searched ancient documents in the British Museum for details of how the medieval ceremony was performed. When it was clear that the inner bailey of the castle would not be able to accommodate everyone who wanted to witness Wales's moment of glory, Lloyd George arranged for the Prince to address the crowds in Castle Square before the ceremony began. His Royal Highness told the cheering masses, 'All Wales is a sea of song,' and offered 'thanks from the bottom of my heart to this old land of my fathers'. Both sentiments were expressed in passable Welsh – thanks to coaching by Lloyd George. The King was said to have been deeply impressed by the Chancellor and Constable choosing to play only a small part in the pageant – handing the keys of the castle to his sovereign as the royal party passed through the water gate. Knollys sent a message saying that 'the King is most pleased'.[8]

Throughout the day of rejoicing, relations with Germany must have been the silent preoccupation of both King and Constable. Later in the year, when Lloyd George was a guest at Balmoral, the King was perturbed by what he regarded as the Chancellor's general antagonism to Germany – a nation led by his cousin. He reported his feelings to Churchill when the Home Secretary arrived at Balmoral shortly after Lloyd George had left. Perhaps he had a guilty conscience. According to the gossip of the time, the Kaiser and King had discussed Morocco when the two grandsons met at the unveiling of the Victoria Monument.[9] The Kaiser asked if the King would object to a German gunboat being sent to Agadir, and the King gave his approval, subsequently 'forgetting' to tell the Foreign Secretary of the conversation.[10] On the other hand, Lloyd George may have offended by repeating the view he had expressed to Balfour. If Germany meant war, 'wouldn't it perhaps be better to have it at once?'[11] On his way to Balmoral, he had met Henry Wilson and told him that he was 'quite in favour of war now' – though the probability is that 'now' appeared at the wrong point of the sentence and Lloyd George was 'now in favour' rather than anxious for immediate hostilities. Wilson also 'asked him if he would give us conscription and he said that, although he was entirely in favour . . . he dare not say so until war broke out'.[12]

Writing to Margaret from Balmoral, Lloyd George announced

I am not cut out for court life. The whole atmosphere reeks of Toryism. I can breathe it and it depresses and sickens me. Everybody very civil to me as they would be to a dangerous wild animal whom they fear and perhaps just a little admire for its suppleness and strength. The King is hostile to the bone to all who are working to lift the working man out of the mire.[13]

The hostility was occasionally reduced by royal flattery. But it was real and lasting. Beaverbrook's complaint that he did not 'pay the King very much attention' understated his antagonism.[14] He refused to carry the Sword of State at the opening of Parliament on the grounds that he was not a court flunkey.[15] Even when Lloyd George was Prime Minister, 'he always got out of going to the palace if he could and constantly refused invitations to Windsor.'[16] Balmoral was more of a penance than a pleasure.

Royal duty done, Lloyd George set out with Alexander Murray on a Scottish tour. They met Grey at Fallodon and Asquith at Archerfield in East Lothian and on both occasions took the opportunity to argue for McKenna to be replaced by Churchill at the Admiralty. Lloyd George did no more than reinforce the Prime Minister's judgement that McKenna must be moved and the First Sea Lord retired. Asquith had already written to the First Lord complaining that, when he attempted to pursue the question of troop transport to Belgium, he had found that the whole Admiralty was on holiday. Churchill became First Lord and McKenna, with the greatest reluctance, replaced him at the Home Office. Britain's 'blue water strategy'* – in place since Waterloo and wholly consistent with McKenna's 'abhorrence of the use of British troops in France' – was abandoned.[17] The Admiralty cured Churchill's passion for 'economy'. The new ruler of the King's navy demanded an expenditure on new battleships which made McKenna's claims seem modest.

By the early autumn of 1911, even the most chauvinistic of British newspapers were beginning to doubt the wisdom of Lloyd George's Mansion House speech. The progressive papers had always doubted the wisdom of challenging Germany so aggressively. C. P. Scott, editor of the *Manchester Guardian* and former Liberal MP, feared that the Chancellor was not 'immune from the microbe of Germanophobia'.[18] But Lloyd George rose – if only temporarily – in Asquith's esteem when he once more rescued the country from a national rail strike.

Increases in the cost of living – which had combined with the militancy of the manual trade unions' leadership to precipitate the Tonypandy riots in 1910 – had continued into the following year.† Pay was the immediate cause, but the unions' bitterness was increased by their long-running dis-putes over recognition. The heatwave of August was popularly assumed to have shortened tempers on both sides of the several arguments.

On 8 August, the London dockers walked out. During the next few

---

*The belief that the sea and the navy were all that Britain needed to resist invasion.
†Churchill became, in trade union folklore, the Home Secretary who 'sent in the troops' to subdue the striking miners at Tonypandy in South Wales. The evidence suggests that he did his best to avoid the confrontation.

days they were followed by both the other traders in the Port of London and the women in the sweated factories of the East End – many of whom were dockers' wives. The employers met their demands. But, five days later, the dockers struck in Liverpool, supported by the railwaymen and power station labourers. The dispute spread to Glasgow and South Wales. Strikers rioted, troops were called in and, as was usual at the time, the government began to fear Red Revolution. A more imminent danger was a national rail strike, which would paralyse the whole British economy. On 13 August, the four railway unions agreed to empower their executives to call a strike at thirty hours' notice.

The strike threat was considered by the Cabinet on 16 August. It agreed – as Asquith reported to the King – that 'there is no doubt that the men have a real grievance'.[19] As the employers had smugly predicted, the 'conciliation committees', which had been the centrepiece of Lloyd George's settlement in 1907, had not worked. That did not, in Asquith's estimation, justify the unions shutting down the whole railway system – particularly at a time when tension between Britain and Germany had escalated to a point at which war, if not probable, was certainly possible.

Asquith himself met the railway unions on 17 August and offered to set up a Royal Commission to consider their members' wages and conditions of service. But – without explaining his concern about the international situation – he added that the railways must be kept running and that he would 'employ all the forces of the Crown' to ensure that they did so.[20] The union leaders had begun the meeting hoping that a strike could be avoided. But after receiving what they took to be an ultimatum, their attitude hardened. Royal Commissions took years to report. And the threat to use troops, which was what they assumed the Prime Minister proposed, seemed to be intentional provocation. When they rejected the offer, the Prime Minister closed the meeting with the words, 'Then your blood be on your own heads.'[21] The strike began the next day.

Asquith left London for the country. In his absence Lloyd George – believing, 'I could have stopped them if I had been at the negotiations' – decided to intervene. There is no evidence that he either sought the Prime Minister's permission or even told Noel Buxton (the President of the Board of Trade) that he proposed to trespass on his territory. Encouraged by Rufus Isaacs, the Solicitor General, he persuaded Ramsay MacDonald to find the railway union leaders who were still in

London and shepherd them to the Treasury. By the time that they arrived, during the afternoon of 19 August, the railway employers had been browbeaten into agreeing to meet the workers' representatives (without granting them formal recognition) and to re-employ without victimisation all the railwaymen who were already on strike. Lloyd George assumed that, added to the promise that the Royal Commission would report within weeks, he had done enough to end the dispute. He was wrong.

Southern trains were still running but in the North and Midlands the stoppage was so complete that no goods trains had left the sidings for twenty-four hours. The Lord Mayor of Manchester claimed that, in the absence of food supplies, his city was starving.[22] On 18 August, while Asquith was attempting to conciliate, Churchill had told the King, 'the railway strike will now be fought out'.[23] Determination turned to despair. 'The men have beaten us. We cannot keep the trains running . . . We are done.'[24] Next day, after rioters attacked a train outside Llanelli, troops opened fire. Two men were killed.

Lloyd George, though not despairing, was certainly exasperated. At dinner in the National Liberal Club he told Masterman, 'The men are the damndest fools. I have got them everything they want and yet they are now sticking out for recognition before the strike ends. It is not possible.'[25] The railwaymen were wiser than he recognised. Next day they went back to work. Lloyd George took the credit. 'Hardest struggle of my life but I won. I cannot even now realise how.'[26] The probability is that, at some point, Lloyd George, unlike Asquith, appealed to the railway union leaders' patriotism and encouraged their cooperation by confiding in them 'secret' details of the military preparations.

The end came suddenly. Lloyd George burst into a War Office planning meeting, which was considering how best the army could 'come to the aid of the civil power', and cried, 'A bottle of champagne! . . . The strike is settled.' Haldane was mystified as well as impressed. 'From that day to this, I have never known and none of his colleagues has even known how it was done.'[27] Margaret was delighted but not surprised. 'We knew it would be done once you got in touch with the employers' men and their leaders. To think that S Bux[ton] and the PM would settle it. I knew it was hopeless in their hands.'[28] The Prime Minister himself wrote an even more fulsome letter commending the Chancellor's 'indomitable purpose, untiring energy and matchless skills'.[29]

The Agadir Crisis ended in what Edward Grey called 'a patched up peace' with the signing of a Franco-German accord on 4 November. But for Asquith's government the turbulence of 1911 continued until the end of the year. On 7 November, the Prime Minister made the statement to the House of Commons which Lloyd George had promised the Albert Hall Women's Liberal Federation rally. Being a reasonable man, Asquith believed it would delight the suffrage movement. The government proposed to introduce a new Reform Bill. If, on a free vote, it was amended to include complete women's suffrage, the government would ensure that it completed all of its remaining stages. Lloyd George wrote in *Common Cause*, the suffragists' magazine, that at last 'the carrying of a woman's suffrage amendment on broad and democratic lines' was not in doubt.[30] But that happy day was two years distant. The militants of the movement saw issues of principle which moderates did not identify. They wanted votes now – and they wanted them provided by a bill of their own, not as the result of an afterthought tacked on to other legislation.

At the meeting of the Liberal Federation in Bath on 24 November, Lloyd George made one of his portmanteau speeches which approached his subject from every point of the compass. The claim which was made by the supporters of women's suffrage was as modest as it was moral. 'All we ask is that the custodian of the cupboard should have the weapon to defend her children's bread.' Opponents of a universal franchise hoped 'to destroy the Liberal Party by further packing the register'. The suffragettes who opposed the comprehensive change were motivated by political malice. Extending the limited franchise to women would have been 'grossly unfair to Liberalism. Now that Bill has been torpedoed the way is clear for a broad and democratic amendment to the suffrage . . . which will enfranchise not a limited class of women chosen just to suit the Tory canvass. That explains the fury of these anti-Liberal women.'[31]

That speech guaranteed Lloyd George an eventful December. In London, as he entered the Horticultural Hall in Vincent Square on his way to address the Women's Liberal Federation, he was struck on the temple by a stone thrown by a male sympathiser with the women's cause. It was a symbolic end to a bruising year – a year in which public aggression had been invariably matched with private conciliation in twelve months of extraordinary achievement and effort.

It was also a year in which, although he had little time to spare for his family, he did devote some attention to one pressing domestic problem. Megan was beginning to occupy the place in his affections which had been filled by Mair, and he increasingly feared that as a child in a house of adults, she would become lonely and introspective. The remedy was boarding school, for which she had to be prepared by a summer of private coaching. The chosen tutor was a young woman called Frances Stevenson.

CHAPTER 20

ENTER MISS STEVENSON

Frances Stevenson and Lloyd George were lovers for more than thirty years. What began as an 'affair' evolved into a permanent relationship and eventually became a marriage. Yet for all the time of their irregular union only a handful of intimate associates knew how close they were. He never spoke – even to those who knew the truth – about his love for Frances. She was so discreet that it was only in her autobiography – published more than twenty years after her husband's death – that the second Countess Lloyd George of Dwyfor described her feelings for the man who was to dominate her life. The purple prose of the passages which describe first sight and first meeting should not undermine faith in their accuracy. They may not give an accurate impression of how Lloyd George appeared to less infatuated observers. But they leave no doubt about how Frances Stevenson felt when she came face to face with her destiny.

On the last Sunday in June 1911, Frances Stevenson was taken by a friend to morning service at the essentially Welsh Baptist Church in Castle Street, Covent Garden. Lloyd George preached the sermon and she 'Instantly fell under the sway of his electric personality. I listened to his silver voice, observed his mastery over his audience . . . Although he spoke almost entirely in Welsh, I felt myself in some mysterious way drawn into the orbit of his personality.'[1]

The first meeting had an even greater impact. It came about by the strange working of fate. Megan Lloyd George, about to start full-time school, was thought to need a private tutor who could improve her grasp of basic subjects. Margaret's first suggestion was that her daughter should be coached by the sister of the woman who had been Megan's occasional tutor. Her husband was emphatically opposed. 'I do not know Miss James's sister, but if she is as surly a creature as Miss James, then I don't like her for Megan.'[2] He had an alternative in mind, 'an excellent governess . . . A nice German Swiss – simple, straight, kind but not good looking'.[3] Despite possession of all those virtues, the paragon was not appointed. In desperation, Lloyd George asked Mrs Woodhouse, the headmistress of Clapham High School, which Mair had attended, if she knew a suitable candidate. Mrs Woodhouse's first recommendation declined. She had already arranged her summer holidays. It was then suggested that the Lloyd Georges approach Miss Stevenson, a twenty-three-year-old teacher at Allenswood School in Wimbledon who had been one of Mair's classmates in Clapham. She was interviewed in Downing Street 'one day towards the end of July 1911' and appointed there and then. Fifty years on the candidate wrote

> His image as I saw him then is graven on my mind: the sensitive face, with deep furrows between the eyes: the eyes themselves, in which were all knowledge of human nature, grave and gay simultaneously.
>
> There was something more even than this which distinguished him from all other men I had ever met – and from all whom I ever met thereafter – a magnetism which made my heart leap and swept aside my judgement.[4]

It was not how, at that time, everybody saw Lloyd George. Lucy Masterman – on holiday with her husband in Criccieth – watched him 'as he posed in his Chancellor's robes' for Christopher Williams, the portrait painter. She found the scene 'extraordinarily comic: He is so very short and so very broad in the shoulders and his enormous, untidy head, rising out of the mass of gold embroidery, had something very incongruous about it'.[5] Lucy Masterman, although an undoubted admirer, did not feel about him as Frances Stevenson felt.

Frances Stevenson was in Criccieth with the family that summer. She travelled to Wales two days after her appointment as tutor-governess and was still there when the civil servants came down from London to discuss the National Insurance Bill. W. J. Braithwaite recorded her presence with the admission, 'I never found out who she was.'[6] Lucy Masterman remembered, 'Miss Stevenson going down to bathe with the rest of the family,' without being sure what her role might be.[7]

When the summer holidays were over and Megan was safely installed in school, Frances returned to the life of schoolmistress. But, from time to time, she was invited to do odd jobs at 11 Downing Street. At Easter 1912, the Chancellor of the Exchequer asked her to translate a book which described the pattern of landownership in France and, as a result, she offered what help she could in promoting his land campaign. To her surprise, he began to write to her almost every day. Despite their initially innocent character, at first Frances 'burned the letters after reading them' as she imagined Lloyd George burned her letters to him.[8] Fortunately she abandoned the discipline that he never followed. Her letters are in the careful hand of a schoolmistress. His – many of them written in bed to avoid discovery and, in the years which followed, interspersed with endearments in Welsh – are a pencil scrawl which has to be deciphered. Frances wrote with care, Lloyd George with confidence.

In the autumn of 1912, Lloyd George asked Frances to work for him in the Treasury. She was certainly well qualified for the job. However, her professional status may not have been uppermost in the Chancellor's mind when the offer was made. In 1907, his private secretary at the Board of Trade had received a revealing note from A. E. Widdows of the War Office. 'I enclose a copy of the Regulations which govern the appointment of lady typists at this office. I am afraid that even if the lady in whom Mr Lloyd George is interested possesses the necessary qualifications, it is impossible to hold out the hope of early employment.'[9] Finding jobs for personable young women became a habit which persisted into old age. Lloyd George became permanently attached only to one of them.

Frances Stevenson was born in the year that David Lloyd George married Margaret Owen. Her maternal grandparents – French and Italian – left Montmartre for London during the siege of Paris in 1871. Their daughter met and married a God-fearing Lowland Scot. Frances, initially privately educated, was sent to a board school in the hope that she would win a scholarship to something better. She obliged by gaining a place at Clapham High School, where she became a close friend of Mair Lloyd George, whom she described as 'gentle and charming. She would often come to my help in my mathematical difficulties.'[10]

Whatever these difficulties were, they did not prevent her from matriculating 'first class' and, following the classic pattern of clever girls from working families, she was encouraged to aspire to higher education by a far-sighted teacher who took her on a day trip to

Cambridge. Her ambition was a place in Newnham or Girton. But she was persuaded to sit a scholarship for London University – a scholarship which she 'had no intention of taking up'.[11] Her parents encouraged her to change her mind. What if neither of the Cambridge colleges accepted her? Could she be sure that the cost of Cambridge was within the family's means? In the end she accepted a place at the Royal Holloway College and read classics. Subsequently she was appointed assistant mistress at Allenswood, the school which it had been decided Megan would attend after suitable preparation.

The Stevensons harboured only conventional ambitions for Frances. They hoped that she would 'preserve a prim, even forbidding, countenance . . . The right sort of man would somehow discern beneath this unprepossessing appearance qualities of sterling worth.'[12] They did not know their daughter. She joined the Fabian Society, listened to Bernard Shaw's lectures, attended Christabel Pankhurst's rallies and spent her holidays on walking tours. Although an ardent supporter of women's suffrage, she never joined the Women's Social and Political Union because she disapproved of its inclination to violence – an indication of a gentle character which caused her colleagues in the Allenswood staff room to call her 'Pussy'. That was the name by which Lloyd George addressed her in his letters. Her parents were wrong to describe her appearance as 'unprepossessing'. She was not a great beauty. But she was certainly warmly attractive and she displayed a magnetic spark of vitality.

With the years, her reading habits had changed. As a girl she had 'read *Quo Vadis* and longed to be a Christian martyr'.[13] At college her favourite author was H. G. Wells – *Tono-Bungay*, *The New Machiavelli* and *Ann Veronica*, the gospel of female independence. She had become what Edwardians called a 'New Woman'– while clearly retaining her penchant for martyrdom. Perhaps she did not realise the price she would pay for dedicating her life to Lloyd George. From the start, she was even denied the status of exclusive mistress. And, when the real nature of the association seemed likely to become public, she agreed – or at least acquiesced – to a bogus marriage with another man which, Lloyd George hoped, would prevent his exposure as a virtual bigamist.

Margaret – tied to Lloyd George by sentiment and the need for stability as well as the protection she provided against scandal – remained a looming presence in both their lives. She neither provided the material comfort which Lloyd George craved nor shared his obsessive interest in politics. But for forty years he wrote to her, almost every day, with often exaggerated accounts of his achievements. And he was deeply distressed if she did not write to him just as frequently. The tone of the letters did not change between his election to Parliament in 1890 and the end of her life. Their style, as well as their content, was significant. They were jocular, patronising, inconsequential – and barely distinguishable from messages to his mother written in letters home after he left Wales for London. Frances Stevenson accepted Margaret's publicly pre-eminent position without complaint.

When they met, Lloyd George was forty-six and Frances twenty-three. She was a schoolteacher who hurried home each weekend to her family. He was the Chancellor of the Exchequer with four children – Dick (a twenty-four-year-old engineer with a Cambridge degree), Olwen (at twenty-one the product of a Dresden finishing school), Gwilym (an eighteen-year-old, about to go up to Cambridge) and Megan, the child in need of a tutor. His eminence and her age would, in themselves, have been enough to make a relationship of equals impossible. But their temperaments, being exactly opposite, fitted together. She believed that 'nothing I could do would ever be so worthwhile as to help this man'.[14] He, sure of his destiny, was willing to let others – uncle, brother, wife as well as mistress – pay whatever price was necessary to ensure that his fate was fulfilled. Megan Lloyd George likened Frances to 'a thick pile carpet into which one's feet sank gratefully'.[15] The metaphor was as inaccurate as it was cruel. She was a woman of courage and ability who, because of love and admiration, allowed Lloyd George to trample her underfoot.

It has been argued – in the words of Megan Lloyd George – 'that she loved her seat in the front row of politics' and that she knew that she shared his life more fully as secretary-mistress than she would have done had she been his wife.[16] The theatre metaphor described her attitude exactly. Frances remained a political observer rather than a participant. The comments confided to her diary were far more trenchant than the messages which she sent to the Prime Minister. Her letters provided reassurance rather than advice. Even in his darkest days they contained predictions of his eventual vindication. In 1922, as he resigned the premiership, he was 'still a towering figure among the little pigmies who are strutting about at present'.[17] Nine years later, with the country in the depths of recession, she told him, 'things will begin to come your way very soon, my darling, and it will make things all the simpler because you are not in a hurry. Things will just fall into your lap.'[18] The truth is always best. But after 1922, Lloyd George was

not in a mood to accept it, and Frances Stevenson was never prepared
to force it on him.

Had she not been personally attracted to Lloyd George, the prospect
of working for the Chancellor of the Exchequer would still have been
irresistible. But after she 'began to realise that he looked forward to
seeing [her]', she recognised the full implication of the job offer. 'LG
made it clear that he would like to have me as his secretary in the
Treasury. But I realised that would be on terms which were in direct
conflict with my essentially Victorian upbringing.'[19] So, being sensible
as well as clever, she went to Scotland to stay with friends and consider,
in comparative calm, what her future should be.

Lloyd George's parting gift was eloquent testimony to his ruthless
ambition, his supreme self-confidence and his crass insensitivity. It was
a biography of Charles Stewart Parnell, the lost leader of Irish
Nationalism who sacrificed his own career and the short-term interests
of his party for the love of Katherine O'Shea. The parallel was not
exact. Parnell was single, Katherine O'Shea married. But the comparison was close enough to enable Lloyd George to make his point. 'No
man has the right to imperil his political party and its objective for the
sake of a woman.'[20] Frances, who in her 'heart wanted to marry and
have children', knew that she could look forward only to a life of
devoted subterfuge and constant humiliation. When William George
came to write his brother's biography he could not bring himself – or
thought there was no necessity – to write about his second sister-in-law
until the narrative arrived at 1943, more than three decades after her first
meeting with the Chancellor. By then Frances Stevenson, mistress, had
become Countess Lloyd George, wife.

In Scotland, Frances met, by accident or design, a man she knew to be
in love with her. He proposed marriage. Frances 'wrote and told Lloyd
George about him'. The reply was the only response she could have
expected. 'He replied at once that I must do what I thought right' – the
classic opening gambit in a campaign of moral blackmail.[21] Lloyd George
was provided with an opportunity to heighten the drama. 'Almost immediately [Frances] received another urgent letter. It simply said something
terrible had happened.'[22] The crisis was genuine, but Lloyd George
exploited it to ensure that Frances surrendered. After she received the
news that he was in trouble, she travelled south as soon as she decently
could. 'When I returned to London from Scotland, after Christmas 1912,
in response to LG's letter, I returned to place myself in his hands unconditionally – that is to say, on his conditions.'[23]

Lord Riddell had made Lloyd George the gift of a house at Walton Heath in Surrey – doubly convenient because it was close to a golf course and allowed long days and nights away from Margaret. Frances Stevenson's diary – noting the second anniversary rather than the occasion itself – suggests that they became lovers on 21 January 1913. She described that day's event as their 'marriage'. Three days after it occurred, David and Margaret Lloyd George celebrated, in public splendour, their silver wedding anniversary.

CHAPTER 21

RULES OF PRUDENCE

The letter which brought Frances Stevenson hurrying down from Scotland has not survived. But, although the precise date is uncertain, there is no doubt that the 'something terrible' which had happened during the dying days of 1912 was the result of developments in what was already called the 'Marconi Scandal'. By the time the *cri de coeur* was written, the allegations of corruption – which threatened the Chancellor's career as well as reputation – had been public for several months and rumours, about which Lloyd George must have known, had been circulating in political society for most of the year. It is unlikely that he had only just realised that he teetered on the brink of political ruin. The letter was moral blackmail but the risk of destruction was real.

The Marconi saga, as distinct from the scandal, had begun on 7 March 1912 when Herbert Samuel, promoted into the Cabinet as Postmaster General, accepted – subject to the approval of Parliament – the tender submitted by the Marconi Company for the construction of the 'wireless chain' which the Sixth Imperial Conference, meeting the previous year, had decided was essential to the security and cohesion of the Empire. No technical expert doubted that Marconi was the company best equipped to do the work.

The managing director of the Marconi Company was Godfrey Isaacs, brother of Rufus, who had been appointed Attorney General in Samuel's place. Godfrey Isaacs was also a director of the Marconi Company of America, in which he, in consequence, held shares. The American company was not a shareholder in the associated British company, so it gained no material benefit from the government contract. But the British company did hold half the shares in American Marconi. So the relationship between the two companies was close and complicated. Even so, the contract – signed in July 1912 – would have passed parliamentary scrutiny with only a handful of objections had not the *Eye Witness* – an openly anti-Semitic magazine edited by Cecil Chesterton, the brother of G. K. – begun to hint that there was something improper about the government's relationship with what it loosely referred to as the 'Marconi Company'. Its August issue went a step further and denounced the 'abominable business of Samuel, the Isaacs and the Marconi Company'.[1] The 'abominable business' to which it referred involved the alleged purchase of Marconi shares. Lloyd George was not mentioned in the *Eye Witness*'s original exposé – probably because Chesterton wanted to use it as an indictment of Jewish politicians. However, rumours that the Chancellor was engaged in some dubious financial transaction had circulated around political London during the New Year and by March had travelled north to Birmingham. George Cadbury was sufficiently concerned for him to send a warning, and slightly presumptuous advice. 'I would not write if I did not feel that I had a definite duty to convey to you my own desire, which I believe represents that of millions, that you should hold fast your integrity.'[2]

Lloyd George – whose Patagonia escapade had demonstrated his lack of financial scruples – had already been accused, in a letter to the *Daily Mail*, of insider dealing in Port of London Authority shares. The newspaper could find no evidence to support the claim. In that instance, as in his purchase of American Marconi shares, Lloyd George had kept just within the law. But he was willing to cut corners in his search for additional income and he was a victim of the suspicions which were aroused by the general assumption of untrustworthiness to which Harold Nicolson had so famously referred. On 15 April, he had written to Margaret, 'So you have only £50 to spare. Very well. I will invest that for you. Sorry you have no more available as I think it is quite a good thing I have got.'[3] Clearly he believed that he had been offered something of exceptional value. The 'good thing' was an investment in the Marconi Company of America. Two days after his letter home was posted he agreed to buy a thousand shares at a cost of £2 each.

The Marconi Company of America had made a new share issue in early April and Godfrey Isaacs had guaranteed that the British company

would buy or dispose of a hundred thousand and that he would personally do the same with fifty thousand. The pre-issue price of £1 a
share was quoted in New York at £1:1:3. Godfrey Isaacs sold shares –
either his own or those acquired by his company – to both of his
brothers before they were available on the London Stock Exchange.
They paid £2 a share, the pre-sale price quoted at the time the transaction was made. Nothing illegal had taken place.

Rufus Isaacs – for no discernible reason other than a laudable desire
to share good fortune with his friends – offered a thousand shares, at the
price which he had paid for them, to both Lloyd George and Alexander
Murray. The deal was done on 17 April, when the shares were still not
available on the British stock market. But it was already clear that their
value would swiftly increase. On the night of 14–15 April, the *Titanic*
had sunk, six hundred miles south of Newfoundland. When the
Carpathia landed the seven hundred survivors in New York, Guglielmo
Marconi was waiting on the Cunard pier to explain to the reporter from
the *New York Times* that the lives had been saved by the miracle of wireless telegraphy. When sales of his $10 million share issue opened, success
was guaranteed. On 19 April, the first day that shares in the Marconi
Company of America were available in London, they opened at over
£3 and ended the day at £4.

Lloyd George was later to argue that his intention was not to make
a speculative profit, but to provide a little security for his old age. If that
were the case, he failed to achieve his objective. On 22 May, he sold his
shares at a profit and used the money to buy fifteen hundred more.
Murray did the same. Both men had made the elementary error of
buying at the top of the market. Within weeks the price had fallen back
to £2. During the furore which was to follow, part of the Chancellor's
not altogether relevant defence was that he had lost on the deal. The
Liberal Party did better. Murray had also bought two thousand shares
on its behalf. They were allowed to fructify in the party's pocket until
the general election.

Rumours that ministers of the Crown had entered into a corrupt relationship with the Marconi Company reached the Postmaster General
almost two months before the *Eye Witness* made its public allegations.
Samuel was told that there was 'something worrying about the Marconi
contract. Members of the Government, having private information that
it was pending, had been buying shares in the company expecting the
price to rise when the contracts were concluded.'[4] The allegations were
unjustified and the rumours were wrong. The stories confused the

British and American Marconi companies and knowledge of the government contract had had no bearing on the share purchasers' decision. But, by pursuing a false hare, the hounds unearthed another quarry.

On 7 August, when Samuel commended the Marconi contract to the House of Commons, no one suggested that the arrangement was tainted by corruption. Twenty-four hours later, the *Eye Witness* allegations were published. The House rose for the summer on the same day, preventing any immediate parliamentary assault on the accused ministers and providing time for them to consider legal action. Asquith advised against. 'I suspect that [*Eye Witness*] has a very meagre circulation. I notice only one page of advertisements and then by Belloc's publishers. Prosecution would secure it notoriety which might yield subscribers. We have broken weather. But for Winston there would be nothing in the papers.'[5]

Silence emboldened other minority publications. In August, a periodical called *Outlook* repeated the allegation and included Lloyd George in its indictment. He too wanted to prosecute. The recently employed and then unknown Frances Stevenson was sent to 'newspaper offices in an endeavour to find out whether there had been any public mention of American Marconi shares which would have made them available to the general public'.[6] It is by no means certain that previous publication would have, as he believed, 'exonerated him'. He abandoned the idea of a libel action after F. E. Smith told him that defence counsel would suggest that anyone who attacked his enemies so violently should not complain about being attacked and the jury would agree.[7]

It was clear to ministers that, once the House of Commons reassembled, the Unionist Opposition would return to the charge. So the government decided to pre-empt the anticipated debate and demonstrate its faith in the ministers' innocence by itself proposing that a select committee enquire into the decision to sign the Marconi contract. The debate, on the motion for its creation, took place on 11 October. It began reasonably enough with Samuel asserting that Marconi was the company best qualified to do the job and the Opposition spokesman agreeing. But it deteriorated into innuendo as the afternoon wore on, and George Lansbury – speaking with the irresponsibility of the truly pious – asserted, quite wrongly, that there had been 'scandalous gambling in Marconi shares'.[8] Lloyd George rose to the bait.

The Honourable Member said something about the Government and he has talked about rumours. If the Honourable Member has any charge to make against the Government as a whole or against individual Members of it, I think it ought to be stated openly. The reason why the government wanted a frank discussion before going to Committee was because we wanted to bring here these rumours, these sinister rumours that have been passed from one foul lip to another behind the backs of the House.[9]

Later in the day, Rufus Isaacs made his personal statement. He chose his words with care.

Never from the beginning . . . have I had one single transaction with the shares of that company. I am not only speaking for myself but also speaking on behalf, I know, of both my Right Honourable Friends the Postmaster General and the Chancellor of the Exchequer who, in some way or another, in some of the articles, have been brought into this matter.[10]

The operative phrase, as Isaacs well knew, was 'the shares of that company'. The assertion was irrefutable. But in failing to mention his investment in American Marconi he was − in the traditional phrase − 'being less than frank with the House'. When the contrivance was unravelled, Isaacs's obvious intention to divert attention from the American deal created the clear impression that the ministers had something to hide. They had been reckless rather than corrupt. But, as is always the case in the Commons, attempts to hide an indiscretion elevated the offence into a major scandal.

By the time that the select committee met, the truth − though not yet common knowledge − was well known to the avenging angels of the major newspapers who were prevented from publishing only by the fear of libel. Leopold Maxse, editor of the National Review, gave evidence in language which was as carefully chosen as Isaacs's refutation of all wrongdoing.

One might have conceived that [the Ministers] might have appeared at the first sitting clamouring to state in the most categorical and emphatic manner that neither directly nor indirectly, in their names or other people's names, have they had any transactions whatsoever . . . in any Marconi company throughout the negotiations with the Government.[11]

Ministers realised that the truth could not be concealed for much longer. They were then presented with what they believed to be an intervention by Providence. *Le Matin*, ostensibly reporting Leo Maxse's evidence to the select committee, claimed that Samuel had endorsed the Marconi contract without consulting Parliament and that he, together with the Isaacs brothers, had secretly bought the company's shares at two pounds and sold them at eight. The newspaper published a retraction and an apology the following day. The gift from heaven was not spurned. It provided all the involved ministers, including Lloyd George, with an opportunity to admit an association with American Marconi. Rufus Isaacs and Samuel sued *Le Matin* for libel.

Le Matin was represented by James H. Campbell KC, a former Attorney General for Ireland and the Member of Parliament for Trinity College, Dublin. His only task was to repeat the apology and retraction. The barristers appointed to accept it were two of the most famous and feared King's Counsels in England – Sir Edward Carson for Rufus Isaacs and F. E. Smith for Herbert Samuel and Lloyd George. Smith – then in partnership with Isaacs – had been chosen to represent Lloyd George in his libel case against the *People* because of his aggressive style. But his second appearance was the result of more than his fearsome courtroom reputation. Winston Churchill – Smith's gambling friend – had suggested that if he acted for Lloyd George, Carson would be encouraged to act for Isaacs – producing an extraordinary double coup. The public was bound to notice that the integrity of two Liberal ministers was being defended by normally partisan members of the Unionist Party, and their appearance on behalf of Isaacs and Samuel would make it impossible for them to attack either man in the House of Commons debate which would surely follow. Carson's first duty was to perform the task which the trial made possible. The purchase of shares in the Marconi Company of America had to be placed on the public record in a way which so emphasised the propriety of the deal that the damage caused by the revelation would be minimised. In what he admitted to the court was a long digression, Carson explained that Isaacs had 'insisted' on the purchase of the American shares being made public.[12] Smith's task was less contrived. He simply had to assert Samuel's complete innocence, which, since it was true, was easily accomplished.

Carson's revelation, as must have been anticipated, excited rather than dampened interest. But the *Daily Mail*, which might have been expected to lead the howling pack, was strangely subdued. Northcliffe had been nobbled by Churchill, who had taken the considerable risk of telling him, in advance, what Carson was to reveal in court. Northcliffe, no doubt flattered to be taken into Churchill's confidence, accepted that the ministers had done no serious wrong and agreed to treat them gently. A week later he told Lord Riddell, 'Winston was very much agitated when he came to see me. I did not know until then how much he was attached to Lloyd George.'[13] The First Lord supported the Chancellor in every way he could. In September the *Enchantress*, the Admiralty Board yacht, sailed to Criccieth, picked up Lloyd George, his wife and daughter, and took them on a morale-building week's cruise.

The select committee spent four months examining the technical aspects of the Marconi contract before it called Isaacs, Samuel and Lloyd George to give evidence. Murray was called but could not come. He had left the government, been elevated to the peerage and, in the hope of reviving his family's fortunes, become Lord Cowdray's representative in the Colombian goldfields. 'Gone to Bogotá' became a rebuke with which Unionists in the Commons tried both to ridicule and to incriminate what they hoped to portray as corrupt Liberal politicians.

Lloyd George appeared on 28 March 1913. The notes he made in preparation are in the National Library of Wales.

> I can throw no light on negotiations other than that given by papers.
>
> Claim no special privileges as Member or Minister.
>
> Claim only the elementary right of fair play accorded to any subject of the King's,
>
> Though he may be of the criminal classes

At that point the witness changed from supplicant to adversary.

> Charge of theft or fraud?

Then he proposed to dismiss the allegations with contempt.

> Yes, whole evidence upon which the charge is built . . .[14]

The notes did not prove adequate for two full days of evidence and cross-examination. But Lloyd George solemnly asserted that he held no shares in any company which did business with the government and that he had never made improper use of official information. He ridiculed the charges which were made against him – some of which he invented. He had never made £60,000 on a speculative investment, nor did he own a villa in France. His total investment income was £400 per annum. To prove the point he presented the committee with his bank book. What success he might have achieved in winning public sympathy for the ministers was undermined by a piece of simple bad luck. Murray's stockbroker was declared bankrupt and, in consequence, his account books and business papers were open for public examination. They revealed an element of the Marconi Scandal which had, until then, remained secret even from Lloyd George and Rufus Isaacs. Murray had invested £9000 in Marconi shares on behalf of the Liberal Party.

The Liberal Party's investment prompted another, albeit minor, deception. On 8 June 1913, Percy Illingworth, Murray's successor as government Chief Whip, 'seemed much disturbed' by the revelation which he described as exposing 'a right mess'. Next day it became clear that 'Illingworth [had] known these facts for some time'.[15] Together with Murray, he was a trustee of the fund in the name of which the shares were held.

The select committee – as select committees often will – divided on party lines. The majority exonerated the ministers. The minority, while making no allegations of fraudulent or illegal conduct, censured their lack of discretion and propriety. The chairman – who had threatened to resign when he believed, with some justification, that Lloyd George had 'fed' prejudicial information to sympathetic members of the committee – produced a report of his own. It dealt more with the way the inquiry had been conducted than with what it had concluded. The divisions within the committee guaranteed an acrimonious debate on the floor of the House of Commons. There has been much speculation about why it was not on a government motion. Papers only recently made available provide the answer.

Percy Illingworth drafted a motion. Other ministers sought to improve upon it. Asquith himself made a series of changes – all of which suggested that ministers were not wholly confident of their colleagues' innocence. The assertion that the House 'accepts and approves' the statements made by Lloyd George and Isaacs was first changed to the contention that both men 'acted in the sincere belief that their actions were not in conflict with their'. There the amendment ended and was replaced by the 'acceptance' though not the 'approval' of their pleas of innocence. More significantly, in the fourth and final attempt to strike the right note, someone crossed out 'desire further to put on record the undisputed fact that there is no ground whatsoever for any imputation of corruption, undue influence or want of good faith'.[16] In the absence of agreement, no government motion was tabled.

Strangely, considering the mood of the moment, the Opposition motion on which the Marconi debate took place complained of no more than 'lack of frankness'. Lloyd George offered the Prime Minister his half-hearted resignation and, it being rejected as anticipated, prepared for the battle which had already been presaged by some of the more bellicose Unionist MPs. John Kebty-Fletcher had put down the question 'To ask Mr Chancellor of the Exchequer if there are any emoluments or allowances attached to his office other than his salary'. On being told, 'The answer is in the negative', he asked a supplementary question which was as ingenuous as it was offensive. 'Is not the Right Honourable Gentleman's salary sufficient to prevent him from wrongfully and improperly gambling?'[17] Lloyd George had again taken refuge in the tried and true formula beloved by Members of Parliament accused of personal wrongdoing. 'If he has anything of that kind to say about me he had better say it in a place where he will be subject to cross-examination.' The threat of libel prevented open comment in the Commons. But it did not stifle the rumbles of suspicion in the country. The rumours continued even after Cecil Chesterton was sued for a further libel by Godfrey Isaacs and the court concluded that he was not a 'vile conspirator, a thief and a knave, attempting to obtain public plunder' and awarded him £100 damages with costs. By 18 June, when the first of the two days of debate was held, most people who thought about the Marconi Scandal at all were sure that something disreputable had happened, though few of them knew what it was.

Margot Asquith, writing – we must assume – with her husband's approval, had written to Lloyd George to advise him how to conduct himself in the debate. 'This debate must show that nothing of the kind can ever happen again and that when you realised the folly you apologised (that part of yr speech sd be broad and simple, in no way rhetorical: it will have much more effect).' Then, she said, the Prime Minister would 'let the opposition have it'.[18]

Lloyd George took Mrs Asquith's advice and her husband was as good as his word. The Chancellor was as near to penitent as his character allowed.

I am conscious that I have done nothing which brings a stain on a Minister of the Crown. If you will, I acted thoughtlessly. I acted mistakenly but I acted innocently. I acted openly and I acted honestly. That is why, with confidence, I place myself in the hands not merely of my political friends but of Members in all parts of this great assembly.[19]

When the Prime Minister had told the King that the conduct of some of His Majesty's ministers was 'difficult to defend', he spoke figuratively to emphasise his judgement that their behaviour had been 'lamentable'.[20] For he defended them to the House of Commons with plausible conviction – after making a distinction between the 'rules of obligation', which they had observed, and the 'rules of prudence', which they had flouted. But, paradoxically, the figurative description of his attitude almost certainly represented his true feelings. All Asquith's history suggests that he viewed his colleagues' conduct with deep distaste. But the demands of practical politics required that he defend them – not out of loyalty but in the knowledge that if Lloyd George were forced to resign, his government would lose its vitality. So he proclaimed:

> Their honour, both their private and their public honour, is at this moment absolutely unstained. They have, as this Committee has shown by unanimous verdict, abused no public trust. They retain, I can say with full assurance, the complete confidence of their colleagues and their political associates.[21]

When the House divided the resolution of censure was defeated by a margin of seventy-eight votes – twenty fewer than the nominal majority of the government and its allies.

The formal proceedings being completed, Lloyd George felt able to turn on his tormentors. His friends told him to let the subject drop. Northcliffe told Winston Churchill that in April, immediately after the Marconi Scandal was revealed in all its sensation, the number of letters received by his newspapers was 'exactly three, one of which was printed – the other two were foolish'. He took the view that 'the whole Marconi business looms much larger in Downing Street than among the mass of the people'.[22] And the message from the provinces was that 'outside of London Clubs and London Press the campaign against yourself and some of your colleagues in the Cabinet is exerting little influence'.[23] But Lloyd George was temperamentally incapable of leaving the last word to his adversaries. At the National Liberal Club on 1 July 1913, he made a speech which was a combination of special pleading and an attempt – not completely successful – to change the terms on which the debate on parliamentary impropriety was being conducted.

He began with the entirely spurious complaint that the hallowed conventions of the House of Commons had prevented him from defending himself while the select committee was examining his conduct. However, his tormentors had been free to continue the campaign of denigration – 'hitting a man when he is down, hitting a man when his hands are tied behind his back and he cannot hit back'. He had suffered the 'least endurable martyrdom of all . . . where the victim has his hands tied and arrows are shot into his body and he could not protect himself nor sling them back'.[24] Leo Amery, building on the metaphor, was to describe Lloyd George as the 'St Sebastian of Limehouse' – proof of how much the Unionists had enjoyed the discomfiture of the man who had attacked the landed interests during his speech in that borough. By the end of the National Liberal Club speech, Lloyd George had given them more reason to be fearful.

The theme of his speech was, again, the land. His audience was invited to consider 'the millions of acres . . . the inheritance of the people, bartered away by Parliament when landlords governed both the Upper and Lower Houses'. Then came the almost obligatory biblical analogy. In 'the greatest of all Books' Samson had been 'assailed by a hideous monster' which he slew. Returning to the scene a few days later he found the carcass filled with honey.

> My right honourable Friend and myself have been assailed by a hideous monster which sought our lives. Not with our own right arm alone, but with the help of our friends we have slaughtered it and, unless I am very much mistaken, out of its prostrate form will come something that will sweeten the lives of millions who hitherto have tasted nothing but bitterness and the dust of the world.[25]

Land reform was back on the agenda.

The Marconi drama preoccupied Parliament and part of the press from April 1912 until June 1913. Thereafter, it had no significant effect on the careers of the principal *dramatis personae*. It was accepted that Herbert Samuel was in no way implicated. Rufus Isaacs, ennobled as Lord Reading, became Lord Chief Justice of England. Lloyd George, barely more than three years after the censure debate, was Prime Minister of the United Kingdom of Great Britain and Northern

Ireland. He had escaped the consequences of behaviour which was disreputable though not dishonest as he had so often escaped the consequences of personal folly. He was not an introspective man, but Marconi – and the risk of disgrace – must have made him wonder, no matter how briefly, if the time had come to act with greater circumspection. If he seriously considered treading the straight and narrow path, he quickly discarded the idea. Conformity was not in his character. The rules were for ordinary mortals. The remedy to his damaged reputation was new campaigns and more speeches. The subject would be the land.

CHAPTER 22

_____

BACK TO THE LAND

New party leaders feel an obligation to justify their elevation by taking the fight to the enemy. Bonar Law, abrasive by nature and appointed to replace the emollient Arthur Balfour, responded to Conservative hopes by announcing that he would lead the resistance against what he described as 'a revolutionary committee . . . an example of destructive violence without parallel since the Long Parliament'.[1] As he walked with the Prime Minister in procession from the House of Commons to the House of Lords to hear the Speech from the Throne with which the King opened the 1912 Parliament, he gave Asquith a courteous warning. 'I am afraid I shall have to show myself very vicious, Mr Asquith, this year. I hope you will understand.'[2] It was not altogether clear what he proposed to be vicious about. When the Prime Minister trapped him into making an unthinking nod of the head which implied that he would repeal the National Insurance Act – the contentious issue of 1911 – he quickly made clear that he had no such intention. However, as is so often the case in politics, 'events' transpired to make it an eventful session. One was anticipated in the King's Speech, which expressed the pious hope that a 'reasonable spirit would prevail on both sides' of the looming dispute between the coal-mine owners and the Miners' Federation of Great Britain.

Back in October 1911, the MFGB – as loose an alliance as the name suggests – had met in Southport and agreed to demand a minimum wage for both men and boys in each of the regions where miners were members of its constituent unions. In mid-December, the owners rejected the idea and, before the end of the month, a strike ballot had demonstrated, by 445,800 votes to 115,271, that the men were willing, indeed determined, to fight their corner. On 2 January 1912, they decided what the minimum rate should be – 5/- a shift for men and 2/- a shift for boys. Five days later, negotiation between men and management broke down. Worried ministers saw the impending strike as the climax of the years in which industrial unrest had spread from industry to industry and was likely to spread even further.* The Prime Minister decided to intervene. On 2 February – together with Edward Grey, Lloyd George and Noel Buxton, the President of the Board of Trade – he met the miners' leaders.

The solution which the government proposed was a system of regional conferences at which both sides of the industry should meet and determine a minimum wage, with the government standing by to arbitrate if there were no agreement. Lloyd George, whose sympathy for organised labour was strictly limited, had begun his ministerial career fundamentally opposed to the government becoming involved in fixing pay rates. But his experience at the Board of Trade had changed his view and, with his assistance, a grudging settlement was obtained on the promise that a minimum-wage bill – which stipulated the 5/- and 2/- rates – would be introduced into Parliament. The significance of ministers intervening so directly in the economy had not escaped him. It had 'sounded the death knell of the Liberal Party in its old form'.[3]

On 23 May, the dockers employed by the Port of London Authority came out on strike in support of the lightermen, who had claimed victimisation and the breach of agreement as the result of the employment of non-union labour. Lloyd George, by then an enthusiastic convert to government intervention, proposed that ministers either impose or attempt to negotiate a settlement which both sides would tolerate even if neither side would welcome it. Other ministers reverted to the view that, until there was a national emergency, industry was best left to its own devices. Dockers in ports outside London refused to 'come out in sympathy'. So did the railway unions. The strike petered out in the bitterness of defeat and the government, vindicated in its reassertion of Old Liberal principles, could concentrate on two essentially Old Liberal issues – the Church in Wales and Irish Home Rule.

Reginald McKenna introduced the bill to disestablish the Welsh

---

*Chapter four of George Dangerfield's *The Strange Death of Liberal England*, 'The Workers Revolt', gives a comprehensive, though controversial, account of the previous disputes.

Church on 23 April 1912. Lloyd George held the passionate belief that the important issue was not the Church's legal status but the future of its most precious possession – Welsh land. When the bill was first presented to Parliament, Lloyd George, characteristically but perversely, chose to make an attack on the distribution of spoils during the Reformation – assets which the Church no longer possessed.

> Most of the property was given to laymen as bribes for selling their faith. There are laymen now enjoying these endowments and they are the people who, when I tried to take a halfpenny in the pound, called me a thief . . . There is no-one more bitter against Disestablishment and Disendowment.

Foolishly the laymen – in the form of the brothers Lords Robert and Hugh Cecil, two Unionist Members of Parliament – chose to take issue with him. If, said Lord Hugh, 'the suggestion is that my family received church lands . . . he is, as he generally is when discussing historical questions, entirely wrong'.[4]

Two days later Professor A. F. Pollard, an eminent Tudor historian and Liberal activist, wrote to *The Times* with details of church land acquired by Lord Burghley, the 'greatest ancestor' of the Cecils. The brothers struck back with letters of their own. Lord Robert was reckless enough to ask, rhetorically, if Pollard believed that 'descendants of men who received property in the sixteenth century should be precluded from attacking Disendowment proposals in the twentieth?' He was told that while 'descent from a thief should debar no-one from denouncing theft . . . retention of stolen property should'. In the course of the correspondence Pollard convincingly included the 'ducal houses of Somerset, Bedford, Devonshire, Rutland and Norfolk' in the lists of thieves and added that 'the restitution to the Church of a tithe of the property that was taken from it by their ancestors would richly compensate it for the disendowment of the four Welsh dioceses'.[5] Lloyd George must have felt that Pollard was trespassing on his territory. During the bill's second reading he reasserted ownership.

> The Duke of Devonshire issues a circular applying for subscriptions to oppose this Bill and he charges us with the robbery of God. Why, does he not know – of course he knows – that the very foundations of his fortune are laid deep in sacrilege, fortunes built out of desecrated shrines and pillaged altars.

He then widened his attack from one duke in particular to dukes in general.

> They robbed the Catholic Church. They robbed the monasteries. They robbed the altars. They robbed the almshouses. They robbed the poor. They robbed the dead. Then they come here when we are trying . . . to recover some part of this pillaged property for the poor for whom it was originally given, with hands dripping with the fat of sacrilege, to accuse us of robbery of God.[6]

F. E. Smith, leading the opposition to the bill, claimed that the disendowment proposals 'shocked the conscience of every Christian community in Europe' – provoking G. K. Chesterton to write 'Anti-Christ or the Reunion of Christendom: An Ode'. It suggested that the Balkan Christians ravaged by the Turks would be reconciled to the murder of 'their kin and kith' because a Cardiff curate's pension had been 'saved by Smith'. It ended with a line which has echoed down the years, 'Chuck it, Smith'.

F. E. Smith was a man of mercurial brilliance and louche habits whose relationship with Lloyd George changed over the years. Before the war, he led opposition to the Liberals' social programme and supported the Ulster rebellion against Home Rule. He served, without much genuine commitment, in the 1916 coalition, but two years later (as Lord Birkenhead) became Lord Chancellor and helped to negotiate the 1921 Irish Treaty. When the coalition broke up he was one of the few Conservatives to support Lloyd George – who neither liked nor trusted him but, true to character, admired his caustic oratorical brilliance.

Smith's single line of rhetorical excess was, when compared with some of the speeches made on and about the Disestablishment Bill, a model of restraint. Lloyd George was the most exuberant of its supporters. In Swansea on 28 May, he compared the social provision which was available in towns and the country and concluded that, although the state Church

> never carries a cup of cold water to the parched lips of the fevered shepherd in the hills, Nonconformity is there. It has erected its infirmaries and dispensaries and sanatoria for the bruised soul . . . These are the people who, for forty years, have stood patiently at the bar of parliament with the humble petition that . . . their faith

should be freed from the bondage of the state and that the inheritance of the poor should be restored to them.[7]

By 'state' he meant the Established Church.

The Disestablishment Bill was given a second reading in May but the committee stage, which did not begin until November, dragged on – delayed by fierce opposition – until February 1913. In the hope of making progress and disarming the Lords, the government modified its disendowment proposals. The Church lost the tithe but kept glebe money (the proportion of rent on land within some parishes which was paid to the local church), Queen Anne's Bounty and grants made during the nineteenth and twentieth centuries. Despite the concessions, the Lords defeated the bill in the spring of 1913 and again, months later, when it was returned to them by the Commons. They were considering it for the third (and last) time under the provisions of the Parliament Act when war broke out in 1914.

According to Lucy Masterman, disendowment was 'really the question [Lloyd George] was keenest on' with the land next in order of importance.[8] She was wrong. Disestablishment was the passion of his youth and the lingering obligation of his middle age and what real interest he retained in the subject almost entirely related to its connection with farming incomes. The land was his enduring preoccupation – political, emotional and, insomuch as, for once, he proposed ways of righting wrongs rather than only denouncing them, intellectual. It was the subject to which he always returned as proof that he was the best radical of all.

On 27 May 1912 – 'with the dock strike at full blast' – he had spoken to Lucy Masterman, with all the zeal of a recent convert to interventionism, about his colleagues' reluctance to mediate.[9] 'They make me wonder if I am a Liberal at all.'[10] Then he added, 'I am convinced that the land question is the real issue. You must break down the remnants of the feudal system . . . Radicalism needs a great stimulus. The Radical cause has fallen into an abyss of respectability and conventionality. Something must be done to put life into dry bones.'[11] He had no doubt what that something was. The land tax had never been expected to change the pattern of tenure or stir Liberal blood, but 'the land and the agricultural labourer are at the root of the whole social evil' – by which he meant the neglect of one and the exploitation of the other.[12] To Lloyd George, the farmworker typified the down-trodden employee who needed the protection that only the government could provide.

Land reform, he had no doubt, could be made the burning issue of the day. But he made his plans against the background of a year which had been disrupted by industrial action. The experience encouraged him to argue that a living wage should be fixed for all of the industries which were prone to sudden disruption. This owed as much to his desire for economic stability as his belief in social justice. He wanted the 'thrust' of Bismarckism to stabilise relations between management and men. Far better an arrangement which was negotiated by the government than one which had been imposed on employers by the trade unions. For that reason he 'tried very hard to induce [the Cabinet] to agree to introduce legislation which would enforce payments of a scale of wages on all employees in the trade within a given area, if associations of masters and men stood outside the agreeing associations'.[13]

Only Haldane and Buxton (enthusiastically) and Runciman (half-heartedly) supported him. The Prime Minster was strongly opposed. Friends in the government found Lloyd George 'evidently growing out of sympathy with other members of the cabinet'. He was, Riddell suggested, advocating 'a minimum wage or some other form of state interference – a sort of mild Socialism, although he would not admit it'.[14] If Riddell included the land reform in his list of new ideological heresies, he was wrong. It had the most respectable Old Liberal antecedents. Gladstone's two Irish Land Acts had increased the income of tenant farmers by reducing the power of the landlords – thereby denying the sanctity of freely negotiated contracts. It was Gladstone's one major deviation from 'classical liberalism'. Lloyd George intended to move the balance of agricultural power further in the same direction throughout Great Britain. But it was the state, not the workers' own organisations, that he advocated as the proper engine of change. He proposed these changes during what he grandly called the 'Land Campaign'.

The tentative plan which Lloyd George put to Asquith in June 1912 was intended to guarantee 'Breaking down the relics of Feudalism. Land courts [would] fix fair rents and tenure for agricultural land and decide upon new terms for leaseholders who improved their property' while 'tribunals [would] fix agricultural wages in the various districts'. The proposals 'obviously involve[d] a minimum wage for agricultural workers and the establishment of a rule that in fixing agricultural rents regard must be had not to wages paid but to wages which should be paid'.[15] It was a plan which might have been formulated – indeed, in a less coherent way, had been formulated – in the valleys of Wales twenty years earlier.

Age had brought a degree of caution. The land campaign had to be based on and justified by incontrovertible evidence which would convince politicians and the people that reform could not be delayed. So Lloyd George set up an unofficial inquiry under the chairmanship of Arthur Acland – a Liberal former minister who had befriended Lloyd George during his early years in Parliament. The membership included E. G. Hemmerde, who had just won a by-election in North-West Norfolk – according to political wisdom, very largely because Lloyd George had sent him a message which, more or less, promised the implementation of the land policy. Jesse Collings – Joseph Chamberlain's acolyte who had led the 1886 campaign for 'three acres and a cow' – asked rhetorically, 'How different from the actions of our own Leaders was that of Lloyd George [who] on the eve of the poll wrote a stirring letter in support of Mr Hemmerde and of his land proposals.'[16]

For no very good reason except the plaudits he had received after the North-West Norfolk victory, Lloyd George began to fantasise about leaving the government – first to 'devote himself to carrying on the land movement', then 'to do something for the underpaid people of Bethnal Green'. Masterman described him as 'very restless'.[17] The Land Campaign became the focus of his turbulent energy.

It had got off to a near-perfect start. A few wealthy Liberals objected to the enquiries and questionnaires from which Acland's committee obtained its evidence. The information which it required provoked Violet Markham – wealthy sister of a Liberal MP and coal owner – to complain of 'a secret enquiry, the methods of which Liberals would have been the first to condemn if adopted by their political opponents'.[18] But it was what the inquiry revealed about the state of rural England that stole the headlines.

The first volume of the committee's report was published on 15 October 1913.[19] Its findings left no doubt that agriculture was in steep decline and that, in consequence, farm labourers lived on starvation wages. More than 60 per cent of them were paid less than 18/- a week and between twenty thousand and thirty thousand received less than 16/-. The real wages of farm labourers – which had risen at the turn of the century – had fallen during the previous ten years, while in the economy as a whole the increases of the 1880s and 1890s had been followed by nothing worse than stagnation. The result in industrial employment was strikes and unrest. In agricultural Britain the youngest and most ambitious men looked for work in the towns. Most of the farmworkers who remained lived in tied cottages. Many of the cottages were, by the standards of the towns, unfit for human habitation. The tenants could be evicted at a week's notice. The inquiry's final observation confirmed an allegation which Lloyd George had often made, more as a result of class antagonism than the product of supporting evidence. Land which could be successfully cultivated was being left wild so it could be used for various 'country sports'.

Ministers examined the report three days after its findings were made public. In those days there was no Cabinet secretariat and no one kept Cabinet minutes.* The only record of decisions was the letter which the Prime Minister sent to the King after each meeting. However, 'at the suggestion of the Colonial Secretary [Lewis Harcourt]', Lloyd George sent 'colleagues notes of the points upon which decisions were taken during our discussion on the land question'. So, thanks to his prudence, there is no doubt what they agreed. The proposals – built around the creation of a Ministry of Lands and Forestry – were radical to the point of being revolutionary. They included 'New powers for dealing with waste land and under-cultivated land, reclamation, afforestation, land purchase, condition of the agricultural labourer (wages and hours), differences between landlord and tenant that interfere with the effective development and cultivation of the soil.'

The new ministry was to possess 'powers to acquire and develop land where uncultivated or under-cultivated'. There was to be 'no interference with landlords' powers to fix rents' – except when rent was increased or conditions of service changed. However, the free market was not sacrosanct. 'Wages and hours of labour' were to be determined by wages boards of the new ministry which – in a proposal denounced as near revolutionary – would include representatives of the farmworkers. The towns were not forgotten. Municipalities were to be given the power to acquire land in town and country 'for present or prospective uses'. The value of land, 'at the present moment capricious and extravagant', was to be determined not by supply and demand but by commissioners. Indeed, commissioners – a good Cromwellian concept – were to be the final arbiters in all disputes over the exercise of the proposed powers. If conciliation failed, the decisions rested with them.[20]

Lloyd George and his followers clearly thought that the Land Campaign – putting aside its intrinsic merits – would be the salvation

---

*Lloyd George remedied both omissions when he became Prime Minister.

of the Liberal Party. 'An autumn campaign of a thousand speeches . . . on the blessings of Free Trade, Home Rule and Disestablishment' would, Masterman predicted, reveal 'the nakedness of our programme'. He urged Lloyd George to break away from traditional Liberalism, 'launch the Land Campaign with speeches . . . issue a condensed 1/-summary of the report . . . create an organisation to spread the virus in every village'.[21] National insurance had sounded the death knell of Old Liberalism – free-trade *laissez-faire* and the minimal state. The Land Campaign offered an opportunity to dance upon its grave.

Lloyd George accepted Masterman's advice. On 11 October, he made two speeches at the Bedford ice rink to Liberal audiences. Both of them dealt exclusively with the land. The Acland Committee's report had not been published and the Cabinet was yet to pronounce upon it. But that was only one reason why the speech, instead of setting out the details of land reform, was almost entirely destructive. Lloyd George reverted to type. Lord Beauchamp, the chairman, began each meeting with the announcement that the Chancellor spoke with the full authority of the Prime Minister. As a result, Asquith was associated with the complaint that mangold-wurzels, needed to sustain a starving peasantry, were being eaten by pheasants and partridges. *The Times* for 13 October spared the Chancellor nothing.

> Disappointment was undoubtedly the feeling of many, even of the Liberal delegates who were present. Mr Lloyd George spoke with all his old accustomed skill and made his points effectively. He was not personally vituperative (except when he called Mr Leo Maxse, 'the cat's meat of the Tory Party') but his address was inspired throughout by what it is only possible to call a savage rancour against the landowners, the House of Lords and the Tories.[22]

At Swindon on 22 October, after the Cabinet had considered his proposals, Lloyd George announced the creation of the new Ministry of Lands and Forests. He set out its powers in a speech at Middlesbrough on 8 November which emphasised the importance of land reform to the lives and prosperity of the families who lived in towns – an argument which was essential to the Land Campaign's prospect of inspiring a national Liberal recovery. In the Oxford Union on 21 November – speaking against the motion 'This House has no confidence in the Land Policy of His Majesty's Government', he almost apologised for the extremism of Bedford.

I am represented as a very violent partisan, making partisan speeches simply drenched with partisanship. Let me say this to you, speaking as an old man to young men. This country is governed by party. Party has become an essential part of government. Many men have tried to get their ideas through without associating themselves with party and they have always failed because party government is an essential part of the government of this country . . . I sometimes honestly deplore it. There are many things which, if you could get a party truce for five years, you could get through and transform this land.[23]

The motion was defeated. But the interesting aspect of Lloyd George's speech is what it reveals about his attitude to the importance of the party system. It is the basis of the British system of democracy. But it can also be an obstacle to progress. Lloyd George achieved much by manipulating it to his own advantage. But it never moved fast enough for him. In 1910, he had tried to break the party system and failed. In 1916, he succeeded in neutralising it while he fought the war. In 1920, he tried to reshape it to his own advantage. In 1922, it destroyed him.

Lloyd George made two more major Land Campaign speeches. At Holloway in London on 29 November, he promised 'leasehold enfranchisement' – an aspiration which became reality fifty years later, after Harold Wilson's Labour government passed an act which Welsh backbenchers continually reminded their Scottish and English colleagues was all Lloyd George's idea. In Glasgow on 3 February 1914, he promised legislation to introduce the principle of rating site values. At the time, it sounded like another piece of flesh put on the skeleton of a developing policy. In fact it was the last stand of the first Land Campaign, which only Lloyd George had prosecuted with any real conviction. War, and the threat of war, combined with the sceptical inertia of most of the Cabinet to ensure its collapse. But Lloyd George had not given up his hopes of land reform. He never did.

There were still battles to be fought over national insurance. The Northcliffe newspapers had abandoned their usual pious calls to support the rule of law in order to lead a campaign to persuade employers not to buy national insurance stamps. On 29 July 1912 – two weeks before the scheme came into force – Lloyd George had told a rally at Woodford

They write letters to the papers threatening to reduce the wages of their servants, threatening to lengthen their hours – I should have thought that almost impossible – and, in the end, threatening to dismiss them. They are always dismissing servants. Whenever any Liberal Act of Parliament is passed they dismiss them. I wonder that they have any servants left. Sir William Harcourt imposed death duties: they dismissed servants. I put on a super-tax: they dismissed more. Now the Insurance Act comes, and the last of them will have to go. You will be having, on the swell West End houses, notices like 'Not at home – her ladyship's washing day'.[24]

Two days before the act came into force on 15 July he was more magisterial – in a populist sort of way.

Defiance of the law is like the cattle plague. It is very difficult to isolate it and confine it to the farm where it has broken out. Although defiance of the Insurance Act has broken out on the Harmsworth [Northcliffe] herd, it has travelled to the office of the *Times*. Why? Because they both belong to the same cattle farm. The *Times*, I want you to remember, is just a two penny-halfpenny edition of the *Daily Mail*.

The battle over national insurance – ending as it did near to outright victory – had given him perhaps even more pleasure than the People's Budget of 1909 and the defeat of the despised House of Lords the following year. Together they had made him the greatest radical in British history. After 1912, though, the blazing light began to dim.

CHAPTER 23

FULL OF FIGHT

It was Lloyd George's habit to turn his mind to a subject only when there were urgent decisions to be taken, imminent advantage to be gained or pressing danger to be averted. So despite his seniority within the Cabinet, some great issues escaped his attention. In January 1912, John Redmond wrote to him in anguish. 'I want to urge you to take an early opportunity of making a speech on Home Rule. I need not say I do not misunderstand your silence so far, but others do. Our people are eagerly looking for a promise direct from you.'[1] Redmond did him more than justice. His position on Home Rule was accurately described by Lucy Masterman as 'not very keen. He admits it as an abstract proposition but he has a good deal of the protestant in him.'[2] So when the Liberal Party promised to complete Gladstone's 'mission' his almost cynical detachment was illustrated in a Delphic letter to his wife. 'Home Rule launched. Went off quite well. But no enthusiasm. My own opinion . . . is that the Liberal Party will, by and by, be looking in the direction of the Welsh hills for another raid to extricate them out of the troubles.'[3]

The letter also confirmed his inclination to see life through the narrow prism of his own interests. Two days earlier in the other Balmoral, a prosperous suburb of Belfast, one hundred thousand men and women had demonstrated against Home Rule under the largest Union Flag ever made. Sir Edward Carson and James Craig had been supported on the platform by Andrew Bonar Law. The leader of His Majesty's Loyal Opposition had promised that, if Ulster refused to accept the will of Parliament, they would not lack 'help from across the water'.[4] Back in London he committed a constitutional outrage of even greater proportion by formally advising the King that, because the Parliament Act had removed the House of Lords' 'buffer' between sovereign and Commons, he was not under an obligation to sign the Home Rule Bill into law.[5]

By the autumn of 1912, Ireland was on the verge of civil war. On 28 September, the Solemn League and Covenant to Reject Home Rule was inaugurated in Belfast Town Hall. Within a week, 218,200 men had signed the roll and 228,991 women had signed a petition in their support. In the House of Commons on New Year's Day 1913, Carson moved an amendment to the Home Rule Bill. It proposed that the nine counties of Ulster remain within the Union. The Protestant demands were reinforced by the recruitment of a Volunteer Force of one hundred thousand men between the ages of seventeen and sixty-five, which was organised around the Orange Lodges. Earl Roberts, the senior field marshal of the British Army, was consulted about its organisation. He provided the names of two retired officers who he thought suitable to organise training and manoeuvres. Meanwhile Alfred (now Lord) Milner suggested that the Lords, by defeating the Army Act, could force Asquith to call a general election.

The Cabinet – with the notable exception of Winston Churchill, who thought 'the time [had] come to put these grave matters to the test' – believed that it was best to compromise, even though the Home Rule Bill had been passed by the House of Commons, rejected twice by the House of Lords and therefore had to pass the Commons only once more to become law. Asquith had secret meetings with Bonar Law.[6] It was Lloyd George who suggested 'a scheme which would remove all moral purpose from under Carson's rebellion' – a temporary exclusion of Ulster from Home Rule with permanent inclusion guaranteed to follow. Neither Redmond, whose opposition was encouraged by Augustus Birrell, the Irish Secretary, nor Carson, who refused to accept 'a sentence of death with stay of execution', supported the idea.[7] Asquith decided that the government must insist that the law, as passed by Parliament, be obeyed.

The 1914 session of Parliament opened with a King's Speech which spoke of the Irish dilemma being solved in 'the spirit of mutual concession' in the hope of laying the 'foundations of a lasting settlement'. Lloyd George's speech, ten days later, attacked Carson but, at the end, contained a hint of concession and compromise.

Sir Edward Carson owes everything to the law . . . If people had anticipated his action and taken the law into their own hands there would have been nothing for Sir Edward Carson to do. He would have been looking forward to the advent of Old Age Pensions – which, by the way, he voted against. We are confronted with the gravest issue raised in this country since the days of the Stuarts. The British Government . . . [will] confront the defiance of popular liberties with a most resolute, unwavering determination. When we have exhausted the means of conciliation, we shall have a perfectly free conscience.[8]

Unfortunately conciliation was not to everybody's taste. In March, Colonel J. E. B. Seely (Haldane's successor as Secretary of State for War) discussed with General Sir Arthur Paget (the Commanding Officer of British troops in Ireland) the disposition of troops in the event of an armed uprising by the Ulster Volunteers. They also considered how to deal with officers who refused to obey an order to take the necessary action against their rebellious kith and kin. It was agreed that officers with homes and families in Ireland would be given leave. The rest, if they disobeyed orders, would be dismissed. Back in Ireland, Paget described the conversation in a way which convinced some of his officers that they were to be subject to draconian and arbitrary discipline. Brigadier Hubert Gough, commanding the 3rd Cavalry Brigade at the Curragh racecourse, announced that he and sixty of his officers would accept dismissal rather than 'initiate active military operations against Ulster'.[9] The 'Curragh Mutiny' had begun.

The situation was complicated by Seely, who – in a combination of incompetence and cowardice – told the mutinous soldiers that they would not be ordered to enforce the provisions of a Home Rule Bill. At the same time police and customs officers watched sympathetically as 24,000 rifles and 300,000 rounds of ammunition – financed in England but bought from Germany – were landed at Larne and Bangor for use by the Ulster Volunteers. Seely was dismissed, Asquith himself became the Secretary of State for War and the government pressed ahead with a new form of Home Rule which contained a concession, similar in spirit to the one which Lloyd George had unsuccessfully suggested to the Cabinet a month earlier. On 23 June 1914, an amending bill was introduced into the House of Lords. It offered each Ulster county the right to vote against joining the devolved province and remain a full part of the Union for six years. Lloyd George prepared the way by preaching the gospel of constitutional propriety.

They say that they are called upon to submit to a Government
which they loathe and detest. Well, we have all had to do that in
our time . . . Bide our time and vote them down when we get the
chance. This is the very essence of democracy . . . Whilst they
think it an intolerable act of oppression to force Home Rule on a
corner of Ireland where sixty per cent of the inhabitants protest
against it, they think it is great Imperial statesmanship to refuse
Home Rule to a part of Ireland where ninety per cent of the
inhabitants do ask for it.[10]

The idea of seeking yet another negotiated settlement was raised by
Lord Loreburn (a former Liberal Lord Chancellor) in a letter which
The Times published on 11 September 1913.[11] Two weeks later, F. E.
Smith wrote a confidential letter to Lloyd George supporting the idea
and expressing the 'strong opinion that a Conference should be summoned by the King'.[12] Lloyd George – taking advantage of the
reputation as a coalitionist which he had acquired among a select
group of politicians in 1910 – sent a positive reply: 'You know how
anxious I have been for years to work with you and a few others on
your side.'[13] Asquith had, initially, been reluctant to accept the idea.
But pressed by the King he eventually agreed. A conference was convened under the chairmanship of Speaker Lowther. Ulster (in the
form of Carson and Craig) was afforded the same representation as the
rest of Ireland (Redmond and Dillon), the Opposition (Bonar Law and
Lansdowne) and the government itself (Asquith and Lloyd George).
The conference was opened by the King, who called for compromise.
Everybody realised that it would have to be built around a special
status for Ulster. That notwithstanding, there was no agreement on the
number of counties to be excluded from Home Rule and no discussion on the period of possible exclusion. The contents of a possible
amending bill were left for future discussion. The Home Rule Bill did
not receive royal assent until September 1914. Its operation – like decisions about exclusions – was postponed for a year or the duration of
the First World War, which had just begun. The Battle of the Marne
had been won – convincing many Irish Nationalists that victory was
less than twelve months away. They had to wait for four years – by
which time the character of Irish Nationalism had changed, Lloyd
George was Prime Minister and Carson, Milner and Bonar Law (the
three most vehement opponents of Home Rule) had served in his
Cabinet.

It was not only Home Rule which had to yield precedence while politicians made fighting and winning the First World War their overwhelming priority. 'Votes for women', popularly supposed to be the result of women's contribution to victory over Germany, was postponed rather than promoted by the four-year conflict. Their cause would have been successful before 1914 had it not been for what history suggests was an error by the Speaker. Asquith – not himself a supporter of women's suffrage – introduced a bill to extend the franchise to all adult men with the promise that, if the House of Commons amended it to include women, he would guarantee that the government would provide enough time to prevent it being 'talked out', the fate of previous attempts to secure votes for women. In January 1913, to Asquith's astonishment and against all precedent, the Speaker ruled the amendment out of order.

Lloyd George's involvement with the franchise campaign was most notable for the interruption of his public meetings by militant suffragettes who took particular exception to politicians who were, or in private claimed to be, on their side but seemed reluctant to say so in public. He was certainly a supporter of votes for women. But his commitment could not be described as passionate conviction. 'There are two ways of dealing with them. My way – give them the vote – or firm administration of the law.'[14]

Lloyd George's detachment from the cause of women's suffrage was, in itself, inconsistent with his claim to be a genuine radical. It was made all the more remarkable by his growing attachment to Frances Stevenson – not a suffragette, because she opposed violent protest, but certainly a convinced suffragist. But no matter how close they became, she never aspired to influence his attitude towards great issues. Although she was a 'new woman' – confident enough in her own view of right and wrong to tell her parents that she had become the Chancellor's mistress – the idea of a partnership of equals never crossed her mind, and she accepted public humiliations that Margaret, 'Old Mair' sitting at home in Wales with the children, would never have tolerated.

Both women provided Lloyd George with the constant boosts that his ego required. But they performed their tasks in different ways. At the end of an Opposition debate which proposed to censure the Chancellor for his 'gross and personal attacks on individuals' – mostly dukes who had either exploited increases in land values or opposed Welsh disestablishment – Frances 'hurried into the ante-room behind the Gallery to scribble him a message of excited congratulation'.[15]

Margaret, on the other hand, waited at home for the hero's own account of his achievement. 'I cannot do without my round little wife. I am so disappointed you were not in the House . . . By common consent I scored the greatest triumph of my parliamentary life.'[16] The added endearments were a usual – and, at the moment of writing, no doubt sincere – feature of the self-congratulation. In the summer of 1914, while eagerly awaiting the arrival of Frances, the Chancellor of the Exchequer wrote to Margaret, 'I hate facing Downing Street, now that you have all departed.'[17]

Budget statements offer fewer opportunities for putting opponents to the sword. After the heroics of the previous four years, the Budget of 1913 was an anticlimax. The passage of the Miners' Minimum Wage Bill and the assumption that the coal strike would soon be over combined with good news about the national balance sheet to create an atmosphere which gave the Chancellor an easy passage. The Admiralty had spent less than its estimate allowed and the Revenue had collected more than had been anticipated. The People's Budget had raised so much revenue that – despite the demands of health and unemployment insurance – there was no need to increase tax. The only contentious proposal was the announcement that the surplus would be held ready to meet unforeseen contingencies rather than diverted to the sinking fund. And true to form, Lloyd George – who had no strong views on the issue – amended the proposal to meet his critics more than halfway.

Despite there being no tax increases in the 1913 Budget, Lloyd George still took the opportunity to deplore the 'sterile expenditure on rearmament' which he attributed not to 'the will of the government or the House of Commons so much as the concerted, or rather competitive, will of a number of great nations'. He was growing restless. Maintaining fiscal stability did not have the attraction of raising taxes to finance reform. He was clear about his aim – amassing 'large sums which give promise of strength and happiness to the nation'.[18] While they accumulated, he had to wrestle with procedural innovation. In order to take advantage of the Parliament Act, it spawned two Finance Bills. One was strictly limited to raising revenue and could not, therefore, be touched by the House of Lords. The other dealt with what, it was feared, the Speaker would designate 'social legislation' and, in consequence, rule that it could be amended and delayed in 'the other place'. The stratagem was necessary but inconvenient and it reawakened old antagonisms. Irritation led to irresponsibility. In Caernarvon on 31 July 1913, Lloyd George made a promise which he must have known would not be kept.

There is one reform which the action of the House of Lords has made essential and that is the abolition of the present Second Chamber. The Prime Minister has already announced that next year he will introduce a measure for a new Second Chamber. It is not for me to say what it will be. One thing I can predict, it will be a Chamber in which all parties, all sections, all creeds will have equal treatment.[19]

Apart from a testy aside about the 'need to deal with the House of Lords', there is no evidence that Asquith had any real intention of embarking on another round of the fight against the Upper House, though it was clear enough that the Lords were determined to exercise to the full the limited rights over new legislation that the Parliament Act allowed them.[20] Despite that, or perhaps because of it, Lloyd George was determined that in 1914 he would introduce what he thought of as a second People's Budget.

On 12 November 1913, Lloyd George had given dinner to Asquith, Grey, Haldane and Crewe. He described it as 'one of the most important gatherings I have attended . . . So important that I made a note of what took place, a thing I have never done before.* It was an historic occasion.'[21]

The note was headed 'the financial situation' – an anodyne title which did not do justice to the gloomy conclusions which followed. The books had moved out of balance in a year.

There is a deficiency of 10 millions on the assumption that Pease [President of the Board of Education] was given an additional 2 million for Capital Education Grants: that Churchill's Naval Estimates would reach £52,300,000 . . . Feeling, unanimously expressed, was in favour of postponing the (£2 millions) construction until next year, pressing Churchill to knock at least 1½ millions off his estimates by slowing down construction and postponing increase in Education Grants until the great educational scheme is introduced. Very strong feeling against increased taxation before the election.

---

*He had taken notes previously. Fearful that his colleagues would renege on the decision to implement his land reforms he had circulated a note of their agreement after a meeting almost a year earlier. It is in the Illingworth Papers.

There was also some discussion of the election date. 'Prime Minster clearly leaning towards a 1914 dissolution.'[22] Christmas intervened to prevent further immediate discussion.

The year 1914 began badly. On New Year's Day Lloyd George gave an interview to the *Daily Chronicle* which – probably intentionally – confirmed that there were disagreements within the Cabinet about the size of the naval budget. 'Our relations with Germany,' Lloyd George told the reporter, 'are infinitely more friendly now than they have been for years.' He then went on to warn that there would be an increase in taxes 'unless there is an effort made to reduce the overwhelming extravagance of our expenditure on armaments'. Grey – who had learned of the *Daily Chronicle* démarche only when he read the interview in the paper – was furious. Lloyd George's excuse was that his intervention had been provoked by Churchill's intolerable conduct. Initially reluctant to pick a fight with his old friend, the Chancellor of the Exchequer had accepted the proposed Naval Estimates for 1914–15 (£50,694,000) without amendment on the understanding that there would be substantial reductions in the following year. But less accommodating members of the Cabinet had complained about his generosity. They were led by McKenna, who, having moved from the Admiralty to the Home Office, had become a disciple of prudence just as Churchill, who had moved in the opposite direction, had become convinced that the need to create an invincible navy transcended all other considerations.* Lloyd George suggested the construction of two new Dreadnoughts rather than four. Churchill responded, with infuriating insouciance, that he could cut his estimates to £49,910,000 without reducing his building programme and then added that his supplementary estimate for 1913–14 would have to be increased from £1,400,000 to £3,000,000. The *Daily Chronicle* interview was the product of Lloyd George's frustration.

After some days of uncertainty – during which Asquith called Lloyd George home from a holiday in Algeria – an agreement was reached on an increase of £5 million in the Naval Estimates rather than the £8 million about which ministers had been warned in November. The revised figure was accepted only after Lloyd George had, dramatically, threatened to resign – a gesture which, according to C. P. Scott, the editor of the *Manchester Guardian*, McKenna greeted with 'Homeric laughter'.[23] The proposed education grants were also reduced. But when a draft

---

*Proof of the rule of government, laid down by the Institute of Politics at Harvard when I was there in 1971–2: 'Where you stand depends on where you sit.'

Budget was presented to the Cabinet in April 1914, the proposed total expenditure was £9.8 million higher than in the previous year – almost as much as the increase which ministers had found unacceptable at their November meeting.

Without consulting colleagues, Lloyd George had decided to use his Budget to implement one part of his Land Campaign. Rating was to be on site values rather than the estimated value of properties – the recommendation in the Acland Committee's report which most benefited town and city dwellers. The proposal became the main feature of a speech in Glasgow which was intended to convince wavering Liberals that the Land Campaign was concerned with more than improving the lot of tenant farmers and agricultural labourers. Making site rather than property values the basis on which the local tax liability was calculated transferred some of the burden from tenant to landlord. It also enabled the householder to improve his premises without incurring a rate increase. The new calculation was meant to be 'an integral part of the system of local taxation'. To achieve that aim, and to soften the blow to landlords, the Exchequer grant to local authorities would eventually rise to £11 million in a full year – reducing the rate burden by ninepence in the pound. Part of the need for increased revenue would be the result of an interim grant which prepared the way for the full introduction of the new system.

Lloyd George proposed to raise all the necessary extra revenue from direct taxation. Income and super-tax were both to be graduated – 9d in the pound on the first £1000 of earned income (which was itself an increase of 2d), rising to 1/4 for earned income of more than £2500 and an additional 5d in the pound for earnings over £3000, rising to 1/4 in the pound for earnings of more than £8000. All unearned income was to be taxed at the top rate. Death duties were to be increased – on a sliding scale – to a maximum of 20 per cent on estates of more than £1 million. The total additional income from tax changes was estimated to be £8.8 million. The £1 million gap was to be closed by raiding the sinking fund.

The Cabinet, anticipating an election in the autumn, was not prepared to 'soak the rich' – and the not so rich – as thoroughly as the Chancellor proposed. McKenna, who by then had become Lloyd George's implacable enemy, clearly rejoiced at the confusion which resulted from demands that the Budget must be revised.

The whole thing has been a shocking muddle. The Budget Committee knew nothing of LlG's proposals until their meeting shortly before the introduction of the budget. LG spoke for three hours explaining his scheme which left no time for discussion. The bill as drawn was very complicated, many of its chief provisions being in the schedules. It would have required three months to pass it. LG talked of passing it in a week, which was absurd. The House is not in the mood for heavy tedious bills.[24]

Initially, the Cabinet made only one major change – though it tore the heart out of the Budget. The basic increase in income tax was reduced from twopence to a penny. Many more changes were to follow.

Lloyd George's determination to insist on the introduction of a long and controversial Finance Bill was made all the more surprising by a warning which he – and other ministers – had received from Percy Illingworth, the Chief Whip, in a memorandum dated 4 May 1914.

The Cabinet should realise at once that an Autumn Session is impossible . . . I do not think that the Cabinet realises the tremendous strain which constant attendance at the House places on private Members . . . I hope, therefore, that every effort will be made to reduce the Government programme to the smallest necessary dimensions.[25]

It was not a hope which Lloyd George was prepared to gratify.

The Chancellor's Budget statement on 4 May 1914 was generally agreed to have been a complete disaster. The complex proposals which it contained were never fully explained to the House of Commons – largely, Lloyd George's critics suggested, because he did not fully understand them himself. However, the damage done to the Liberal Party's morale by the inadequacy of a single day's performance was an insignificant threat to the government's future when compared with the possible consequences of the protracted procedural wrangles that the Finance Bill's complications created.

The Provisional Collection of Taxes Act (1913) required the Finance Bill to become law within four months. But a Tory backbencher raised its whole status with the Speaker. Did the change in local government finance qualify for inclusion in a Finance Bill which was protected from rejection, amendment or delay in the House of Lords? The Speaker ruled that it did not. If the peers rejected it, the Finance Bill (1914) would become law only after it had been passed by the House of Commons on three separate occasions. To add to the government's woe, fifty Liberal backbenchers, led by Sir John Jardine and Sir Richard Holt, announced their opposition to the Budget proposals.

The result was a multiple humiliation. On 22 June, Herbert Samuel – President of the Local Government Board and therefore capable of claiming that he had been chosen to break the news for better reasons than sparing the Chancellor's embarrassment – announced a change in the legislative timetable. The original Finance Bill would be divided in two in accordance with the practice which had been pioneered the previous year. A new Finance Bill – which dealt exclusively with the raising of revenue – would be introduced at once. A bill to reorganise local government finance would follow at some unspecified date. After some haggling with Jardine and Holt about the timing of the two bills, the permanent increase in the government's grant to local authorities was postponed and the interim increase was abandoned. To guarantee the passage of the new (and truncated) Finance Bill, the increase in tax on unearned income was halved in line with the adjustment to the income tax increase.

Lloyd George insisted that 'the Parliamentary draughtsmen let me down badly. They should have found out beforehand what the Speaker's decision would be.'[26] Few other people thought that the blame lay with them. 'LG has had a bad week. His stock stands low with the party. The Budget has been a fiasco. Nevertheless he seems in excellent spirits and full of fight. His courage and powers of endurance are wonderful.'[27] In the four years that lay ahead he was going to need all the heroic qualities which Lord Riddell identified.

CHAPTER 24

THE PATRIOT

Politicians who want to avoid war have always taken refuge in wishful thinking. Speaking at the Mansion House banquet on 17 July 1914 – three weeks after the assassination of Archduke Franz Ferdinand in Sarajevo – Lloyd George reassured the City of London that the peace could be preserved.

> There are always clouds in the international sky. You never get a perfectly blue sky in foreign affairs. There are clouds, even now, but having got out of the greater difficulties, last year, we feel confident that common sense, the patience, the goodwill, the forbearance which enabled us to solve the greater and more urgent problems last year will enable us to pull through these problems at the present moment.[1]

The Chancellor's historical analysis was no better than his powers of prediction. The great powers of Europe had not 'got out' of the difficulties of 1913. The Austrians – alarmed by the military strength of Serbia which it demonstrated in its defeat of Turkey – had been persuaded not to declare war. But the underlying causes of tension remained and it seemed likely that Germany – despite having urged Austria not to make the pre-emptive strike – was determined eventually to expand to the west. The number of recruits conscripted into the German Army each year was increased from 280,000 to 343,000 men. A capital levy of 1000 million marks was devoted to the cost of military preparations. The Berlin General Staff was preparing to implement the Schlieffen Plan – six weeks to defeat France after an invasion through Belgium. Then a combined attack on Russia and the Slav states before the winter set in. On 23 July – six days after Lloyd George's Mansion House speech – the Austrians issued an ultimatum to Serbia. It was more extreme than the Germans had anticipated. Even the milder original version would have made a general European war inevitable. Grey attempted to buy time by proposing a four-power conference but asked for the Cabinet's agreement to announce that, if France were invaded, Britain would come to her support. The Cabinet refused to endorse his proposal.

Lloyd George provided C. P. Scott with a reassuring footnote for his diary.

No question of our taking part in any war in the first instance. Knew of no minister who would be in favour of it. But he admitted that a difficult question would arise if the German fleet were [*sic*] attacking French towns on the other side of the Channel and France sowed the Channel with mines.

The Chancellor then offered a bizarre suggestion which he did not claim represented the general ministerial view. Britain 'might pair' with Italy – an ally of Germany and Austria – in a mutual agreement to remain neutral.[2]

Asquith's thoughts on the role Britain would play were barely less confused. On 24 July, in his letter to the King, he described the impending conflict as 'the greatest event for many years past' but he added 'happily there seems no reason why we should be anything other than a spectator'.[3] However, he instructed the War Office to effect the emergency procedures set out in Haldane's 'war book'. Five days later, his daily message to the palace was intentionally ambivalent. Reaction to the invasion of Belgium would, 'if the matter arises, be rather a matter of policy than legal obligation'. Grey had been 'authorised to inform the French and German ambassadors that, at this stage, we were unable to pledge ourselves in advance either under all conditions to stand aside or in any conditions to join in'.[4]

The opposition was less equivocal than the government. Bonar Law told Asquith, 'It would be fatal to the honour and security of the United Kingdom to hesitate in supporting France and Russia at the present juncture.'[5] Redmond pledged the Irish Nationalists' support for resistance to aggression,* and when Ramsay MacDonald refused to

*A year later, Redmond was to make clear that his offer of a carte blanche did not include agreement to conscription in Ireland.

accept the possibility that Britain might wage a just war, he was forced to resign the leadership of the Labour Party.

The government's divisions had been described by the Prime Minister in one of the flood of letters that was the manifestation of his strange, though unconsummated, infatuation for Venetia Stanley – a friend of his daughter to whom he wrote several times each day, sometimes during Cabinet meetings. Some ministers believed 'that we should declare now and at once that in no circumstances would we take a hand. There is no doubt that, for the moment, that is the view of the bulk of the party. Ll-G – all for peace – is more sensible and statesmanlike, keeping the position open.'[6] In fact the Chancellor of the Exchequer was 'in a difficult position – bombarded with telegrams from friends like [C. P.] Scott of the *Manchester Guardian* who had wired to say that any Liberal who supported war would never be allowed to enter another Liberal Cabinet'.[7] Lloyd George was attempting to reconcile instinct with judgement, ambition with conviction and two conflicting principles. Liberals do not go lightly to war. But they also defend the integrity of small nations. A man who had supported the Boers' right to self-determination could not easily sacrifice the independence of the countries which Germany was likely to absorb.

Most ministers were equally ambivalent. But the speed of events concentrated minds. There were two Cabinet meetings on Sunday 2 August. Both accepted the possibility of British involvement and ended with resignations – first John Burns, President of the Board of Trade, and then John Morley, Lord President of the Council. At dinner that night, Lloyd George loyally – and no doubt with conviction – defended the day's decisions after John Simon, the Attorney General, had shown the assembled guests his draft letter of resignation.

> Lloyd George brought out the official war map and, putting it on the end of the dinner table, graphically described the position of various forces. He said that as a compromise the Government had determined to tell Germany that England would remain neutral if Germany undertook not to attack the coast of France or enter the English Channel with a view to attacking French shipping. He said that if the Germans gave this undertaking in an unqualified manner and observed the neutrality of Belgium, he would not agree to war but would rather resign.[8]

It was a naive assertion that as long as Britain's security was protected, what happened to the rest of Europe was of no immediate concern. Lloyd George was no less prepared for war than the rest of the Cabinet. The state of readiness was illustrated by an extraordinary incident which had occurred during a Riddell dinner party.

> The telephone bell rang. It was Sir John French [Chief of the Imperial General Staff] with whom [Riddell] was on intimate terms. He said, 'Can you tell me old chap whether we are going to be in this war? If so are we going to put an army on the continent and, if we are, who is going to command it?'

Riddell took advice from his guests and then told French that he 'thought we should be in the war, that we should send an army to the continent and that he would be in command'. He added, 'Lloyd George says "Be at Downing Street tomorrow at ten o'clock sharp".'[9] It was good advice. On 3 August, ministers were told that Belgium had refused to allow the passage of German troops into France and on 4 August – at the fourth Cabinet meeting in three days – the news that Belgium had, in effect, been invaded was followed by reluctant agreement to issue an ultimatum. If, by midnight, Berlin had given no assurances that its army would be withdrawn from Belgium, 'a state of war would exist between Britain and Germany'. Lloyd George no longer doubted the justice of the cause. Nor, it seems, did his sons Richard and Gwilym. On 15 August their father received, on their behalf, a telegram from Churchill: 'Please forward your application direct to Colonel Fitzwilliam, War Office, stating units in which you wish to serve.'[10] The Chancellor's sons had asked for advice about joining the Territorials.

On the day before the ultimatum was issued Lloyd George had told his wife,

> I am moving through a nightmare world these days. I have fought hard for peace and succeeded, so far, in keeping the Cabinet out of it, but I am driven to the conclusion that if the small nationality of Belgium is attacked by Germany all my traditions and even my prejudices will be engaged on the side of war.[11]

That was an honourable and, to an objective observer, wholly convincing explanation of a gradual shift in position. However, Charles Hobhouse – who had once been employed to report on the new

Chancellor's conduct – regarded the call to arms as no more than the reassertion of instincts which had been suppressed for purely political reasons. 'At first LlG was very anti-German . . . but as Liberal papers were very anti-war he veered round and became peaceful.'[12] Then he reverted to his true beliefs. Frances Stevenson, whose bias was in the other direction, shared the Hobhouse view and described the transition from peace to war in even more unflattering terms. 'My own opinion is that LG's mind was really made up from the first, that he knew that we would have to go in and that the invasion of Belgium was, to be cynical, a heaven-sent opportunity for supporting a declaration of war.'[13] The truth is more to Lloyd George's credit.

Lloyd George was motivated by a combination of idealism and self-interest – not an unknown partnership in politics – and his strategic judgement was changed by briefings he received in the Committee of Imperial Defence. He recalled, with a mixture of self-satisfaction and apprehension, what he described as 'the experiences of 1899 to 1902' and added that he 'had had enough of standing out against a war-inflamed populace'.[14] He was so obviously a reluctant warrior that he was able to persuade some of the pacifists to postpone their resignations from the government. But, because he did not argue for peace at any price, he also felt able to warn his 'gung-ho' colleagues that they risked splitting, and therefore destroying, the government. A stern note passed to the temperamentally bellicose Churchill urged moderation: 'If patience prevails, and you do not press us too hard tonight, we might come together.'[15] And so they did. Only Burns and Morley stood out against the eventual view that war was inevitable. The *Punch* cartoon of the gallant youth defending his property against his overbearing neigh-bour – captioned 'Bravo Belgium' – caught the national mood. Great Britain must go to the rescue. A formal proclamation of war against Germany was signed by the King at 10.45 a.m. on 5 August. War was declared against Austria on 12 August and against Turkey on 5 November.

When hostilities began, Asquith was still Secretary of State for War, a temporary expedient to re-establish the authority of the government after Colonel Seely's unintended encouragement of the Curragh 'muti-neers'. The obvious candidate to replace him was Lord Kitchener of Khartoum, a national hero because of victories won in the colonies. His status, which was to become a major factor in the prosecution of the war, was described by Lord Beaverbrook – at the time Max Aitken MP. 'The People did not reason about Kitchener, they just trusted, and that mere trust was a priceless asset in days when life was being torn up by its roots and the firmest mind might fall into doubt and fear. Men simply said, "Kitchener is there. It is all right".'[16]

No doubt Beaverbrook was right about 'men' in general. Lloyd George was not among the idolatrous majority. Kitchener had hunted down the Boer commandos and imprisoned Boer women and children. But that was not the real reason for Lloyd George's antagonism. He was instinctively hostile to authority – the outsider who challenged the establishment and regarded deference as self-humiliation. He would have set out to diminish the new, authoritarian Secretary of State for War even if Kitchener had offered advice which he judged to be correct in every detail. Often Kitchener was wrong. Fortunately for Great Britain – and particularly for British soldiers – Lloyd George was willing to break through the aura of invincibility and first expose, before eventually rectifying, the errors of a man he regarded as 'a good poster but a bad general'.

It says much for Lloyd George's confidence that he was prepared to challenge the strategic judgement of a field marshal of the British Army. Kitchener – contemptuous of politicians and reluctant to accept the disciplines of Cabinet government – was a difficult colleague. But it is easy to understand the irritation he felt when his plans were challenged by the Chancellor of the Exchequer, a Baptist lawyer from Wales who had spent a week at camp with the local militia, and the First Lord of the Admiralty, who had been a junior cavalry officer at the Battle of Omdurman when Kitchener was commander-in-chief of the Anglo-Egyptian forces. Not surprisingly, Lloyd George's alternative strategy – opening up a second front outside France and Flanders – did not find favour. Churchill's parallel plan did. It ended in a disaster not entirely of Churchill's own making.

Lloyd George's first battle was against neither the Germans nor the General Staff, but the prospect of financial collapse. The City of London had begun to panic in late July.

By August 1, the foreign exchange market had practically ceased to operate, the Stock Exchange was closed, it was impossible to get bills accepted or discounted, the accepting houses and bill brokers were in grave danger of having to stop payment and the Bank of England itself found the demands upon it increasing and its reserve near exhaustion.[17]

Lloyd George's own description of the crisis, although florid, was accurate.

I saw Money before the war, I saw it immediately after the outbreak of war. I lived with it for days and days and did my best to
steady its nerve, for I knew how much depended on restoring its
confidence and I can say that Money was a frightened and trem-
bling thing.[18]

'Money' was 'steadied' by a series of emergency measures. The fidu-
ciary issue (the amount of currency that the Bank of England could
print and circulate)* was enlarged and the bank rate was increased to
10 per cent. Markets were closed for a full week by the statutory
extension of the August Bank Holiday. Parliament authorised the
printing of treasury notes which could be used as legal tender if economic activity was imperilled by the hoarding of gold sovereigns.
The postponement of contracted payments was legalised – with a
number of essential exceptions – and the insurance of shipping against
damage and destruction from enemy action guaranteed by the Bank of
England.†

The speed with which Lloyd George acted and the decisive nature of
his 'special measures' deservedly did much to repair the reputation
which had been damaged by the Budget fiasco. In his diary Charles
Hobhouse, who had once found the Chancellor woefully negligent of
detail, endorsed Walter Runciman's encomium.

The way Lloyd George has picked up financial questions is marvellous. He knew nothing originally of commerce and trade and
bills of loading or exchange, holders, drawers, acceptors had no
meaning for him. Notwithstanding all this, he has mastered these
problems and captivated the bankers and the measures taken have
been wise, prudent and far seeing.[19]

Lloyd George wrote home to Wales in jubilation.

I have launched my great scheme – the boldest financial experiment any government has ever launched . . . Just received a letter
signed by the Rothschilds congratulating me on the way I had
tackled the greatest difficulty that has ever occurred in the finances

---

*The term 'quantitative easing' had not then been invented.
†The exceptions to postponement included wages, national health insurance, rates,
taxes, workmen's compensation and debts of less than £5.

of this country★ . . . PM told me it was the greatest success the government has yet scored.[21]

Austen Chamberlain was added to the Treasury's Panel of Advisers. It is hard to believe that he contributed much to the collective wisdom. But his presence in itself added to stability and helped to preserve the party truce which was in desperate danger of collapse when – despite the introduction of suspensory legislation which delayed implementation until the war was over – the Unionists walked out of the Commons chamber rather than hear that the Home Rule Bill had received royal assent. Lloyd George, the pragmatist, had realised the importance of keeping the Liberal Party together before the war began. Once it had started, he had no doubt that some form of coalition was necessary for victory.

As late as 18 August there was still talk of the government disintegrating. Simon, the Attorney General, mentioned, as an aside to dinner guests, that he was still minded to resign his office and volunteer for the front – the honourable course for a patriot who disagreed with government policy.[22] It may have been Simon's doubts which prompted Lloyd George to agree to his host's suggestion that he should 'make a speech explaining why we are at war and appealing to the patriotism of the whole nation'.[23] He prepared for the call to arms with a visit to France two days later. 'Went right to the front. The Germans were shelling a village close by. We got into the French trench.'[24]

It was decided that the appeal should be made in the Queen's Hall on the afternoon of 19 September. The audience – mostly London–Welsh Nonconformists – was carefully chosen. Despite that, while eating an early lunch, Lloyd George – realising that he was to act out of character – was 'terribly nervous, feeling, he said, as if he was about to be executed'. However, when he spoke, he 'did not give any sign of perturbation'. Nor did he betray the slightest doubt that Britain was fighting a necessary and righteous war.

There is no man in this room who has always regarded the prospect of engaging in a great war with greater reluctance and with greater repugnance than I have done through the whole period of my political life. There is no man inside or outside this

---

★The compliment was delivered in an anatomically confused metaphor: 'You grasped the situation with a masterly eye and solved it with the same masterly hand.'[20]

room more convinced that we could not have avoided it without national dishonour . . . They think we cannot beat them. It will not be easy. It will be a long job. It will be a terrible war. But in the end we will march through terror to triumph. We shall need all our qualities – every quality that Britain and its people possess – prudence in counsel, daring in action, tenacity in purpose, courage in defeat, moderation in victory, in all things faith.[25]

The speech concluded with a passage which was built around a quintessentially Lloyd Georgean metaphor.

I know a valley in North Wales between the mountains and the sea. It is a beautiful valley, snug, comfortable, sheltered by the mountains from all the bitter blasts . . . We have been living in a sheltered valley for generations. We have been too comfortable and too indulgent – many, perhaps, too selfish and the stern hand of fate scourged us to an elevation where we can see the great everlasting things that matter to a nation – the great peaks which we had forgotten. Honour, Duty, Patriotism and, clad in glittering white, the great pinnacle of Sacrifice pointing like a rugged finger to heaven. We shall descend into the valley again. But as long as the men and women of this generation last, they will carry in their hearts the image of those great mountain peaks whose foundations were not shaken, though Europe rock and sway in the convulsions of a great war.[26]

According to Frances Stevenson, Lloyd George 'was very depressed after it was over'. The speech might have been a success had the audience not been such a complete failure that they 'made him sick. They were far too stodgy and comfortable', requiring him to 'talk his way through layers of fat'.[27] His colleagues judged the result differently. Grey wept when he read the peroration. An equally lachrymose Asquith told him that it was a wonderful speech and Masterman judged it to be 'the finest speech in the history of England'.[28] The newspapers 'were loud in their praise – Tory papers loudest of all'.[29] Lloyd George had established his reputation as a British patriot in a speech which, in its language, was pure Baptist bethel.

However, when the opportunity to serve was presented to his own family, Lloyd George had not endorsed the poet Rupert Brooke's view that death in battle was 'a rarer gift than gold'. He had written home to Margaret with an urgent request.

They are pressing Territorials to volunteer for the War. [Gwilym] mustn't do that yet . . . I am dead against carrying on a war of conquest to crush Germany for the benefit of Russia . . . I am not going to sacrifice my nice boy for that purpose. You must write, telling him he must on no account be bullied into volunteering abroad.[30]

The speech and the letter can be reconciled with the explanation that new recruits were essential to the war effort and that a desire to protect his son was an understandable, indeed admirable, reaction to the risk of Gwilym's feeling an obligation to 'do his bit'. But there are aspects of his letter home that reveal Lloyd George at his most devious. Although normally an obsessive letter writer, he asked his wife to urge caution on their sons rather than writing directly to them himself – presumably because of his reluctance to put his own name to such an unpatriotic suggestion. And the accusation of double standards is given extra force by a reply he wrote to a letter which congratulated him on the Queen's Hall speech. 'I was so sorry to hear the news about your nephew's death, but I know you are too good a patriot to grudge even the life of one to whom you are attached in the service of your country.'[31] That sentiment did not represent his attitude towards his own family. He remained 'protective' towards both his sons throughout the war.[32] But he also took great pleasure in being the father of two soldiers. 'The young warriors have started. They look the part . . . Saluted by every Tommy on the street.'[33] Happily – although both of them served in France – they survived.

The Queen's Hall speech – initially intended to appeal to Welshmen living in London – was meant as a contribution to Kitchener's recruitment campaign. The Secretary of State for War had called for 100,000 volunteers. More than 120,000 men had responded, but he still told the Cabinet that unless another 600,000 enlisted before April 1915, it would be necessary to introduce conscription. It was not a step which Kitchener – a soldier with a low opinion of reluctant warriors – wanted to take. And when the time came to accept its necessity, both he and Lloyd George – whose objections were based on quite different considerations – supported compulsion with great reluctance. The two men agreed on little else.

Their first dispute – the subject of a heated Cabinet discussion on 28 September 1914 – concerned Lloyd George's insistence that Nonconformist chaplains should, like Anglicans, be allowed to accompany troops into battle. Kitchener was eventually persuaded to allow them in the front line and, despite initial objections, agreed to withdraw the order which forbade the speaking of Welsh in barracks or on parade. But he was more obdurate in his rejection of another proposal which Lloyd George thought a necessary sign of respect to Welsh nationhood – the creation of a purely Welsh division which would allow new Welsh recruits to serve together rather than be absorbed into the English county regiments. Lloyd George also contended that a Welsh division was the best way of stimulating recruitment within the principality. He supported his argument with two recruitment speeches which were part a challenge and part a rebuke to his countrymen.

On 24 September, he told a meeting in Criccieth,

> In recruiting, Scotland comes first in numbers. England is second. Wales is third. Mr Asquith is in Dublin tomorrow. If Wales does not wake up, we shall be last. That is not the position for a nation which has turned out more soldiers than any in the Continental wars of the past. At Crecy and Agincourt, where the British were eminently successful, half the soldiers were Welsh.[34]

At Cardiff, five days later, he made an admission. 'In proportion to our population, it is incumbent upon us to raise at least 40,000 to 50,000 in the Principality . . . All we are asking is to escape conscription.'[35] After a battle in the Cabinet – described as a 'stand up fight with Kitchener'[36] – there was a 'most satisfactory meeting'[37] in which the Secretary of State 'conceded everything' that Welsh nationhood demanded,[38] including Lloyd George's right to nominate the brigadier who would command the North Wales contingent. Richard Lloyd George, the Chancellor's elder son, became his aide-de-camp.*

On 26 August – when asking the House of Commons to approve a War Loans Bill which superseded the Vote of Credit which had financed the first weeks of hostilities – Lloyd George had warned the Commons that the enemy would 'probably fight to the very end before he will accept the conditions upon which we can possibly make peace . . . That is where our resources will come in, not merely men but cash.'[39] By November cash was beginning to run out. An

---

*During the Battle of the Somme, the Welsh Division – as a whole – suffered four thousand casualties during a failed assault on Mametz Wood. Various commanders, including Lloyd George's brigadier, were replaced. A renewed assault was successful.

emergency War Budget was necessary. Lloyd George had already demonstrated his prudence. Although he had argued, successfully, for married men's allowances to be paid to common-law wives, he had attempted to limit the widows' war pension to 5/- a week and rejected suggestions that financial help should be provided for Belgian refugees. The Cabinet agreed to be hard on the Belgians but insisted on a widows' pension of 6/6. Winston Churchill argued for a shilling more.

The Budget was preceded by Parliament approving a second Vote of Credit – just £25 million rather than the £100 million which had been raised during the first week of hostilities, but enough to fuel the engines of war until the taxes were levied. Income tax was doubled (from 1/4 to 2/8 in the pound), beer duty was almost quadrupled (from 7/9 to 25/- a barrel). War loans were to be raised from patriotic citizens. The first – a bad bargain for lenders from the start – was quickly over-subscribed. But it was an apparently uncontroversial Treasury proposal which followed the Budget that led to one of the earliest battles of the war – between the Treasury and the War Office. Lloyd George provided £20 million for private companies manufacturing munitions to invest in expanded capacity. General Sir Stanley von Donop, the Master-General of Ordnance, chose not to pass on the money. Indeed, he kept its existence secret. He was not, he later said, a man to encourage extravagance.

The British Expeditionary Force, under its Commander-in-Chief Sir John French, had been short of shells from the very beginning of the war – and particularly short of the essential high explosives. In Lloyd George's opinion, the High Command was 'fighting the last war'. The 'military mind', he wrote, 'makes up in retentiveness what it lacks in agility'. Generals – who had made their names in campaigns against Afrikaner guerrillas were 'still preparing to slug . . . Boers, hiding behind bushes and boulders'.[40] In September and October 1914, 'the War Office was supplying only shrapnel for field guns and of the shells and seventy per cent of the ammunition provided for field howitzers and 66-pounder was shrapnel'. Throughout the autumn General Headquarters in France continually asked for more high explosives. The requests were refused. 'Even more serious than the failure to supply high explosives was a general shortage of shells of any kind whatso-ever . . . The shortage of ammunition for the larger guns became the theme of almost daily telegrams from Sir John French.'[41]

During the early weeks of September, Lloyd George felt able to write home: 'News from front remarkably good. Just had a wire from [Sir John] French that Joffre [Commander-in-Chief of the French

Army] there today and tomorrow. They think the Germans are dis-
couraged by the last few days' fighting. They suffered frightful casualties.
So did we, but the French are bringing reinforcements up.'[42] The war
of attrition had begun. For the moment, Lloyd George accepted the
generals' argument that victory would go to which of the opposing
armies had the greater capacity to accept, absorb and replace its losses.
In fact, the French counter-attack on the Marne had done no more
than stabilise the front after the retreat from Mons, and the Russian
Army advancing on East Prussia had been virtually destroyed at
Tannenberg. The entry of Turkey into the war in November required
the already overstretched British Army to send reinforcements to Egypt
and Mesopotamia. The ammunition shortage increased the risk of
defeat on every front.

To Lloyd George's relief – premature, as it turned out – a Cabinet
committee was set up to supervise arms production. It agreed to aim at
producing 1600 rather than 800 field guns by April 1915, to place orders
for ammunition in the United States and to persuade the ordnance factories to employ subcontractors. Sensible though those measures were,
they were unlikely to turn the tide. Lloyd George – accompanied by
Rufus Isaacs (who had become Lord Reading, Lord Chief Justice of
England) and John Simon – visited France to make a personal assessment
of the situation. He returned, on 19 October, dispirited. He would have
been even more depressed had he stayed longer. The Battle of Ypres was
about to begin. It ended a little more than a month later. By the end of
1914, half the British Expeditionary Force of 160,000 men had been
killed, captured or wounded.[43] The news was equally bad from sea and
land. German submarines menaced British shipping. The *U-9* sank three
British cruisers in one day. At the Battle of Coronel off the coast of
Chile – the first British naval defeat for a hundred years – two ships, the
Monmouth and *Good Hope*, were sunk with all hands, 1600 sailors in all.

On New Year's Eve, Lloyd George wrote to the Prime Minister to
express his 'unease about the prospects of the War unless the
Government take some decisive measures to grip the situation'. His language grew increasingly intemperate as the letter progressed.

> I can see no signs anywhere that our military leaders and guides are
> considering any plans for extracting us from our present unsatis-
> factory position. Had I not been witness to the deplorable lack of
> provision, I should not have thought it possible that men so
> responsibly placed could have so little forethought.

Ministers had increased the number of field guns on order. But 'rifles are not yet satisfactory owing to von Donop's stupidity'.[44] Next day he sent Asquith a long memorandum, setting out his alternative plan of battle. It began with a warning that 700,000 men in the volunteer army 'were drawn almost exclusively from the better class of artisan, the upper and middle classes . . . If this superb army is thrown away upon futile enterprises such as those we have witnessed during the last few weeks, the country will be uncontrollably indignant.'[45] He then set out his plan to break the deadlock. It amounted to the opening of a second front. France should be left to the French – allowing 300,000 British troops to be brought home so that 200,000 of them could join with 400,000 recent recruits to form a new army. Together with 300,000 Serbs – and possibly 500,000 Romanians, Greeks and Montenegrins – they would land on the Dalmatian coast and attack Austria through Salonika. It was one of several schemes considered by the War Council – a committee of ministers and service chiefs set up by Asquith in November 1914 to coordinate policy. A landing at Zeebrugge, the invasion of Schleswig–Holstein and the forcing of the Dardanelles narrows by the Royal Navy were all approved. The Salonika proposal was rejected. Lloyd George continued to argue in its favour for the next two years.

Lloyd George's first attempt to revive the idea of invading Salonika was preceded by the proposal that the Foreign Secretary visit the region in the hope of persuading its governments to cooperate in the venture. Grey declined to go. Then – believing that only the creation of a new front could end the stalemate in Europe – Lloyd George offered to visit the region himself with a mandate to persuade the neutral states to enter the war. Grey would not agree. Lloyd George continued to argue his case with a determination which justified Churchill's accolade: 'LG has more true insight and courage than anyone else and really sticks at nothing – no measure is too far-reaching, no expedient too novel.'[46]

It was his determination to extend the war to another front that made him agree to the Churchill-inspired Dardanelles campaign – even though he was doubtful about its prospect of success from the very beginning. The plan, insomuch as anything so premeditated existed, was for the Royal Navy to fight its way through the straits, force the surrender of Constantinople and, by knocking Turkey out of the war, relieve pressure on Russia in the Caucasus and persuade Greece, Romania and Bulgaria to support the Allies. Lloyd George's doubts

about the feasibility of the plan were expressed on 24 February 1915 at
a meeting of the War Council when he asked if

> in the event of a naval attack failing (and it was something of an
> experiment) it was proposed that the Army should be used to
> undertake an operation in which the Navy had failed? Mr
> Churchill said that was not his intention . . . Mr Lloyd George
> hoped that the Army would not be required, or expected to pull
> the chestnuts out of the fire for the Navy.[47]

He was anxious not to reinforce continual failure. Churchill did not
regard failure as a possibility.

It may have been frustration – or perhaps it was real conviction – that
made Lloyd George change his mind about what his best contribution
to the war effort would be. He continued to advocate opening another
front. But he turned most of his attention to the need to improve war
production. He was particularly determined to increase the output of
shells. The extent of his commitment to that objective was illustrated by
what he regarded as an essential step towards its achievement. Alcohol
consumption must be reduced and, in some industrial areas, sales prohibited altogether. Asquith, speaking to McKenna of courage, 'marked
Lloyd George rather low in this respect'.[48] He then went on to make a
more legitimate criticism of the Chancellor's 'versatile and volatile'
personality. On 2 March 1915, the Prime Minister set out the cause of
his complaint in an aide-mémoire. 'After midnight Lloyd George completely lost his head on the question of drink.' It was a subject about
which the two men were unlikely to agree.

> His mind apparently oscillates from hour to hour between the two
> poles of absurdity: cutting off all drink from the working man,
> which would lead to something like a universal strike; and buying
> out (at this moment of all others) the whole liquor trade of the
> country and replacing it by a huge state monopoly.[49]

On 29 March 1915, Lloyd George told the Shipbuilding Employers'
Federation, 'We are fighting Germans, Austrians and drink and as far as
I can see the deadliest of these is drink.' He decided to battle against the
greatest of the nation's enemies with the assistance of an unexpected and
almost cerainly reluctant ally. In the belief that 'all classes would hasten
to follow the lead of the sovereign' he asked George V to set an

example.[50] On the afternoon of the Shipbuilding Employers meeting he 'had three quarters of an hour with the King – mostly on the Drink question' and, according to Lloyd George's letter home, 'He was impressed.' Whatever the King's real feelings, he agreed to 'give up all alcoholic liquor himself and issue an order against its consumption in the Royal Household'.[51] The House of Commons was less cooperative and refused, outright, to close its bars.

According to Asquith, Lloyd George was 'engaged in his usual process of roping in everybody – Opposition leaders, Labour, temperance men etc – and he is persuaded that he will succeed in getting them all' to support what he called 'The King's Pledge'.[52] In itself, an assault on alcohol consumption did not warrant the use of Lloyd George's time. But the method he used to pursue his trivial objective was deeply significant. Politicians of all parties were to combine in using the instruments of the state to create – by persuasion or statute – the outcome which was in the national interest. The idea of 'war socialism' – which was to dominate his thinking for years – was born. It was a rare political example of a mouse bringing forth a mountain.

Bonar Law, on the other hand, had still to be convinced that a nation at war needed to abandon party politics. He warned that the Unionists would oppose statutory interference with the drinking classes. And the Irish Nationalists – for whom whiskey sales had an importance second only to Home Rule – reacted to the idea of prohibition with scandalised fury. Lloyd George was forced to retreat. Selective powers to take action in areas of special concern were included in the Defence of the Realm Act (DORA) and (more out of pride than necessity) the public houses of Carlisle were nationalised. There was no increase in alcohol duties in the Budget.*

Asquith dismissed the 1915 Budget as 'a humdrum affair'. But by then the Prime Minister had become both impatient with, and suspicious of, Lloyd George. His disenchantment led to an extraordinary charge. Complaining that the Chancellor was 'kept at Walton Heath by one of those psychological chills which always precede his budgets, when he does not feel altogether sure of his ground', he added, 'He would like to see me take his budgets for him'.[53]

---

*Lloyd George claimed that exhortation and example had some effect. Between 1913 and 1917 convictions for drunkenness fell from 3482 a week to 929. Alcohol consumption fell from 89 million gallons annually to 37 million gallons between 1914 and 1918. It may have been the result of so many men being away at the Front.

There are several possible explanations – apart from nerves – for Lloyd George's delay in returning from Walton Heath. One of them is that Frances Stevenson was pregnant and about to have an abortion. About the pregnancy there is no doubt. Her diary is explicit:

> C and I have wanted so long to have a child and we thought this week that our wish was about to be realised.★ But when I told Mamma of what was going to happen she was so terribly upset and still is. She says she would rather see me dead than that such a thing should happen.

Frances wrote that she would 'be proud to have his child and would be willing to suffer for it'. But a sacrifice of a different sort was necessary. 'It is not to be. I fear that if I insisted upon this, [my mother] would be so upset that people would see what had happened and I cannot be responsible for the ruin of C's career.'[54]

Frances's willingness to lose the baby rather than risk damage to Lloyd George's career was not the ultimate proof of her selfless devotion. That was provided by the gratitude and guilt she felt about his 'goodness', as demonstrated, during her time of physical and emotional trauma, by his willingness to interrupt his busy life by visiting her. There was no danger of his being damagingly distracted from his great work. The pregnancy was on the margin of his life. His real concern was war aims – his and the nation's.

War requires the revision of domestic policies. Lloyd George embarked on a 'great new chapter in the history of labour and its relations with the state'.[55] The DORA allowed the government to commandeer factories and workshops, required the acceptance of technically unskilled labour in theoretically skilled jobs and prohibited continued strike action when an industrial dispute was judged to be damaging to the war effort. Industrial relations 'reforms' are quickly implemented only when they are supported by the workers they affect. Within ten days of the second DORA becoming law, the trade unions had signed what came to be called the 'Treasury Agreement'. It was a tribute to organised labour's patriotism and Lloyd George's negotiating skills as well as a rebuke to the politicians who, even in the face of the enemy, could not agree among themselves.

Frances Stevenson described the trade unionists who spent three days

---

★'C' is for 'Chief' – a rather strange choice of sobriquet.

'overrunning the Treasury' as 'a very unsatisfactory lot of people ...
essentially selfish and narrow minded'.[56] Balfour (wisely invited to attend
the discussions) was surprised 'to find the workmen's representatives
talked so well'.[57] Lloyd George had enough common sense and vision
neither to despise nor patronise. He was not instinctively on the unions'
side. And he failed to implement his promise to curb war profiteering
with the rigour which he led them to expect. But in order to obtain
their cooperation, he accepted – indeed promoted – a crucial change in
their status. The unions negotiated with the government. They were
accepted as a power in the land.

The day after the Treasury Agreement was signed, the Battle of
Neuve Chapelle began. Its reverberations did not ricochet around
Whitehall for some weeks, but the multiple failures of organisation and
personal performance which it came to typify had become increasingly
obvious since the first weeks of the war – even though, as later events
revealed, Kitchener had not shown the Cabinet the despatches from the
front which undermined his claims of success.

The problem remained the shortage of arms and ammunition. The
Cabinet committee, set up in October 1914 to supervise procurement,
rarely met. On 5 March 1915, an ad hoc meeting was called by the Prime
Minister to brief ministers about progress. They learned that many of the
new recruits – enlisted during the 'Kitchener Wants You' campaign –
would not be given rifles until an indeterminate date in the following
year. Lloyd George threatened to resign unless a new Munitions
Committee – which Kitchener did not chair – was set up at once.
Asquith agreed and made Lloyd George the chairman. The infighting had
only just begun.

Kitchener contended that the new committee's role must be purely
advisory. 'If the responsibility in regard to the provision of munitions of
war is to be transferred from the Secretary of State for War, I am told
that an Order in Council, and perhaps legislation, would be necessary.'[58]
Lloyd George said that he would resign if the new committee were
purely advisory. Kitchener responded that he would resign if it were
given executive powers. Indeed he actually did resign in the middle of
one Cabinet meeting but his dramatic walkout was interrupted by J. A.
Pease, by then Postmaster General, who closed the Cabinet Room
door in his face and refused to let him leave.[59] Denied his moment of
drama, he returned to his seat and resumed his unhappy relationship
with his political colleagues. His complaint was that ministers did not
behave like soldiers. 'They discuss military secrets with their wives – all

except one who discusses them with other people's wives.' It was Asquith whom he had in mind.

While the Whitehall bickering was going on, the war in the Dardanelles was being lost. On 19 February 1915, Churchill asked to modify his original plan. He still insisted that what remained a predominantly naval operation would succeed. But troops would be necessary to consolidate the success. Kitchener agreed to make the 29th Division available and then changed his mind. The Royal Navy would have to rely for support on an ANZAC division which had yet to see action. On 18 March, Admiral J. M. de Robeck – after two days in command of a combined British and French fleet – decided that the time had come to force his way through the narrows into the Sea of Marmara. Two British and one French battleship were sunk by mines. Three more were damaged. The Admiralty agreed that the attack should continue. But, in consultation with General Sir Ian Hamilton – the commander of the (yet to be completed) land forces – de Robeck postponed further engagement until the army – no longer a consolidating force – had invaded and captured the Gallipoli peninsula and destroyed the Turkish guns which protected the narrows. Local commanders, on their own initiative, had transformed the Dardanelles from a sea to a land battle.

Winston Churchill, First Lord of the Admiralty, wanted the navy to press on. But Admiral of the Fleet Lord 'Jackie' Fisher – the formidable First Sea Lord – supported de Robeck's caution. Uncharacteristically, Churchill chose not to insist that his judgement should prevail. A week after the failed assault on the narrows, he was caught up in another Westminster intrigue. On 25 March, Asquith asked Lloyd George whether Churchill was manoeuvring to force Grey out of the Foreign Office and replace him with Balfour – a Unionist but co-opted to the Committee of Imperial Defence. He replied that he believed the story to be true.[60] Lloyd George was probably trying to demonstrate his loyalty – to his Prime Minister rather than to his friend. Stories about his own determination to replace Asquith were already circulating in the Westminster hothouse.

Much of the gossip was of Lloyd George's own making. He was pathologically incapable of discretion. Modest stillness was not within his power. He believed that Asquith was failing in his duties and there can be little doubt that he openly repeated the criticism which he made to George Riddell. Asquith, he said, 'lacks initiative and takes no steps to control, or hold together, public departments, each of which goes its own way without criticism'.[61] In the feverish atmosphere of wartime politics, complaint swiftly becomes conspiracy. The allegations were given added force by the general acceptance that, whether or not Lloyd George was plotting, he certainly wanted and intended to become Prime Minister.

On 29 March 1915, the *Daily Chronicle* condemned what it described as 'innuendo and suggestions' made about the Prime Minister's conduct. Later that day, Reginald McKenna – recently the recipient of Lloyd George's scorn because of the way in which he had mishandled the attempt to postpone Welsh disendowment – visited Asquith and volunteered his view that 'LlG and perhaps Winston' were the miscreants to whom the paper referred. He also claimed that he possessed 'a certain amount of evidence as to LlG to go on'.[62] Unusually, Asquith decided on confrontation. Lloyd George was summoned into the Prime Minister's presence that evening. His reaction to the accusations was reported by Asquith to Venetia Stanley. 'I have never seen him more moved. He made a most bitter onslaught on McKenna whom he believes, through his animosity against Winston, to be the villain of the piece and the principal mischief-maker. He vehemently disclaimed having anything to do with the affair.' Lloyd George made a parenthetical complaint about Kitchener's failure to provide adequate ammunition for the army and the not wholly relevant (or logical) suggestion that the newspapers, reluctant to attack a field marshal, attacked him as a surrogate. Then the emotional refutation of disloyalty continued.

> As to himself, he declared that he owed everything to me, that I had stuck to him and protected him when every man's hand was against him and that he would rather break stones and dig potatoes, be hanged and quartered (metaphors used at different stages of his broken but impassioned harangue) than do any act, or say a word, or harbour a thought that was disloyal to me.[63]

Next day Lloyd George indignantly insisted, 'I have never intrigued for office. I have intrigued to carry through my schemes, but that is a different matter.' Advice 'not to allow the subject to worry him' was ignored. McKenna was confronted and accused and, although he did not confess his guilt, he agreed to tell Asquith that his suspicions had been unfounded. Meanwhile – as the bickering in London continued – the Cabinet agreed to send Allied troops to invade Gallipoli in the hope of capturing the shore batteries and giving the battleships free passage to the Sea of Marmara. On 25 April, a division – largely consisting of New Zealand and Australian troops – was sent to the Dardanelles. It landed at Suvla Bay. After two days of advance, the Allies failed to push home their advantage and were driven back to the beaches. The news from the Western Front was no better. The Battle of Neuve Chapelle had been brought to an inconclusive end with 11,652 Allied soldiers killed or wounded. German casualties were barely two-thirds that number.[64]

The argument about procurement rumbled on. Kitchener set up an Armaments Output Committee (manned by soldiers) to rival the committee (composed of ministers) which Lloyd George chaired. When the Chancellor proposed a tour of armament factories, there was a dispute about which he should visit and who should accompany him. The tour never took place. On 12 May, the day he would have left to inspect the factories, he met – at their request – Brinsley Fitzgerald, secretary to Sir John French, and Captain Frederick Guest, the Commander-in-Chief's ADC.* They brought with them copies of telegrams sent by the French to the War Office. They all asked, in increasingly dramatic terms, for more ammunition and had all been rejected or ignored.

Kitchener never accepted that shells were in short supply. A passage from Frances Stevenson's diary puts his position in stark perspective.

> Kitchener was discussing Neuve Chapelle with Balfour and C. 'I told French', he said, 'that he had wasted the ammunition. He told me that he would want 5,000 shells and he used 10,000. He is far too extravagant'. 'And consider the casualties' said Balfour. 'There must have been nearly 10,000 men lost in these engagements'. 'Eight thousand seven hundred at Neuve Chapelle' said K 'but it isn't the men I mind. I can replace the men at once, but I can't replace the shells so easily'.[65]

More recent authorities have shared his assessment of the ammunition situation without endorsing his view that men were more expendable than shells.† Sir John French had good reason to look for exonerating explanations for the failure to take the Aubers Ridge – an assault which,

---

*Guest was Winston Churchill's cousin and was to become Lloyd George's Chief Whip.

†John Keegan, in *The First World War*, writes, 'the British artillery had ample stock', while in one important salient 'the German batteries had little ammunition available'.

had it succeeded, would have turned Neuve Chapelle from stalemate into victory. But at least one contemporary authority – admittedly close to French – believed the claim to be justified. Colonel Charles Repington, military correspondent of *The Times*, visited the Commander-in-Chief 'not as a correspondent, for no war correspondents were permitted, but as a friend'.[66] In both those capacities he initiated a news story which was printed under the banner headline 'Need for Shells. Attack Checked: Limited Supply the Cause'.[67] It was a story which was immediately exploited by one of Kitchener's most bitter enemies – not Lloyd George but Lord Northcliffe, the owner of both *The Times* and *Daily Mail*. The campaign 'Kitchener Must Go' was overtaken by a crisis of greater political magnitude when the Dardanelles Campaign claimed its two most illustrious casualties – Admiral Lord Fisher and Winston Churchill.

On the morning of Saturday, 15 May 1915, Lloyd George was surprised to find Fisher in the entrance hall of 10 Downing Street and was 'struck by a dour change in his attitude. A combative grimness had taken the place of his usual genial greeting.' The cause of his change of mood was quickly revealed. 'I have resigned,' Fisher said, 'I'm going to Scotland.' According to Lloyd George's own version of events, Fisher complained, by way of explanation, 'Our ships [on other seas] are being sunk while we have a fleet in the Dardanelles which is bigger than the German Navy. Both our Navy and Army are being bled for the sake of the Dardanelles Expedition.'[68] In his second version of the conversation – published in his war memoirs – Lloyd George loyally defended Churchill by reminding Fisher that the First Sea Lord had never told the War Council that he was opposed to the Dardanelles Campaign. Fisher was said to have rebutted the reproof by insisting that the rules of naval discipline prevented him from criticising a superior officer in public though he had, privately, urged the Prime Minister to veto the adventure. Lloyd George's plea that he should stay at his post – later reinforced by McKenna – was rejected. But he agreed not to make a public announcement for forty-eight hours. After repeating that he was leaving for Scotland, he took a back room in London's Charing Cross Hotel.

That morning Asquith was at a wedding. According to Lloyd George, he had 'a great liking for weddings and funerals'.[69] So it fell to the Chancellor of the Exchequer to give the Prime Minister the bad news on his return. At first it was brushed aside as the product of a typical and therefore brief Fisher tantrum.[70] Then, when Asquith was convinced that nothing would change Fisher's mind, the Prime Minister decided to stand by Churchill and promote the Second Sea Lord to fill the sudden vacancy. It was decided that on Monday 17 May Churchill himself would announce the changes to the House of Commons.

On the evening of 16 May, an envelope was pushed under the door of Bonar Law's house in Edwardes Square. It was addressed in Fisher's unmistakable hand and it contained a press cutting from the *Pall Mall Gazette* which reported that 'Lord Fisher was received in audience by the King and remained there for about half an hour.'[71] Bonar Law had little doubt about the message which the cutting was intended to convey. Early on the following morning he arrived, uninvited, at the Treasury and asked if Fisher had resigned. Lloyd George had no choice but to confirm Bonar Law's suspicions and describe the circumstances which had brought about the resignation. Bonar Law's reaction was instant and categoric. His sympathies were entirely with Fisher. If Churchill remained at the Admiralty, the Unionists would divide the House of Commons against the government.

Lloyd George's meeting with Fisher in the foyer of 10 Downing Street had been fortuitous. Bonar Law's decision to ask Lloyd George, rather than the Prime Minister, about Fisher's intention was calculated and deeply significant. In his *War Memoirs*, Lloyd George describes the Unionist leader as a 'personal friend' with whom he was 'on terms of greater cordiality . . . than is usual between political adversaries'.[72] That was certainly true. Despite their political differences, they had more in common with each other than with many members of their own parties. Both men were, in their different ways, outsiders. Bonar Law, Canadian by birth and Scottish by upbringing, was no more part of London 'society' than was Lloyd George. They had made their perilous ascents to the tops of their parties despite lacking the qualifications which in early twentieth-century Britain normally propelled men into high office – aristocratic connections, academic distinction, or, as in the case of Balfour, both. The characteristics which attracted Lloyd George to Bonar Law made Asquith less than at home in his company. Bonar Law, the Glasgow iron-master, had read Gibbon's *Decline and Fall of the Roman Empire* three times before he was twenty-one, but he felt out of sympathy with Asquith's conscious intellectualism as well as what he regarded as the foolish side of the Prime Minister's character – the love of parties and the company of young women. Asquith, for his part, preferred to do business with Balfour and Curzon. They understood his Latin tags and Greek aphorisms. Asquith's neglect of the man who was now the Unionist Party leader was to cost him dear.

In his *War Memoirs*, Lloyd George describes the outcome of his historic meeting with Bonar Law in language which, no doubt intentionally, does not correspond to its importance. 'After some discussion we agreed that the only certain way to preserve a united front was to arrange for more complete co-operation between the parties in the direction of the war.'[73] Lloyd George then 'went alone to see Mr Asquith and put the circumstances plainly before him. The Prime Minister at once recognised that it was necessary . . . to reconstruct the cabinet and admit into it some of the leaders of the Unionist Party. The decision took an incredibly short time.' The Prime Minister's subsequent meeting with Bonar Law was similarly brief. It took 'less than a quarter of an hour'.[74]

Thus came into being the coalition which Lloyd George had always believed essential to the prosecution of great causes – and ended the great reforming Liberal administration that had come to office and power in 1906.

CHAPTER 25

ARMS AND THE MAN

The Unionists demanded concessions before they joined the coalition. Their demands concerned personalities not policies. Churchill the political turncoat – whose recklessness had, they claimed, been checked by Fisher – must leave the Admiralty. Two other demands were less categoric. Haldane, whose reforms had greatly improved the efficiency of the British Army, was said – for no better reason than the direction of his academic interests – to be 'pro-German'. McKenna, who had become Lloyd George's *bête noire*, was accused of being too soft-hearted towards aliens – all of whom, in the first years of the war, were assumed by the popular newspapers to be potential spies. Much to Lloyd George's chagrin, McKenna was saved and Haldane sacrificed.

Churchill – supported by angry letters from his wife – fought to stay at the Admiralty. The news that the German Grand Fleet had left port postponed his departure by a day. But there could be no reprieve. Lloyd George suggested that he be given the Colonial Office, an offer so much beneath his dignity that he responded to the proposal with the accusation, 'You don't care if I am trampled underfoot by my enemies.'[1] In the end he accepted a greater demotion and became Chancellor of the Duchy of Lancaster. Nobody expected him to tolerate the indignity for long.

Frances Stevenson's accounts of events are reliable only when they reflect her own experiences rather than rely on Lloyd George's reports. So 'Balfour and Bonar Law suggested that he should be the next PM, but he absolutely refused the proposal as being unfaithful to the present PM' may exaggerate both their enthusiasm and his loyalty. But it is true that, when there was talk of a reshuffle, 'on all hands . . . he was begged not to give up the Exchequer'.[2] The City of London had been impressed by the way he had managed the financial crisis of September 1914. It reacted to rumours that he was to replace Kitchener with the insistence that sterling was more important than the war effort.

When the war was over, the idea that the 'shell scandal' had brought down the government was invented by Churchill to protect him from the accusation that his breach with Fisher had destroyed the Liberal ministry. The shortages of arms and ammunition had, however, done immense damage to Kitchener's reputation within the Unionist Party. By the summer of 1915, Bonar Law was prepared to see him go. But the Secretary of State for War was still immensely popular with the people. When, on 21 May 1915, Lord Northcliffe's newspapers published a vituperative attack upon him – hoping to speed his exit – a copy of the *Daily Mail* was ceremoniously burned on the floor of the Stock Exchange. During the next two weeks, the paper's circulation fell by a quarter of a million copies. Kitchener was safe.

Asquith's original plan was to give Lloyd George control over munitions production by making him Secretary of State for War. When that was judged impossible, the Prime Minister proposed that he should make a temporary move from the Exchequer, which was a great office of state, to a Ministry of Munitions which – since it possessed only the prestige provided by necessity – had none of the status which comes with antiquity. When Churchill had complained about his own demotion, Lloyd George told him, 'all that matters is that we can win the war'.[3] The time had come for Lloyd George to accept that precept himself. Not even the prospect of McKenna's becoming his temporary replacement altered his resolve. The Prime Minister was fulsome in his gratitude. 'I shall never forget your devotion, your unselfishness, your powers of resource and what, after all, is the best of all things, your self-forgetfulness.'[4]

Selflessness is not an attribute with which Lloyd George is usually associated. But in 1915, preferment and promotion were not his only objectives. His ambition was, in a sense, still essentially personal. He believed he was the man – perhaps the only man – who could win the war. No doubt he hoped and expected to be rewarded for that achievement. But winning the war had become an object in itself, an aspect of his destiny which had to be fulfilled. Others, prompted by less Messianic impulses, accepted lowlier positions in the coalition government than they were entitled to expect. Bonar Law, who might have insisted on the Treasury, took the Colonial Office and Balfour – who had, of course, been Prime Minister – agreed to replace Churchill at the Admiralty.

Much has been made of the new Ministry of Munitions not being ready for its minister. There was very little furniture in Whitehall Gardens – the house which was to become its home – and, on the morning of Lloyd George's arrival, workmen came to remove the chairs and table from what passed for his office. But too little has been said about Lloyd George's being ready for his new ministry. The task was ideally suited to fit his idea of life and politics. It was more than his chance to win the war. It was an opportunity for the 'cottage-bred man' to succeed where the establishment had failed, and it enabled him to put into practice his most cherished principle of politics. He believed that national aims were most easily achieved when men of talent combined – irrespective of their political allegiances. In May 1915, Lloyd George began the first 'talent search' in the history of British government and pioneered the introduction of businessmen into Whitehall.

Initially he was supported by Christopher Addison, a politician imported from the Education Department, and Sir Hubert Llewellyn Smith, late of the Board of Trade. They were reinforced by important appointments from outside Whitehall and Westminster. Some were mistakes. Sir Percy Girouard – a railway engineer, soldier and colonial governor who had worked for Kitchener – became a hesitant and indecisive Director General of Munitions Supply. But one rank below him, the 'outsiders' were a great success. Glyn West (from Armstrong Whitworth), G. M. Booth (previously a Liverpool shipowner), Charles Ellis (a director of John Brown and Company) and Eric Geddes (deputy general manager of the North Eastern Railway) met each morning at the Reform Club to coordinate the use of powers which had been transferred to them with surprisingly little opposition, from the War Office. Perhaps Kitchener did not realise how much of his empire he had lost. On the day of Lloyd George's appointment, the Secretary of State for War sent him a message: 'Delighted to hear you are coming to help me.'[5] That was not how the new minister saw his job, nor how the job was done.

Lord Esher wrote that Lloyd George 'adopted with marked success the plan of cutting away red tape and of placing reliance upon personal responsibility by bestowing extended powers upon individuals selected for their capacity, vigour and courage'.[6] In his pursuit of men who possessed those qualities, 'the best find from the business world' and one of his 'luckiest discoveries' was – in Lloyd George's estimation – Eric Geddes.[7] He was appointed after an unconventional interview. Lloyd George 'asked me if I knew anything about munitions. I did not. He asked me what I could do. I said I had a faculty for getting things done. "Very well", he said, "I will make you head of department".' Geddes became one of the four deputy directors in the 'craziest department ever organised by mortal man'.[8] He took charge of the Woolwich Arsenal, where, he said, working practices 'were like eating soup with a fork'.[9] Six months before the Battle of the Somme began, he was persuaded, with some difficulty, to take charge of shell filling – a process which, until then, was usually carried out by ladies who, using ladles, scooped high explosives into the shell cases like grocers measuring out sugar.

The Minister of Munitions' talent for identifying first-class organisers was not always matched by his man-management techniques. One new recruit complained, 'Nearly everybody . . . is in such an unhappy state by being harried by LG that they cannot do their work . . . LG has now turned against Geddes and the shell-filling department and the position is most unhappy.'[10] The cause of friction was the new minister's impatience and fierce determination to demonstrate the success of the new enterprise. Geddes was accused of 'taking a rather pessimistic view of our [shell] filling arrangements'.[11] But Lloyd George did not allow one disagreement, no matter how unpleasant, permanently to prejudice him against a man of such obvious ability. When, after he became Secretary of State for War and Geddes was sent to GHQ in France as Director General of Military Railways and Inspector General of Transportation, Lloyd George insisted that the job carry the rank of major-general.

Lloyd George performance at the Board of Trade – ending the railway and dock disputes – confirmed that his attitude towards the trade unions was, like his position on so many other matters, flexible. When, therefore, he began his campaign to end restrictive practices in arms-manufacturing companies, his speeches and his inclinations escalated between exhortation, which he enjoyed, and threats of the compulsion which he thought necessary. For a year he persisted in his unrewarding efforts to persuade the industrial workforce to make a larger contribution to the war effort. In Manchester he argued for the greater mobility of labour and an end to rules of demarcation.

The enlisted workman cannot choose his locality of action. He cannot say 'I am quite prepared to fight at Neuve Chapelle but I won't fight at Festubert'. He cannot say 'I have been in the trenches ten hours and a half and my trade union won't allow me to work more than ten'. He cannot say 'You have not enough men here, and I have been doing the work of two men. My union won't allow men to do more than their own share'.[12]

In Liverpool he tried to combat trade union hostility not by recanting his call for change but by making jokes at the expense of solicitors, which, he hoped, would make clear that he was opposed to restrictive practices in the professions as well as in the trades.

I happen to belong to about the strictest, the most jealous trades union in the world . . . But if, during the period of the war, there were any particular use for lawyers – I know it requires a good deal of imagination – do you suppose that even the Incorporated Law Society . . . could stand in the way of bringing in outside help.[13]

Before it was clear what the response to his appeal would be, he had decided that the Treasury Agreement, which he had negotiated during the previous year, must be given statutory authority. On 16 June 1915 he showed the Trades Union Congress a draft of his Munitions of War Bill. The gesture was a threat rather than a courtesy. A week later, he told the House of Commons that the trade unions had seven days to agree procedures by which the vacancies in ammunition factories could be filled. 'Tomorrow morning the seven days begins . . . If we cannot, by voluntary means, get the labour which is essential to this country in a war on which its life depends we must use, as an ultimate resort, the means which every state has at its command to save its life.'[14] Although he never used the word 'compulsion', that was the expedient which his impatience demanded and which he chose to justify in an inexplicable outburst of political philosophy. 'We talk about the state as if it were something apart from the workman. The workman is the state.'[15] In calmer moments he remembered how few workmen had a vote.

In September 1915, he addressed the TUC's annual conference in Bristol. 'The government', he told them, 'cannot win without you.' Unfortunately the blandishments were not matched by the slightest understanding of the time-served craftsman's psychology. It was true that, because there was a shortage of skilled labour, there was no 'question of turning out the skilled workmen in order to put cheaper workmen in his place'. But 'a good deal of work which [was] being done by skilled workmen [could] just as easily be done by those who had only a few weeks or a few days' training'.[16] Craftsmen do not want to hear that their jobs do not require as much skill as they claim. Pride, though it comes second to pay, is something to be protected, like employment, against dilution.

The speech ended with the promise that sacrifices by working men would not 'inure to the enrichment of individual capitalists, but entirely to the benefit of the state . . . We have declared 715 establishments, producing munitions of war, to be controlled establishments . . . They are only to get standard payments, based on the profit made before the war.' That arrangement was augmented by the excess-profits tax which McKenna introduced in his autumn Budget. Nevertheless, arms manufacturers became the archetypal hard-faced men who did well out of the war.

As is often the case with government pleas for trade union cooperation, the response of the leadership in London was much more helpful than the reaction of the members in the provinces. A miners' strike – a dispute over pay rather than working practices in an industry outside the Treasury Agreement – was not a major challenge to the government's authority. But general reluctance – and in some cases absolute refusal – to alter the working practices in shipbuilding on the Tyne and the Clyde had to be taken seriously. Lloyd George decided on personal intervention. A meeting with various Tyneside works committees was adjudged to be a success. So he moved on to Clydeside, where he knew, or should have known, that converts would be more difficult to make. Housing was poor. Rents were high. The union leaders were ideological socialists with a deep suspicion of the ruling classes in general and the London ruling classes in particular. The Clyde should have been treated with particular sensitivity and care. The organisation of Lloyd George's visit guaranteed that what was always likely to be an embarrassment turned into a fiasco.

The ground was to be prepared during preliminary discussions with shop stewards. The ministry party arrived forty-five minutes late. David Kirkwood, the trade unionist who chaired the meeting, dispelled all thought of a quick and easy agreement by claiming that the Munitions Act 'had the taint of slavery about it'.[17] The meeting with the men – three thousand inside Glasgow's St Andrew's Hall and a thousand outside – was held on Christmas Morning 1915. It could not have been organised more maladroitly. A Union Jack covered the speakers' table. Women workers – dressed in khaki uniforms – stood in line at the back

of the platform. The police presence was substantial and visible. Before
the speeches began, a choir sang patriotic songs. At Lloyd George's
approach a band struck up 'See the Conquering Hero Comes'. Then
'he rolled off burning sentences about love of country and the awful
struggles against the enemy'.[18]

There was an immediate uproar of resentment. Lloyd George was
shouted down to the accompaniment of 'The Red Flag'. Thomas
Johnston, the editor of the left-leaning *Forward*, whose paper was suppressed and his printing press impounded by the government, thought
that the mayhem had been caused by no more than 10 per cent of the
assembled workers. 'On the whole, the feeling of the meeting was with
Lloyd George' – as were the feelings of the patriotic nation.[19] So Lloyd
George waited for suitable opportunities to manifest the national will. He
did not have to wait for long. By late January 1916 the stockpile of munitions was large enough to guarantee supplies to the army during a
six-week Clydeside strike. When men at Lang's engineering works went
on strike against the employment of women machinists, he gave police
protection to strike breakers and met the cost out of national funds to
protect the rates. The strike ended in a week. On the day that they
returned to work, the three leaders of the Clyde Workers' Committee
were arrested – allegedly for inciting violence. Sympathetic strikes broke
out sporadically and, equally sporadically, came to unsuccessful ends. In
March, three more members of the Workers' Committee were required –
under powers provided by the Munitions of War Act – to leave Glasgow.
They spent the next two years in exile in Edinburgh – their deportation
supported by the official leadership of their trade union, who, like Lloyd
George, had been waiting for a chance to put them in their place.

It was during a House of Commons speech on industrial manpower
that Lloyd George revealed his general frustration with the way the war
was being run.

> Too late moving here. Too late moving there. Too late in coming
> to this decision, too late in starting with enterprises, too late in
> preparing. In this war the steps of the allied forces have been
> dogged with the spectre of too late and unless we quicken our
> movements, damnation will fall on the sacred cause for which
> much gallant blood has flowed.[20]

Frances Stevenson proudly noted that 'the speech created a sensation.
His words seemed like those of a prophet.'[21] The immediate cause of

the Messianic moment was the government's refusal to introduce conscription. Lloyd George had changed his view on the merits of compulsory service – both as a military necessity and as a sign of nationhood – soon after the war began. The 1910 Memorandum, in which he set out the advantages of a coalition, had canvassed the idea of a 'Swiss militia system' in which 'those liable to serve might be chosen by ballot'. But in February 1915, a Cabinet minute in which he denounced the press for 'treating the progress of the war as one of almost unbroken success', ended with a note which asserted that he was still not arguing for conscription. By the summer he was. On 10 August, he told a Cabinet committee, 'the longer you delay, the nearer you get to disaster'.[22] Kitchener disagreed. For a while the soldier's view prevailed.

In October of that year the subject was again raised in Cabinet. Kitchener was still opposed but had to argue against a War Office minute which reported a severe manpower shortage. Lloyd George, Curzon, Churchill, Walter Long, Lansdowne and Selborne (President of the Board of Agriculture) all threatened (or hinted at) resignation unless Kitchener was overruled. The Prime Minister asked, and was granted, twenty-four hours to consider an alternative to general conscription. Without further consultation he appointed Lord Derby Director of Recruiting, with the remit to prove, within six weeks, that the voluntary system could be made to work. Asquith had begun to feel the political ground move under him. He told Maurice Hankey, 'Lloyd George is out to break the government on conscription if he can.'[23] Kitchener was warned, 'I should like you to know that what is going on now is being engineered by men (Curzon, Lloyd George and others) whose real object is to oust you.'[24] The Prime Minister must have known that Christopher Addison – one of Lloyd George's most loyal lieutenants – was working his way through the House of Commons' bars and tearooms, nominally counting those in support of conscription but in the knowledge that the information he obtained might serve another purpose as the months progressed. Whether or not Lloyd George was manoeuvring to strengthen his position, Asquith was certainly intriguing to maintain his. He was supported in his opposition to conscription by both Bonar Law and Balfour, in defiance of most Unionist opinion. Lloyd George, in favour, was in a minority among Liberals.

According to Frances Stevenson, the radical papers 'lost their head [sic] and conceal their rage no longer at finding that D. is among the Conscriptionists'. He defended his position in an echo of the Queen's

Hall speech. A total commitment to the war was, he implied, necessary to the spiritual welfare of the nation. That sentiment was expressed explicitly in the foreword to *Through Terror to Triumph*, a collection of his early war speeches.[25] It was released to the press before the whole book was published: 'If the nation hesitates when the need is clear to take the necessary steps to call forth its manhood to defend honour and existence . . . then I can see no hope.'

The Prime Minister, who saw conscription in less spiritual terms, changed his position from opposition to vacillation. His mind was not even made up by the figures of voluntary recruitment – 135,000 for May but only 95,000 for August 1915. Derby, or the civil servants working for him, contrived a scheme which became the last hope of avoiding compulsion. All men between the ages of eighteen and forty-one were invited to 'attest' their willingness to serve by signing a register. The 'volunteers' were divided into forty-six groups, depending on age and domestic obligations. The youngest and those with fewest dependants would be 'called up' first. The oldest – with family to support – might not be 'called up' at all. Four groups of unmarried men were recruited under the scheme before its weakness was recognised. Only 840,000 single men attested, while 1,345,000 married men signed up in the belief that they would never have to join the colours.

Lloyd George renewed his threat of resignation. Asquith – with all the evidence and much of the Cabinet against him – promised general conscription but Lloyd George doubted if the promise would be kept. 'PM and his gang trying to sneak out of the pledges. If they do, I wash my hands of the position and come out.'[26] Fortunately, on 28 December 1915, the 'PM dropped on right side. Compulsion for unmarried men'.[27] The Military Service Bill was introduced by Asquith himself on 21 January 1916. But there was still strong opposition to compulsion within the Cabinet – Simon on principle, Grey, Runciman and McKenna because of anxiety about the loss of manpower on the home front. Simon resigned. So did Henderson, who had represented Labour in the coalition government. He believed that while he held office he must represent the will of his party. He supported conscription from the backbenches.

On 21 February 1916 – as the Battle of Verdun began with French requests for more British support – the army was 78,000 men below strength and the Territorials were 50,000 men short of their target. A dispirited Lloyd George was a frequent absentee from Cabinet meetings. 'D not at all well. I think he is very depressed about things in general.'[28]

He may have really believed himself to be sick. Frances dismissed his condition as hypochondria. 'He always thinks that he is dying when he has a bilious attack.'[29] But she also recorded the fundamental cause of his malaise. 'Heartily sick of the present government.'[30] Recovery was swift enough to allow participation in discussions of Asquith's last attempt to avoid a general conscription which included married men. Despite the General Staff's belated conclusion that it was necessary, Asquith suggested the final decision be postponed until it was seen if 50,000 married men had volunteered by 27 May. Lloyd George argued for complete conscription there and then. 'He was the first to make a stand and it was naturally thought that he would be supported by the Conservatives in the Cabinet. They ratted to a man.'[31]

The Unionists in the Commons were more reliable. Under the leadership of Edward Carson – recently resigned from the coalition government in protest against what he described as the betrayal of Serbia – they staged a revolt of such magnitude that the 'wait-and-see' scheme was dropped and replaced with all-out conscription within forty-eight hours.* Asquith blamed the Chancellor for the government's embarrassment and told Lady Scott, the widow of the polar explorer, that Lloyd George and Churchill 'were the most distrusted men in the party'.[32] That was a view shared by many influential Liberals. A. G. Gardiner, the editor of the *Daily News*, wrote an open letter to his own paper describing Lloyd George 'as one of the chief architects of the fall of the Liberal Government and of the establishment of the Coalition' and accusing him of precipitating a conscription crisis in order to supersede Asquith.[33] Lloyd George replied to the growing chorus of Liberal disapproval with a speech to his constituents. On 6 May 1916, he told a meeting at Conway that 'you cannot run a war as you would run a Sunday school treat'.[34] It concluded with a declaration of loyalty to Asquith.

> I have worked with him for ten years. I have served under him for eight years. If we have not worked harmoniously (and we have) let me tell you at once it would have been my fault and not his . . .
> Freedom of speech is essential everywhere but there is one place where it is vital and that is in the Council Chamber of the

---

*It was an early example of the paradox which modern politicians call the West Lothian Question. Carson was the Member for Dublin University. His constituents would not be conscripted.

nation. The councillor who professes to agree with everything that falls from his leader betrays him.[35]

But it was clear that he was growing increasingly impatient with the way the war was being run – and increasingly detached from the Liberal Party. He was mistrusted by both Liberals and Conservatives – the price he paid for his ambition being so recklessly displayed. Politicians much prefer bogus humility. Bonar Law, the leader of the Unionist Party, was probably not as antagonistic as Max Aitken – who never poured oil on troubled waters – made out. But he had 'formed the opinion that in matters of office and power LlG was a self-seeker and a man who considered no interests except his own'.[36] No doubt Bonar Law remembered that, despite their alliance, Lloyd George had attempted to have him passed over for the Colonial Office in favour of Churchill. The attempt to provide Churchill with that consolation prize had been dismissed, by the demoted First Lord himself, as a betrayal which, for a time, ended their friendship. 'LG, by all accounts, is isolated,' wrote Churchill gleefully. 'He has been very foolish in his relations with me, Bonar Law, FE [Smith] and Curzon. He might have combined with us all. As it is he has earned the deep distrust of each.'[37] Clementine Churchill held Lloyd George in even lower esteem. In a letter sent to her husband at the front, after he resigned from the government and resumed active service, she described Lloyd George as 'the direct descendant of Judas Iscariot', whose hand she would take only after acquiring protection from 'charms, touch-woods and exorcisms' and by crossing herself.[38] His attitude to conscription, about which he had acted with conviction, increased the distrust. He was beginning to pay the price for his reputation – the assumption of dishonesty when none existed.

As early as November 1915, Lloyd George had told Seebohm Rowntree that – in order to release men for the front – it was his ambition 'to have a million women in industry before the war is over'.*[39] Rowntree had replied, 'It is time enough to talk like that when you are treating properly the women who are already there.'[40] One woman already in the munitions business – whose treatment by Lloyd George might have been improved – was Frances Stevenson.

---

*Rowntree had advised Lloyd George during the preparation of the National Insurance Bill. When businessmen were recruited to the Ministry of Munitions, he was made head of the Welfare Department.

She had joined the Ministry of Munitions as one of the minister's secretaries – a task for which she was eminently qualified and would have carried out with distinction even if she had been appointed by the Civil Service Commission.

Her diary leaves no doubt that she revelled in her proximity to great events. Politics excited her and, had she lived fifty years later, she would have been a substantial politician in her own right. As it was, she played a vicarious part in government through her personal and professional association with Lloyd George. Whether or not she would have loved him had he remained a Welsh lawyer, there can be no doubt about her absolute self-sacrificial devotion to the man she first saw in the Baptist Church on Castle Street on Flower Sunday, 1911. The three decades that followed were a mixture of elation and sadness, punctuated by humiliations which she seemed to accept (and Lloyd George seemed to inflict) without qualm or question.

Her parents were never reconciled to the relationship. And the demands of wartime government added to the tension. 'The last fortnight has been too dreary and unhappy to write of . . . My people have been trying to separate us – trying to make me promise that I will give up his love, the most precious thing in my life.'[41] Precious it certainly was, but it had to be celebrated in a fashion which was too furtive for a woman of spirit to enjoy without some shame. On the evening that she recorded her parents' continual concern she went, with Lloyd George, to Walton Heath. They met for the journey after she received a message which was more appropriate to a conspiracy than to a love affair. 'Go *now* a little beyond the House of Lords.'[42] A month later, there was a rare admission that sharing Lloyd George with his wife caused unavoidable pain. 'I had Muriel's company for the weekend, as I got terribly lonely.'[43]

The most poignant, and perhaps the most pathetic, diary entry of the year was a comment on an evening which she and Lloyd George had spent as the guests of a Mr Murray. 'We enjoyed it thoroughly. I think that Mr Murray must know of our relationship.'[44] The account of the dinner at Murray's flat after a performance of Messager's operetta *Véronique* leaves no doubt about her joy that, for once, they were recognised as a partnership.

Occasionally, circumstances forced Lloyd George to accept the responsibility, as well as enjoy the pleasures, of the relationship. In May 1915 – while they were together at a performance of J. M. Bowrie's play *Rosy Rapture, the Pride of the Beauty Chorus* – he had been brought a message to say that Paul Stevenson, Frances's brother, had been killed in action. After he broke the news, he took her home to her parents – not an easy task for a man who, in even the most propitious of circumstances, could not have felt at ease in their company. But the little kindness – always welcomed with an excess of gratitude – did not excuse the indignities, great and small, which he expected her to accept without complaint.

In October 1915, he had brusquely told her that when she joined him at Walton Heath she would have to travel to Surrey alone and by train. 'D does not like taking me about in his Gov car in case people fix on it for a scandal. I am rather sick about it as I love driving with him.'[45] But that was nothing as compared with the humiliation that would have been the consequence of a plan he proposed to avoid people 'fixing on a scandal' ever again. Lloyd George wanted Frances to marry an infatuated admirer as cover for their continued relationship. And she came very close to agreeing: 'I've had a talk with D. His view is that O is moved by a consuming desire to *get on*. That is the line. I believe he would do it unconditionally. There is peril and pollution in the other course. I love my pure little darling.'[46]

The lucky man was Captain Hugh Owen, former station master at Holyhead and, no doubt as a result of intervention from on high, a recently appointed liaison officer between the army and the Ministry of Munitions. His passion for Frances was sincere and his desire to 'get on' – reported to Lloyd George by his private secretary – clearly incidental. David Lloyd George seized on the idea of exploiting both emotions. Owen spent a weekend at Walton Heath and discussed marriage arrangements with which Frances seems to have agreed without objection. None of the letters or diary entries explains how 'genuine' the marriage was supposed to be. But there is no doubt that Owen was expected to accept that Frances's relationship with Lloyd George would continue unchanged. During the summer of 1915, Owen and Frances were engaged at Lloyd George's suggestion. The Stevenson family believed that the engagement was genuine and welcomed their daughter's being 'married to a good man who cared for [her]'.[47] Their disappointment at the end of the relationship was tempered by the knowledge that Frances 'did not care sufficiently for Owen to marry him'.[48] In fact she barely cared for him at all. Frances was part of a complicated charade in which each participant dissimulated.

By 5 October, Frances believed that 'D was making himself miserable about my belonging to somebody else if only in name.'[49] In fact, Lloyd

George was pressing for the arrangement to be completed while counterfeiting increasing distress at the prospect of his wish being granted. 'Several times he cried and sobbed as a child when speaking of it, begging me all the time to take no notice of him.'[50] The stratagem failed because Frances took him at his word and broke off the engagement. Lloyd George persisted in discussing what he then began to describe as the benefits which marriage offered Frances. On 23 October, he was 'on the marriage tack again' and arranged for Frances and Owen to dine together.[51] Briefly, she was convinced of the 'many advantages to be gained' by becoming Mrs Owen.[52] But Lloyd George's deception had been so successful that she believed that, when he promoted the idea, he was offering to sacrifice himself for her. So Owen's offer was finally rejected. He was posted to Canada to buy ships for the Royal Navy and was quickly forgotten. Frances, who moved from her parents' house to a flat of her own in Chester Square, was free to devote herself entirely to Lloyd George, consoled by what she regarded as 'sharing his reflected glory'.

The letters Lloyd George wrote during the discussion of the Owen marriage illustrate an affection that is patronising to the point of condescension. 'Pussy do be good. Don't be miserable. I would rather you got naughty (within decent limits).'[53] Yet Frances received and read them without apparent damage to her self-respect. The entire episode is inconsistent with her claim to be a 'liberated' woman who identified with the suffragist movement and rejoiced at the opportunity to meet Mrs Pankhurst after the leader of the Women's Social and Political Union 'offered to recruit women to the munitions factories'.[54] Lloyd George promoted the idea by addressing a 'pageant' of thirty thousand female enthusiasts. He told them, as he had told the Trades Union Congress, that the war could not be won without them and, having learned the lesson of Clydeside, he also addressed some of their anxieties. Women in war work would be paid the same piecework rates as men.

Women certainly contributed to the improved output of arms and ammunition which followed the creation of the Munitions Ministry, but the principal cause of the increase was what the official war history describes as Lloyd George's 'length of vision. He created confidence in the industry with orders that guaranteed work for two years and ordered more big guns than the War Office thought necessary as an inducement to accept less profitable work.'[55] It was the triumph of the political will – the determination not to be constrained by the cautious military establishment and a belief in his right to take decisions which had been the legitimate province of professional soldiers.

In two major areas – the importance of mortars and the need to increase the number of machine guns available to each battalion – he was right and the soldiers wrong. But the most eloquent testimony to his success at the new ministry were the figures of production. At the end of his tenure, it took eleven days to produce the number of medium shells which, when he became minister, had been regarded as reasonable annual output. The improvement was typical of what he achieved over the whole range of armaments. Churchill – who inherited the ministry in 1917 – described Lloyd George's achievement in typically purple prose. 'Production of every kind was already on a gigantic scale. The whole island was an arsenal . . . The keenest spirits in British industry were gathered as state servants in the range of palatial hotels which housed the Ministry of Munitions. The former trickles and streamlets of war supplies now flowed in rivers rising continuously.'[56]

The sinews of war were increasingly available but their manipulation remained woeful. One problem was the division of responsibility between the War Committee (the successor to the War Council and the Dardanelles Committee which had superseded it) and the Cabinet itself. Another was ministers' reluctance to countermand Kitchener's plans, even when they knew them to be misconceived or in direct defiance of Cabinet decisions.

In late June 1915, Lloyd George had met his French opposite number, Albert Thomas, and warned him that the Allies did not possess sufficient guns and shells to mount a successful major offensive. When heads of government met at Chantilly on 7 July, the French and British prime ministers agreed that, for the time being, energy and resources should be concentrated on renewed efforts in the Dardanelles while the Allies did no more than hold the line on the Western Front. General Joffre, Commander-in-Chief of the French forces, did not agree. Not only did he prepare to mount a major attack, he persuaded Kitchener to support his defiance of ministerial authority with the meaningless explanation, 'Unfortunately we have to make war as we must, not as we would like it.'[57] Lloyd George was absent from the committee which considered the Secretary of State for War's conduct. The following day he asked for, and obtained, a copy of the letter in which the Prime Minister had told the King of the decision.

Lord Kitchener reported on his recent visit to France. General Joffre is quite determined, both on political and military grounds (the main element in the former being the situation in Russia) to take the offensive without delay and on a considerable scale. Sir J French agreed with him as to the urgency of the step from the military point of view. Lord K, though far from sanguine that any substantial military advantage will be achieved, is strongly of the opinion that we cannot, without serious and perhaps fatal injury to the Alliance, refuse the co-operation which Joffre expects . . . After much consideration, the Cabinet adopted Lord K's view.[58]

At the next Cabinet meeting, Lloyd George raised the question of available guns and ammunition – no doubt, unless politicians changed over the next half century, causing much irritation to colleagues who regarded his preoccupation with armaments as a self-serving obsession. He was assured that supplies were adequate. Joffre's offensive was postponed until late September. Its climax was the Battle of Loos. The Allied artillery failed to breach the enemy barbed wire. So the infantry was trapped. 'Never had machine-guns such straightforward work to do.'[59] The British losses were sixteen thousand dead and twenty-five thousand wounded. No ground was gained. One of the casualties was Kitchener's reputation. The Secretary of State for War had endorsed an offensive which he knew was likely to end in failure and certain to result in heavy Allied losses.

The immediate result was another of the resignation threats which had become a feature of Asquith's government. Lloyd George and Bonar Law threatened to go unless Kitchener was either removed from the War Office or his formal powers radically reduced. Asquith chose the easier course and sent him on a fact-finding mission to the Eastern Mediterranean in the hope that a prolonged absence might stifle the calls for his removal. As if to confirm his weakness, Asquith took advantage of Kitchener's absence to make new appointments lower down the chain of command – desirable in themselves but not an adequate substitute for changes at the top. Sir John French, whose attempts to portray Loos as a victory had fooled the newspapers but not the Cabinet, was replaced as Commander-in-Chief of the British Expeditionary Force by Sir Douglas Haig – the Commander of the First Army who had spent some months undermining French's position by sending confidential critical letters to Kitchener and telling the King that his superior officer was 'a source of great weakness . . . and nobody has confidence in him any more'. He had then added that he was 'ready to serve in any capacity'.[60] Sir Archibald Murray resigned as Chief of the Imperial General Staff and was replaced by Sir William Robertson, previously the Chief of Staff in France. Robertson was the army's equivalent of a 'cottage-bred man' – the first general to rise from the ranks. His origins were not enough to endear him to Lloyd George.

Kitchener returned from his tour of inspection sooner than Asquith hoped or expected – almost certainly because he realised that he maintained only a precarious hold on office. By January 1916, he was sufficiently chastened to accept – indeed, formally to propose as Secretary of State – that the Chief of the Imperial General Staff should, in future, be responsible for 'issuing the orders of the Cabinet in regard to military operations'. He had been demoted from 'saviour of the nation' to regulation Secretary of State for War.

Two months later an Austrian-German army – supported by Bulgarians – advanced in Serbia. Two Anglo-French divisions landed at Salonika but were too late to turn the tide. King Constantine of Greece dismissed Eleftherios Venizelos, his pro-Allies Prime Minister, as a sign of his personal support for the Central Powers. Venizelos was to play a crucial part in Lloyd George's eventual downfall, but in 1916 he was just another complication in a series of catastrophes which inevitably divided the Cabinet and were intensified by Grey giving an unequivocal pledge of support to Serbia which he knew the Allies were unable to honour. Uncertain what to do next, ministers agreed to send a force of 150,000 men to Egypt, from where they could be redeployed to whichever part of the region the Cabinet eventually decided. Lloyd George and Bonar Law, believing that Carson had been proved right to claim that Serbia would be betrayed, considered – or talked of considering – following him out of the government. They decided, as politicians who agonise over resignation often do, that the national interest required them to stay at their posts.

Governments which are about to fall apart are rent with disagreements about trivia as well as disputes about issues of real importance. So it was inevitable that Asquith's preference for Curzon over Bonar Law caused the sort of irritation which can easily precipitate the collapse of a whole administration. Bonar Law – offended by his omission from the Cabinet committee set up to consider the necessity of conscription – was not mollified by the explanation that he had been excluded at Curzon's suggestion. Attempts to heal his wounded ego resulted in

Lloyd George's standing on his dignity in a way which – as well as being uncharacteristic – risked a break with the man who was, in his attitude towards the war, a natural ally. On 15 September 1915, he told Bonar Law

> the PM whom I have just seen tells me what you said to him yesterday on the subject of the Deputy Leadership of the House which you were anxious to secure. As you are aware, I have held the position for 8 years. I have no objection to surrendering it to you. I wish however you had mentioned the matter to me. It would have been more friendly – and, having regard to our conversation yesterday, more candid.[61]

The letter went on to say that the 'fate of the Empire' was more important than 'personal considerations', which raised the question of why it was written in the first place. Part of the answer is to be found in Frances Stevenson's diary entry for the same day. Lloyd George was becoming exasperated. 'Things are going very badly with us and whenever he draws attention to it he is greeted with a chorus of indignation from Liberals and Liberal journalists.'[62] But his reaction also illustrates a political truth. The distinction between 'wanting to do something' and 'wanting to be somebody' is false. Most successful politicians want both.

The disintegration of the government continued with the resignation of Churchill, who realised that, since evacuation from Gallipoli was only a matter of time, he would be held responsible for a miscalculation which had been allowed to develop into a catastrophe. Despite the public protestations of loyalty, Lloyd George continued to talk about resignation. On one occasion he got to the point of asking C. P. Scott to help him compose a suitable letter – only to fall asleep while discussing the draft. If he hoped that fear of the government's collapse would force Asquith into making him 'a sort of executive officer charged with the duty of listening to suggestions and exercising general supervision', he was mistaken.[63] The Prime Minister was prepared to see him go and had warned the King of his likely departure. The prospect was taken sufficiently seriously for Stamfordham, Knollys's successor as the King's private secretary, to tell Lloyd George of the royal anxiety which the possibility of the government's disintegration caused. The flurry of concern came at a time when the news from every front sapped morale. In Mesopotamia the British garrison at Kut-al-Amara had surrendered to the Turks and almost half of the captured men had died on their way to imprisonment in Baghdad.

On Easter Monday 1916, the Prime Minister was wakened with the news that a number of armed men – calling themselves Irish Volunteers and soldiers of the Citizens' Army – had occupied the General Post Office in Dublin, and that one of their number had appeared on the steps and read a proclamation which announced the foundation of the Irish Republic. Nobody in London took the Easter Rebellion very seriously. The Irish – a handful of Fenians aside – were a loyal people. Ninety thousand Irish Catholics were serving as volunteers with the British Army. The 3rd Royal Irish Rifles and the 10th Royal Dublin Fusiliers had willingly moved on the Post Office – and the other public buildings which were subsequently occupied – to re-establish the rule of law and King George. When it was all over, the captured rebels were jeered and spat at as they were led away. In London, it seemed that there was nothing to worry about.

The official Whitehall assessment might have been correct had it not been for the brutal blunders of General Sir John Maxwell, General Officer Commanding. His response to armed insurrection against the Crown – in which 134 members of His Majesty's forces had been killed – was the court martial of the rebellion's leaders. Some of the fifteen men who were condemned to death were barely involved in the uprising. Three days after the executions began, Asquith telegraphed Maxwell with the suggestion that commutation to life imprisonment was a more appropriate punishment. Maxwell took no notice. James Connolly was shot by firing squad after the Prime Minister's message was received. Asquith then issued an order. There was to be no more killing. It was too late. The mood of the Irish people had changed. The cause of independence had been provided with martyrs and Ireland unfree would never be at peace.

Augustine Birrell, the Irish Secretary since 1907 – who, it was said, should have anticipated the uprising – resigned, but Asquith could not find a suitable replacement. So for a while he did the job himself and 'spent long hours sitting in Dublin Castle'.[64] According to Lloyd George, 'he brought back absolutely nothing. He had no plan and he funked the task of making a settlement.'[65] He did, however, think that a final settlement was necessary to preserve the peace. That required a permanent appointment. But there was still some difficulty in finding a man who was both willing to take the risk of making the final push and was not anathema to one (or both) of the opposed Irish factions. Lloyd

George was not the Prime Minister's first choice but Asquith consoled himself with the thought that he 'was an ambitious man [who would] stand or fall by the success he made'.[66] He told Lloyd George, 'It is a unique opportunity and there is no one else who could do so much to bring about a permanent solution.'[67]

Some of his friends warned Lloyd George that he was being lured into a trap, but Lord Riddell told him, 'This appointment gives you the reversion of the Premiership.'[68] He accepted the appointment after carefully considering the warning and responding to the prediction with wild optimism. Asked if he could bring it off, he replied, 'You know I am that kind of beggar. I always do think that I can bring it off.'[69] But he still protected his future by insisting on remaining Munitions Minister. 'I don't mean to let somebody else take the credit while I have undergone all the anxiety and criticism.'[70]

Lloyd George got very near to succeeding. After negotiations with some of the most intractable men in politics – Carson, Craig, Redmond, Dillon and O'Connor – he proposed to the Cabinet what amounted to the implementation of the 1914 settlement, with the proviso that it was to remain in force for a year after the war had ended and longer if Parliament so decided. There was some disagreement over what the proviso actually meant. Lansdowne called the arrangements 'permanent and enduring'. Redmond described them as 'temporary and provisional'. Such ambiguities were an invariable feature of settlements negotiated by Lloyd George.

The Cabinet was not unanimous in its support. Indeed some ministers – the Irish landowners in particular – were deeply opposed. But once reminded of their patriotic duty they accepted Lloyd George's scheme with one addition. Westminster must maintain direct control of everything – from the use of land to law and the administration of justice – which affected the armed forces. Dillon and Redmond did not like it, but they reluctantly agreed. Then Lansdowne, speaking in the House of Lords, repeated his view that the arrangement was permanent and added that a draconian Defence of the Realm Act would have to be accepted by the new Dublin government. That was not quite enough to alienate the Nationalists. But a House of Commons amendment to the plan, which deprived Members from the Home Rule counties of full rights in the Imperial Parliament, was. There would be no settlement.

The recriminations began at once. Dillon blamed Lloyd George. 'In his endeavour to be too artful, he over-reached himself. The failure is the nemesis of his method of negotiation.'[71] Even Frances Stevenson, who believed that he 'would have done himself less harm by leaving the government', judged that he had 'not quite played the game'.[72] Two days later she changed her mind. 'I think, after all, D is right in the course he is taking with the Irish.'[73] Right or not, he was certainly lucky. Until he had agreed to hold the fort in Dublin, he had planned to join Kitchener on a military mission to Russia.[74] On 5 June, the *Hampshire*, on which the Secretary of State for War sailed, struck a mine in the North Sea and sank. There were only twelve survivors.

Lloyd George's Delphic, but certainly less than solemn, reaction was recorded in a letter to his brother. 'What a tragedy. Poor K at the best possible moment for the country and for him.'[75] Ten days later he was slightly more explicit about his attitude to the lost leader. 'I used to get on well with Kitchener. Great driving force but no mental powers . . . Hard eyes – relentless – without a glimmer of human feeling.'[76] In truth, the two men did not 'get on' at all. They were temperamentally incompatible. Kitchener personified authority. Lloyd George resented all authority but his own.

Asquith wanted Bonar Law to succeed Kitchener as Secretary of State for War. Bonar Law declined and recommended Lloyd George, who accepted with one proviso. In order to reduce Kitchener's powers, the Chief of the Imperial General Staff had been given direct access to the Cabinet and the sole right to implement its instructions. Lloyd George was therefore caught in the trap which he had helped to set for his predecessor. The constraint must be removed. The demand was rejected, but the job was, nevertheless, accepted. He clearly realised its potential. So did Margot Asquith. 'We are out,' she wrote in her diary. 'It can only be a question of time before we leave Downing Street.'[77] Lloyd George's friends realised that it would not be long before he and Asquith came into head-to-head collision. Frances Stevenson must have feared that the Prime Minister's supporters suspected the truth about the carefully concealed relationship. 'George Riddell says that the Asquithians are still plotting to get D out of power . . . They would put poison in his cup. They would stoop to the trick that was played on Parnell.'[78]

The Allies had begun their doomed offensive on the Somme four days before Lloyd George became Secretary of State for War. He therefore escapes all responsibility for that tragedy. Indeed his one major contribution to the Allied effort during his brief tenure at the War Office was his insistence on the appointment of Geddes to reorganise behind-the-lines transport in France and Flanders. But it was during those five months that Lloyd George and Haig's relationship changed from dislike to the mutual loathing that certainly influenced the course of the war.

The two men had first met in January 1916, before Lloyd George became Secretary of State for War. The meeting had gone well. Dick and Gwilym had been brought from their units to meet their father, who was impressed by more than the Commander-in-Chief's great courtesy. He left with the 'feeling that everything which the assiduity, the care and the trained thought of a great soldier can accomplish is being done'.[79] Haig, on the other hand, thought Lloyd George 'astute and cunning with much energy and push but ... shifty and unreliable'.[80] Haig believed that his suspicions had been confirmed after he discovered that Lloyd George had visited General Foch, Joffre's replacement as French Commander-in-Chief.

> General Foch asked me to leave the others and go into the garden ... He then spoke to me of Mr Lloyd George's recent visit to his HQ. Lunch was at 12 noon and LG said he would be bringing 2 or 3 with him. He arrived at 1.45 and brought 8 persons! ... He wished to know why the British, who had gained no more ground than the French, if as much, had suffered such heavy casualties ... LG also asked his opinion of the British generals.

Haig, an officer and a gentleman, was scandalised. 'Unless I had been told of this conversation personally by General Foch, I would not have believed that a British minister could be so ungentlemanly as to go to a foreigner and put such questions regarding his subordinates.'[81] No doubt he felt even more aggrieved when General Sir Henry Wilson related Joffre's unexpurgated account of his own meeting with Lloyd George. 'He did not think that Haig's seat was very secure.'[82] He was not alone in that. The British Ambassador to Paris reported, 'most sensible people admit that our failing is competent leadership as compared with the French'.[83]

Haig was the most political of soldiers. At his prompting Lord Northcliffe advised the Secretary of State for War to spend more time with the troops. Then he provoked Northcliffe into such rage against Lloyd George that he stormed into the War Office, shouting for the Secretary of State to be told, 'I hear that he has been interfering with strategy and that if it goes on I will break him.'[84] For the next four years, the relationship between Haig and Lloyd George was, at best, armed neutrality. Often it was open warfare.

The *Morning Post* – basing its allegations on the undoubted fact that Lloyd George was still arguing in favour of reinforcing the army in Salonika – was the first newspaper openly to claim that Lloyd George wanted to usurp the generals' power. Robertson – conscious of the special powers conferred on him as Chief of the Imperial General Staff – had the temerity to suggest that military matters were best left to the soldiers. Lloyd George's reply illustrated the mistake he often made in dealing with the military establishment. Instead of calmly exercising his authority, he argued with them as if they were rival politicians. He was, he complained, being asked to become 'a pure advocate of all the opinions expressed by my military advisers . . . You must not ask me to play the part of a mere dummy. I am not in the least suited for the part.'[85] He was certainly unsuited to dealing with the generals. He despised them too much even to attempt to understand them.

On 28 November, Lord Derby, Undersecretary of State for War, told the House of Lords ('with the full authority of Mr Lloyd George') that 'the reports that friction existed between the Army Council and individual Members were untrue'. Nor were 'changes insisted on and individuals imposed on Sir Douglas Haig without his consent and approval'.[86] Derby ended by asserting ministers' unqualified admiration for Robertson and Haig. The whole statement was a succession of lies.

Lloyd George's disenchantment with the generals was matched by his impatience with his fellow ministers – and contempt for those who were arguing for a negotiated peace. There had, for some time, been a group within the Cabinet which wanted to encourage President Woodrow Wilson of the United States to arbitrate between the Allies and the Central Powers. McKenna thought that opposition to such an idea was 'sheer lunacy'.[87] Lansdowne saw no merit in 'slowly but surely killing off the best of the male population'.[88] Even Asquith and Grey were not sure that Britain could afford to fight a war which cost £5 million a day. The Liberal newspapers, particularly the *Manchester Guardian*, saw Bonar Law and Lloyd George as warmongers-in-chief – with Lloyd George the real villain because he should have known better.

Lloyd George usually bent with the wind rather than risk it breaking him. In autumn 1916, he was not in a mood to compromise. In an interview with Roy Howard, the director of the United Press of America, he expressed his determination to fight on in language which was so aggressive that he must have known (or perhaps intended) it to be offensive. The full tract was published in *The Times*.[89] 'Britain has only just begun to fight. The British Empire has invested thousands of its best lives to purchase future immunity for civilisation. This investment is too great to be thrown away.' Britain, he said, was growing 'suspicious' of America. 'The feeling seems to be directly attributable to a notion, generally entertained by the man in the street, that President Wilson might be induced to "butt in" for the purpose of stopping the European War.' He had been asked to use simple language to describe the British attitude towards Wilson's peace initiative. He chose an elaborate metaphor about sportsmanship which ended: 'The British, now that the fortunes of the game have turned a bit, are not disposed to stop because of the squealing done by Germans [and] . . . done for Germans by probably well-meaning but misguided sympathisers and humanitarians'. The rest of the Cabinet – led by the recently elevated Lord Grey – were furious. Even those who sympathised with his point of view had grown impatient with Lloyd George's inability – to steal his sporting metaphor – to play as part of a team. But they were nothing like as angry with him as he was contemptuous of them. In his view they had neither the will nor the capacity to win the war. They would have to change or he would have to go. For once, he meant it.

CHAPTER 26

THE FALL OF THE
ROMAN EMPEROR

Prime ministers rarely leave office in a way and at a time of their own choosing. During the twentieth century only three – Salisbury, MacDonald and Baldwin – determined their own departure dates, and even they were influenced by the knowledge that their erstwhile supporters thought that it was time for them to go. Balfour, Attlee, Home, Heath, Callaghan and Major were summarily evicted by the electorate. Campbell-Bannerman, Bonar Law, Eden, Macmillan and Wilson resigned on grounds of health – Eden in the knowledge that his Cabinet colleagues were on the point of revolt, and Macmillan in the mistaken belief that his doctors were sparing him the news that he was fatally ill. Churchill and Thatcher were deposed as a result of pressure from their parties. Asquith was the victim of a palace revolution – the process by which Lloyd George both rose and fell.

Asquith contributed to his own downfall with a lethal mixture of pride and desperation. His errors were compounded by Curzon's perfidy, Bonar Law's high-minded public spirit, Max Aitken's obsessive manipulation and Lloyd George's ruthless determination to assume, in one capacity or another, the direction of the war. But despite the weeks of growing dissatisfaction with his leadership, Asquith would – had it not been for a series of miscalculations – have remained the tenant of 10 Downing Street. During his final week in office, 'the last of the Romans' – like Mark Antony – failed even to fall on his sword with either competence or grace.

It was the backbench Unionists – led by Edward Carson, an embittered Asquith critic – who first made public the growing concern about the management of the war. The news was uniquely bad. The stalemate on the Somme had cost some four hundred thousand casualties. Romania, whose entry into the war had been hailed as proof that the tide was turning, had collapsed and been occupied. The U-boat offensive was putting British food supplies in jeopardy. As is so often the case in parliamentary politics, the dissidents chose to demonstrate their dissatisfaction by rebelling against a decision which did not, directly, concern the issues which had brought them to the brink of revolt.

On 1 November 1916, during the debate on the disposal of assets acquired by the occupation of German West Africa (Nigeria), Carson moved an amendment which would have had the effect of limiting the sale to British subjects. In theory the argument was between a variant of free trade and a hybrid version of protection. In practice, the debate provided an opportunity for dissidents to demonstrate their dissatisfaction with the management of the war – particularly the willingness of Bonar Law, the Unionist Party leader and Colonial Secretary, to support what they regarded as a failing ministry.

Bonar Law won the Nigeria vote, thanks to the near-unanimous support of the Liberal Party – though Lloyd George, who had dined that night with Carson, missed the division and Churchill, who had returned to Westminster after an interlude in the trenches, voted with the dissidents. But the government's majority included only 73 Unionist Members; 65 voted in the opposition lobby and 148 were absent or abstained. Bonar Law's future as leader of the Unionist Party and the continuation of the coalition were clearly both in doubt. To his credit, Bonar Law would, undoubtedly, have tried to improve the government's performance, whether there had been a Unionist rebellion or not. But the Nigeria vote concentrated his mind on the need to rectify two failures in the machinery of government.

The War Committee was too big. It had begun, after the formation of the coalition, as a three-member executive – Asquith, Lloyd George and Balfour. Soon after its creation, McKenna and Bonar Law were added to its ranks. Then Grey and Kitchener were made members and Curzon, Austen Chamberlain and Edwin Montagu were 'invited to attend'. The Chief of the Imperial General Staff and the First Sea Lord 'attended as necessary'. Colonel Hankey acted as secretary. It had become just another Cabinet committee which held long and inconclusive meetings and, even when it came to a decision, often thought it necessary to report to the full Cabinet before issuing an executive order. The whole operation was compounded by disagreement and mistrust. In the summer of 1916, Asquith had, insouciantly, spoken of 'six resignations looming'.[1]

Carson, who had left the coalition government because of what he claimed was the betrayal of Serbia, used his resignation statement to advise the Prime Minister about the need to change his ways. 'What is wanted for carrying on the war is a small number, the smaller the better, of competent men . . . The whole question is one of concentrating ability.'[2] It was not only politicians who felt the need for change.

On the evening of 15 November 1916, Lloyd George and Maurice Hankey – in Paris for a ministerial conference – walked in the Place Vendôme and discussed the government's lack of direction. Hankey was sure what needed to be done.

> You ought to insist on a small War Committee being set up for the day-to-day conduct of the war, with full powers. It must be independent of the Cabinet. It must keep in close touch with the PM, but the Committee ought to be in continuous session and the PM as Head of the Government could not manage that.[3]

Lloyd George had long believed in the need to change the way in which the government worked. He had already asked Max Aitken – then a young Member of Parliament close to Bonar Law – to put the idea to his Canadian compatriot, but it was in the Place Vendôme that he decided that the change must be made at once. The two men agreed that 'it is important that Mr Asquith should continue to be Prime Minister'.[4] But Lloyd George must become the man who seized the reins of the chariot and guided it to victory. His immediate reaction to Hankey's suggestion was to wire Max Aitken and ask 'him to arrange a meeting between Bonar Law and myself the following evening'.[5]

Max Aitken (not yet Lord Beaverbrook as Lloyd George's *War Memoirs* claim) had come to London from Canada in 1908 as a bond salesman and persuaded Bonar Law to invest in a company he was promoting. Two years later he returned a millionaire, renewed his acquaintance and became, in effect, Bonar Law's protégé. His patron – in an act of remarkable self-sacrifice – had agreed to abandon his safe seat in Dulwich and lead the battle for tariff reform in free-trade North-West Manchester. Aitken followed him to the North-West and became a candidate in Ashton-under-Lyne. Although Bonar Law lost, Aitken won. When his mentor returned to the Commons as Member for Ormskirk Aitken assumed the duties of chief of staff, adviser and acolyte. He was to play a central part in the drama that Lloyd George's message from Paris initiated.

Critics of the government's performance agreed that a series of related problems must be overcome. The War Committee needed to be reduced in size and its powers to be increased in a way which allowed its decisions to be implemented with greater despatch. Asquith was temperamentally incapable of imposing the necessary discipline on his colleagues – or accepting it himself. In July 1916, Bonar Law had written to the Prime Minister with suggestions that he 'should have, for every Cabinet meeting, an agenda and not permit any of our colleagues to raise any subjects, not previously submitted to you, until the agenda has been completed'. To members of more recent Cabinets, that proposal amounts to no more than one step away from anarchy. But it was regarded by Asquith as a 'counsel of perfection'. He tried 'as far as possible to rule out secondary discussion' but found it 'very difficult'.[6] Lloyd George knew that to be true. His resolve was hardened by a conversation with Sir Robert Donald, the editor of the *Daily Chronicle*, who spoke to Lloyd George on the advice of the CIGS and suggested 'that a committee of three or four be appointed to control the country, the members to be relieved of their departmental duties'.[7] Lloyd George liked the idea but told him 'it would not work' under the chairmanship of the Prime Minister. 'The Committee would never decide anything. Asquith is too judicial.'[8] And he went on to imitate the Prime Minister's technique – calling witnesses, pro and con, with equal impartiality and postponing a verdict until the following Thursday. If the new committee were to work, it had to have a new and dynamic chairman. He had no doubt who that should be.

During his conversation with Lloyd George, Bonar Law accepted the need for change but was less enthusiastic about joining a campaign to bring the desired end. He was motivated by a combination of loyalty and suspicion. Honour prevented him from being 'drawn into anything like an intrigue against Asquith' and he recalled his unhappy 'experience of what flows from this sort of a conversation' with Lloyd George, who would, he suggested, 'do better to go quite openly to the Prime Minister and tell him what he has told us'.[9]

Aitken regarded Bonar Law's position as honourable but futile. If Lloyd George approached the Prime Minister alone, he would receive vague and eventually unfulfilled assurances about improving the War

Committee's performance. With Bonar Law, on whose support the coalition depended, he might make some progress, even though there was one, unspoken, objection to the changes which he proposed. It would be assumed that Lloyd George was scheming for power and position. Even his criticism of the new Chief of the Imperial General Staff was seen as a preliminary skirmish in anticipation of a larger power battle. 'Of course,' said Asquith, 'I see his scheme really goes further than eliminating Robertson.'[10] Bonar Law could not contradict the Prime Minister's interpretation of why the call for reorganisation was being made.[11]

However, another element had entered into the calculation. Asquith had invited members of the Cabinet to prepare papers which set out their views on the future conduct of the war. Lord Lansdowne – Minister without Portfolio, leader of the Unionists in the House of Lords and ex-Foreign Secretary – had circulated his thoughts on 13 November, the day before Lloyd George and Asquith set out for the Paris conference during which Lloyd George's mind-concentrating walk with Hankey took place. When ministers grasped the implications of Lansdowne's paper, they realised that they were being presented with the need to make a crucial decision. Lansdowne began by considering the consequences of a prolonged war.

> The financial burden which we have already incurred is almost incalculable. All this is, no doubt, our duty to bear, but only if it can be shown that the sacrifice will have its reward. If it is to be made in vain, if the additional year or two years or three years finds us still unable to dictate terms, the war with its nameless horrors will have been needlessly prolonged and the responsibility of those who needlessly prolong such a war is not less than those who have needlessly provoked it.

It ended with what amounted to a call for a negotiated peace. 'The prospect of a "knock-out" [is] to say the least of it, remote'.[12] It added up to the insistence that without a real chance of victory, continuing the slaughter was indefensible. That was no more Asquith's view than it was Lloyd George's. But it probably commanded a majority in the War Committee as it was composed during the last weeks of November 1916. That meant that the need to revitalise the war effort diverted Bonar Law's attention from the dubious motives of the man who was most likely to bring that revitalisation about. Aitken persuaded him to consult other discontented Conservatives. On the night of 20 November, the first meeting took place between the four men who were to change the course of the war and, albeit inadvertently, the pattern of British party politics. Lloyd George, Bonar Law and Carson (known to their host as the 'Triumvirate') met in Max Aitken's rooms in the Hyde Park Hotel.★

It was the first in a series of meetings which took place almost every day for the next three weeks. The participants changed, but Max Aitken was always the glue which held them together and the lubricant which kept their initiative moving forward. Without him, Bonar Law's doubts about Lloyd George's motives might well have held him back from full participation in the campaign to reinvigorate the government. Even on 20 November, after the initial meeting, he remained of the view that 'Lloyd George's plans boiled down to one simple proposition – to put Asquith out and himself in'.[13]

For the next four days, while Asquith was preoccupied with the business of government – a coal strike in South Wales, the appointment of a 'food controller' and the renegotiation of American loans – the Triumvirate and Aitken manoeuvred. On Saturday 25 November, Bonar Law, Carson and Lloyd George – meeting at Pembroke Lodge, Bonar Law's house – decided that the time had come for a formal démarche. It took the form of a memorandum which they proposed to invite the Prime Minister to circulate in his own name. After complimenting the War Committee on its 'devoted and invaluable service' it proposed the creation of a 'civilian general staff' to 'consist of myself as president and three other members of the Cabinet who have no portfolio and will devote their whole time to the consideration of day-by-day problems'. The sentence which began 'The three members who have undertaken to fulfil these duties' was not completed. But it was followed by the announcement that 'Lloyd George was to be chairman' and preside in the Prime Minister's absence. The memorandum concluded with the proposal that 'the body should have executive authority', subject only to the right of the Prime Minister to refer its decisions to the Cabinet. It was not the memorandum which, given a free hand, either Carson or Lloyd George would have drafted. They wanted Asquith – whatever his

---

★In his much admired biography of Andrew Bonar Law, the distinguished historian Robert Blake based his account of the three weeks which followed on 'Lord Beaverbrook's book'. In fact *Politicians and the War* misses out one of the incidents on which the drama turns. It happens to reflect badly on Bonar Law.

formal status – to lose all influence over the progress of the war. But the concession to the Prime Minister's pride kept the Triumvirate united. And during the desperate days which lay ahead, the contents of the memorandum were to prove less important than its existence.

Asquith received the memorandum on the afternoon of the 25th. It was, in itself, evidence of his diminished authority. The Prime Minister's reaction – which could not have been more damaging to his own interests – was confirmation that he no longer felt entirely in charge. In conversation with Bonar Law he raised some potential objections and promised a definite response within a couple of days, but he sent a strangely personal letter to Bonar Law next morning. It conceded that although his own opinion of the War Committee was 'less disparaging' than the view taken in the memorandum, he was 'open to suggestions for its improvement'. He realised that 'the essence of the scheme' was 'a body of four – myself, yourself, Carson and Lloyd George'. He was not prepared 'to pass over Balfour or Curzon or McKenna' in favour of Carson and, as to Lloyd George,

> you know as well as I do both his qualities and his defects. He has many qualities which would fit him for the first place but he lacks the one thing needful – he does not inspire trust . . . There is one construction, and one construction only, that could be put on the new arrangements – that it has been engineered by him with the purpose, not perhaps at the moment but as soon as a fitting pretext can be found, of displacing me.[14]

Asquith ended his letter with a *cri de coeur* of the sort that prime ministers should not even make to their wives. 'Nor need I tell you that, if I thought it right, I have every temptation (especially now) to seek relief from the intolerable daily burden of labour and anxiety.'[15]

It was the letter of a man who had lost his zest for office and was weighed down by personal sorrow as well as public obligation. On 15 September, his son, Raymond, had been killed on the Somme. 'Whatever pride I had in the past,' he wrote, 'and whatever hope I had for the future – by much the largest part of both was invested in him. Now all that has gone. It will take me a few days more to get back my bearings.'[16] They had not completely returned by November. Nor had he quite recovered from the trauma which followed the news that Venetia Stanley – the object of his strange but almost certainly unconsummated passion – was to marry Edwin Montagu. He described his anguish in a letter to Sylvia Henley, Venetia's sister. 'This is too terrible. No Hell can be so bad . . . I miss (more than I could say) what has helped and guided me so often during these last three years. I cannot describe to you the depth of the unbridged gulf.'[17]

Bonar Law – who was to lose two sons during 1917 – was likely to be sympathetic about the death of Raymond Asquith but unmoved by Miss Stanley's decision to end her emotional correspondence with the Prime Minister. Lloyd George – although he had felt genuine grief when his daughter Mair Eluned died – was temperamentally incapable of understanding how a politician could allow personal feelings, no matter how strong, to deflect him from his duties. And the Venetia Stanley affair must have left him bewildered. He believed that women existed to serve men's purposes. In the summer of 1916, when Frances Stevenson could rejoice at spending 'a very quiet and happy weekend alone with D at Walton Heath', he was sending urgent messages home to Wales about Richard Lloyd's medical treatment.[18] 'I also want *you* to see Doctor Brocklebank and tell him how anxious I am about Uncle Lloyd's condition . . . Do, old darling, put your back into this job and I will love you ten times as much.' Margaret did as requested. Her husband received her next report on Richard Lloyd's health with so much 'relief and satisfaction' that he was moved to describe himself as 'very grateful'.[19] Uncle Lloyd's welfare was one of the rare domestic concerns that could have deflected his attention from the stern business of winning the war.

Asquith's letter to Bonar Law was headed: 'intended for your eyes only'. It was, however, clearly a response to a joint initiative and had to be examined – no doubt with embarrassment – by all the instigators of the memorandum. The Triumvirate discussed it on Monday 27 November and agreed that Lloyd George should seek a personal interview with the Prime Minister. Aitken, however, was growing impatient. Carson had persuaded the *Morning Post* – normally a bitter opponent of Lloyd George and all he stood for – to describe its previous *bête noire* as the potential saviour of the nation. And the *Daily Chronicle*, without prompting, had criticised Asquith's direction of the war. Aitken wanted *The Times* and the *Daily Mail* to be encouraged to follow suit. Lloyd George, asked by Aitken to cultivate Northcliffe, refused on the grounds that he would 'as soon go for a sunny evening stroll round Walton Heath with a grasshopper'.[20]

The flurry of press interest, and Aitken's clear determination to promote more, made Bonar Law realise that it would be wise to tell the other Unionist ministers what he had done and what he proposed.

There followed a series of gatherings which, because of their Byzantine complexities and bewildering frequency, left even the most intimately engaged participants doubtful about what they had decided. The initial meeting took place on 30 November. All the Unionist Cabinet ministers were present.* Despite some concern about the progress of the war, they were all both astonished and affronted by Bonar Law's failure to give them early warning of his initiative. None of them wanted to promote Lloyd George. Had they known that Carson was involved in the preparation of the memorandum on reform of the War Committee they would have been more antagonistic still. Whereas Bonar Law preferred the continuation of the Asquith premiership, albeit with reduced powers, the initial reaction of the Unionist ministers appeared to be insistent upon it. F. E. Smith referred contemptuously to 'the intrigue'. Lord Robert Cecil said that Bonar Law was 'dragging the Conservatives along at the tailcoats of Lloyd George'.[22] On the same evening, Lansdowne wrote to Bonar Law to say that the final meeting had 'left a nasty taste in his mouth'. Only Walter Long had any sympathy for the Bonar Law proposal for a small executive authority. Instead the ministers wanted two Cabinet committees – one to take charge of the war effort, the other to supervise domestic policies. The idea had already been considered, and rejected, by the Cabinet. Bonar Law reverted to his original idea. Lloyd George should personally put his plan to the Prime Minister.

Lloyd George saw Asquith on Friday 1 December. In the knowledge that his preferred solution had attracted only hostility from the Unionist Cabinet members, he took with him a memorandum which was, in effect, the proposals of the Triumvirate revised – but not by very much. The War Committee was still to consist of three members – Lloyd George, Carson and Bonar Law – who were to possess executive authority. The exclusion of the Prime Minister was, in itself, enough to guarantee Asquith's opposition. But Lloyd George did make one material concession to the Prime Minister's view. The First Lord of the Admiralty and the Secretary of State for War should both be members – as long as Carson replaced Balfour at the Admiralty.

Almost a century later, it is impossible to know whether Lloyd George wanted the acceptance of his 'revised' plan or hoped for its rejection. If he wanted to force the Prime Minister into the reassertion

---

*Some accounts say that Balfour was absent with flu. They are wrong. He missed a subsequent meeting on 5 December.[21]

of his supreme authority – a recipe for continuing inertia which even Asquith's most devoted supporters would not accept – his stratagem was entirely successful. Asquith's definitive reply, sent after 'time to reflect', was categoric. 'In my opinion, whatever changes are made in the composition of the War Committee, the Prime Minister must be its chairman. He cannot be relegated to the position of arbiter in the background or a referee to the Cabinet.'[23] It was an entirely proper position for Asquith to adopt. But it also made his downfall inevitable.

Neither the participants nor their biographers agree about the sequence of events. But it seems likely that Lloyd George – through the agency of the indefatigable Max Aitken – told Bonar Law of Asquith's initial response shortly after he saw the Prime Minister, and that Bonar Law immediately announced that he must see Lloyd George at once. Aitken, who had 'means of finding Lloyd George at any hour of night or day', knew that the Secretary of State for War was dining with the governor of the Bank of England at the Berkeley Hotel and offered to take him a message.[24] That was not enough for the agitated Bonar Law. He insisted on travelling in Aitken's taxi and waiting outside the hotel while his messenger entered the restaurant and signalled, as discreetly as he could, that he had a message for Lloyd George – who left the startled governor to finish his dinner alone and joined Bonar Law in the cab. Together they made their way to the Hyde Park Hotel, where, in the privacy of Aitken's rooms, they discussed, almost certainly inconclusively, what the next step should be. One fact of their conversation is beyond dispute. Bonar Law claimed that Lloyd George's revised proposals represented a greater reduction in the Prime Minister's role than the original agreement had demanded.

According to Aitken's account, the next day Lloyd George sent Bonar Law a copy of Asquith's formal, written rejection of the plan – accompanied by a covering note which was as brief as it was dramatic. 'The life of the country depends on resolute action by you now.'[25] Bonar Law responded by calling together the Unionist members of the Cabinet. The meeting was fixed for Sunday 3 December. 'They all arrived at Pembroke Lodge with copies of *Reynold's News* in their hands.'[26] It was not the first newspaper which the Unionist ministers usually read on a Sunday morning. But that day's edition became a major influence on their deliberations and therefore on the future of the government, the war and the country. Other papers had published criticisms of Asquith in articles which were clearly sympathetic to Lloyd George. But their comments seemed to be based on rumours and speculation. As Aitken himself admitted – while denying all responsibility – the *Reynold's News* story read 'like an interview with Lloyd George written in the third person'.[27] It described his proposals for the reorganisation of the government and announced that he would resign unless they were implemented – possibly taking Carson and Bonar Law with him. It is impossible even to guess if affront at the article really hardened the Unionist ministers' opposition to Lloyd George, or whether it was merely a pretext to justify a long-standing antagonism. It is, however, certain that Bonar Law – despite regretting its publication and realising the damage which it did to his cause – was not to be deflected from what had become his mission. His colleagues were persuaded to press the Prime Minister to face the need for change. After much discussion they agreed a statement – written in the form of a message to Bonar Law – to be presented to Asquith. It made clear that they were united in their demand for a change in direction. However – as it turned out, disastrously for Asquith – it made no attempt to describe how that change should be brought about.

> We share the view expressed by you to Mr Asquith some time ago that the government cannot continue as it is.
>
> It is evident that a change must be made and, in our opinion, the publicity given to the intentions of Mr Lloyd George makes reconstruction from within no longer possible. We therefore urge the Prime Minister to tender the resignation of the government. If he feels unable to take that step we authorise Mr Bonar Law to tender our resignations.[28]

Bonar Law had no doubt that its object was the protection of Asquith at the expense of Lloyd George.

> The course proposed . . . was not one which I desired to adopt. What I wished to say to the Prime Minister was that we considered it absolutely necessary that there should be a change in the conduct of the war and that, as Lloyd George was the only alternative, the change should consist in practically putting the conduct of the war in his hands.[29]

The most widely accepted – though barely credible – explanation of what the ministers hoped to achieve is provided by Aitken. A call for 'reconstruction' of the government would have been little more than a demand for a reshuffle. Resignation would require the King to invite another politician to form a new administration. According to Aitken, the Unionists had no doubt that it would be Lloyd George who was called to the palace and that, because of the antagonism he had attracted, he would be unable to fulfil the royal commission. Asquith would then be reinstated with his authority restored and Lloyd George could either be sent to the backbenches or allowed to occupy some ministry which reflected his diminished status. The plan was for Asquith to relinquish office in order to regain it with enhanced authority.

There were other interpretations of the ministers' intentions. Curzon wrote to Lansdowne immediately the meeting was over with his assessment of what had taken place. Despite a sentimental inclination to support the Prime Minister, the assembled ministers knew 'that with him as chairman, either of the Cabinet or the War Committee, it is absolutely impossible to win the War'.[30] As Roy Jenkins points out in his biography of Asquith, the resolution contained neither a message of direct support nor anything which could be interpreted as implying that the Unionist ministers would stand by the Prime Minister. Asquith certainly regarded the resolution as an ultimatum and feared that it prepared the way for Lloyd George. And for that, Bonar Law – intentionally or by mistake – was responsible.

It was Bonar Law's duty, as titular leader of the Unionists, to take the ministers' message to the Prime Minister – even though he had made plain that it was not altogether to his liking. Even after the meeting which drafted it was over, he agonised about the paragraph which referred to Lloyd George's manipulation of the press. No one could be sure that he had inspired the *Reynold's News* article. Aitken fed Bonar Law's fears that it would be wrong to go to the Prime Minister with a statement based on an assumption. F. E. Smith was called in to focus his legal mind on the propriety of ignoring the contentious paragraph. He ruled that, since the Unionist ministers had seen fit to castigate Lloyd George, Bonar Law must report their view, justified or not, to Asquith. And so he did, but in a way which – whether the result of duplicity or incompetence – gave the Prime Minister a confused impression of their intention. According to Lord Crewe, the Liberal leader in the Lords, 'the message was curtly delivered but in further conversation it was implied that the demand for resignation was not made in Lloyd George's interest'.[31] Perhaps. But the implication was not as clear as the situation demanded and not as clear as it would have been had Asquith actually been handed a copy of the resolution. 'I told him of the decision we had come to but, although I had the resolution in my pocket, as I had not begun by handing it to him but had simply announced its contents, I forgot to hand him the actual document.'★[32] Reading the text, with its explicit criticism of Lloyd George, would surely have prevented the Prime Minister from being 'not only greatly shocked but greatly surprised by [the] communication'.[33] It would have seemed inconceivable that ministers who had denounced Lloyd George were plotting to serve under him. As it was, Asquith, seeing the word 'resignation', thought that his only hope of survival was an accommodation with Lloyd George. The Secretary of State for War was summoned to Downing Street from Walton Heath to discuss the terms of an armistice.

Lloyd George took the invitation to meet the Prime Minister 'very coolly. He lit a cigar and considered impartially the invitation which lay before him . . . He considered that what he had to avoid was a settlement which was not really a decision . . . He finished his cigar quietly and left for Downing Street.'[34] The conversation which followed was 'long and friendly' and ended with the agreement that, although 'The Prime Minister [is] to have supreme and effective control of War policy', Lloyd George would become chairman of the War Committee. There was some disagreement about the committee's membership but, Asquith having obtained the appearance of power and Lloyd George having secured the reality, both men were satisfied. Bonar Law was sent for and told the good news. He, in turn, reported to the other Unionist ministers, who agreed to leave their resignations in suspension.

It was Bonar Law who recognised the danger that the ministers' initial, rather than final, decision would be reported by the newspapers. He advised Asquith that 'the only way to prevent the danger resulting from this is . . . that it should be formally stated tonight that you have decreed to reconstruct your government'.[35] Edwin Montagu – Lloyd George's successor as Minister of Munitions and the sort of politician who believed that he had a mission to reconcile the irreconcilable – suggested that the arrangement should be confirmed in writing. Asquith declined but accepted the need for a press statement. 'The Prime Minister, with a view to the most active prosecution of the war,

---

★Although it is salient to Asquith's understanding of the ministers' intention, Aitken omits this fact from his account of Bonar Law's conversation with the Prime Minister. In consequence, so does Blake in his biography of *The Unknown Prime Minister*.

has decided to advise His Majesty the King to consent to a reconstruction of the government.'[36] On the following day, Monday 4 December, a *Times* editorial dealt with the state of the government.

> The testimony of Mr Asquith's closest supporters – even more perhaps than the testimony of those who have no politics beyond the war – must have convinced him by this time that matters cannot possibly go on as at present. They must have convinced him too that his own qualities are fitted better, as they are fond of saying, 'to preserve the unity of the nation' (although we never doubted its unity) than to force the pace of the War Council.

The leader had been written by Geoffrey Dawson, the editor of *The Times*, after a briefing from Edward Carson. But Asquith assumed that it was Lloyd George's work – an error which Montagu compounded (in history if not in Asquith's mind) by later announcing that Lord Northcliffe had visited the War Office on the day before publication.[37] In fact the editorial and the assumption about its inspiration was deeply damaging to the cause it sought to promote. Lloyd George's enemies were able to represent demands for a reorganisation as less the determination to win the war than a way of replacing Asquith.

Whether or not the *Times* editorial would, in itself, have made the Prime Minister change his mind must forever be in doubt. He certainly regarded Dawson's version of events as a public humiliation, but it was one which he might have been prepared to accept had he not been subject to other pressures. While he was still digesting the bitter fruits of Printing House Square he was visited by a deputation of angry and bitter Liberal Cabinet ministers. They complained, with every justification, that they had read in the morning papers that their portfolios had been put at his disposal as the result of an agreement about which they had not been consulted. McKenna was the most vocal. The Prime Minister should reassert his authority.

The Unionist ministers were equally angry. They had called for a resignation – in order, many of them hoped, to dispose of Lloyd George – and discovered, through newspaper reports, that the government was to be reorganised in order to accommodate him. The anger – and apparent opposition to Lloyd George – of two factions within his Cabinet persuaded Asquith that he could defeat his tormentor. His decision was influenced by his typically lofty misjudgement of the situation. He had no doubt that 'the "crisis" [showed] every sign of following its many predecessors to an early and unhonoured grave'.[38] But he could also claim to have been misled. One of the signatories of the Sunday night memorandum had sent him a message which he thought threw new light on the Unionists' intentions. Lord Curzon had told Lord Lansdowne that with Asquith's chairmanship of the War Committee 'it was absolutely impossible to win'.[39] Twenty-four hours later he wrote to assure the Prime Minister that the proposed resignations 'were far from having the sinister purpose' which some people had suggested.[40]

Pride and overconfidence prompted Asquith to make the last blunder in a week of blunders. It was embodied in a letter to Lloyd George.

> Such productions as the first leading article in today's Times, showing the infinite possibility for misunderstanding and misrepresentation of such an arrangement as we considered yesterday, make me at least doubtful as to its feasibility. Unless the impression is at once corrected that I am being relegated to the position of an irresponsible spectator of the war I cannot possibly go on.[41]

It was clear which of those alternatives he proposed to pursue. In the reorganised government 'The Prime Minister [was] to have supreme and effective control of war policy.' Lloyd George's reply, despite its disingenuous beginning – 'I have not seen the *Times* article' – could not have been more conciliatory. 'I have had these representations to put up with for months. Northcliffe, frankly, wants to smash you. Derby and I do not . . . I cannot restrain nor, I fear, influence the attitude of Northcliffe. I fully accept in letter and spirit your summary of the suggested arrangements – subject, of course, to personnel.'[42] Lloyd George could afford to sound reasonable. Whether or not he was genuinely satisfied, there was no hope of the ministers who wanted to fight a more aggressive war agreeing to Asquith's retaining responsibility for its management. It is unlikely that he felt as submissive as he sounded. But the offer of obedience was on paper. Had Asquith accepted it, he would have seized the initiative. But, like Northcliffe, he – or those who advised him – wanted a smash. Lloyd George had to be broken, not just beaten.

On Monday 4 December, Bonar Law, still principally concerned with reorganising the machinery of government and suspicious that the Prime Minister was going back on the Sunday night agreement to streamline the War Committee, approached Asquith in the House of Commons. His suspicions were confirmed but, before he had time to express his concern, Asquith was called away to answer questions in the chamber and – with an uncharacteristic fleetness of foot – made his escape from the Palace of Westminster before the conversation could be completed. Bonar Law pursued him to Downing Street, where a group of Liberal Cabinet ministers was waiting audience. The Unionist leader insisted on precedence and walked into the Cabinet Room. Asquith was not asked to confirm his change of mind. Bonar Law, without any preliminaries, announced that if the War Committee scheme – with Lloyd George as effective leader – were abandoned, he would resign and withdraw his support from the government. Despite his disagreement with his colleagues, he remained leader of the Unionist Party and to continue the coalition without both him and Lloyd George would be a formidable task. But Asquith thought it could be done. Buoyed up by what he believed to be Curzon's message of support – and the belief that it represented the view of other Unionists – he wrote to Lloyd George. The letter was delivered the following morning. Only one paragraph mattered. 'The King gave me today authority to ask and accept the resignation of all my colleagues and to form a new government on such lines as I should submit to him. I start, therefore, with a clean slate.'[43]

Lloyd George replied with what he clearly regarded as a reasoned argument in favour of a new start. 'We have', he wrote, 'thrown away opportunity after opportunity.' His only object, he insisted, was to avoid 'the disaster which is inevitable if the present methods are longer persisted with'.[44] He added, quite unnecessarily in light of the Prime Minister's decision, that 'as all delay is fatal in war, I place my office without further delay, at your disposal'.[45] From then the fate of the country and Lloyd George's future were in the hands of the Unionist Party.

On Tuesday 5 December, the grandees of the Unionist Party – Long, Curzon, Chamberlain and Cecil – met at the India Office. The intention was to castigate Bonar Law for his failure fully to inform the Prime Minister of their intentions, but the miscreant refused to attend. Balfour, meanwhile, was confined to bed with flu. He sent Asquith two letters from his sick room. The first made it clear that he had no idea of what had gone on during the previous twenty-four hours – apart from Lloyd George's proposal that Carson should succeed him at the Admiralty.

I am aware that you do not personally share Lloyd George's view in this connection. But I am quite clear that the new system should have a trial under the most favourable of circumstances; and the mere fact that the new Chairman of the War Council did prefer and, as far as I know, still prefers a different arrangement is, to my mind, quite conclusive.[46]

Balfour was in Lloyd George's camp. But the Prime Minister was still uncertain about the position of the men Aitken called the 'Three Cs'. They were sent for. Curzon, Cecil and Chamberlain arrived in Downing Street at three o'clock on 5 December. Asquith asked them questions which betrayed his insecurity. Would they join a government in which Lloyd George and Bonar Law refused to serve? According to Chamberlain, their response 'was evidently a great blow to him'. They replied that their only object was to secure a government of such vigour, and

with such a prospect of stability, that it might be reasonably expected to be capable of carrying on the war; that in our opinion his government, weakened by the resignation of Lloyd George and Bonar Law and all that had gone on during the previous week, offered no such prospect and we answered the question therefore with a definite negative.[47]

When Asquith asked his second question – would they join a Lloyd George administration? – the Three Cs were brutally frank. If it looked like succeeding and prosecuting the war to victory, they would. When a Prime Minister is driven to ask such questions, he is not destined to remain Prime Minister for long.*

Many years later, Chamberlain claimed that the behaviour of the Three Cs proved that the Sunday night memorandum was not intended to offer Asquith the chance to re-establish his authority. Aitken, however, reports that Bonar Law, after refusing to attend the meeting at the India Office, summoned his critics to the Colonial Office and persuaded them that a Prime Minister who would not follow the death-or-glory route which they had proposed was unlikely to defeat either Lloyd George or the Germans.

Asquith's doubts about his own position must have been resolved by the receipt of a second letter from Balfour – written at four o'clock on

---

*Margaret Thatcher, behaving in similar fashion, sealed her own downfall in November 1990.

the same day as the first in response to the rejection of his resignation. It offered the view that the government 'could not go on in the old way' and added 'an open breach with Lloyd George would not improve matters . . . I am therefore still of the opinion that my resignation should be accepted and that a fair trial should be given to the new War Council, a la George.'[48] Then even Asquith realised that Balfour was lost to his cause. In fact Balfour had come to believe that Lloyd George was, potentially, the saviour of the nation. For the rest of the war, he was the most loyal of allies.

It seems that both the Prime Minister and the Unionists who had abandoned him took an almost simultaneous decision that matters must be brought to a head. When Unionist ministers were told the outcome of the Three Cs' meeting with Asquith they agreed without dissent yet another resolution.

> C C and C have reported to us the substance of what passed at your meeting with them this afternoon. After full consultation we are unanimously of the opinion that the course which we urged upon you on Sunday is a necessity and it is imperative that the course should be taken today.
>
> We hope that you arrive at the same conclusion but, if this is not so, we are obliged to ask you to accept our resignations.[49]

Curzon was deputed to take the resolution to Downing Street – though what self-serving gloss he would have put on it is impossible to guess. The message was never delivered. Asquith had lost his nerve and already resigned.

The King followed precedent and sent for Bonar Law – a member of the coalition government, but leader of the official Opposition after the most recent general election – and invited him to form a government. Bonar Law's response was confirmation of his selfless preoccupation with the national interest. His only concern, he said, was in creating or supporting a stable and effective government. In his view that object would best be achieved if both Lloyd George and Asquith remained in office. If he could secure that outcome he would accept the King's commission; otherwise the job was best left to Lloyd George – who was more likely to succeed in forming a government if Asquith refused to serve.

When Asquith was approached he declined to give a definite answer but left the impression that he was unlikely to accept Bonar Law's offer. Bonar Law then consulted Balfour, Lloyd George and Henderson, the senior Labour Party member of the coalition government. One of them suggested a Buckingham Palace conference under the chairmanship of the King. When it was convened, each of them claimed credit for the idea. The high hopes were dashed when Asquith ended the discussions with a rhetorical question. 'What is proposed? That I, who have held first place for eight years, should be asked to take a secondary position?'[50] Bonar Law was not ready to compromise. Balfour summed up the proceedings as 'an agreement that Mr Asquith should consider the proposal made to him and let Mr Bonar Law know, as soon as possible, whether he would join the government under him. If the answer was in the negative Mr Bonar Law would not form a government but Mr Lloyd George would endeavour to do so.'[51]

Asquith must have been tempted to deny Lloyd George the chance of reaching the top of the greasy pole. But pride overcame resentment and he declined to serve – without thanks. So Lloyd George began the task of forming a government, reinforced by the support of Balfour. 'If he thinks he can win the war, I am all for him having a try . . . I have no prejudices in favour of Lloyd George. I have opposed every political principle that he holds . . . but I think that he is the only man who can, at this moment, break down the barriers of red tape and see that the brains of the country are made use of.'[52]

That view was not shared by every member of the coalition. Led by the increasingly antagonistic McKenna, with the sole exception of the vacillating Montagu, the Liberal Cabinet ministers all proclaimed their loyalty to Asquith. When Lloyd George told Frances Stevenson, 'I am not sure that I can do it. It is a very big task,' he was speaking, with bogus modesty, about the premiership itself.[53] But he might well have been expressing doubts about his chances of forming an administration.

Wednesday 6 December was one of those days in politics when the future is decided not by great acts of daring or bursts of oratorical brilliance but by the prosaic business of counting heads. Christopher Addison – with the benefit of having run a similar exercise during the conscription crisis – divided Members of Parliament into 'doubtful' and those who were 'thought to be – for LlG' and 'arranged for a small band of men to canvass round'.[54] He was derided at his club as the only Liberal left in the government. It was not quite that bad. But the Unionists were more easily won over than the Liberals. Balfour turned the tide by accepting the Foreign Office – greatly influenced by the view (expressed by both Bonar Law and Lloyd George) that his example 'would greatly help with the rest of our Unionist colleagues'.[55]

Aitken claims that Balfour's response to Bonar Law was 'Well, you hold a pistol to my head. I must accept.'[56] Balfour's own version of events was less dramatic. His one proviso was that he be allowed 'a reasonable time to recuperate from a sharp attack of flu'.[57]

Support from the Labour Party was essential if the new administration were to be regarded as a 'government of national unity'. Henderson was personally sympathetic but, once again, would not accept office unless his National Executive Committee gave its approval. On 6 December, Lloyd George addressed the full Labour Party NEC. The war, he told them, was going badly. Victory could be won only with the assistance of the trade unions. What was more, he wanted the workers' representatives to help in the work of two new ministries – Labour and Pensions – and in planning the virtual nationalisation of the mines and shipping. The shrewder members of the NEC – Ramsay MacDonald, Philip Snowden, Ernest Bevin and Sidney Webb – were sceptical about his sincerity. Jimmy Thomas, the railwaymen's leader, and Henderson were impressed. A resolution to support the new coalition was carried – by one vote.

Although Balfour's support had opened the way to Unionist participation in the coalition, the party as a whole would not confirm its membership until it received three specific assurances. Churchill would not return to office. Northcliffe would not be offered a ministry. Haig would remain Commander-in-Chief in France and Flanders. Lloyd George acquiesced and, on the afternoon of 7 December, he told the King that he was able to form a government. He kissed hands at Buckingham Palace at 7.30 p.m. that evening. The cottage-bred man had become Prime Minister.

The War Committee and the Cabinet were merged into a single body under the chairmanship of the new Prime Minister. Maurice Bonham Carter, Asquith's private secretary and eventual son-in-law, called it 'In essence a democratic form of constitutional dictatorship.'[58] Curzon was made a member. So, to general surprise, was Lord Milner – confirming Lloyd George's preference for men of action. The Cabinet was reduced to just five members. The Prime Minister was its only Liberal. But the party provided the heads of five departments – including the Board of Education, to which H. A. L. Fisher was called from the dreaming spires of Sheffield. Altogether, there were fifteen Unionists in the government, twelve Liberals, three members of the Labour Party and three ministers who were officially unaligned. All the most important posts were occupied by Unionists – as much because Asquith's supporters refused to serve as because of Lloyd George's desire to keep the Unionists loyal.

As always with government reshuffles, there were disappointments. Carson, despite the help he had given Lloyd George at the start of the reorganisation campaign, did not get his expected place in the War Cabinet. Aitken – whose assistance had been invaluable throughout the turbulent six days – thinking that he was to become President of the Board of Trade, heard that he might be made Postmaster General and declined before he received the offer. The nearest he got to office was the request – which he accepted – that he take a peerage in order that his seat in Parliament could be given to the man who had been selected for the job to which he aspired. Max Aitken thus became Lord Beaverbrook. Winston Churchill felt humiliated and betrayed and was not mollified by the promise that, one day, he would be a minister again. Lloyd George was not the man to allow gratitude or friendship to stand in the way of his success.

Asquith and his followers – some motivated by personal loyalty, others old-style Liberals with doubts about the social policies which Lloyd George had come to epitomise – never doubted that the new Prime Minister was driven by personal ambition rather than patriotism. That was a simplification of the truth. Lloyd George was certainly determined to seize control of the war effort and that meant, in effect, running the country. He risked the impotence that would have followed his resignation not as a matter of principle but as a dangerous – perhaps desperate – way of putting pressure on Asquith and Bonar Law. But he did not much care what he was called. As long as he had the power, the glory could wait until the war was over.

Asquith, on the other hand, wanted the status but lacked the will to use it to the nation's advantage. By 1916, he was incapable of the vigorous leadership that the nation needed. He was an incompetent Prime Minister and fought an incompetent campaign to remain in office. Lloyd George thought his vacillations might be the result of 'losing his memory' or 'not knowing what he was saying'.[59] That was an exaggeration of his mental deterioration. He had simply lost his zest to govern without losing his desire still to lead the government. In times of crisis zest is essential. Lloyd George possessed it in abundance.

CHAPTER 27

FRONTAL ASSAULTS

If, as he often claimed, Lloyd George was the 'Man Who Won the War', he secured the Allies' victory at least as much by his work before he became Prime Minister as by his efforts after he took command of the coalition government. At the Ministry of Munitions he achieved far more than an end to the shell famine, the introduction of a tank-building programme and a reorganisation of the army's procurement policy. He infused the General Staff with a sense of urgency and purpose and forced the War Office to accept the advice of men, from outside its ranks, who thought efficiency was more important than protocol. When he became Prime Minister, his indomitable spirit played an essential part in maintaining both the army's and the politicians' morale. Admiral David Beatty, Commander-in-Chief Fleet after April 1917, said that Lloyd George was 'the one man in the whole rotten crew who had his heart set on winning'.[1] But during his wartime premiership, strategic direction rarely, and then only briefly, changed in the way he wanted. It well may be that, but for him, the insistent demands for an early neegotiated peace would have become irresistible. Yet the war that went on was not fought on his terms.

The war might have ended sooner, and casualties would certainly have been lighter, had Lloyd George succeeded in imposing his will on Field Marshal Sir Douglas Haig. But he led a coalition which was mostly composed of old enemies turned into reluctant friends. Political insecurity made him unwilling to challenge Haig head-on. To change the course of the war would have required him to risk his premiership. But the risk was not as great as he imagined.

During his December meeting with the Unionist leaders, Lloyd George had promised that Haig would remain at the head of the British Expeditionary Force. An attempt to dismiss the Commander-in-Chief would have ended Lloyd George's premiership. But Haig could have been overruled. And had he chosen to resign, Lloyd George might well have won the trial of strength which followed. The Prime Minister depended upon Unionist support. But the Unionists were also dependent on him. They had rallied behind him as the man most likely to bring victory. Deposing him would have fatally undermined the whole war effort. But instead of challenging Haig's strategy head-on, Lloyd George tried to undermine his authority and obstruct, rather than oppose, those of Haig's initiatives with which he disagreed. His excuse for not overruling decisions which he knew to be wrong was the conviction that he had a duty to lead Britain to the victory which would elude other politicians. The alternative explanation is that anything was better than riskily losing office.

It must be said in Lloyd George's defence that politicians rarely feel competent to disregard the advice of professional soldiers, and Haig's position was strengthened by his assiduous cultivation of the establishment. Paradoxically, Lloyd George might well have dealt with him more successfully had there been less personal antagonism between them. But the two men were chalk and cheese. Douglas Haig – Clifton College, Oxford, and Sandhurst – had been commissioned into the 7th Hussars, a regiment which was happy to allow him to indulge his passion for polo. He married the Honourable Dorothy Maud Vivian, Maid of Honour to Queen Alexandra, and become a personal friend of the King. His background alone would have antagonised the cottage-bred man who became Prime Minister. But his patronising manner, his stubborn certainty and his role during the Boer War, in which he commanded a special unit created 'to act vigorously with the object of clearing the [Cape] Colony of the enemy as soon as possible', converted dislike and disapproval into aversion.[2] The feeling was reciprocated.

Haig's antagonism to Lloyd George did not begin with the discovery that, during his first visit to Allied headquarters, the new Secretary of State for War had cross-examined French generals about the competence of their British counterparts. Back in 1908, Haig had sent a friend, the military secretary to Richard Haldane, his opinion of the Liberal government. He wished Haldane well, but 'What a pity it is that he has to associate with such a pack of rascals as Lloyd George and Co. They seem to be running the country.'[3] It was personal animosity, as well as self-protection, which prompted Haig to have the story of Lloyd George's 'disloyal' conversations with the French reported first to Northcliffe (whose papers responded with articles in praise of the British Expeditionary Force and its Commanding Officer) and, more explicitly, to the *Morning Post*, which referred directly to 'what the French call [a] "gaffe" which must not be repeated'.[4] From then on, Haig briefed the press far more often against Lloyd George than Lloyd George briefed them against him.

The new Prime Minister, leading a fragile coalition and at odds with the Commander-in-Chief of an army that seemed to be losing the war, needed a colleague on whom he could rely – a politician of almost equal status and seniority whose support was prejudiced by neither envy nor ambition. Fortunately for Lloyd George, Andrew Bonar Law was such a man. Each morning, Lloyd George walked along the corridors which joined 11 to 10 Downing Street and, in a haze of pipe smoke, discussed the business of the day with the Chancellor of the Exchequer. It was part of what Stanley Baldwin – a future Conservative Prime Minister not notable for extravagance of language – called 'the most perfect partnership in political history'.[5] It was all the more remarkable because 'the two men constituted such a contrast in temperament and mental equipment'.[6] Bonar Law, in an echo of Robert Cecil's rebuke, described his role as 'hanging on to the coat tails of the little man and holding him back'.[7] Lloyd George confirmed that definition of the relationship in more eloquent language.

> He had an incomparable gift of practical criticism. When he had finished marshalling his objections, I knew there was nothing more to be said against my plans . . . I never failed to listen to his views and give full weight to them. Once I had secured his consent, I had no more loyal supporter.[8]

Without Bonar Law's support Lloyd George could not have reorganised the government on a businesslike, if not entirely warlike, footing. It was thanks to him that Unionists as distinguished as Chamberlain and Carson, reinforced by Balfour's example, were prepared to head major departments without serving in the five-man War Cabinet – for two years the only Cabinet there was.★ The creation of the War Cabinet did not change the course of the war. But it did alter the machinery of British government for ever.

Colonel Maurice Hankey, a Royal Marine who had been in government service since he had been seconded to the Committee of Imperial Defence, became the first Cabinet Secretary. There followed changes which, strange as it now seems, were looked upon at the time as bold innovations. Hankey kept official minutes of the War Cabinet's proceedings. After some protest from the palace, they replaced the Prime Minister's letters to the King, which, until then, had been the only records of what had taken place. Ministers outside the Cabinet attended by invitation when matters which related to their departments were under consideration. Decisions were to be implemented at once. And, whenever possible, discussions were to be based on previously circulated papers. In only one particular did its procedure vary from the conduct of Cabinets during the next ninety years: it met on every weekday. Between 12 December 1916 and 31 December 1917 it held 308 meetings.[9]

Hankey, like every Cabinet Secretary who has succeeded him, became (when dealing with other ministers) a reflection of the Prime Minister's views and was therefore able to speak on Lloyd George's behalf with unquestioned authority. On the day before the War Cabinet's first meeting, he prepared a thirty-page paper on prospects and priorities. It focused ministers' attention on the issues which Lloyd George thought of vital importance – the defence of British shipping against U-boat attack, reinforcement of the army in Egypt, the supply of heavy guns to the Italians. The Allies' conference at Chantilly – held the month before Lloyd George had become Prime Minister – had agreed to authorise another large-scale offensive on the Western Front. So Hankey's paper properly accepted that decision as irrevocable, although he realised that the new Prime Minister wanted to switch the emphasis away from France and Flanders. Lloyd George's war strategy was based on opening a second or third front rather than relying on a breakthrough in Western

---

★The five members were Lloyd George himself, Bonar Law (Chancellor of the Exchequer), Lord Curzon (Leader of the House of Lords), Lord Milner and Labour's Arthur Henderson (Ministers without Portfolio). The War Cabinet evolved from the Committee of Imperial Defence via the War Council, the Dardanelles Committee and the War Committee. After December 1916 it was, in itself, the supreme political authority.

Europe. What was more, he believed, with an unshakeable confidence which owed more to temperament than to his brief tenure at the War Office, that he knew where the battles should be fought and won. An offensive on the Italian front would knock Austria–Hungary out of the war. Reinforced with two divisions, the army in Egypt could be in Jerusalem in two months and Baghdad would fall in three. Turkey would be forced to capitulate. Whatever the strategic merits of his proposals, they were built on much needed optimism. Meanwhile, the Germans thought the war already won.

Lloyd George inherited the leadership of a war which was going badly. The hoped-for Italian advance had been held on the Isonzo River. Romania had been overrun. The Austrians, reinforced by Germany, had halted the Russian advance. And U-boats were taking a terrible toll of British shipping. The French Army had suffered such losses that it needed time to rebuild itself into a fighting force and the United States was yet to enter the war. On 12 December 1916, Theobald von Bethmann-Hollweg, the German Chancellor, presented a note to the American Ambassador in Berlin which he asked to be passed on to the leaders of the Allied Powers. He believed that he was making an offer of a negotiated peace from a position of unchallengeable strength. The note said that Germany and Turkey, although on the point of victory, were prepared to discuss a negotiated peace. Should their pacific overtures be rejected, they would press on to total victory 'while solemnly disclaiming any responsibility before mankind and history' for the slaughter which followed. The symbol of Germany's strength was the Central Powers' capture of Bucharest on the day that the offer was made.

The War Cabinet read the text of the note in the newspapers before it was formally presented to the Foreign Office. On 18 December, it was agreed – as required by the 1914 London Pact – to consult the other Allies before making an official response. But ministers accepted that to negotiate peace at a time of weakness would be the equivalent of surrender. The following day, Lloyd George – in his first speech as Prime Minister to the House of Commons – dismissed the German démarche in the words of Abraham Lincoln. When the war began 'we accepted this was for an object and a worthy object and [it] will end when that object is attained. Under God, I hope it will never end until that time.'*[10]

---

*It is assumed that he meant what he said, and that – when, as he was forming his government, he told Labour MPs that he favoured a negotiated peace – he had been deceiving them.

Lloyd George had admired Lincoln since his boyhood and as the years passed he increasingly identified with the man who had progressed from log cabin to White House. No doubt he had learned of Lincoln's battle cry from Uncle Lloyd. But sincere though his admiration was, the reference to Lincoln was primarily intended to impress President Woodrow Wilson. It did not have the desired effect. The next day, Wilson responded to the German initiative by asking both London and Berlin to state their peace terms. His appeal contained the offensive conclusion that Germany, no less than Britain, sought 'to make the rights of weak peoples and small states as secure against aggression and denial in future as the rights and privileges of the great and powerful states now at war'.[11] Initially the French wanted to ignore the President's initiative. But they were persuaded that the Allies could not afford to alienate him. They relied on the United States for arms, needed to raise loans on Wall Street and hoped that Congress would eventually vote for the declaration of a just war. So it was agreed that France and Britain would send a carefully worded joint reply setting out possible peace terms. As well as demanding the evacuation of all occupied territories and the return of Alsace-Lorraine to France, it described the purpose of the peace negotiations as 'the rescue of Europe from the brutal encroachment of Prussian militarism' – thus disposing of the German peace initiative.[12]

French and British ministers had met in London on 26 and 27 December. Lloyd George's letter to Criccieth on Christmas Eve explained that he 'could not dream of leaving things until the Asquith muddle had been sorted out' even though 'it would have been such happiness to me to spend my holiday in the midst of my family' – a joy which, for a variety of less plausible reasons, he had denied himself for most of the previous decade.[13] On the second day, the ministers moved from consideration of the German peace note to examination of future policy. France, like Britain, had attempted to improve the efficiency of its war effort by giving supreme authority to a five-man Cabinet. But it had also replaced Joseph Joffre, its Commander-in-Chief, with Robert Nivelle, whose recapture of the Douaumont and Vaux fortresses at Verdun had become the symbol of French resistance against superior forces. Lloyd George remained certain of the dubious proposition that reinforcing in the Eastern Mediterranean would guarantee that Greece remained a staunch ally and, by threatening Turkey, divert German attention from France and Flanders.

The 1916 Christmas conference was the beginning of regular meetings proposed and promoted by Lloyd George, partly because he found them congenial and in part because of his determination to coordinate Allied policy. The process continued in Rome on 2 January 1917. The Prime Minister interrupted his journey in Paris in order to meet Lord Northcliffe – who warned him that if he agreed to transfer two British divisions from France to Salonika his newspapers would bring down the government. Perhaps by coincidence, the British memorandum to the conference expressed regret that a shortage of shipping would prevent the troop movement to which *The Times* and *Daily Mail* objected and suggested that Italy should reinforce Salonika by land. As a practical exercise in cooperation, Lloyd George offered to send guns and ammunition, but not men, to assist the Italians. When he was told that they could not be returned, he explained that changes which he had made in the royal arsenal had so increased production that he was able to offer a gift rather than a loan. Cadorna, the Italian Commander-in-Chief, remained reluctant to accept, and Lloyd George took it for granted that his initiative had been sabotaged by Haig. Robertson, the Chief of the Imperial General Staff, responded to renewed pressure from the French to send more British troops to Greece with a formal warning which illustrated Lloyd George's need to overcome an obduracy which was close to insubordination. 'I do not know what effect [French Prime Minister Aristide] Briand's oratory may have had on you in regard to this wretched Salonika business, but it seems right and fair that I should tell you now that I could never bring myself to sign an order sending further British Divisions to Salonika.'[14]

The conference concluded with agreement to take a harder line against the pro-German King Constantine of Greece, who was attempting to depose his pro-Allies Prime Minister. In November – a month before Lloyd George had succeeded Asquith – Eleftherios Venizelos had formed a provisional government in Athens, declared war on Germany and asked for British support. Robertson – intruding into politics despite his resentment of politicians' involvement in military matters – attributed France's interest in Salonika to a desire to dominate a Venizelos-led Greece when the war was won. In the meantime it seemed likely that the country to which Lloyd George was being urged to send reinforcements was about to be convulsed in civil war.

On the way home from Rome, Lloyd George met Nivelle in Paris, but prudently refused to discuss the French plans in the absence of Haig. He 'returned safely [to England] after a dreadful crossing. Owing to a blunder on the part of the Foreign Office there was no packet boat ready for the party at Calais and they had to cross in a destroyer that happened to be there.'[15]

During the weekend that followed Lloyd George's homecoming, Colonel Hankey told Frances Stevenson that 'she must be ready to go next time there is a journey' to meet the other Allied leaders.[16] In Rome there had been no one who could 'write and translate French'. The Cabinet Secretary may have known of her close relationship with the Prime Minister but he was not the sort of man who allowed personal considerations to influence office policy. Miss Stevenson fully justified her place on the Number 10 staff. But the status which she rightly enjoyed in Lloyd George's public life was not replicated in their private relationship. As soon as he returned from Rome, the Prime Minister was reunited with his wife at Walton Heath. Frances was understanding. 'D said he would have sent for me only that he felt it would not quite be playing the game with Mrs LlG. "She is very tolerant", he said, "considering that she knows everything that is going on. It is not right to try her too far".'[17] Around that sentence, and many more like it, was built the classic defence of Lloyd George's conduct. He hurt both women but deceived neither of them.

Lloyd George returned from Rome with his desire to depose Haig increased by his growing admiration for Nivelle. The Prime Minister's detractors attributed his enthusiasm to one of the impetuous judgements which had resulted in his involvement in the Marconi Scandal and the 1914 Budget fiasco. In fact Nivelle attracted him partly because he was not Haig and partly because he was personable and plausible.*
At the meeting after the Rome conference, Nivelle had been invited to address a meeting of the War Cabinet. He attended two, on consecutive days – 15 and 16 January 1917. His performance confirmed the Prime Minister's low opinion of his own Commander-in-Chief. On the day Nivelle left London, Hankey wrote in his diary, 'Lloyd George would like to get rid of Haig, but cannot find an excuse.'[18]

The War Cabinet was impressed by Nivelle's 'vigour, strength and energy'.[19] And he possessed one other supreme virtue. He had a plan of attack which would not require the level of British casualties which had been incurred on the Somme. Nivelle, like Haig, believed that the war could be won by one crushing blow, but he was determined that it

---

*Nivelle also possessed a large head – according to Lloyd George, a sign of intellect and character. Neville Chamberlain, on the other hand, had a head so small that Lloyd George never trusted him.

should be delivered by the French Army. He proposed to abandon the Haig–Joffre plan for another Anglo-French offensive on the Somme and replace it with assaults on the 'shoulders' of the old battlefield. The major attack – mounted by the French – would be in the southern salient around the department of Aisne, with Chemin des Dames as the first objective. The British would be responsible for a less comprehensive action on the northern salient at Arras, and would occupy a greater part of the front line – thus releasing French troops for their great advance. Nivelle promised a 'hard and brutal offensive' in which, during forty-eight hours, the Germans would be overwhelmed by three successive assaults.[20]

Nivelle's plan met none of Lloyd George's aims except a reduction in British casualties. The reinforcement of sectors outside Europe was postponed or abandoned. The idea of a decisive breakthrough on the Western Front was revived. But Lloyd George believed that 'Nivelle has proved himself to be a Man at Verdun, & when you get a Man who has proved himself why, you back the Man!'[21] Frances Stevenson hoped that 'D will not go too far in the backing of the French against the English'.[22] He did. During a meeting with Haig before the 15 January War Cabinet, 'The PM proceeded to compare the success obtained by the French Army during the last summer with what the British had achieved. His general conclusion was that the French Army was better all round and was able to gain success at less cost of life.'[23]

Support of the Nivelle plan provided an opportunity to argue that the new strategy required the Allies to establish a unified command. Since the French were to mount the main assault, and had far more men in the battle-line than the British, Field Marshal Haig would be required to act, for the duration of the spring offensive, on the orders of General Nivelle. Lloyd George told the French Ambassador in London that Nivelle should prepare a paper, describing a new and unified command structure.

According to Lord Northcliffe, Lloyd George's dislike of Haig – fuelled, no doubt by his inability to remove him – was so obsessive that the Prime Minister tried to enlist support from *The Times* and the *Daily Mail* for the dismissal of the Commander-in-Chief. Early in 1917, Haig, on the advice of Major Neville Lytton, his staff officer in charge of press relations, had given an interview to selected French journalists. The interview caused little stir in France. But its English translation – published in *The Times* on 15 January – was denounced by critics of the war effort as bombastic and vainglorious. According to Northcliffe,

Lloyd George hoped that the minor indiscretion would be the excuse he needed.

> The little man came to see me some weeks ago and told me that he would like to get rid of Haig but could not do so as he was too popular. He made the proposition that I should attack him in my group of newspapers and so render him unpopular enough to be dealt with. "You kill him and I will bury him". Those were his very words.[24]

If the story is true, it raises disquieting questions about Lloyd George's judgement – not least because Northcliffe was known to be, and remained, a Haig supporter.

The idea of a 'unified command' had been in Lloyd George's mind for months. The ground had been prepared in Downing Street on 15 January 1917. Commander Bertier de Savigny, the representative of the French high command in London, had been told that reorganisation was necessary but that a straightforward attempt to establish supreme French authority would fail. 'The prestige which Field Marshal Haig enjoys with the public and the British Army will make it impossible to subordinate him purely and simply to the French Command but if the War Cabinet realises that this measure is indispensible [sic], they will not hesitate to give Field Marshal Haig secret instructions to this effect and, if need be, replace him.'[25] The French Ambassador was told that Nivelle should be ready to describe how a unified command would be organised. The subsequent War Cabinet had not acted with the robust determination which the Prime Minister predicted. But it had agreed that coordination of forces was 'indispensible'.

The creation of a unified command was not formally agreed until a War Cabinet meeting on 22 February. Lord Derby (the new Secretary of State for War), General Robertson and Field Marshal Haig did not attend the meeting. Lloyd George argued with conviction that the proposed reorganisation was necessary to the successful prosecution of the war but did not add that it also provided an opportunity to bypass what he regarded as a major obstacle on the road to victory – the immovable presence of Douglas Haig. For the moment attempts to get rid of him were abandoned, partly because he retained the rest of the Cabinet's confidence and partly because the Prime Minister had, capriciously, come to the 'eventual conclusion' that 'Haig is the best man we have got, but that is not saying much and that between Haig and Nivelle [he would] support Nivelle.'[26]

Five days later Lloyd George travelled with Robertson to an Allied conference in Calais – ostensibly to discuss behind-the-line transport during the Nivelle offensive – but he did not think it necessary to tell him of the plan to put Haig under the command of a French general of junior rank. The Prime Minister – hoping that he would not be recognised as the architect of the humiliation – had persuaded Nivelle himself to make the proposal as if the idea of giving the Frenchman supreme authority was his own.

Nivelle tried, but failed, to persuade Aristide Briand, the French Prime Minister, to propose the adoption of Lloyd George's plan. Obliged to advocate his own elevation, Nivelle 'floundered about most hopelessly and had to be helped out'.[27] The discussion was abandoned in order to give Nivelle the chance to put his ideas on paper. He circulated copies of the plan which had been drafted, days before, at his headquarters. They amounted to command of the British Expeditionary Force being handed over to the French. According to Lieutenant Colonel Spiers of the British Military Mission to French headquarters, they were 'terms which might be imposed on a vassal state'.[28] Even Lloyd George was alarmed and 'Robertson showed every signs of having a fit'.[29] According to Frances Stevenson – who, despite Hankey's suggestion, had not travelled to France – 'Haig objected but D "remained firm" and forced the Commander-in-Chief to endorse the new arrangements with the words "Either Haig signs it or he goes or I go".'[30] Eyewitnesses to the event, who did not have to rely on Lloyd George's own account of the proceedings, told a less heroic tale.

On the first evening of the Calais conference, Lloyd George – claiming to be unwell – ate in his room with Hankey, while Haig and Robertson, unwary of their doom, enjoyed a convivial dinner with their French comrades-in-arms. As the dinner concluded, Nivelle gave Robertson the document which he had been invited to circulate. Its title, 'A Proposal for the Organisation of a Unified Command on the Western Front', did not adequately describe its contents. As well as giving Nivelle overall command of the British forces, it proposed that a British officer on his staff should report directly to the London War Cabinet without the inconvenience of going through the CIGS. Robertson and Haig, outraged and amazed, abandoned dinner and burst into Lloyd George's room to be told that the plan had already been agreed by ministers. They replied that the British soldier would never accept orders from an alien commander. Lloyd George retorted, 'I know the British soldier very well. He speaks more freely to me and there are people he criticises a good deal more strongly than General Nivelle.'[31] Stung by the implication of Lloyd George's riposte and seething with righteous anger, they insisted that it 'would be better to be tried by Court Martial than agree . . . [to be] placed under the French' and that they 'must resign rather than be parties to the transaction'. They 'went to bed thoroughly disgusted with our Government and the Politicians'.[32]

Soldiers stick together. Early the following day Nivelle asked Haig to join him in his room. Pride notwithstanding, Haig made the journey and received an apology for the 'insult' which, Nivelle assured him, had been entirely the work of Briand – thus abetting the theory that Lloyd George had been no more than an accessory to French ambitions. It is inconceivable that Haig believed him. At half past nine the Commander-in-Chief received a second summons. In Robertson's room, he was shown a paper which had been described to the CIGS as 'giving LlG's solution' to the impasse.[33] The description was a second misrepresentation of the Prime Minister's role in the affair. The new plan had been written by Hankey, who, horrified by the strength of the British reaction to the unification plan, had prepared a compromise. Lloyd George, who had been shaken by the passion with which Haig and Robertson had rejected the scheme, had agreed that Nivelle should have supreme command solely for the spring offensive.

Haig claimed that the clause which gave him 'a free hand to choose the means and methods of utilising the British troops in that sector allotted by the French C-in-C' was inserted in the document after the circulation of the revised draft at his insistence.[34] Whether or not that was true, the proviso – together with agreement that Haig could appeal to the British government against orders which he regarded as unreasonable – saved the Commander-in-Chief's face. Had he been wise, he would have declared a victory over Lloyd George. He chose, instead, to complain to the King about a humiliation which had confirmed his view of the Prime Minister. 'It is indeed a calamity for the country to have such a man at the head of affairs in this time of great crisis. We can only try to make the best of him.'[35] Robertson went further. Perhaps the calamity would be averted by a revolt against the 'awful liar. His story to the War Cabinet gave quite the wrong impression. He accused the French of putting forward monstrous proposals and yet you know he was at the bottom of it. I cannot believe that a man such as he can for long remain the head of any government.'[36] It was – for Lloyd George if not for the army – a time to withdraw and regroup. On 8 March, Haig was told that he 'enjoyed the full confidence of the War Cabinet' and promised that his relationship with Nivelle would be further clarified. An Allied conference, a week later, endorsed what had become a written agreement on the unified command, including the words 'The British Army and its C-in-C will be regarded by General Nivelle as Allies not subordinates.' While the politicians and generals argued about status, the war went on.

The Nivelle offensive ended in a defeat which amounted to a near disaster. The Germans had captured copies of the French battle plan and moved their reserves into place before the big push began. However, on 4 April the combined British and Canadian forces at Arras achieved an initial victory which might have been turned into a lasting triumph. Within a few hours they had advanced along the whole front – at some points to a depth of three miles – and taken nine thousand German prisoners. In a single charge, the Canadians captured Vimy Ridge – leaving them convinced that 'nothing at all could prevent the breakthrough – nothing except the weather'.[37] For once, the British papers had genuine, if brief, cause for jubilation. However, the failure to drive home the early advantage before the Germans brought up their reserves reduced what might have been a rout to a stalemate. The spring offensive was halted with only Vimy Ridge in Allied hands. The French Army mutinied and Nivelle was replaced by Philippe Pétain.

Aristide Briand had lost office even before Nivelle was relieved of his command, but the strategic balance was altered by greater upheavals than a change in either Prime Minister or general. On 3 March, the Tsar of Russia abdicated. Although the social democrats who formed the subsequent government announced their intention of fighting on against Germany, the Allied leaders were sceptical about the extent of their determination. A month later, though, the good news was beyond doubt. On 2 April 1917, the United States of America declared war on Germany. President Wilson's instinctive pacifism had not survived Berlin's approaches to Mexico – offering to reunite Texas, Arizona and New Mexico with the nation from which they were detached by the United States. In return Mexico was expected to offer the German fleet a safe haven within sailing distance of the South Atlantic where the indiscriminate U-boat war was having a devastating effect on American merchant shipping.

Until then American participation in the war had largely consisted of unhelpful interventions by the President and the sale to Britain, at strictly commercial terms, of food and essential raw materials in increasing quantities. But supplies from neither America nor the Empire were getting through. Merchant ships were being sunk at an accelerating rate – almost always by submarines. To make good the losses, the rate of shipbuilding was increased to 3 million tons a year. But although the torpedoed ships were replaced, the loss of their cargoes imperilled both food supply and morale. The threat was eventually neutralised by the organisation of protected convoys. The belated adoption of the system owed much to Lloyd George's willingness to challenge conventional thinking and Hankey's dogged determination. But it was not the clear-cut triumph for courage and determination that Lloyd George claimed.[38] The story of the convoy system's introduction is an almost perfect paradigm of the way in which the last two years of the war were fought in Whitehall. Convoys (like Lloyd George's proposed changes in strategy) were right, essential and opposed by the service chiefs, whose judgement was supported by the political heads of their departments. The new Prime Minister – fearful that his support within the coalition was fragile at best – flinched from head-on confrontation. Essential changes were, in consequence, abandoned or postponed.

Throughout 1916, both the Allies and the Central Powers had struggled to deny their adversaries vital food supplies. Britain had mounted a successful blockade and Germany had employed its U-boat fleet to sink British merchantmen to such effect that on 9 November Walter Runciman – the President of the Board of Trade – warned colleagues that there was a real danger of a serious food shortage.[39] A week earlier Lloyd George, supported by Bonar Law, had proposed the organisation of convoys, but Admiral Sir John Jellicoe, the First Sea Lord, had rejected the proposal. The role of the Royal Navy, he said, was to search out and destroy, not provide passive protection. It was not a duty which they had performed with conspicuous success during the year. In 1916, only 15 of Germany's 140 submarines were sunk.

On New Year's Day 1917, the German high command issued a warning. U-boats would attack all ships in and around British waters – whatever flag they flew. The aim was to sink 600,000 tons of Allied shipping each month. By February, the losses had risen to over 540,000 tons. In April, they were more than 870,000 tons. Jellicoe resisted any change in tactics and Lloyd George responded by being offensive rather than decisive. Foolishly, he told Carson, the First Lord of the Admiralty, that he would be better advised by 'fresh men with sea experience'. Six months earlier, Jellicoe had been in command of the Grand Fleet. Carson, fearing that the Prime Minister was about to insist on the formation of convoys, issued what amounted to a public warning. 'I advise the country to pay no attention to amateur strategists . . . Sailors will not be interfered with by me and I will not let anyone else interfere with them.'[40] Hankey, free from the political pressures which inhibited Lloyd George, did not accept the warning. He prepared a paper which urged the Prime Minister to reopen the convoy question. A meeting at Downing Street followed. Jellicoe accepted the logic of Hankey's proposal, but said it was logistically impossible. The Royal Navy did not have enough ships to provide the escorts. A subsequent meeting of merchant-ship captains supported Jellicoe's technical reservations. They doubted their ability to 'keep station' in a convoy.

Although Lloyd George was later to deride the merchant navy meeting as rigged, at the time he accepted that Jellicoe had won. Hankey did not. His diary records, 'I have many ideas on the matter but cannot get at Lloyd George in regard to it as he is so full of politics.'[41] However, Lloyd George was – as always – thinking of ways of outmanoeuvring his adversaries. In defiance of convention he asked for second opinions from junior officers without the knowledge of their superiors. His devious tactic paid dividends. Commander R. G. Henderson from the Board of Admiralty staff had discovered that his superiors' assertion that it lacked the necessary ships was based on a misunderstanding. Although some 2500 ships left British ports each week, no more than 150 were ocean-going cargo ships in need of protection.[42] On 23 April, Lloyd George played this trump card in the War Cabinet, adding that he had hopes that America would contribute six destroyers to the fleet of escort vessels. The ministers changed policy and Carson was told that a decision had been taken. Hankey, in evident relief, wrote, 'At last Ll-G has set himself to tackle the submarine problem seriously – when it is almost too late.'[43]

An experimental convoy set out from Gibraltar. But the description 'experiment' was no more than a device to avoid embarrassment to the Board of Admiralty. The navy had capitulated. Two days after the effective decision was taken, Lloyd George visited the Board of Admiralty in full session and, according to his *War Memoirs*, insisted that 'at any rate an experiment in this direction should be made'.★[44] Perhaps the origin of the new policy was less important than its result. What the Prime Minister described as 'Germany's expectation of bringing us to our

---

★According to A. J. P. Taylor, the story was invented by Lord Beaverbrook.

knees by August' evaporated.[45] The *War Memoirs* contain pages of statistics which prove that the introduction of the convoy system resulted not only in a dramatic reduction in the loss of merchant shipping, but a gratifying increase in U-boats destroyed.*

For the first six months of Lloyd George's premiership, the fortunes of war ebbed and flowed. Elation at the entry of America into the war was matched by doubts about the prospects of continuing the campaign in the east. In February 1917, the Russian Revolution had begun. Initially Lloyd George had regarded the overthrow of the Tsar as 'Worth the whole war and its terrible sacrifices' but within a month he had changed his mind.[46] On 17 March, two weeks after Lenin's return to Moscow, he told Lord Riddell that Russia was 'not sufficiently advanced for a republic'.[47] Two days later the Tsar asked for asylum in Britain. Lloyd George was surprisingly sympathetic towards a man he called a 'virtuous and well-meaning Sovereign [who] became directly responsible for a regime drenched in corruption, debauchery, favouritism, jealously, sycophantic idolatry, incompetence and treachery'.[48] Paradoxically it was the King who could 'not help doubting . . . on grounds of general expediency whether it is advisable that the Imperial Family should take up their residence in this country'.[49]

No doubt the Prime Minister sympathised with the King's reluctance. Lloyd George was not a man to allow the demands of friends and family to stand in the way of his destiny. But on 28 February 1917, the day on which he returned from the Calais conference, he was near to incapacitated by genuine grief. Richard Lloyd had died of bowel cancer. Two weeks earlier he had preached his last sermon. He had chosen as his text 'Yea though I walk through the valley of the shadow of death'. *The Times* wrote an eloquent account of the funeral mostly dealing with the sorrow of the 'most highly placed man in the world's greatest empire' as he 'buried his foster father and uncle, the village cobbler'.[50] Lloyd George wrote to his brother William in language which it is difficult to justify even after making allowances for both his highly emotional nature and his understandable desire to offer comfort and consolation. 'The interest in what he did will long survive any interest there may be in what I have or ever can achieve.'[51] William George – a sensible man whose pain was, no doubt, as great as his brother's – could

---

*German figures were quoted – twenty-two in 1916, sixty-three in 1917 and sixty-nine in 1918.

not have found much solace in such obvious nonsense. But only the modesty was false. The pain was real.

In death as in life, those around Lloyd George were allowed to be no more than a reflection of him. Frances Stevenson wrote a chilling comment on the consequences of Uncle Lloyd's death.

> D is very upset and will be until after the funeral takes place. It is a great strain for him coming at this time. He will miss the old man very much and he says I am his only devoted friend now. That I shall have to fill the old man's place. God knows I shall try. D needs so much someone who will not hesitate to give him everything and if necessary give up everything and whose sole thought and occupation is for him. Without that it is hopeless to try and serve him.[52]

A month later – when Lloyd George speculated about death – she was provided with an opportunity to demonstrate how complete her self-abnegation was. The Prime Minister was recognised – even his closest friends agreed – as a physical coward. Tom Jones, the Assistant Cabinet Secretary, noticed that, on one occasion after a meeting was interrupted by a call to 'take cover', Lloyd George was 'all of a tremble'.[53] Later in the year, when Zeppelin raids were at their height, the *Star* and the *Westminster Gazette* published – under the heading 'Mr Lloyd George's Country Retreat' – the allegation that on 17 September 1917 the Prime Minister had left London for Walton Heath 'about the time it became known that raiders were approaching London'. But the papers withdrew the claim and its implications of cowardice unreservedly. They had made the elementary mistake of nominating the wrong date. But there was no doubt that Lloyd George was afraid – afraid of dying and afraid of death itself. Frances Stevenson, it seems, was not. She was, in consequence, willing, literally, 'to give up everything'. On 22 April 1917, she wrote in her diary,

> D says that ours is a love that comes to very few people . . . It is a thing that nothing but death can harm and even death has no terrors for me now for D asked me yesterday if I would come with him when he went. He begged me not to stay behind but for both of us to go together and I promised to do so unless I had any children of his to claim me. So I am not now of the misery if D is taken away for I shall go too and his end will be my end.[54]

There was, however, one cause for possible concern. 'I hope by any chance I shall not go first for I know his misery would be great and he could not leave his work which is a great one.'[55] Lloyd George could add to his many other achievements the distinction of being the only British Prime Minister – indeed one of the very few human beings – to be party to a one-sided suicide pact.

The 'arrangement' has to be put into context and perspective. The reported conversation took place on the day after Lloyd George had returned from one of his frequent visits to France – on this occasion pursued by German destroyers with his life at risk. Jennifer Longford – Frances Stevenson's daughter, who spent much of her childhood with Lloyd George and believes him to be her father – does not regard either the request or the acquiescence as genuine. According to her judgement, that afternoon the lovers wanted to increase the emotional tension. Whatever its cause, it is not an incident which does Lloyd George much credit.

Two weeks before Frances welcomed the idea of selective suicide, Richard Lloyd George had married Roberta McAlpine, the daughter of the cement manufacturer and civil engineer. She was neither Richard's nor his father's first choice. Richard had hoped to marry Dilys Roberts but she had broken off their engagement. Lloyd George had been sentimentally inclined towards his son's marrying a Welsh girl and politically opposed to a union with Conservative money. The bad start to the marriage was symbolised by the Prime Minister's insistence that the ceremony – held in Bath Abbey – should be ostentatiously austere and that the 'King's pledge' to avoid alcohol should be respected at the reception. However, Lloyd George was full of joy. Megan, fit and well, was able to take her place as a bridesmaid. A month earlier she had contracted measles and her father had been convinced that he would lose her as he had lost Mair Eluned.

For all her forbearance, the pictures of the happy family must have been wormwood and gall to Frances Stevenson. Two months later, she was to face the pain of exclusion again when Olwen Lloyd George married Thomas Carey Evans, a young surgeon serving with the Medical Corps. If Lloyd George recognised Frances's unhappiness, he made no apology for it – or even acknowledged her suffering – in his letters. He had a war to win. Everything else was incidental.

CHAPTER 28

A WAY ROUND

Within weeks of becoming Prime Minister, Lloyd George had radically revised the machinery of government. The War Cabinet had become all-powerful and even its most independent-minded members expected Lloyd George to dictate its decisions. In December 1916, Bonar Law told Walter Long, 'I agree with you about Dictatorship. This is essentially Lloyd George's government and my own intention, like yours, is to back him to the full extent I can'[1] – a declaration which makes the reluctance to challenge Haig head-on all the more extraordinary. Without such loyalty the administration would not have survived, but Lloyd George's role within it placed a huge burden upon him. Between 20 March and 17 May 1917, the War Cabinet met on fourteen occasions, and the Prime Minister was expected to take the lead in all of its discussions. Lloyd George would not have allowed business to be conducted in any other way. But the strain was immense. Fortunately he had devised a support system which provided both advice and reassurance – though, occasionally, an appointment made in haste was regretted at leisure.

A week after he became Prime Minister, Lloyd George told the House of Commons that he intended to 'mobilise the whole of the labour strength of this country for war purposes'. To give his promise substance, he appointed a Director General of National Service on the morning of his speech. It was Neville Chamberlain, sometime Lord Mayor of Birmingham and son of his old hero-turned-adversary Joseph. Four days into the job Chamberlain told his wife,

I have never had even a scrap of paper giving me any idea where my duties begin and end. I don't know whether I have Scotland and Wales as well as England. I don't know if I have munitions volunteers. I believe I have a salary but I don't know what. I suppose I can be dismissed by someone but I don't know who.[2]

The bad start was better than the rest of the relationship. Chamberlain continually complained about being 'hustled' as he struggled to perform impossible tasks. He resigned after a year. From then on, both men behaved towards each other with an unconcealed animosity.

The supreme politician of his age was most confident when he could rely on the services of men who were not politicians – men he believed he could trust because they existed only as extensions of himself. When he became Minister of Munitions, he recruited businessmen to reorganise arms production. In the last year of the war he enlisted young men of conspicuous ability to help him pilot the country towards victory and peace. Lord Milner – in Lloyd George's estimation 'much the best all-round brain that the Conservative Party contributed to [Britain's] councils' during the war – had been supported in his imperialist ventures by a 'kindergarten' of exceptional talent.[3] Two of its members – Leopold Amery and Philip Kerr – became the nucleus of an independent 'secretariat' which Lloyd George created when he became Prime Minister. It was housed in huts at the back of 10 Downing Street and because of its location was known as the 'garden suburb'. Its head was W. G. S. Adams, Gladstone Professor of Political Theory at Oxford and, at forty-three, the oldest member of the team. Leo Amery became a Tory MP and one of Lloyd George's fiercest critics. Philip Kerr changed both religious and political convictions but remained true to Lloyd George. He had been a member of Milner's 'round table' of young intellectuals – predecessor to the 'kindergarten' – and he retained its philosophy of foreign and colonial policy. In consequence, his advice to Lloyd George was invariably 'imperial'.

The garden suburb turned its fine collective mind to more than the need to win the war. In 1917, Home Rule was still a running sore. It was not a wound which Lloyd George felt an emotional need to heal. But the Irish parties, as always, believed it had paramount importance and the American public – which had to be kept on Britain's side – gave sentimental support to anything that Ireland wanted. The Prime Minister's first plan – rejected out of hand by Redmond – had been Home Rule for all of Ireland except the six 'Protestant counties' of the North and an all-Irish council to coordinate policy north and south of the border. At Easter, a year after the 1916 uprising, the initiative was taken out of Lloyd George's hands. Horace Plunkett – Papal Count, landowner and father of an Easter rebel – convened what he called the 'Irish Convention' at Dublin's Mansion House. The delegates agreed to submit Ireland's demand for independence to the post-war peace conference. The assumption that Ireland was a nation in its own right gave the Home Rule movement a new dimension. Nationalists were being replaced by Republicans.

In January 1917, the Speaker's Conference on Electoral Reform reported. It proposed an end to the property qualification and virtually universal male suffrage, votes for women over thirty years of age, an end to plural voting and general elections held on a single day rather than spread over several weeks. Inevitably the reforms were not acceptable to the whole Unionist Party, but Lloyd George 'made clear' to the doubters within the Cabinet that he was 'not going to be dragged at the heel of the Tory reactionaries who supported them . . . I impressed them enormously and swung them round,' he told his brother. 'So far I have carried Minimum Wage to Agricultural Labourers, Adult and Women's Suffrage in a Cabinet described as being "predominantly Unionists" with a suggestion that I had come over to the Tories. Not a bad start for a renegade Radical in a Tory camp.'[4] Lloyd George was beginning to re-examine his political position. A month later he announced that the war had 'revealed fundamental facts which it is necessary to recognise'. It was not a revelation that the old Liberal Party would have welcomed. The time had come to examine the practical merits of applying Imperial Preference to all imports save food. Lloyd George defended himself against the charge of apostasy by claiming that Reginald McKenna – his old enemy and an anti-coalition Liberal – had abandoned the principle of free trade by imposing duties on imported food in his first Budget as Asquith's Chancellor of the Exchequer.[5] He felt no obligation to mention that it was the submarine scare that had made ministers accept that desperate expedient.

Agreement that some tariffs might be necessary was first conceded during a conference at which dominion prime ministers and a representative of the Indian government met under Lloyd George's chairmanship. The meeting, called to convince the Empire that its leaders could influence the course of the war to which it was contributing so many men and so much *matériel*, was given the grandiose title of Imperial War Cabinet. One of the participants was Jan Christiaan Smuts – a Cambridge graduate who, fifteen years earlier, had been a

Boer commando leader fighting to expel the British from South Africa. Lloyd George – who regularly, and often disastrously, came to immediate conclusions about people of whom he knew nothing – was quickly convinced that he had found a man whose judgement and loyalty he could trust and a soldier whose professional experience could be employed to illustrate the inadequacy of Robertson and Haig. It was a conclusion which could have been based only on Lloyd George's obsessive antagonism towards his own generals. He had rightly accused Kitchener of arming the British artillery with shrapnel because, in his mind, the Secretary of State for War was still fighting against Boer guerrillas. Smuts had been one of their commanders. He knew nothing of mighty armies locked in land battles that spread across the continents. Yet Lloyd George offered him command of the Allied army in Egypt and, when he wisely declined the honour, made him a permanent member of the War Cabinet.

From 6 June 1917 until the end of the war, Smuts was Lloyd George's confidant and counsellor. His duties ranged from ending a coal dispute in South Wales – when he asked the striking miners to sing to him – to making a tour of the Western Front 'to report . . . on the condition of affairs generally' and, in cooperation with Colonel Hankey, 'to see for themselves whether among the Generals they met there was one who they considered might fill the first place'. They came back with the disappointing conclusion that they could find no more competent a Commander-in-Chief than Haig.*[6] Once again Lloyd George had to content himself with frustrating Haig's attempts to initiate new offensives. So he turned his attention to removing Robertson, the Chief of the Imperial General Staff.

Lloyd George's hopes of victory, perhaps even in 1917, had been encouraged by news that Austria, tired of war, was prepared to abandon Germany and conclude a separate peace. But the terms on which it would have been agreeable to Italy were too severe for Vienna to accept. The idea of ending the war without demanding unconditional surrender – suppressed since Lloyd George became Prime Minister – again seemed attractive to some ministers. The Prime Minister remained obdurate – still certain that the way forward was success outside Europe.

---

*According to A. J. Sylvester, then shorthand writer in the Cabinet Office, Smuts and Hankey *did* suggest an alternative – General Claud Jacob, an Indian Army general who had become a Western Front corps commander. He was not thought worth 'a tremendous fight' with the Cabinet.[7]

Robertson agreed to the transfer of troops from Salonika to Egypt, where General Sir Edmund Allenby had accepted the command which Smuts had rejected. He was promised more reinforcements and told to aim at capturing Jerusalem by Christmas. At the same time, Haig and Robertson were planning another major offensive on the Western Front. It had been in their minds since the beginning of 1917.

Frances Stevenson's comments on the war always concerned the way in which its prospects and progress affected Lloyd George. By the middle of 1917, the Prime Minister had become so committed to a new strategy that his personal fortunes and an Allied change of course were inextricably linked – each one influencing the other.

> Nivelle has fallen into disgrace, and let D down badly after the way
> D had backed him up at the beginning of the year. Sir D Haig has
> come out on top in this fight between the two chiefs and I fear D
> will have to be very careful in future in backing the French against
> the English.[8]

There were, however, grounds for hope that the Allied strategy would change. Pétain, Nivelle's successor, shared Lloyd George's determination to avoid the pointless sacrifice in offensive actions which, when they failed, did not even capture a few miles of desolate ground. Pétain wanted to hold the line and wait for the Americans to arrive in Europe. His reluctance to mount a 'big push' was reinforced by the state of the French Army. A mutiny at Chemin des Dames was put down only after forty-nine rebellious soldiers had been summarily executed. The full extent of French disarray was kept secret even from France's allies. But Lloyd George realised that morale was low. Yet he needed the French to keep up some pressure on the Arras front to make sure that Haig did not again turn his attention to Flanders. In early May, he visited Paris 'to ginger up' the French.[9] But, conscious that Nivelle's failure had, at least temporarily, reduced his chances of confounding Haig, he took the opportunity to – it is the only word to use – ingratiate himself with the Commander-in-Chief.

On Friday 4 May, there was a meeting in Pétain's office. Lloyd George 'stated that he had no pretensions to be a strategist and that he left that to his military advisers, that [the] C-in-C of British Forces in France had full power to attack where and when [he] thought best'.[10] Before he left Paris Lloyd George had lunch with Lord Esher, who then reported to Haig. 'He has entirely changed his point of view as to the respective merits of the chiefs of the Allied army staff and powers of offence. For the moment I do not think you could do wrong.'[11]

The Paris meeting ended in unanimous agreement to 'attack vigorously'.[12] But despite Lloyd George's protestations of confidence in Haig he had asked General Smuts to make an independent appraisal of the likely outcome of a new offensive. It was a job to which the Boer commando leader was wholly unsuited. But it must be assumed that Lloyd George commissioned his investigation less because of his experience than in the hope that he would recommend that Haig be overruled. Smuts disappointed. He concluded that a defensive operation would be disastrous. 'I see more advantage in an offensive intended to recover the Belgian coast and deprive the enemy of their advanced submarine base.'[13] Hankey had already argued the same case and the Admiralty Board remained convinced that only the capture of Zeebrugge and Ostend could reduce shipping losses to acceptable proportions. Another Flanders offensive seemed inevitable.

Only Robertson among Lloyd George's professional advisers even considered the need for caution. He warned Haig against an offensive which 'will probably entail heavier losses than will justify the few hundred yards of trench or village gained'.[14] But the Chief of the Imperial General Staff believed that his duty lay in first advising the Commander-in-Chief and then defending him whether the advice was accepted or not. Lloyd George, lacking both evidence and allies, was driven back on a stratagem which he was to use for the next eighteen months. He tried to delay a 'big push' by denying Haig reinforcements.

In preparation for the great Flanders assault, Haig and Robertson asked for another half a million men. Derby, the Secretary of State for War, sought to meet their demand by 'combing out protected occupations'. Men who had previously been excused war service would be conscripted. Lloyd George persuaded the War Cabinet to reject the proposal. Robertson and Derby, at a private meeting with the Prime Minister, were told that they 'must be content with the scrapings ... He further added that we must very much limit our attacks and wait until America changed the strategic balance.'[15] It was to prove a long wait.

Haig ignored the advice. During the first week in June, the British forces mounted a preliminary offensive south-east of Ypres. It was a stunning success. Tunnels had undermined the German lines with galleries packed with a million tons of high explosive. The noise of the

detonation was heard in England. The explosion preceded three weeks
of bombardment. When the infantry advanced, they met negligible
resistance. The case for a new major assault on the same salient was
becoming irresistible.

A committee was created to examine what had become the General
Staff's formal decision to resume the Flanders campaign. It was called
the War Policy Committee and its members – Lloyd George himself,
Curzon, Milner and Smuts – met on 19 June to consider a plan which
'up to that date had never been submitted to the examination of the
government by the Chief of the Imperial General Staff or the
Commander-in-Chief'.[16] In his *War Memoirs*, Lloyd George insists that
he 'remained sceptical' about the idea of a new offensive although he
did not impose his view on his colleagues. However it was arrived at,
the committee came to a conclusion which men of their experience
should have realised could have only one outcome. The formal
endorsement of Haig's proposal was qualified by the instruction which
should have been unnecessary. The attack was not to begin 'unless the
situation [was] sufficiently favourable when the time came'.[17] Lloyd
George feared that Haig would announce that the time was right and
the army was ready, whatever the realistic appraisal of the prospects. So
it turned out. Lloyd George devotes twenty pages of his *War Memoirs* to
a description of his doubts and Haig's near-fraudulent insistence that the
German Army was short of men and ammunition. The despairing prediction turned out to be an accurate description of what happened. 'A
brilliant preliminary success [was] followed by weeks of desperate and
sanguinary struggle, leading to nothing except driving the enemy back
a few bare miles – beyond that nothing to show except a ghastly casualties list.'[18] A question remains. Why was the admirable prescience not
matched by sufficient courage to insist that the soldiers kept their
promise?

Lloyd George had persisted in the belief that the defeat of Austria
would deal Germany a fatal blow and returned to the idea of sending
heavy guns to boost the firepower of the Italian Army. Haig, determined not to reduce the forces available for his impending Flanders
offensive, urged Robertson to 'play the man and, if need be, resign if
Lloyd George should persist in ordering troops to Italy against the
advice of the General Staff'. Robertson stayed in post. But in 1917 there
was a summer of resignations. Haig – who showed less loyalty than he
expected to receive – reinforced Lloyd George's suspicion that the
Admiralty needed the total overhaul which could come about only if

the First Sea Lord were replaced. But Carson, the First Lord of the Admiralty, remained doggedly faithful to Jellicoe. Lloyd George – whose changes were usually made with more caution than his fiery reputation has encouraged history to believe – prepared the way for reorganisation by 'promoting' Carson to the War Cabinet and making Eric Geddes First Lord of the Admiralty – an appointment which required him to find a seat in Parliament.

Austen and Neville Chamberlain resigned within a month of each other. Austen left the government after the report of the Select Committee on Mesopotamia had concluded that the surrender of the British forces at Kut-al-Amara had been the constitutional responsibility of the India Office. His brother's departure from the Manpower Directorate was less a matter of honour than incompatibility. He had been appointed in haste to a job he found uncongenial by a Prime Minister he loathed. Arthur Henderson – Labour's representative in the War Cabinet – resigned on principle enhanced by pique. He had been sent, at the outset of the Russian Revolution, on a goodwill mission to St Petersburg and, on his return, had caused great offence by reporting to the National Executive of the Labour Party before he reported to ministers. Worse was to come. Henderson accompanied Ramsay MacDonald – general secretary of the Labour Party and an out-and-out opponent of the war – to a meeting in Paris which had been called to arrange a Stockholm 'peace conference' of all belligerent nations, including Germany. Summoned by the Prime Minister to account for his behaviour, Henderson was kept outside the Cabinet Room for an hour while his colleagues considered his conduct. He had returned from France opposed to the idea of a peace initiative. But, offended by his treatment at Number 10, he decided to assert his independence. He resigned from the government and, on the same day, moved a Labour Party National Executive resolution which supported participation in the conference.

But it was an appointment, not a resignation, which created the greatest storm in the already wind-tossed government. Christopher Addison was moved from the Ministry of Munitions to become Minister of (post-war) Reconstruction. The vacancy thus created was filled by Winston Churchill.

A variety of reasons have been suggested for Churchill's recall – including the fear that he would support Asquith's long-anticipated, but never realised, attempt to regain the premiership. Quite the opposite was true. Churchill had spoken 'responsibly' – that is to say, in support of Lloyd George – during a secret session in the House of Commons and when, as a result of his constructive moderation, he had taken part in a subsequent government-sponsored visit to France, his demeanour was much admired by the generals he met. It seemed that he could be trusted. And, as Frances Stevenson recognised, Lloyd George wanted a Cabinet colleague who was a friend, 'someone who will cheer him up and help and encourage him and who will not be continually coming to him with a long face and telling him that everything is going wrong . . . D feels he must have someone a little more cheerful to help him cope with all these mournful faces.'[19] The appointment, when it was made, did not have a similarly uplifting effect on the Unionist Party and its representatives in the government.

Bonar Law was not told of Churchill's reappointment until after it had taken place. Then, before he had an opportunity to protest against either the appointment or the discourtesy, Lord Beaverbrook was sent to smooth the ruffled feathers. He managed to prevent a public disagreement, though not profound apprehension. The Tory leader made clear to the Prime Minister that his loyalty would not survive Churchill's becoming a member of the War Cabinet or his being allowed to interfere in the service ministries. Walter Long – Colonial Secretary and self-appointed custodian of Tory interests – wrote to the Prime Minister expressing the anxiety of the Tory Party and was greatly relieved by the receipt of assurances on both points. However, he still insisted that 'the real effect has been to destroy all confidence in LlG. It is widely believed that, for purposes of his own quite apart from the war, he has deceived and jockeyed us.'[20] The assurances were not as effective as Long would have wished. Within weeks of his return to government, Churchill was, according to Geddes, interfering in naval matters. At the First Lord's suggestion, Bonar Law asked the Prime Minister to reinforce his insistence that reincarnation had not made the Minister of Munitions omnipotent. He told his friend, the editor of the *Scotsman*,

> There is no doubt that our party is very seriously disaffected at the moment mainly on account of Churchill but as regards the Government as a whole, especially as regards the Prime Minister. I confess I am surprised that after six months in which nothing has gone particularly well in the war his unpopularity has not become greater than it is . . . Lloyd George has been a better Prime Minister so far than I expected. He has devoted every minute of his time and all his energy to the war and has shown greater patience than I would have given him credit for.[21]

Bonar Law's judgement that 'nothing had gone particularly well in the war' was an understatement. Almost everything had gone spectacularly badly, as might have been expected from a campaign conducted by generals in whom their political masters had no faith and a Cabinet of ill-assorted talents backed by an uneasy coalition. Lloyd George had feared, and therefore failed to make, the changes which he knew to be necessary. His *War Memoirs* contain both an apology and an excuse – albeit venial – for his decision not to go 'further and take more drastic action in replacing Haig and Robertson'. It is a reflection of the less heroic aspect of the Man Who Won the War.

Lloyd George had no doubt that Haig and Robertson were fighting the wrong campaign. But both of them

> had a considerable backing in the press and in the House of Commons and inside the Government. The Asquithian opposition was solidly behind them. Northcliffe strongly supported both. They could also count on the support of a strong contingent of Conservatives, of whom some were members of the ministry. It was an incongruous combination but too strong to challenge at this stage.[22]

The explanation, although correct in every detail except its conclusion, reveals a failure of both nerve and judgement. Once more, had Lloyd George done what he knew to be right, he would – almost certainly – have succeeded in imposing his views on policy, either by insisting on a change in strategy or making a change in the high command. He was certainly not loved on the benches behind him. But he was needed. A palace revolution – in effect a regicide – would have jeopardised the whole war effort. Members of Parliament, being less heroic than they claim, take desperate action only when the path ahead is clear. In 1917, Lloyd George would not have suffered the fate which befell Neville Chamberlain in 1940 because there was no Winston Churchill waiting and determined to replace him.

Lloyd George justified his caution with what amounts to an admission of pathological timidity. He 'never believed in costly frontal attacks either in war or in politics'. Because he shirked a political frontal attack in 1917, he allowed the military frontal attack to go ahead – with thousands of Allied soldiers killed and wounded. The *War Memoirs* claim that he found 'a way round' which 'in the end achieved the purpose'. The solution, if solution it was, came late.

On 20 July 1917, Lloyd George, Balfour, Smuts, Hankey and Robertson were in Paris to attend another of the Allied conferences which, in the First World War, were perhaps too regular events. The overt purpose of the meeting was to consider withdrawing men and munitions from Salonika and transferring them to Italy. The generals were again opposed – this time on the grounds of logistic difficulty. But, in the margin of the discussions, Foch, the French Chief of Staff, suggested that the Allies set up, in Paris, some machinery for coordinating policy. It was certainly Lloyd George's view that 'the comparative failure of the Allies in 1917 [was] also in some measure due to the defects of their mutual arrangements for conducting the war'.[23] But as Robertson recognised, Foch's idea also provided a way of reducing the power of the British General Staff. 'I can see Lloyd George in the future wanting to agree to some sort of organisation so as to put the matter in French hands and take it out of mine.'[24] The discussions on the possibility of creating a Joint Allied War Council were to continue throughout the summer and into the autumn with the French Prime Minister and sometimes (by means of long and detailed letters or via Colonel House, Sancho Panza to Woodrow Wilson's Don Quixote) with the President of the United States. Another catastrophe in Flanders made the reorganisation inevitable. Haig's new offensive began while the discussions were taking place. Officially it was the Third Battle of Ypres. But the name which was to become embedded in the public memory was Passchendaele.

Four million shells were fired at the German lines during the fifteen days which preceded the first assault. Then, at ten minutes to four on the morning of 31 July, the British Second and Fifth armies – supported by the French on their left flank and accompanied by 136 tanks – moved forward. The ground, although pock-marked with craters, was dry and for almost twelve hours the advancing troops made steady progress. Then the Germans counter-attacked with a bombardment. And the rain began. It did not stop for three days and nights. On 4 August – as much because of the state of the ground as the ferocity of German resistance – Haig called a temporary halt. In the first few days of fighting the Allies had suffered about 35,000 killed and wounded. Haig described the situation as 'highly satisfactory' and 'the losses slight' – as indeed they were when compared with the Battle of the Somme, in which 59,000 British casualties had been sustained on the first day.[25] The battle was resumed on 16 August. By early September, British losses were around 18,000 killed or missing (many of them drowned in the mud) and some 50,000 wounded. 'As the futile massacre . . . piled up the ghastly hecatombs of slaughter', Lloyd George 'repeatedly approached Sir William Robertson to remind him of the condition attached to the Cabinet's assent to the operation. It was to be abandoned as soon as it became evident that its aims were unattainable.'[26] Robertson insisted that the battle could be won and that, because of the near collapse of the Russian and French war efforts, it was essential for it to continue. The Prime Minister, who knew that the battle was wasting men's lives, felt that he did not possess the political power to overrule him.

In September, Lloyd George – staying with Lord Leverhulme after attending the Birkenhead Eisteddfod – was taken suddenly ill. True to the pattern of his medical history, the high temperature quickly passed, but he remained 'feeble as a kitten'. The convalescence which followed was notable for a letter – written to Frances Stevenson on the 13th – which illustrates the nature of their relationship. It was headed with the warning 'Kerr opens *all* letters – so beware.' Philip Kerr was the Prime Minister's foreign affairs adviser and for many years one of his inner circle. Lloyd George was clearly still determined to keep the truth from even his closest friends. Discretion was matched by passion. 'How I miss you every hour of the day & every wakeful hour of the night. When I see beautiful sights, my thoughts always fly to you my darling.' A description of his illness concluded with the explanation that unless he recuperated in Cheshire, 'Pussy will soon have to find another Tom Cat'. But, since he 'longed more than ever to see' her, he had a 'proposal to make. Couldn't you and Muriel [Frances's sister] come down hear and stay in the Marine Hotel. We might snatch one or two walks along the riverside . . . I could meet you on the cliff under Murian beyond Marine Terrace.' A paragraph, which was crossed out before posting, began, 'I will pay the fares.'[27]

A month later, on 12 October, New Zealand and Australian infantry attacked Passchendaele village itself. Caught in the uncut barbed wire, 3000 men were mown down by machine-gunfire. The general commanding the Canadian division on the Ypres salient protested about the instruction to take the Anzacs' place in an operation which, he estimated, could be successful only at the cost of 16,000 casualties, but he accepted his orders. By 10 November, the village was captured, at the expense of 15,634 killed and wounded.[28] It was the only Allied 'success' of the whole battle.

There might have been a resounding victory at Cambrai, where 300 tanks – supported by eight infantry divisions – advanced on a 10,000-yard front over a distance of four miles in as many hours. But they were halted when the German counter-attack separated them from the infantry and, although British newspapers rejoiced at the news of what they had prematurely decided was a triumph, the Germans reclaimed most of the lost ground and even occupied the British positions. The Third Battle of Ypres was halted at a point when the generals could declare that their strategic judgement, if not vindicated, had not been confounded. Little ground had changed hands. British casualties had been more than 300,000 killed and wounded; the Germans fewer than 200,000. Haig looked forward to renewing the offensive in the spring of 1918.

Lloyd George was opposed to the third Ypres offensive from start to finish. Unfortunately, he said so only in private. In public, he was the loyal Prime Minister who criticised neither the performance of the army under fire nor the decisions of the generals who were squandering the soldiers' lives. Indeed, he expressed his full support for what he chose to represent as a great British victory. On 16 October, with the battle almost over, Field Marshal Haig received a telegram from Downing Street.

> The War Cabinet desire to congratulate you and the troops under your command upon the achievement of the British Armed Forces in Flanders . . . Starting from the position in which every advantage rested with the enemy, and hampered and delayed from time to time by most unfavourable weather, you and your men have nevertheless continuously driven the enemy back with such skill, courage and pertinacity as to have commanded the grateful admiration of the people of the British Empire.[29]

Haig wondered why the Prime Minister – who had been notably sparing with his congratulations – should have chosen that moment to send a message of such fulsome praise. He decided – in a combination of conceit and cynicism – that public support for his endeavours was so great that Lloyd George had no alternative but to reflect the country's admiration. That was certainly part of the Prime Minister's motive. But he also judged that it would be easier to make another attempt to reduce Haig's power if the major reorganisation of the war's direction were proposed against a background of openly expressed admiration. The new idea was the creation of a Supreme War Council.

CHAPTER 29

THE MAN WHO WON
THE WAR

Paul Painlevé – the French Prime Minister, who had succeeded Briand and promised a 'government of caution' – gave his support to the creation of a unified Allied War Council in September, and an interim meeting between the British and French was arranged for Chequers, to begin on 12 October 1917. General Sir Henry Wilson and General Sir John French were asked to supply papers on the future of the war effort. Neither man was a wholly objective commentator. French was still deeply resentful that he had been succeeded as Commander-in-Chief by Haig. Wilson wanted to succeed Robertson as CIGS. Both papers supported the established policy of concentrating on the Western Front and discounted Haig's view that Germany was on the point of collapse. French criticised Robertson so robustly – particularly for being 'Haig's agent' rather than the government's adviser – that his paper was rewritten by Hankey before it was shown to the object of his scorn. Lloyd George passed on both documents to the French and then asked Wilson, who had become his favourite general, to add his comments.

Wilson – in the great tradition of telling ministers what they want to hear – reconciled his judgement on the importance of the French and Flanders campaign with the Prime Minister's enthusiasm for initiatives in other theatres. He suggested that greater attention be paid both to the Italian campaign and the prospect of dealing Turkey a mortal blow in the Middle East – while still concentrating men and materials on the

Western Front. Lloyd George suggested the change of strategy to Painlevé and received, in return, a proposal for an amphibian assault on Syria and the request that Britain relieve the overstretched French Army by taking responsibility for another 60 to 100 miles of the Flanders front line. Lloyd George welcomed the suggestion and expressed sympathy for the request, which he recognised would guarantee that Haig could not mount a spring offensive. Crucially, both prime ministers reiterated the view that an Allied Supreme War Council, in which *political* leaders agreed common positions, must be created without delay.

On 2 November, the War Cabinet – in the absence of Robertson – approved the creation of a Supreme War Council which would be supported by its own General Staff. To avoid the alienation of the army, Lloyd George asked General Sir Frederick Maurice (the Director of Military Operations, who deputised at the meeting for Robertson) to draft a constitution. Thus prepared, Lloyd George left for Rapallo, where, on 6 and 7 October, there was to be a general reappraisal of Allied strategy. By then the situation had been transformed by the Germans. Six divisions had been moved from the Western Front to reinforce the Austrian Army in Slovenia. The combined force had inflicted a crushing defeat on the Italians at Caporetto and advanced several miles into north-eastern Italy.*

On his way to the conference, Lloyd George stopped in Paris to warn Haig of the proposed changes to the command structure. The Commander-in-Chief gruffly told him that 'the proposals had been considered for three years and always dismissed as impractical'.[1] Lloyd George replied that the decision had already been taken and moved the conversation on to press attacks which, he claimed, had been orchestrated by the military high command. Haig speculated in his diary that the Prime Minister was inventing complaints about the General Staff's conduct in order to divert attention from 'the enormity of which he is meditating' and 'in an attempt to put the people against the military and pose as the saviour of his country'.[2] Haig did not have long to wait for confirmation of his suspicions.

After Rapallo, the Italians – grateful for Allied reinforcements which had halted the German advance, and following the logic of the coordinated action which had provided their salvation – became enthusiasts for the creation of a Supreme War Council. On his way home – in Paris on 11 November – Lloyd George made a public appeal for an integrated

---

*The German tanks were under the command of Colonel Erwin Rommel.

war effort in a speech which was as much an admission of past failures as the promise of future success. He began by recalling Caporetto. 'There is no good minimising the extent of this disaster. If you do, then you will never take adequate steps to repair it.' And exaggerating the scale of the occasional success was equally damaging. 'When we advance a kilometre into enemy lines, snatch a small village out of his cruel grip, capture a few hundred of his soldiers we shout with unfeigned joy.' How, he wondered, would the patriotic press describe a true victory? Many of the defeats suffered by the Allies were the result of inadequate organisation and even the successes exacted a heavier price than was necessary. 'We have won great victories. When I look at the appalling casualty lists I sometimes wish it had not been necessary to win so many.' There was a desperate need for 'strategic unity' to replace the piecemeal initiatives of the past. 'Stitching is not a strategy. So it came to pass that when these plans were worked out in the terrible realities of war, the stitches came out and the disintegration was complete.'[3]

The public call for unity of purpose and command was accompanied by private negotiations with the Allied governments. The United States did not need to be convinced of the need for a radical change in direction. Over dinner on 13 November, Colonel House told Lloyd George, 'We not only accede to the plan for a single war council, but insist on it and think that it does not go far enough.' But there were still formidable obstacles in the path towards its practical operation. Georges Clemenceau – the new French Prime Minister who had replaced Painlevé – was opposed to what he feared would be a mechanism for imposing political control over decisions which should be taken by soldiers, and Haig and Robertson continued to tell their supporters in the press and Parliament that Lloyd George was plotting to usurp the power of his generals.

On 19 November, Conservative backbenchers – who traditionally hold a simple view of what they call British sovereignty – accused Lloyd George of betraying the British Army by denigrating its commanders in preparation for their being made subservient to politicians, some of whom were foreign. Lloyd George retorted that he had backed the troops with deeds not words. Speeches were 'No substitute for shells'. Admittedly, he had acted against the advice of soldiers. He had insisted on the manufacture of more guns and ammunition than the generals thought necessary.[4] The allegation that he was trying to undermine Haig and Robertson was virtually ignored. Congratulated on his

Field Marshal Earl Kitchener – 'A good poster but a bad general.'

MEPL

General Sir William Robertson, who resented working for 'an awful liar'.

Topham Picturepoint/Press Association Images

General Sir Henry Wilson, who told Lloyd George: 'I do not like your politics, but do admire you as a man.'

Topham Picturepoint/Press Association Images

Marshal Foch – scandalised to be asked his opinion of British generals.

Getty Images

Field Marshal Haig makes an emphatic point to an unimpressed
Lloyd George.

Getty Images

The amateur strategists – Winston Churchill and Lloyd George, 1915.

Getty Images

THE MAN WHO WON THE WAR

Lloyd George with Welsh troops at Rhyl.
Getty Images

AND THE MEN WHO LOST THE PEACE

Seated with Lloyd George: Vittorio Orlando, Georges Clemenceau
and Woodrow Wilson.
Bettmann/Corbis

Lloyd George at home with his family six months before the coalition ended.

Bettmann/Corbis

Back to work.

Mrs Jennifer Longford

Launching the Land Campaign.
Getty Images

Taking his plan for reducing unemployment to Downing Street.
Getty Images

HAPPY FAMILIES

Margaret had just told her husband of Frances Stevenson's 'infidelity'.

Associated Newspapers

A toast to Lloyd George. Frances was excluded from the eightieth birthday photograph.

Getty Images

With his 'daughter'
Jennifer Stevenson.
Mrs Jennifer Longford

Buying a postcard,
reproduced below,
for Hitler to sign
'To Jennifer'.
Mrs Jennifer Longford

Mrs Jennifer Longford

Lloyd George – 'I don't like it. It makes me look lecherous.'
Countess Lloyd George (née Stevenson) – 'You are lecherous.'
Mrs Jennifer Longford

Peace at last.
Mrs Jennifer Longford

performance by Addison, he replied in military language. 'Yes, the camouflage wasn't bad was it?'[5]

The Tory newspapers were less easily fooled than Tory MPs. 'Hands Off the British Army', cried the *Star*. Lloyd George responded with an attempt to ingratiate himself with Lord Northcliffe, the most powerful as well the most assertive of the press barons and, thanks to his volatility, a dangerous man with whom to do business. The plan did not merely fail. It ended in humiliation. Northcliffe was obsessed with aeroplanes. So Lloyd George invited him to head the recently created Air Ministry – without warning Lord Cowdray, the incumbent and another press baron. Northcliffe not only spurned Lloyd George's advances but published his letter which rejected the offer in *The Times*. 'I feel that, in the present circumstances, I can do better work if I maintain my independence and am not to be gagged by loyalty.' Cowdray read the letter and resigned. From then on his newspaper, the *Westminster Gazette*, was implacably opposed to Lloyd George and all his works. Chagrin at Northcliffe's conduct – embarrassment and shame being out of the question – was, to a degree, mitigated by news of the capture of Jerusalem on 12 November. The Holy Land had been freed from the Turks, thus 'achieving something which generations of chivalry had failed to achieve'.[6] General Allenby's victory came just three weeks after Arthur Balfour, the Foreign Secretary, announced that 'His Majesty's Government view with favour the establishment in Palestine of a Jewish national home' – a policy which Lloyd George endorsed because he had 'always supported the idea of reuniting the Jewish people with the land of their forefathers', and in the hope that it would ensure a permanent British presence in the region.[7]

Despite the affectionate acquaintance with the Tribes of Israel which his Baptist boyhood had provided, Lloyd George's real interest in the Jewish homeland was strategic. Asquith wrote that 'Lloyd George who, I need not say, does not care a damn for the Jews or their past or their future . . . thinks it would be an outrage to let the Christian Holy Places . . . pass into the hands of Agnostic, Atheist France.'[8] But he was less worried about that country's theological position than its influence in the Middle East. The secret Sykes–Picot Agreement – negotiated in 1915 – gave France control of Syria and the Lebanon. The creation of a Jewish state would, in Lloyd George's opinion, strengthen Britain's position in Mesopotamia and Palestine. In his *War Memoirs*, he substituted romance for Realpolitik. During the early years of the war, Chaim Weizmann, Israel's 'founder', was a research scientist in

Manchester. He had discovered a method of producing acetone – an essential ingredient in high explosive – from wood alcohol. Asked how he could be rewarded, according to Lloyd George he asked for 'nothing' for himself but suggested the creation of a Jewish state in Palestine. The story was an invention.

Autumn 1917 was the season in which Lloyd George's confidence in victory increased, encouraged by the conviction that the coordination which would follow the effective operation of a Supreme War Council would speed its achievement. But he was surrounded by pessimism. George Barnes – who had replaced Henderson as Labour's representative in the coalition – wrote from the Cabinet Office, 'Last week the casualty list was 26,000. The killed and missing were some 8,000. That means probably 7,000 killed. It is a mere matter of arithmetic calculation that we cannot go on for long at that rate.'[9] Lord Lansdowne – who had advocated a negotiated peace when he was a member of Asquith's Cabinet – renewed his call for an armistice in a letter to the *Daily Telegraph*.

> We are not going to lose this war, but its prolongation will spell ruin for the civilised world and an infinite addition to the load of human suffering which already weighs upon us . . . What will be the value of the blessings of peace to a nation so exhausted that they can scarcely stretch out a hand with which to grasp them?[10]

Lloyd George immediately announced that he read the letter 'with as much surprise as anyone else', and the ever-reliable Andrew Bonar Law put friendship aside and, in a speech to the Conservative Party conference, repudiated the idea of peace without victory. Calls for a negotiated peace, while men were fighting and dying at the front, he said, damaged national morale and undermined the government's authority. The Allies needed to demonstrate their capacity to bring the war to a successful conclusion. That, Lloyd George accepted, required victory in a major European land battle. But Haig, he had no doubt, would only waste lives in a doomed offensive. So he must be prevented – by the denial of reserves – from making another 'big push' in the spring. Haig could not be deposed. But Robertson – who would support the Commander-in-Chief's plan but did not share his hero status – was not invincible.

Derby – a minister held in justifiable contempt by Lloyd George – had to be persuaded that Robertson must go. His resignation would, it was assumed, precipitate a landslide of Tory defections from the coalition. So Lloyd George told Derby that the CIGS had tried to sabotage the Jerusalem campaign. It was not true and Derby, knowing that Lloyd George was lying, was emphatic that if Robertson were forced out, he would follow him. Derby also rejected the alternative proposal that Haig should be 'promoted' to 'generalissimo' – thus, at one stroke, removing him from Flanders and diminishing the influence he exercised, through Robertson, on Whitehall. Only one expedient was left.

Lloyd George certainly believed in the general necessity of greater Allied cooperation. But the effective operation of the Supreme War Council also offered the only remaining hope of preventing another Haig-inspired 'big push' on the Western Front. Its creation was making uncertain progress. When the Allies met at Versailles on 22 November, Clemenceau was still dubious about the merits of a Supreme War Council and was persuaded to discuss it at his first bilateral meeting with Lloyd George only after he was told that, unless the subject were on the agenda, the talks would not take place. He eventually 'agreed' to preside at the council's first meeting. As it was held in Versailles, he would have regarded any other arrangement as intolerable. Lloyd George and Milner represented Great Britain on the council itself. General Henry Wilson became the British military representative. Clemenceau proposed that Foch should be France's military nominee but remain the French Army's Chief of Staff. Convinced that, to make the council work, power had to be drained away from the national governments, Lloyd George vetoed the appointment and General Maxime Weygand was nominated as the French representative with the announcement that Foch had more important work to do. Clemenceau's attitude did not augur well for the council's future, but Lloyd George remained convinced that it could become the catalyst of change and improvement. Wilson was told of his duty in Messianic language. 'The whole future of the war rests upon your shoulders. You must get us out of the awful rut we are in. I do not like your politics but I do admire you as a man and a soldier.'[11] Lloyd George was still fighting on two fronts – against the Germans abroad and the generals at home. The second battle was eventually won by exploiting Clemenceau's acceptance of the advantages provided by a unified command – as long as it had a French general at its head.

While the Allies were considering how better to prosecute the war, moves were afoot to bring it to a sudden end. Dissident Austrians in London suggested, in a secret meeting with Smuts, that Britain should force Germany to the conference table by publishing the terms on which it would end the war. Leon Trotsky – acting on behalf of what was to become the Soviet Union – had begun discussions with the Berlin government in the hope of negotiating a treaty which guaranteed that peace and international justice went hand in hand. In late December 1917, the Labour Party endorsed a 'Memorandum on War Aims' which reflected many of the noble propositions which Trotsky was urging the Germans to accept. The notion that the Bolsheviks might want to 'export' their revolution was to haunt the British establishment – and influence both its domestic and foreign policies – for the next twenty years. It was a fear that Lloyd George shared. But when he addressed leaders of the Trades Union Congress at Caxton Hall on 5 January 1918, his object was less to dissuade them from rising up in bloody revolt than to convince them that, since the war was just, their members should redouble their efforts to secure a victory.

> The settlement of the New Europe must be based on such grounds of reason and justice as will give some promise of stability. Government, with the consent of the governed, must be the basis of any territorial settlement to this war . . . In these conditions the British people would welcome peace. To secure those conditions its people are prepared to make even greater sacrifices than those they have yet endured . . . A great attempt must be made to establish some international organisation as an alternative to war as a means of settling international disputes.[12]

The speech had been seen and approved by the King, Asquith and the dominion prime ministers and was meant to be the definitive statement of British war aims. But, although it was well received inside the hall, it attracted little publicity outside – leaving the field clear for President Woodrow Wilson, who, three days later, set out the 'Fourteen Points' on which he hoped to build a 'new world order'. His speech – with its noble hopes of self-determination, the resolution of conflict by negotiation rather than war and the creation of a forum for international cooperation – was first the contentious and then the forgotten aspiration on which the eventual peace conference was founded.

Arguments about the Supreme War Council's role and status were resolved, as was so often the case with disputes during the First World War, by the pressures of events. Fearful that a new German advance would threaten Paris, Pétain warned Haig that the French Army would concentrate all its forces on defending Amiens. In order to prevent the division which would result in defeat, the council agreed that Foch should coordinate the action of the French and British armies. The practical utility of the arrangement was reduced by the initial refusal of both Pétain and Haig to place any of the forces under their command at the disposal of the general Allied reserve which the Versailles conference had agreed was an essential feature of coordination. But a dispute about how much more of the Allies' front line was to be defended by British troops was solved by Haig's agreeing 'voluntarily' to Pétain's request rather than accept the indignity of being ordered to change his line of battle. Robertson – in disagreement with the Versailles conference decisions – considered both rebellion and resignation.

The Chief of the Imperial General Staff was, Lloyd George knew, close to a number of military journalists. Robertson's complaints about the way in which he was treated certainly prejudiced some newspapers against the Prime Minister, though – since he observed the duties of an officer and a gentleman with all the solemnity of the first general to have risen from the ranks – it is hard to believe that he actually broke King's Regulations. The Versailles meetings of the military committee were secret. It was therefore unlikely that the story which appeared in the *Morning Post* on 8 February came directly from him – even though it was written by Charles Repington, a journalist well known for supporting Robertson against the interference of his political master and a close friend of Major-General Sir Frederick Maurice, Director of Military Operations at the War Office and devoted supporter of the CIGS. 'Decisions of a recent Inter-Allied War Council regarding the control of British troops in the field [were] of such a strange character that Parliament . . . should examine them at once and take the opinion of our General Staff concerning the new arrangements.' A second article placed the blame for the bypassing of the War Office on the Prime Minister and called for his resignation.

Lloyd George took it for granted that the story had come from Robertson – a view that was given some probably spurious credence by the fact that, on the evening before the offending article appeared, the CIGS had written privately to the editor of the *Morning Post*. 'The little man is after my blood and is trying to isolate me . . . My intention is to isolate him. If he wants me to go, he should tell me so. But he doesn't. He is, therefore, trying to make my situation impossible.' Whatever the origins of the article, it strengthened Lloyd George's resolve to finish Robertson once and for all with a plan which he had already put to

Bonar Law. The CIGS would be asked to replace Wilson as Britain's military representative on the Supreme War Council in Versailles. Wilson would then replace him as Chief or the Imperial General Staff. If he refused – as was anticipated – 'he would put himself in the wrong and nobody would have any sympathy with him'.[13]

The ground was prepared with great care. Haig was asked to come to London. He was met at Victoria Station by an unusually compliant Lord Derby, who set out the proposed rearrangement and added that Robertson had 'become most difficult and lost his temper very quickly'.[14] Derby and Haig travelled together to Lloyd George's house at Walton Heath. It reminded the field marshal of 'summer lodgings at the seaside'.[15] Haig 'warned the PM and Derby of the distrust in which Henry Wilson [was] held in the army' and the 'shock' his appointment would cause.[16] He made no attempt to defend Robertson or to argue for his retention as CIGS. During the journey to Downing Street and in subsequent conversations with the Prime Minister and other members of the War Cabinet, the best Haig could do for the man who had defended him so robustly was to put on record that Robertson's new appointment did not have his formal endorsement and suggest that his old friend and champion should not be made Commander-in-Chief in India but, instead, should become General Officer Commanding Ireland. Then he argued with far more passion against the creation of a permanent general Allied reserve (which would remove British troops from his command) and the whole idea of a Supreme War Council.

The Undersecretary of State for War was then sent to give Robertson the news that he was to become the British military representative in Versailles and that, since he would also be Deputy CIGS, it amounted to demotion. Robertson refused to see him. When he was told the Prime Minister's decision by a more appropriate messenger, he formally declined to take up the new post. Derby lost his nerve and – supported by Curzon and Balfour – suggested that the order be rescinded. Lloyd George – supported by Milner and Barnes – stood firm. Balfour, converted to Lloyd George's cause by Robertson's intransigence, swung the balance of influential opinion the Prime Minister's way. Robertson's resignation was accepted.*

---

*The right to report directly to the Cabinet – granted to the Chief of the Imperial General Staff in 1914, for no better reason than to bypass Kitchener, the Secretary of State for War – was formally rescinded. Ministers believed that they were back in charge.

Parliament wanted – indeed demanded – to be told how and why the changes in the line of command had been made. The debate took place on 19 February 1918. Lloyd George spoke highly of Robertson but at more length about the Supreme War Council, an institution based on the assumption that the Allies had hitherto suffered through lack of concerted and coordinated effort. Asquith – who was critical of the decisions but did not divide the House – knew so much about the details of Robertson's removal that the ever-proper Austen Chamberlain wondered 'whether such a brief should ever have come into his possession'. But the most telling contribution to the whole debate was a one-line intervention from the virtually unknown James O'Grady, the Labour Member for Leeds East. 'Men are dying at the front while all this is going on.'

Men were not, however, dying at the front in Russia. Although the new Soviet government was split over the propriety of accepting aid from the Western powers, it united behind Lenin's insistence that a swift negotiated peace was essential to the survival of the revolution. The Treaty of Brest-Litovsk was signed by the Soviets and the Central Powers on 3 March 1918. From then on Germany was able to concentrate its forces on the Western Front without the constant fear that a resurgent Russia would pose a significant threat in the east.

The Allies, although formally united in the Supreme War Council, were still deeply divided over strategy. So were the French. Pétain wanted to hold firm and wait for the arrival of the American Army. Foch wanted to mount a new offensive or, at least, prepare to make a massive counter-attack if the Germans struck first. Haig – still resentful that he had been left with no alternative but to extend the British line – supported Pétain for the very good reason that he had been denied the reserves he regarded as essential to his plans.

Haig's submission to the Manpower Committee of the Cabinet had set out his needs in detail – 615,000 'Class A men' in addition to the 450,000 already training in Great Britain. Meeting the full extent of his demands was, ministers said, 'not feasible' in the light of demands from the Royal Navy and the absolute necessity of maintaining the civilian workforce needed for munitions. Instead they agreed to raise 100,000 Class A recruits and supplement them with 120,000 men from lower categories and 120,000 'youths' who could not go to the front. The Allies, the committee pointed out, had outnumbered the forces of the Central Powers in both 1916 and 1917 – most recently by 3,420,000 to 2,536,000, excluding the 12,000 Indian troops at Haig's disposal. At

General Headquarters no one doubted that the real reason that the recruits were being denied was the Prime Minister's determination to frustrate preparations for a spring offensive. Lloyd George would have described his position as the righteous refusal to be party to the squandering of more lives on an enterprise which was doomed to fail.

On the home front the war was going badly. A sudden fear of food shortages had swept the country – almost creating, through panic buying, the disaster which the rumours had wrongly prophesied – and forced the government to introduce sugar and meat rationing. Ireland, as always, seethed with discontent. At the beginning of 1917, a new crisis loomed. Should military conscription – in force in Great Britain since May of the previous year – be extended to all of the United Kingdom? The most devout Orangemen believed it should, as a symbol of the imperishable Union. So did many British families which, disrupted by the call to arms, thought that there should be equality of suffering on both sides of the Irish Sea. But to meet their demands was to risk a general uprising. On 21 March all other preoccupations were put aside as the Germans opened an offensive which, they hoped, would guarantee eventual victory.

Neither the Allied politicians nor the generals who advised them could agree about the Germans' likely intention. Haig complained that Lloyd George and Bonar Law 'did their best to get me to say that the Germans would not attack'. He had, in fact, said that he would not attack were he in their position, and his political masters wanted to know what practical conclusion he drew from that judgement. The answer, unhelpfully, was none. 'The German Army and its leaders seem drunk with their success in Russia . . . So it is impossible to foretell what they might not attempt.'[17]

Haig was wrong about the Germans' motivation. 'Operation Michael' – conceived by General Ludendorff in January 1918 – was an entirely rational attempt to win the war before the arrival of the Americans. The plan was built around what, in the Second World War, was called a blitzkrieg – a sudden and massive attack on a limited front which, having breached the enemy lines, would allow a swift infantry advance. The assault would be concentrated on the south flank of the British sector with the object of forcing the abandonment of Flanders and effecting a strategic separation between the French and British forces.

On 2 March, Haig was warned by his chief of intelligence that the Germans were 'preparing to attack on the Fronts of our Third and Fifth

Armies'. Haig 'told Army Commanders that [he] was . . . only afraid that the enemy would find our Front so very strong that he would hesitate to commit his Army to the attack with the almost certainty of losing heavily'.[18] Three weeks later, on the morning of 21 March, 'a compact mass of seventy-six first class German Divisions fell upon twenty-eight British Divisions of unequal quality'.[19] The attack had been preceded by a barrage from 3500 mortars and 6600 guns of various calibres – some of which had fired chlorine-, mustard-, phosphine- and tear-gas shells. Within three and a half hours the whole of the Fifth Army was overrun and the Third was in retreat. By the end of the day, the Germans had captured a hundred square miles of territory. Fifty more square miles were being evacuated. By the standards of the Somme, casualties were light. The speed of the German advance meant capture, rather than death, for the defending army. Twenty thousand British soldiers were taken prisoner.

Haig, who had slept through the bombardment, was told of the German offensive while dressing. He judged that 'having regard to the strength of the attack . . . the result of the day was highly creditable to the British Army'.[20] Wilson (in London) thought that 'although we have fallen back we ought to be able to kill them all off'.[21] Lloyd George's letter home to Wales mixed anxiety and hope. The British had 'been forced to retire from our front line' but 'that always happens in an attack of this kind'.[22] The Prime Minister was whistling in the dark. 'The news', he told Lord Riddell, 'is very bad. I fear it means disaster.'[23] On the following evening he blamed the defeat, which he took for granted, on the failure of Haig and Pétain to contribute to a combined Allied reserve. His Paris speech had called for greater Allied cooperation because he believed that only a united effort could win the war. There was no mention of his refusal to send reinforcements to France, though it was clear that he had changed his mind on the subject: 'I must send all the men I can.'[24]

On 'Black Saturday' – 23 March – Lloyd George took charge of the War Office's attempts to find reinforcements for the Western Front. He instructed that 170,000 troops in Britain be sent to France at once. They were to be followed by two divisions from Palestine and one from Italy. Conscription would have to be extended. On 9 April he introduced into the House of Commons the Military Service Bill. Men were to be liable for conscription between the ages of eighteen and a half and fifty, rather than nineteen and forty-two. Consideration was being given to extending the call-up to Ireland. Were that to happen then Home

Rule would be introduced at the same time. The offer was as offensive as it was doomed and particularly resented by the friends and families of the 150,000 volunteers (90,000 of them Catholics) who were already serving with the colours. Introducing the bill, Lloyd George told the House of Commons, 'When the young men of Ireland are brought into the firing line, it is imperative that they should not feel that they are fighting for a principle abroad which is denied them at home.'[25] In 1914, Redmond had made the same claim on behalf of the Irishmen who had volunteered to fight in Kitchener's army and it had been rebuffed by Lloyd George. The sudden change of attitude created outrage throughout Nationalist Ireland and consternation at the thought of Home Rule among Unionists. Before the bill had passed all its stages in the House of Commons, a member of Roger Casement's★ Irish Brigade emulated his leader by landing on the Irish coast from a German submarine and being instantly captured. His folly provided Lloyd George with the excuse to drop his proposals for both Irish conscription and Home Rule.

The offer to Ireland was a mistake which was instantly exposed. But the speech in which it was made contained another passage which – although allowed to pass at the time – was to prompt a parliamentary scandal that almost brought down Lloyd George and the government. The Prime Minister had been justly accused of denying Haig the reserves which he needed and of diverting to other sectors the troops which were urgently needed in France. Lloyd George replied that the army in France had increased in size during 1917 and that many of the forces stationed in the Middle East were unsuitable for service in Europe.

> In Mesopotamia there is only one white division at all and in Egypt and in Palestine there are only three white divisions. The rest are either Indian or mixed with a very small proportion of British troops in those divisions. I am referring to infantry divisions.[26]

The figures were initially accepted by both press and parliamentarians. Meanwhile, more urgent matters commanded the Cabinet's attention. On 9 April, Ludendorff launched a second offensive, code-named 'Georgette'. It was directed against the northern flank of the British

---

★Casement had made a similar landing in anticipation of the 1916 rising's success. He had been captured, convicted of treason and shot.

front and was instantly successful. It seemed that Boulogne, Calais and Dunkirk would fall. Haig issued an Order of the Day which may have inspired some of his troops but must have depressed many more.

There is no course open to us but to fight it out. Every position must be held to the last man. With our backs to the wall and believing the justice of our cause, each one of us must fight on to the end. The safety of our homes and freedom of mankind alike depend on the conduct of each one of us at this critical moment.

The British line held – largely due to the superiority of its artillery.

On 14 April, Foch was formally made Commander-in-Chief of the Allied armies in France. Haig accepted the arrangement with surprisingly good grace. His forces facing the enemy at last included Americans. Woodrow Wilson had agreed to despatch 120,000 men a month if Britain provided the troopships. He was better than his word. By the end of July there were 943,000 American soldiers in Europe. The risk of sudden defeat had passed – but not the danger that Lloyd George might be held responsible for a shortage of manpower which brought the Germans perilously close to victory.

On 7 May 1918, a letter from Major-General Sir Frederick Maurice, by then the former Director of Military Operations, was published in *The Times* and, simultaneously, in the *Morning Post*, *Daily News* and *Daily Chronicle*. It had also been offered to the *Daily Telegraph*, where it had been adjudged unsuitable for publication. It accused Lloyd George and Bonar Law of misleading the House of Commons. On 23 April Bonar Law had assured a Unionist backbencher that the decision to extend the British front line had been taken by Haig rather than forced upon him by the Supreme War Council. That, Maurice said, was untrue. So, the letter claimed, was Lloyd George's assurance – given to the House of Commons – that the size of the British forces in France had increased during 1917 and his assertion that there were only four 'white' divisions in Mesopotamia, Egypt and Palestine.

Lloyd George instantly suspected a conspiracy – a view reinforced by a series of parliamentary questions which had been tabled in the days immediately before the letter was published. For once it seems that there was at least some justification for his suspicion that the establishment was plotting to bring down the government . Maurice, who had been approached, both in France and at the War Office, by soldiers who doubted the government's honesty, was almost certainly genuinely concerned about what he called 'distrust of the Government . . . impairing the splendid morale of troops at a time when everything should be done to raise it'. It is hard to see how exposing the Prime Minister as a liar would have improved the spirits of soldiers in the trenches. Maurice – Robertson's man who had been replaced as Director of Military Operations as soon as Wilson became Chief of the Imerial General Staff – had asked his old chief how best to respond to the approaches of 'concerned officers' who wanted to force the government into admitting that the Prime Minister had initially refused to reinforce Haig and was, therefore, at least as responsible as the generals for the Ludendorff defeat.

Very properly, Robertson advised that, as a first step, Maurice should present his accusations – together with what he believed to be the correct facts and figures – to Wilson. Only if no correction were made should he write to the newspapers and consider briefing Asquith. The advice was accepted. Wilson ignored his letter. Maurice was then encouraged to write to the press by a message from Robertson which – being from one serving officer to another – constituted a court martial offence. 'Everyone I see swears that the days of LG are numbered, but I don't attach much confidence to these statements . . . Be quite sure of your facts and do not say a word that cannot be conclusively substantiated or that can be twisted to your disadvantage. You are contemplating a great thing – to your undying credit.'[27] The 'great thing' was the absolution of the army from all blame for the defeats of March and April.

Lloyd George told the Cabinet that he must respond to the Maurice allegations with an immediate statement to Parliament and a subsequent vote of confidence. Bonar Law would not agree. A House of Commons vote would be cast on party lines. Only a judicial inquiry could meet the demands of honour. Lloyd George was reluctant to nominate three judges who would be given the power to make or break his government, but Bonar Law insisted. So Asquith was told an inquiry would be set up, composed of judges of his nomination. To Lloyd George's relief, the offer was rejected. Asquith proposed to table a motion calling for the appointment of a select committee to 'inquire into allegations of incorrectness in certain statements of Ministers of the Crown'.

Parliament debated Asquith's motion on 9 May. Early that morning he received a letter from H. A. Gwynne, the editor of the *Morning Post*. It predicted that the 'almost immediate effect' of General Maurice's letter and the House of Commons debate would be 'the dissolution of the present government and disappearance from it [*sic*] of Mr Lloyd

George and Bonar Law'. Gwynne went on to recant the support he had given to the coalition of December 1916. Asquith was the man 'to guide and lead the spirit of victory to its goal'. In eighteen months, Lloyd George had become to Gwynne and many others 'the man who is losing the war'. Gwynne's call to arms no doubt reflected the view of Asquith's friends and Lloyd George's foes. But it failed to inspire Asquith himself. He made a tediously technical speech which was less concerned with the substance of Maurice's allegations than with the constitutional role of select committees. It began with a revealing, some would say incriminating, disclaimer: 'I know there are people, gifted with more imagination than charity and with more stupidity than either, who think of me as a person who is gnawed with hungry ambition to resume the cares and the responsibilities of office.' It ended with an unwise rhetorical question. 'What', he asked 'is the alternative' to a select committee? To cheers, C. B. Stanton, the Labour Member for Merthyr Tydfil, told him, 'Get on with the war'.

Sustained by a resolution of support from the munitions workers of Woolwich Arsenal – a rare example of organised labour rallying to his cause – Lloyd George went on the parliamentary offensive. That would have been his preferred style whatever the background to the debate. But on this occasion aggression was wholly justified. Maurice's department had prepared the statistics on which the whole argument was based. 'He was', said Lloyd George, 'as responsible as anyone else' for the information and the figures which had been given to Parliament. Why, if he subsequently found them to be wrong, did he fail 'to come to ministers whom he has since impugned' and tell them of their (and his) error? In any event, the strength of the fighting army *had* increased during 1917 – an indisputable fact on the basis of Lloyd George's carefully chosen definition of combatants – and the figures for 'white divisions' in Egypt, which Maurice disputed, were based on information given to ministers in his presence. Ministers could have been told of their errors 'quite nicely'.

The allegation that the Supreme War Council had forced Haig, against his wishes, to extend the British front line had still to be refuted. The accusation was untrue insomuch as he had made the adjustment 'voluntarily' rather than accept the indignity of having it imposed upon him. But Lloyd George had another point to make. Maurice's letter suggested that he had been at the meeting which agreed to impose its will on the British Commander-in-Chief. That was simply wrong. Maurice was in the building, but not in the room when the decision about stabilising the Allied front took place. The extent of the British sector had not even been considered. The implication was clear. Maurice was a liar as well as a conspirator and the House must understand the consequence of his conspiracy succeeding. 'Make no mistake. This is a vote of Censure upon the Government. If it were carried we could not possibly continue in office and the Right Honourable Gentleman who is responsible for the motion would have to be responsible for the government.' Asquith had lost all appetite (and therefore capacity) for office, and the House of Commons, if not the editor of the *Morning Post*, knew it. It was the realisation that the nation needed Lloyd George, as much as the merits of his argument, which produced the defeat of Asquith's motion by 293 votes to 106. But the large number of abstentions illustrated the extent to which Lloyd George was disliked, even by those who knew that he was indispensable.[28]

Bonar Law – not sure that his honour had been fully redeemed – fretted on about the need for some sort of inquiry. 'Poor old Bonar,' said Lloyd George. 'He felt it very much. He didn't like being called a liar. I don't mind. I've been called it all my life.'[29] That was not what they called him after the Maurice debate. Lloyd George himself made the cleverest and most apposite comment on his performance. 'They have caught the little devil telling the truth.'[30] But that specific truth conceded a wider deception. Maurice had attempted to prove that Haig had been *unnecessarily* starved of reserves and that he was constantly subject to political pressures which forced him to modify his plans in order to avoid being forced to change them. *That* was true – though Lloyd George sought to frustrate the Commander-in-Chief in the good cause of avoiding more slaughter in yet another failed offensive.

The Maurice debate was the last challenge to Lloyd George's authority before the end of the war and, in the spring of 1918, his power was enhanced by more than his bravura performance in the House of Commons. At the end of April, Roger Keyes, in command of the Dover Patrol, had led a daring raid on Zeebrugge and Ostend. Its object – blocking the canals along which the U-boats made their way from their bases to the sea – had not been achieved. But escapades of reckless daring do wonders for morale whether or not they succeed in their purpose. And the U-boat threat was being contained by the use of convoys. For two months, every troopship carrying American reinforcements to the British Expeditionary Force had arrived safely. There was also what seemed to be a more conventional victory to celebrate.

The Germans had been held at Arras. However, the German High

Command believed that they could turn the stalemate to their advantage by veering west towards the Aisne and threatening Paris. The variation in plans became 'Operation Blücher', the third Ludendorff offensive. It began at one o'clock on the morning of 27 May, exactly as American intelligence – relying on information obtained from captured prisoners – had warned. The warning came too late. French troops had been taken out of the line to prepare for an attack in another sector which never took place. After a four-hour bombardment the Allied army offered little resistance. The retreat turned into a rout. In four days the Germans (having taken fifty thousand prisoners) were within thirty-seven miles of Paris. In the Champs Élysées, thunder or the sound of gunfire made Parisians hurry home and prepare for the second German occupation in half a century.

Salvation seemed to lie in the hands of the newly arrived Americans but, according to Anglo-French military opinion, they – and particularly their officers – were not ready for battle. It was suggested that their battalions might be 'brigaded' – integrated into other units. But their commanding officer, General 'Black Jack' Pershing, was prepared only for his men to fight under American command. So another Allied general was at odds with Lloyd George. Their antagonism, unmitigated by old-world courtesy from the start, increased with acquaintance. Pershing said that he would rather the Allies be driven back to the Loire than commit American troops before they were ready. Lloyd George threatened to refer his obstinacy to the President. Pershing replied, 'Refer it to the President and be damned.' Relations were further impaired when Lloyd George described himself to Pershing's liaison officer as 'a trusted member of the relatively small squad of Pershing admirers'.[31] Major Lloyd Griscom, United States Army, did not see the joke. Lloyd George's impatience was easily explained. After a year at war – with French and British casualties in the hundreds of thousands – America had lost 800 men killed, 3598 wounded and 203 missing.[32]

Ludendorff's third offensive was such an initial success that there was talk in the British Expeditionary Force Headquarters of the French Army disintegrating and leaving British troops trapped. Haig's Chief of Staff, though not Haig himself, even contemplated abandoning the Channel ports and retreating behind the Somme – a desperate expedient which Lloyd George dismissed out of hand. Once again, Ludendorff was first held and then chose to pause. Fifty German divisions waited in reserve. It seemed likely that the battle would soon be resumed. As they waited, the Allied generals argued over rights and responsibilities. Lloyd George, fearing that the power – which he had fought so hard to give to Foch – was being abused to protect the French Army, suddenly became an opponent of collective responsibility. Haig, angered by troops under his command being moved before he had been consulted, was urged by the Prime Minister to 'appeal to his national government' – a last resort which Lloyd George had conceded with reluctance when the Supreme War Council was created. Wilson was proving a broken reed. At the height of the battle he had canvassed the idea of Haig's being transferred from France to the Home Forces Command. Before ministers could consider the idea he lost his nerve. On 20 May he told the Commander-in-Chief that the 'Cabinet had no desire to replace [him] in France'. He added that they would 'not consider Robertson for . . . C-in-C Home Forces' because he 'is thought to be mixed up with Maurice'.[33] The appointment was announced two days later.

Lloyd George was still haunted by contradictory beliefs – that it was essential to replace Haig and that it was politically impossible for him to do so. During a discussion on the Third Battle of Ypres he had spoken to a conference of dominion prime ministers in the language of a man who needed to make excuses for his conduct.

> The government could have stopped it if they had had the moral courage to do it. Had they done so, however, the Military Authorities would have insisted that they had been on the point of breaking through, that the enemy was demoralised and that, at the last moment, they had been stopped by civilian politicians.[34]

One scapegoat had been identified and punished. After the initial success of the third Ludendorff offensive, General Sir Hubert Gough – who had commanded the Fifth Army – had been removed, without much protest from Haig. But the Commander-in-Chief remained, despite increasing doubts, untouchable. After Gough's dismissal he actually wrote to Derby, offering to go.

> Personally I have a clear conscience and feel that I have done the best with the means at my disposal and am prepared to continue here as long as the Government wishes me to do so. But I have more than once said to you and to others in the government that the moment they feel they would prefer someone else to

command in France I am prepared to place my resignation in your hands.[35]

The War Cabinet declined the offer. Haig was secure for the rest of the war. Emboldened by the vote of grudging confidence, he began to plan a new offensive.[36]

Ludendorff had pushed on towards Paris but a swift counter-attack – with 28,000 fresh and eager American troops, despite earlier reservations, under French command – drove the German Army back across the Marne. The German losses suffered in the retreat were so great that the next stage of Ludendorff's plan – an attack on the British in Flanders – had to be abandoned. Foch was promoted to Marshal of France and Haig prepared his new offensive. It was launched on 8 August. The balance of early casualties – 9000 to 27,000 – was, for once, in the Allies' favour and, unlike Cambrai, the ground captured was held and consolidated. Ludendorff spoke dramatically of the blackest day of the German Army in the history of this war and offered his resignation to the high command.

To replace the losses of the summer campaigns, the German Army needed 200,000 new recruits each month for the rest of the year. In a desperate bid to fill the gap, military hospitals were instructed to return convalescent casualties to the ranks. But the strength of the army had fallen from 5,100,000 to 4,200,000 men.[37] Ludendorff conceded that, after August 1918, the Allies would always outnumber the Central Powers. 'The attempt to make the nations of the Entente incline to peace before the arrival of the American reinforcements by means of German victories had failed.'[38] The subsequent German defeat at Amiens was 'not the loss of a battle but the loss of the war'.[39]

So it was that France and Britain won an unintentional war of attrition. The Allied generals, squandering their men on ill-devised offensives and adding to the losses in tactically inept retreats, had contrived for the enemy to run out of men first. The Americans had tipped the strategic balance. But the slaughter, before their arrival in Europe, had sapped the military strength of all the belligerent nations and made Germany vulnerable to the sudden influx of a new fighting force. Haig's optimism had been vindicated at the cost of more than a million dead soldiers of the British Empire.

The effective German defeat on the Western Front reduced the fears that, after Brest-Litovsk, the Kaiser would come to some agreement with the new Russian government and, in conjunction with

Turkey, begin to menace British India. But it did not prevent the Allies hoping, albeit in vain, for the victory of the Tsar's 'White Russians' over the forces of the new regime. There were material as well as ideological reasons for their opposition to the revolutionary government. The West needed Carpathian and Ukrainian oil and millions of tons of military stores had been landed at Murmansk and Archangel. The stores became the pretext for the despatch of expeditionary forces which offered moral support and military assistance to the remnants of the Russian Imperial forces. The true attitude of the West was revealed by Clemenceau, who, in August 1918, told his Cabinet that he proposed 'not only to continue the struggle against the Central Powers but to encircle Bolshevism and bring about its downfall'.[40] Lloyd George's policy was more romantic but equally unrealistic. His hope was that a democratic rising in Siberia would lead to an irresistible demand for the creation of a representative government. All that was 'needed was somebody to help organise and inspire such a movement, someone like Chinese Gordon* with a streak of genius in him'.[41]

In the absence of such a hero, the future of the Tsar and his family grew ever more precarious. It was the Prime Minister who initiated the meeting with George V's private secretary at which, for a second time, 'it was generally agreed that the proposal that we should receive the Emperor in this country . . . could not be refused'. When Lloyd George proposed that the King should place a house at the Romanovs' disposal he was told that only Balmoral was available and that it was 'not a suitable residence at this time of year'.[42] But it transpired that the King had more substantial objections to the offer of asylum. He 'begged' (a remarkably unregal verb) the Foreign Secretary 'to represent to the Prime Minister that, from all he hears and reads in the press, the residence in this country of the ex-Emperor and Empress would be strongly resented by the public and would undoubtedly compromise the position of the King and Queen'.[43] It was the hereditary monarch, not the radical politician, who left the Russian royal family to the mercy of the Bolsheviks and execution in Ekaterinburg.

August 1918 had not – despite the imminence of victory – been one

---

*General Charles Gordon had made his reputation working for the Emperor of China. He became a British hero by disobeying orders and dying in Khartoum rather that evacuating the garrison.

of Lloyd George's happiest months.★ Hankey found him 'in a curious frame of mind' – which he attributed to the most unworthy of causes. 'I believe at bottom he is supremely jealous of the position which Clemenceau has won in consequence of recent French success. He is also jealous of the position which President Wilson will achieve when the peaces comes.'[45] They were the men with whom he would have to negotiate the 'new world order' and decide the place which, when the war was won, the defeated Central Powers should occupy in the community of nations. In the black mood of August in London he took up the position which he was to pursue, with disastrous consequences, during the treaty negotiations in Paris. Even Hankey was shocked.

> Lloyd George, under the stimulus of our remarkable military success, showed a very hard attitude, talking of judgements and penalties. I fear he may over-rate our power and miss securing a good peace which will, as far as possible, remove bones of contention . . . [He] is out for blood and wants to give Germany a thorough hiding. In fact he actually used the term 'destroy Germany' as punishment for the atrocities by land and sea.[46]

In Manchester, on 12 September, he was in a more conciliatory mood. Germany 'freed from military domination' must be a member of the League of Nations which President Wilson hoped to create. The more emollient passages of the Manchester speech – delivered when he accepted the freedom of the city in which he was born – did not attract public attention. Newspapers noted the aphorism which followed the promise to improve the nation's health: 'You cannot maintain an A1 Empire with a C3 population.' However, they ignored the strange image which implied that, when the war was over, politics would take on a new shape and form. He did not propose to return to 'the sheds where the various party machines have rusted'.

After December 1916, Lloyd George had no party machine – rusty or burnished bright – at his disposal. By the time of the Manchester speech he had made up his mind to lead 'a Lloyd George coalition' into a general election which would not be long delayed, had decided how to

---

★All in all, August 1918 was not Lloyd George's finest hour. During the month he wrote a series of particularly toe-curling 'love letters' to Frances Stevenson, one of which ends with the hope that she will grow to love him 'as much as if [he] were a grilled kidney swimming in fat'.[44]

identify the MPs who would go to Westminster on his coat-tails and had begun to marshal his forces. Perhaps he intended to deal with the future of party politics during the evening speech which he should have made to the Manchester Reform Club, an essentially Liberal organisation. But, during the afternoon, Lloyd George declared himself too ill to complete the day's programme. He had caught influenza. The flu epidemic of 1918 claimed some 150,000 lives in Britain. Fortunately Lloyd George recovered after being confined to bed for nine days – spent in a committee room at the front of Manchester Town Hall which had been turned into his exclusive sanatorium. He left before he had fully recovered and travelled to London in the care of Sir William Milligan, an ear, nose and throat specialist, and wearing a respirator to assist his breathing. It was in Manchester that he received the news that the troops in the Salonika bridgehead – whom, he had long believed, could play a decisive part in the war – had routed the Turks and Bulgarians in a major contribution to the now inevitable victory.

For the next six weeks the Allies made steady gains. On 3 November, Prince Max of Baden – the new and moderate Chancellor of Germany – telegraphed a message to Woodrow Wilson. He was ready to negotiate peace terms on the basis of the Fourteen Points. It took some days for the Allies to decide how punitive the armistice should be. The European leaders, afraid that Wilson would act alone and conscious that the Fourteen Points might be used to justify a peace which did not dismantle the German war machine, sent the President a message which Lloyd George had drafted. It began with a tribute to the 'lofty sentiments' on which American policy was based and then expressed concern that an interim agreement might 'not prevent the enemy from taking advantage of the suspension of hostilities to place himself, at the expiration of an armistice not followed by peace, in a better situation than at the moment of suspension of hostilities'.[47] In the War Cabinet, he described his position in less diplomatic (and clearer) language. He believed that

> We ought to go on until Germany is smashed, that we ought to force our way into German soil and put Germany at our mercy, that we should actually dictate terms on German soil . . . The enemy should be shown that war cannot be made with impunity.[48]

The armistice, punitive but signed on French soil, was still two days away when the Prime Minister spoke at the Lord Mayor of London's banquet. He was in good health and humour. The Allied advance was, he said, moving forward at such speed that the Kaiser's emissaries – hurrying to surrender to Marshal Foch – had lost their way in a Europe where maps changed by the minute. Thirty-six hours later, encouraged by the Archbishop of Canterbury's sermon, which described the subdued mood of Sunday as 'the hush before the dawn', a small crowd assembled in Downing Street and was rewarded by an impromptu statement from the Prime Minister. 'At eleven o'clock this morning, the war will be over. We have won a great victory and we are entitled to a bit of shouting.'[49]

The official announcement was made in the House of Commons. In contravention of all precedent and in clear breach of the standing orders, the whole House – including Asquith, whom he had deposed almost two years earlier – rose and cheered the entrance of the Prime Minister. There were more cheers as he summarised the terms of the armistice. Clause XIX, headed 'Reparation for Damage Done', was received with particular enthusiasm. The brief precis completed, he explained the brevity of the statement. 'This is no time for words. Our hearts are too full of gratitude to which no tongue can give adequate expression.'

Then the House of Commons, followed by the House of Lords, marched in solemn procession to St Margaret's, the parish church of Parliament, and gave heartfelt thanks for victory. At the head of the column, Lloyd George and Asquith walked side by side. Together they listened to Isaiah's promise: 'He hath sent me to bind up the broken hearted, to proclaim liberty to the captives and the opening of the prison to them that are bound.'

The war was over, but one battle had yet to be won. The final phase in the war of attrition between Prime Minister and Commander-in-Chief is described in Field Marshal Haig's war diary. It follows news of his invitation to the victory parade.

Later I heard that I was to be in the fifth carriage along with General Henry Wilson. I felt that this was more of an insult than I could put up with, even from the PM. For the past 3 years I have effaced myself because I felt that to win the war, it was essential that the British and French Armies work well together. And in consequence I have patiently submitted to Lloyd George's conceit and swagger . . . I have no intention of taking part in any triumphal ride with Foch and a pack of foreigners . . . merely to add to LG's importance and help him in his election campaign.[50]

If contributing to Lloyd George's importance and winning a general election were the objects of the victory parade, it was an unnecessary addition to what was the already inevitable result of Germany's defeat. Lloyd George was a hero and, for the moment, politically invincible.

CHAPTER 30

A LAND FIT FOR HEROES

Neither of the wartime coalitions – Asquith's in 1915 or Lloyd George's a year later – had been formed in circumstances which allowed much time for speculation about the future. The principal aim of both governments had been victory over Germany. The politicians calculated what influence immediate events would have on their long-term success and survival. But the long term was not something about which – from the beginnings of their bipartisan leaderships – Asquith and Lloyd George plotted and pined. Asquith expected the normal party battles to resume with the peace and assumed that he would lead the Liberals into the post-war general election. Lloyd George – disowned by almost the entire Liberal leadership – seemed to occupy a lonely eminence. When Germany was defeated, the Unionists would not need him and the Liberals would not have him back. The idea of retiring like a Welsh Cincinnatus had no appeal. He did not see his wartime leadership as his own version of supreme sacrifice. Instead he dreamed of a new political order. Bringing it about had to wait until the Kaiser was defeated.

Lloyd George was a coalition man. And, despite setbacks which he blamed on the generals, it seemed, as the war progressed, that the coalition had proved a success. Not only had politicians worked together, the people had followed their lead. Old prejudices and outdated practices had been abandoned in the pursuit of victory. The argument for realignment and the emergence of the 'new politics' was strengthened by the condition of the Liberal Party – 'in its old form a thing of the past [which] cannot be galvanised into life'.[1] The danger was not the

death of Liberal England – an idea which gained currency without the
support of much compelling evidence – but the absorption of its radical element into the Labour Party. The eliminating bout to decide who
challenged the Tories in a general election 'might', Lloyd George
believed, 'come to a fight between Henderson and me'. But if, in the
immediate future, people were to be asked to vote for him, he needed
a party. 'You must have candidates. You cannot vote without having
someone to vote for.'[2]

It is not clear when he began to make plans. The end of the war was
sudden and unexpected. In the spring of 1918 – with victory barely six
months away – Lord Northcliffe made the gloomy prediction that
'none of us will live to see the end of this war', a judgement which was
no more than an exaggerated expression of the pessimism which
afflicted much of the nation.[3] In July, General Henry Wilson forecast
(with more authority) that the decisive battle was still a year away.[4]
During the following month, Jan Christiaan Smuts told the War
Cabinet that, to obtain a ceasefire on acceptable terms, Britain would
have to fight on until 1920.[5] But, as early as July 1917, Lloyd George was
preparing policies for peace and, since it is inconceivable that he
expected them to be implemented by anyone else, he was already planning to lead a post-war coalition.

In July 1917 a new Ministry of Reconstruction had been created with
Christopher Addison at its head. It was a demotion from the Ministry
of Munitions. His annual salary was reduced from £5000 to £2000 a
year. But he was the right man for the new job. He was a genuine radical – a status confirmed by his evolution into a Cabinet minister in
both the MacDonald and the Attlee governments. So he was temperamentally suited to formulating idealistic plans which were unlikely to be
realised. In the autumn he began to examine the repeal of the Poor Law
and its replacement with what Beatrice Webb described as 'all the conclusions of the Minority Report of the Poor Law Commission'.[6] The
decision to endorse her views on the future of social security did not
change her opinion of the Prime Minister, who 'did not impress
favourably in spite of his flattering friendliness. He is a blatant intriguer
and every word he says is in the nature of an offer to "do a deal". He
neither likes you nor dislikes you. You are a mere instrument, one
among many, sometimes of value, sometimes not worth picking up.'[7]
But the radical instinct, although dormant, was not dead. By the
summer of 1918, Addison, with Lloyd George's approval, was working
on a scheme to extend unemployment insurance to all industries and

trades and had overcome opposition to his proposal to subsidise council house building.

Some reform could not wait for the war to end. H. A. L. Fisher, who had made the perilous journey from academe to Parliament, had a distinct philosophy of education. 'The young should not be trusted to the care of sad, melancholy, careworn teachers. The classroom should be a cheerful place.'[8] That conviction inspired his first estimates as President of the Board of Education. An increase of £4 million enabled him to double the pay and triple the pension of every elementary-school teacher. The Education Act which bears his name made fourteen the mandatory 'rather than the permissive' leaving age and gave permission to local education authorities to extend it to fifteen. Pupils who chose to leave at the first opportunity were required to attend 'continuation schools'. It aimed to ensure that 'children and young persons shall not be debarred from receiving the benefits of any form of education by which they are capable of profiting through inability to pay', and it gave practical effect to that noble aspiration by abolishing primary-school fees. After Lloyd George's fall from grace, Fisher attracted the criticism of his New College colleagues for the enthusiasm with which he defended the excesses of the post-war coalition. The economist Lionel Robbins said that Fisher reminded him of 'a man who had unwittingly entered a brothel – and found that he rather enjoyed it'.[9] In fact Fisher represented the progressive spirit which characterised Lloyd George before December 1916. He saw the best in the Prime Minister. 'His animated courage and buoyancy of temper . . . his easy power of confident decision in the most perilous of emergencies injected a spirit of cheerfulness and courage which was of extraordinary value during those anxious years . . . During the war he was at the summit of his brilliant powers.'[10]

The Fisher Education Act had received royal assent on 8 August 1918. The Germans were in full retreat from Amiens. Lloyd George was on his way to attend the National Eisteddfod, an event which he never missed, whatever the demands of politics and Parliament. He remained in Wales for almost three weeks – attending local gatherings and collecting his thoughts about the general election which would swiftly follow the peace. By then he was certainly considering a programme for the post-war government which, he believed, provided an opportunity to abandon both old party alignments and – with the exception of Ireland – outdated divisive policies.

Lloyd George's closest advisers were called to Criccieth. They spent

21 and 22 August discussing a parliamentary programme. The gathering was remembered by the participants for a bathing expedition in the Dwyfor – the Prime Minister in his pink underpants and Lord Milner fully dressed. But the choice of participants was more surprising than their method of recreation. Although a Coalitionist Liberal Group had been formed after the Maurice debate, Addison was the only practising Liberal politician among the planning group which met in Criccieth. Leo Amery had become a Tory MP for Birmingham Sparkbrook but he, like Philip Kerr, was invited to the meeting in his capacity as Milner's protégé. Hankey was highly political but not a politician. The rest were 'experts'. They concluded that when the war was over, politicians and public should be reunited behind a programme based on public health.

Lloyd George returned to London on 28 August, where the police, for the first and only time in their history, were on strike. The issue which underlay the dispute was pay, which had fallen behind wages in comparable occupations. But the occasion of the walkout was the dismissal of PC Tommy Thiel, an old soldier who had become a voluntary organiser of the technically illegal police union. The Metropolitan Commissioner was confident that the strike call would be ignored. He was wrong. Guardsmen were diverted from ceremonial duties to protect public buildings and the War Cabinet was called into emergency session. Unhelpfully it insisted that the strike must be ended without the union being recognised. By the evening of 30 August, twelve thousand policemen had 'withdrawn their labour'. Lloyd George decided on a personal intervention. A meeting was arranged through the good offices of an intermediary, Charles Duncan MP, chairman of the General Workers Union and honorary president of the 'illegal' National Union of Police and Prison Officers. The Prime Minister employed the technique which he had perfected when dealing with strikes at the Board of Trade – make the least concessions necessary and give assurances which, on careful analysis, turn out to offer less than first seemed the case.

If the men returned at once to work, pay would be generously increased and Thiel would be reinstated, but *in wartime* the police were as vital as the armed forces to national security. So the 1918 strike must end. The policemen – certainly patriotic and equally naive – accepted their special obligation and assumed that the Prime Minister's analysis meant that trade union membership and the possibility of strikes which went with it would be acceptable when the peace returned. After the meeting, the union leaders – some of them policemen, others advisers from longer-established organisations – addressed the strikers. James Carmichael, the chairman of the London Trades Council, told them – in awed tones – 'You have been received by the Prime Minister of England.'[11] He was clearly not in a mood to cross-examine Lloyd George about the real meaning of the government's assurances. So when he addressed a mass meeting on Tower Hill, he promised no more than that an 'authorised organisation . . . framed on your present union . . . will deal with every grievance you have got'.[12] The assembled policemen cheered and returned to work.

After 'settling the police strike, Lloyd George was in the highest of spirits'. Earlier in the day, there had been 'much talk of a general election' fought on the issue 'who is to run the war?' By the evening, in more sober mood, he had begun to consider the problems of peace. He had just received the results of the new recruiting drive. 'Only 750,000 out of 2,000,000 men are fit for service . . . In the districts devoted to the Cotton industry, the men showed distinct signs of decay after 30 instead of after 50.' His thoughts were turning to post-war reconstruction. 'I shall make it plain that I shall not be a party to the continuance of such a condition of affairs.'[13] By then, he had no doubt that he would be chosen to lead the nation in peace as he had led it in war.

That summer – when victory seemed far away – ministers had considered the possibility of Britain going to the polls before the fighting ended. In September, a National Election Committee was set up. Eight years had passed since the last general election and the franchise had been radically changed by the 1918 Representation of the People Act. The additions to the register – including women over thirty years of age – had almost trebled the size of the electorate. The Parliament which was leading the nation's fight against 'the Prussian military junta' was no longer representative of the people it claimed to serve – including many servicemen who had been too young to vote before the war. Universal adult suffrage – always, for Lloyd George, an aspiration if not an imperative – had become irresistible. The prospect of a wartime general election hardened the idea, already in Lloyd George's mind, that the coalition might be given an extended, even indefinite, life. His experience at the Ministry of Munitions – when the recruitment of businessmen to head ministries had much improved the government's performance – had reinforced the old belief that competence is sometimes more important than party allegiance.

Lloyd George was not alone in believing that the old order must change. On 5 May 1918, Bonar Law – writing to Arthur Balfour about the continuation of the coalition – told him, 'Our party, on the old lines, will never have any future in this country.'[14] That convinced him that, despite the Prime Minister's holding views on Irish Home Rule and tariff reform with which he did not agree, the Unionists should fall in behind Lloyd George's leadership. The alternative was a realignment which might destroy the Conservatives. 'It would obviously suit his view if the Party's solidarity all round was broken and I fancy that he would personally like nothing better than that there should be a split in our party and that a majority should support him.'[15] That was the defensive – the negative – argument for keeping the temporary partnership alive. But there were more positive reasons for hanging together – and one precedent. Lloyd George 'would have the same attitude towards the Conservatives as Joe Chamberlain – with the difference that he would be leader of it [sic]. He brings to his new party fresh blood and extended appeal.' Bonar Law was inclined to think it 'would be not a bad thing for our Party and a good thing for the nation'.[16]

So the ground was prepared for Lloyd George to lead an ecumenical ministry committed to 'war socialism' – a term invented by Alfred Milner, who thought of the government's extended role in the economy as comparable to the policies by which Bismarck had reinvigorated Germany. The economist J. A. Hobson judged that 'The war has advanced state socialism by half a century.'[17] Whether or not an extension of state power amounts to 'socialism' – whatever the qualifying adjective – is the subject of a different book. It is the adjective itself that needs examination. Ignoring it contributed to Lloyd George's downfall. The war had made respectable both government intervention in the economy and public ownership of some essential industries. But in wartime, restrictions on the free economy – like restrictions on personal liberty – are accepted as an unfortunate necessity which should be abandoned whenever peace returns. Bismarck had not impressed either the British trade union movement or British management in the way that he had impressed Lloyd George and Winston Churchill.

Watkin Davies, in a biography published immediately before the Second World War, argued that Lloyd George's radical spirit had died with his uncle in 1914. 'The foundations of his old life at Criccieth were sapped . . . and he was left to his own devices and surrounded by characters whose grip on political principles was even weaker than his own.'[18] The explanation is romantic but unconvincing. Criccieth – as an idea rather than a place – had lost its hold over him long before

Richard Lloyd's death. But one change did come with the war. Until then, ambition had been justified by the belief that it was his destiny to eradicate the grinding poverty which, for the working classes, followed illness, unemployment and old age. In 1916, he found another 'great cause' to sustain his grip on power. His determination to win the war was noble and necessary. But it had nothing to do with the dreams of Criccieth. When the war was over the purpose of his political existence was not so easily defined, and the politician without a philosophy was left without a star by which to steer. From time to time, the radical flame of Lloyd George's early years spluttered back into life. The Land Campaign was briefly revived. He advocated Keynesian remedies for unemployment earlier and with more vigour than any other politician. But there was no consistent objective and no great cause.

The political preparations for peace were certainly built around what eventually became the promise of a 'land fit for heroes'. Addison proposed the complete abolition of the old Poor Law and its replacement with a comprehensive system of social insurance – the minority recommendation of the Royal Commission which had been successfully opposed by John Burns and the Local Government Board in 1908. The renewed attempt at reform was quietly dropped, much to the fury of William Beveridge, and the Local Government Board concentrated on frustrating the introduction of a slum clearance programme built around subsidised local authority houses. The programme survived for a time, largely thanks to Addison. But by announcing that the 'country is ready for a bold move forward under state inspiration', Lloyd George proclaimed the central theme of government policy.[19] 'Bismarckism' and 'war socialism', were the order of the day. By the summer of 1918 – with the duration of the war still in doubt – the official Committee on Policy for Government had agreed a programme which was essentially a continuation of the interventionist programme. There would be subsidies for essential industries and public investment in housing and transport – the policies which had united the nation and would, it hoped, keep the coalition alive.

When the time came to take election preparations seriously, Lloyd George – assuming that his manifesto would be 're-elect the man who won the war' – had to recruit six hundred candidates who would support him. He had always known that support could be solidified by the identification of a common enemy. So he disqualified the ninety-eight Liberals who had voted against the government at the end of the Maurice debate and therefore jeopardised the war effort by calling his integrity into question. It was a clear indication that he was preparing to cut the painter which, with varying degrees of tension, had moored him to the Liberal Party for thirty years.

Deciding on which MPs to reject was easier than selecting which candidates to support. Unionists who had been selected to fight vulnerable Liberals resented and resisted the proposal that they should step aside. In the end the decision was taken seat by seat in a process which was supervised by Freddie Guest – one of the officers who, in the early years of the war, had reported the shortage of shells but was now the Liberal Chief Whip within the coalition – and Sir George Younger, the chairman of the Conservative Party Organisation. Candidates who received their endorsement received what Asquith, taking his metaphor from wartime food rationing, called 'the coupon' and were not opposed by official nominees from the other coalition party. Timothy Davies wrote a strangely personal letter to Lloyd George, 'begging' for endorsement. It was refused.[20] An exception was made for Asquith who – despite his role in the Maurice debate – was thought to qualify for re-election because of his distinction. When the election came, the electors of East Fife took a different view. Asquith lost his seat.

Initially, 'coupons' were to be offered to ninety-eight Liberals. At Lloyd George's insistence the Liberal quota was increased to one hundred and fifty, and the Labour apostates who stayed in the government were added to the list. The Labour Party had been uneasy about participation in the coalition since the beginning of the year. It was attracted by Addison's reconstruction proposals but unhappy about the suppression of the Irish Nationalists, the clear antagonism towards the Soviet Union and the pressure which had been exerted on the trade unions in order to secure the abandonment of rights and responsibilities which were, traditionally, theirs. There was also an ideological objection to cooperation. At the beginning of the year, the Sheffield Trades Council had submitted a resolution to the 1918 Labour Party conference which expressed the position of much of the rank and file. 'Seeing that the chief political function of the working class is the destruction of the ruling capitalist order . . . no member of the Labour Party should accept any position in any government representative of the capitalist parties.'[21] As a compromise, the National Executive had endorsed Henderson's recommendation that Labour members should leave the coalition as soon as the war ended and, when approached about peacetime cooperation, the party had accepted Bernard Shaw's advice and replied, 'Nothing doing.' Lloyd George's public wrath against the Labour leadership was terrible. 'They pulled Labour out of the Government . . . What they really believed in was Bolshevism.'[22] But when the election came, he told his wife, 'I hope the Labourites will get more [seats] than the Asquithians.'[23]

There were still individual egos to be massaged. Asquith was sounded out to see if – after the election was won – he would join the reformed coalition. His refusal 'to take second place' in 1916 cannot have made Lloyd George optimistic about the chances of the invitation being accepted. There are three versions of the way in which the approach was made. Lloyd George wrote that he *offered* Asquith the office of Lord Chancellor and a place in the peace conference delegation. It seems more likely that, at most, he made a neutral enquiry about Asquith's inclinations. Margot Asquith claimed that he merely said, 'I understand that you don't want to take a post in the government.'[24] Whatever message went from the Prime Minister to his predecessor, Asquith denied all interest in returning to government.

Winston Churchill, the stormy petrel of that and several other administrations, did not emulate Asquith's calm dignity. On 6 November, with peace less than a week away, he and Edwin Montagu – the government's two most senior Liberal members – were invited to Downing Street to discuss the political prospects. 'Winston', wrote Montagu, was 'sulky, morose and unforthcoming' – the result of his fear that the peacetime Cabinet would be no larger than its wartime predecessor and that, as a result, he would still be excluded.[25] When Lloyd George assured him that he meant to return to the traditional numbers, 'the sullen look disappeared and smiles aerated the hungry face. The fish was not quite landed.'[26] Next day, anxiety combined with arrogance still prompted Churchill to warn the Prime Minister that 'I feel I cannot choose my own course without knowing who your chief colleagues would be.'[27] Lloyd George's reply was one of history's great political rebukes.

> Your letter came upon me as an unpleasant surprise. Frankly it perplexes me. It suggests that you contemplate leaving the government and you give no reason for it beyond an apparent dissatisfaction with your own personal prospects . . . I have fully recognised your capacity and you know that at the cost of a great deal of dissatisfaction among many of my supporters I placed you in the Ministry of Munitions.

Then, having reminded Churchill of his precarious position within the government, Lloyd George made the damning accusation. Churchill's letter, he wrote, made clear that, for him, 'National interests are completely overshadowed by personal concern.'[28]

Churchill should have realised that the Prime Minister had begun to govern with the confidence which came from the knowledge that he was, at least for the moment, in indisputable command. A week earlier, Lloyd George had discovered that the electoral register had not been brought up to date, and, in consequence, proposed to dismiss W. Hayes Fisher, the Unionist President of the Local Government Board, with a letter of calculated brutality. When Bonar Law suggested that the deed might be done more delicately, he replied, '[I] don't mind if he is drowned in Malmsey Wine, but he must be dead chicken by midnight'.[29] Lloyd George was in charge. All that was left was for the parties formally to endorse a continuing agreement.

The path had been prepared by a letter which Lloyd George had sent to Bonar Law on 2 November 1918. It was not overburdened with policy details. 'I recognise that there must be some statement of policy and a statement of such a nature as will retain, to the greatest extent, the support of your followers and mine. My fundamental object will be to promote the unity and development of the British Empire.' However, he did 'not think it necessary to consider in detail how the programme is to be carried out' – except for three items about which it was essential for the Liberal Prime Minister to reassure his Unionist followers. 'The policy of Imperial Preference as defined in the Resolution of the Imperial Conference' would continue. The Welsh Churches Bill could not be repealed, but some of its financial clauses – the abolition of what the young Lloyd George had denounced as a free people's subsidy of an alien Church – could be re-examined. Home Rule, as agreed, had passed into law before the war began, but Ulster would not be coerced into subservience to Dublin. Bonar Law, realising the impact that the reassurances would have, kept the letter and its contents secret until the Unionist MPs met on 12 November, the day after the armistice was signed. Then he read it to them. As he anticipated, its contents were unanimously endorsed. But he made sure of its acceptance with a speech which implied both that the Prime Minister had become the Unionists' creation and that he was too powerful to disown.

> We have made Lloyd George the flag bearer of the very principles on which we should appeal to the country. It is not his Liberal friends, it is the Unionist Party which has made him Prime Minister. Remember that at this moment Mr Lloyd George commands as

great an amount of influence in every constituency as has ever been exercised by a Prime Minister in political history.[30]

On the same day, at a gathering of Liberal MPs and party activists, H. A. L. Fisher, whose political purity was beyond question, moved a resolution proposing continued membership of the coalition. Lloyd George supported it in a speech that gave his own interpretation of the November letter – which, unlike Bonar Law, he did not read to his followers. It was, he said, 'the reactionaries who I'm afraid of'.[31] And he justified his fear with a thoroughly Liberal – indeed Nonconformist – view of the peace negotiations which were to follow. 'We must not allow any sense of revenge, any spirit of greed, any grasping desire to overrule the spirit of righteousness.'[32] No doubt he had changed his mind since, a week earlier, he had dined with General Wilson, Winston Churchill and F. E. Smith. According to Wilson, they 'discussed many things but principally the general election' and the CIGS added, 'Lloyd George wants to shoot the Kaiser. FE agrees. Winston does not.'[33]

The King wanted the general election to be delayed until the public bitterness towards Germany and the desire for revenge had faded. But the Prime Minister insisted on going to the country in the warm afterglow of victory. The election was held on 12 December after a brief campaign which concentrated on the record of the wartime coalition. Lloyd George's few speeches vacillated between severity and emollience. Other members of the coalition did not match his ambivalence. George Barnes, once a Labour man, wanted to hang the Kaiser, and Eric Geddes promised to squeeze Germany 'until the pips squeak'. Even though he made only six speeches, there were moments when the voice of the old Lloyd George was heard in the land. At Wolverhampton, his first meeting, he asked and answered the question which was to characterise the election and haunt him for the rest of his premiership. 'What is our task? To make Britain a fit country for heroes to live in.' In Newcastle he commended the record of the coalition but also complained of being 'surrounded by a reactionary bodyguard [which kept him] from moving too far'.[34] He made obeisance to the newly enfranchised women by insisting that Mrs Pankhurst be allowed to speak on Liberal platforms.[35]

Only two speeches dealt in any detail with the treatment of the vanquished foe. In London he promised 'a sternly just peace', and in Bristol he extended the idea with a promise which, during the years ahead, was to cause him endless anguish. It was then that he guaranteed that

Germany would be required to pay compensation or reparations (the Allies were not sure which) 'to the limit of its capacity'.[36] His sin was not so much making the speeches – which were never worse than exaggerations of what was right and possible – but his failure either to forbid or disown the expression of opinions which he knew represented the desire for punishment and revenge.

Seventeen parties claimed to be represented in the 1918 Parliament. Included among them were the Coalition Conservatives (332 Members), Coalition Liberals (127 Members), Coalition National Democrats (9 Members) and Coalition Labour (4 Members). Sinn Fein's 93 Members did not take their seats; Labour held 57 seats and Independent Labour 2 more. For the moment, Lloyd George was invincible – adding to Hankey's October fear that he was 'assuming too much the role of a dictator [and] heading for very serious trouble'.[37] But his dictatorial instincts – neglecting the House of Commons and ignoring the Cabinet – were constrained by the reality of the strange alliance which he had fashioned. Lloyd George held the Unionist Party captive. But he was also the Unionist Party's prisoner.

CHAPTER 31

SPOILS TO THE VICTORS

The destroyer which carried the British delegates to France and the peace conference on 11 January 1919 was heavy laden. Lloyd George, Balfour and the variety of ministers and dominion prime ministers who set out for Paris were accompanied by 750 civil servants and expert advisers.* One of them was John Maynard Keynes of the Treasury. For the rest of the century Keynes was to have a dominant influence on history's judgement on the eventual treaty. His analysis of its results was coloured by his patrician contempt for the principal peacemakers. Clemenceau he regarded as a savage who 'took a different view as to the nature of civilised man' from the one which was accepted in polite society.[1] Wilson he regarded as 'a blind and deaf Don Quixote'.[2] But it was Lloyd George – the man who held the balance between the idealistic but unrealistic Wilson and the pragmatic but vengeful Clemenceau – who, in Keynes's view, carried the greatest burden of guilt for imposing a 'Carthaginian peace' on the defeated Germans. Keynes later modified his opinion of both the treaty and Lloyd George. But it was too late to moderate the damage done by the absurd rhetorical question which he asked about the Prime Minister. 'How can I convey any just impression of this extraordinary figure of our time, this siren, this goat-footed bard, this half-human visitor to our age from the hag-ridden enchanted woods of Celtic antiquity?'[3] His less colourful description of the delegates *en masse* was more accurate.

---

*At the end of the Napoleonic Wars, Wellington and Castlereagh took seventeen advisers to the Congress of Vienna.

The future life of Europe was not their concern. Its means of livelihood was not their anxiety. Their preoccupations, good and bad alike, related to frontiers and nationalities, to the balance of power, to imperial aggrandisement, to the future enfeeblement of a strong and dangerous enemy, to revenge and to the shifting, by the victors, of their own unbearable financial burdens on to the shoulders of the defeated.[4]

Lloyd George's conduct during the negotiation of the peace treaty is difficult to defend. He went to Paris with no clear idea of what was either desirable for the future peace of the world or necessary to recompense Britain for the cost of the war and neutralise the demands for retribution. He possessed neither a guiding principle nor the full confidence of the politicians on whom he depended. So he veered wildly between attempts to create a new world order and endorsement of a settlement designed to propitiate the vengeful victors, incapacitate 'the Prussian war machine' and ensure that Germany was never again a threat to peace. Temperament as well as judgement allowed him only one way of dealing with the popular demand that Germany should pay the full cost of the war. He tried to broker a compromise between reason and prejudice. It was that which made Keynes find 'in his company, that flavour of final purposelessness, inner irresponsibility, existence outside or away from Saxon good and evil, mixed with cunning, remorselessness and love of power' which fascinated even his most bitter critics.[5]

It is not necessary to agree with Keynes's bitter analysis of Lloyd George's character to accept that he was temperamentally unsuited to the demands of a long and tedious peace conference. He was not at his best in a council of equals. He liked to be firmly in charge or to lead an open rebellion against the establishment. Paris allowed neither. Yet, because of his domination of his own delegation, history has, rightly, held him responsible for the British position.

Lloyd George had not wanted the conference to be held in Paris, but France – reminding the Allies which nation had suffered most in the war – insisted on deciding the venue. In consequence Georges Clemenceau was in the chair and, at the first meeting of the Council of Ten (the Supreme War Council plus representatives of Japan and, in effect, the conference's executive arm) announced an immediate adjournment until he had decided the order of business. From then on power was concentrated in fewer and fewer hands. Small nations were relegated to membership of commissions that reported to the council, which shrank to eight (when Italy walked out after its claim to Fiume★ was rejected), six (when Japan simply ceased to attend) and three when Lloyd George, Woodrow Wilson and Clemenceau decided they could make better progress without the support of their foreign ministers. The rules were made up as the meetings went along. The delegates had arrived in Paris with nothing to guide them except the knowledge that Germany had signed the armistice in the belief (and after the assurance) that the peace treaty which followed would be based on Woodrow Wilson's Fourteen Points. It was an assurance which the delegates, eventually including Wilson himself, chose to betray.

The Fourteen Points were never, in their entirety, accepted by America's allies. Point Two demanded 'the freedom of the seas' – a direct denial of the Royal Navy's historic right to stop and board ships anywhere in the world. Point Three called for the 'removal of trade barriers' – far too dangerous a concept to be endorsed by the leader of a coalition which hung together because of the half acceptance of Imperial Preference. And seven of Wilson's points demanded or implied support for 'autonomous development' or 'self-determination'. Nobody in Europe believed in that. It would create a dangerous instability and prohibit the spoils of war being distributed among the victors.

The French plan for the emasculation of Germany redrew the boundaries of the Fatherland without reference to the ethnic origins or historic allegiance of the people whose nationality was changed. Italy expected to acquire parts of the Dalmatian coast. Britain anticipated confirmation of its control over the Mesopotamian oilfields and had agreed to French suzerainty in Syria as a quid pro quo. The dominion governments had laid claim to various territories in Africa and the Pacific Ocean. Many of the proposed boundary changes had already been enshrined in small treaties. 'Sykes–Picot' had divided up Asia Minor between Britain, France and Russia. 'London' had guaranteed Italy its share of the Ottoman Empire. 'St-Jean-de-Maurienne' had added parts of Austria to Italy's booty. Japan had been promised the Chinese province of Shantung in return for a Japanese destroyer squadron supporting Mediterranean convoys. Most of the treaties had been negotiated in secret, in direct defiance of Woodrow Wilson's Point One – the obligation for relations between states to be determined by 'open covenants, openly arrived at'.

The Europeans' concerns had been increased by a speech which the

---

★The seaport that, today, is known as Rijeka and belongs to Croatia.

President had made to clarify his intentions. 'Self-determination is no mere phrase. It is a principle of action which statesmen ignore at their peril.' The disturbing discovery that Woodrow Wilson meant what he said alarmed the already resentful Europeans, who, even when they had thought the talk of a new world order was just window dressing, had been affronted by his presumption. Clemenceau confirmed that, like him, Lloyd George had not been consulted about the President's prescription for lasting peace and asked 'Fourteen points? Why fourteen points? The Good Lord only needed ten.'[6] They joined with Prime Minister Orlando of Italy to send a warning letter to the White House. It was far from frank. There was no explicit rejection of the proposition that the boundaries of the new Europe should be determined by the wishes of the people within them. At Britain's request, the letter recorded reservations about 'freedom of the seas' and it reaffirmed the demand that 'compensation be made by Germany for all the damage done to civilian property of the Allies and their families'.[7] The letter ended with the qualified assurance that, although the signatories' support should not be taken for granted, subject to their stated reservations and requirements being accepted, the European leaders were willing 'to make peace with the Government of Germany on the terms of peace laid down by the President's Address to Congress of July 8 1918 and the principles of peace laid down in subsequent addresses'.[8] That was a lie. The commitment to self-determination was enough in itself to ensure that the Fourteen Points would never be accepted in undiluted form.

Within weeks, Clemenceau had made his true position brutally clear. A settlement of European boundaries which left Germany in more or less her pre-war shape and size would never be agreed by France. When he suspected that Lloyd George was sympathetic to the Fourteen Points, he told him,

> If I accepted what you propose as ample for the security of France after the millions who have died and the millions who have suffered, I believe – indeed I hope – that my successor in office would take me by the nape of the neck and have me shot.[9]

Lloyd George was forced to clarify his position by the discovery that the loosely worded proposal for compensation produced a payment formula which worked against British interests. 'Reparations' are defined as 'compensation for war damage . . . the act of repairing or being repaired'. More than a quarter of France's productive capacity had been destroyed and 40,000 square miles of French territory had been devastated. Britain had lost merchant shipping and the property which had been damaged and demolished by sporadic Zeppelin raids and the occasional (and generally ineffective) bombardment of coastal towns. France would be awarded 90 per cent of reparations. Lloyd George therefore argued for 'indemnities' instead.

So, the disputes over boundaries and compensation – with Woodrow Wilson insisting that there could be no treaty unless it included the creation of a League of Nations – ensured that the peace conference droned on. And while the politicians argued, Germany starved. British troops were demanding demobilisation and French soldiers were leaving their units and returning home. The only way in which the Allies could ensure that Germany accepted the terms of the eventual treaty was to maintain the naval blockade. General Plumer, officer in command of the British Army of Occupation, telegraphed the War Office with desperate news. 'The mortality among women, children and the sick is most grave and sickness, due to hunger, is spreading. The attitude of the population is becoming one of despair and people feel that an end by bullets is preferable to death by starvation.'[10] Frances Stevenson, in Paris as Lloyd George's secretary and therefore an official member of the British delegation, feared that in Germany 'the rations allowed for a whole day are not enough to make what we should consider a decent breakfast. The people have practically no clothes and their mental capacity has decreased by 60% owing to privation.'[11] What Frances – by then the Dowager Countess Lloyd George – wrote fifty years later about life in post-war Europe suggests that Lloyd George was not oppressed by concern for the starving enemy. 'LG used to say that the happiest time of his life was the six months he spent in Paris during the Conference . . . He enjoyed the fray of the conference table and was able to indulge to his heart's content in entertaining.'[12] No doubt. But he also found the company in which he had to do six or eight hours' business every day extremely uncongenial.

Lloyd George heartily disliked Clemenceau. At their first meeting he had picked an unnecessary quarrel with the French Prime Minister in the hope that a demonstration of aggression would act as a deterrent to future disagreements. The trick – which was invariably effective in Welsh magistrates' courts – had not worked and dislike had escalated into animosity. He thought Clemenceau a 'disagreeable and bad-tempered old savage' who, despite his large head, 'had no dome of benevolence, reverence or kindliness'.[13] Clemenceau had an equally low opinion of Lloyd George, who – he believed – knew nothing about the world beyond Great Britain, lacked a formal education and 'was not an English gentleman'.[14] Both men, however, were united by their irritation at the high moral tone of the 'little sermonettes' with which Wilson accompanied every declaration of American policy. But, as with every other aspect of the Paris conference – policy as well as personalities – Lloyd George's attitude towards the American President was bewilderingly ambivalent. When Wilson had doubts about attending the peace conference, Lloyd George told him that his 'presence [was] necessary for the proper organisation of the world which must follow the peace'.[15] When the President arrived in Paris, Lloyd George rejected his definition of reparations and, as often as not, sided with Clemenceau in the arguments over national boundaries.

No doubt Lloyd George – the champion of small nations during 'Joe's War' in South Africa – retained some residual sympathy for the minorities whom Wilson aimed to protect. But his real concern was with an aspect of the Paris negotiations with which both the Ten Commandments and the Fourteen Points dealt only obliquely – money. Somehow a way had to be found of adding indemnities to reparations. A possible solution was proposed by General Smuts, who had established a reputation for common sense as well as compassion. His piety so annoyed Lloyd George that, after one of his speeches on the virtues of clemency, the Prime Minister had suggested that he set an example by abandoning Pretoria's claim to German South-West Africa. However, Smuts devised a payments formula which satisfied both Britain and France. The Germans should be asked for no more than recompense for damage done and injury caused, but the calculation should include the cost of pensions paid to war widows and the separation allowances which had been received by the families of soldiers serving overseas. It was an example of the 'web of sophistry and Jesuitical exegesis' which, Keynes wrote, was 'finally to clothe with insincerity the whole treaty'.[16] But if President Wilson could be persuaded to agree, it would solve the problem. It also required the calculated cost of the newly defined reparations to be increased from a reasonable sum to the largest amount possible.

As early as 1916, the British Treasury – apparently more confident of victory than the British generals – had examined the principles on which a calculation of German indebtedness should be based. In the autumn of 1918, it had estimated that an application of those principles might produce a bill as high as £4 billion, but added that Germany was probably incapable of paying more than £3 billion.[17] Keynes, who had led the investigation, suggested that the Allies should demand no more than £2 billion – at 5 per cent rate of interest, £100 million a year until the debt was discharged.* 'If Germany is to be milked, she must not at first be ruined.'[18]

During the general election campaign Lloyd George had spoken of reparations in bellicose generalities. In Bristol he had promised to make Germany pay 'up to the limit of her capacity'. Pressed to be more precise, he had replied, 'I am not going to mislead the country on the question of capacity until I know more about it', but he added, 'if Germany has any greater capacity she must pay to the very last penny'.[19] It was enough to excite hopes of vast subventions. On 26 November, the day after Parliament was dissolved, the War Cabinet agreed to set up a committee to examine the question which the Prime Minister had been unable to answer. Lloyd George's choice of chairman must have been influenced by the knowledge that polling day was less than a month away. He chose William 'Billy' Hughes, the Prime Minister of Australia and the hardest of hardliners, whose idea of a just peace would, according to Lloyd George, 'mean that for two generations we made German workmen our slaves'. Hughes had been infuriated by the Treasury's view that Australia's claims should not be included in the calculation of German indebtedness and, in consequence, had launched a 'Make Germany Pay' campaign which, inevitably, was taken up by the popular press.

Lloyd George must have known that – despite its membership including Lord Cunliffe, an ex-governor of the Bank of England – the committee would come to a wholly unrealistic conclusion. And so it did. On 10 December 1918, fourteen days after Hughes was given the complicated task, he announced that the Allies were entitled to between £24 billion and £25 billion of reparations and that Germany was capable of paying the bill in full at the rate of £1.2 billion a year. Lloyd George's stratagem had created expectations which could not possibly be gratified but which Hughes's committee thought it possible to assuage. Too late, the Prime Minister realised the danger. 'I regarded the conclusion of the Report as a wild and fantastic chimera . . . I was repelled and shocked by the extreme absurdity of this document. In view of the election then proceeding, I decided not to publish it.' What Lloyd George dismissed as 'insane hopes that the enemy would shoulder

---

*Fifty years earlier, the French reparations to the Germans following the Franco-Prussian War had totalled £212 million.

the whole or even a substantial proportion of our heavy war burdens' had become conventional wisdom – even though there was no agreement about what the total burden was.[20] The estimates of total indebtedness had become absurd. France put the figure at £44 billion, the Americans made it £4.4 billion.[21] During discussions of the distribution of reparations, held in the Council of Ten on 20 March 1919, Lloyd George – agonising about reconciling reality and expectation – reminded his colleagues of how difficult it would be 'to disperse the illusions which reign in the public mind. Four hundred Members of Parliament have sworn to exact the last farthing of what is owing to us. I will have to face up to them.'[22] Woodrow Wilson offered a solution to his dilemma which Lloyd George found unattractive. 'Nothing could be finer than to be put out of office during a crisis of this kind for doing what is right. I could not wish for a more magnificent place in history.'[23]

In conversation with Wilson's confidant Colonel House, Lloyd George had already explained that he 'had to have a plausible reason for having fooled [the British people] about the questions of war costs, reparations and what not . . . Germany could not pay anything like the indemnity which the French demanded.'[24] Even the British calculation was wholly unreasonable. So, two arguments proceeded along parallel lines. One, largely theoretical and mostly for public consumption, concerned the total reparation payment. The other, real and earnest, was a dispute about how the total (whatever it was) should be divided between the Allies. France asked for 72 per cent, with Britain receiving 18 per cent and the smaller nations what was left. Britain wanted 30 per cent and suggested that France should receive only 50 per cent. In the end, after four years of haggling, France accepted 52 per cent and Britain accepted 28 per cent – without knowing the value of 100 per cent.

The total sum was to be decided by yet another subcommittee. It reaffirmed that Germany could pay £25 billion but proposed that the Allies should accept £8 billion if the Americans agreed. Wilson would not go beyond £6 billion. Britain wanted to increase the demand to £9.4 billion. Experts devised a new formula by which the total would be set between £5 and £7 billion, but now Lloyd George would not accept a solution that mentioned the lower figure unless it was endorsed by the two financiers on the British delegation – Lord Cunliffe and his equally exacting collaborator Lord Sumner, a partnership known in Paris as 'the heavenly twins'. Otherwise he would be 'crucified'.[25] Eventually it was agreed to omit a total from the treaty. Germany would go on paying until it had discharged its debt – still estimated, in the imagination of the British public, as between £24 billion and £25 billion.

Some progress seemed possible when President Wilson accepted the Smuts suggestion that the definition of reparations should be extended to include war pensions, disability allowances and separation payments, with the explanation, 'Logic! Logic! I don't care a damn for logic. I am going to include pensions.' He realised that 'it was not in the minds of those who drew up the armistice', but including them within the reparations formula was necessary to win Lloyd George's support for the overall package.[26] But there was still an argument about how to share out the total amount. Lloyd George, in turn, accepted France's demand that, if necessary, the repayment period should be extended beyond the initially agreed thirty years. Frances Lamont, the wife of a banker on the American delegation and an assiduous diarist of the conference, recorded her husband's discovery that 'LG does not want anything put in to limit the capacity of the Germans to pay.' Billy Hughes's 'wild and fantastic chimera' had become a member of the British peace conference delegation.

Lloyd George, reflecting British public opinion, was more concerned with money than with boundaries. He had grave doubts about French territorial proposals and feared that they would be accepted by the United States as the price to be paid for agreement on a treaty which included the creation of a League of Nations. Everyone accepted that Alsace–Lorraine should return to France. Indeed, rectifying the wrong done to France in 1871 was the eighth of the Fourteen Points. But France also claimed the coalfields of the Saar and, as part of its policy of protecting its strategic borders, wanted to give away large parts of Germany (and large numbers of Germans) to old allies and the new countries which the treaty would create. The coalfields of Upper Silesia (and four million ethnic Germans) were to be incorporated into Poland. So was Danzig (with half a million German citizens), and the port was to be connected to Warsaw by a 'Polish corridor' which ran through East Prussia. There was some disagreement about how many Germans lived in the Sudetenland. France, and eventually the peace conference, accepted the Czechoslovak calculation and included it in Czechoslovakia.

The most audacious French proposal was that the west bank of the Rhine should become French, be controlled by France or be under French occupation. Marshal Foch canvassed the British delegation. His representations were reported to Curzon (in temporary charge of the Foreign Office while Balfour was in Paris) by Robert Cecil.

Marshal Foch came to see me this afternoon (principally about
Poland) but went on to speak about the necessity for France to hold
the Rhine. He said that the Germans had a population of 75,000,000
and the French and the Belgians combined of 48,000,000.

Very large proportion of male population trained for army.

An excellent general staff.

There was therefore an imminent danger that France might be
attacked in a few years' time.

Russia practically finished.

GB and USA would come to France's aid – but too late.[27]

Foch's demand illustrated the difference between French and British
priorities. His concern was that 'Once more Belgium and Northern
France will be made a field of battle – a field of defeat . . . There is no
English or American help which can be strong enough and arrive in
sufficient time to prevent disaster.'[28] Lloyd George saw the new map of
Europe in economic rather than strategic terms. 'If the Poles won't give
the Germans the product of the mines on reasonable terms the
Germans say they cannot pay the indemnity. Therefore the Allies may
be cutting off their noses to spite their faces.'[29] It had become necessary
to attempt to change the conference's direction towards a conciliatory,
rather than a punitive, settlement.

On 22 March 1919, Lloyd George took his closest advisers – including Kerr, Hankey and Henry Wilson – to Fontainebleau, the pleasant
Paris suburb in which the defeated Napoleon Bonaparte had said his
farewell to his Old Guard. There, in the aptly named Hôtel de France
et d'Angleterre, he plotted another French defeat. His strategy did not
prove as successful as that which Wellington had employed at Waterloo.

In a little over two days, Lloyd George formulated a new policy
from which Kerr constructed what came to be called the 'Fontainebleau
Memorandum'. A prediction of brilliant prescience was followed by a
forecast which (whatever its validity at the time) now seems fatuous.

You may strip Germany of her colonies, reduce her armaments to
a mere police force and her navy to that of a third rate power, all
the same if she feels that she has been unjustly treated in the peace
of 1919, she will find means of exacting retribution from her con-
querors . . . The greatest danger that I see in the present situation
is that Germany may throw in her lot with Bolshevism and place
her resources, her brains, her vast organising powers at the disposal

of the revolutionary fanatics whose dream is to conquer the world for Bolshevism by force of arms.[30]

Lloyd George's Fontainebleau proposals amounted to an adjustment of the French proposals rather than their radical revision. France should annex part, rather than all, of the Saar. The occupation of the Rhineland should be temporary, and France should be compensated for the consequent loss of security by a non-aggression pact with Britain and America which would guarantee their immediate military support were German troops to invade again.

The memorandum offered the Hungarians self-determination. 'There will never be peace in South Eastern Europe if every state now coming into being is to have a large Magyar Irredenta within its boundaries.' The 'corridor' between Warsaw and Danzig should be narrowed but not eliminated. Germany should be admitted to membership of the League of Nations, and the Allies should agree to strict limitations on their armament programmes. Lloyd George had still to make his final disposition on the payment of reparations. At Fontainebleau he contented himself with generalities – knowing that no reasonable figure would satisfy the House of Commons. He did, however, make a concession to reality which he was later to abandon. Germany's obligations should last only for the lifetime of 'the generation which made the War'. Frances Stevenson had no doubt that Lloyd George would impose his wishes on the peace conference. He

arrived back from Fontainebleau with his plans all made. He meant business this week and will sweep all before him. He will stand no more nonsense from French or Americans. He is taking a long view about the Peace and insists that it should be one that will not leave bitterness for years to come and probably another war.[31]

Keynes's congratulations were more guarded. 'LlG was, at least for the time being, taking a turn towards a heaven place and away from a hell place.'[32]

Copies of the memorandum were sent to Woodrow Wilson and Georges Clemenceau. The American President endorsed the proposed revisions with virtually no reservations. The French Prime Minister rejected them with the justified allegation that Lloyd George had proposed a reduction in the spoils of war to be received by France, but not a moderation of the benefits to be enjoyed by Britain. 'If you find the peace too harsh, let us give Germany back her colonies and her fleet and let us not impose upon the continental nations alone – France, Belgium, Bohemia and Poland – the territorial concessions required to appease the beaten aggressor.'[33] What was more, he had no doubt that Lloyd George's claim that Germany would respond to a moderate settlement was 'a sheer illusion'.[34]

Lloyd George was wrong to believe that terms which were 'stern and even ruthless' could be so just 'that the country on which they are imposed will feel in its heart that it has no right to complain'.[35] But he was entitled to hope for 'a peace which, while just, will be preferable to all sensible men to Bolshevism'.[36] Unfortunately other Allied leaders believed that there were better ways of containing Russian Communism. Among them was Winston Churchill – a dove in his attitude towards the defeated Germany, but a hawk in his reaction to the threat which he believed emanated from Moscow. Clemenceau was merciless equally towards Germany and Russia. During the last month of the war he had told the French General Staff, 'The main line of the plan of action which should be adopted is not only to continue the struggle against the Central Powers but to encircle Bolshevism and bring about its downfall.'[37]

The Allies had what the most bellicose among their leaders argued was a legitimate reason for intervening in Russia's domestic affairs. Before the Treaty of Brest-Litovsk had ended the war in Eastern Europe, millions of tons of stores had been landed in Murmansk and Archangel to provide for the Tsarist forces, an Allied base had been established in the east at Vladivostok, and British troops had been transferred from Mesopotamia to occupy Batum on the Black Sea and Baku on the Caspian. The Allied expeditionary forces had landed in Vladivostok, Murmansk and Archangel theoretically to protect and repatriate the armaments and stores. In fact they were intended to give moral support to three White Russian generals – Kornilov, Alexeev and Denikin – who, in defiance of the Moscow Soviets, were fighting on against Germany and were ready to turn on the new Communist government.

The expedition was as unsuccessful as it was misconceived. The British troops grumbled about their demobilisation being delayed. There were fears that the French Army would refuse to fight. 'Not one soldier who saved his head at Verdun and the fields of the Marne will consent to losing it on the fields of Russia.'[38] Foch evacuated Odessa and Sebastopol but proposed a full-scale invasion of Russia by a mixed force of Greeks, Poles, Finns, Czechs and Russian prisoners-of-war.

Lloyd George, who might have objected to the idea on grounds of principle or practicability, chose instead to argue that the cost would be prohibitive. Britain had spent £100 million on the Russian campaign – almost twice as much as France – and it seemed unlikely that Clemenceau would contribute much more. 'I am sure [France] cannot afford to pay. I am sure we cannot. Will America bear the expense? Pin them down on the cost of any scheme before sanctioning it.'[39] His scepticism was fuelled by suspicions about French motives for wanting a return of the Tsarist regime. Russia's pre-war debt to France was 25,000 million francs – to which half as much again had been added in war loans.[40] 'There is nothing they would like better than us to pull their chestnuts out of the fire for them.'[41]

The alternative to containing the spread of Communism by force of arms was a negotiation which ended with an agreement to live in peaceful coexistence. Lloyd George and Woodrow Wilson suggested a meeting. Balfour reported that Clemenceau was 'quite unmoved and unmovable with regard to either inviting or allowing Bolshevik representatives to [visit] Paris'.[42] The meeting eventually took place in Principo, one of the Princes Islands in the Sea of Marmara, where, it was hoped, both White Russians and Communists would meet with low-level representatives of Great Britain and the United States. The Communists accepted the invitation to attend, but ignored the proviso that the negotiations must be preceded by a ceasefire in the various wars between Russia and its neighbours. As a sign of goodwill, they offered the Allies trade agreements and raw materials at preferential rates. Woodrow Wilson was profoundly affronted, Lloyd George almost equally so. He told Philip Kerr, 'We are not after their money or the concessions, or their territory.'[43] They wanted an agreement, tacit or formal, that Moscow would not undermine the governments of democratic Europe.

Clemenceau, using the Paris émigrés as intermediaries, urged the White Russians to boycott Principo. The Unionists within the British coalition – for once in harmony with Churchill – openly expressed their horror of the Moscow Communists being afforded what they called 'official recognition'. Wilson and Lloyd George lost whatever enthusiasm they had for negotiations with the Communists. The President left Paris for a brief visit to Washington. The Prime Minister had to return home to intervene in an industrial dispute. 'Principo', which had been a concept as well as an island, was quietly abandoned.

Churchill occupied the vacuum. At first he told Lloyd George that he

wanted no more than firm leadership – either direct military engagement with the Communists or complete withdrawal from Russia. But,
mercurial as always, he developed a sudden fear of capitulation. While
Lloyd George was in London, he made a dramatic dash to Paris where
he urged Wilson not to take a decision which meant 'No further armed
resistance to the Bolsheviks in Russia and that an interminable vista of
violence and misery was all that remained for the whole of Russia.'[44]
When the Prime Minister returned to Paris, Churchill became 'an
exceedingly pernicious influence on the Cabinet'.[45] Lloyd George's
response to the unauthorised initiative did not reflect the master-and-
servant relationship which was said to be the basis of the two men's
partnership. Indeed it was not consistent with a Prime Minister's proper
attitude towards a member of his Cabinet. When Churchill told him
about his Paris initiative, instead of ordering an immediate return home,
he merely expressed 'alarm at [the] . . . telegram about planning a war
against the Bolsheviks. The Cabinet has never authorised such a proposition.' He then 'begged' rather than instructed Churchill 'not to commit
the country to what would be a mad enterprise out of hatred for the
Bolsheviks'.[46] Prime ministers who beg are unlikely to get their way.

Lloyd George was growing weary of the long negotiation process.
His complaint against Churchill – 'He wants to conduct a war against
the Bolsheviks. That would cause a revolution. Our people would
never permit it' – does not suggest that he had any strong view on
either the morality or practicality of intervention.[47] His attitude was a
symptom of a more general disease. During the Paris peace talks Lloyd
George was not debilitated by the need to reconcile conflicting political pressures – a task at which he was adept. The problem was his lack
of commitment. He was at his best when he had a cause for which he
was willing to fight and, if necessary, perish. The Man Who Won the
War and the great radical of the Insurance Bills was lost when he could
not identify with the struggle he was leading.

Intellectually he knew that intervention in Russia was 'not merely
none of our business . . . but would be positively mischievous' as it
would 'strengthen and consolidate Bolshevik opinion'.[48] Yet – having
been attacked by the *Daily Mail* and *The Times*, which described the
Principo initiative as an attempt simultaneously to appease the
Communists, propitiate the Germans and ingratiate himself with the
Jews – he could only wonder, 'As long as the British press is doing this
kind of thing, how can you expect me to be sensible about Russia?'[49]
Steering a steady course – determining objectively what the level of

reparations should be, forming a principled view on relations with Russia and sticking to his conclusions come wind, come weather – was not a solution which he considered.

The Northcliffe papers' campaign against Principo was only part of what amounted to their 1919 vendetta against Lloyd George. Northcliffe himself had aspired to be a member of either the War Cabinet or the Paris peace conference delegation. Neither wish had been gratified. Lloyd George was therefore held guilty – among other misdemeanours – of gross ingratitude. In Northcliffe's opinion, he could never have become Prime Minister without the support of the *The Times* and the *Daily Mail*. The price he had to pay for his supposed disloyalty was a campaign of denigration which inevitably climaxed with the claim that, because of his affection for Germany and the Germans, he was betraying British interests by proposing a level of indemnities and reparations which was below both the French demand and the German ability to pay. Lloyd George cabled Northcliffe, 'You are quite wrong about France STOP No ally has named figure STOP Allies in complete agreement as to demand for indemnity STOP Don't always be making mischief.'[50]

There are always Members of Parliament – usually unknown until their brief moment of glory – who are prepared, indeed desperate, to add such weight as they possess to newspaper campaigns. The Northcliffe offensive gained speed for a few weeks and then accelerated towards a House of Commons confrontation when Colonel Claude Lowther, a Sussex landowner and Unionist who sat for Eskdale in Cumberland, circulated a note to all Members which claimed to demonstrate that the full cost of the war was £25 billion and that the Germans could afford to make recompense of the full amount. Had not the Prime Minister quoted a similar figure during the general election campaign which he said had been calculated by an ex-Governor of the Bank of England?

Cunliffe's estimate that Germany could afford £24 billion had been the headline of the speech. The small print which followed expressed doubts about the possibility, as well as the moral propriety, of reclaiming so large an amount. The device – bold assertion qualified by less newsworthy reservations – is an old trick which almost invariably backfires. The headline has such an impact on public opinion that, when the time comes to rely on the more moderate sub-clauses, the reservations are of no value. The Prime Minister had talked of £24 billion. How could he now dismiss £25 billion as a preposterous overestimate?

In the first debate on reparations and indemnities, Bonar Law tried, loyally, to concentrate attention on that part of the Prime Minister's election speech which, on the day of its delivery, Lloyd George had hoped would be ignored. 'The one point that [Lowther] did not mention was the part which was the basis, I believe, of all the Prime Minister's speeches. That was not that he would make Germany pay the whole cost of the war but that we would exact from Germany whatever Germany was able to pay.' He concluded with a much stronger point – a rejection of the 'curious idea that if you have doubts about the arithmetical figures you are friendly to the Boche'.[51] The logic of that assertion notwithstanding, Bonar Law's speech was badly received in the House of Commons. On the following day, he wrote to tell Lloyd George, 'I had a bad time about indemnities last night. I do not think I convinced anyone and probably nine out of ten Unionist Members at least were very disgusted.'[52] He was right. Three days later, in Paris, Lloyd George received a telegram from 370 Unionist MPs. It urged him to 'stand firm' – an encouragement which is always based on the fear that retreat is being contemplated.

> Our constituents have always expected and still expect that the first edition of the peace delegation would be, as you repeatedly stated in your election pledges, to present the bill in full, to make Germany acknowledge the debt and then discuss ways and means of obtaining payment. Although we have the utmost confidence in your intentions to fulfil your pledges to the country, may we, as we have to meet innumerable inquiries from our constituents, have your renewed assurances that you have in no way departed from your original intention.[53]

Fortunately he was provided with an opportunity to reply by Kennedy Jones, a Unionist MP who had worked for the *Daily Mail* before his election and had remained faithful to his old employer. Jones initiated another reparations debate in the House of Commons and, to the Prime Minister's delight, claimed that his calculations of Germany's ability to pay had been obtained from a 'reliable source'. Lloyd George replied with his favourite metaphor for Lord Northcliffe. 'Reliable! That is the last adjective I would use. It is here today, jumping there tomorrow and there the next day and I would as soon rely on a grasshopper.'[54] Thus enabled to turn a defence of his own conduct into an attack on his tormentors, Lloyd George accused Northcliffe of seeking revenge for his exclusion from the government and the peace delegation. 'The war was won without him. There must be something wrong.'[55] He tapped his head in what can only have been a suggestion that Northcliffe was deranged.

> Under these conditions I am prepared to make allowances, but let me say that when that kind of diseased vanity is carried to the point of sowing dissension between great allies whose unity is essential to the peace of the world . . . then I say, not even that kind of disease is a justification for so black a crime against humanity.

He feared that Britain's allies took the complaints seriously. '*The Times* is still believed in France to be a serious organ. They do not know that it is merely a threepenny edition of the *Daily Mail*' – a paper which, only a month ago, had set out 'essential peace terms' which were less exacting than those which it now condemned as inadequate.[56]

It was the attack on Northcliffe that caught the public's attention. But another section of the speech – though less sensational – was equally extraordinary. Lloyd George appealed for the sympathy of the Commons and the nation. He doubted if 'any body of men with a difficult task have worked under greater difficulties – stones clattering on the roof and crashing through the windows and sometimes wild men screaming through the keyholes'.[57] Politicians rarely attract support by appealing for sympathy. But Lloyd George believed that the speech had been an unequivocal triumph. Frances Stevenson, in Paris, was told on the telephone that 'it was a wonderful performance'. On the following day, Lloyd George returned 'very pleased with himself'. He was, as usual, unstinting in his praise of his own performance and equally uninhibited about the way he had avoided discussing the real issue. 'He had a wonderful reception and gained complete mastery of the House while telling them absolutely nothing about the peace conference.'[58]

The draft peace treaty was published three weeks later. Clemenceau, although accused by his political opponents of being too sympathetic towards Germany, expressed his satisfaction in a job well – if not perfectly – done. Wilson, back in America, hoped – in a rare burst of humour – to read it in full during his lifetime. He concluded, from the parts with which he was familiar, that the Paris delegates had completed 'in the least possible time the greatest work that four men have ever done'.[59] Frances Stevenson – no doubt reflecting Lloyd George's feelings – was ecstatic. 'Everyone seems delighted with the peace terms and there is no fault to find with them on the grounds that they are not severe enough. Someone had described it as "a peace with a vengeance".'[60]

That was certainly the German view and, instead of meekly accepting both the terms and the implication of guilt which the penalties implied, they argued that they had been promised a peace built around the Fourteen Points and that the promise had been broken. Germany was to lose 13 per cent of its territory and 10 per cent of its population. So much for boundaries based on nationality rather than the interests of the Great Powers. But, the Germans argued, the greatest outrage was Article 231 of the treaty:

> The Allied and Associated Powers attest and Germany accepts the responsibility of Germany and its allies for causing all the loss and damage to which they and their nationals have been subjected as a consequence of war imposed on them by the aggression of Germany and its allies.

For Germany, rejection of that article was a matter of honour. Acceptance amounted to an admission of guilt which they did not feel. For the Allies, accepting it was a political necessity. 'I could not accept the German point of view,' Lloyd George wrote ten years later, 'without giving away our whole case for the war.'[61] In short, no guilt, no reparations.

In Britain the mood outside Parliament began to change. The Archbishop of Canterbury, speaking for 'the great central body which has no representation in the ordinary channels of the press', declared himself 'very uncomfortable' with the draft treaty.[62] The coalition candidate in the Central Hull by-election lost to a Liberal who called for a 'good, early and non-vengeful peace'.[63] Members of the British delegation, who had long harboured doubts, began to express their misgivings. 'The present financial proposals, which in my opinion are not workable, should not be withdrawn, but an alternative should be added, fixing a lump sum . . . Unanimous opinion of British delegation that at this critical juncture you should have the solid backing in making concessions to the Germans to bring about peace.'[64] Doubts about the draft treaty were expressed by ministers too. Smuts seemed to disagree with every article – except the annexation of South-West Africa. He described the reparation clause as certain 'to kill the goose which is to lay the golden egg' – even though his idea of including pensions and separation allowances had increased Germany's liability. Then the British delegation – meeting as a whole in Paris on 1 June – considered the draft treaty and, with Lloyd George's agreement, asked for, indeed demanded, three major changes. Unless the articles governing the new Polish frontier (effectively the annexation of Upper Silesia), the occupation of the Rhineland and the size and payment period of reparations were radically revised, Great Britain should not sign the treaty and, in the event of Germany refusing to sign, should neither provide an army of occupation nor maintain the naval blockade.

Woodrow Wilson, the peacemaker, was adamant that no change was possible and, with justification, told his delegation, 'It makes me a little tired for people to come and say now that they are afraid the Germans won't sign and their fear is based upon things that they insisted upon at the time of writing the Treaty.' In more restricted company he added that Lloyd George had no principles whatever of his own but reacted according to the last person who talked to him, with expediency as his sole guide.[65] Keynes wrote a cruel postscript to the disagreement.

To his horror, Mr Lloyd George, desiring at the last moment all the moderation he dared, discovered that he could not in five days persuade the President of error in what it had taken months to prove to him to be just and right. After all it was harder to de-bamboozle this old Presbyterian than to bamboozle him.[66]

During the heated discussions which followed, Lloyd George won one major concession: Upper Silesia was not ceded to Poland. Its citizens were allowed, by plebiscite, to determine their own future. It was, in itself, a significant improvement and its achievements, together with the doomed attempt to do better, rehabilitated Lloyd George in the opinion of some of his delegation. Harold Nicolson wrote that he was 'trying his best to alleviate the terms imposed upon Germany. The French are furious with him nor does Wilson give him any support. Can't understand Wilson. Here is a chance to improve the thing but he won't take it. LlG is, however, fighting like a little terrier all by himself.'[67] Nicolson should have realised that, by June, it was too late to correct the errors of March and April. His disillusion with the treaty was complete but – in a way – understated. 'We came to Paris confident that the new order was about to be established. We left convinced that the new order had merely followed the old. We arrived, fervent apprentices in the school of President Wilson. We left renegades.'[68] It was an accusation which would be repeated, time after time, for the rest of Lloyd George's life.

CHAPTER 32

THE PERILS OF PEACE

Lord Riddell – proprietor of the *News of the World* and, for many years, Lloyd George's confidant and companion – expressed in a single sentence what history has come to say at greater length about the fall from public grace of the Man Who Won the War. On 27 March 1920 – with the post-war government barely fifteen months old – he wrote in his diary, 'I notice that LG is steadily veering over to the Tory point of view.'[1] He justified his contention by quoting the Prime Minister's opinion on the just wage. 'He says one Leverhulme or Ellerman [soap manufacturer and shipping magnate, respectively] is worth more to the world than 10,000 sea captains or 20,000 engine drivers and should be remunerated accordingly.' Riddell added, by way of mitigation, 'He wants to improve the world and the condition of the people but he wants to do it in his own way.'[2]

The most startling example of the policy differences between Lloyd George the post-war Prime Minister and Lloyd George the pre-war Chancellor of the Exchequer was his opposition in 1918 to levying excess profits tax at a level which would penalise 'the hard-faced men who did well out of the war'. The change of policy was made particularly unattractive by the Cabinet minute which described a high rate as 'likely to incur immense odium, particularly among [the government's] principal supporters'. His agreement to the abolition, in 1920, of the land taxes which he had introduced with such satisfaction in 1910 is partly explained by the practical measures of land reform which replaced a largely declaratory statute – including the creation of the Forestry Commission and increased powers to local authorities which needed to acquire house-building land.[3] There were echoes of his pre-war radicalism – though they were as much the result of political necessity as conviction. The housing drive, the most ambitious of the government's social policies, was hurried forward by Christopher Addison. His enthusiasm was to prove his undoing.

The shift in attitude if not instinct was calculated. Lloyd George argued that the justification 'for the existence of the present form of government [is] that it attempted to hold the balance evenly and fairly between all classes of the community'.[4] It is around that idea – a desire to build a national consensus – that the most intellectually distinguished analysis of Lloyd George's peacetime premiership is based.* Cynics will say that the leader of a recently formed and highly unstable coalition had a vested interest in seeking to accommodate his natural enemies. But unity of a sort was Lloyd George's genuine inclination – witness his doomed attempt in 1910 to create a coalition which would drive his national insurance policies through the House of Commons. In opposition, the party battle had made him. In government, he often saw it as an obstacle to the achievement of the public good. But the consensus which he hoped to build was meant to be a reflection of his own ideas, with as few concessions to other opinions as were essential to secure majority support.

In the early years of peace, that consensus was difficult to achieve within a coalition which had been created to win the war. The Unionists, on whom it depended, disliked and distrusted a Prime Minister whose temporary leadership they had accepted as essential to an Allied victory. When the government began to grapple with the problems of peace, it became increasingly clear that the leader and the led were incompatible. Much of Lloyd George's time was spent attempting to reconcile the irreconcilable. When a temporary accommodation was achieved, it was usually at the expense of principles which, ten years earlier, he had claimed to hold dear.

Although he still prided himself on being the great conciliator, by 1918 Lloyd George had grown impatient with the disciplines of democracy. Even when the Paris talks were over, he rarely attended the House of Commons, and although he eventually, and reluctantly, extended the Cabinet to something like its normal size, he still preferred to work with small ad hoc groups of supportive ministers. In that, as in his appointment of businessmen to 'advise' ministers, he pioneered new,

---

*Consensus and Disunity by Kenneth O. Morgan.

but not necessarily desirable, techniques of government. His attitude to colleagues – as illustrated by his letters – was correspondingly dismissive, and he devoted much time to rest, recovery and recuperation after his frequent minor illnesses.

The prestige which victory had ensured had certainly been sustained and probably increased by the part he had played in the Paris peace talks. He had 'made the Germans pay', at least appeared to be the pivotal element on which the decisions turned and had, in consequence, appeared to dominate the conference which redrew the map of the world. In the opinion of the nation he was a hero and, in his own estimation, an international statesman. In effect, he was his own Foreign Secretary. Much to Curzon's disgust, Balfour had 'abdicated all power in favour of Lloyd George', allowing 'the practical suppression of the [Foreign] Office and the total domination of the Prime Minister which was later to have such deplorable results'.[5]

Prime ministers always revel in the glories of international conferences, where – treated like potentates – they can briefly ignore the intrigues and indignities of domestic politics. In difficult times, they provide a refuge from the cares of home, a particularly welcome respite in post-war Britain. Despite the groundless optimism of November 1918, within eighteen months the economic outlook was bleak. The post-war boom collapsed in the spring of 1920. The bank rate was raised from 6 to 7 per cent. Investment fell away with predictable consequences for employment. 'In April 1920 all was right with the world. In April 1921 all was wrong.'[6] And it was not only the depression from which Lloyd George found relief in Cannes, Geneva and Paris. The Prime Minister was required to confront problems which ranged from new trade union militancy to Ireland's ancient demands for independence. And all his difficulties were compounded by his unique political position. He was a Prime Minister without a party.

Lloyd George was at his best when he could concentrate on a single issue – Welsh denominational education, the Boer War, old-age pensions, the reorganisation of armament manufacture. In peacetime, prime ministers have to do everything at once – an obligation which is most easily fulfilled by politicians who are guided by a consistent and coherent philosophy. Lloyd George dealt with each issue individually – relying for guidance on instinct and rough calculation of what would meet the needs of the moment. He cannot have welcomed the news that it was necessary for him briefly to abandon discussion of the peace treaty in order to meet Jimmy Thomas, the secretary of the

National Union of Railwaymen, who had flown to Paris for urgent talks about an imminent strike. Thomas was, in Frances Stevenson's judgement, 'an amusing creature, not very reliable and very open to flattery and coaxing'.[7] These were two qualities which Lloyd George was to exploit during the next two years when the miners called on their partners in the Triple Alliance – the loose confederation of dockers', railwaymen's and miners' trade unions which, in theory, would stand together to support each other's demands – to support their fight for higher wages and improved conditions. It was the time when it became clear what Lloyd George had meant by his declaration to Lucy Masterman, 'I know which side I am on.'[8] He was for the men, but he had little sympathy for the trade unions which aimed to protect their interests.

The war had changed both the pattern of industrial relations and the balance of power between employers and employees. In shipbuilding and engineering, the workers had accepted – as a result of a combination of persuasion and coercion – both the suspension of free collective bargaining and the 'dilution' of skilled labour. Conversely, coal had been in such great demand that the government – recognising the unpopularity as well as the incompetence of the mine-owners – had, in effect, nationalised the pits and limited the distribution of profits while rewarding the miners for their extra effort. With the war won, both the engineering workers and the colliery companies expected a return to what they regarded as the natural order of things. And, with the relief and relaxation which followed victory, all sorts of pent-up grievances exploded into sporadic strike action. At the end of 1919, there were disputes in the docks and gas and electricity companies. And once again, a national rail strike threatened. Clydeside, as always, was particularly militant. It was there that the Bolshevik revolution – which the government feared – seemed most likely to begin.

Lloyd George's plan to defeat the imagined threat required moderate working men to be convinced that the government had their interests at heart at the same time as it stamped down hard on their extremist workmates. That justified an extension of the social legislation which had made his radical reputation, and it enabled him to persuade the Unionists within the coalition that it was necessary – if not in itself desirable – to increase both public expenditure and the involvement of the state in the lives of individual citizens.[9] A Ministry of Health was created to build 'homes for heroes', and the argument for new insurance legislation was reinforced by the return of servicemen and the economic decline which increased the level of unemployment from a million at the end of 1920 to two and a half million by July 1921.

So the flurry of initiatives included a new National Insurance Act. It extended protection against unemployment to 8 million workers who had not been covered by the 1911 act – virtually everybody earning less than £250 a year except domestic servants, agricultural labourers and civil servants. Six months later, the rate of male benefit was increased from fifteen to twenty shillings a week to ensure that unemployed ex-servicemen were not disadvantaged when they moved from the demobilisation 'dole' to the national scheme. Six months after that, though – when the cold wind of recession had begun to blow – it was cut to twelve shillings and hedged about with provisos that the recipient must be able to demonstrate that he was genuinely seeking work. Nevertheless – although Lloyd George had lost some of his abrasive zeal – his last excursion into social policy continued the process he had begun in the glory years before the First World War. Unemployment 'relief' had become an almost universal right. The Poor Law was effectively dead.

The idea of a comprehensive insurance system had been discussed and commended by a National Industrial Conference which had been held, at Lloyd George's instigation, in Westminster Central Hall on 27 February 1919. Its object was the demonstration that masters and men had identical economic interests and that progress and prosperity depended on cooperation rather than conflict. It was a success of sorts – despite the absence of the Triple Alliance – and it encouraged the Prime Minister in the belief that his hard line against extremism must be balanced by a constant demonstration of his own moderation. The formula – whatever its intrinsic merits – required an accurate identification of extremism. That Lloyd George was unable to provide. There were certainly a handful of would-be Communists among the leadership of the Miners' Federation of Great Britain. But although the coal dispute that bedevilled the first two years of his peacetime administration was inspired by a need for security, not hope of revolution, the spectre of a Bolshevik uprising haunted the government. Conventional wisdom left no doubt that the miners would be the first at the barricades. In February 1920 – during a period of comparative industrial peace – Lloyd George was preparing for the most desperate contingency. Ninety years on, his fears seem absurd. But extensive notes made during a ministerial meeting on industrial relations by Tom Jones – Assistant Cabinet Secretary – illustrate how seriously Lloyd George took the prospect of revolution and how determined he was to suppress it. After cross-examining the Adjutant General about the number of troops stationed in Great Britain and Ireland, he turned to Air Marshal Sir Hugh Trenchard, Chief of the Air Staff, and asked,

> How many airmen are available for the revolution? Trenchard replied that there were 20,000 mechanics and 2,000 pilots, but only a hundred machines which could be kept going in the air . . . The pilots had no weapons for ground fighting. The PM presumed they could use machine guns and drop bombs.[10]

The vanguard of the feared revolution would, in Lloyd George's opinion, be the Triple Alliance. He determined to beat the miners in what – with the mines still in public ownership – would amount to an exemplary show of strength. 'Once the state begins, it is imperative that the state should win. Failure to do so would undoubtedly lead to a Soviet Republic.'[11]

The miners wanted assurances about their future. They were demanding security at a time when the enthusiasm for deregulation was virtually universal. During the war, government control of the mines and the need to maximise output had kept 'uneconomic' pits in operation and, thanks to the government subsidy, the men who worked them had been paid a living wage. If, as the mine-owners expected and demanded, the coalfields were returned to private control, the subsidy would end and both the price of coal and wages would be determined by the market. Inevitably some collieries would close. Others would reduce their pay rates. At the first skirmish in the battle for permanent nationalisation, the Miners' Federation proposed that the price of domestic coal be reduced by 14/2 a ton, wages increased by 2/- a shift and the extra cost – £63 million in all – be borne by the Treasury. When ministers rejected the proposals, the union's executive prepared for strike action by balloting its members.

Before the ballot was conducted, Lloyd George had left for what – despite the entourage which accompanied him – he described as a holiday in Lucerne. He intended, while he was there, to forge a friendship with the new Italian premier, who, he hoped, would become an ally in his machinations against the French. But he remained by the lake for two weeks after the meeting had taken place. In London Robert Horne, the President of the Board of Trade – fearing imminent action by the whole Triple Alliance – was preparing to rush an Emergency

Powers Bill through Parliament. Lloyd George thought that was the wrong approach. On his return to England, he took personal command. 'I was', he complained disingenuously, 'only called in after the battle lines had been set . . . Everyone said "Let him have a free hand" so I stood aside and now I have to shoulder the whole burden.'[12] He lightened the load by abandoning all thought of confrontation and agreeing to pay the additional 2/- a shift until a long-term settlement had been agreed. Time, he believed, was on his side. So, when the miners made their claim – a 30 per cent increase in basic pay, a six-hour day and nationalisation – he offered to set up a Royal Commission under the chairmanship of Sir John Sankey, a High Court judge. Both owners and workers believed that the terms of reference had been designed to meet their needs.

There are different views about how the confusion arose and some suspicion that they were the result of Lloyd George's calculated deception of the miners. The Miners' Federation leadership certainly thought that the whole future of the industry – ownership as well as wage rates – was to be considered in one report. Sankey, with the government's agreement, divided his work into two parts. On 20 March, the commission published its first recommendation – a permanent wage increase of 2/- a shift and a seven-hour working day. Lloyd George accepted the proposals, which he regarded as vindication of 'what he had been saying for years, but nobody paid any attention. The owners are making a very poor show.'[13] The exploitation of unearned increments in land values had once provoked his righteous anger. It still offended his sense of justice. He was 'going to be made the cat's paw of the landlords'.[14]

The first Sankey Report averted the prospect of an immediate strike. But there could be no lasting peace while the prospect of public ownership remained in doubt. To the miners' delight, the second Sankey Report – representing a bare majority of the Royal Commission – recommended permanent nationalisation. The minority, in its separate report, proposed an immediate and complete return to private ownership.* Lloyd George, if not an enthusiast for public enterprise, clearly did not oppose it root and branch. In April, when Bonar Law had expressed the fear that it might be unavoidable, the Prime Minister had replied, 'It has to come. The state will have to shoulder the burden sooner or later.'[15]

---

*One member of the commission added a dissenting note, advocating private ownership *after* reorganisation and amalgamation.

But during the next three months he abandoned the idea of state control and government subsidy. On 19 July, at the end of the parliamentary session, he announced that the government had accepted the recommendation of the minority report.

The speech lasted for almost three hours and began with a gloomy assessment of Britain's economic prospects. The adverse trade balance had increased in five years from £150 million to £800 million. Over the same period, the national debt had risen from £645 million to £7800 million – incurring annual interest charges of £400 million. The fall in national output had been 'almost sensational' – a strange and unhappy phrase which typified a strange and unhappy speech. 'We are', he told the Commons, 'spending more and earning less. We are consuming more and producing less.'[16]

The coal industry was excoriated as an example of national failure. A reduction in the working week – which the Miners' Federation had promised would guarantee higher levels of output – had, as the critics of the bargain predicted, produced the opposite effect. Despite the increase in the labour force, annual production had fallen during the war from 280 million tons to 200 million tons. Nationalisation would not solve the industry's problems. The coalfields would be returned to private ownership. But mineral rights would be acquired by the state and subventions from the increase which they produced would contribute to improved wages in the barely economic pits.

While the miners decided how much of the loaf they had been offered and whether it was worth accepting, Lloyd George – unusually with his wife and more typically with a large retinue of acolytes – left on what the Prime Minister insisted was a medically essential holiday on the Normandy coast. After ten days, Margaret returned home and Frances Stevenson and the Astors joined the party in Deauville. Frances described Lady Astor – who was about to become the Member of Parliament for the Sutton division of Plymouth – as 'treacherous and not to be trusted'. Poor Frances – more sensitive to her anomalous status than either she or her biographers allow – complained that 'in spite of her protestations of friendship, she takes every opportunity of saying spiteful things about D and myself'.[17] Being close to power was not a complete compensation for the indignities of having to wait to join the party until Mrs Lloyd George had left.

By the time the Prime Minister arrived back in a Britain, there was an uneasy peace in the coalfields but a series of other disputes. The iron moulders had begun a strike which was to last until the end of the year and, far more serious, the long-threatened national railway stoppage had begun. Months earlier Auckland Geddes – Eric's brother, who had first succeeded Neville Chamberlain at the Manpower Directorate and then preceded Horne at the Board of Trade – had suggested, in the spirit of the true businessman, that wages should be rationalised on a formula which required some workers to accept reductions of 20 per cent. In the circumstances, it is hard to believe that the strike took Lloyd George by surprise 'like a thief that comes in the night' or that he believed it to be 'the most serious labour war this country has ever seen'.[18] He eventually decided that the dispute was not, as he had first supposed, the consequence of an 'anarchist conspiracy'.[19] And, brushing aside Eric Geddes – in charge of the newly created Ministry of Labour – he settled down to bringing it to an end before the other members of the Triple Alliance came to the railwaymen's aid. In fact none of the three unions – including the National Union of Railwaymen itself – wanted to extend the strike beyond the railways. Jimmy Thomas, the railwaymen's secretary, was anxious to display his 'moderation'. When Lloyd George offered him a deal which allowed him to save face with his members, he accepted it at once. Railway wages were to be held at their current levels until the autumn of 1921 while new rates were negotiated – with the assurance that minimum pay would not fall below 51/- a week. The Prime Minister told his wife that 'the railwaymen have been thoroughly beaten and they know it. It will save much trouble in future.'[20] Colleagues were not so sure. They feared that, by agreeing to a settlement which 'appeared' to concede the railwaymen's case, the government had set a dangerous precedent.

The Miners' Federation leadership brooded throughout the summer. By the beginning of autumn – frustrated by abortive negotiations and reinforced by the result of the ballot which had approved strike action by 602,000 to 235,000 – they had decided to wait no longer. The strike would begin on 27 September. It was time for Lloyd George once more to employ the calculated ambivalence which was central to his negotiating technique. On 24 September, at a meeting held at his request, the Prime Minister persuaded the Miners' Federation leadership to wait for another week. During the discussions which followed, the magic – by which he had managed to postpone earlier strike action – deserted him. After the initial meeting, 'he was not so good, getting into figures which he did not really understand'.[21] He 'gave the impression that he would rather like a strike'.[22] It is possible that his apparent incompetence was a ruse to generate failure. But there is a second possible explanation. It may well have been a symptom of a steady decline not in his capacity but in his enthusiasm for government. A year before the meeting with the miners' union, Hankey had written in his diary,

Lloyd George's erratic, inconsequent and hasty methods are the negation of organization. Owing to his personal habits (sleeping after lunch for instance) involving late evening meetings and very discursive talks on every question, he exhausts to an extraordinary degree, not only his own colleagues and his immediate subordinates, but the whole executive of state.[23]

He was not alone in his concern. A. J. Sylvester – the expert shorthand writer who progressed through the Cabinet secretariat to become first Hankey's and then Lloyd George's personal secretary – grew so concerned about his neglect of state papers that he left unopened envelopes on the Prime Minister's desk, knowing that they would be examined out of curiosity and that then there could be no dispute about them having been sent to the Cabinet Room.*[24]

If Lloyd George did want a strike, his complicated strategy succeeded. The miners chose to fight on the enemy's ground. Coal stocks were high. The Emergency Powers Bill would keep the railway system working. The Miners' Federation executive was divided. But although the owners and the government could have won, after two weeks ministers persuaded the Mining Association of Great Britain, the mine-owners' alliance, to use some of the profits to finance an interim pay increase while – once more – the government supervised the search for a lasting solution. The miners returned to work on 2 November convinced that the government was on their side and that, in consequence, public ownership and the subsidy which it provided would continue until at least the summer of 1921. Perhaps that undertaking would have been honoured had not the slump dramatically reduced the demand for coal at a time when cheap exports from the Ruhr and Silesia were again available on the British market. Between January and March 1921, coal industry losses rose to £5 million a month.[25] The government decided to cut and run. The Coal Mines (Decontrol) Bill became law on 24 March.

---

*Sylvester also had the distinction of being the first man to make a note of a Cabinet or Cabinet committee meeting. Before Lloyd George's premiership, no note was taken.

The mine-owners immediately announced the need for wage reductions and published proposed new rates which amounted to 50 per cent pay cuts in uneconomic pits. The Miners' Federation talked vainly of pooled profits and a national minimum wage. The aims of the owners and miners were irreconcilable. The coal mines were returned to private ownership at midnight on 31 March. Next day, the anticipated strike was pre-empted by a lock-out. In a change of tactic, Lloyd George determined to demonstrate that the coal industry was no longer the government's business and, therefore, tried to encourage a settlement without becoming directly involved. So, although he regarded the demand for wage cuts 'absurd', he neither denounced it in public nor criticised it privately to the employers.[26] And he continued to promote the double image – emollient to the reasonable and obdurate to the intransigent. It was not a tactic which always had the intended result. Aristide Briand, reinstalled as the French Prime Minister, warned him that he was 'dealing with Bolsheviks'.[27] But while Lloyd George urged moderation and caution on both parties, Lord Birkenhead, the Lord Chancellor, was drawing up plans to suppress – with the aid of troops who were kept on standby – what he still thought might be an incipient revolution.

He need not have worried on that account. Neither the transport workers nor the railwaymen felt much sympathy for the miners, and what little enthusiasm for the fight they had was reduced by the Miners' Federation's assumption that the other unions would simply do what they were told. The dispute escalated. First in Fife and then in Yorkshire and South Wales 'safety men' – who protected the pits from fire and flood – broke the usual rules of engagement by joining the strike. Their action provided another opportunity for Lloyd George to appear reasonable. If safety cover was restored he would convene another conciliation meeting. The unions would not accept any invitation which was issued subject to preconditions. Lloyd George made his last conciliatory offer. The government would restore the subsidy for a limited period if the men returned to work first and negotiated afterwards. The miners – always proud that they preferred to break rather than bend – rejected the offer.

The transport and railway unions asked for a meeting to discuss a plan of action. Herbert Smith – the president of the Miners' Federation – told them, 'Get on t'field. That's thy place.'[28] Until the other members of the Triple Alliance joined the strike and manned the picket lines they had, in Smith's opinion, no rights in the dispute.

Jimmy Thomas, always dubious about the merits of direct action in despair begged the Prime Minister to intervene once more. Tom Jones, who transmitted the request, was shocked by Lloyd George's reaction: 'I think we better have the strike. Let them kick their heels for a week or a fortnight. It will help the moderates against the extremists.' Then he added, 'What I most wish is that I had some conference abroad to go to urgently. Then I could come back in a fortnight and take up the negotiations again.'[29]

If the strike had not ended in a resounding defeat for the miners, Lloyd George's tactics – conciliatory on some occasions and unyielding on others – might have been heralded as the reasonable man's response to a complex and changing situation, or it might have been dismissed as the vacillation of a politician with no fixed principles. But whatever chance there was of a union victory disappeared on 14 April 1921 as the direct result of the ineptitude of the Miners' Federation leadership. Frank Hodges, the union's general secretary, had agreed to address a group of backbench MPs. In the course of his speech he said – without thought or authority – that the Miners' Federation was prepared to abandon the demand for a profit pool to equalise wages. He was immediately repudiated by his own executive, which confirmed, by a majority of one vote, that its demands were unchanged and unchangeable.

The next day, the Transport and General Workers' Union and the National Union of Railwaymen announced that, since the miners were divided about which course to follow, they would neither endorse nor support a strike. The Triple Alliance was dead and the miners were doomed. But they fought on long after what they came to call 'Black Friday'. Pit by pit, they were starved back to work as their wages fell – on average – by 47 per cent of the pre-war rate.[30] As a result, Lloyd George, although he gained little credit from the mine-owners, became the enemy of organised labour and the political party which it had created.

Cabinet minutes make clear that throughout the mining dispute, political considerations were never out of Lloyd George's mind. The leader without a party and the Prime Minister who believed in coalition was defining himself by reference to his enemies.

> If the working class is united against us, the outlook is grave and the gravity would be intensified if what I call intellectual liberalism unites with Labour against us. The great struggle which is coming must not be partisan . . . I have become more and more

convinced that the time has arrived for coming to grips with the conspiracy which is seeking to use Labour for the purpose of overthrowing the existing organization of the time. The opportunity will show itself over the miners' demand.*[31]

Lloyd George feared that continued industrial militancy would stimulate an upsurge in support for the Labour Party. The coalition which he led had won a landslide majority. But it was an essentially unstable alliance of convenience. Political security lay in the creation of something more permanent. The obvious answer was a new centre party. That was an idea which was clearly in his mind as early as December 1919 when he told a Manchester meeting that the differences between the Liberals and Conservatives were much exaggerated and that the time had come for men of moderation and goodwill to unite in the battle to defeat socialism. He claimed that he agreed with every resolution that had been passed at a recent meeting of the National Liberal Federation – a meeting which he said he had not been invited to attend. By expressing regret that his old friends had ignored him, he won the sympathy of his audience. But – like so many politicians before and after him – he paid for a moment's support with long-term embarrassment. The Liberal Party announced that he had been invited but had not replied, and the Unionists told him he *had* no business either endorsing the Liberal programme or admitting a desire to renew old friendships.

That augury of troubles in store did not diminish Lloyd George's enthusiasm for creating a new party. And in February 1920, his hopes were reinforced by necessity. After much doubt and deliberation Asquith had agreed to contest a by-election in Paisley. His return to the House of Commons increased the prospect of a Liberal revival, in which Lloyd George would be allowed to play no part. So the Prime Minister edged to the left in the hope of reclaiming his old radical following. 'Some of your people', he told a Unionist junior minister, 'want to tie me to the Tory Party pure and simple.' That was not his way.

I want a national party, but I want Liberals in it. I should be quite content if I got such a party by dropping some of the people at

---

*Lloyd George can take some credit for the invention of Cabinet minutes. So he should be allowed a degree of latitude about what they might properly contain. CAB/63/29 is, however, strangely party political.

both ends who would not agree. A Labour Government would land the country in a revolution because it would resist direct action by talk, not force . . . I want strong government. I want private enterprise. But private enterprise must give workers a chance and certainty.[32]

Lloyd George argued with some justification that, under his leadership, a coalition which largely consisted of Conservatives had – despite a couple of aberrations about tax policy – inherited some of the principles which he had espoused before the war. Eligibility for national insurance had been extended and the old-age pension had been increased from £26:5/- to £47:5/- a year. There had been a massive increase in school building. The Agriculture Act, which guaranteed prices and enforced a minimum wage, was the achievement of one of his long-held ambitions. The disestablishment of the Welsh Church – admittedly on terms more generous than the young Lloyd George would have regarded as acceptable – delighted the principality. Yet those achievements had not commended the coalition to the new electorate that he was determined to capture. Its post-war popularity had faded with the post-war economic boom. In March 1919, when the coalition candidate was defeated at West Leyton in Essex, he had claimed to welcome the warning message which it had sent to his Unionist followers. 'The country is in no mood to tolerate reactionaries, high or low.'[33] Bonar Law warned of more conflicts to come. The Budget would require dangerous decisions on the future of the mining industry and 'the question of fiscal policy'. Lloyd George refused 'to meet trouble half way' in the belief that the government 'would scrape through with the revival of trade'.[34] But he must have begun to doubt the durability of a coalition of parties built on the needs of the day. He believed in the coalition of ideas. His ambition was to create a single party which could bring about such a coalition.

The portents were not encouraging. Asquith's return to the House of Commons had made the Liberals within the coalition feel a need to demonstrate their independent identity and encouraged those outside the coalition – the 'Wee Frees', so-called because they had sheltered under the temporary leadership of Donald Maclean – to believe that the political pendulum was swinging back in their direction. After some tentative private discussion among the coalition leaders, Winston Churchill had (typically) broken ranks and on 14 July 1919 publicly advocated the creation of a unified party. Liberals within the coalition – who had always regarded him as a gadfly – were offended by both the sentiments of the speech and the speaker, whom they assumed Lloyd George had chosen to lead the charge towards realignment. Then, after Lloyd George returned to the subject in his Manchester speech, the wounds of 1916 were reopened by the coalition's insistence on fielding a candidate in the by-election in Spen Valley. The natural Liberal vote was split and John Simon was defeated by the Labour nominee. Lloyd George contemplated the possibility of political extinction.

> I am faced with a serious crisis and I must make up my mind how to act. I have told Bonar Law that I am not going on like this. We are losing by-election after by-election. There is no proper organization in the country and no enthusiasm.[35]

There were, he decided, three courses of action – honourable retirement, leadership of a coalition rump outside the government, and the promotion of 'fusion between the two branches of the coalition'. Fusion was certainly possible. 'Bonar Law and Balfour favour it.'[36]

Fusion required the nomination of ideas around which members of a new party could coalesce. Half a dozen of Lloyd George's closest allies spent the first weekend in February 1920 considering what they should be. H. A. L. Fisher agreed to produce a draft manifesto in the form of a speech with which Lloyd George could argue the case for realignment. Before it was made, he had to reply to a House of Commons motion by which the Labour Members of Parliament called for the outright and permanent nationalisation of coal mining. He chose to ridicule as well as reject the idea. He was so well received on the Tory benches that he convinced himself that the way ahead was clear. 'I think I am forming a new party,' he told Frances Stevenson.[37]

Fisher's draft of the defining speech was sent to Balfour, whose reaction revealed the insoluble dilemma which was to confound the whole idea. Balfour was sympathetic to the underlying principle, which he defined as 'reform without revolution', but was worried about the policies which Fisher (still a natural radical) regarded as the inevitable consequences of that precept – votes for women over the age of twenty-one, proportional representation and social welfare legislation. Perhaps Lloyd George should have realised that more people always want to create a centre party than are able to agree about its purpose. Instead – loyalty not being his most conspicuous virtue – he disowned Fisher and emphasised what the new party would be against rather than what it should be for. 'I am in complete sympathy with the criticism of Fisher's draft. It struck me when I read it that there were too many challenging details.' Then he rode on his current hobby-horse. 'The Socialist movement has behind it most of the organized labour in the country. A more serious development, however, is the tent into which it is already attracting the lower middle classes and, unless there is a concerted effort made to arrest this tendency, very grave consequences may ensue for the whole country.'[38]

Despite there being no agreement on its purpose, a scheme was devised for launching the new party on the waiting world. First, Balfour would write to the chairman of the Conservatives in the City of London, his constituency, advocating its creation. Then, with Unionist support clearly established, Lloyd George would present the coalition Liberals with a plan that would give them a fighting chance at the next election. It was decided that expediency, as well as courtesy, required that the Liberal meeting – arranged for 18 March – should be preceded by a briefing for the twenty-five Liberals who were (mostly junior) members of the government. The ministers, who were told of Lloyd George's plan on 16 March, were unanimously opposed to the whole idea. It was time for some quick – if not, as it turned out, very nimble – footwork. MPs at the meeting of coalition Liberals were told that their colleagues, who had met the Prime Minister two days earlier, had misunderstood his intention. He wanted 'closer co-operation, not fusion'. *The Times,* reporting the private meeting two days later, revealed that Lloyd George had been forced to change tack. The idea of a new party was, for the time being, abandoned and coalition Liberals began to form local associations. In October, the idea of an independent political identity was reinforced by the publication of the *Lloyd George Liberal Magazine.*

For much of the spring and summer of 1920, the miners' dispute and the accelerating economic decline dominated domestic politics. The Treasury's remedy for recession was, as always, a balanced budget and a reduction in public expenditure. As usual, the government's attempted savings were denounced as inadequate by its critics. While Lloyd George wrestled with the problems of a still-unsettled Europe – and was increasingly drawn into the still-unsolved conundrum of Irish Home Rule – Lord Rothermere was inciting the public against government profligacy. In January 1921, he founded the Anti-Waste League and promoted it in his newspapers. The candidate who won the January by-election in Dover fought under its colours. Gradually the sin of waste came to be personified by Christopher Addison – Minister of Health and architect of the plans for post-war reconstruction.

Addison's most ambitious proposal was a housing drive which owed more to post-war euphoria than careful calculation of cost and feasibility. In 1919, the government had announced that it would build 100,000 new houses during 1920 with another 200,000 under construction as soon as land could be obtained and the contracts signed. Priority was to be given to slum clearance. More than 400,000 houses – the homes of 1.5 million men, women and children – had been condemned as unfit for human habitation. For a brief idealistic moment, clearing the slums caught the public's imagination.

The targets were never realised, although between 1919 and 1922, 213,000 low-cost houses were completed. Over 170,000 of them were built by local authorities and partly financed by subsidies provided by the Addison Act.[39] However, the complaint against Addison was not that he built too little but that he spent too much. In November 1920, Austen Chamberlain – Chancellor of the Exchequer for the second time – told the Cabinet Finance Committee that every house built under government sponsorship cost the Treasury (and therefore the taxpayer) between £50 and £75 a year and would continue to do so for the next sixty years.[40] Within a year what had begun as a symbol of the government's radical zeal had become evidence of both its incompetence and its profligacy.

During the first six months of the programme, the government had received enough site applications to build 450,000 houses, but only 10,000 were actually under construction. The trade unions were asked to persuade their members to improve productivity by abandoning restrictive practices. They refused outright. Addison's last resort was to switch the emphasis away from local authority construction by offering a government subsidy to private builders. The Cabinet agreed to subscribe £150 towards every house completed in 1920, up to a total of 100,000.

The plan was doomed. Addison – with more ideals than commercial experience – was partly to blame. So was the nature of his scheme and the economic climate of the time. Interest rates had risen, the building industry was disorganised and local authorities were reluctant to do more than make a gesture in the direction of clearing the slums. In some areas, both builders and builders' merchants were inflating their prices in the belief that lax local authority accounting would enable them to make a quick fortune. John Tudor Walters, a coalition Liberal with a claim to be a housing expert, estimated that the few houses under construction were costing the government £5 million more than they were worth. He was made Paymaster General with the explicit remit of holding down costs. It was the first stage of the abandonment of both the housing programme and Christopher Addison.*

Although cuts were made in the Army Estimates and the Royal Navy's capital-building programme, the housing programme – alongside the proposed increases in school building and teachers' salaries – survived. Unionists within the Cabinet – most notably Chamberlain in a spirited House of Commons speech – largely defended policies which were becoming anathema to his party supporters in the country and on the backbenches. But he did not hold out for long. When, on 17 March 1921, ill health forced Bonar Law to leave the government and Chamberlain succeeded him as the leader of both the House of Commons and the Unionist Party, the pressure to represent grassroots Tory opinion became irresistible. Within two weeks of Bonar Law's resignation, Addison was replaced at the Ministry of Health by Sir Alfred Mond. The news of his demotion to Minister without Portfolio was conveyed by a message from the Prime Minister. Lloyd George was too embarrassed to speak to him.

Perhaps the Unionists would have been satisfied with Addison's exile into the ministerial wilderness had an Anti-Waste candidate not won the by-election against an orthodox Tory in the St George's division of Westminster. But, fearful that the demands for economy would sweep them all away, the Tories needed another ritual sacrifice. Addison, as Chamberlain explained in a letter to Lloyd George, fitted the bill exactly. Tory backbenchers had put down a motion to reduce the Minister without Portfolio's salary from £4000 to £2500 a year – the traditional House of Commons method of execution. Chamberlain feared the worst.

> I am being pressed to name a day for the discussion of Addison's salary and I think I must appoint today fortnight for the purpose. But I am really concerned about the result. My Whips give me a worse report of the feeling of my party in respect of this matter than of anything else . . . The only chance of averting defeat is that you yourself should undertake the defence.[41]

---

*Both were rehabilitated by the Labour Party. Housing was the one success of the first MacDonald government. Addison became a minister in the second. He also served in Attlee's Cabinet from 1945 to 1951.

Lloyd George – according to his doctor, again in need of rest and recuperation – accepted no responsibility for Addison's receiving a salary but
not having a real job.

> I have been only too conscious for some time that the defence of
> his appointment would be difficult if not impossible. In fact I
> quite anticipated defeat over it and the only question in my mind
> was whether it was better for the House of Commons to get rid of
> him or for us to anticipate parliament's decision.[42]

He hoped that the debate could be postponed until he was well enough
to return from Wales to London. Then he would 'put the facts of the
case squarely before' Addison. But he feared that the Minister without
Portfolio – regarding himself as a martyr to public health and housing –
would refuse to resign. And so he did, arguing not for his own future
but for the need to revitalise the flagging slum-clearance drive. In the
debate on Addison's salary, the Prime Minister nobly accepted his obligation to speak for the government. Addison's appointment, he said, was
always meant to be temporary. While he remained in post his salary
should be cut not to £2500 a year as the motion demanded but to
£2000. The following week the Cabinet decided that only the houses
for which building contracts had already been let should receive a
Treasury subsidy. Addison resigned from the government on 14 July
1921.

There can be no doubt that Addison was a reckless Minister of
Health. His manifest failings were set out in an angry letter which
Lloyd George sent to Winston Churchill in reply to the complaint that
the Prime Minister had deserted a comrade. Addison, the Prime
Minister wrote, 'let contracts far in advance of the trade's ability to
assimilate. The market was glutted with offers . . . Prices soared, higher
and higher.'[43] That was undeniable, but the method of his removal
made many genuine Liberals fear that Lloyd George identified with his
new allies more than with his old friends. The administration was about
to implode under the pressure of its internal contradictions. And, like all
prime ministers whose end is near, he imagined that, on all sides, there
were plots to bring it nearer.

Bonar Law – who had returned reinvigorated from convalescence in
Paris – was suspected of planning a coup after Lord Salisbury wrote to
The Times expressing his personal view that Unionists should abandon
the coalition. When he heard of the Prime Minister's suspicions, Bonar

Law visited Chequers – presented to the nation for the use of prime ministers by Lord Lee of Fareham on 8 January 1921 – to swear his fealty. His assurances were accepted but then irrational doubts developed about the loyalty of Churchill and Birkenhead. A story was planted in the *Manchester Guardian* with the hope of smoking them out. Birkenhead, not altogether characteristically, condescended to contradict the rumours. The fears about both men were unjustified. They chose to go down with Lloyd George's sinking ship.

Whether or not Lloyd George was in real need of continual rest and recreation, he increasingly demanded breaks from the routine of Westminster, Whitehall and the conference circuit. In August 1921 – barely two months after the sojourn in Wales which had been disturbed by the Addison demotion – he again felt the need for a clean break from affairs of state. Bernard Dawson, who was what amounted to 'physician by appointment', said that nothing less than a month would have the necessary recuperative effect. The Prime Minister decided that two weeks would be enough. He moved to Scotland, first as guest of the Duke of Athol and then to Flowerdale House in Gairloch, which he rented with the announcement to his staff that it would be the seat of government during the summer.* He travelled with the usual entourage, to which was added (unusually) both Margaret and Frances. The fortnight provided another example of the chaos which Lloyd George's casual methods created. The Cabinet secretariat tried 'to do the work as if they were in No 10 with one not very efficient shorthand typist. There [was] one room as an office into which everybody crowded, no telephone and a P[ost] O[ffice] with a single line one mile away.' They were 'thirty miles from the nearest station which it [took] four hours to reach' and had 'only one car'.[45] The civil servant who sent that plaintive message home must have been horrified by the discovery that events in Ireland required the Cabinet to meet, and that rather than the Prime Minister returning to London, ministers would gather in Inverness Town Hall.

The arrangements were complicated by Lloyd George suddenly developing an abscess on his jaw of such a size that the local dentist dare not remove the offending tooth. Dawson was summoned from London and a bolder dentist brought from Inverness. Before the full Cabinet

---

*He was pursued, first to Inverness and then to Flowerdale House, by a group of London mayors, led by the young Herbert Morrison. He agreed to discuss increased grants for local authorities' relief work, but the delegation 'left disappointed'.[44]

meeting, the still-suffering Prime Minister met a selection of ministers to discuss ways in which unemployment could be reduced and the unemployed helped. The Prime Minister returned to London to announce the Cabinet's conclusions, but Frances had developed so serious a chill that she was adjudged too ill to travel. From Downing Street Lloyd George wrote what, in the emotion of the moment, he no doubt believed to be true. 'Sleep dreaming of an old man who loves you more than anything and anybody in the world and would gladly if need be give them all up for you.'[46]

The 'package' which the Cabinet agreed was eventually set out in a statement made to the House of Commons on 19 October 1921. It included extra grants for ex-servicemen who wanted to emigrate to the colonies, an extension of export credit guarantees and an increase in investment on relief work. The announcement of the government's plans was accompanied by a homily on the need to reduce wage levels.

> Trade will never be restored to this country, certainly not for years and years to come, unless this problem is courageously faced. Face it with the employees. They are bound to make their case and, if they make their case, it is surely in the interests of the workmen as well as their employers that something be done to enable trade to begin again.[47]

Lloyd George, his critics claimed, had no clear view of how best to deal with the depression. The newspapers, on the other hand, had no doubt about what was the proper remedy. The economy would revive only when a prudent government balanced the nation's books. That view was shared by a majority of the coalition's backbench supporters. Perhaps Lloyd George could have stood out against their combined forces. But he either did not wish or did not dare to do so. The 'economy drive', which had been set in motion before the Prime Minister left for Scotland, was accelerated. On 19 August, Eric Geddes was made chairman of a committee – largely made up of businessmen – which was to devise ways of cutting public expenditure, and the 'Geddes Axe' was forged.

The committee produced three reports. In total they recommended public expenditure cuts of £86 million, which, after the anticipated pressure from departmental ministers, were reduced to £64 million. The blows fell hardest on the Admiralty and the Ministry of Education. Even at their revised level the reductions ended Britain's hopes of naval superiority over the United States and emasculated Fisher's Education Act. Lloyd George was more opposed to cuts in the education budget than to reductions in the naval shipbuilding programme, but he agreed to an increase in minimum class sizes. 'He was sure that the brighter children would learn as readily and as quickly in a class of seventy as they would in a much smaller class.'[48] Presumably, he was equally certain that the middle classes needed an extra incentive to stimulate their contribution to economic recovery. The standard rate of income tax was reduced from 6/- to 5/- in the pound. The Geddes Axe saved only £226 million, but it was enough – even after the tax cut – to produce a budget surplus of £101 million.

Perhaps Lloyd George had honestly abandoned his old beliefs. When his government abolished the Agricultural Wages Board and the excess profits tax – two measures he had himself introduced to fulfil the hopes of his radical past – there was, naturally, a suspicion that his only concern was placating his Unionist critics within the coalition. But there had been a shift in his private opinions which was as seismic as the change in his public policy. 'The truth is that the House of Lords is not unduly obstructive, it is not a bad second chamber.'[49] That had not been his view in 1910. But, whether the conversion was genuine or counterfeit, by 1920 Lloyd George had accepted the domestic agenda of the Unionists who dominated the coalition. It did not make his leadership secure. His future was to be decided not by his tactics on the home front but by his strategy for revising the map of Europe and his success in solving the ancient conundrum of Irish Home Rule.

CHAPTER 33

GOD HELP POOR IRELAND

Lloyd George did not possess any clear or strong view on either the justice or the necessity of Home Rule. He had expressed grave doubts about Gladstone's 1886 bill but, despite his admiration for Joseph Chamberlain, he had deeply disapproved of the rebellion which had destroyed the Liberal government. On the other hand, he had little sympathy for Gladstone's determination to complete his 'mission to pacify Ireland', and he had never hidden his view that the future of Ireland was less important than the electoral success of the Liberal Party and the progress of legislation which was held back by Home Rule's monopoly of parliamentary time. The closest he had come to positive views on the subject was half-hearted support for Home Rule All Round – a feeble federation which satisfied neither the Irish Nationalists nor the English Unionists. To him, Ireland was not a cause but a problem which had to be solved. He did not choose to negotiate an Irish settlement. History left him no choice.

A Home Rule Bill had been passed in 1914 under the provisions of the Parliament Act after it had been defeated in the House of Lords. Asquith had introduced an amending bill which allowed the Protestant counties of the north to remain, at least for a time, within the Union. But it was agreed that the shape and size of the partitioned provinces should be decided after the war was won. During the four years which followed, Irish politics changed. Home Rule, on the Gladstone model, was no longer enough. Nationalists were brushed aside by Republicans. The Irish Parliamentary Party of Charles Stewart Parnell was superseded by Sinn Fein. In October 1917, that party's convention had elected

Eamon de Valera as its president and vowed 'to complete by force of arms the work begun by the men of Easter week' 1916.[1]

In February 1918, Addison – chairman of the Cabinet's Ireland Committee and rightly regarded as sympathetic to Irish aspirations – had been privately warned that partition was 'a policy to which a vast majority of Irish people will be opposed' and that, by espousing it, 'Lloyd George has driven all moderate men in the country, for the moment, out of politics'.[2] But the Prime Minister, lacking either time or inclination, was not in a mood to do more than respond to events. When it was suggested to John Redmond – the leader of the largest Irish Party in the Commons – that the government call a conference at which the Republicans of the south meet the Unionists of the north in an attempt to find a mutually acceptable way forward, he agreed to attend on the understanding that Lloyd George would accept and implement any plan that enjoyed the 'substantial agreement' of all the parties. Relying on the disparate Irish elements remaining irreconcilable, the Prime Minister made the required promise. Indeed he went further. If a proposal were found that commanded support from everyone except the northern Unionists, he 'would use his influence with colleagues' to persuade them 'to accept the proposal and give it legislative effect'.[3] It was too late.

On the day before the armistice was signed, and with the 'coupon' or 'khaki' election pending, Edward Shortt, Chief Secretary for Ireland since May, wrote to warn the Prime Minister against accepting 'suggestions in Tory quarters that Home Rule, for the present, is impossible due to changes in circumstances in Ireland' and that if he were 'ever seen to lend countenance to such proposals, the result will be deplorable'.[4] The old Home Rule formula – regurgitated on 22 December 1918 in a bill which became the Government of Ireland Act – had much the same result. According to the *Irish Times*, plans for two separate parliaments, united by a Council of Ireland and separated by redrawn borders, was 'hateful alike to Unionists and Nationalists'.[5]

Sinn Fein won seventy-three seats in the 1918 election and the Home Rule Party lost all but six of the constituencies which it had held since before the war. Although twenty-five Sinn Fein candidates were returned unopposed, the party polled twice as many votes as the Nationalists. Twenty-nine of its new Members of Parliament were in prison – convicted of subversion. Those who were still at liberty declined to take their seats at Westminster. Instead they assembled in Dublin Mansion House on 21 January 1919 – the day after the Paris peace conference began – and issued a declaration of independence in the name of Dáil Éireann, the Parliament of Free Ireland. Eamon de Valera, in Lincoln Prison, was appointed Prime Minister in his absence. After an escape which might have featured in a *Boy's Own Paper* adventure story, he went to America to raise both morale and material support while his 'government' demanded that the Paris peace conference must treat Ireland like any other oppressed small nation and insisted that it be allowed the right to self-determination which had been promised in Woodrow Wilson's Fourteen Points. Although the Viceroy, Lord French (by then retired from the army), remained the legal governor of Ireland and, in those counties which he designated 'special military areas', imposed what amounted to martial law, the administration of the twenty-six Catholic counties was effectively in the hands of the Dáil.

A negotiated peace might still have been possible if the Republicans – some of whom clearly killed for killing's sake – had not been afraid that the leadership would settle for too little. In the week of the Dáil's first meeting, two policemen – escorting a lorryload of dynamite to a quarry – were shot dead. From then on, violence escalated week by week. Often the police – many of whom preferred retaliation and reprisals to prosecutions – were as guilty as the recently formed Irish Republican Army. Yet most of Ireland was still opposed to violence. In the municipal elections of 1920, Sinn Fein – the only party which supported it – won only 550 seats out of 1806. But revolution does not respect the rules of democracy.

The attacks on police and public servants escalated. Then, in January 1919, the *Daily Chronicle* – effectively Lloyd George's paper – predicted, and came close to endorsing, arbitrary retribution. 'It is obvious that if those murderers pursue their course much longer, we may see counter clubs spring up and the life of prominent Sinn Feiners becoming as unsafe as the prominent officers.'[6] The predicted counter-attack began on 20 March 1920, with the murder of Tomás MacCurtain, the moderate Sinn Fein Mayor of Cork. The Viceroy and the Prime Minister both thought it necessary to issue an immediate statement asserting that neither the police nor their auxiliaries had been involved in any way. But the jury in the coroner's court – which included Unionists – came to the unanimous conclusion that the 'wilful murder was organized and carried out by the RIC [Royal Irish Constabulary] officially directed by the British Government'.[7] It gave the names of the men and women it held responsible for commissioning and carrying out the capital offence. The list included Lloyd George and Lord French.

The Catholic hierarchy condemned the violence without reference to its origins. Cardinal Logue, Primate of All Ireland, said that 'Ireland would never be regenerated by deeds of blood' and that 'among the body of the people, those crimes inspire horror, contempt and reprobation'.[8] And, after the first assassination of a policeman, Monsignor Ryan of St Michael's in Tipperary prayed, 'God help Ireland if she follows this path of blood.'[9]

Not even its bitterest enemies ever accused the Royal Irish Constabulary of cowardice. So it must be assumed that the resignations – 10 per cent of the force between August 1918 and August 1920 – were the result of disagreement over policy and tactics. Whatever the reason for the manpower crisis, the shortage of officers forced the RIC to look for new and temporary recruits in Great Britain. It enrolled ex-servicemen – 4400 in all – at such a speed that they could not be supplied with regulation uniforms. So they wore police tunics and army trousers and were, in consequence, called Black and Tans. They undoubtedly performed their duties with great brutality. But auxiliaries (officially known as cadets and paid, like casual labour, a pound a day) behaved far worse. However, lacking a nickname to establish their place in Irish folklore, they escaped much of the odium.

In the spring of 1920, the Restoration of Order in Ireland Act increased the power of the police and army to suppress rebellion by interning suspects without trial. But the greater the repression, the more the people of Ireland turned against the British and towards the Republicans. Sinn Fein began openly to exercise the powers of government. By the summer of that year, Sinn Fein 'courts' were operating in two-thirds of the Irish counties. During the first two weeks of June, Sinn Fein 'police' made eighty arrests. Sinn Fein 'civil servants' were collecting income tax and a Sinn Fein Land Commission was examining 'land hunger'. According to the *Irish Times*, 'the King's government [had] virtually ceased to exist south of the Boyne and west of the Shannon'.[10]

In August, the army, mistakenly believing that a Cork council meeting was a Sinn Fein court in session, raided the City Hall and arrested Terence MacSwiney, the Sinn Fein Lord Mayor, and held him without trial under the provisions of the Restoration of Order Act. When he was transferred to Mountjoy Prison in Dublin, he immediately began a hunger strike and announced that his death would be a victory in the war for Irish freedom. The Viceroy responded with the announcement that he would not be released, no matter how long his fast continued. MacSwiney died in Wormwood Scrubs Prison in London on 25 October.

The King had sensibly suggested to Lloyd George that 'the probable result arising from MacSwiney's death will be far more serious and far more far-reaching than if he were taken out of prison where his wife could look after him' while he was 'kept under close surveillance so that he could not return to Ireland'.[11] But instead of accepting that wise advice, ministers had tried to diminish the admiration in which he was held by telling friendly newspapers that food was being smuggled into his prison cell. One of the more unlikely stories was that bread had been found hidden in a visiting priest's beard.

Lloyd George had been inundated with messages begging for MacSwiney's release. Some argued the case on humanitarian grounds. Others echoed the King's warning about the damage that his death in custody would do. The clamour became so great that the Prime Minister was persuaded of the necessity to explain the long-term consequences of capitulating to moral blackmail. The warning that subversion threatened the kingdom was, to a degree, undermined by his statement being sent to newspapers from Lucerne, where he was spending an extended holiday. The subsequent explanation of the decision – which he sent to Bonar Law – suggested that he was less than comfortable with the whole episode.

> When I sent my wire I had been definitely informed that if I let him go it would completely disintegrate and dishearten the police force in Ireland and the military. Apart from that it struck me that if we released him we might as well give up attempting to maintain law and order in Ireland.

His conclusion that 'not enough has been done to put our case before the British public' was the typical response of a troubled politician.[12] It is always easier to blame the presentation than the policy itself. No doubt he believed that the speech which he made in his constituency in October 1920 would help to reconcile the public to the excesses of the army and the police. 'There is no doubt that at last their patience has given way and there has been some severe hitting back. But take the conditions . . .'[13] There was no need for him to finish the sentence. Civilians, Lloyd George said, were shooting at troops and the RIC without warning. No wonder they sometimes shot to pre-empt attack. Herbert Samuel, an ex-Home Secretary, took a different view. He told the St Albans Liberal Association, 'If what is going on in Ireland was going on in the Austrian Empire, England would be ringing with the tyranny of the Hapsburgs.'[14] In fact, Lloyd George and his Irish Secretary were acting to reduce police retaliation, but they thought it inexpedient to admit that it was necessary to tighten discipline. In the first three months of 1921, twenty-four members of the RIC and their supporting forces were convicted of brutality by the legitimate courts. Two hundred and sixty-seven more were dismissed from the service. There was, however, only one conviction for murder. The officer was found guilty but insane.

Winston Churchill addressed the subject with the same reckless demagoguery that he had employed during the constitutional crisis. 'Surrender to a miserable gang of cowardly assassins like the human leopards of West Africa would be followed by passionate repentance and fearful atonement.'[15] Lloyd George, speaking at the Lord Mayor of London's banquet, chose to proclaim a victory rather than justify a continuation of the war. On 9 November 1920, he told the City what it wanted to hear. He denounced the insurgency as 'organized assassination of the most cowardly kind' but assured his audience, 'We have murder by the throat.'[16] Perhaps he was thinking of the 'Cairo Gang', a network of army officers which had been set up in Dublin to locate and kill Michael Collins – the boldest and most ruthless of the IRA gunmen operating in the city. Their existence was revealed to the IRA by an informer and their lodgings identified by Republican-sympathising maids and porters. On the morning after the Lord Mayor's banquet, IRA volunteers burst into eight Dublin houses and shot dead eighteen British soldiers, among them most of the Cairo Gang. Horror piled on horror. That afternoon, Black and Tans surrounded the Croke Park stadium where a Gaelic Athletic Association football match was due to take place. Ostensibly the irregulars were looking for the morning's murderers. According to the official inquiry, the first shot came from the crowd and the security forces did no more than return fire. They killed twelve spectators and a woman was crushed to death by the stampede that the shooting provoked. That night, three men – one of whom had been arrested by mistake – were shot 'while trying to escape' from Dublin Castle, the headquarters of the British administration. They had been beaten and bayoneted before they died.

While the murder and mayhem continued, a variety of peace plans were initiated, promoted and withered away. On 21 October 1920, Patrick Moylett, a London-based Irish businessman, asked H. A. L. Fisher to pass a message from Sinn Fein to Lloyd George. Peace could be secured on the basis of proposals set out in a letter to *The Times* by Brigadier-General Cockerill MP. Its crucial paragraph had claimed that 'if Ulster would join [them] . . . in a spirit of conciliation to seek a settlement by consensus, there was practically no limit to the concessions [they] would be prepared to make'.[17] In November, the Archbishop of Perth, on a visit to Britain from Australia, visited Arthur Griffith in gaol. Griffith, a veteran Republican who had fought with the Boers against the British, told the archbishop that Sinn Fein would negotiate a settlement if there were 'a mutual cessation of armed activity, a moratorium on prosecutions and agreement that the Dáil should meet without interruption'. Lloyd George, anticipating the mistakes of future generations, refused to negotiate with Sinn Fein until it surrendered its arms and ammunition.

General Sir Nevil Macready – once Lloyd George's choice to bring discipline to the Metropolitan Police – was made Commander-in-Chief with instructions not to compromise with terror. The assumption has always been that he was appointed to act towards Republicans with a ferocity which his predecessor would not contemplate. His communiqués, sent to Lloyd George via Frances Stevenson, suggest that, if that were the intention, the government chose the wrong man. 'Ever since my days in Ulster in 1913–14 I have always looked on the [Orange] movement as rebels . . . In the ranks of Sinn Fein are men of substance and deep religious feeling . . . here and there will be unauthorised reprisals, due entirely to the fact that certain police officers have not got full control over their men.'[18] He even echoed Addison's warning against introducing a 'bill which is not acceptable to any party', and opposed martial law.[19] The advice of the policeman who had been sent to intimidate Ireland was far too conciliatory to appeal to either the general public or the Unionist Party. In consequence, the Prime Minister rejected it.

The best that can be said of Lloyd George's view on combating terror with terror is that he was ambivalent and that, although he deplored the brutality, he thought it the only way to reduce attacks upon the police and the army. Winston Churchill was, typically, more uninhibited. He wanted 'the substitution of regular, authorized and legalized reprisals for unauthorized reprisals by police and soldiers'.[20] The Cabinet considered the suggestion but decided to keep clean hands. The refusal to denounce the brutality which had become commonplace ended – albeit briefly – Lloyd George's twenty-year friendship with C. P. Scott, the editor of the *Manchester Guardian*.[21] It also did nothing to endear him to those members of the Cabinet who wanted him to go further along the road to repression of the kind which he had condemned during the Boer War.

Ian Macpherson, the hardline Chief Secretary for Ireland who had succeeded Shortt, complained that he 'never had a word of sympathy from the PM. He preferred to have the views of a man who was notoriously a Jesuit, whose views on Irish affairs I should listen to but never accept.' The adviser about whom he complained was 'the stupid egoist Sir Horace Plunkett', the Unionist landowner who had warned Addison against adopting a policy which alienated all of Ireland.[22] Lord Salisbury's succinct comment on Lloyd George's Irish policy – 'the PM makes me sick' – confirmed that, by attempting to avoid being wholeheartedly associated with either Home Rule or the continued Union, Lloyd George had created a consensus of disapproval.

The Government of Ireland Act had created two parliaments in Ireland and had been tacitly accepted by Sinn Fein as an opportunity to legitimise the Dáil. It had been accompanied by what Lloyd George hoped would be seen as concessions to moderate Republican positions. The replacement of Lord French by Lord Fitzalan was greeted by Cardinal Logue with what could not be described as even a qualified welcome. A Catholic Viceroy was no more acceptable than a Catholic hangman. Lord Derby was sent – disguised in horn-rimmed spectacles and registered in his hotel as 'Mr Edwards' – to make secret contacts with Sinn Fein. He was confounded by de Valera's dialectical technique. When he asked if the Dáil would negotiate about a settlement without the principle of independence being accepted by Lloyd George, the Taoiseach responded by asking if the British government would negotiate without it being abandoned. But Lloyd George had become convinced that the Republicans would never be suppressed. Since he had no strong feelings about maintaining the Union he was happy enough for them to be accommodated. Neville Macready's request for more troops was rejected. Conciliation would begin with the King's opening the Northern Ireland parliament on 22 June 1921.

The elections that the Government of Ireland Act required were held on 12 and 24 May 1921. The idea of calling for a truce during the campaign was considered by the Cabinet and rejected as a sign of weakness. In the north, the Unionists won forty seats out of fifty-two, and in the south they lost every constituency except Trinity College. In Dublin, Republicans celebrated their victory by burning down the

Customs House. It was the last hurrah of the armed revolt. The IRA – desperately short of arms, ammunition and men – was overstretched and exhausted. Once more, peace was being promoted by attrition.

The first draft of the King's Belfast Speech – prepared by George V's advisers – simply repeated the government's outdated determination to crush terror. Lloyd George rejected it. General Smuts – an authority in the conversion of rebels into patriots – supervised the composition of a new version. It was agreed by the King and accepted in both northern and southern Ireland with astonished delight. 'I appeal to all Irishmen to pause, stretch out the hand of forgiveness and conciliation, to forgive and forget and join together in making for the land they love a new era of peace, contentment and good will.'[23] Newspapers of every opinion described the speech as a triumph. Lloyd George was at Euston Station to greet the King on his return. George, encouraged by the discovery that he was an expert on Irish affairs, advised his Prime Minister, 'When dealing with a quick-witted, volatile and sentimental people it is necessary to seize the moment', and urged him to prevent Churchill and Birkenhead from making bellicose speeches.[24] He did not, as the *New York Times* reported, ask Lloyd George, 'Are you going to shoot all the people in Northern Ireland?' Nor did he, on being assured that genocide was not government policy, insist, 'You must come to some agreement with them. This thing cannot go on. I cannot have my people killed in this manner.'[25] The imagined – or invented – expression of opinion represented Lloyd George's reconsidered view about policy towards both north and south. On 11 July 1921, British troops in Ireland were returned to barracks. The way was open to negotiations. Lloyd George did not expect to enjoy the process. He found the Taoiseach an uncongenial companion. Arguing with de Valera was, he said, 'like sitting on a roundabout and trying to catch up with the swing in front'.[26]

Lloyd George's hopes of an Irish settlement were inseparable from his aspiration to secure his own political future. On 21 June, he told Frances Stevenson that the time had come 'to commit suicide as a coalition and, like the phoenix, rise from the ashes of a new party'.[27] He was more than ever convinced – perhaps with some justification – that half the Cabinet, including some Liberals, was conspiring against him. Smuts, despite his success in redrafting the King's Speech, was accused of being 'tiresome' over Ireland – a fault which Frances (who detected 'intrigues seething everywhere') attributed to his 'running with Asquith and Co in case the government fails'.[28] Churchill was 'very hostile'.

Beaverbrook was 'clearly engineering for a coup'.[29] F. E. Smith, by then Lord Birkenhead, was said to be prevented from inciting rebellion only by the quick-witted Prime Minister, who blocked what Frances Stevenson described in a contradiction in terms as 'a sensational speech on fiscal autonomy'.[30] It was then that the plot was mysteriously revealed in an 'amazing article' in the *Manchester Guardian*, forcing Birkenhead into 'denying the whole thing' in a fashion Frances Stevenson regarded as 'protesting too much'.[31] As one threat was being averted, another arose. The suspicion was resuscitated that Bonar Law had returned from his convalescence in France only 'for a specific purpose' – his assumption of the premiership in place of Lloyd George. The coup was said to be orchestrated by Lord Beaverbrook, who, because of damaging (but unspecified) information in his possession, was able 'practically [to] blackmail' the Unionist leader.[32] Throughout the turbulent summer of 1921, the claustrophobic secrecy of Lloyd George's 'other life' encouraged Frances Stevenson to think that she alone stood between the Prime Minister and a world of would-be assassins. Her suspicions fuelled, rather than dispelled, his fears. An unusually insecure Lloyd George began to negotiate a treaty which, he knew, would satisfy nobody.

The Sinn Fein delegation met Lloyd George for preliminary discussions on 18 July. They agreed about nothing except the name of the country which they proposed to create. According to de Valera's version of events, Lloyd George asked about the heading of the paper on which the letter confirming the meeting had been written. He was told that *Saorstát n hÉireann* meant 'The Free State of Ireland'. The alternative to *Saorstát*, de Valera explained, was *Poblacht* or 'Republic'. After some banter about Celts never having been republicans, Lloyd George accepted *Saorstát n hÉireann*, encouraged by the precedent of the Orange Free State, which Smuts claimed to have drawn to his attention.[33] It was certainly Smuts who suggested that Sinn Fein accept dominion status and persuaded Lloyd George, who had initially dismissed it as an Asquith manoeuvre, that it offered the best hope of a settlement.

On 20 July 1921, the Cabinet agreed what its minutes describe as the government's final position. Twenty-six counties were to be offered dominion status. The Six Counties of the north would remain part of the Union for as long as that was their wish. The Royal Navy would defend Irish coastal waters and have free access to southern ports. The *Saorstát n hÉireann* army was to limit its activities to the Free State. The Dáil would accept responsibility for part of the United Kingdom's national debt and would undertake not to raise tariff barriers against British imports. After much discussion it was reluctantly agreed that the new arrangement should be embodied in a treaty. Balfour, Curzon and Birkenhead were bitterly opposed to what they regarded as an admission of Irish sovereignty. Lloyd George said that no other form of agreement would be acceptable to de Valera.

Sinn Fein rejected the proposals without quibbling about their legal status. For them, nothing but 'amicable, but absolute, separation' would do.[34] The Irish delegation left London after an afternoon of point scoring, interspersed with a passage of verbal brutality about the consequences of disagreement which ended with Lloyd George asking de Valera, 'Do you not realise that this means war? Do you not realise that the responsibility for it will rest on your shoulders alone?' De Valera replied, 'No, Mr Lloyd George. If you insist on attacking us it is you, not I, who will be responsible: You will be the aggressor.' The Prime Minister changed tack. Threats replaced the allocation of blame. 'I could put a soldier in Ireland for every man, woman and child in it.' De Valera told him, 'Very well. But you would have to keep them there.'[35] And so the British government did, in one way or another, for ninety years.

When the House of Commons rose for the summer recess, Lloyd George left for his recuperative holiday in Scotland. He had been at Flowerdale House in Gairloch for a week when he received a note from de Valera. It suggested more discussions. Ministers were summoned north to attend the Cabinet meeting which was to be held in Inverness Town Hall on 2 September. It was not a journey on which they embarked with either enthusiasm or even calm resignation, as Baldwin recalled:

> Looking along the train the first familiar figure to meet my eye was the Lord High Chancellor, seated not on a woolsack but on a cane bottomed chair with a cigar a foot long in his mouth and a case of cider at his feet . . . His vocabulary was singularly limited. 'This bloody journey'. Those, for an hour, were the only words I could clearly distinguish.[36]

There were cheers from the waiting crowd when the Prime Minister – who, on the previous day, had been featured on the front page of the *Tatler* in a picture to which Stanley Baldwin had added his own caption, 'Goat on a pony' – arrived at Inverness Town Hall.[37] In the certain knowledge that the ceasefire would not hold much longer, the Cabinet quickly agreed terms of reference for a new meeting with Sinn Fein. They were constructed in a way which implied a small but significant relaxation of the British position. The new talks would 'ascertain how the association with the community of nations known as the British Empire can best be reconciled with Irish national aspiration' – a formula which was general enough to secure initial agreement and guarantee eventual breakdown.

The final round of meetings between Sinn Fein and British ministers began on 10 October 1921. Lloyd George was supported by Churchill and Birkenhead. The Irish delegation – defined in its credentials as 'plenipotentiaries' – was led by Arthur Griffith, supported most notably by Michael Collins. De Valera refused – despite Collins's entreaties – to attend. There are two possible explanations for his absence. One is that it would have been certainly inappropriate and possibly improper for the President-cum-Prime Minister of the Free State to risk being forced into making concessions which some of the citizens he represented did not support. However, constitutional propriety had not inhibited his behaviour in the past. The other possible reason why he remained in Dublin is less honourable but more plausible, and it accounts for his insistence that Michael Collins – increasingly his rival – should act as deputy to Arthur Griffith. He knew that the negotiations were bound to end in failure.

The discussions were long and tedious – a certain recipe for growing complaints from Ulster 'loyalists' who had never wanted them to begin. Although the Unionists' parliamentary leadership, in the form of Austen Chamberlain, accepted the need for unconditional discussions, there was profound opposition on the Tory backbenches to negotiations with men who, only months before, had been in rebellion against the Crown. A motion of censure was put down for 31 October. Lloyd George announced that the motion would be regarded by the government as a vote of confidence and told Frances Stevenson that he 'was anxious to go out and this would be a good moment and a good excuse'.[38] He did not mean it. To ensure their continued loyalty, he reminded Churchill and Birkenhead that, if the vote were lost, the Bonar Law administration which followed would have no room for them. The vote was won – very largely because Chamberlain rallied the Unionist forces – by 439 votes to 43.

On the night before the coalition's House of Commons victory, the Prime Minister had met Arthur Griffith – according to Lloyd George's invitation, simply in order to clear away some of the obstacles on the path to unity. During discussions between the rival Irish politicians, James Craig, the Prime Minister of the nascent Northern Ireland province, had been amazed by Griffith's willingness to meet Lloyd George without a third party present. Indeed, he had warned him of the dangers of doing so.[39] No doubt the leader of the Sinn Fein delegation should have realised that he had little to gain and much to lose from a conversation which he was asked to keep secret from his colleagues. But Griffith was flattered by the invitation to talk to the Prime Minister man-to-man and, when the meeting took place, was equally convinced of both the wisdom and sincerity of the offer which he received. Griffith was told that if he would urge his delegation to accept 'Irish recognition of the crown . . . and a free partnership with the United Kingdom', Lloyd George would 'go to the House of Commons and smite the diehards' who opposed Home Rule.[40] Griffith promised to do his best and signed a document signifying his personal agreement to dominion status.

Griffith took it for granted that the Ireland of which Lloyd George spoke would be united under a single parliament. And that, at the time, was certainly the Prime Minister's preference. Lloyd George was determined to avoid a renewal of repression at *almost* all costs. On 12 November, he wrote to Herbert Lewis, now the Liberal Member for the University of Wales, with apparent sincerity. 'I have made up my mind that I will not coerce Southern Ireland. I may lose everything but I shall save my soul anyway.'[41] But, two days later, Bonar Law's opinion on the Irish negotiations – reported, verbatim, in the *Scotsman* – changed his mind.

> I did not intend to have anything to do with politics till the beginning of next session. But it now looks as if I might. If LlG goes on with the present proposals I shall oppose them. I shall try to get the Conservative Party to follow me.[42]

It was, he added, his intention to see Lloyd George that night. He proposed to repeat the advice he had given him a couple of days earlier. 'Don't confine your bullying to Ulster. Try it on the Sinn Feiners too.'[43] Wisely or cynically, Bonar Law played no part in the meeting of the National Union of Conservative Associations which was held on 17 November to debate a motion calling on Unionist supporters of the coalition to reject Home Rule. The 'loyalist' motion was heavily defeated. When Lloyd George heard the news, he marched up and

GOD HELP POOR IRELAND

down the Cabinet Room playing 'See the Conquering Hero Comes' on an imaginary trumpet.[44] Then he was told that the vote had been won only because Chamberlain had once more appealed for loyalty to the leadership.

Lloyd George at last realised the truth of what Tim Healy – an unofficial adviser to the Sinn Fein delegation – had told his countrymen. 'You can get a fresh deal for Ireland but you can only get as much as the Conservative Party will give you. The Prime Minister himself is in chains to the Conservatives in this matter.'[45] Lloyd George had come to accept that the Unionists would never agree to the incorporation of Ulster into an Irish Free State. Another adjustment of tactics was necessary.

Because he was not yet reconciled to full and permanent partition, Lloyd George suggested that an all-Ireland parliament should be established but that the Six Counties of the north should be given the right to leave after a year. His hope was that the hard-headed Ulstermen would choose to pay Dublin taxes rather than the higher Westminster alternative. When that proposal was rejected by the Unionists, he suggested a variation. Ulster should, initially, be separated from the south but should be offered the right, after six months, to amalgamate with it and enjoy its comparatively low tax rates. That proposal was also rejected – as Lloyd George should have known it would be. He had begun his consideration of possible solutions in the mistaken belief that no one would 'die for Tyrone or Fermanagh'.[46] Only desperation or self-delusion could have made him imagine that the patriots of Ulster's Six Counties would abandon their identity and heritage for sixpence in the pound off the basic rate of income tax.

The last hope of reconciling the two conflicting demands – already canvassed with Sinn Fein by Tom Jones, the author of the scheme – was ingenious enough, or some would say sufficiently devious, to have been invented by Lloyd George himself. The Six Counties would have their own parliament. But, in an adaptation of the 1918 proposals, the boundary which divided them from the south would be redrawn to ensure that Catholics from the Border counties were included in the Free State. This, Jones argued, made the separation 'essentially temporary'. Much of Londonderry, Fermanagh and Tyrone would choose to go south. What remained of the Six Counties could not survive as an independent province. Eventual, if reluctant, absorption into the Free State would be inevitable.

The proposal was exactly suited to Lloyd George's negotiating technique – which had not changed since, as President of the Board of

Trade, he had employed it so successfully with the railway unions. Whatever he said, or meant, each party to the discussion was left with different interpretations of his intentions. Michael Collins believed that 'very large areas' would be moved south.[47] James Craig claimed that the Prime Minister had assured him that the Boundary Commission 'would not leave Ulster less than it was under the Government of Ireland Act'.[48]

Lloyd George and Lord Birkenhead met Arthur Griffith and Michael Collins on 25 November to discuss a draft of the proposed treaty's opening paragraphs. There was no agreement on any of the contentious issues. Two more draft treaties were examined with no more success and Griffith, unsure how to move on from the stalemate, returned to Dublin, where he was instructed by de Valera to accept no other status for the Free State than 'external association' with the Commonwealth. He returned to London on 28 November. On the following day, Lloyd George – conscious that his opponents within the coalition were gaining strength – decided that the negotiations must be moved on. James Craig was authorised to tell the Belfast parliament that Ireland's future would be determined by 6 December. The stage was set for the fateful meeting which, by design, took place on the day before the deadline which Lloyd George had set.

In a last attempt to find agreement, the British ministers moved as far as party and public opinion would allow. A suddenly and surprisingly accommodating Winston Churchill agreed to negotiate with Dublin about the future of British bases within the Free State, and the proposed oath of allegiance had been constructed to minimise offence to Republican opinion.* But as de Valera and his followers insisted that *any* mention of the King was an affront to Irish sovereignty, there seemed little hope of defining the Free State's relationship with the Empire in a way which was acceptable to both Sinn Fein and the Unionists within the coalition. However, at the 'ground-clearing meeting' on 29 October, Griffith – alone with Lloyd George – had agreed to accept full dominion status and accepted that the King was head of the whole Empire. Unless he went back on his undertaking, the Sinn Fein delegates' unity of purpose had been shattered. Lloyd George exploited the split on 5 December with his first *coup de théâtre*.

As the argument dragged on, he produced from his pocket the

---

*'I do solemnly swear true faith and allegiance to the Constitution of the Irish Free State – and will be faithful to HM King George V, his heirs and successors.'

statement which Griffith had signed – claiming that he had forgotten about its existence until the suit that he had worn on the day of the preliminary meeting had been sent to the cleaners. The trick worked. Griffith, affronted by the implication that he was going back on his word, took the bait. 'I have never let a man down in my life and never will.'[49] He could not speak for the rest of the delegation, but he would sign the treaty.

The meeting was adjourned to enable the Sinn Fein delegation to regroup. Gradually, as the day wore on, it edged closer and closer towards acceptance but, after eight hours of agonising, it still hesitated. It was time for the second contrived moment of drama. Lloyd George produced two more letters – by some accounts holding one in each hand above his head – and explained their contents.

> I have to communicate with Sir James Craig tonight. Here are the alternative letters which I have prepared, one enclosing Articles of Agreement reached by His Majesty's Government and yourselves and the other saying that Sinn Fein representatives refuse to come within the terms. If I send this letter, it is war and war within three days. Which am I to send? Whichever you choose travels by special train to Holyhead tonight and by destroyer to Belfast. The train is waiting, steam up, in Euston. We must know your answer by 10 p.m. tonight. You have till then, but no longer, to decide whether you give peace or war to your country.[50]

He waited to hear their decision until two o'clock on the morning of Tuesday 6 December. Then the Sinn Fein delegation signed the treaty. Back in his hotel Michael Collins wrote in his diary, 'I tell you this, early this morning I signed my death warrant.'[51]

Tom Jones told Sir Maurice Hankey, 'It was a wonderful day', and that view has been held, with some justification, by Lloyd George admirers ever since. The immediate consequence was a year of civil war in the Free State. It was followed by an uneasy peace until the Catholics of the north – condemned to second-class citizenship by partition – rose up in the civil rights movement and gave the IRA the confidence to renew its guerrilla campaign against the Stormont parliament. But the outline of a new Ireland had been sketched out in a deal which Lloyd George's cynicism and Sinn Fein's naivety had made possible. Whether or not the Sinn Fein delegation believed that Lloyd George would ensure that the Boundary Commission became the agent of

Irish unity, they accepted – apparently without question – the story of the express train, waiting 'steam up' at Euston and the destroyer, ready to sail, in Holyhead dock. Nobody asked or, it seems, thought it necessary to ask why the Prime Minister could not use the telephone or telegraph to send James Craig the fateful message of peace or war. Sinn Fein had been overwhelmed by a combination of charm, ruthless determination, ingenuity and, when necessary, dishonesty. They had fallen victim to Lloyd George's negotiating technique. But the victory which he believed he had achieved also owed much to his defining political characteristic. He set about his task uninhibited by either prejudice or principle. He was neither a Unionist nor a Home Ruler. All he wanted was a deal – any deal – which, at least for a time, removed Ireland from the political agenda. He had succeeded in obtaining a settlement where Pitt, Peel and Gladstone had failed. They had struggled to achieve what they thought right. He had achieved what he judged to be possible.

According to A. J. Sylvester – who had by then become one of his secretaries – Lloyd George greeted Sinn Fein's agreement 'like a man in a dream, a smile of elation over his features'.[52] But the victory was not complete. Bonar Law, supporting the treaty's endorsement when it was debated in the House of Commons, spoke for most of the Unionist MPs who were essential to its acceptance. 'When I say I am in favour of the Treaty, I do not mean that I like it.'[53] That represented Lloyd George's view as well – though his reservations were different from Bonar Law's. The justification for his conduct – including the double-talk and the dissembling – is that he secured the best deal that he could. Perhaps no one could have done better. But had he kept his promise to redraw Northern Ireland's boundary, eighty years of bloodshed might have been avoided.

Like all compromises, the Northern Ireland settlement satisfied neither of the rival factions. Coalition Tories believed that the Union had been betrayed. Their support for the coalition was diminishing and Lloyd George knew it. He was far more popular in the country than in Parliament. He concluded that the time was fast approaching for a general election in which the people's support would make him invincible in his continued battle with the Unionists within the coalition.

Birkenhead, more realistic and therefore apprehensive, told Michael Collins, 'I may be signing my political death warrant tonight.' Both men's fears were to prove justified. Collins was to die in an ambush at Béal na mBláth. Birkenhead perished with Lloyd George and the coalition government.

CHAPTER 34

THROWN TO THE WOLVES

A year after he lost office, Lloyd George – not a man who was usually haunted by regret – confided in Lord Hardinge, a former Viceroy of India, and permanent head of the Foreign Office, 'If I had to go to Paris again, I would conclude a quite different treaty.'[1] He meant that, given a second chance, he would have negotiated terms far less punitive than those which he had allowed Clemenceau to dictate. But he might well have felt equal regret that he had agreed to Britain accepting so many additional international commitments. The 'blotches of red' on the map of the world – which Lloyd George had insensitively drawn to de Valera's attention – had spread. German South-West Africa and Tanganyika were absorbed into the British Empire. New kingdoms in the Middle East – ruled by Arab princes chosen by the Great Powers at the Paris peace conference – were, in form if not in international law, British protectorates. Among them, Mesopotamia (soon to become Iraq) had oil at Mosul. But Palestine and Transjordan offered little except confirmation that Britain was a world power, and world power is expensive. When Arab tribesmen rose up to insist that the government of Iraq was a matter for them – rather than the British – their rebellion was suppressed by the RAF bombing their villages.

British troops were stationed in Persia, Constantinople (to defend the straits), Egypt (to protect the Suez Canal against nationalist saboteurs) and Germany (as part of the occupying forces). Egypt's status changed. Milner – by then Colonial Secretary – proposed to replace the 'mandate' (supervision on behalf of the League of Nations) with a treaty. The idea was initially rejected by the Cabinet, largely on the advice of Lloyd

George, who feared the emergence of what Philip Kerr called a 'Pan-Islamic Sinn Fein'.[2] But, although Egypt's virtual independence was accepted in fact if not in form, the obligation to guard the Canal Zone remained. Other imperial obligations were gradually relinquished, not so much because of the Prime Minister's instincts – he remained at heart a radical imperialist – but because circumstances allowed no other possibility. Money and willing troops were scarce. There were many demands on limited resources. It was assumed that the Bolshevik Soviet Union was no less a threat to India than Tsarist Russia had been.

In India Gandhi, who had refused to campaign for independence during the war, renewed his call for *satyagraha* – the 'soul force of passive resistance'. In 1917 Edwin Montagu, the Secretary of State for India, and Lord Chelmsford, the Viceroy, had produced a report which recommended a limited (and highly complicated) measure of self-government. It was incorporated in the 1919 Government of India Act. At the same time, a committee of enquiry, led by Mr Justice Rowlatt, examined the workings of 1915's Defence of India Act and judged that its powers of arbitrary arrest needed to be strengthened. Neither act quietened the demand for change. At Amritsar on 10 April 1919, two Indian Nationalist leaders were arrested on suspicion of subversion. A mob swept through the town, burned down the Town Hall, cut the telephone wires and murdered four Europeans. Martial law was declared but four days later – on the day of the Baisakhi festival – a peaceful crowd assembled in Amritsar's Jallianwala Bagh. Brigadier-General R. E. H. Dyer ordered the crowd to disperse. When it refused, he ordered his troops to open fire. They fired 1650 rounds in ten minutes. The Indian Army's official statement, generally thought to underestimate the casualties, reported 379 dead and 1208 injured. Dyer was dismissed. When the House of Commons debated his conduct, Unionist Diehards – the Tories who preferred Opposition to government under Lloyd George – defended Dyer as a man pilloried for doing his duty, and Montagu was heckled with openly racist comments about his race and religion. Dyer's treatment was added to the list of complaints that the right wing of the Tory Party made against Lloyd George.

Chelmsford was succeeded as Viceroy by Lord Reading, who, like Montagu, thought that – in the face of renewed agitation from the largely Hindu Indian National Congress movement – it was necessary to win the support of moderate Muslims. Both men were emotionally committed to making progress towards Indian independence – a feature of their genuine radical instincts which in March 1922 led them to commit the indiscretion which cost Montague his job. Pious Indian Muslims – distressed by the collapse of the Turkish Caliphate after the dispersal of the Ottoman Empire – wanted the Sublime Porte, which had once enjoyed suzerainty over all Islamic Asia Minor, to regain its authority over Jerusalem's holy places. On the morning of 1 March 1922, Montagu received a telegram from the Viceroy. It proposed that, in order to placate Muslim opinion, Allied troops should be withdrawn from Constantinople. The Cabinet would never have agreed to ignore Britain's treaty obligations. But before it had an opportunity to reject the idea, a combination of incompetence and bad luck resulted in the Viceroy's telegram being published – in an outraged yellow press – as though it were a *fait accompli*. Curzon, Foreign Secretary since October 1919, told the House of Lords that 'a subordinate branch of government, six thousand miles away, [had] dictated to the British Government' and had to be put in its place. Montagu resigned. It was a victory for the Tories who were counting the days before the now expendable Lloyd George could be ousted.

Montagu responded with a speech which demonstrated that the Prime Minister had lost essential authority even with his long-standing supporters. Two days after he left the Cabinet, he addressed the Cambridge University Liberal Club on the subject of collective responsibility, the obligation which he was said to have ignored. He accused Lloyd George of what, sixty years later, was called 'sofa government'.

> We have been governed by a great genius – a dictator who has called together from time to time conferences of Ministers, men who had access to him day and night, leaving all those who, like myself, found it impossible to get to him for days together. He has come to epoch-making decisions, over and over again. It is notorious that members of the Cabinet had no knowledge of those decisions.[3]

The public description of Lloyd George's autocratic style of government – well known to those who endured it and probably of no consequence to the general public – caused only brief damage. The real harm was done by the demonstration of disrespect. The awe had gone. Montagu, once a Lloyd George acolyte, had called the Prime Minister a genius but clearly viewed him as a flawed and fallible human being. Anger at his dismissal had provoked him into revealing Lloyd George's diminished status within his own Cabinet. The decline in reverence was

clear even in the conduct of those who remained loyal to the end. Lord
Birkenhead contested Lloyd George's choice of new Lord Chief Justice
in a letter which the Prime Minister resented because of its length as
well at its tone. And long after Lloyd George had determined to give a
degree of formal recognition to the Russian revolutionary government,
Winston Churchill continued to complain in Cabinet about doing 'this
supreme favour and patronage to the Bolsheviks' and 'taking sides
against Russia as a whole with a group of dastardly criminals'.[4]

Curzon behaved true to character by criticising Lloyd George
behind his back but fawning on him when they met face-to-face.
However deplorable his duplicity, there is no doubt that he was entitled to resent being regarded as no more than one of what Walter
Bagehot called the 'dignified' parts of the constitution. At the conclusion of the Paris peace talks, Lloyd George had taken command of
foreign policy – ignoring both Foreign Office advice and the Foreign
Secretary. The result was an object lesson in the dangers of hubris. The
coalition was destined to survive for only a year or two, but the Prime
Minister's excursion into foreign policy brought forward the date of its
destruction.

Lloyd George really believed that he needed neither diplomatic
advice nor political support. In April 1921, when the prime ministers of
France and Britain had held a private meeting in Kent at Lympne – one
of several houses owned by Philip Sassoon, Lloyd George's parliamentary private secretary – the French Foreign Minister was invited to
attend but his British counterpart was not, occasioning a letter from
Curzon to his wife which announced, 'I am getting tired of working,
or trying to work, for that man. He wants his For. Sec. to be a valet,
almost a drudge.'[5] However, Curzon never became so tired of humiliation that he seriously contemplated resigning. His desperation to
remain Foreign Secretary – whatever indignity was heaped upon him –
was one of the reasons why the Prime Minister's wartime admiration
had turned into peacetime contempt. But it was not just his low opinion of the incumbent that prompted Lloyd George to be his own
Foreign Secretary. He wanted to be everything because he believed that
nothing was beyond him. So he initiated a practice which subsequent
prime ministers copied – often with similarly disastrous results. Lloyd
George was a pioneer of personal diplomacy.

There were some indisputable, and undisputed, diplomatic successes.
A week after the Anglo-Irish Treaty was signed, the Washington
Agreement between Britain, the United States, Japan and France

defined those countries' roles and rights in the 'insular possessions and dominions' of the Pacific. In the margins of the negotiations, the ground was prepared for the declaration – in which Italy joined – of a ten-year moratorium on naval shipbuilding. The pact was formally agreed in February 1922. But, although more than three years had passed since the end of the war, the Allies could still not agree about the size of Germany's reparations bill and the speed at which it was to be paid. Lloyd George had come to believe that real progress towards a lasting European settlement depended on Russia and Germany being involved in the discussion of the continent's future at a conference which he would initiate and, if possible, convene. The League of Nations, emasculated by America's absence, was not, in Lloyd George's estimation, up to the task. And an 'independent' conference was a forum in which he would be guaranteed to shine. In January 1922, he met the French Prime Minister in Cannes with the hope of preparing the ground for what would now be called a 'summit', at which Russia and Germany would be welcomed into the international community.

The immediate need was to solve the dispute between France and Germany – occasioned by the announcement that the Berlin government could not afford to pay the January and February instalments of its reparations liability. Aristide Briand was, it seemed, ready to forgo his country's dues if he could negotiate a treaty which pledged Britain's military support in time of war. Such a treaty would provide the protection which President Wilson had promised but been unable to deliver after the United States Congress had declined to ratify the Versailles Treaty. For a hundred years, the avoidance of continental 'entanglements' had been a principle of British foreign policy. But Lloyd George was not a man to respect precedents. The proposal was accepted on the understanding that the arrangement applied only to France's eastern boundaries and that help would be guaranteed only if the hypothesised enemy (Germany was never mentioned by name) actually invaded French territory. His offer was endorsed by the Cabinet, comforted by the Foreign Secretary's assurance that British 'military policy would remain unaffected'.[6] The French National Assembly – having come to the same conclusion – accused Briand of sacrificing the reparations payments for nothing in particular. The Paris newspapers added – with supporting photographs – that he had made himself ridiculous by taking golf lessons from Lloyd George. Briand was replaced by Raymond Poincaré, who demanded commitments to military cooperation which Lloyd George was unable to give. Anglo-French relations deteriorated. After the two men met in Boulogne, Poincaré lunched with his staff, leaving Lloyd George to eat alone in the railway station. Although the auguries suggested that a second conference would be no more successful than Cannes, Lloyd George pressed on – according to an increasingly cynical Lord Riddell, in order 'to restore his star to its zenith'.[7]

The conference at Genoa, in April 1922, was certainly intended to revive the reputation of both the coalition and its leader. But it also had a desperately serious purpose. Lloyd George hoped for a conclusion which amounted to a revision of the Versailles Treaty. The temperamentally aggressive Poincaré had reacted to Germany's failure to pay the required indemnities by threatening invasion. Lloyd George, knowing that the repayments were beyond Germany's means, proposed to negotiate a new pattern of reparations. Germany's liabilities should be reduced, but France's share of the total payment should be increased so that her total receipts remained more or less the same. An international loan should be raised to save Germany from complete economic collapse, and the repayment of French war debts to Britain should be suspended. Britain would become a willing loser – receiving less in order that the payment to France should not be reduced.

The offer, which the Prime Minister made without the approval of the Cabinet, confirmed the Unionist backbenchers' fears that the obsession with becoming an international statesman would lead Lloyd George to sacrifice British interests. Their suspicions were increased by his hope that the conference would also regularise relations with the Soviet Union. He took the practical view that recognition was necessary for European stability and trade. The backbenchers were opposed on principle to legitimising a Communist government.

It was a wish to reassure his critics, rather than the anticipation of good diplomatic advice, that prompted Lloyd George – in defiance of his usual practice – to invite Curzon to accompany him to the Genoa conference. But the Foreign Secretary was unwell, so there was no one in the delegation who wished or dared to act as a restraining influence on the Prime Minister's single-minded determination to negotiate some sort of deal. At home, Churchill's animosity towards the Moscow government transcended all feelings of loyalty towards the Prime Minister. According to Austen Chamberlain, Churchill had become 'more Tory than the Tory ministers' in his attitude to Russia and was about to threaten, and perhaps even seriously consider, resignation.* Lloyd George's response was that 'the Cabinet must choose between Winston and me'.[9] There is no doubt what their choice would have been. But *The Times* was justified in announcing that 'The coalition is dying before our eyes.'[10]

Only self-delusion could have convinced Lloyd George that the Genoa conference might be the government's salvation. Yet he told Frances Stevenson, 'I mean to fight on Genoa . . . If I win, the Coalition is definitely Liberal in the real, and not the party, sense.'[11] The auguries were not good. The Cabinet would not endorse a mandate which included the conference recommending full recognition of the Soviet Union. A chargé d'affaires would, ministers reluctantly agreed, be enough to promote the trade links that the Prime Minister said were a crucial object of improved relations. Even that was denounced by Churchill as 'A supreme favour and patronage to the Bolsheviks.'[12] Lloyd George was becoming dangerously short of friends.

Genoa began with an eloquent address from Lloyd George about reconstruction and reconciliation. But the conference was already doomed. Only Britain was represented by its head of government and America did not attend. The plenipotentiaries of the Great Powers which did send delegates signed a generally meaningless Pact of Peace. Good work on currency stability and transport coordination was done in the margins. But no progress was made on the main issues which the conference was called to resolve and – as if to emphasise the futility of the formal proceedings – Russia and Germany met at Rapallo and signed a bilateral treaty of friendship which formalised agreements made during long weeks of previously secret discussions. It amounted to a declaration of international independence. Both countries could survive without the approval of the Allies. The reparations formula was not revised, and Germany remained on the verge of an economic collapse which would imperil the world.

Lloyd George was determined to retrieve something from the ruins of Genoa. Two more conferences were planned – one with Russia in attendance, one without. But Lloyd George's hopes of fighting and winning a general election as the man who brought order out of

---

*The King also had his doubts – especially about his Prime Minister meeting Bolsheviks. Lloyd George replied that he met all sorts of undesirables. Sami Bey, the Turkish representative in London, 'was missing for a whole day and eventually found in a sodomy house in the East End'. He added, for good measure, that Kemal Atatürk himself had 'taken up unnatural sexual intercourse'.[8]

European chaos had been destroyed. By the end of the year, he could not even represent himself as the Man of Peace. Ironically he was to encompass his own final destruction by clinging to a principle – an indefensible principle but a principle nevertheless. Lloyd George insisted on backing the Greeks against the Turks in Asia Minor.

His antipathy to Turkey is not easy to explain. It is unlikely – as some of his admirers suggest – that his beliefs had been set in stone when, at the age of thirteen, he had heard that Gladstone, in response to what came to be called 'the Bulgarian atrocities', had demanded that the Turks should leave the 'province that they had desolated and profaned'. Whatever its cause, his antagonism was intensified by his admiration of Eleftherios Venizelos, the Greek Prime Minister who, during the war, had opposed the attempts of King Constantine to give moral and material support to Germany. Lloyd George would have supported Greek plans to expel the Turks from Constantinople had the Cabinet not insisted that the idea was intolerable as well as absurd. He had argued that sentiment and gratitude combined with Realpolitik. A strong Greece would confirm the freedom of the straits, strengthen European influence in the Middle East and provide a degree of insurance against the dreaded Russo-Turkish Alliance threatening India. Despite his fierce arguments in London and Paris, Greece had to be satisfied with the acquisition of Eastern Thrace.

The Allies had made a theoretical peace with Turkey in 1920 when they signed the Treaty of Sèvres with the Sultan in Constantinople. The straits were declared neutral with their status guaranteed by an Allied garrison. France and Italy annexed a large area of what had been the Ottoman Empire. Then it became belatedly clear that the Sultan was no longer in control of the country. Mustafa Kemal – the victor of the Dardanelles campaign – was the effective government and had to be accommodated or defeated. Although France and Italy chose to negotiate and Russia signed a formal treaty of friendship, Lloyd George chose the second option. Then fate, in the form of King Alexander's pet monkey, took a hand. A bite turned into blood poisoning from which the King – who had succeeded the deposed Constantine – died. The Greek people voted for the restoration of his pro-German predecessor against whom Lloyd George's friend Venizelos had campaigned so valiantly.

Churchill, Curzon and Birkenhead all wished to make peace with Kemal – as did Balfour, temporarily in charge of the Foreign Office while Curzon recovered from a near nervous collapse which he attributed to

Lloyd George's brutal treatment. But Lloyd George could not be detached from Greece, and despite his antipathy to Constantine, determined to support a new settlement imposed on Turkey by force of arms. For a time the Greeks advanced against an apparently passive enemy. Then, at the gates of Ankara, Kemal made his stand. The tide turned. Within two months, most of the ground which Turkey had lost had been reclaimed and France, having decided that the Greeks were beaten, had begun to sell arms and ammunition to the Turks. Constantine was defeated at Inonu in January 1921 and the campaign in Angora was lost. Honour – Constantine believed – might be restored in Thrace. An army of fifty thousand men was assembled. The planned counter-attack was supported on 4 August in what was destined to be Lloyd George's last House of Commons speech as Prime Minister. The finale was a disaster. As well as accusing the Turks of wartime atrocities, he gave the impression – possibly intentionally – that Britain would go to Greece's assistance. Lord Derby asked, with justification, 'How could you expect the Turks to negotiate with a man who made a speech like that?'[13]

The Greeks were defeated at Afium Karahissar and Kemal's army – pausing only to massacre some 120,000 Greeks in Smyrna – pressed on towards the Dardanelles. All that stood in their way was the British garrison at Chanak. It was in place because none of the other Allies was prepared to replace America in the peace-keeping role which the President had first accepted and then abandoned. On 27 August, a surprisingly militant Cabinet took the decision to reinforce the small British force with troops from all the Mediterranean commands. It also instructed the Mediterranean Fleet to set sail for the straits and ordered the Royal Air Force to prepare two squadrons of bombers for action in the Bosporus. Curzon was ignored again. He read the statement of government policy in the newspapers – not having been invited to assist in drafting what he regarded as a 'flamboyant manifesto' of folly.[14] In the end, even he was infected by war fever. An appeal to the Empire was answered only by New Zealand and Newfoundland. When France withdrew her forces from the region, Curzon complained that two years of disloyalty had concluded with the 'abandonment of' her allies. Under pressure he amended 'abandonment of' to 'retreat from'.[15] France was surprisingly satisfied with his 'clarification'.

The irrationality of Lloyd George's conduct is difficult to understand. He might have been right in his insistence that 'the freedom of the Straits is vital. We cannot accept the Turkish guarantee. They broke faith once and they may do it again.' But it is harder to justify his reproof of Lord Riddell: 'You say the country will not stand for a fresh war. I disagree. The country will willingly support our action by force of arms if need be.'[16] The man who, for so long, had understood exactly when to change course had lost his bearings. The newspapers said he was a warmonger and the British people agreed – their view reinforced by the failure of the erstwhile Allies and most of the Empire to join in the defence of Europe against a new Ottoman invasion.

The Turks were still at the gates and Lloyd George – supported by the perpetually bellicose Churchill – decided that they could not be left to advance at will. On 29 September, Churchill – the Secretary of State for War since January 1919 – sent a telegram to General Sir Charles Harrington, the commanding officer of British forces in the straits.

> The Kemalists are obviously continuing to move up troops and are making efforts to net you in . . . It has therefore been decided by the Government that immediate notification is to be sent to the local commander of the Turkish forces around Chanak that unless his troops are withdrawn at a time fixed by you . . . all the forces at our disposal . . . will open fire on the Turks.

Harrington, reluctant to start a world war, delayed implementing his orders and Kemal, who could have destroyed the Chanak garrison, held his fire and withdrew his forces. There was much indignation in the Cabinet – particularly from Churchill, Birkenhead and the Prime Minister himself about 'soldiers who act as statesmen'. Curzon thought that the soldier had shown more wisdom than the politicians.

It took a week to reach a final settlement. The Turks made unreasonable demands. France capitulated. Britain negotiated a compromise which required the Turks to withdraw from the disputed territories around Chanak until their future was finally determined and allowed the Allies to administer Eastern Thrace for a month of peaceful resettlement before the Turks returned. Kemal – soon to become Atatürk – had won. The loser was Lloyd George.

Three days after the talks ended, Lloyd George, speaking at the Manchester Reform Club, turned on his tormentors. 'We have not been war-mongers. We have been peace-makers . . . Whilst we were engaged in a most difficult task we have been assailed with misrepresentations, with abuse, with innuendo.' He was always at his eloquent best when attacked and outnumbered. The Turks, 'according to official testimony', had 'slaughtered in cold blood a million and a half Armenians – men, women and children – and five hundred thousand Greeks . . . It was right that, before the Turkish army should be allowed to cross into Europe, in the first flush of victory with the blood of Smyrna on its hands, it should have time to cool.' In a corner, he always fought back with unrestrained brutality. Lord Gladstone, son of the Grand Old Man, denounced him as no longer fit to call himself a Liberal. Lloyd George asked what gave him the right to excommunicate party members and answered his own question. Lord Gladstone possessed one characteristic that made him indispensable: 'He is the best living embodiment of the Liberal doctrine that quality is not hereditary . . . There is no more ridiculous spectacle than a dwarf strutting before the footlights in garments he has inherited from a giant.' But he ended on a sombre note. 'If I am driven alone into the wilderness, I shall always recall with pride that I have been enabled, with the assistance of loyal colleagues, in the dark hours of this nation's history, to render it no mean service.'[17] Lloyd George knew that he might not be Prime Minister at the end of the year.

The road which led to Lloyd George's downfall in the autumn of 1922 was littered with complaints from allies who had never been his friends. Some of the criticisms had inspired rebellions before and were to do so many more times before the century ended. The new Aliens Act was said to allow too many undesirable foreigners into Britain. By the time it was presented to the House of Commons, Lloyd George was facing all the dangers that confront a wounded politician when his enemies have smelled blood. Most backbench Unionists within the coalition had always regarded his leadership as a necessary but temporary expedient, and they had come to believe that the time had come when they could win without him. It was too late for him to save himself by embracing Unionist policies, though it was still possible for him to add to the antagonism and bring forward his own political demise by offending against long-held Liberal principles and prejudices.

The newspapers – wrote Edward Grigg, his newly appointed and, at the time, unequivocally devoted private secretary – 'are a disgrace . . . As if the ousting of the PM would be the cure for all the evils which the nation is suffering! We should certainly be more up to our necks in the mess than we are now.'[18] And he was not alone in contemplating what life would be like after Lloyd George had left office. Montagu, embittered by his dismissal, claimed that the Prime Minister was so conscious of the risk of being deposed that survival had become the mainspring of policy. 'There he stands – the greatest strategist in the history of the world – scenting the air, waiting for the pursuit and throwing to the wolves the most convenient cargo.'[19]

That prospect of the coalition's sudden collapse had been immensely increased by a letter, from Bonar Law, which had been published in *The Times* and the *Daily Express* on 7 October. Its cunning – indeed its dishonesty – was so uncharacteristic that it is reasonable to assume that it had been written by Lord Beaverbrook. The opening paragraphs endorsed the decision to prevent the Turks from entering Thrace and perpetrating 'horrors similar to those which occurred in Anatolia'. But 'the British Empire, which includes the largest body of Mohammedans in any State, ought not to show any hostility or unfairness to the Turks'. Having both supported Lloyd George's decision and rejected what he insinuated were the unworthy motives which prompted it, Bonar Law then delivered the political *coup de grâce*. The peace settlement's provisions for Constantinople and the straits must be preserved. But it was not right that the 'burden . . . should fall on the British Empire alone'. There was no suggestion of how the load might have been lightened, just the assertion that 'We cannot alone act as the policeman of the world.'[20] The rubric was calculated to appeal to the rank and file of the Unionist Party and provide a ready-made headline for the other newspapers. It was also a declaration of intent. A year earlier, Lloyd George had accused Bonar Law of 'taking up the crown, trying it on his head and then . . . putting it down again'.[21] The 'policeman of the world' letter left no doubt that he had reached for it once more. Bonar Law had returned. The Tory Party had a standard-bearer and a potential Prime Minister again.

CHAPTER 35

NEMESIS

The coalition's landslide victory in the election of 1918 had left Lloyd George dominant but insecure. In the shifting sands of post-war Westminster, he commanded a majority in the House of Commons which fluctuated between three hundred and four hundred. But he also attracted undisguised animosity from the Liberals who had not received the 'coupon', which was the coalition's endorsement, and the Labour Party, which, when asked to join the all-party post-war government, had refused. But the danger to his future lay less in the depleted ranks of his open enemies than in the massed ranks of his ostensible supporters. The Unionist Party, in the country and on the backbenches of the House of Commons, did not like him and would, he knew, dispense with his services as soon as they no longer needed his reflected glamour.

From 1918 onwards the idea of forming a 'centre party' – which would win power on a combination of consensus policies and the reputation of its leader – was in his mind. When it became clear that the Liberal Party could neither forgive nor forget his apostasy, he vacillated wildly between the thought of leaving politics completely (which was a fantasy) and schemes for engineering another general election at a time and in a way which would ensure his continued leadership of the coalition – the creation of a new party by default. But the opportunity to make a dash for safety never arose. International events which he thought would be a suitable prelude to the dissolution of Parliament did not become the personal triumphs which he had anticipated. And he was caught in the trap into which leaders of disparate coalitions always fall. The more he 'succeeded', according to his own criteria of success, the more he alienated an indispensable number of notional supporters.

The idea of a more or less permanent coalition was not Lloyd George's alone. As early as the spring of 1920, Balfour – in Nice with the Prime Minister – had written home to his local party officials to say, 'Of one thing it [the coalition] is still urgently in need, namely a unity of organisation in the constituencies corresponding to its unity of purpose and organisation.'[1] But each of its constituent parts continued to behave like separate entities, reinforcing their own positions whenever they could. At the end of the year, Lloyd George, feeling the need for young, enthusiastic and unquestionably loyal supporters, arranged a peerage for Mathew Vaughan-Davies so that he could be succeeded as Member of Parliament for Cardiganshire by Ernest Evans, a Welsh private secretary at Number 10. Evans won the by-election by a gratifying majority of three and a half thousand, after a campaign which confirmed that Margaret Lloyd George – whether or not she had wanted to become a political wife – had become deeply committed to her husband's success. Against what were commonly supposed to be all her instincts, she agreed to deputise for her necessarily absent husband. Between 8 and 11 February, she made twenty-one speeches, returned to the constituency to speak at more meetings on the 15th and was back again on the 18th for polling day.[2]

Serious discussion of a possible general election date began in late 1921. Charles McCurdy, the new Liberal Chief Whip, had been in favour but thought it important to get Bonar Law back into the government before it was held. Austen Chamberlain was opposed in all circumstances. So was Churchill – according to Lloyd George, in a moment of bitter irrationality, because he feared the coalition would win and, in doing so, extinguish his chances of the premiership.[3] Lloyd George's suspicions were increased by the subsequent discovery that Lords Northcliffe and Rothermere had urged Churchill to leave the coalition, abandon his association with Liberals and Liberalism and seize the leadership of the Unionist Party.[4]

There had been one major diversion from politics to domesticity that autumn. Frances Stevenson knew that Lloyd George was looking for a house with a view and land to cultivate. In September, she believed that she had found the ideal site on a Surrey hill near Churt. Lloyd George was still in Scotland, deciding how to deal with de Valera and Sinn Fein, and the land was about to be auctioned but, on being assured that the house would have a southern aspect, he authorised a bid. It was his for £3000. He visited his acquisition a week later and discovered that the hillside faced due north. He made the best of it. He called the house Bron-y-De – Slope (or Breast) of the South.

The fruit trees which were to occupy so much of his time in retirement had to wait. There was a government to save. The Unionists – realising that Lloyd George's plans were as inimical to their interests as to the independent Liberals' – mobilised their grandees to prevent a precipitate dissolution and the consequent continuation of the coalition. During the days of the New Year, as he was preparing to leave for the Cannes conference, Lloyd George had received three letters from Lord Derby expressing his escalating opposition to an early election. A fourth letter pursued him to France. It was a declaration from George Younger, the Conservative Party chairman. He could see no justification for a general election. So, were one to be called, he would probably oppose the government. It was not only constitutional propriety which made him issue his warning. A memorandum from Sir Malcolm Fraser, the Conservatives' chief agent, was attached to Younger's letter. It forecast that the coalition would lose at least a hundred seats in an early poll. On 5 January 1922, the *Morning Post* made Younger's view public. The early election would be pure opportunism, and if one were called, he and several of his colleagues would refuse to stand as coalition candidates.

On 10 January, Lloyd George – back from Cannes and incandescent with rage at what he believed to be a conscious betrayal – told Austen Chamberlain that Younger had 'behaved disgracefully' in making public 'information which would never have been imparted to him unless we had depended on his being gentleman enough to keep counsel'.[5] Younger, far from being chastened by Lloyd George's strictures, responded by writing to all the Tory agents, setting out the arguments against a general election. As he must have known would happen, the contents of his circular were reproduced in all the national newspapers.

Throughout the Cannes conference, Lloyd George had continued to plot and scheme. Bonar Law – on holiday in the South of France – visited the Prime Minister out of courtesy and was offered, for the second time, the Foreign Office if and when the coalition won the general election. Although the first offer had been declined, Bonar Law had supported the idea of an early general election. But a few days before the second offer he had been told by J. C. Davidson – a long-time opponent of the coalition – that 'Derby in the Lords and you as leader and PM in the Commons has been mooted widely'.[6] Lloyd George's renewed overtures were rejected without an endorsement of the coalition. Bonar Law had begun to contemplate backing into the limelight.

The senior members of the coalition government were forced to the conclusion that, when the election came, they might have to fight it without help or support from either their old or new friends. Under the ever-active leadership of Winston Churchill, they formed a National Liberal Council to coordinate what they assumed would be an imminent campaign. Lloyd George, back in Britain, chose to wait. Parliament would not be dissolved before the summer. 'There has been', he told a coalition Liberal rally in Central Hall, Westminster, 'a good deal of talk recently about a general election. Who started it? I did not. I never started the idea and I have certainly not made up my mind about it. It is my business not to do so until the last moment.'[7] Not even the faithful in the audience believed him.

Prime ministers who complain about the burden of office and claim that they sacrifice themselves on behalf of an ungrateful nation are usually, whether they know it or not, near to the ends of their political careers. Perhaps, from time to time, Lloyd George faced reality. Throughout 1922 he expressed, and probably even felt, resentment at the ingratitude of the nation as reflected in its press. Herbert Lewis, at lunch in Downing Street on 2 February, found his host 'old and lonely in the midst of them all'.[8] Three weeks later the resentment had turned into self-pity.

> Why should I be weighed down by all these cares? I have had five years of strenuous life and hardly a minute to myself. I have been in office for sixteen years. Why should I now not have an opportunity to enjoy the glorious sunshine without feeling that I am snatching two or three hours which might be employed on my work?[9]

Lloyd George had always enjoyed the good life. One of the unflattering comparisons he made between Margaret and other women who entertained him invoked his wife's reluctance to provide the fresh fruit which was available in the houses which he visited. In the difficult final days of his premiership, little luxuries became a solace. Hankey's 'rather disagreeable feeling that the PM is getting too fond of high living' exaggerated the growing love of comfort which meant the Cabinet Secretary 'much preferred him in the simple surroundings of Criccieth or Cobham'.[10] But the Prime Minister had developed a more serious fault. For the first time, he was allowing his personal problems to interfere with his public duties.

Sometime during 1920, his daughter, Megan, had discovered that Frances Stevenson, who had joined the family as her governess, had become the other woman in her father's life. Her response was bitter resentment – both on her mother's behalf and on her own. Until then she had believed herself to be the centre of her father's attention.

Megan Arvon Lloyd George had taken the place in her father's affection which had previously been occupied by Mair Eluned, and she had been able to enjoy the political role that early death had denied her sister. When she was barely ten, Lloyd George had offered Bonar Law the choice of sharing her company at lunch or the two men dining à deux. Bonar Law had chosen to dine without her, but from then on she was rarely denied involvement in her father's political affairs. At the age of sixteen, she was by his side at the Paris peace conference, acting as his 'hostess', as she did three years later at the first weekend party at Chequers after it had become the Prime Minister's official residence. Even before the 'revelation', she was difficult and demanding. Afterwards – although she remained her father's political protégée – she mixed obsessive attention to his welfare with occasional outbursts of criticism about every aspect of his life and work. They continued until his death.

The year 1920 was a bad one for the coalition as well as for Lloyd George's family relationships. It began with Austen Chamberlain complaining, 'Younger humiliates the PM . . . FE attacks Younger personally. Bonar Law tries on the crown but can't make up his mind to seize it, won't join us and share the load but watches, not without pleasure, the troubles of his friends and the Diehards, instead of responding to my advances, harden their resistance.'[11] The Diehards had reacted in the way which he should have expected. They wanted a return to the old party structure and feared that Lloyd George intended permanently to rearrange it to their disadvantage. Stanley Baldwin, the underestimated the new President of the Board of Trade, vacillated. On the one hand, there was the belief that 'he is trying to get the old Liberal Party united under his leadership and then throw us over'.[12] On the other, Baldwin suspected that 'he might resign under the impression that he would be recalled'.[13] He had, in his quiet way, become Lloyd George's most implacable enemy. Austen Chamberlain, who, according to Lloyd George, 'always played the game and always lost it', had told his party the truth – acceptable to him but anathema to many of his followers – that Lloyd George wanted to fuse both coalition factions into a single party.[14] Increased hostility from the Unionists did not inspire compensating loyalty from coalition Liberals who were expected to defend both the Geddes Axe and the Anglo-Irish Treaty – neither of which they supported. Worse still, they were expected to vote for the Safeguarding of Industry Bill which Baldwin was piloting through the House of Commons.

The bill had its origins in a wartime measure which was designed for an economy under siege. Its peacetime adaptation had two parts. The first allowed the government to impose a $33\frac{1}{3}$ per cent tariff on imports which undercut goods produced by the 'essential' industries. The second allowed an additional $33\frac{1}{3}$ per cent to be levied on 'dumped' goods or imports sold in Britain below the cost of production because of currency depreciation. Free-traders regarded the bill as barely disguised protectionism. Inside the government, Fisher, Montagu and Churchill were against it from the start. From the backbenches, William Wedgwood Benn, the Liberal Member for Leith, moved for repeal within days of it passing into law. Only eighteen coalition Liberals voted with the government. Eighty-seven were absent or abstained.

The bill's second part was invoked in January 1922 to reduce the import of 'fibre gloves' – foreign competition to a small British industry which used as its raw material fabric made and exported by the Lancashire cotton trade. Lord Derby, the 'uncrowned King of Lancashire', put county before party and expressed his violent opposition. Lloyd George postponed the promulgation of the necessary statutory instrument and then capitulated to the Conservatives within his Cabinet. The Order in Council was approved by the House of Commons on 31 July 1922, with seventy-six Liberals abstaining or voting against. The 'split' over protectionism was far more fundamental – though less dramatic – than the disagreement about foreign affairs. It demonstrated that, in peacetime, the parties in the coalition were irreconcilable. Lloyd George, suffering from severe neuralgia, retired to Criccieth.

On his return to health and London, the Prime Minister decided to bring matters to a head by inviting Austen Chamberlain to succeed him as Prime Minister. The proposal was made by letter – giving the offer far greater force than would have been conveyed by a casual conversation. 'I have been driven to the conclusion,' the sixteen-hundred-word bombshell began, that I can no longer render useful service to my country by retaining office under existing conditions. I am conscious of the tremendous difficulties with which governments are confronted at this hour. Were it not for that fact, I would have insisted on resigning long ago but I was anxious not to rest under the imputation of running away from trouble . . . I have offered Mr Bonar Law and I repeated the offer to you when you succeeded him [as Unionist leader] to go out and give loyal support to a government formed by either of you. I suggest in all sincerity to you that the time has come to accept that offer.[15]

There is no way of knowing if Lloyd George wanted Chamberlain to accept the offer or hoped that he would reject it and thereby end, albeit briefly, the uncertainty which surrounded the coalition's future. It was probably bluff, though Lloyd George certainly thought about giving way to a successor whose failure would be so spectacular that the whole nation would demand the return of the Man Who Won the War – a fantasy that had echoes of the 'plot' to revive the Asquith administration by proving that there was no alternative. Chamberlain took the offer at face value. The condition which Lloyd George attached to his resignation – the agreement of his successor to continue to search for a permanent settlement in Europe and endorse the Anglo-Irish Treaty – was easily met. Chamberlain declined to become Prime Minister for reasons which were honourable and selfless. He believed that the coalition was essential to the national interest and that only Lloyd George could keep it alive.

Bonar Law, on the other hand, had changed his mind. In his estimation the coalition was doomed. In February, he had told Balfour that, when he returned to London from France, 'he found a compete change of opinion in the party . . . It was impossible that things should go on as they were.'[16] The rank and file of the Tory Party wanted a change of Prime Minister.

The Prime Minister and the Members of Parliament who were to decide his fate had become so incompatible that what Lloyd George exulted as his triumphs were dismissed by the government backbenchers as failures. He had returned from Genoa to a hero's welcome. But the Tory Diehards regarded the outcome of the conference as a craven capitulation to the Russian Bolsheviks and the defeated Germans. The Anglo-Irish Treaty – which he believed to be an historic achievement – was anathema to coalition Unionists, whose hostility turned into open contempt after the outbreak of the Irish Civil War in 1922. Their attitude was dramatically illustrated after Henry Wilson – who on leaving the army had become Member of Parliament for North Down – was assassinated by IRA gunmen outside his house in London. When Austen Chamberlain called on Lady Wilson to express his condolences, the grieving widow called him 'Murderer' and asked that no member of the government attend the funeral.[17] The campaign of assassination was being coordinated by the 'Anti-Treaty Sinn Fein', but the ministers who had negotiated the treaty were being held responsible for the mayhem.

Field Marshal Wilson was shot on the morning of 22 June 1922. On the same afternoon a question asked in the House of Lords began a debate which added a new dimension to the difficulty of finding a propitious election day. Why had Sir Joseph Robinson, a South African mining magnate, been nominated for a peerage in the Birthday Honours List when, as was well known, he had been convicted of fraud in South Africa and fined £500,000? A letter from Robinson, asking for his name to be withdrawn from the list of nominees, was subsequently read to the House. But their Lordships had tasted blood. The debate on which they insisted was held on 17 July. On the same day, the House of Commons agreed to set up a select committee to examine 'the present method of submitting names to His Majesty' with the intention that 'honours should only be given as a reward for public service'. That, Lloyd George hoped, would end the embarrassment. But the damage was done in the House of Lords – principally by the Duke of Northumberland, whose father had been excoriated by Lloyd George for exploiting land values which had been increased by actions of the community rather than by his own efforts.

> The Prime Minister's party, insignificant in numbers and absolutely penniless four years ago, has, in the course of those four years, amassed an enormous party chest, variously estimated at anything from one to two million pounds. The strange thing about it is that this money has been acquired during a period when there has been a more wholesale distribution of honours than ever before, when less care has been taken with regard to the service of the recipients than ever before and when whole groups of newspapers have been deprived of real independence by the sale of honours and constitute a mere echo of Downing Street from where they are controlled.[18]

After providing some figures to justify his claim that newspapers had been seduced and suborned, he read from letters from what he called 'touts'. Some read like a price list – £12,000 for a knighthood and £35,000 for a baronetcy. One might have been a model for the 'special offer' furniture advertisements which, eighty years later, became a feature of commercial television.

> There are only five knighthoods left for the June list. If you decide on a baronetcy, you may have to wait for the Retiring List . . . It is not likely that the next government will give so many honours and this is an exceptional opportunity. But there is no time to be lost if you wish to take it . . . I assure you that all inquiries regarding yourself have been made and satisfactory answers received. So you can be sure there will be no difficulty.

The letter ended with a justification which was almost an apology. 'It is unfortunate that Governments must have money, but the party now in power will have to fight Labour and Socialism, which will be an expensive matter.'[19] Honours had been distributed out of gratitude for political donations ever since the beginning of the eighteenth century. But no Prime Minister – not even Walpole, the most notorious recipient of rich men's generosity – had behaved as blatantly or distributed distinctions so extensively.* On Lloyd George's recommendation, the King had created 294 new knights in eighteen months and ninety-nine new hereditary peers in six years – twice the annual rate of any other period in history. A new honour, the Order of the British Empire, had been invented. Twenty-five thousand had been awarded during Lloyd George's premiership. He was in a hurry. The parties which would oppose him in an election had accumulated funds for years. He had to fill his empty coffers quickly.

Northumberland was right about the lavish rewards received by newspaper owners and editors – forty-nine in all since 1918. Lloyd George had ennobled six proprietors in three years, not including Beaverbrook, who had been elevated to make room in the House of Commons for a new recruit to the coalition Cabinet. But it was wrong

---

*The one award about which no one complained was the DBE – Dame Commander of the British Empire – given to Margaret Lloyd George. She had raised £200,000 for war charities. More importantly, she was the sort of woman about whom everyone felt an obligation to speak well.

to argue that they had responded by giving their support to the government. The three viscounts – Northcliffe of *The Times* and *Daily Mail*, Rothermere of the *Daily Mirror* and *Sunday Pictorial* and Burnham of the *Daily Telegraph* – had shown admirable ingratitude. The others responded to events of the day according to what they claimed was their objective judgement – though it was usually a judgement about what would sell most papers. All of them believed that they had been promoted on merit. None of them – while complaining about other awards – drew attention in their papers to the honours which their industry had received.

The difficulties other parties had found in raising funds were, according to the Duke of Northumberland, clear proof that the coalition's gains had been ill-gotten. His real complaint was that Lloyd George's high-pressure salesmen had poached donors who should have remained the exclusive property of the Tory Party and that – when the coalition broke up – their generosity might be so exhausted that the Conservatives would be short of cash. Sir George Younger had complained, 'Freddie Guest is nobbling our men.'[20] In January 1923, three months after Lloyd George had lost office, the upright Andrew Bonar Law, who succeeded him, insisted that some of the tainted funds be put at his disposal.[21] Earl Farquhar refused to use funds which he had accumulated – part of a gift from Lord Astor – to pay for the running costs of Conservative Central Office. It had, he said, been intended for use by the coalition. After some days of argument, Farquhar, only recently appointed, was replaced as treasurer of the Tory Party.* The eventual destination of the disputed money was never revealed.

Lloyd George responded to the cries of 'scandal' as those who knew him would have expected. He made an audacious speech in the July 'Honours for Sale' debate. 'Selling honours to the highest bidder[s]' was, he said, 'a discreditable system'. But he insisted that making donations to a political party should not exclude the receipt of an honour which was justified by the good works of the nominee. He accepted, with good grace, the proposal to set up a Royal Commission with a remit to recommend how the honours system could be insulated from even the suggestion of corruption. However, all thought of holding a snap summer election had to be abandoned. 'It would', he told Riddell 'be impossible to go now, much as I should like it.'[22]

Perhaps there were times during 1922 when Lloyd George briefly

---

*After 1921, the term 'Unionist' was rarely used.

hoped to escape the cares of office. In the early months of the year, some of his most devoted associates – most notably Edward Grigg – had urged him to retire with dignity and honour, at a time of his own choosing.[23] He rejected the idea in January but in June, according to Frances Stevenson, he would not have 'minded resigning if he could become editor of the *Times* at a decent salary and with a decent contract'.[24] The newspaper was sold to Lord Astor, who had different plans. But before the end of the month there was at least some financial consolation. He planned to write the book 'for which he has had very big offers'.[25] Two months later, the *Evening Standard* revealed that a US publisher had offered £90,000 for the American rights to his memoirs.[26] Lloyd George had been offered the chance to make a fortune out of the war in which so many men had died. The public outcry far exceeded the expressions of shock and horror which were provoked by the 'honours scandal'. Two weeks of embarrassment followed. Then an announcement was made by Downing Street. The Prime Minister had decided that the advance was to be 'devoted to charities connected with the relief of suffering caused by the war. He feels unable to take any personal advantage for himself out of the story of the struggle and suffering of the nation.'[27]

Throughout the summer of 1922, Lloyd George's thoughts were never far away from the need to call an election before the coalition disintegrated and consigned him to political oblivion. He was in a sombre mood when, during the last week in August, Tom Jones visited him in Wales. As they walked by the river, Lloyd George told him, 'Bury me here. Don't put me in a cemetery. You'll have trouble with the relatives and there would be controversy if the Abbey were suggested.'[28] His wishes were respected. But it did not avoid the trouble about which he warned.

Despite the growing unpopularity of the government, Birkenhead believed that, in a presidential election, Lloyd George would have won easily.[29] But the coalition was falling apart. Lord Derby wrote to Austen Chamberlain – pointedly sending his letter to the leader of the Tory Party rather than to the Prime Minister – informing him that he could no longer support the coalition but would 'join Salisbury in his new party', the association of anti-coalition Conservatives which he hoped to create.[30] Bonar Law's 'policeman of the world' letter had given Tories the hope that he would become the leader behind whom they could rally. Clearly, the government could not survive for long. Lloyd George's only hope was a quick election and the victory which enabled him to claim a renewed mandate.

According to Lord Beaverbrook, the crucial meeting which decided the coalition's fate took place at his house on 9 October 1922. Austen Chamberlain and Churchill had already endorsed Lloyd George's decision to call an early election. Birkenhead had yet to decide. Bonar Law's position was still unclear. Beaverbrook's account of the meeting needs to be treated with some caution. As was the case with every historic event which he reported, his role is depicted as crucial to the outcome and the whole story is coloured by his hope that somebody (anybody) would take up the cause of Imperial Preference. According to his version of events, before the Prime Minister's arrival, 'Bonar Law indicated clearly that he had made up his mind to do everything possible to destroy Lloyd George and the Coalition'.[31] If that is so, Bonar Law was less than honest during the lunch itself, when he did no more than warn that Lloyd George had been 'misled, no doubt unwittingly, by his Conservative colleagues as to the temper of the Conservative party. They did not want another Coalition.'[32] His own implacable hostility was not mentioned.

The Conservative backbenchers did want a coalition – it was the sure way to perpetuate their party's power – but they wanted it led by someone other than Lloyd George. Even George Younger, who had done so much harm to Lloyd George's prospects, had told a meeting of Scottish Tories that he 'trembled to think what might happen if the Unionists . . . had differences with those with whom we have acted so long and will form . . . a bulwark against the Socialist Party'.[33] Accused of inconsistency, he had explained, 'the Coalition ought to be saved, but even I cannot save it now'.[34] Lloyd George deluded himself into believing that he, and he alone, could.

The meeting at Beaverbrook's house made half-hearted attempts to find an alternative to the dissolution of Parliament and the destruction of the coalition. Birkenhead suggested that Lord Derby should become Prime Minister with Lloyd George appointed Lord President of the Council and Leader of the House of Commons. The bizarre proposal was canvassed with the nominees and accepted (or so he said) by Lloyd George but rejected by Derby. Once it was clear that everything had to be gambled on an early election, Lloyd George chose to increase the stakes. He made no attempt to compromise with his critics. Instead, he went out of his way to demonstrate his contempt for their concerns. The outstanding issue was relations between Greece and Turkey. While Curzon and the Foreign Office were negotiating a permanent peace, Lloyd George was engaged in secret discussions which, he hoped, would secure Greece's position. Despite Curzon's urgent plea for cautious moderation, when Lloyd George spoke in the Manchester Free Trade Hall on 14 October he attacked Turkey and accused its army of committing new atrocities. In passing he denounced the French government as craven. At the time, Curzon was trying to persuade France to assist in his attempts to placate the Turks. Not surprisingly, Curzon did not attend a dinner arranged by Churchill to discuss what, by then, had become the inevitable general election.

The original decision to appeal to the country had been taken by the Cabinet meeting at Chequers on 16 September. The reason for an autumn poll had been openly admitted and frankly discussed by ministers who – despite the increasing opposition of their parties' rank and file – had grown too comfortable in coalition to give it up without a struggle. The Chanak crisis had prevented the election being held in October. Then the choice of date was taken out of the Cabinet's hands. A meeting of the National Union of Conservatives had been called for 15 November. It evolved into a party conference which, it was universally anticipated, would call for withdrawal from the coalition unless it had already been re-elected. The eventual decision to call a general election was a desperate and doomed attempt to frustrate that demand.

George Younger told Austen Chamberlain that he was 'frankly appalled' by thought of the civil war which lay ahead inside the Tory Party, and Leslie Wilson, now Conservative Chief Whip, warned that, if the coalition went to the country as a united force, at least 184 Tory candidates would describe themselves as 'Independent Conservatives'. But there was no going back. The decision was confirmed by a less than unanimous Cabinet meeting on 10 October. When Younger and Wilson – who believed that a realignment within the Commons could create a stable Conservative government – threatened to repudiate his leadership, Chamberlain suggested what seemed to him a compromise. Tory wishes would be assessed at a party meeting. Opinions differ about whether the idea was forced on Chamberlain, or whether the suggestion was made in the misguided belief that his opponents would be confounded as he had confounded them before. The decision about its date was certainly tactical. It was to be held on 19 October at the Carlton Club. On the previous day, the result of the Newport by-election would have been declared. Nobody doubted that it would be won by the Labour Party as a result of anti-coalition Tories splitting the coalition vote.

On 14 October, Curzon, Baldwin and Arthur Boscawen (the Tory

Minister of Agriculture) met and agreed that, whatever their colleagues decided, they would resign from the government rather than support the coalition in an immediate general election. The coalitionists decided to challenge the dissidents head-on. In the hope of rallying old allies, Lloyd George included a paeon of praise for traditional Liberalism in his Manchester speech and, on the following day, Austen Chamberlain addressed a meeting of Tory ministers. 'The government must at once appeal to the country as a Coalition, though individual private Members could call themselves what they liked and there would be a reshuffle of the ministry and consideration of who was to be leader after the general election.'[35] The speech was hardly a ringing endorsement of Lloyd George's premiership and, if it were meant to reconcile opinion to the continuation of the coalition, it failed in its purpose. The party grandees were, and remained, in favour of the coalition. But the junior ministers led by Leo Amery (a Lloyd George apostate) had met the day before Chamberlain made his plea for unity and had agreed to demand a general election. They met again the following day – reinforced by Younger and Baldwin – and confirmed their opposition to the coalition. Even the most loyal newspapers find it hard to stay on board a sinking ship. In the *Observer*, J. L. Garvin called for Lloyd George to resign.[36]

Bonar Law's attitude remained in public doubt right up to the last day. According to his admirers, he was torn between the duty of loyalty which he felt he owed the Prime Minister and the obligations of leadership which had been impressed upon him by dozens of rank-and-file Tories. He had been inundated with letters which demanded that the party return to the purity of purpose and efficiency of operation which, they claimed, had been its hallmark before it was corrupted by Lloyd George. On the evening before the party meeting, he left Baldwin with the impression that he was too ill to contemplate the premiership. In fact his only complaint about a recent medical diagnosis related to its optimistic certainty. If he was in perfect health, as the doctor had assured him he was, only conscience and personal preference could determine a decision about his future.[37] Earlier in the day, he had drafted a resignation to the chairman of his constituency party. It announced that he was leaving politics.[38] But despite the apparent vacillation, his mind was steadily moving towards attending the meeting at the Carlton Club and, if it was decided not to fight the election as part of the coalition, to offer himself as the leader of the Conservative Party.

On 18 October, the day before the fateful meeting, Bonar Law was visited by a series of influential Tories – all of whom pleaded with him to break with Lloyd George and lead a government of his own. Among them was Curzon, whose vow of fealty must have convinced Bonar Law that opinion was strongly running in his favour. Later, Curzon was to claim that he had been asked to comment only on the substance of the speech which Bonar Law proposed to make.[39] But, whatever his role, Bonar Law assured Curzon that he would remain Foreign Secretary if the Tory leader formed a new government.[40] On the same evening Wickham Steed, the editor of *The Times*, told Curzon that Bonar Law would attend the next day's meeting and, in consequence, make plain his candidature. Archibald Salvidge, a coalition supporter, was told that there was a 'tidal wave of feeling in favour of a united Conservative Party' and hurried round to Downing Street to tell Lloyd George that Bonar Law was lost to his cause.[41]

According to Stanley Baldwin, Bonar Law's Aunt Mary convinced him where his duty lay, but Beaverbrook took credit for the Tory leader's decision by claiming that his 'plea, concluding on a high imperial note'[42] had been decisive. He was certainly the recipient of the simple message – 'I am going to the meeting' – and he made sure that the news was reported in all the next day's papers.[43] They also reported the result of the Newport by-election. The Conservative vote had not split. It had rallied behind the independent Tory who had won with a majority of over two thousand. The coalition Conservative had come a bad third.

Austen Chamberlain opened the meeting with a speech which was described by both friend and foe as 'stiff' and was universally regarded as too long. It dealt in part with the importance of the coalition – necessary to save the nation from the ravages of socialism now that Labour was 'the second largest party in the state' – but chiefly with the virtues of Lloyd George, 'a man who has led us through these troubles and has acted throughout with a loyalty to which my friends will testify as warmly as I do'. The hoped-for assurances about a government reconstruction after victory were never made, and he seemed to suggest that the coalition would continue for all time – making it indistinguishable from a new party. Balfour was the only other speaker to defend the coalition. Chamberlain was followed by Baldwin. To general surprise, he began with what was taken as a joke. 'Speaking for a minority of the Cabinet, that is myself and Sir Arthur Griffith-Boscawen . . .' His subsequent eloquence was as unexpected as his humour. In eight minutes – entirely devoted to the character of the Prime Minister – he made the death of the coalition certain.

The Prime Minister was described this morning in *The Times*, in the words of a distinguished aristocrat, as a live wire. He was described to me and others in more stately language by the Lord Chancellor as a dynamic force. I accept those words. He is a dynamic force and it is from that very fact that our troubles, in our opinion, arise. A dynamic force is a terrible thing. It may crush you but it is not necessarily right.[44]

After a motion to dissolve the coalition had been moved and seconded, there were cries for Bonar Law. He rose with apparent reluctance, asserted that he attached 'more importance to keeping the party together than winning the next election' and concluded that object was best achieved by ending the coalition.[45] It was not a good speech, but Baldwin had put the result of the vote beyond doubt. The motion to withdraw from the coalition was carried by 187 votes to 87.

Back at Number 10 – the news having been received in a message from Philip Sassoon – Lloyd George's parliamentary private secretary – the Prime Minister seemed genuinely to believe that his premiership had been interrupted rather than ended. His wife was even more optimistic about the future. She wrote to tell her daughter that the family was leaving Downing Street for a furnished house in Vincent Square. 'Tada is in such a fever [of] haste to get there, but I am not going until I return from Wales . . . I hope we shall have a house of our own by then or back in Number 10. I can't see Bonar Law lasting too long.'[46]

There was some recrimination – mostly initiated by his friends – about the Tory ministers who had sat in his Cabinet in the morning and plotted against him in the afternoon. Over dinner he pronounced the *Nunc Dimittis* on his five years in Downing Street. 'I have not concealed my own Liberal views in the least from my colleagues in the cabinet and I have thrown my emphasis on that side. Dizzy finished up a sycophant of Mayfair. The language of Mayfair is not my language. Joe Chamberlain, in the end, went right over. I have not done so and I will not do so.'[47]

It was not quite true. The parable of the Eskimo, with which Lloyd George followed his reaffirmation of the true faith, more adequately described his record. Life in an icehouse was hard to manage. If the temperature were too high, the igloo melted. If it were too low, the occupants froze. Lloyd George had lost the Liberal Party without gaining the Tories. In his pursuit of permanent coalition government he had veered wildly from side to side of the political divide and, in the end, had been swallowed up by the gulf which separated the parties. But, although he had adopted many of the establishment's policies, he had never shared its values. He had exploited it without joining it and he left Downing Street as he had arrived – an outsider.

Lloyd George returned his Seals of Office to the King on 23 October after a morning of official farewells and an afternoon in which he mimicked how Bonar Law would behave when the Welsh MPs – led by the Member for Caernarvon Boroughs – petitioned him for increased spending in Wales. 'Everyone was in gales of laughter except Miss Stevenson who could hardly conceal her sadness at parting with No 10.'[48]

Winston Churchill issued a statement which a less emotional man might have thought fulsome. 'Today when men who fawned upon him, praised his errors, who climbed into place in parliament upon his shoulders have cast him aside . . . I am still his friend and lieutenant.'[49] He was pronouncing the last rites of Lloyd George's ministerial career, which – having lasted for sixteen years and included over six as Prime Minister – was never to be revived. Lloyd George was fifty-nine.

CHAPTER 36

THE RADICAL'S RETURN

As the day of the Carlton Club meeting approached, Lloyd George must have realised that, in one way or another – disintegration before or defeat in a general election – his administration would come to an end. Anticipating defeat is not the same as being prepared to meet it – particularly if, as was the case in 1922, the scale of the disaster is overwhelming. The newspapers rejoiced at his humiliation. They had, he told himself, always represented the views of his irreconcilable enemies. But their judgement about his performance in the election, although prejudiced, was basically correct. He was handicapped by short-term anxiety and long-term insecurity. He could not attack his opponents with the vehemence which was his political forte. Many of them had served in his government and some of the coalition Liberal candidates, on whose support his future depended, needed coalition Tory votes to return them to the House of Commons. And he had no idea what his role would be in the new Parliament.

There were moments when he came to life with outbursts of old-style vituperation. In Leeds, he described Bonar Law as 'honest to the verge of simplicity'.[1] And there was much talk of 'Belgravia conspirators' and 'titled Judases'. But the old flame never burned brightly enough to set alight the men and women who came to hear him speak. Between 26 October and polling day, Lloyd George spoke at only a handful of meetings. Often they were attended by men and women who came to see and hear an almost mythic figure from British history rather than for the chance to listen to a future leader of the country. The young C. P. Snow was in the audience at Leicester.

He thought Lloyd George's speech 'already seemed high flown and old fashioned'.[2]

Lloyd George had approached the election with no strategy and confused tactics. On 1 November, he had told H. A. L. Fisher that he expected to win more than fifty seats and hold the balance of power in the House of Commons. In that event, he would keep Bonar Law in office for two or three years and turn him out when the numbers of unemployed began to fall. However, he would prefer the Conservatives to win an outright majority and absolve him of responsibility for making a Tory government possible.[3] Two weeks later, he explained to his wife, 'My chief aim is to keep the Tory numbers down. I don't care much who gets in as long as Bonar does not get a working majority.'[4] In the same letter he announced that he was 'working for a break, 2 or 3 years hence after we have formed a Centre Party with a strong pro-gressive bias'.[5] This hope was encouraged by the persistent fantasy that all the most dynamic members of the coalition government were Tory in name rather than conviction.

There were moments when it seemed that he had lost the zest for power which had driven him for so long. On 19 October, as he left for speaking engagements in the north, he had told reporters on the station platform, 'I travel with the burden off my shoulders but a sword in my hand.' But the following day, his speech in Yorkshire so lacked lustre that *The Times* was able cruelly to extend the metaphor. 'Somewhere between St Pancras and Leeds there must be lying a sword. It may be that, on reflection, it has been restored to its scabbard and forgotten amidst the luggage on the special train.'[6]

The result of the November general election was a conclusive victory for the Tories. The Conservative Party and its allies won 344 seats, Labour 138, Asquithian Liberals 60 and coalition Liberals 57. Four of Lloyd George's most loyal lieutenants – including Churchill – were defeated. So were several of his natural, though temporarily alienated, allies – among them Montagu and Addison. There was disagreement about whether the voters supported the Conservative manifesto or, as Philip Guedalla (a Liberal-supporting biographer and historian) believed, 'Mr Bonar Law . . . became Prime Minister of England for the simple and satisfying reason that he was not Mr Lloyd George.'[7] A hair's-breadth majority would have provided an incentive for the two Liberal groups to work together. A landslide did not have the same effect, but it did encourage the reconciliation of Bonar Law and senior Tory members of the coalition – whose talents the Cabinet so obviously needed. One by one the ministers who had served in Lloyd George's government returned to office in the new administration. At the same time, Liberal reunion was held back by an obstacle more formidable even than personal animosity. Lloyd George's election fund, which he had regarded as essential to his political survival, made reconciliation with diehard Asquithians impossible.

Lloyd George and his family remained irrationally indomitable – only doubtful about how to pass the years before the new government – whose members he held in the utmost contempt – was destroyed by what he regarded as its inherent inadequacies. A letter, sent by Megan to her sister-in-law, expressed the feelings of Lloyd George's inner circle. 'The people are absolutely with him, altho' very tired of the government, more particularly because it is a coalition than anything else. Whatever happens, Tada will be in power. He will be tremendous in opposition – and Bonar knows it.'[8] The phrase 'will be in power' was not meant to be qualified by the proviso 'one day in the future'. Megan – and Lloyd George himself – believed that his mere existence would unnerve the government and influence its policy. And they were, to a large extent, correct. There were, during the next nine years, periods of minority government when the little band of Liberals – 'Nationals' and 'Independent', first separately and then united – could have brought down a Prime Minister. They chose not to do so. That they remained influential – forcing adjustments if not changes in government policy – was less the result of the two factions holding the balance of power than of the reawakening of the turbulent spirit within Lloyd George. His restless energy and unashamed opportunism kept the government in constant fear that he was ready and able, somehow, to seize power again. When policy was influenced it was the result of personality not strength of numbers.

There were still plaudits for wartime achievements to be received. A lecture tour of America enabled the people of the United States to express, and Lloyd George to enjoy, the admiration of a grateful nation. It included a ticker-tape parade and Freedom of the City in New York, dinner with the President, adulation at mass meetings and admission to a tribe of Native Americans with the title 'Chief Two Eagles, War and Peace'. In Vermont he met Robert Lincoln, the son of his hero, as part of a pilgrimage that took him to Gettysburg, the Louisville cottage in which the martyred President was born and the courthouse in Springfield, Illinois, where Lincoln's political journey began. Only two disagreements marred the triumphant progress. His itinerary included more opportunities for receiving the adulation of his American admirers than he could stand. So, after some argument, the programme was culled. Then he moved on to Canada, where he discovered that the fifteen thousand people who attended one of his mass rallies would hear him only if he spoke with the aid of an electric microphone. At first he refused. Then, having been persuaded to test the system, he became an enthusiastic and accomplished performer. All paid speaking engagements were declined as incompatible with his hero status – and because, with an estimated annual income of £35,000, he did not need the money. Andrew Carnegie had bequeathed him an annuity of £2000 a year, and he had been commissioned by the United Press Association to write a fortnightly article which would be syndicated in the United States and sold to the highest-bidding newspaper in Britain. Frances Stevenson agreed to accept 10 per cent of his income from journalism in lieu of salary. In the first year she was paid £3000.

Bonar Law's administration survived for barely six months. The man who had both made and broken Lloyd George's premiership resigned – through ill health – on 22 May 1923 and was succeeded by Stanley Baldwin, the hero of the Carlton Club meeting. According to Tom Jones, Lloyd George 'had become something of an obsession with the new Prime Minister' – a view he illustrated with an anecdote about a visit to Chequers.[9] Mrs Baldwin showed Jones an album of photographs taken in earlier ministerial days. When Lloyd George was included in a group picture, his image was defaced.[10] The story added strength to Megan Lloyd George's view that her father would be the inescapable ghost at the Tory feast. Other Tories shared Baldwin's obsession, but exhibited their neurosis in different ways. In October 1923, when Beaverbrook acquired the *Evening Standard* by bidding for the Hulton newspaper empire with £5 million which he did not posses, H. A. Gwynne, the editor of the *Morning Post*, warned Baldwin that the change of ownership was part of a plot to reinstate Lloyd George as Prime Minister.[11] Baldwin did not even know that the transaction had taken place.

Baldwin had promised 'no fundamental change in [the] fiscal policy' which Bonar Law had set out in the 1922 general election campaign. Within weeks of becoming Prime Minister, he told the National Unionist Association, 'The unemployed problem is the most crucial problem facing the country . . . I can fight it. I am willing to fight it. I cannot fight it without weapons. I have come to the conclusion myself that the only way of fighting this subject is protecting the home market.'[12] He had come to that conclusion before he formed a government and his change of heart was reflected in his Cabinet. His first choice for the Treasury had been Reginald McKenna, who, when Asquith's Chancellor, had edged away from the sacred principle of free trade. McKenna failed to find a suitable constituency to return him to the House of Commons. Baldwin remained interim Chancellor for three months before he appointed Austen Chamberlain, by then an unapologetic protectionist. Even so, the sudden announcement took the Cabinet by surprise. Some attributed it to pressure from dominion prime ministers. Others suggested, not altogether seriously, that Baldwin had experienced a Pauline conversion while on holiday in Aix-les-Bains.

A third explanation is more probable, even though it qualifies for only two sentences in Baldwin's most authoritative biography. Lord Rothermere's newspapers had 'bred the strong suspicion that Lloyd George was about to steal the clothes which the Conservative Party was so delicately putting on'.[13] Tom Jones recorded a conversation in which the Prime Minister made the same point less delicately.

> I felt it was the one issue which would pull the party together, including the Lloyd George malcontents. The Goat was in America . . . I had information that he was going protectionist and I had to get in quick . . . Dished the Goat, as otherwise he would have got the Party with Austen and FE and there would have been an end to the Tory Party as we know it.[14]

Lloyd George, leading a rump of dissatisfied Liberals, may have inadvertently succeeded in changing the government's policy and reuniting the Tory Party behind protectionism. But he had also provoked Baldwin into providing a great incentive for the warring Liberal factions to bury their differences in support of a common cause. They might not agree about how best to harry the government on other issues – Bonar Law had escaped unscathed when he went back on his promise not to repay any part of the American war loan until European debtors had begun to repay Britain. But an assault on free trade was an attack on the ark of the Liberal covenant.

That did not mean that Lloyd George – still hoping to recruit Birkenhead and Austen Chamberlain into a new centre party – was not prepared at least to consider committing the act of ultimate sacrilege. Some of his closest colleagues shared Baldwin's suspicion that he was about to turn protectionist. On 9 November, the day of his return from America, a group of Liberal free-traders – led by Sir Alfred Mond, the former Minister of Health who had replaced Addison in 1921 – travelled to Southampton and joined him on board ship to make sure, before he disembarked, that he realised the importance of standing firm against tariffs. Churchill did not make the journey himself but sent, with one of the delegates, a letter which endorsed the deputation's view. Lord Birkenhead, who cabled his hope that Lloyd George would 'not commit himself' until after they had met, may have wanted to dissent from the view of the delegation which greeted Lloyd George in port. During the Atlantic crossing, Beaverbrook had bombarded Lloyd George with cables which urged him to build a new centre party around Imperial Preference – an idea with which Birkenhead sympathised. If Birkenhead did hope that Lloyd George was about to abandon free trade, he was disappointed. At a press conference in the *Mauritania*'s ballroom, Lloyd George denounced protectionism as 'unutterable folly' and described himself as an 'unrepentant and convinced Free Trader'.[15] Beaverbrook did not give up easily. He invited Lloyd George, Birkenhead and Chamberlain to spend a weekend at Cherkley, his country house in Surrey, to discuss the idea.[16] Lloyd George accepted, but even the most flexible politician of his age could not abandon, within days, a principle which he had espoused with a Messianic fervour.

Lloyd George's robust support for free trade was prompted by a mixture of political calculation and conviction. The battle against protectionism had, in his view, been elevated from a matter of principle to a practical necessity if the ailing European economies were to be revived. He also wanted to distance himself from Baldwin's Tories and edge closer towards Asquith's Liberals. He believed that the time had come for reconciliation, but was determined that it should not be on terms which would parallel the offer made to other faiths by the Roman Catholic Church – individual converts welcome, but no amalgamation with organisations which claimed equal status.

Asquith's immediate circle – not prepared to forgive or trust the man who had usurped their chosen leader – preferred oblivion to reconciliation. Margot Asquith told Bonar Law, 'Don't believe a word about reunion. Never was there a greater lie. We would rather be out for ever.'[17] And many Liberals who rejected that wholly self-destructive view nevertheless believed that when the lost sheep returned to the fold, they should do so as penitents. 'There are no Coalition Liberals for there is no coalition . . . In so far as members of Mr Lloyd George's party are free to fight for Liberalism and do in practice fight for it, they will cease to be [members of] a separate party.'[18] The best that Lloyd George could hope for, if reconciliation came about on Asquith's terms, was membership of the rank and file.

Throughout 1923, Lloyd George promoted the idea of a reunion of equals – first by implication and then overtly. In March he told the Scottish Liberal Club, 'While we throw arrows at each other, Labour is walking away with the Ark of the Covenant.' The offer which followed – willingness 'to follow any leader who possesses the necessary vision, resolution, wisdom, courage and inspiration to lead the nation' – was open to more than one interpretation.[19] But he had caught the ecumenical spirit of the meeting and the desire for Liberal unity which was spreading throughout the party.

Later that month, a group of Independent Liberal MPs drafted a letter calling for positive steps to be taken towards reunion. Its seventy-three signatories came from both Liberal parliamentary factions. Two joint meetings – coalitionists and Independents sitting down together – discussed the best way to achieve reconciliation. The second ended with the suggestion that Lloyd George and Mond should meet Asquith and John Simon to prepare a joint policy statement in anticipation of the breach being healed. The idea was vetoed by Asquith. Although the Independent Liberal leadership – with personal political debts to settle – continued to resist the idea of amalgamation, the grass-roots party membership and MPs, whose parliamentary survival depended on winning both sorts of Liberal vote, grew increasingly impatient with what they regarded as mutually destructive fratricide. Lloyd George, despite his increasing resentment of the personal attacks which were made upon him, chose to concentrate his fire on the government and use his speeches to advance the causes which united Liberalism. He was as much moved by self-interest as by conviction. But the strategy resulted in his slow rehabilitation with the Independent Liberal rank and file. It also reawakened his dormant dynamism.

In the early spring, his journalism acquired a sharper cutting edge. The French occupation of the Ruhr – punishment for Germany's failure, or inability, to keep up its reparations payments – was attacked as 'Digging Out Coal with Bayonets'.[20] In the House of Commons he once more preached the gospel of land reform. 'In the revival of rural life . . . in that alone you will find security for the State's prosperity for the land and safety for the Realm.'[21] In the country he again stirred great audiences with speeches which combined his unique blend of polemic and passion. At a meeting in the Manchester Free Trade Hall on 28 March, he identified 'Liberals' Three Great Enemies – Communism, Fascism, Protection'. The 'Four Great Evils' were 'low wages, the low status of workers, unemployment and inequality of opportunity'. The first priority was 'to eradicate slumdom out of British civilisation'. There must be an assault on 'class favouritism', and there must be the 'utilisation of the soil for the people' and free trade. Resistance to protectionism was described as an 'absolute necessity'. That allowed him to move the speech on from the positive advocacy of Liberal policy to an assault on the party's enemies – past and present. The enemies of free trade were identified as supporters of the 'McKenna Duties' – the Asquith government's flirtation with Imperial Preference. Labour Party policies were, he warned, bound to result in the suppression of freedom which blighted the Soviet Union. The example he offered to illustrate how easily liberties are lost was the Defence of the Realm Act, passed into law by the Asquith government in 1914 – when Lloyd George himself was Chancellor of the Exchequer. He ended his speech with the resounding assertions that Liberalism stood for 'Fair play for the underdog' and that 'Capital has been made for Man, not Man for Capital'. It was not the most intellectual speech that he had ever made. But it was an inspiration to Liberals in search of hope and purpose. Whatever had happened during the next six months, his position within the party would have been re-established. But then came Baldwin's decision that, as a man of honour, he must hold a general election before implementing a fiscal policy which his predecessor had promised not to pursue. Party politics was back and survival required Liberals of every stripe to fight under the same banner. It seemed that the gods were on Lloyd George's side again.

As a sign of goodwill, the *Lloyd George Liberal Magazine* – always the cause of suspicion – ceased publication. In a more tangible proof of his determination to work as part of a team, £100,000 from what had been the Coalition Election Fund was provided to finance the joint campaign. Parliament was dissolved on 15 November. The Conservatives nominated 536 candidates, the Liberals 457 and Labour 427. Newspaper reports of a weekend Lloyd George spent at Cherkley with Lord Beaverbrook – the high priest of protectionism – briefly disturbed, but did not destroy, the new-found unity. It was solidified by Lloyd George's travelling to Scotland to support Asquith, who described his speech as 'ragged and boisterous but with an assortment of telling points' and was gratified by his 'friendly and forthcoming attitude'.[22]

The high water mark of the Liberal campaign was the eve-of-poll rally. There was, according to a Liberal spokesman, a crowd of almost ten thousand in the Brighton Drill Hall and another five thousand at an overflow meeting in the Corn Exchange. Lloyd George addressed both gatherings at length and then – stopping along the way to make impromptu speeches to the crowds on the pavements – spoke from the steps of the Grand Hotel to a multitude of supporters on the promenade. Lloyd George was back – once more delighting his old friends and again infuriating his old enemies. The *Observer* described him as a 'miracle of flamboyant energy who threw all the other Liberal leaders in the shade'.[23] *The Times* called his speeches 'a deliberate attempt to stir up irrelevant prejudice'.[24] *The Morning Post* complained of the 'almost insane ferocity of his language'.[25] Had the election produced its expected result, the Liberal revival might have been unstoppable. But Lloyd George and his party had prepared to fight a war to the death against a Tory government which was wedded to protectionism. Instead they were faced with a Labour government which was so committed to free trade that it even abolished the tariffs which Asquith's administration had imposed.

The Tories won 258 seats, about a hundred fewer than Baldwin had anticipated. The Liberals had 158 Members, who included Freddie Guest (the party's Chief Whip), Charles Masterman (after an absence of ten years) and Gwilym Lloyd George. Labour, with 198 seats, did far better than anyone had expected. Asquith's initial preference was to vote with Baldwin to defeat MacDonald and then vote with MacDonald to beat Baldwin in the hope that he would emerge as the head of some sort of alliance. Lloyd George disagreed. 'The Labour Party', he wrote in the *Daily Chronicle*, 'are entitled to fair play from the constitution which they are expected to obey.'[26] That view was shared by George V, who said it was 'essential that Labour's rights under the constitution be in no way impaired' – even though, unlike Lloyd George, he did not have a vested interest in keeping Asquith out of Downing Street. So MacDonald formed a minority government and cracks appeared in the façade of Liberal unity. Lloyd George decided to maintain his independent offices in Abingdon Street and agreed that the *Daily Chronicle*, his only stronghold in Fleet Street, was free to take an editorial line which differed from the official Liberal position. His critics declared the election 'a triumph for Asquith' – a claim based on the calculation that Asquith's followers had won more seats than Lloyd George's supporters. Margot Asquith hammered the message home with the assertion that 'LlG made his usual crowded station tours and lost every seat he spoke for.'[27]

Lloyd George's dislike of 'socialism' – a philosophy that rarely motivated the Labour government, which he condemned for its timidity – was compounded by his contempt for its leader. Ramsay MacDonald had failed to rally to the country's cause during the First World War and, in Lloyd George's opinion, suffered from two irredeemable weaknesses. 'He had no experience of administration, even of a trades union, and he was extremely vain.'[28] According to C. P. Scott, Lloyd George believed that it would have been possible for the new Prime Minister to construct a programme which, item by item, attracted his support. 'The danger', he said, 'was not that Labour would go too fast and far but that it would not go fast and far enough and perish by inaction.'[29] In office, MacDonald confirmed Lloyd George's fears. 'They are all engaged in looking as respectable as lather and blather will make them . . . Ramsay is just a fussy Baldwin.'[30]

MacDonald wanted to cooperate with the Liberal Party over policy, but stubbornly refused to behave in a way which made it possible. The announcement that Labour would nominate a candidate to fight the Caernarvon Boroughs at the next election seemed calculated to sour personal relations. Lloyd George began to attack the new government's programme and then the crucial question of Labour's real attitude towards the Liberal Party. All MacDonald wanted was 'oxen to drag Labour over the rough roads of Parliament for two or three years and at the end of journey, when there is no further use for them, they are to be slaughtered'.[31] Behind the ritual bickering and parliamentary posturing, there was a fundamental reason for the mutual antagonism. Both Lloyd George and MacDonald expected British politics to revert to the two-party system – the Conservatives and one other. They were competing for the title of the radical alternative.

In March 1924, Lloyd George set out in the *Daily Chronicle* what amounted to his formula for Liberal recovery. In its simplistic way, it was a restatement of radical imperialism.

If [the Liberal Party] means to win back England, it must also show that it is proud of her greatness and is resolved to uphold it against all her detractors and foes . . . It cannot rely on resistance to the quackeries of Toryism and Socialism. It must show that it has lost none of its instinct for the needs of the people and none of its daring to supply them.[32]

From then on he devoted more and more time to setting out how those obligations could be met. He determination to offer the Liberal Party as a positive alternative did not prevent assaults on both the government and the official Opposition. They were unhampered by consistency. The Dawes Plan – a new formula for assessing Germany's reparations liability – was, he told the House of Commons, much to be welcomed. And the London conference which endorsed it received his grudging support, though he doubted if the French evacuation of the Ruhr – one of its decisions – would guarantee much of an improvement in the world economy. Then he learned that the plan included a reduction in reparations payments which the United Kingdom would receive. His regret that he had been party to so harsh a peace settlement were forgotten. Political circumstances required that he demanded his pound of flesh. So he attacked what he had previously defended. 'It is time', he said, 'that somebody stood up for Britain.'[33]

Most of his energy was devoted to more constructive endeavours – based on the bold contention that Liberals must prepare for government rather than aspire to no more than influencing the policy of other parties. In July 1924, he published *Coal and Power*, a pamphlet which revived the proposals set out in the one-man note of dissent which Arthur Duckham, an engineer who had advised on munitions supply during the war, had added to the Sankey Reports – the pits to remain privately owned but mineral rights to be nationalised, amalgamations to be imposed by the government and the creation of a national fund to finance improvements in miners' hours and pit-head amenities. A month later he convened at Churt a meeting of what he called the Land Committee. Its purpose was to decide how and when to launch again the Land Campaign which, despite its genuine importance to Lloyd George, had been constantly sidetracked by more urgent considerations – the Marconi Scandal, the Great War and the Irish Crisis. His hopes remained unchanged. All land not under cultivation was to be owned by the state in order to ensure its most productive use. But although the old ideas survived they had acquired a new romantic dimension. He wanted to rehabilitate rural England. Perhaps he was influenced by his new status. He had become a fruit farmer – land around Churt had been turned into a substantial market garden.

By the end of May, Lloyd George had come to the firm conclusion that it was time to bring down the government by supporting a Conservative Opposition motion which held ministers responsible for the increasing level of unemployment. In fact the 1924 total, although higher than that of 1923, was slightly lower than 1922. By 1930 the figure had doubled.* But Asquith refused to support the Tories. His rejection of Lloyd George's proposal owed nothing to the weakness of the Opposition's case. He did not want a general election. In his view, the Liberals were not ready. The party had no money. Lloyd George, however, had. Not unreasonably, the official leadership asked him to come to the aid of the party.

Donald Maclean, who had led the Liberals during Asquith's absence from the Commons, made a direct approach which Lloyd George satirised as a demand to 'give me your dirty money'. The request was refused on the grounds that he had made a major contribution to the previous election campaign – initially estimated to be about £100,000 but, as the discussion went on, inflated to £160,000. Viscount Gladstone, son of the Grand Old Man and a bitter Lloyd George critic, made a second appeal. The party was in desperate need of £20,000 to meet running expenses and to finance the next general election. Lloyd George's response was intentionally offensive. He would not provide a penny until he was certain that it would be efficiently employed by a reorganised party. Asquith humbled himself by agreeing to set up a committee of enquiry under Alfred Mond's chairmanship. Lloyd George, complaining that it was packed with Asquith's cronies, announced that he would not necessarily accept its findings. The 'fund' – though Lloyd George could not say so – was meant to finance the party after he had regained the leadership.

While the Liberal Party was squabbling over money, the MacDonald government was completing one of the policy initiatives which Lloyd George had begun. The government of the Soviet Union was formally recognised and an Anglo-Russian commercial treaty laid the foundations of greater trade between the two nations. Unfortunately the negotiations were bedevilled with disagreements about the repayment of Russia's war loan – resulting in an agreement which Lloyd George described as a 'contract in which the space for every essential figure is left blank'.[34] A vote on the treaty's ratification might well have brought down the Labour government. MacDonald believed that Lloyd George would oppose what he had previously advocated because 'he wants us to fail on the Russian Treaty and deliberately wishes the Liberal Party would split in order to secure his ascendancy'.[35] MacDonald's judgement was never

---

*1922, 1,464,000; 1924, 1,263,000; and 1930, 2,500,000. See Overy, Richard, – *The Morbid Age: Britain between the Wars*, Allen Lane 2009.

tested. Before the combined Liberal and Conservative parties had the opportunity to destroy the government, it destroyed itself.

On 25 July 1924, J. R. Campbell, a Clydeside member of the Communist Party of Great Britain, published an article in the *Workers" Weekly* – a publication unknown outside militant trade union circles. It called on the armed forces not to open fire on striking workers. What prompted the article, apart from the need for a subject about which to write, is not clear. There was no prospect of the slaughter which it sought to avoid. But the Director of Public Prosecutions – who cannot have been a regular reader of the publication and must, therefore, have been prompted into taking action – advised that Campbell, 'a man who had both feet almost blown off during the war . . . and had been decorated for exceptional gallantry', be prosecuted under the Incitement to Mutiny Act of 1797.[36] Sir Patrick Hastings, the Attorney General, a fashionable lawyer without much political background, agreed. Labour backbenchers were outraged.

Hastings – without, according to MacDonald, consulting colleagues – responded to the parliamentary pressure by dropping the prosecution. A failure to announce his decision to the House was followed by a vote of censure tabled by the Conservative Opposition. Asquith, uncertain which way to jump and relying on the precedent of the Marconi Scandal, proposed an amendment which called for a select committee to investigate the whole affair. MacDonald announced that the amendment, no less than the substantive motion, raised issues of confidence. The Conservatives then voted against their own resolution in support of the Liberal alternative and, by a majority of 364 to 198, brought down the government. In the general election which followed, the 'Zinoviev letter' – according to the *Daily Mail*, proof that Moscow anticipated a proletarian uprising in Britain – ensured that the Labour government was annihilated. Mond's committee, which might have modernised the Liberal Party, was suspended, leaving the electorate to carry out the cull of nineteenth-century grandees.

The election was called for 29 October 1924. Lloyd George was asked to provide £130,000 to enable the Liberal Party to contest 400 seats. He refused with the aggressive question, 'Why should we have more than 300 candidates? This election does not count' – an assertion as absurd as the answer to his question was obvious.[37] A party that contests only half of the constituencies cannot claim to aspire to government. And the result confirmed that the Liberal Party was no longer a major influence in British politics. It fielded 339 candidates. Only forty were elected. Asquith was not among them. The Tories, who won 412 seats, had a majority of more than 200 over all other parties, and Baldwin was back in office. So were Lloyd George's closest coalition partners. Churchill, to general astonishment, became Chancellor of the Exchequer. Austen Chamberlain went to the Foreign Office and Lord Birkenhead was made Secretary of State for India. Asquith's associates held Lloyd George responsible for the debacle. Shortage of money and uncontested seats had undermined the party's prospects. For once, he chose to defend himself rather than attack his tormentors. 'The limited number of candidates was not due to inadequacy of funds but the fact that eligible candidates were not available . . . It is no use talking of a Liberal revival unless there is a sincere Liberal reunion.'[38]

It was not an explanation which all his colleagues accepted. When the Parliamentary Liberal Party reassembled, Walter Runciman, a former President of the Board of Trade, suggested that the chairmanship – occupied by Asquith before the election – should be left vacant and that the Chief Whip should preside over future meetings. The idea was defeated by 26 votes to 9 and Lloyd George – elected chairman by 26 to 7 – became the effective leader in the Commons with Asquith – soon to be in the House of Lords – still in supreme command. The Earl of Oxford and Asquith, as he became, had briefly considered looking for another Commons seat. But there were few Liberal fiefdoms left in England and Scotland, and he told Masterman that he would 'sooner go to hell than Wales'.[39] He must have known that his opinion of the principality would reach Lloyd George. But he did not expect the new partnership to bring peace. What was left of Asquith's praetorian guard formed a not altogether appropriately named Radical Group with a statement which ended with a calculated, if only implied, insult to Lloyd George. 'The distinctive characteristic of the Radical Group is that they are not embarrassed by compromise in any direction, Right or Left. They do not regard politics as a game and they do not arrive at understanding with their opponents for the compromise of their principles.'[40] What remained of Asquith's old guard were determined that Lloyd George would never become Liberal leader. Indeed they still hoped to expel him from the party. It took two years for them to find a plausible reason.

By 1925, the subscriptions, raised in various ways to finance the coalition, had become the Lloyd George Fund. The new name did nothing to reduce the tension. Liberal headquarters, despairing of acquiring any of the 'dirty money', launched a Million Fund of its own to attract individual donations. It failed, allegedly because potential benefactors were loath to subscribe their own money when Lloyd George would not relinquish his. The bickering dragged on for most of the year, with Frances Stevenson, wearing the mantle of Lady Macbeth, using a letter – which the confused metaphor does nothing to moderate – to urge her man to be 'bloody, bold and resolute'. 'The Old Man counts for nothing . . . If you are not careful that section of the party is going to be like an old man of the sea about your neck.'[41] Then she became 'Darling Pussy' again, coquettishly 'laying in stores of vitality and energy in order to cope with the vigour of 62 the week after next. Not an easy job, but such a thrilling one.'[42] Wisely Lloyd George, instead of brushing aside the demands for financial help, chose to explain that he had other calls on his fund – all of which supported their common aims. Chief among them was the reborn Land Campaign.

In his radical youth, Lloyd George had been content to argue for land reform almost entirely in the name of social justice. With sixteen years of Cabinet experience to mature his judgement, he added economic necessity to the list of reasons why action was urgently needed. During the war, the U-boat threat had convinced him of the need for self-sufficiency in peace as well as war. The argument fitted very well into his decision to concentrate most of his time on attacking the government's economic policy. Much of his criticism was directed at Churchill, the Chancellor of the Exchequer. The ferocity with which he attacked his old friend in the House of Commons delighted the Labour Opposition – who often gave him the support that many of his grudging 'Honourable Friends' were unwilling to provide.

The land was the theme of his speech in Walsall on 21 February 1925, but it was the last fusillade before an enforced truce in his campaign. Immediately after the meeting he was attacked again by the recurrent throat constriction and spent three days in a Birmingham hospital before returning to rest at Churt. On 23 March, he was sufficiently recovered to speak in the House of Commons on unemployment – the subject which would soon become his major preoccupation. But, after two more speeches that were equally well received, his doctors advised that a rest cure was necessary. On 4 April, he set sail with Margaret on a cruise to Madeira. From Reid's Hotel he wrote to Frances Stevenson in language which justifies some careful analysis. The letter began with the usual description of the surroundings and the equally frequent claim that he could not wait to return. Then, uniquely in twenty years of correspondence, came an apology for his temporary desertion: 'The voyage was necessary.' Next he told her

> Although I have no delusions as to the past – none – neither have I any regrets. It is all to me like a previous existence. A new birth came in October 1922 . . . Before that – to use a legal term applicable to the law of domicile – there was a certain *animus reverend*. More marked in your case than in mine. Since then we have definitely settled our domicile . . . I cannot think of life apart from you now. I could give up everything for you without a qualm – even some relief.[43]

The suggestion that Frances Stevenson was more likely to abandon him than he was likely to desert her may have been no more than flattery. But it is also possible that he was beginning to doubt her fidelity. The bogus marriage, which he had thought necessary to provide as cover for their liaison, was one thing. A relationship into which she had entered on her own emotional initiative was quite another. The man who gave Frances Stevenson *The Life of Charles Stewart Parnell* to explain why there was no hope of regularising their relationship did not expect his Katherine O'Shea to be unfaithful.

Lloyd George was back in Britain for Budget Day and welcomed the increase in old-age pensions to 10/- a week, the extension of national insurance to widows and orphans, and the rise in the level of death duties. The reimposition of the McKenna Duties – which the free-trade Labour government had removed – was denounced in a reproach to the Asquithians as well as a condemnation of the Conservatives. The Budget's major error – the return to the gold standard – had to be ignored. In 1919, Lloyd George's government had described revaluation as the objective of fiscal policy and, a year later, prepared the way by adopting a 'dear money policy', which required the bank rate to be increased from 6 to 7 per cent. Lloyd George was not alone in initially thinking that a 'strong pound' was essential to economic recovery, but he deserves credit for realising, sooner than many others, that it depressed rather than reinvigorated the economy. At Wisbech in Cambridgeshire, on 10 July, he put the position exactly. 'It has made sterling dearer and thus put up the price of British goods in neutral markets . . . At this very hour coal owners and mines have been driven to the brink of a yawning chasm of strife, largely through this deed of egregious recklessness by the Chancellor of the Exchequer.'[44] During the next eighteen months, disagreements over policy towards coal and the miners was first to destroy what hope Lloyd George had of forging a partnership with the Asquithian Liberals and then securing him the formal leadership of the party.

Between January and June 1925, export prices – forced down by revaluation – fell by 25 per cent. In consequence, between March and May, the total value of British coal mined at a loss rose by 40 per cent. The Mining Association insisted that miners' hours would have to be extended or their pay cut and formally ended their agreement with the Miners' Federation of Great Britain. Its new offer – which, in effect, reduced wages by 2/- a shift – was instantly rejected by the Miners' Federation. Other unions, assuming that their members would face similar demands, rallied to the miners' cause, and the Trades Union Congress 'agreed to give complete support to . . . resistance to the owners' proposals'. Neither management nor men wanted a strike. Both hoped that a government subsidy would enable wage levels to be maintained and losses to be reduced. Baldwin first rejected the idea and then recommended it to the Cabinet, where, on the unusual basis of a vote, it was agreed that 'between a national strike and the payment of assistance to the mining industry, the latter course was the least disadvantageous'. The miners' union declared a victory and called 5 July 1925 'Red Friday'. No one was sure whether Lloyd George supported the miners or sympathised with the mine-owners. But it was clear that he was against the government. Ministers, he said, were 'afraid of cold steel' and her claimed that when Tory MPs were 'herded into the lobbies . . . The hand which directs them will be the hand of the Patronage Secretary [the official title of the government Chief Whip], but the voice which compels them will be the voice of Mr Cook', the secretary of the Miners' Federation.[45] What little sympathy he had for the miners was swept away by his passion to score rhetorical points. Churchill, he said, 'was very eager to fight Reds on the Volga. I am sorry to see him running away from them on the Thames and leaving his purse behind.'[46] If Lloyd George really believed that the government had capitulated, he underestimated Baldwin's cunning and failed to recognise the significance of speeches made by the Chancellor and the Home Secretary, Sir William Joynson-Hicks. Churchill told the House of Commons that the government had 'decided to postpone the crisis in the hope of averting it or coping with it effectively when the time came'.[47] Joynson-Hicks was even more explicit. 'Sooner or later the question has to be fought out by the people of this land.'[48] In 1926, the question would be fought out and won by an alliance of ministers and mine-owners.

During the intervening year, Lloyd George extended and expanded the Land Campaign to the point at which his Asquithian critics suspected, with some justification, that he was creating an organisation which at best was parallel to and at worst in rivalry with the Liberal Party. The campaign was supported by a Land and Nation League. It established its headquarters at 25 Old Queen Street, to where Lloyd George had moved his own offices from Abingdon Street – exciting Asquith's fears that it was no more than an extended leadership campaign. Complaints about the League's activities were dismissed with something approaching a declaration of independence. 'The Committee has urged, and is arranging, a very large number of meetings, 10,000 before the winter is over . . . It has never been the practice to discourage unofficial movements among Liberals from promoting particular opinions on moral and social questions.' It was, Lloyd George said, vital to the reinvigoration of flagging Liberal spirits.[49] Margot Asquith thought that the response confirmed that Lloyd George regarded himself as 'quite indispensable to the party and says so himself'.[50] Her husband was less censorious but deeply resented Lloyd George's suggestion that his campaign provided an essential boost to Liberal morale. 'So far as being downcast by the transient electoral disaster of the year, Liberals have everywhere shown . . . a most wholehearted and encouraging willingness to rally round the flag.' He ended his letter by deprecating any activity which 'resulted in dividing our energies'.[51] Altogether it confirmed Asquith's unwillingness, or inability, to face the extent of the Liberal Party's decline.

The public and official launch of Lloyd George's land policy took place at Killerton Park near Exeter on 19 September 1925. It was set out in more detail, three weeks later, in a pamphlet titled *Land and the Nation* – more commonly called the 'Green Book'. It proposed public ownership of rural land and guaranteed security of tenure. Asquith, as Lloyd George no doubt anticipated, was horrified by what amounted to wholesale nationalisation. On 24 November, the companion document *Towns and the Land* (the 'Brown Book') offered a compromise. It proposed to limit public ownership to providing local authorities with the power to buy urban land specifically for housing and the state with the right to buy land on the open market or by compulsory purchase when it was badly managed. At a special conference in February 1926, the compromise became official Liberal policy. So did the Brown

Book's less contentious proposals – rating assessment based on site values and 'leasehold reform', the right of owner-occupiers to buy the land on which their houses stand.* The uneasy peace was temporarily restored to the Liberal Party just as hostilities were being renewed in the coal-fields. But the bitterness persisted. Lloyd George, it was revealed, had offered the party financial help from his fund and then made the gift contingent on the acceptance of his land policy. Alfred Mond – who disliked the policy, with or without the £20,000 that Lloyd George had promised – defected to the Conservative Party.

Stanley Baldwin, enjoying the luxury of leading a united party, reacted to the coal crisis with what he modestly described as 'an attempt towards meeting the situation'. He set up another Royal Commission to enquire into the future of the coal industry. Its chairman was Herbert Samuel, Asquith's Home Secretary. It concluded that 'viability required labour costs to be cut by 10%' and judged it was unreasonable to expect workers – paid less than colliers – to subsidise, through their taxes, a miner's minimum wage. After a couple of weeks of indecision, the government agreed and endorsed the Mining Association's call for a wage reduction. At the end of May, the temporary subsidy was exhausted. The miners were 'locked out'. The General Council of the TUC announced 'coordinated action' in support of Miners' the Federation. Initially the government, fearful of a general strike, pro-posed to intervene. But on the night of 2 May, Baldwin was told that workers at the *Daily Mail* had refused to print an editorial which con-demned the unions' action. He told the House of Commons 'the first, active, overt move in the General Strike was being made, by trying to subvert the press'.[52] Negotiations were broken off – ensuring that the General Strike, which (as Baldwin well knew) had not started that night, began the following day.

Lloyd George – with the confidence and authority which came from his successful mediation in coal industry disputes – had made his first speech on the subject on 1 May in Cambridge. He had defended the government's right to take what steps were necessary to maintain essen-tial services but criticised ministers for not mediating earlier rather than waiting for the mine-owners to win an outright victory. Four days later, he deplored 'the precipitancy which was shown in breaking off negotiations' and, by implication, compared ministers' intransigence unfavourably with the moderation of the TUC, whose members were

---

*A Leasehold Reform Bill was eventually passed by Parliament in 1966.

'most anxious to negotiate a settlement'.[53] He went on to attack the *British Gazette*, a propaganda sheet published by the government and edited by Churchill. 'What we want', he said, 'is news not dope.'[54]

On 6 May, speaking in the House of Commons, John Simon – still notionally a Liberal – condemned the strike out of hand and warned the unions that, since they were breaking the law, they were liable to criminal prosecution. Two days later, the *British Gazette* published messages of support for the government from Asquith and Grey. It made no reference to the call by churchmen – headed by the Archbishops of Canterbury and York – for a negotiated settlement. That morning Lloyd George wrote to the Liberal Chief Whip to say that he was not in agreement with the policy which his colleagues were likely to adopt and that nothing was to be gained by his presence at the meeting of the parliamentary committee which had been called for 10 May.

> I have always deprecated the general strike and I am supporting the government in emergency measures to defend law and order and to enable the nation to carry on without privation . . . but that does not involve a declaration that negotiations for peace should be conditions on an unreserved withdrawal of the General Strike . . . If we support the Government in an absolute refusal to negotiate . . . the struggle may be a prolonged one and the damage to the nation may well be irreparable.[55]

On 21 May – nine days after the TUC had called off the General Strike and left the miners to fight on alone – Lloyd George received a letter from Asquith. It dealt with the meeting of 10 May. 'All my colleagues attended with the notable exception of yourself. The reason for your absence, as set out in a letter dated the same morning, seems to me to be wholly inadequate.' It went on to assert that the chairman of the party in the House of Commons had a particular duty to attend. 'Your failure to do so I find impossible to reconcile with my conception of political comradeship.'[56] That night Lloyd George dined with Frances Stevenson. 'He came in very excitedly so that I could see something had happened. He said to me "I have been expelled from the party" and handed me [Asquith's] letter.'[57]

Expulsion was clearly Asquith's intention. So Lloyd George was entitled to consider his position rather than respond by return of post. He sent a holding message. 'I appreciate fully the gravity of the unprecedented letter you have sent to me . . . I propose to take two or three

days to consider it before I reply.'[58] He took three – including Whit
Monday – and used the time to consult C. P. Scott and Charles
Masterman. On the afternoon that his considered answer was posted, he
received a telegram from Asquith which announced that, in the absence
of a definitive reply, he was releasing the text of his original letter to the
press. Lloyd George's only possible response was the publication of his
own letter – a model of sweet reasonableness which called for reconciliation within the Liberal Party as, a fortnight earlier, he had called for
reconciliation between the mine-owners and the miners. But it was too
late. Asquith – his judgement as faulty as when he lost the premiership –
insisted that the party choose between Lloyd George and him. Twelve
survivors from his government – including Grey, Simon, Runciman and
McKenna – issued a statement endorsing his stand on the grounds that
Lloyd George's 'instability destroys confidence'.[59] Lord Gladstone,
unaccountably overlooked by the 'Twelve Apostles', as they were
known, wrote a public letter of his own. It explained that Lloyd
George – who had refused to finance the Liberals' election campaign –
was the architect of all the party's misfortunes.

Lloyd George's troubled relationship with his party was matched by
turbulence within his own family. His children – Richard and Megan
vociferously, Gwilym and Olwen by way of silent protest – increasingly
resented the way in which their mother was treated and, in consequence, were hostile to Frances Stevenson. Gwilym, who had been
unseated in the 1924 general election, had become managing director of
the *Daily Chronicle* under the chairmanship of Charles McCurdy, sometime Liberal Chief Whip. When, with a thought ahead of his time,
McCurdy decided that the paper should have a woman on the board,
Frances Stevenson was his first choice. Gwilym, much influenced by his
mother and sisters, resigned. Lloyd George, virtually the paper's proprietor, offered the job to Richard, who was, his father knew, in
chronic need of funds. He declined. According to Frances, Lloyd
George – in a fury at the family's concerted opposition – asked Dame
Margaret for a divorce.[60] The claim is unsubstantiated.

The passions raised in Lloyd George by what he thought of as his
family's disloyalty were genuine, tempestuous and brief, and in sharp
contrast to the unemotional judgements he made about his relationships
with colleagues. The hatred and contempt of other politicians left him
unmoved as long as they did not materially damage his plans and
prospects. So the hostility of the Liberal old guard was a matter of no
concern and little interest. He was liked and admired by the New Model

Army of candidates and by grass-roots members. They realised that what new ideas came out of the leadership emanated from him, that only he enjoyed the parliamentary battle, and shared his view on the General Strike. Asquith's behaviour bewildered, as well as angered, them. The London candidates were the first section of the party to declare their support. Then he was told by a delegation of MPs that, if he contradicted the rumour spread by the Asquithians that he was about to join the Labour Party, his chairmanship of the Liberal MPs could be confirmed. On 3 June 1926, he wrote to the Chief Whip to dismiss 'the foolish story that I have been seeking a pretext for joining another party'.[61] Five days later, his chairmanship was renewed. Three days later Asquith suffered a slight stroke. The conference of the National Liberal Federation loyally passed a vote of confidence in his leadership. But the delegates sang 'For He's a Jolly Good Fellow' when Lloyd George appeared on the platform. The Liberal Party – such as it was – belonged to him.

CHAPTER 37

NEW DEALS

Asquith resigned the leadership of the Liberal Party on 16 October 1926 – not on account of ill health but because he thought that Lloyd George's superior forces left him no choice but to capitulate. 'The alternatives are to lead a squalid faction fight against LlG in which he would have all the sinews of war, or to accept his money and patch up a hollow and humiliating alliance. I am quite resolved to do neither.'[1] The battle had been lost long ago. 'The disintegration of the Liberal Party began with the Coupon Election of December 1918. It then received a blow from which it has never recovered.'[2] Its demise was bound to leave a legacy of bitterness. All that the most optimistic Asquithians could say was that 'LlG's time is comparatively short', and that while they must dissociate themselves from 'the personal record of LlG and his corrupting methods', they should 'avoid a schism between us and the party in the country' in anticipation of the day when they were once more in command.[3] Lord Gladstone had no thought except to limit Lloyd George's authority. 'We detest corruption . . . I urge that the public be told . . . that Lord Oxford's retirement has not wiped us out and that we exist as a force. Nothing short of this will stop the flight to LG and his Fund.'[4] Lord Cowdray – the proprietor of the *Westminster Gazette* and the victim of Lloyd George's fumbled attempt to win Lord Northcliffe's favours by the offer of a ministry – judged it 'better for the country that the Liberals should not return to power than that the party should be represented by a Lloyd George Government'.[5] It may have been these continued levels of animosity which prevented the *de facto* leader pressing for his position to be formalised – even after Asquith died on 15 February 1928.

A month after Asquith's retirement, Commander J. M. Kenworthy resigned from the Liberal Party and Parliament and fought the consequent by-election as the Labour candidate. He won and his Liberal opponent lost his deposit. Frances Stevenson, bewailing 'one blow after another', thought that it would be 'a tremendous fillip' if the Liberal Party won the by-election at Market Bosworth – which it did. But radical politics were in a state of flux. Frances compressed speculation about all the possibilities into half a diary paragraph.

> D's idea is to go definitely towards the Left and gradually to coordinate and consolidate all the progressive forces in this country against the Conservatives' reactionary forces. Thus he will get all sane Labour as well as Liberals behind him. D will not leave the Liberal Party. I begged him not to offer himself to Labour, saying he must be solicited by them.[6]

Despite the implication of Frances's entreaties, there was never any serious prospect of Lloyd George joining Labour. What little philosophical basis there was to his policy made him reject what he believed to be the inevitable consequence of socialism. 'Nothing struck me so much in the war as the disappearance of the individual . . . Socialism means transferring into peace the conditions of war.'[7] But his relationship with the Labour Party was to become one of the major sub-plots of British politics during the next five years. There were certainly times when he hoped for an electoral arrangement which would prevent constituencies being won by the Conservatives as a result of a split in the radical vote. Frances Stevenson chose the right personal pronoun when she wrote, 'We take the view very strongly that Labour cannot get into power again without our help and the converse is certainly true also. It would be a tragedy if we could not agree in time to prevent the Conservatives getting a second term.'[8] But Lloyd George also knew that, since both parties competed for support from the same groups within the electorate, a Liberal revival was dependent on a Labour decline. His relationship with the Labour leadership was prejudiced by his contempt for Ramsay MacDonald – who rightly believed that, for Labour to become a party of government, the Liberals must be eliminated from genuine contention for that role. Yet the Liberals had more new ideas than Labour, and the policies which the ideas generated outflanked the Labour Party on the left. On 31 January 1929, R. H. Tawney wrote to warn Arthur Henderson,

Liberals . . . propose to make a big plan for public works the
centre of their election programme. The idea is to create employment until total unemployment is brought down to half a million.
If the Labour election programme is to be any use, it must have
something definite and concrete about unemployment.[9]

No doubt Tawney thought that making his appeal political was the best
way of persuading the Labour leadership to improve its programme. But
while he argued for a more ideological party manifesto, the Liberals
were making serious attempts to find remedies for the scourge of the
age.

The Liberal plan for reducing unemployment had its origins in the
summer of 1920, when Ernest Simon (a Manchester businessman),
Ramsay Muir (Professor of Modern History at the University of
Manchester), Ted Scott (the son of the *Manchester Guardian*'s editor) and
Philip Guedalla spent a week in a Herefordshire farmhouse discussing
how to focus the party's attention on the 'New Liberalism' which had
begun to spring up in the heady days of Asquith's government but had
been extinguished by the war. 'Some party leaders', Simon complained,
'still lived in the old ideas of *laissez faire*. Their only industrial policy was
free trade.'[10] New Liberals wanted to extend the 'war socialism' (which
had prompted Addison's Housing and Town Planning Act and Fisher's
education reforms) and to combine it with a positive industrial strategy.
The weekend meeting evolved into the Liberal Summer School which
met in Grasmere in the Lake District the following year. From 1922
onwards it was held – in alternative summers – in Oxford and
Cambridge. It attracted a thousand students each year and became an
increasingly popular forum for the exploration of new ideas. Both the
Green and Brown Books had been by-products of long Summer School
deliberations.

In 1925, John Maynard Keynes gave a lecture to the Summer School
entitled 'Am I a Liberal?' His speech left his listeners in no doubt that
he was a Liberal of the most advanced kind. 'The hereditary principle
in the transmission of wealth and the control of business is the reason
why the leaders of the Capitalist cause are so weak and stupid' was not
a comment which Gladstone would have endorsed.[11] Equally startling – but more important – was his call for 'a new wisdom for a new
age'. The assumption that economic adjustment can and ought to be
brought about by the free play of the forces of supply and demand had
to be abandoned.[12] In the following year, the Summer School

Committee (which included Keynes) decided to set up an industrial inquiry. Lloyd George subscribed £10,000 from his notorious fund to finance its secretariat and took part in the discussions as chairman of the working group on unemployment. On 25 September 1926, there were '14 professors at Churt'. Keynes – no doubt included in Lloyd George's academic estimate – was as near to ecstatic about the weekend as his temperament allowed. 'The occasion was a gathering of a few trying to lay the foundations of a new radicalism and for the first time for years I felt a political thrill and the chance of something being possible in the political world.' But he still had doubts about Lloyd George. At Churt he had been 'as good as gold. But how long will it last?'[13] It lasted (surprisingly) until the Liberal Industrial Enquiry – the spelling later changed to 'Inquiry' to avoid it being known as the LIE – had completed its work. Lloyd George, a 'hard taskmaster', according to Seebohm Rowntree, drove the work on.[14] On 22 February 1928, the Liberal Party published a policy paper which reflected the inquiry's conclusions. Its official title was *Britain's Industrial Future*. But a precedent had been established and it was known as the 'Yellow Book' – yellow being the Liberals' colour. In fact it was books, plural – five in all. Each one moved the Liberal Party further to the left.

Book One, essentially an introduction, wrestled with the age-old problem of reconciling economic efficiency and social welfare. It concluded that the two objectives were more complementary than incompatible. Book Two (*The Organisation of Business*) was mostly Keynes's work. As well as proposing a whole new swath of instruments by which the government could influence, if not control, the progress of the economy, it recommended the creation of a Board of National Investment to finance new industries. Book Three (*Industrial Relations*) proposed that a minimum wage be negotiated, industry by industry, and advocated profit-sharing schemes to ensure that 'popular ownership of industry promotes the goal of Liberalism in which everybody will be a capitalist and everybody a worker as everybody is a citizen'. Book Four (*National Development*) reiterated much loved Liberal policy – a land policy which guaranteed security of tenure, nationalisation of coal royalties and a massive programme of public works. Book Five (*National Finance*) insisted that 'the control of our credit system . . . should be exercised more deliberately and systematically than hitherto with a view to the maintenance of steady trade conditions'. The Bank of England should be subject to closer regulation and social spending increased to ensure a redistribution of national income. All in all it was

a thoroughly social–democratic document – described by some news-papers as revolutionary extremism and by others as platitudinous. Had it been published ten years later, after the description became fashion-able and to some people pejorative, it would have been called 'Keynesian'. Doubts about the Yellow Book's importance should be dis-pelled by the knowledge that most of its recommendations are as right and as necessary now as they were when the policy proposals were published.

Philip Kerr – Lloyd George's devoted assistant – regarded the Yellow Book as intellectually 'so good that it is a poor electioneering docu-ment'. It lacked 'the impact, from a political point of view, of a simple rallying cry like Nationalisation or Protection'.[15] It certainly did noth-ing to unify the Liberal Party. The Liberal Council, which met on 27 February 1928, refused to accept *Britain's Industrial Future* as official Liberal policy and, although its decision was overturned by the National Liberal Federation in March, Grey insisted that individual members of the party had the right to concentrate on the 'most essential' aspects of Liberal policy – by which he meant the ancient beliefs in *laissez-faire* and free trade. The Liberal Party won by-elections in St Ives and Middlesbrough by small, yet satisfying, majorities. But the spectre of an irresistible Labour Party, elbowing the Liberals aside, still haunted Lloyd George. William Wedgwood Benn had resigned from the Liberal Party in 1927 explicitly because of his reservations about the moral standing of the leadership. He contested, and won, the 1928 Aberdeen by-election as the Labour candidate. The Liberal came fourth behind the Communist nominee.

It is not power but failure and insecurity which corrupt politicians. Lloyd George was certainly debilitated by the mixed reception which his new industrial policy received. The Yellow Book had advocated a reduc-tion in industry's rate burden but when Churchill's Budget proposed rate relief, admittedly in a different form, Lloyd George opposed it and thereby opened himself to the criticism which he could afford the least – the allegation that he would say and do whatever was convenient at the time. Churchill spared him nothing. 'The Right Honourable Gentleman has used on every occasion arguments, many of them flatly contradic-tory, one after another and arguments so unsound and degraded that they will hardly bear reporting.'[16] However, Charles Masterman – a Lloyd George acolyte again after a brief flirtation with the Twelve Apostles – was right to tell his wife, 'When Lloyd George came back to the party, ideas came back to the party.'[17] But the country remained unimpressed. By-elections continued to go badly. The Cheltenham result – held by the Conservatives after Labour split the radical vote – was 'a blow between the eyes' and Frances Stevenson complained, 'if Tavistock goes the same way it means that Labour, in their blind jealousy of Liberalism, are more intent on doing us harm than in putting the Conservatives out'. Once again Lloyd George talked of retirement. If the prospect was 'another five years of Tory domination with a miserable and ragged group of divided and dejected Liberals in the House', his choice would be 'not Westminster but Churt and Pussy (if she can bear me)'.[18] Once again, he did not mean it, or at least he did not mean it for very long.

Had Lloyd George gone into voluntary exile, he would have left behind – and no doubt attempted to live vicariously through – a political dynasty. In 1928 Megan – at the tender age of twenty-seven – was elected Liberal Member of Parliament for Anglesey. She had spent two months on the island campaigning to secure the nomination, accompanied by her mother, there to ensure that 'her health does not suffer' on Lloyd George's instructions.[19] The *Daily Mail* accused her of attending a 'pyjama bottle party' and her rival for the Liberal candidature reminded the selection conference that 'the first farmer in the world was turned out of the Garden of Eden . . . owing to a woman'.[20] But she prevailed. Her father's telegram of congratulation began 'Hurrah! Hurrah!' and ended 'Hallelujah! Hallalujee!' In between, he reminded her that he had predicted the outcome exactly.[21]

By the end of 1928, Lloyd George was considering which combination of forces would – after the next election – provide him with most power and influence. He consulted Philip Snowden, Chancellor of the Exchequer in the brief first Labour government. Snowden – with whom Lloyd George shared a Nonconformist background and, according to his son Richard, Mrs Snowden as well – sent him an estimate of the rival parties' prospects. It examined the result of the fifty-six by-elections since 1924 and concluded that, if the pattern persisted, the Tories would win 307 seats, Labour 209 and the Liberals 98 – a near dead heat between government and combined opposition. If, however, the most recent twenty-four by-elections were taken as a guide, the Tories would still win 307, but Labour would be victorious in only 129 constituencies while the Liberal Party triumphed in 179. The Liberal Party's performance had improved since Lloyd George had assumed control of its organisation and policy. That discovery made Lloyd George only more ambivalent about securing a pact with Labour.

Sometimes he was completely opposed. 'Anything in the nature of a Liberal–Labour combination in the coming Parliament is impracticable. Neither of the two parties is ripe for it.'[22] On other occasions he preached the necessity of some sort of arrangement. 'If we fight each other in the constituencies where Liberal or Labour, as the case may be, has no chance of winning but can only keep the other out, the Conservatives, I fear, will have a good working majority.'[23] His only real policy was to wait and see where and how he could maximise his personal advantage. He was even prepared to consider coming to an arrangement with the Tory Party.

On 18 February 1929, he warned Churchill that 'It was quite on the cards' that, after the next election, 'the Conservatives might be the second party of the state, not the first'.[24] And he set out the terms on which the Liberals would cooperate in keeping Labour out of office – even though he had suggested to Snowden that Liberals and Labour should form an alliance which would prevent 'another five years of Tory rule'. The only thing to be said in mitigation of what was clearly double-dealing is that his offer to support MacDonald's government was made contingent on the acceptance of impossible demands – electoral reform, free trade in iron, steel and other basic commodities, reconstruction of the ministry to remove men he regarded as dead wood and a drive against unemployment based on the policy which he and the Liberal Party had evolved. But he was ready to talk.

The fight against unemployment was to be the centrepiece of the Liberal election campaign which, in effect, Lloyd George launched two months before Parliament was dissolved. His address to 400 candidates and peers at the Connaught Hotel was followed by a speech to a rally in Manchester. At both events he made the reckless claim, 'We are ready with schemes of work which we can put immediately into operation . . . [We] will reduce the terrible figures of the workless in the course of a year to normal proportions.'[25] The speech prepared the way for the publication of *We Can Conquer Unemployment* – the 'Orange [or Little Yellow] Book', in Liberal jargon. Lloyd George – afraid that it would be impossible to fulfil the promise of the title – would have preferred the pamphlet to be called *The Problem of Unemployment*. The caution, though uncharacteristic, was justified.

No other election document in British history has ever made such detailed promises or such precise predictions. A two-year road-building programme would be financed by £145 million of state borrowing. Trunk road construction (£42 million) would employ 100,000 men, ring roads (£20 million) 50,000, bridges and improvements to existing roads (£53 million) 350,000. The Wheatley Housing Act (repealed by Neville Chamberlain after the defeat of the first Labour government) would be revived to provide subsidies which would finance 200,000 houses and provide work for 60,000 builders. Sixty thousand seems to have been the golden number. For it was claimed that land drainage, improvements in London transport and developments of the telephone system would each provide jobs for that size of labour force. The one element in the equation which made the target of reduced unemployment approach credibility was the prediction that the increased purchasing power of men directly employed would create jobs for others. Seven years before the publication of *The General Theory of Employment, Interest and Money*, Lloyd George, with a little help from Keynes, was relying on the multiplier effect. He had become a thoroughgoing Keynesian and, as such, in economic policy, both ahead of his time and a social democrat.

The Tory Party, as represented by the newspapers which supported it, denounced the proposals as 'A Programme of Imposture' (*The Times*), 'Make Believe' (the *Scotsman*) and 'Specious' (the *Glasgow Herald*).[26] But ministers, fearful of its attractions to the general public, employed civil servants to cobble together a White Paper which they hoped would convince voters that the government had a policy which reduced unemployment without bankrupting the nation – the certain consequence, they claimed, of the Liberal scheme. Labour, in the form of a *Daily Herald* editorial, dismissed the plan as 'contributing nothing new to existing ideas and, on the face of it, it appears to be a hasty and rather crude plagiarism of Labour resolution and publications'.[27] Lloyd George responded with the claim, 'The Labour Party cannot make up its mind whether to treat the Liberal plan as a freak or to claim its paternity . . . Mr MacDonald says – often in the same speech – "This is a stunted thing". Then, looking at it fondly, he says, "This is my child".'[28] The attacks on the Liberal economic policy were accompanied by assaults on its author. The Home Secretary could not 'understand how a man of [Lloyd George's] ability could put such a proposal before the people of this country'.[29] Baldwin quoted Thomas Carlyle – 'He has spent his whole life in plastering together the true and the false and therefore manufacturing the plausible.'[30] The White Paper, despite the vacuity of its contents, had a sufficient status to justify a serious response. Keynes and his fellow economist Hubert Henderson published a pamphlet which asked, '*Can Lloyd George Do It?*' They concluded that he could and went on to satirise the government White Paper in an imitation of its stifled language. 'You must not do anything for that will only mean that you cannot do something else . . . We will not promise more than we can perform. We therefore promise nothing.' *The Economist* endorsed the Keynes–Henderson view. So did a hundred well known industrialists who, on the eve of poll, issued a statement supporting the policy.

In April, three weeks before the election was declared, Lloyd George announced that he was determined 'not to carry the ladder and hold it in place for five years while the Socialists are up on the scaffold'.[31] But his letters to Frances Stevenson increasingly betrayed the realisation that the best he could hope for was to hold the balance of power between the larger parties. They also reveal that his ability to deceive himself as well as her was undiminished. In January 1929, in the Mediterranean with his wife and a host of admirers, he wrote Frances a letter which – had it not been for the evidence that he was loving every minute of his walking holiday – might have been taken as proof that he was pining. After speculating about the prospects of the Liberal Party becoming a force again, he added,

> Whether we do or not, I shall not fret. I shall have my little girl. If it is not reserved for me to lead the people for whom I have fought all my life to the promised land, I shall feel a pang of dis-appointment – but what a sweet consoler I shall have . . .[32]

The fantasy was the product of excitement. The letter in return, for which he was 'thirsting', was likely to contain news to which he dare refer only in bogusly insouciant language. 'By the way I shall be expecting an interesting wire from you next Monday week. You know what I mean. If the usual thing happens wire "transactions". If not, then "no transactions". I am hoping for the latter.'[33] 'No transactions' was the coded message which would confirm that Frances was pregnant.

Jennifer Stevenson – now Mrs Longford – was born on 4 October 1929. She takes it for granted that Lloyd George's clear delight at the prospect of her mother's pregnancy is conclusive evidence that he had abandoned all hope of playing a major role in politics again and that Frances Stevenson, who was as ambitious for him as he was for himself, had also recognised that the glory days were over. In 1915, according to her diary entry, Frances's first pregnancy had been terminated – despite the emotional distress the abortion caused – because she feared that her

mother 'would be so upset that people would see what had happened
and [Frances] could not be responsible for the ruin of C's career'.[34] By
1929, her mother (who had known about the first pregnancy and
thought it should be ended) and her father (whom she had hoped to
keep in happy ignorance) were dead. And no one else was likely to
express the degree of outrage which would leave no doubt about the
child's paternity. So it may be that Jennifer Longford is wrong and that
Frances did not regard a baby's arrival as the unavoidable end to her and
Lloyd George's mutual hopes of a return to power. But Jennifer
Longford's belief that she was born thanks to the death of Lloyd George's
ambition is at least plausible. His letters demonstrated an enthusiasm
which, even allowing for the gusto which was his style, must be regarded
as genuine pleasure at the thought of becoming a father again.

A telegram carrying the glad tidings that there were 'no transactions'
arrived on 4 February 1929. The pregnancy which it confirmed was not
always easy. Lloyd George's apology for his neglect, during a March
indisposition, does not equal in sincerity the expressions of pleasure at
the prospect of a baby on the way.

> What a pig I have been . . . My only excuse darling is that I must
> not disappoint those scores of thousands who are looking forward
> to the great meeting tomorrow . . . Will you forgive me my own
> darling for seeming to put the fortunes of battle above you? I have
> never done so in my heart. Had I thought for a moment there was
> danger I would have chucked everything and rushed to my cariad's
> side. You know that, don't you, girl of my heart?[35]

However, despite the artifice of his letters, there was genuine rejoicing
when Jennifer was born, and his affection for her grew with the years.
Indeed, more than seventy years on, she looks back on a childhood in
which she received more affection from Lloyd George than from her
mother. The 'father's name' was not entered on the birth certificate. But
although Frances ('a woman of private means') was named as mother, she
formally adopted her natural daughter – at the time, a common practice
among single parents. Less usual was Frances's decision to leave the adoption papers where Jennifer could find them. For a time, the little girl was
led to believe that she was the daughter of murdered missionaries. Then,
when she was twelve and had discovered that she was Frances's natural
daughter, her mother told her that her father was Colonel Thomas
Tweed, Lloyd George's Chief of Staff. Frances had had a brief affair with

Tweed at about the time Jennifer was conceived. But even after Lloyd
George realised that her parentage was in doubt, he treated Jennifer with
a father's affection. She called him 'Taid' (Welsh for 'grandfather') and
loved him as he showed every sign of loving her. But he never acknowledged her as his daughter and, unlike Tweed, who bequeathed her a few
pounds, he left her nothing in his will.

Jennifer Longford bases her belief that she is his daughter on his
treatment of her when she was a little girl, living with her nanny in a
house close to Churt while her mother lived with Lloyd George – frequently and furtively before Margaret Lloyd George died, and regularly
and publicly after their marriage.

Frances had been pregnant for four months when Baldwin dissolved
Parliament in preparation for the general election of May 1929. It then
became necessary for Lloyd George to make unwarranted claims about
the likelihood of the Liberals becoming the largest single party. Scottish
Young Liberals were told that the Baldwin government was 'about to
give up office' and that their own party 'united and competent, stood
ready to take its place' after a resounding victory.[36] In Bristol he
boasted, 'We have the plans, the men and the determination to form
one of the most steady and experienced administrations of this generation.'[37] His eve-of-poll message could be interpreted as either hopeful
or cautious. 'Nothing will hinder you from having a Liberal
Government if you are resolved to get it.'[38]

Had Lloyd George really believed that there was a prospect of returning to office, he would have fought a more vigorous campaign. As it
was, he spoke outside Wales on only four occasions. At Rochdale,
where he was to address an open-air rally after he had spoken at a
more formal meeting in Darwen, also in Lancashire, he was so dis-
couraged by hecklers that he gave up the unequal effort. He did well
enough in his own constituency, where he won with a majority of over
nine thousand. But the national result for the Liberal Party was a near
disaster – the Liberals won 59 seats, the Conservatives 260 and Labour
288. When he arrived back in London, two days after the votes were
cast, he told the journalists who were waiting at Euston Station, 'It
would be silly to pretend that we have realised our expectations. It looks
for the moment as if we still hold the balance.'[39] That was certainly the
numerical position. But both Baldwin and MacDonald were determined that Lloyd George should be neither kingmaker nor arbiter of
what programme a minority government was able to implement.
Baldwin had to decide whether to resign at once or go to the House of

Commons and wait to be defeated there. Tom Jones, Deputy Secretary to the Cabinet under four prime ministers,

> found him in a great state of nervous tension with the LlG obsession weighing heavily upon his mind . . . He spoke with great rapidity – most unusual with him and only possible when roused by LlG. It was LlG who had put the Socialists in office and it was LlG who throughout the day dominated our discussion. What we all feared was that LlG might keep SB in office for a week or month and humiliate him in every conceivable way.[40]

Baldwin's decision to resign at once was a concession that, even with only fifty-eight Members to lead, Lloyd George was still a force in politics. And after the Labour Party took office, ministers were 'still haunted by the spectre of LlG' Philip Snowden, Chancellor of the Exchequer again, dismissed the section of the King's Speech which dealt with unemployment with the prediction that 'Lloyd George would tear it to pieces'.[41] But, while his opponents continued to fear him, half of his own party rejoiced at what they regarded as his humiliation.* 'The verdict of the country is final on LG anyway . . . The country has demonstrated its view on LG in a way which cannot be mistaken . . . LG was a millstone round our necks.'[42]

The King's Speech included a vague reference to electoral reform – official Labour policy before the party harboured hopes of wining an outright majority. Its reappearance signified MacDonald's wish – part the result of necessity – to hold out a tentative hand of friendship to the Liberals. Lloyd George, in a similar mood, decided to make peace with his own party by contributing to the cost of the headquarters organisation. Then he went off on a tour of Europe, officially to visit the battlefields of the war which people were beginning to forget that he had won. When he got back to Britain he had to decide how to deal with the Coal Mines Bill – a subject about which he had strong feelings, considerable experience and a dilemma. He wanted to endorse neither the government's policy nor the Opposition's alternative.

Lloyd George claimed that, by refusing to consider pit amalgamations, MacDonald had made Liberal opposition inevitable. MacDonald thought the explanation was an excuse.

---

*Sir Ivor Phillips, a Coalition MP deputed to work on plans for reconciliation, was jubilant.

The [Liberals] would look at nothing but compulsory amalgamation. They admitted that it would take at least two years to
complete and that it made no contribution to [solving] immediate
economic difficulties. We informed them that as soon as the Bill
was off the hands of the Department we would proceed to an
amalgamation Bill. They quite evidently did not mean to agree.[43]

However, Lloyd George was not willing to vote against the second
reading of the bill. So Herbert Samuel, on behalf of the Liberal Party,
moved what, in parliamentary language, is called 'a reasoned amendment'. It supported the need for reorganisation but both deplored the
method and regretted the imposition of a seven-hour day which was to
be financed by each pit being given a production quota for which it
would be paid a guaranteed price. The amendment was defeated by
eight votes at the end of a debate in which Lloyd George had
denounced 'an incredibly bad bill', which contained 'the worst features
of Socialism and individualism without the redeeming features of
either'.[44] During the committee stage when the Liberals 'attempted to
improve' the bill, Lloyd George – apparently restored to health and self-
confidence – made a series of speeches which were heralded as a return
to his old form. Only once was he bested. The Labour Member for
Ebbw Vale, Aneurin Bevan, fresh from the collieries of South Wales,
told him that he was exploiting his 'parliamentary position to attempt
to put new life into the decaying corpse of Liberalism' and added,
'better to have slightly dearer coal than cheaper colliers'.[45] Twice Lloyd
George expressed regret at 'having fallen foul of a young countryman of
mine'. As with Lord Randolph Churchill's attack on Gladstone, which
he had witnessed forty-six years earlier, he enjoyed a good speech,
even when he disagreed with its message. In several of the votes, there
were Liberal MPs in both the government and Opposition lobbies,
while others abstained. The Liberal Chief Whip resigned. The Coal
Mines Bill committee-stage debates were a triumph for Lloyd George
and a disaster for the Liberal Party.

The third reading was carried by a majority of fifty-seven. The
Liberals – fearful of again exposing their divisions – abstained on the
transparent pretext that it would be wrong to defeat the government
while it was taking part in a naval disarmament conference. For Ramsay
MacDonald, Lloyd George became 'Samson, shaved of his locks and
bent on destruction'.[46] In fact his performance – dazzling oratory and
selective opposition – had made him again a power in the land.

For a politician bent on notoriety rather than office, irresponsibility has much to commend it. And, by being against almost everything and in favour of not very much, Lloyd George began to restore his reputation as a fearsome debater. He had, according to the *Sunday Times*, 'been so effective as to inspire some observers to believe that he may recapture his former dominating position in British politics'.[47] It was a view which was increasingly shared by the political establishment. Tom Jones wondered about the inclinations of the young Tory MPs who, like Lloyd George, were enjoying Lord Astor's hospitality. 'The tide has turned very much in favour of LlG . . . and think most of this group would follow him if he got into the saddle again.'[48] Oswald Mosley – on his way from the Unionist backbenches to the New Party, via an improbable brief membership of the Labour government – thought much the same. After a meeting with a group of progressive Tories, including the young Harold Macmillan, he wrote, 'If Lloyd George had been able to form an Administration, I do not think that any of the young men who took part in these discussions would have refused to serve.'[49] Both Jones and Mosley stated the obvious and hypothesised the impossible. Had Lloyd George become Prime Minister, all sorts and conditions of politicians would have rallied to his flag. But there was no chance of that happening – even though he was prepared to look for support from both left and right. As 1930 ended and 1931 began, Lloyd George's new popularity combined with the disarray of the Tory Party to argue that his best prospect lay in forging an alliance with the government.

By now Churchill had resigned from the Conservative front bench – formally because of his opposition to Baldwin's India policy, but in part because of his growing conviction that Baldwin was leading the party to destruction. The time had come for Lloyd George to change his relationship with the Labour Party from armed neutrality to uneasy peace. In December 1929, he had defended Snowden's Budget: 'The Chancellor is paying the gambling debts of his predecessor . . . and I think it a little discreditable that his predecessor should taunt him.'[50] But he made electoral reform the price of continued cooperation at a time when MacDonald was moving from positive support through half-hearted acceptance to positive opposition. Labour, he had decided, could hope to win an overall majority. Lloyd George's demands were, he believed, proof that the Liberals believed that too. 'The bargain proposed really amounts to this. We get two years in office from the Liberals and give them in return a permanent corner of the political stage.'[51] He wrote in his diary, 'Let him do his worst. It will break him.'[52] Perhaps Lloyd George realised that fractious opposition would undermine his claim to be a moderating force.

Despite what amounted to a resounding victory in the final Coal Mines Bill division – and his claim that Lloyd George was a spent force – MacDonald· thought it necessary to make another attempt to win Liberal support by proposing the introduction of the alternative vote, the abolition of both the university seats in Parliament and the business vote and a strict limit on election expenditure.* It would, he told Lloyd George frankly, be necessary to justify the proposals to the Labour Party with the explanation that winning Liberal sympathy was the only way to keep the government in office. Then, in April, he appealed for a bi-party approach to the struggle for economic stability. The idea eventually took practical shape with the suggestion that the Liberal and Labour leaderships should form a joint Committee on the Economy – compared, at various times during the negotiations about its creation, with a Council of State, the Committee of Imperial Defence and the Public Accounts Committee. Lloyd George agreed to cooperate as long as he had direct access to Treasury papers and officials. In May, he made his willingness to cooperate public. 'The fact that the Socialist government is shunning socialist ideas in the legislation makes the *rapprochement* the easier.'[53] When the meetings took place, Lloyd George found them pointless.

Unable to convince the Labour Party of the need for – or expediency of – electoral reform, MacDonald included only a vague reference to the subject in the 1930 King's Speech and demonstrated its impotence by failing to carry the bill which would have abolished the university seats. But Lloyd George continued to support the government on the grounds that the only alternative to MacDonald was Baldwin and 'the spectacle of a leader of a great party driven and kicked from pillar to post by a couple of newspaper boys'.[54] It was a gross libel on Baldwin, who stood up to the press barons – in private and public – more than any prime minister in history, and it demonstrated Lloyd George's determination to cling on to the Labour Party as the lifeline

---

*History constantly repeated itself. David Cameron offered a referendum on the alternative vote as a bait to catch Nick Clegg. Jim Callaghan accepted proportional representation in the European elections as the price of David Steel's support. Tony Blair set up a commission on electoral reform to show his sympathy for more Liberal representation. Then Paddy Ashdown agreed to a joint Liberal/Labour committee. Like MacDonald's earlier proposal, it was a confidence trick.

that connected him to power. But he had other demands to make. They related to the protection – and ideally to the increase – of Liberal representation in Parliament. 'While members of the Liberal Party are engaged in supporting the government on great measures in the House of Commons, they should not be assailed by government nominees.' His vain hope was that the Labour Party would give his sitting Members, and some candidates, a clear run.

Lloyd George had told the *Daily Herald* that he was willing to provide 'wholehearted support to secure a sound and dependable majority for emerging measures necessary to wage war on unemployment'.[55] He was expressing both a genuine concern and a reproach to the Labour government, which, he believed, had no clear view of how to put Britain back to work. Rumours persisted that he was still contemplating some formal realliance of political forces. Beatrice Webb (whose husband, Sidney, had become a Labour Cabinet minister) wrote that Labour's 'big four' met Lloyd George 'and his inner Cabinet . . . every week or so and it looks like the preparation for [his] appearance, sooner or later, on the Labour Front Bench'.[56] They certainly met to discuss items of mutual interest – foreign policy and free trade in particular. But the idea of amalgamation, or even federation, was proposed only by men who conspicuously did not speak for the leaderships of their parties.

In January 1931, loose talk of alliances had to be replaced with hard decisions about which side the Liberal Party was on. In the pre-Christmas debate on the King's Speech, Herbert Morrison, the Minister of Transport – speaking on the government's economic policy – had specifically rejected the proposals which Lloyd George had set out in *We Can Conquer Unemployment*, the popular version of the Yellow Book. But on 11 February 1931, when the Opposition moved a vote of no confidence in the government, the real argument was not about alternative proposals for cutting the dole queues. It was whether or not Labour should be replaced in office by the Conservatives. Neville Chamberlain assumed that Lloyd George would come to MacDonald's rescue: 'To put the government out would mean Liberal extinction.'[57] John Simon claimed that the party would 'Carry support to the point of subservience'.[58] The Liberals did rescue the government. The censure motion itself was defeated by 310 votes to 235. But the device by which the Liberal Party hoped to demonstrate its independence eventually destroyed the government and ended, by tragic coincidence, Lloyd George's last hope of office.

The Liberal Party moved an amendment to the censure motion

which – having removed its main clause – called on the government to create 'a small and independent committee to make recommendations to implement forthwith all legitimate reductions in national expenditure'. In the debate, MacDonald spoke warmly about the Yellow Book proposals, and Lloyd George warned the government against 'running away the moment a few volleys are fired from the City of London'.[59] The amendment was carried, with the government's support, by 408 votes to 21. Sir George May, former secretary of the Prudential Assurance Company, was appointed chairman of the proposed committee. The government was safe for the moment and, according to the *Morning Post*, 'the leadership of the far left [had] fallen to Mr Lloyd George'.[60] The ever-susceptible George Lansbury, the First Commissioner of Works, believed the same and suggested that Lloyd George should join the Labour Party. Indeed, without any authority, he suggested that Lloyd George might become its deputy leader if he could 'fling aside all thought of self'. The reply – six carefully written paragraphs – combined political realism with bogus modesty. 'Coming out is not the best way to help. It would antagonise millions of Liberals . . . Personally I have had enough of office . . . I can and will give effective assistance to the government if they mean business.'[61]

MacDonald remained sceptical about both Lloyd George's sincerity and his ability, even if it were his wish, to rally all the Liberal Members behind the government. The Parliamentary Liberal Party had discussed the subject at a meeting which lasted six hours and, after rejecting the idea of a formal pact, had carried a motion to sustain Labour in power by 33 votes to 17. In the Prime Minister's view, Lloyd George could still not be relied upon to resist the temptation to court popularity, or solidify support with his own party, by turning on the government. And he was right. In April 1931, at the National Liberal Convention in Buxton, Lloyd George beat off a challenge from the right wing of his party with an anti-Labour speech that 'moved the audience of 2000 to a remarkable demonstration of enthusiasm'.[62] Yet a month later, 'the people's champion' of Edwardian Britain voted against the introduction of a land tax on the grounds that it was double taxation. It was assumed that he had abandoned one of the great crusades of his youth for no better reason than to convince his Liberal critics that he was not about to defect to Labour or propose a formal alliance.

As Lloyd George jockeyed for power and position, he said and wrote so much which was self-evidently insincere that a letter, clearly written without artifice or affectation, comes as a shock as well as a surprise. But such letters do exist. They concern the progress of baby Jennifer. 'The weight. What did she make last week? . . . I am looking forward to getting the photo tomorrow . . . The photos were the best to date.'[63]

In May, Liberal cohesion was encouraged by the launch of Baldwin's tariff campaign, but the old disagreements – ideological and personal – were too bitter to be obscured for long. When John Simon resigned the Liberal whip – on the surprising ground for a Liberal that he opposed the government's Land Reclamation Bill – he provoked a valediction which was savage even by Lloyd George's standards. 'I do not object to the intolerable self-righteousness. Greater men have done it in the past. But at any rate they did not leave behind the slime of hypocrisy in passing from one side to the other.'[64]

Throughout the spring and early summer, the slow recession, which had begun in America, increasingly depressed the European economies; and the crisis, which had begun with the collapse of the Austrian Credit Bank, created a run on the pound which the Labour minority government doubted its ability to withstand alone. MacDonald met Lloyd George. An account of their meeting exists – described by earlier biographers as a 'memorandum' but most likely a speaking note – dictated by Lloyd George to Frances Stevenson. It is at least possible that it was based as much on wishful thinking as on the actual conversation. 'Generally speaking, Labour would like an alliance. They would be willing to drop certain of their present ministers. Ramsay would be Prime Minister, Lloyd George would be Leader [of the House] at the Foreign Office or the Treasury.'[65]

By then, the cause for concern had turned into crisis. The Treasury warned that the 'gold exodus is unprecedented.' The bank rate was increased from 3.5 per cent to 4.5 per cent. On the same day, the May Committee reported. The brainchild of the Liberal Party estimated that the public accounts were £120 million in deficit. Between 4 and 11 August, while the Cabinet was digesting that unpalatable figure, £11 million of reserves and £10 million of foreign-loan receipts were spent in supporting sterling. Then the Treasury revised the May Committee's estimate of the budgetary deficit. The true total was £170 million. The Opposition was told the original calculation and guessed that it had been superseded by a higher figure. The May Committee's proposed cuts – unemployment insurance, education and transitional benefit – became the test of the government's willingness to save the pound and make the political sacrifice which 'international confidence' demanded.

It was a demand which most of MacDonald's Cabinet declined to meet – though some of the ministers who refused to make the cuts accepted that they would have to be made by the government which succeeded them. The national government that followed included Herbert Samuel – the semi-detached Liberal who helped to justify the claim that what amounted to a Labour–Conservative coalition represented the whole nation. Undoubtedly, had Lloyd George been fit and well, he would have been offered a job of some sort. Whether or not he took it would have depended on his calculation about his future prospects – best inside the national government or better outside. But whatever he might have decided, the character of the administration would not have changed. The restoration of international confidence – that intangible and elusive necessity – required a government which, whatever its composition, was Tory in character.

Lloyd George was spared the temptation to repudiate his Yellow Book and cooperate in implementing the cuts which the May Committee – his idea – proposed. On the 25 July 1931, while spending an evening with Frances Stevenson at Addison Road, he was taken suddenly ill. Within twenty-four hours his prostate gland had been removed in an operation performed in his own bedroom. His recovery was complete, but it was three months before he could play a practical part in politics again. By then the world had changed. Ramsay MacDonald was still Prime Minister, but Stanley Baldwin was his anointed successor and a coalition – with the Conservatives in command – governed the United Kingdom. Lloyd George's last chance of office had gone.

CHAPTER 38

WANDERING IN THE WILDERNESS

Politicians rarely choose the right moment to say goodbye and Lloyd George – who spent almost twenty years jostling and scheming to return to power – was temperamentally incapable of accepting that, after 1922, his day was done. He could console himself with the fiction that, had it not been for his prostate operation, the Liberals he would have led into a national government would have made it a much more progressive administration than the coalition which the Baldwin Conservatives joined. But international opinion – which Ramsay MacDonald's coalition was created to assuage – wanted retrenchment, not reflation. And Lloyd George, although, as he proudly proclaimed, economically far more adventurous than either the Labour government which left office or the coalition which replaced it, would have been forced to accept the reality of the moment. Between 1922 and 1931, he was influential but powerless. After 1931, even his influence began to wane.

Although the prostate operation was a complete success, progress towards full recovery was impeded by his suspicion that he was more seriously ill than the doctors and his wife had told him. And his convalescence was complicated by Dame Margaret's determination that he should not be visited by Frances Stevenson, who, having called the doctors when he was first taken ill, made a discreet exit before the family arrived. After Sir Thomas Carey Evans – Lloyd George's son-in-law, who had assisted in the operation – took Margaret Lloyd George for a drive in his new motor car, he was accused of persuading her to leave the house so that Frances could visit the invalid. Roberta, Richard Lloyd George's wife, was anxious to call but advised not to do so. People were beginning to talk about her relationship with Lloyd George. Later in the year, she divorced her husband on the grounds of infidelity. According to the diary of A. J. Sylvester – by then Lloyd George's private secretary – had Richard cross-petitioned, he would have been entitled to cite his father as co-respondent.[1]

Ramsay MacDonald had promised that the national government would last only until the economic crisis was over. While it lasted, Lloyd George's associates continued to fantasise about his future. Colonel Thomas Tweed MC, the Liberal Party organiser who had become his Chief of Staff (as well as, briefly, Frances Stevenson's lover) believed that 'had he been fit to serve in thes National Government it would have possessed one man of guts, vigour and real leadership and might have transformed the situation'. But – in an apparent change of mind about the propriety of Liberal cooperation with MacDonald – he urged Lloyd George not to 'disavow the actions of Samuel and Co' since 'before many weeks are past the leadership of the Labour Party may be his for the taking'.[2]

The coalition parties had agreed that only once the crisis had passed would politics resume its normal pattern, and they would reform and fight each other in a general election. By September 1931, it was clear that the promise would not be kept. The convalescent Lloyd George did all he could to persuade MacDonald to soldier on and the Liberal members of the coalition Cabinet to use their influence to prevent what amounted to a 'coupon election' of the sort which he had called in 1918. Herbert Samuel, Donald Maclean and Archibald Sinclair – the men who led the party in Lloyd George's temporary absence – visited the sickroom at Churt but did not have the courage to tell him that they had already agreed to the dissolution of Parliament. Liberal ministers endorsed their decision on 2 October and were supported by a resolution of the full parliamentary party on the following day. When the formal announcement was made, four days later, only two parliamentary secretaries resigned. One of them was Gwilym Lloyd George.

Lloyd George's reaction was typical. 'As a consequence of his advice not being followed there would be financial help only for certain candidates.'[3] The decision to dissolve Parliament was described as 'an act of reckless criminal folly' and the 'death warrant of the Liberal Party'.[4] He also had highly personal regrets. 'Think of a fight and me not in it.'[5] In his absence, the campaign in Caernarvon was fought on his behalf by Dame Margaret, augmented by a radio broadcast from her husband in which he denounced MacDonald's call for a 'doctor's mandate' as 'a partisan intrigue under the guise of a patriotic appeal'. He won 60 per cent of the votes cast and a majority of 5387. Seventy-two Liberals were elected – Simonites, Samuelites and Lloyd Georgians – but only four were wholly committed to Lloyd George. The parliamentary party disintegrated. Lloyd George resigned the leadership and the group led by Sir John Simon boycotted the meeting which was called to elect his successor. The split was formal and permanent, and, for a while, it seemed that Lloyd George had accepted the role of distinguished, but retired, elder states-man. After a recuperative visit to Egypt and India – travel being an emotional necessity – he took up residence in Churt, gave audience to visitors of distinction and began, at last, to write his *War Memoirs*.

Ten years earlier, after he had been accused of exploiting the men who had served and died in the Great War, he had announced his intention of donating the proceeds of his memoirs to ex-servicemen's charities. He had been so dilatory in their production that the contract was cancelled. So the donation was never made. At the time that a new deal was arranged, nobody suggested that he should not keep the advance. So he got down to work at once – for less than he would have earned in 1922, but at least keeping the £5000 he was paid for British rights and $12,000 he received from publication in America.* The first two volumes were published in September and October 1933. While he was writing them, the world changed. Japan – in the first of its 1930s aggressions – invaded Manchuria and Shanghai, and Adolf Hitler was elected Chancellor of Germany. There was also an upheaval in the Lloyd George family.

On 11 December 1932, A. J. Sylvester received a message instructing him to 'Come down to Churt early in the morning.'[6] When he arrived as instructed, he was met by Carey Evans – destined, it seems, to be constantly embarrassed by his father-in-law's irregular lifestyle – who warned him to 'look out'.[7] The family were assembled, apparently amicably, in the library – Lloyd George, Dame Margaret, Megan and Lady Carey Evans. Lloyd George suggested that he and Sylvester have a private conversation in his bedroom. The fire having been lit, he then asked him, 'Do you know about Frances and Tweed?'[8]

Sylvester had known for some time that Tweed and Frances had

---

*He was subsequently paid £9000 and $2000 for *The Truth about the Peace Treaties*.

been lovers. But he had felt no obligation to tell Lloyd George, who, in consequence, found out in a way which must have maximised his humiliation. A maid, who had worked for Frances when she lived in Morpeth Terrace in Victoria, but had chosen not to move with her to Worplesdon, near Churt – had taken employment with the Carey Evanses in Wimpole Street. One afternoon, she had told Olwen of Tweed's late-night visits, and Olwen had told her mother. The news of Frances's infidelity was broken to Lloyd George by his wife.

Openly challenged, Sylvester had no choice but to confirm the story, and he added, perhaps gratuitously, that Tweed was with Frances in Devon when Lloyd George was on a Caribbean cruise. So Lloyd George had to face the possibility that Jennifer was not his daughter. For the rest of the day – apart from posing for an official family photograph in which he appears entirely composed – he was debilitated by anguish. Next day, in the London office, Frances, who had clearly spoken to Lloyd George on the telephone, was in tears. Tweed displayed the coolness under fire which had contributed to his receipt of the Military Cross and behaved as if he had not betrayed his employer. Lloyd George, who would not have reached the top of the greasy pole had he been incapable of overcoming misfortune, recovered his composure and, after a day or two, carried on as if nothing had happened. Lord Riddell, no longer an intimate, described the episode with unfriendly accuracy. 'LG, who has had so many affairs, with whom no woman seemed to be reckoned safe . . . finds out that his own mistress has been seduced in his own house, almost by one of his paid men.'[9]

The end of the Tweed affair remains in doubt. There was certainly no ultimatum or demand that Frances make her choice and remain true to one or other of the men in her life. Lloyd George was by then almost certainly incapable of risking losing Frances – whatever the terms on which she stayed. It was certainly not his own irregular arrangement that prevented him from insisting that she remained faithful to him alone. Letters written in 1934 suggest that, for a couple of years, he had accepted, without complaint, that he shared Frances with someone else. When her subsidiary affair ended, the renewed fidelity was welcomed with a letter which revealed both how little he understood her emotional turmoil and his conviction that he was not circumscribed by the rules which constrain mere mortals. 'I was so pleased that you mean to be a good girl. I know you will be happier. The double life is full of worry and apprehension which wrecks the nerves.'[10]

By the mid-1930s, devaluation – the remedy which no one had told the Labour government was available – had rescued the pound, but it had not been able, in a depressed world economy, to stimulate British exports to a point at which unemployment was substantially reduced. In the autumn of 1934, Lloyd George began, once more, to formulate his own plans for industrial revival. It was too late for his ideas – far-seeing though they were – to influence the government. Baldwin dismissed him and his proposals in a single sentence. 'He does not, of course, count for very much in the present House of Commons.'[11] And he had become a hate figure to most Conservatives. The idea that he might replace Samuel as the senior Liberal in the coalition was rejected with the explanation, 'I should have the resignation of half the cabinet in my hands.'[12] But true to character, Lloyd George fought on.

In Bangor on 1 January 1935 – 'going back to Wales because that is where [he] began [his] crusading' – he launched his campaign for what he called a 'British New Deal'.[13] His proposals – more domestic investment, planned migration and developing trade with the Empire, had echoes of the radical imperialism which had attracted him in his youth. But he also called for public control of the Bank of England and – still reliving the glories of 1918 – a 'war cabinet' of four or six ministers who, since they did not have departments to run, could concentrate on the strategy of recovery. His Bangor speech contained a revealing disclaimer. 'I am not here tonight to launch a party campaign. I am neither a party leader nor do I have a strong desire to be one . . . I have had enough of that misery! Whatever happens, I have no intention of manoeuvring, or being manoeuvred, into that again.'[14] Even in an audience packed with devoted supporters, some men and women must have wondered who he imagined was likely to attempt the manoeuvre which he promised to resist. No doubt they concluded that leadership was still on his mind.

Unemployment was still the general preoccupation of the thinking public. That was why Ramsay MacDonald invited Lloyd George to send a résumé of his proposals to the Cabinet and then discuss them with ministers. The meetings, Lloyd George wrote, were 'studiously pleasant but they knew in their hearts that they were going to knife me – what they did not know was that I had a dagger in my sheath for them too'.[15] Before it could be drawn, Baldwin had succeeded MacDonald as Prime Minister.

On 12 July 1935, three weeks after the new Prime Minister 'kissed hands', Lloyd George published a new manifesto, *A Call to Action*. It announced the creation of a Council of Action for Peace and Reconstruction. At first there was talk of the council contesting three hundred seats at the next general election. Then it modified its ambition and threatened no more than a public examination of other parties nominees to see if they subscribed to the council's principles. Those principles appealed to the section of the nation which thought appeasement the right response to the rise of the dictatorships. Lloyd George did not believe that economic sanctions were the right response to Italy's invasion of Abyssinia. But the country's mood changed and Lloyd George's mood with it, and he denounced the assertion that 'it is inconceivable that [Germany and Italy] would bring their countries to the insane challenge' of a European war as the sort of self-delusion which had allowed the dictators to consolidate their power.[16]

Lloyd George turned on Mussolini and the government which would appease him. His campaign was briefly interrupted by the general election which Baldwin thought necessary to endorse his premiership. But, after he had won in Caernarvon with the comfortable majority of 9609 – and seen the Samuelite ranks reduced to sixteen and Samuel himself defeated – he returned to the charge. A week after the election, Samuel Hoare, the Foreign Secretary, signed with Pierre Laval – his French opposite number – a pact which required Abyssinia to cede sixty thousand square miles of territory to Italy and grant Rome the rights to 'develop' the south and west of the country. The national outrage was so great that Baldwin repudiated the Hoare–Laval Pact and accepted the enforced resignation of his Foreign Secretary. But Italy had to be placated. In June 1936, the government announced that it would no longer impose the commercial sanctions which the League of Nations had hoped would force Mussolini to abandon his Abyssinian adventure. Lloyd George, again the champion of small nations, made a speech which Churchill – in his time an admirer of Mussolini – described as 'one of the greatest Parliamentary performances of all time'.

> The choice before us is whether we shall make a last effort . . . for peace and security, or whether by a cowardly surrender we shall break all the promises we have made and hold ourselves up to the shame of our children and their children's children . . . Tonight we have had the cowardly surrender.[17]

With a cause for which to fight, Lloyd George was reinvigorated. When Harold Nicolson happened to meet him in Derby's Midland Hotel, 'He was absolutely bursting with vitality, roguishness, wit and reminiscences.' The adrenalin created by his rapturous reception at a packed meeting in the local Drill Hall was still pumping. 'Gladstone', he announced, 'went on until he was eighty and I shall do the same.'[18] Memories of more powerful days must have been rekindled by the brief threat of renewed scandal. He was warned that his enemies were planning to damage his son Gwilym and daughter Megan by claiming they were party to the half-forgotten 'sale of honours scandal'. The threat was averted in typical Lloyd George style. He prepared a list of Conservative beneficiaries from honours sales and threatened to publish it.

Despite the eloquence of his denunciations of appeasement, Lloyd George's opposition to the dictators and aggressors was unattractively selective. Throughout 1935, Joachim von Ribbentrop, the German Ambassador to London, had mounted a campaign of attention and flattery which was designed to prepare the way for a visit to Germany and a meeting with Adolf Hitler. Ribbentrop's efforts were assisted by Lloyd George's sudden loss of interest in unemployment and its replacement as a subject for articles and speeches by foreign affairs. When Harold Macmillan, then a backbencher, invited him to attend a rally which would launch another campaign for economic regeneration, he replied, 'I cannot attend any gatherings in this country between 7th and 20th of September as I have made arrangements for a continental journey.'[19] He had accepted an invitation to visit Munich and Hitler's 'eerie' high in the Bavarian Alps. He took with him Megan, Gwilym, (his doctor, the recently ennobled) Lord Dawson, Sylvester and Tom Jones, by then attached to Baldwin and therefore living proof that there was no intention of undermining or upstaging the Prime Minister. There would have been much justification for his doing so. Germany had, illegally, reoccupied the Rhineland and France's pleas for help had been rebuffed by Anthony Eden, the Foreign Secretary. Britain was 'not prepared to go to war in order that Germany should be compelled to go out of the Rhineland one week and allowed to come in the next'.[20] The nearest Lloyd George got to commenting on Germany's flagrant breach of the Versailles Treaty was the surprising suggestion that the security pact signed at Lucerne in 1925 should be renegotiated to obtain international recognition of Germany's eastern borders. The Lucerne Treaty also confirmed the Rhineland's neutral status.

On the night of their arrival in Munich, Lloyd George's party had dinner with the Ribbentrops – an unsuccessful occasion in the estimation of the principal guest, who resented his host's insistent complaint that Britain underestimated the strength of the 'Red Menace' which emanated from Russia. No doubt this is what prompted Lloyd George to make the extraordinary suggestion that Ribbentrop should try to convince Churchill – Britain's leading anti-Bolshevik – that Hitler deserved his support. 'If you could get Winston into your new church, it would be worthwhile.'[21]

The first meeting with Hitler began at 3.45 on the afternoon of 4 September 1936 and – prolonged by the need for translation – lasted for two hours. Hitler returned to the subject of the Soviet threat but described it in terms of German vulnerability rather than British indolence. His fear was that Germany would be surrounded by Communist states. That was why it was so important for General Franco to replace the elected government in Spain. Surprisingly, in light of the speeches which he was soon to make in London, Lloyd George endorsed Britain's decision to maintain a strict neutrality in the Spanish Civil War – a policy which he seemed to believe Germany also followed. There were many platitudes about the need for mutual understanding and a shared desire for peace before the meeting ended with a practical discussion about autobahn construction and its effect on employment levels. Lloyd George's reaction to the two-hour audience was described by A. J. Sylvester.

LG returned from his interview with Hitler in great form, very delighted with his talk and obviously very much struck with Hitler. 'He is a great man' said LG. 'Fuhrer is the proper name for him for he is a born leader, yes, and a statesman'.[22]

The panegyric ended with the firm conclusion that Hitler was in favour of neither rearmament nor conscription and an acknowledgement that he had explained how the loss of African colonies had denied Germany essential raw materials. Perhaps Lloyd George was convinced that Hitler was a man of sound judgement by a paragraph from *Mein Kampf*. It dealt with the criticisms made of Lloyd George's speeches by a 'German quill-driver [who] did not in the least understand these psychological masterpieces in the art of influencing the masses'. In Hitler's opinion, they were

Most wonderful achievements, precisely because they showed an astounding knowledge of the soul of the broad mass of the people.

The primitive quality itself of those speeches, the originality of his expression, his choice of clear and simple illustration, are examples which prove the superior political capacity of this Englishman.[23]

No doubt Lloyd George forgave the confusion of nationality. And it is unlikely that he believed himself to possess the power that made the 'people carry out his will absolutely'. But no doubt he was flattered. Twenty years earlier, Lenin had described him as 'a popular orator, able to make any kind of speech, even Revolutionary speeches before labour audiences'.[24] He was the only British politician to be commended by tyrants of both the left and the right.

Even in the Berghof, 'four thousand feet up the mountain', Lloyd George retained enough sense of political perspective to decline an invitation to attend the National Socialist rally at Nuremberg. But when he got home he repeated (in the *Daily Express*) that Hitler was 'a born leader of men' and added that he had a 'dynamic personality'.[25] The account of the visit which he gave young Jennifer Stevenson was less elegiac. Hitler's house, he told her, had a massive window from which he could see across the Bavarian mountains as far as distant Strasbourg. He had a similar window built into his house at Churt.

It would be easy to dismiss the whole episode as the aberration of a prematurely old man who had been seduced – as many younger and still active politicians have been seduced by the charms of a foreign visit, far away from the pressures of domestic politics – and flattered by the attentions of a famous host. But his faith in Hitler persisted. In December 1937, eighteen months before the outbreak of war, he wrote to T. P. Conwell-Evans (the Welsh professor at Königsberg University who had arranged the itinerary for his German visit), 'I have never doubted the fundamental greatness of Herr Hitler as a man, even in moments of profound disagreement . . . I only wish we had a man of his supreme quality at the head of affairs in our country.'[26]

Foreign affairs now dominated Lloyd George's attention, interrupted only briefly by a peripheral involvement in the abdication crisis. He felt a sentimental attachment to Edward VIII, whose installation as Prince of Wales he had organised and for whom, at the height of his enthusiasm for economic regeneration, he had interrupted his New Deal campaign and accompanied on a visit to Cardiff. Six months later, back in the principality, the King – after meeting unemployed steelworkers at Dowlais in South Wales – had told the *Daily Mail* 'something must be done to find them work'. Lloyd George's emotions were aroused and, since Baldwin was regarded as Edward's nemesis, so were his prejudices. So he insisted, 'The nation has a right to choose its Queen but the King has a right to choose his own wife.' And he added, 'if Baldwin is against them, I am against Baldwin'.[27] He probably meant 'if Baldwin is against them, I am for them'. He left Gwilym and Megan in no doubt about their duty – or his belief in their duty – to accept his advice. 'Do not join the harriers in hunting the King from the throne.'[28]

In January 1938, he visited France. Frances Stevenson, who accompanied him, wrote in her diary, 'We took with us to Paris my small adopted [sic] daughter.' He met Léon Blum, to whom he took an instant dislike, and was infuriated by the refusal of Edouard Daladier to meet him. By then he had changed his mind on 'non-intervention' and he urged the French to change theirs too. After his old adversary Neville Chamberlain succeeded Baldwin as Prime Minister in May 1937, Lloyd George had become even less disposed to look for the best in the government. 'The dictators', he told the House of Commons, 'are taking at the present moment a rather low view of the intelligence of our government – very low.'[29]

He had no great sympathy for Czechoslovakia, whose claim to the Sudetenland he had never accepted, and during the Paris peace conference he had developed a deep dislike for Edvard Beneš, the Czech representative at Versailles and future Prime Minister and President. As always, he was unable to separate his personal feelings from his political judgements. But his contempt for Chamberlain transcended all other emotions. So after the Prime Minister had flown to Munich, in a last desperate attempt to prevent war, Lloyd George became appeasement's greatest enemy. Free churchmen, lunching at the City Temple, were invited to consider a litany of retreats. 'China, Abyssinia, Spain, Czechoslovakia! We have descended during these years a ladder of dishonour rung by rung. Are we going, can we go, any lower?'[30]

On 1 September, Germany invaded Poland and, two days later, Britain was at war. Patriotism required Lloyd George to give Chamberlain his support though it was worded in highly ambiguous language. 'The Government could do no other than what they have done.'[31] But then came another sudden change of direction. On 6 October, Hitler told the Reichstag that he was willing to negotiate an immediate peace 'to spare my people suffering'.[32] Chamberlain rejected the offer out of hand. But Lloyd George – who, in the week which followed Munich, had excoriated appeasement and in 1916 had stoutly resisted Lord Lansdowne's call for compromise with Germany – became the national champion of a negotiated peace. He told an astonished House of Commons that Hitler should be asked on what terms peace was possible. Sylvester telephoned Churt with the news that the response to Lloyd George's speech was 'the greatest [he] had ever known'. But although 'all the letters cry out for peace, none of them say on what conditions'.[33] Sylvester wrote that 'the bags of letters have literally turned LG's head. Every day he's crazy about letters – not what is in them, but how many are there?'[34]

On 14 October, Lloyd George spoke in favour of negotiation at a meeting of the Council of Action in Caxton Hall, Westminster, and because of the Council's association* endured the humiliation of being monitored by a Metropolitan Police officer who was preparing evidence for the government on the need to take strong action against defeatism and subversion. Five days later, he returned to the subject at a meeting of six thousand of his constituents in Caernarvon. While he was in Wales, Lloyd George completed the purchase of land in Llanystumdwy which, together with his orchard at Churt, qualified the cottage-bred man for the title of landowner. When he returned to London, he asked Lord Dawson to give him a general medical examination. He was preparing for a campaign – or for office. He believed that he had become an expert on food production, and his advice on how to make the beleaguered country self-sufficient would, he thought, be his first contribution to the war effort.

Chamberlain – his government reinforced by the return of Churchill as First Lord of the Admiralty – lasted, precariously, until the spring of 1940. As Lloyd George waited, without being sure what he was waiting for, the signs of age were pressed upon him. On 20 April, he celebrated the fiftieth anniversary of his election to Parliament at a rally in the Criccieth Pavilion. He was agitated, rather than gratified, by the BBC's decision to broadcast his speech live and spoke so softly that half of the audience in the hall (nine thousand strong) could not hear him. On the way back to Churt next day, his companions provoked him into speculation about a recall to office. As they anticipated, he did not dismiss the idea as a daydream, but laid down the terms on which he would accept not a ministry but the premiership. Those terms confirmed that he had lost touch with reality. 'It would have to be made perfectly clear that I

---

*Ivan Maisky, the Soviet Ambassador, launched a campaign for a British–Soviet alliance and – brushing aside Polish fears about Russia's territorial ambitions – called for a joint guarantee of Poland's territorial integrity.

could not bring a decisive victory as I did last time. We have made so many mistakes that we are not in nearly so good a position.'[35]

On 2 May, Chamberlain, still Prime Minister, announced that British troops were being withdrawn from Norway. Colonel Tweed, who had been ill since February, had died four days earlier and was to be cremated on 3 May at Golders Green after a funeral service at which, according to Sylvester, Lloyd George's behaviour and dress had been 'a studied insult to the dead'.[36] Later that night, Frances accused him of 'persecuting her to death' with complaints about her 'being upset' and questions about how 'upset she would be when he died'. His behaviour was not solely attributable to senile decay. He had succeeded as a politician and failed as a human being because, since childhood, he had expected the world to revolve round him. By then Sylvester, although still the obedient servant in public, made no pretence of loyalty. After he was asked to obtain a copy of Boccaccio's *Decameron*, his diary entry may be a definitive comment on Lloyd George's final years. 'If LlG gave his mind to thinking how best he could help his country, instead of thinking cunt and women, he would be a better man.'[37] Jennifer Longford thinks that Sylvester's irritation was caused by the behaviour of the young women in Lloyd George's office – some of whom tried to avoid close contact with their employer, while others assumed an air of knowing superiority. It may have had deeper psychological origins. He had allowed himself to speculate about the causes of his employer's unusual sexual appetite. 'There he stood as naked as when he was born with the biggest organ I have ever seen. It resembled a donkey's more than anything else . . . No wonder they are always after him and he after them.'[38]

Neville Chamberlain's premiership came to an inglorious end on 10 May 1940 following a bitter two-day debate in the House of Commons which revealed that he had lost the confidence of the Conservative Party. When Herbert Morrison announced that the Opposition would 'divide' against the government, Chamberlain called on his 'Friends' in the House to support him and added, 'I have friends in this House.' Perhaps he was just using parliamentary jargon. But it sounded self-loving. Lloyd George was in the House but, strangely, not in the chamber when the Prime Minister used the unhappy phrase, and there is a dispute about who hurried to his room behind the Speaker's chair to tell him that his moment had come. Both his daughter Megan and Clement Davies (who, after the war, was to become Liberal leader) claim the credit. But there is no doubt about what followed. 'The vigour and violence of Mr Lloyd George's personal attack on the Prime Minister astonished the House.'[39] Dingle Foot, then a Liberal backbencher (who claimed to have told Megan to find and fetch her father), wrote that the speech which Lloyd George made displayed 'the accumulated dislike and contempt of twenty-five years'.[40] He began by urging Churchill not 'to be converted into an air-raid shelter to stop the splinters hitting his colleagues'. Then

> It is not a question of who are the Prime Minister's friends. It is a far bigger issue . . . He has appealed for sacrifice . . . The nation is prepared for sacrifice as long as it has leadership. I say solemnly that the Prime Minister should give an example of sacrifice because there is nothing which can contribute more to victory than that he should sacrifice the seals of office.[41]

When Chamberlain resigned, there was no doubt who his successor would be. Frances Stevenson's diary records what did not need recording. 'LG realises that Churchill must be chosen and that he himself is out of the running.'[42]

The Churchill coalition took office on 10 May sustained by goodwill that Lloyd George had never enjoyed. The new Prime Minister – certain of his destiny to save Britain – had longed for the premiership. But he had not intrigued in order to obtain it. The opposition parties endorsed his appointment and their Members agreed to serve in his government. Chamberlain became Lord President of the Council and Leader of the House of Commons. But there was one painful reality which both he and Churchill had to face. To keep their coalition intact, they had to avoid offence to their senior colleagues and that required agreement on the allocation of the Cabinet portfolios. In 1916, Lloyd George had felt unable to offer Cabinet office to Churchill. In 1940, Churchill was not sure that – even if he wanted to recall Lloyd George, which was by no means certain – the Conservatives would let him.

There is no doubt that Lloyd George longed for an invitation to join the War Cabinet, which, he rightly assumed, would be like the one he had led – half a dozen ministers with no departmental responsibilities. But at first he accepted hard reality. 'I do not think that Winston will approach me. I think it will be the old coalition of parties and their nominees. In that I would not have a place . . . Neville would have far more authority than I would have and he would oppose everything I proposed . . . It would be far better for me to go on with the food production part of it.'[43] He had become convinced – thanks to his recent expansion of interests into arable as well as fruit farming – that he should chair a council of ministers which would make sure that agriculture met the needs of an island nation under siege.

He was, however, determined to be ready for the call, whenever it came and whatever form it took. When, on 12 May, the new Prime Minister invited him to lunch, Lloyd George summoned Lord Dawson to Churt and asked for medical confirmation that neither age nor health would stand in the way of a return to government. The meeting took place at Admiralty House on 16 May – three days after Churchill had offered the nation 'blood, sweat, tears and toil'. Lloyd George told Sylvester that the Prime Minister had confirmed his gloomy diagnosis and added that he was 'glad to be out of the War Cabinet', would not serve with Chamberlain and was not prepared to face the daily routine required of a departmental minister.[44] It was not clear that any of those prospects were on offer.

Lloyd George heard nothing more for over a week. Then, on 28 May, Churchill asked to see him in the House of Commons and invited him, subject to one proviso, to join the War Cabinet. Lloyd George set out the reason for his refusal in a letter which reflected the collective view of the family:

> You were good enough yesterday to ask me if I would be prepared to enter the War Cabinet if you secured the adhesion of Mr Chamberlain. It is the first time that you have approached me personally on the subject and I can well understand your hesitancy, for in the course of the conversation you made it quite clear that if Chamberlain imposed his veto on the grounds of resentment over past differences, you could not proceed with the offer. This is not a firm offer. Until it is, I cannot consider it.[45]

Both men must have heard ironic echoes of Lloyd George, almost a quarter of a century earlier, telling Churchill that pique or pride was an unworthy consideration when the national interest called.

There were harsh critics who thought that Lloyd George was no longer capable of making a contribution to the war effort. On 6 June, Cecil King visited Churt to discuss an extension of Lloyd George's *Sunday Pictorial* contract. King judged that 'from his eyes you can see that he is really past it, though now and then you catch a glimpse of his glance as it must have been. He eats very untidily, though this may be due to the deplorable set of false teeth which clicked and rattled in conversation, even when he was not eating. His conversation is more about the last war than this one.'[46]

Later that day, Lloyd George was made an unconditional offer of a seat in the War Cabinet. The offer came at an urgently arranged meeting, about which Lloyd George was given only two hours' notice. He hurried to London in an unusual state of anxiety but was reassured by the discovery that 'the PM gave instructions that someone else should be kept waiting for half an hour to enable them to finish their talk . . . He had never known [Churchill] more friendly'.[47]

Churchill agreed to give him time to consider his decision. Tom Jones, who urged him to accept, thought his membership would give the Cabinet authority and courage. 'I find him far more alive and stimulating than any Cabinet minister I ever meet and he would be much better inside instead of chafing and stamping among his family in impotent fury.'[48] But, after a week of consideration, chafe and stamp is what he chose to do – though not so much in fury as in frustration. He believed that the war was being lost and that the composition of the Cabinet would prevent him from guiding it onto a winning path. Frances Stevenson had no doubt that it was his duty to accept the call. But he told her that he would not share in the guilt of defeat.

A year later, Lloyd George wrote another letter which suggests that his decision was based less on hurt pride than careful calculation. Jennifer Stevenson, then aged twelve, wrote from boarding school to ask 'Taid' to explain why he was playing so small a part in the war effort. For all his life, Lloyd George had used private letters – to his uncle, his brother and Frances – to leave messages for posterity. No doubt his reply to Jennifer was meant to do the same. 'I do not believe in the way we entered the war – nor the methods by which it has been conducted . . . I do not believe in the way or in the persons with which the War Cabinet is constituted.'[49] Whatever his motives, his devious reputation encouraged the belief that he was waiting for Churchill to fail.

The summer of 1940 was Britain's most desperate, as well as its finest, hour. France fell, Dunkirk was evacuated. The Battle of Britain was fought and won. The concern for personal safety, of which Lloyd George had been accused during the First World War, was now too obvious for even his closest friends to ignore. The claim that 'LG talks of nothing but bombs and invasion' was an exaggeration.[50] He also talked about how much the government needed him. Churchill's numerous failings were an equally frequent topic of conversation. They were said to extend well beyond his record as a war leader. 'Winston is not a real democrat. His real interest is in the governing classes. He does not want a strong proletarian party . . . He would rather be at the head of a sort of plutocratic state.'[51] His articles for the *Sunday Pictorial* were suitably, though fraudulently, optimistic. But sometimes his real opinions disturbed the patriotic prose. After paragraphs praising the courage of the armed forces and rejoicing that Britain was protected by 'the stormy moat which surrounds our castle', he concluded, 'We have first to prove to Hitler's satisfaction that this combination is invincible. Then we shall be in a position to discuss terms with him.'[52] He still believed in a negotiated peace.

His judgement may have been influenced by his preoccupation with his personal security. In October, he wrote to Frances Stevenson with the claim that the Germans had 'been bombing various parts of Caernarvon for a week' and the admission that he did not propose 'to run the gauntlet of the incessant bombardment in and around London merely for the privilege of hearing a speech from Winston . . . with a handful of ministers listening with one ear cocked up to the ceiling for an air raid warning'.[53] During the First World War he had strongly denied that he was afraid of air raids. During the Second he used his anxiety to justify his growing alienation from the people and places which had dominated his life.

After 1940, Lloyd George spoke rarely in the House of Commons. For the sake of his reputation, it would have been better had he not taken part in the vote of confidence debate on 6 and 7 May 1941. The result was not in doubt – the motion was carried by 477 votes to 3 – but it was an opportunity to reiterate the message of defiance in the face of further military setbacks. Rommel's Afrika Korps was sweeping through Cyrenaica towards Egypt, and the British Expeditionary Force in Greece had been withdrawn with heavy losses. For reasons which must have been more connected with seniority than sympathy with the government, Lloyd George was selected to open the second day from the Opposition front bench. He spoke of the urgent need for allies (he meant America) to join the fight for freedom, maintained that talk of Britain invading the European mainland was 'fatuous', argued that it was more important to conscript men for the land than for the army, and demanded a smaller War Cabinet with – as had been the case in 1916 – unfettered executive powers.

Churchill was entitled to be angry. It was later argued by Lloyd George's friends that the Prime Minister's reference to the puppet leader whom Hitler had installed as titular head of Vichy France was not meant to be as brutal as it sounded. But the words themselves make that hard to believe. 'I must say that I did not think the speech by my Right Honourable Friend, the Member for Caernarvon Boroughs, was particularly helpful. It was the kind of speech with which I imagine the illustrious and venerable Marshal Pétain might well have enlivened the closing days of M. Reynaud's cabinet.'[54] Lloyd George left the House of Commons without facing the embarrassment of the division lobby. He never spoke in the Commons again. From then on suggestions that he should join the Cabinet came only from known eccentrics. His family and friends occupied more and more of his attention. But it was not Churchill's cruel jibe that brought the long career to its appointed end. At last Lloyd George was tired and, perhaps more surprisingly, he knew it.

An alert and perceptive Lloyd George would never have made a speech which so defied the national mood and allowed the less than scrupulous Churchill to make public a suspicion that had long been whispered in private conversation. To Lloyd George's enemies it was obvious that the Man Who Won the First World War hoped to benefit from defeat in the Second. They offered in evidence more than his well-known hunger for power and lack of scruples. The recent record, they claimed, spoke for itself. He was, or had been, an open admirer of Adolf Hitler. His scepticism about the hopes of victory was well known and he had publicly advocated a negotiated peace. In January 1943, with the outcome of the war still in doubt, Harold Nicolson, at lunch with Aneurin Bevan and Kingsley Martin, the editor of the *New Statesman and Nation*, said 'that Ll.G, if he had not been so gaga, would have been our Petain' and 'they agreed'.[55]

The truth was more complicated. He did not *hope* for defeat and the chance to become Hitler's satrap in London. But a suspicion must remain that if defeat had come and an offer had been made, what Anthony Trollope described as the passion to be back 'where the trumpets played' would have been too strong to resist.

CHAPTER 39

PEACE AT LAST

Frances Stevenson had, for some months, wondered whether Lloyd George was still able to play a major part in politics. 'LlG has some idea he is coming in on a peace settlement . . . But when you see him in the state he is you wonder if he would be capable.'[1] It was a question which he had to answer for himself after the unexpected death of the Ambassador to Washington – Philip Kerr, the confidant and trusted adviser of his premiership who had become the Second Marquis of Lothian. Lloyd George, Churchill's first choice to fill the vacancy, discussed the appointment with the Prime Minister first at a formal meeting and then over lunch. Before the second meeting he asked Lord Dawson if his health would stand the strain. The diagnosis must have been a fraudulent attempt to avoid bad news. The great conciliator was said to be physically probably up to the job but temperamentally unsuited to diplomacy. Lloyd George showed Dawson's opinion to Churchill to explain his decision to decline. 'He showed genuine pleasure at having been invited. "I tell my friends" he said "that I have honourable offers made me by the Prime Minister".'[2]

Dame Margaret Lloyd George – in 1940, as usual, without her husband at Christmas – spent the holiday with her sister-in-law. Back home for tea after a meeting of the Women's Institute, she slipped while hurrying to answer the telephone, fell and fractured her hip. After a fortnight in which her general health deteriorated and her husband arranged for a Liverpool bone specialist to see her, the consultant pronounced her condition serious. Sylvester and Lord Dawson, the all-purpose physician, set out for Wales by train. En route, they discussed

Lloyd George's own health and applauded his decision to decline the Washington Embassy. At Bridgnorth in Shropshire, there was no car to meet them. The road to Criccieth was blocked by snow. They spent the night in a local hotel. At breakfast they learned that Lloyd George was being driven from Churt to Wales. He got as far as Cerrig-y-Druidion. Then the car was buried in a snow drift. After he was dug out, he too took refuge in a local inn. It was there that he received the news that Margaret had died at twenty minutes past ten that morning.

It was Sylvester who suggested that if Lloyd George could get to Betws-y-Coed – retracing his steps of the previous day – he could catch a train to Criccieth. It was some hours before even that seemed possible. Then the news of David Lloyd George's proposed odyssey reached Cerrig-y-Druidion. 'All classes of men from the mountain village, including the Wesleyan minister, the school master and the local garage proprietor . . . cut a way through the deep snowdrifts', all the way to Corwen where, for a moment, David Lloyd George and Richard – his disinherited son – were reunited by grief.[3]

Lloyd George chose not to see his wife in her coffin. It was not his way to look death in the face. But his grief was genuine if – since he had chosen to see so little of his wife while she lived – the product of complex emotions. Margaret Lloyd George met few if any of her husband's needs – physical, social or intellectual. But he needed her to exist. She represented stability, continuity and the years of hope when he was young in Wales.

The day after the funeral, his talk was all of politics – and what a 'damn fool' Neville Chamberlain had been to declare a war he had no chance of winning. But despite his swift emotional recovery – a replica of his behaviour after Mair Eluned was buried – there was a gap in his life which would not be filled. There would be no more letters from London explaining why he could not come home to Criccieth, or from exotic holiday locations assuring her that he wished that she were there.

In January 1941 – perhaps as a reaction to Margaret's death – Lloyd George began to adopt an old man's habits. He 'stayed in bed for the greater part of each day'.[4] Yet an eventful year later – Germany had invaded Russia, Japan had attacked Pearl Harbor and America had entered the war – there was still talk among the political classes of his joining the government. Despite his increasing infirmity, he would have gladly done so. But Churchill – by comparing him with Pétain – had forfeited his political support. In January 1942, he told Richard Stokes, a Labour MP, that he although he 'would not go in with

Winston' he would 'serve with Eden as Prime Minister'.[5] The dark days at the New Year – culminating with the surrender of Singapore to the Japanese – necessitated a vote of confidence in the government. Lloyd George did not attend and he advised Megan to abstain. In political matters she dutifully respected her father's wishes. But she felt no obligation to obedience where family matters were concerned. Brynawelon, always recognised as her mother's house, was left to her. Lloyd George, without a house in Wales, bought Ty Newydd, a Criccieth farm.

In March 1942, more than a year after Margaret's death, the manager was told that the house must be prepared for Easter visitors. The whole establishment – London and Wales – was consumed by anxious curiosity. If he meant to take Frances and Jennifer Stevenson home for the holiday, the family would be in turmoil, and Megan might sever all connections with her father. At the back of all their minds was the thought that Frances might become the second Mrs Lloyd George – a proposal which none of them would welcome and Megan would find intolerable.

Megan was undoubtedly devoted to her mother. But her views must have been influenced by a love affair which, although it mirrored Frances Stevenson's relationship with her father, had no prospect of a happy ending. For years, she had been in love with Philip Noel-Baker, a married Labour MP. It is not clear whether the relationship ended because of the impassioned entreaties of her mother or whether, when Noel-Baker's wife died, he was too overcome with guilt to continue with it. Whatever the reason, the end came at just about the time when her father became free to marry Frances – whom Megan loathed. But Lloyd George did not rush into his second marriage. The fears of Easter 1942 proved unfounded. Frances still had to wait. Jennifer Longford remembers her mother asking her to raise the subject of marriage with Taid – which the little girl of thirteen dutifully did, and received an inconclusive response. But on 6 May 1942, Frances telephoned Sylvester with positive news and an extraordinary request. Would he break the news to Megan that the marriage was about to take place? The date had not been decided. Frances later discovered that he 'wanted to wait for two years for the sake of appearances'.[6] But it would definitely happen. Megan already knew – Lady Astor had told her. On 28 June, Lloyd George presided, for the last time, at the Castle Street Flower Service. It was there, thirty-one years before, that Frances Stevenson had fallen in love with him.

His political behaviour became increasingly unpredictable. On 1 July, he excused his absence from the House, during another confidence debate, with the explanation that, when the Prime Minister spoke, he would have felt compelled to walk out of the chamber.[7] Two weeks later, he accepted the Prime Minister's invitation to join him in an inspection of the bombed House of Commons.[8] Uncertainty about his public role and responsibility was compounded by increasing anxiety about his private life.

For the next six months there was much manoeuvring about the marriage – complicated by Megan, in one respect, filling her mother's role. Frances had to leave Lloyd George's house when his daughter arrived. Now Lord Dawson was asked to reconcile Megan to the prospects of the wedding. He concluded that 'You cannot talk to her like a normal woman.'[9] Megan asked Dawson to speak to her father – to warn him about either the objections of the family or the risks to his health. Next day, Lloyd George responded with a request that Dawson make another attempt to reconcile Megan to his decision. She was irreconcilable. The rest of the family were no more than hostile. They kept Dawson busy – mediating and moderating their antagonism. In January 1943, he persuaded Megan and her sister, Olwen, that it was their duty to visit Lloyd George on his eightieth birthday whether or not Frances Stevenson was at Churt. Megan arrived late and was publicly rebuked by her father.

The wedding eventually took place on 23 October 1943. Dinner the night before was interrupted by a telephone call from Megan, who made a last desperate attempt to change her father's mind. It failed. The ceremony – which prudence dictated should be in Surrey rather than Wales – was kept as secret as possible. Not even the chauffeur knew why he was driving into Guildford. Only the two witnesses – Sylvester and Frances's sister Muriel – were present at the wedding. On the return to Bron-y-De, only Jennifer was waiting to drink their health. Gwilym and his wife attended the wedding breakfast. The world reacted differently from the family. On 24 October, Sylvester could report, 'Splendid press for LG and Frances on their wedding.'[10]

Frances, much to her credit, made one last desperate attempt of her own to persuade Megan to

> put her own feelings on one side and act generously . . . I am depriving you of nothing in becoming his wife – neither of his affection, nor of any material benefits now or in the future. You must realise how much you owe to him and how estrangement

will hurt him. Even if you cannot see your way to burying the past as far as I am concerned, I hope you will make this concession to him and establish yourself even more firmly in his heart.[11]

Megan did not reply.

It was age and disenchantment, not the delights of domesticity, that kept Lloyd George away from Parliament, and on the rare occasions that he did attend the House of Commons, he took no part in the debates.* He did not speak in the chamber for over two years, and when, in October 1944, a day had been devoted to Welsh affairs, he was not even present. The announcement, made the following week, that he proposed to contest the general election expected sometime in 1945 was received with some surprise by his colleagues and considerable apprehension by local Liberals. The *Caernarvon and Denbigh Herald* suggested that, as a sign of respect and gratitude for his services to the nation, Conservative and Labour candidates should not contest the seat. Both parties rejected the idea. The Boroughs had, they said, been virtually disenfranchised since 1942. After the war, they would need another MP. The electorate agreed. Soundings among the new voters who had changed the character of the constituency since the 1935 election left no doubt that Lloyd George could not win.

Sylvester decided, on his own initiative, to promote the idea of a peerage. Archibald Sinclair, leader of the Liberal Party and Secretary of State for Air, agreed to put the proposal to the Prime Minister. Frances judged that 'he would accept if offered' but strongly urged that Megan should not be told. While the family waited, she discovered that – unbeknown to her – Lloyd George himself had written to Churchill to ask for a knighthood. On the morning of 18 December, a message to Ty Newydd said that a Royal Marine courier would arrive in Criccieth that night with a letter from the Prime Minister. It said, in the traditional phrase, that Churchill was 'minded' to recommend the receipt of an earldom in the New Year's Honours List. Lloyd George decided to sleep on the offer and, according to his brother, who was summoned to the farm next morning, 'passed a restless night' of indecision.[12] Frances, either impatient or worried that he was distressed by the dilemma, suggested that 'If you have any doubts, why not send a telegram refusing –

---

*However, some youthful characteristics persisted. On the way home from Carmarthen, Lloyd George complained to his second wife that the bust which he had just unveiled 'made him look lecherous'. She replied, 'You are lecherous.'

that would be an end of the matter.'[13] He sent a telegram which read 'Gratefully accept' and, after the ritual argument with Garter King at Arms about a suitable title, became Earl Lloyd George of Dwyfor. There was one more vote in the House of Commons. The pioneer of social security supported a Labour Party amendment to the King's Speech calling for the adoption of the Beveridge Report, which proposed the extension of Lloyd George's work into a full 'welfare state'.

In September 1944, Frances and David Lloyd George moved into Ty Newydd. Lloyd George had gone home to die. In mid-January 1945 – two weeks after his eighty-second birthday – it was announced that, because of an attack of flu, he would not take his seat in the House of Lords for some time. Dawson wondered whether he was suffering from cancer but did not recommend an investigation. 'His weakness increased, but his patience and serenity with it.'[14] The family paid regular visits. 'Megan', Frances wrote, 'came every day with a show of friendliness to me . . . LG was pleased that she and I – to all appearances – were friends.'[15] During the last month he spoke, often barely coherently, of the faith he had lost but which he claimed had been restored by reading Carlyle's *Sartor Resartus*. Then, on 26 March, it became clear that the end was only hours away. The family were assembled round the bedside.

Jennifer Longford remembers the last moments with the clarity of a sixteen-year-old schoolgirl. Her account might be entitled *Sic Transit Gloria Mundi*. It records the death of an old man, not a hero passing into history. She recalls the day and time because she thought that, had she not been called to witness the moment, she would have been listening to *Monday Night at Eight O'Clock* on the wireless. She stood at the foot of the bed with Ann Perry, Lloyd George's Welsh private secretary, to keep her company. Her mother and Megan stood on either side of the dying man, each holding one of Lloyd George's hands. Other family members were near the window. Lord Dawson watched and waited as the pauses between the deep breaths grew longer. Jennifer was astonished by the perception with which he identified the last deep sigh and hurried forward to close the sightless eyes.

Frances, though 'very distraught', described the feeling in prosaic language. 'I felt', she told her daughter, 'as if I had been knocked off my perch.' Jennifer admits to being 'totally unmoved' – apart from being relieved that she had washed her hair that morning – something which she felt appropriate to important family occasions. That day she was accepted as a member of the Lloyd George family. She had endured a difficult year. Taid had grown increasingly possessive: 'If I went out at all he would object.' And there was residual resentment – which must have increased with understanding – of how he had treated her mother. Jennifer's recollection is not of Frances's poised acceptance that to be with Lloyd George on any terms was enough. She recalls her mother running home in tears and claiming, 'Taid and I have had an argument' – by which she meant that Margaret had arrived at Bron-y-De.

Megan was 'very decent' on the day of death and remained so until – though not after – the funeral. The body was borne through the woods on a farm cart, with a village ancient who had known Lloyd George as a boy in Llanystumdwy sitting guard by the coffin. The grave was on the bank of the River Dwyfor – the place which Lloyd George had chosen back in 1922, when he had told Tom Jones, 'Don't put me in a cemetery.'[16] The choice of last resting place was right, for reasons far removed from the reservations of the Church and the divisions within his family. To bury him with all the pomp that accompanies the funerals of state would have been denial of his greatness. He had exploited the establishment but he had never joined, admired or imitated it. His great achievements – the six years at the Treasury when the welfare state was born and the four in which, as Minister of Munitions and Prime Minister, he had 'won the war' – would not have been possible if he had accepted the decent conventions or played by the respected rules. His fall – the demeaning search for a return to power through the creation of unlikely alliances – was another feature of his contempt for convention. But, because he was in all things the Great Outsider, he was also the authentic radical of British history.

APPENDIX I: LLOYD GEORGE'S HOMES

'His wife was effectively a visitor in his house, except in
Criccieth where he was a visitor in hers' – Frances Stevenson

Born 17 January 1863	5 New York Place, Chorlton-upon-Medlock	Father schoolmaster
1863–4	Bullford, Haverfordwest, Pembrokeshire	Father moved into a smallholding to try farming
7 June 1864	Highgate cottage, Llanystumdwy, near Criccieth	Father died. Moved in with Rebecca (grandmother) and Richard Lloyd (uncle)
1879	Lodgings in Portmadoc while articled	Lloyd George on his own
10 May 1880	Morvin House, Criccieth	Whole family moved
24 January 1888	Mynydd Ednyfed, Criccieth	Married Margaret Owen – lived with her parents
10 April 1890	Lodged with R. O. Davies and family in Acton	Elected MP and moved to London
Later in 1890	Lived with friends or at National Liberal Club	Margaret only visited
Late 1890	Bryn Awel (or Brynawelon)	Built by Margaret's parents, next to their house

Early 1891– August 1892	Verulam Buildings, Gray's Inn	Margaret stayed until May 1891 and for a few weeks in June and July, but not at all in 1892
August– September 1892	Davies family, Acton	
September– November 1892	National Liberal Club	
End 1892	5 Essex Court, the Temple	Leased for six months, Margaret only visited
Late autumn 1893	30 Palace Mansions, Addison Road, Kensington	Remained tenant for six years, although the property was often sub-let or empty
Late 1894– April 1895	National Liberal Club	
Early 1897	Rooms at Bingham Hotel, Chancery Lane	
Towards end 1899	179 Trinity Road, Wandsworth Common	Margaret lived in London for the first time
1904	3 Routh Road, Wandsworth Common	
December 1907	5 Cheyne Place, Chelsea	
6 April 1908	11 Downing Street	
1908–9	Built the second house (Brynawelon) in Criccieth	
1913	House at Walton Heath, Surrey	Gift of Lord Riddell
November 1916	Flat in St James's Court (11 Downing Street closed)	Lived there for short time – then Prime Minister
December 1916–22	10 Downing Street The Firs, Cobham (instead of Walton Heath)	Moved in at the end of January 1917
1920	Chequers	Bequeathed to the nation by Sir Arthur Lee on 8 January 1921

Summer 1922	Built house at Churt, Surrey – called Bron-y-De	Moved there on 23 October 1922
October 1922	86 Vincent Square	Temporary lease, having resigned as Prime Minister and left Downing Street
1923	Cheyne Walk, Chelsea	
Summer 1927	2 Addison Road, Kensington	
1940	Ty Newydd, Llanystumdwy	Moved there on 19 September 1944; died there on 26 March 1945

APPENDIX II: FOREIGN TRAVEL

'He never visited cathederals or galleries . . . but liked to be in places where there are bands, functions and a general feeling of gaiety' – Lucy Masterman

August 1892	Switzerland
November 1892	Paris
Summer 1894	Switzerland
21 August–end October 1896	Argentina
21 December 1897–2 January 1898	Italy
December 1898	Mediterranean
24 August–13 October 1899	Canada
September 1900	France
Summer 1901	Austria
Summer 1902	Switzerland
Christmas 1902	France
September 1903	Italy
August 1904	Switzerland
16 December 1904–January 1905	Italy
Mid-November–4 December 1905	Italy
Summer 1906	Portugal
Christmas 1906	France
September 1907	France
20 December 1907–January 1908	France
14–26 August 1908	Austria and Germany
April 1909	France
End August 1909	France
October 1909	Motoring holiday on the Continent
February 1910	France
Summer 1910	Italy and Switzerland
End September 1910	Italy
20 December 1910–January 1911	France
2–20 January 1912	France

August 1912	France
February 1913	France
September 1913	At sea on *Enchantress*, Admiralty Board yacht
January 1914	Algiers and Sahara
August–10 September 1919	Deauville
Summer 1920	Switzerland
November 1920	France
December 1922	Spain
8 April–19 May 1922	Italy
22 December 1922–23 January 1923	Spain
29 September–9 November 1923	United States of America
April 1925	Spain
New Year 1926	Italy
27 December 1926– 28 January 1927	South America
January 1929	France and Italy
Summer 1929	French and Italian battlefields
Winter 1931	India, Ceylon and Egypt
1935	Morocco
2–16 September 1936	Germany
December 1936–February 1937	Jamaica
December 1937–January 1938	France
February–March 1939	France

NOTES

ABBREVIATIONS

Daniel = D. R. Daniel, unpublished memoir, trans. Prys Morgan, National Library of Wales, Aberystwyth

HofL = Lloyd George Papers (Beaverbrook Collection), House of Lords Archives

NLW = Lloyd George Papers, Political Archives, National Library of Wales, Aberystwyth

PRO = Public Record Office

CHAPTER 1: THE LAND OF MY FATHERS

1. Lloyd George, Richard, *My Father, Lloyd George*, p. 17.
2. George, William, *My Brother and I*, p. 2.
3. Du Parcq, Hubert, *The Life of David Lloyd George*, Vol. I, p. 9.
4. George, W. R. P., *The Making of Lloyd George*, p. 43.
5. Du Parcq, *The Life*, Vol. I, p. 9.
6. George, W. R. P., *The Making of Lloyd George*, p. 41.
7. Ibid., p. 44.
8. George, William, *My Brother and I*, p. 2.
9. Du Parcq, *The Life*, Vol. I, p. 9.
10. Ibid.
11. George, William, *My Brother and I*, p. 5.
12. Lloyd George, Richard, *My Father, Lloyd George*, p. 19.
13. George, William, *My Brother and I*, p. 20.
14. *Mainly About People* magazine, 10 August 1998.
15. George, William, *My Brother and I*, p. 27.
16. George, W. R. P., *The Making of Lloyd George*, p. 178.
17. Ibid., p. 45.
18. Davis, Walker W., *Lloyd George 1863–1914*, p. 26.
19. Grigg, John, *The Young Lloyd George*, p. 31.
20. George, W. R. P., *The Making of Lloyd George*, p. 71.
21. George, William, *My Brother and I*, p. 13.

22. Ibid.
23. Ibid.
24. George, William, *My Brother and I*, p. 19.
25. Gilbert, B. B., *David Lloyd George: A Political Life*, p. 25.
26. *Mainly About People* magazine, 10 August 1998.
27. Du Parcq, *The Life*, Vol. I, p. 14.
28. George, William, *My Brother and I*, p. 11.
29. *Mainly About People* magazine, 10 August 1998.
30. Gilbert, *David Lloyd George*, p. 28.
31. George, W. R. P., *The Making of Lloyd George*, p. 69.
32. Ibid.
33. Ibid.
34. George, William, *My Brother and I*, p. 33.
35. NLW FCW 2/1.
36. Jones, Thomas, *Whitehall Diary*, Vol. I, p. 169.
37. Campbell, John, *Lloyd George: The Goat in the Wilderness 1922–1931*, p. 5.
38. Julie Dawnes, *Welsh History Review*, December 1974, quoted in Gilbert, *David Lloyd George*.
39. George, William, *My Brother and I*, p. 16.
40. Lucy Masterman, *C. F. G. Masterman: A Biography*, p. 173.
41. Du Parcq, *The Life*, Vol. I, p. 21.
42. Daniel.
43. Masterman, Lucy, *C. F. G. Masterman*, p. 209.
44. Taylor, A. J. P. (ed.), *Lloyd George: A Diary by Frances Stevenson*, p. 7.
45. George, W. R. P., *The Making of Lloyd George*, p. 74.
46. Ibid.
47. *Review of Reviews*, September 1904, p. 369.
48. Spender, Harold, *The Prime Minister*, p. 29.
49. George, William, *My Brother and I*, p. 40.
50. Ibid., p. 41.
51. George, W. R. P., *The Making of Lloyd George*, p. 73.
52. George, William, *My Brother and I*, p. 43.
53. Ibid.
54. Ibid.
55. Daniel.
56. Gilbert, *David Lloyd George*, p. 35.
57. Taylor, A. J. P. (ed.), *Lloyd George*, p. 77.
58. Daniel.
59. Riddell, Lord, *Lord Riddell's War Diaries*, p. 350.
60. NLW 2253A, Notes for Education Debate, 9 July 1902.
61. NLW 1C/230, conversation, 8 September 1908.
62. George, William, *My Brother and I*, p. 43.
63. Ibid., p. 44.
64. Ibid.
65. Ibid., p. 46.
66. Du Parcq, *The Life*, Vol. I, p. 25.

67. George, W. R. P., *The Making of Lloyd George*, p. 22.
68. George, William, *My Brother and I*, p. 53.
69. Du Parcq, *The Life*, Vol. I, p. 31.
70. George, William, *My Brother and I*, p. 51.

CHAPTER 2: THE FEVER OF RENOWN

1. George, W. R. P., *The Making of Lloyd George*, p. 29.
2. George, William, *My Brother and I*, p. 108.
3. George, W. R. P., *The Making of Lloyd George*, p. 93.
4. Ibid., p. 100.
5. Ibid.
6. Du Parcq, *The Life*, Vol. I, p. 53.
7. Ibid., p. 54.
8. George, W. R. P., *The Making of Lloyd George*, p. 93.
9. Ibid.
10. Ibid.
11. George, William, *My Brother and I*, p. 82.
12. George, W. R. P., *The Making of Lloyd George*, p. 101.
13. George, William, *My Brother and I*, p. 114.
14. George, W. R. P., *The Making of Lloyd George*, p. 100.
15. Ibid., p. 101.
16. George, William, *My Brother and I*, p. 116.
17. George, W. R. P., *The Making of Lloyd George*, p. 104.
18. George, William, *My Brother and I*, p. 121.
19. George, W. R. P., *The Making of Lloyd George*, p. 102.
20. Ibid., p. 112.
21. Du Parcq, *The Life*, Vol. I, p. 41.
22. George, William, *My Brother and I*, p. 33.
23. *North Wales Express*, 24 November 1882.
24. Du Parcq, *The Life*, Vol. I, p. 42.
25. George, W. R. P., *The Making of Lloyd George*, p. 117.
26. Ibid.
27. Du Parcq, *The Life*, Vol. I, p. 43.
28. George, W. R. P., *The Making of Lloyd George*, p. 115.
29. Ibid., p. 99.
30. Ibid., p. 116.
31. Ibid.
32. Ibid., p. 115.
33. Daniel.
34. George, W. R. P., *The Making of Lloyd George*, p. 115.
35. George, William, *My Brother and I*, p. 83.
36. Ibid.
37. George, W. R. P., *The Making of Lloyd George*, p. 120.
38. Ibid.

39. Rowland, Peter, *David Lloyd George*, p. 39.
40. Du Parcq, *The Life*, Vol. I, p. 51.
41. Morgan, Kenneth O., *Wales in British Politics 1868–1922*, p. 86.
42. Du Parcq, *The Life*, Vol. I, p. 49.
43. Ibid., p. 48.
44. George, W. R. P., *The Making of Lloyd George*, p. 113.
45. Ibid. (Speech in London in 1885.)
46. George, W. R. P., *The Making of Lloyd George*, p. 133.
47. Ibid., p. 129.
48. Ibid., p. 131.

CHAPTER 3: NOT A GENTLEMAN . . .

1. George, W. R. P., *The Making of Lloyd George*, p. 136.
2. Ibid.
3. Ibid., p. 138.
4. Ibid., pp. 138–9.
5. NLW 204036, 22 May 1886.
6. Ibid.
7. Hague, Ffion, *The Pain and the Privilege*, p. 80.
8. NLW 204037, 8 January 1887.
9. Ibid., 2 September 1886.
10. Ibid., 7 August 1887.
11. Morgan, Kenneth O. (ed.), *Lloyd George Family Letters 1885–1936*, p. 14.
12. George, W. R. P., *The Making of Lloyd George*, p. 141.
13. *Observer*, 12 November 1961.
14. Morgan, *Family Letters*, p. 17.
15. George, W. R. P., *The Making of Lloyd George*, p. 142.
16. Morgan (ed.), *Family Letters*, p. 19.
17. George, William, *My Brother and I*, p. 92.
18. NLW 20433C.
19. George, William, *My Brother and I*, p. 99.
20. Ibid., p. 100.
21. Owen, *Tempestuous Journey*, p. 56.
22. George, W. R. P., *The Making of Lloyd George*, p. 121.
23. Ibid.
24. George, William, *My Brother and I*, p. 139.
25. George, W. R. P., *The Making of Lloyd George*, p, 134.
26. George, William, *My Brother and I*, p. 135.
27. Ibid.
28. Du Parcq, *The Life*, Vol. I, p. 63.
29. Ibid.
30. Ibid., p. 67.
31. Ibid.
32. Ibid., p. 70.

33. Ibid., pp. 70–1.
34. Daniel.
35. HofL A/12/1/69, David Lloyd George, *British Monthly*, June 1904.
36. George, W. R. P., *The Making of Lloyd George*, p. 132.
37. Morgan (ed.), *Family Letters*, p. 20.
38. George, W. R. P., *The Making of Lloyd George*, pp. 152–3.
39. NLW 20443A.
40. Ibid.
41. Ibid.
42. Du Parcq, *The Life*, Vol. I, p. 83.
43. Ibid.
44. George, W. R. P., *The Making of Lloyd George*, p. 157.
45. Ibid., p. 158.
46. *The Times*, 9 April 1890.
47. Interview with Dame Margaret Lloyd George, April 1940, quoted in Grigg, *The Young Lloyd George*, p. 78.
48. Ibid.
49. Du Parcq, *The Life*, Vol. I, p. 95.
50. Ibid.
51. Ibid., p. 99.
52. Lloyd George, Richard, *My Father, Lloyd George*, p. 72.
53. Ibid., p. 41.
54. Hague, *The Pain and the Privilege*, p. 107.
55. Walker Davies, *Lloyd George 1863–1914*, p. 162, quoted in Grigg, *The Young Lloyd George*, p. 84.
56. Du Parcq, *The Life*, Vol. I, p. 97.
57. Morgan (ed.), *Family Letters*, p. 23.
58. George, W. R. P., *Backbencher*, p. 2.
59. Lloyd George, Richard, *Dame Margaret Lloyd George*, p. 228.
60. Interview – Morgan, Humprey Collection (April 1940), National Library of Wales.

CHAPTER 4: A FAILURE IN THE HOUSE

1. Morgan (ed.), *Family Letters*, 17 April 1890, p. 25.
2. Du Parcq, *The Life*, Vol. I, p. 102.
3. Morgan (ed.), *Family Letters*, p. 25.
4. Spender, Harold, *The Prime Minister*, p. 90.
5. NLW 10/231, 8 January 1905.
6. HofL A/6/3/3, *Caernarvon Herald*, 18 October 1889.
7. Morgan (ed.), *Family Letters*, p. 25.
8. Ibid., p. 27.
9. HofL A/6/4/14, 13 June 1890.
10. *The Times*, 28 May 1890.
11. Churchill, Winston, *Life of Lord Randolph Churchill*, Vol. II, p. 432.

12. George, William, *My Brother and I*, p. 43.
13. Hansard, Vol. CCCXLV, col. 873, 13 June 1890.
14. Morgan (ed.), *Family Letters*, p. 29.
15. NLW, 14 June 1890, quoted in Grigg, *The Young Lloyd George*, p. 103.
16. Ibid., p. 102.
17. Daniel.
18. Hansard, Vol. CCCXLVIII, cols. 904–6.
19. Owen, Frank, *Tempestuous Journey: Lloyd George, His Life and Times*, p. 61.
20. Gilbert, *David Lloyd George*, p. 81.
21. Ibid.
22. Morgan (ed.), *Family Letters*, p. 35.
23. HofL A/6/4/22, *St Helens Advertiser*, 4 October 1890.
24. NLW 204039, 2 February 1891.
25. Morgan (ed.), *Family Letters*, p. 28.
26. Ibid., p. 31.
27. Hague, *The Pain and the Privilege*, p. 98.
28. Morgan (ed.), *Family Letters*, p. 28.
29. Du Parcq, *The Life*, Vol. I, p. 107.
30. NLW 20462C, 27 December 1907.
31. Riddell, *War Diaries*, 7 March 1915.
32. HofL A/1/7/1, Alfred Thomas to David Lloyd George, 4 October 1905.
33. NLW 20462C, 3 October 1898.
34. Morgan (ed.), *Family Letters*, p. 38.
35. Ibid., p. 39.
36. Ibid.
37. Ibid., p. 40.
38. Ibid., p. 39.
39. Lloyd George, Frances, *The Years That Are Past*, p. 52. (Some editions give the author as Countess Lloyd George.)
40. HofL A/6/4, *Caernarvon Herald*, 13 June 1890.
41. Du Parcq, *The Life*, Vol. I, p. 122.
42. NLW 8316 D/498.
43. Hansard, Vol. CCCLIV, col. 135, 24 June 1891.
44. Du Parcq, *The Life*, Vol. I, p. 130.
45. Ibid.
46. Morley, John, *Life of Gladstone*, Vol. III, p. 463.
47. Gilbert, *David Lloyd George*, p. 96.
48. George, W. R. P., *The Making of Lloyd George*, p. 171.
49. Ibid., p. 173.
50. George, William, *My Brother and I*, p. 86.
51. NLW 20403E, DLlG to MLlG, 21 July 1883.
52. *Review of Reviews*, October 1904.
53. Gilbert, *David Lloyd George*, p. 100.
54. Morgan, *Wales in British Politics*, p. 117.
55. *Caernarvon Herald*, 1 July 1892.
56. HofL A/7/1/27, 24 July 1892.

57. Du Parcq, *The Life*, Vol. I, p. 156.
58. Churchill, Winston, *Great Contemporaries*, p. 1.
59. Ibid., p. 7.

CHAPTER 5: A WELSH PARNELL

1. 22 July 1892, in Grigg, *The Young Lloyd George*, p. 117.
2. Morgan (ed.), *Family Letters*, p. 56.
3. Lloyd George, David, *War Memoirs*, Vol. I, introduction, pp. 1–5.
4. George, William, *My Brother and I*, p. 162.
5. Ibid.
6. *The Times*, 13 September 1892.
7. Grigg, *The Young Lloyd George*, p. 129.
8. HofL 22515c.
9. NLW 22521E.
10. NLW 20411C/350.
11. Gilbert, *David Lloyd George*, p. 108.
12. Du Parcq, *The Life*, Vol. I, p. 156.
13. Gilbert, *David Lloyd George*, p. 108.
14. Morgan (ed.), *Family Letters*, p. 60.
15. NLW22826C, DLlG to MLlG, 13 February 1893.
16. Du Parcq, *The Life*, Vol. I, p. 188.
17. NLW 2360, 7 March 1894.
18. NLW 686, 11 August 1892.
19. HofL A/19/7/3/4.
20. HofL A/19/3/7.
21. Hansard, Vol. XXII, col. 32, 12 March 1894.
22. *British Weekly*, 19 April 1894.
23. HofL A/20/4/7.
24. Jenkins, Roy, *Asquith,* p. 84.
25. George, W. R. P., *Backbencher*, p. 137.
26. NLW 20462C.
27. *The Times*, 24 May 1894.
28. Morgan (ed.), *Family Letters*, p. 74.
29. Ibid.
30. HofL A/7/3/19, *Caernarvon Herald*, 1 June 1894.
31. Ibid.
32. Gilbert, *David Lloyd George*, p. 134.
33. HofL A/8/1/18, *South Wales Daily News*, 6 June 1895.
34. *Manchester Guardian*, 17 May 1895.
35. George, W. R. P., *The Making of Lloyd George*, p. 165.
36. Ibid.
37. NLW 20477C.
38. Morgan (ed.), *Family Letters*, p. 87.
39. Ibid.

40. HofL A/8/2/38, *North Wales Observer*, 12 July 1895.
41. Evans, Beriah, G., *The Life Romance of Lloyd George*, Vol. III, p. 124.
42. Morgan (ed.), *Family Letters*, p. 88.
43. HofL A/8/135, *Caernarvon Herald*, 2 August 1895.
44. *Manchester Guardian*, 12 November 1895.
45. Morgan (ed.), *Family Letters*, p. 90.
46. Ibid., p. 92.
47. Ibid., p. 94.
48. NLW A/8/1/19, *North Wales Observer*.
49. Morgan (ed.), *Family Letters*, p. 94.
50. Gilbert, B. B., *David Lloyd George: Architect of Change*, p. 41.
51. Spender, Harold, *The Prime Minister*, p. 13.

CHAPTER 6: ALL THAT GLISTERS

1. Ensor, Robert, *England 1870–1914*, p. 285.
2. *Caernarvon Herald*, 4 January 1898.
3. Hansard, Vol. XL, cols. 237–42.
4. Morgan (ed.), *Family Letters*, 22 May 1896, p. 103.
5. HofL A/8/2/13, *Caernarvon Herald*, 29 May 1896.
6. George, W. R. P., *Backbencher*, p. 200.
7. Ibid.
8. Du Parcq, *The Life*, Vol. I, p. 178.
9. Ibid., p. 177.
10. George, W. R. P., *Backbencher*, p. 201.
11. HofL A/7/3/24, *South Wales Observer*, 7 September 1894.
12. George, William, *My Brother and I*, p. 86.
13. Grigg, *The Young Lloyd George*, p. 176.
14. Ayerst, David, *Manchester Guardian: Biography of a Newspaper*, p. 290.
15. George, William, *My Brother and I*, p. 87.
16. HofL A11/82/18.
17. George, W. R. P., *The Making of Lloyd George*, p. 201.
18. Ibid., p. 108.
19. Ibid.
20. Ibid.
21. Ibid., p. 116.
22. NLW 20469, 5 December 1892.
23. NLW 20469, 4 January 1893.
24. George, W. R. P., *The Making of Lloyd George*, p. 115.
25. NLW 20411C/309.
26. 16 August 1893, quoted in Grigg, *The Young Lloyd George*.
27. 19 September 1893, quoted in ibid.
28. 21 September 1893, quoted in ibid.
29. 28 September 1893, quoted in ibid.
30. George, W. R. P., *Backbencher*, p. 125.

31. NLW 23296D.
32. George, W. R. P., *Backbencher*, p. 128.
33. Ibid.
34. Ibid., 5 January 1894, p. 130.
35. Ibid., 4 January 1894.
36. Ibid., 19 February 1894, p. 132.
37. Ibid., p. 131.
38. Ibid.
39. George, W. R. P., *The Making of Lloyd George*, p. 201.
40. Ibid., p. 200.
41. NLW 26339C2.
42. George, W. R. P., *The Making of Lloyd George*, p. 203.
43. Lloyd George, Richard, *My Father, Lloyd George*, p. 55.
44. Ibid.
45. George, W. R. P., *The Making of Lloyd George*, p. 210.
46. Ibid.
47. Ibid., p. 211.
48. Ibid.
49. Ibid., p. 215.
50. Ibid., p. 216.
51. Ibid., p. 114.
52. George, W. R. P., *The Making of Lloyd George*, p. 225.
53. Ibid., p. 226.
54. Grigg, *The Young Lloyd George*, p. 231.
55. Ibid., p. 236.
56. Lloyd George, Richard, *My Father, Lloyd George*, p. 132.
57. NLW 2329.
58. George, W. R. P., *The Making of Lloyd George*, p. 250.
59. Ibid., p. 216.
60. Ibid., p. 243.
61. Ibid., p. 278.

CHAPTER 7: AN END TO HIRAETH

1. Lloyd George, Richard, *My Father, Lloyd George*, p. 60.
2. NLW, DLlG to MLlG, 11 February 1896.
3. Morgan (ed.), *Family Letters*, p. 111.
4. Grigg, *The Young Lloyd George*, p. 241.
5. Morgan (ed.), *Family Letters*, 18 August 1891, p. 111.
6. Ibid., p. 112.
7. Grigg, *The Young Lloyd George*, p. 244.
8. NLW 24327, 19 August 1901.
9. Morgan (ed.), *Family Letters*, p. 109.
10. HofL A/5/3/12, *North Wales Observer*, 7 May 1897.
11. Gilbert, *David Lloyd George*, p. 154.

12. *British Weekly*, 14 May 1896.
13. Hansard, Vol. XLVIII, cols. 479–88, 16 March 1897.
14. NLW 20464C, 3 October 1898.
15. Morgan (ed.), *Family Letters*, p. 116.
16. *North Wales Observer*, 23 February 1898.
17. HofL A/8/4/28, *South Wales Daily News*, 3 November 1898.
18. Morgan (ed.), *Family Letters*, 17 August 1898, p. 114.
19. Grigg, *The Young Lloyd George*, p. 222.
20. Ibid., p. 223.
21. Margin note in Memorandum by Mr Lloyd George MP: Appendix 21, Select Committee on Aged, Deserving Poor, quoted in Gilbert, *David Lloyd George*, p. 177.
22. Morgan (ed.), *Family Letters*, p. 118.
23. Hansard, Vol. LXXIII, cols. 1006–72, 29 June 1899.
24. NLW 22518E, 27 May 1892.
25. Morgan (ed.), *Family Letters*, p. 99.
26. Grigg, *The Young Lloyd George*, p. 256.
27. George, William, *My Brother and I*, p. 177; also Grigg, *The Young Lloyd George*, p. 256.

CHAPTER 8: GO FOR JOE

1. Rhodes James, R., *The British Revolution 1880–1939*, p. 182.
2. Morgan (ed.), *Family Letters*, p. 99.
3. Ibid.
4. Speech in Cardiff, 4 February 1898, in Grigg, *The Young Lloyd George*, p. 258.
5. Rhodes James, *The British Revolution*, p. 192.
6. Ibid., p. 175.
7. Ibid., p. 189.
8. Ibid.
9. Du Parcq, *The Life*, Vol. II, p. 216.
10. Pakenham, Thomas, *The Boer War*, p. 115.
11. Wilson, John, *Sir Henry Campbell-Bannerman*, p. 307.
12. Morgan (ed.), *Family Letters*, p. 125.
13. Jenkins, *Asquith*, p. 115.
14. Du Parcq, *The Life*, Vol. II, p. 216.
15. Owen, *Tempestuous Journey*, p. 103.
16. Hansard, Vol. LXXVII, col. 782.
17. George, W. R. P., *Backbencher*, p. 299.
18. Ibid.
19. Wilson, *Sir Henry Campbell-Bannerman*, p. 300.
20. George, W. R. P., *Backbencher*, p. 300.
21. Grigg, *The Young Lloyd George*, p. 260.
22. Du Parcq, *The Life*, Vol. II, p. 221.

23. Ibid., pp. 222–3.
24. Ibid., p. 223.
25. Speech in Criccieth, 1 January 1900, in Grigg, *The Young Lloyd George*, p. 262.
26. Cecil, Lady, *Life of Salisbury*, Vol. III, p. 191.
27. Hansard, Vol. LXXVIII, cols. 758–67.
28. Hansard, Vol. LXXVIII, col. 758.
29. George, William, *My Brother and I*, p. 179.
30. Ibid., p. 178.
31. Ibid.
32. Du Parcq, *The Life*, Vol. II, p. 226.
33. Ibid.
34. George, W. R. P., *Backbencher*, p. 316.
35. Ibid., p. 317.
36. Du Parcq, *The Life*, Vol. II, p. 232.
37. Ibid.
38. HofL A/9/2/4, *North Wales Observer*, 19 January 1900.
39. Hansard, Vol. LXXVII, cols. 1199–1213, 25 July 1900.
40. George, William, *My Brother and I*, p. 73.
41. Edwards, J. Hugh, *David Lloyd George: The Man and the Statesman*, p. 204.
42. Marsh, Peter T., *Joseph Chamberlain*, p. 181.
43. Hansard, Vol. LXXXVII, cols. 1005–14.
44. George, W. R. P., *Backbencher*, p. 321.
45. Jenkins, *Asquith*, p. 119.
46. Morgan (ed.), *Family Letters*, p. 126.
47. George, W. R. P., *Backbencher*, p. 322.
48. NLW 20462C, 26 September 1900.
49. Grigg, *The Young Lloyd George*, p. 272.
50. NLW 20462C/2389.
51. Spender, Harold, *The Prime Minister*, p. 127.
52. *Caernarvon Herald*, 12 October 1900.
53. George, W. R. P., *Backbencher*, p. 302.
54. Morgan (ed.), *Family Letters*, p. 127.
55. NLW 204626/2292.
56. George, W. R. P., *Backbencher*, p. 327.
57. Ibid.
58. Wilson, *Sir Henry Campbell-Bannerman*, p. 342.
59. Ibid.
60. Grigg, *The Young Lloyd George*, p. 277.
61. Hansard, Vol. LXXXIX, cols. 391–405.
62. Wilson, *Sir Henry Campbell-Bannerman*, p. 346.
63. Taylor, S. J., *The Great Outsiders*, p. 70.
64. *The Times*, 25 May 1901.
65. Gilbert, *David Lloyd George*, p. 200.
66. Jenkins, *Asquith*, p. 14.
67. Grigg, *The Young Lloyd George*, p. 286.

68. Du Parcq, *The Life*, Vol. II, p. 292.
69. *The Times*, 19 December 1901.
70. *Review of Reviews*, October 1904.
71. Du Parcq, *The Life*, Vol. II, p. 305.
72. *New Liberal Review*, III, January 1902, pp. 767–74.
73. Hansard, Vol. CL, col. 537, 20 January 1902.
74. Ibid.
75. Hansard, Vol. CL, col. 541, 21 January 1902.
76. Ibid.
77. Wilson, *Sir Henry Campbell-Bannerman*, p. 384.
78. Ibid.
79. Gilbert, *David Lloyd George*, p. 262.
80. NLW 20462C 10/231.
81. Grigg, *The Young Lloyd George*, p. 284.
82. Gilbert, *David Lloyd George*, p. 202.
83. HofL 5/13/13/2.
84. Du Parcq, *The Life*, Vol. II, p. 318.
85. *The Times*, 21 February 1902.
86. *North Wales Observer*, 28 February 1902.
87. Gilbert, *David Lloyd George*, p. 181.
88. Morgan (ed.), *Family Letters*, p. 131.

CHAPTER 9: NONCONFORMITY'S CHAMPION

1. Morgan (ed.), *Family Letters*, p. 132.
2. NLW 20462/181, 24 March 1902.
3. *Western Mail*, 25 March 1902.
4. *Daily News*, 25 March 1902.
5. Ibid., 8 May 1902.
6. Grigg, John, *Lloyd George: The People's Champion 1902–1911*, p. 40.
7. Ibid., p. 30.
8. George, W. R. P., *Backbencher*, p. 357.
9. Morgan (ed.), *Family Letters*, p. 134.
10. George, W. R. P., *Backbencher*, p. 354.
11. Ibid.
12. Morgan (ed.), *Family Letters*, p. 134.
13. Ibid. p. 135.
14. Ibid.
15. George, W. R. P., *Backbencher*, p. 360.
16. Ibid.
17. Ibid.
18. Ibid., 29 April 1899.
19. *British Weekly*, 12 June 1902.
20. Hansard, Vol. CVII, cols. 1113–17, 8 May 1902.
21. *Caernarvon Herald*, 30 May 1902.

22. Rowland, *David Lloyd George*, p. 166.
23. Herbert Lewis Diary, 11 November 1902, quoted in Morgan, *Wales in British Politics*, p. 187.
24. Morgan (ed.), *Family Letters*, p. 132.
25. Du Parcq, *The Life*, Vol. II, p. 348.
26. Hansard, Vol. CXV, col. 437, 25 November 1902.
27. *British Weekly*, 11 September 1902.
28. Hansard, Vol. CXV, cols. 1175–80, 3 December 1902.
29. Morgan (ed.), *Family Letters*, p. 135.
30. Rowland, *David Lloyd George*, p. 166.
31. Ibid.
32. *The Times*, 31 December 1902.
33. Quoted in Gilbert, *David Lloyd* George, p. 222.
34. Grigg, *The People's Champion*, p. 39.
35. Du Parcq, *The Life*, Vol. II, Appendix III, p. 412.
36. *British Weekly*, 13 November 1903.
37. George, W. R. P., *Backbencher*, p. 373.
38. Grigg, *The People's Champion*, p. 43.
39. Gilbert, *David Lloyd George*, p. 236.
40. Du Parcq, *The Life*, Vol. II, p. 412.
41. George, W. R. P., *Backbencher*, p. 375.
42. NLW 10/230, 13 March 1903.
43. HofL A/11/1/40, 30 May 1903.
44. Grigg, *The People's Champion*, p. 45 note.
45. *Illustrated Mirror*, 11 March 1904.
46. Gilbert, *David Lloyd George*, p. 246.
47. George, W. R. P., *Backbencher*, p. 390.
48. A/12/1/25, 10 March 1904.
49. HofL A/12/1/31, *South Wales Daily News*, 15 March 1904.
50. NLW 20462A/41.
51. George, William, *My Brother and I*, p. 171.
52. Ibid.
53. Gilbert, *David Lloyd George*, p. 245.
54. NLW 20462C 10/231, diary, 10 August 1904.
55. *The Times*, 10 August 1904.
56. 'Chieftain of Wales', *Review of Reviews*, September 1904.
57. 'The Rising Power of Mr Lloyd George', *The Times*, 11 August 1904.
58. Gilbert, *David Lloyd George*, p. 251.
59. Ibid.
60. Ibid., p. 253.
61. *Christian World*, 2 February 1905.
62. Gilbert, *David Lloyd George*, p. 260.

CHAPTER 10: PROTECTION, PROPERTY AND PUBLICANS

1. George, William, *My Brother and I*, p. 176.
2. George, W. R. P., *Backbencher*, p. 391.
3. Ibid.
4. Morgan (ed.), *Family Letters*, p. 133.
5. *The Times*, 17 May 1902.
6. Marsh, *Joseph Chamberlain*, p. 550.
7. PRO, Cabinet Paper 4/29, No. 8.
8. Balfour Papers, British Library H66471, 27 August 1903.
9. Gollin, Alfred, *Balfour's Burden*, p. 37.
10. Ibid., p. 35.
11. Du Parcq, *The Life*, Vol. II, p. 618.
12. Ibid., pp. 617, 626.
13. Ibid., p. 620.
14. Ibid., p. 625.
15. Ibid., p. 617.
16. Hansard, Vol. CXXIII, col. 1549, 22 May 1903.
17. Ibid., col. 1553, 22 May 1903.
18. Grigg, *The People's Champion*, p. 62.
19. Hansard, Vol. CXXIII, col. 185.
20. Grigg, *The People's Champion*, p. 63.
21. Gilbert, *David Lloyd George*, p. 268.
22. Ibid.
23. Churchill, Winston, *My Early Life*, p. 362.
24. Churchill, Randolph, S. and Martin Gilbert, *Winston S. Churchill*, Companion Vol. II, Part 1, p. 104.
25. George, W. R. P., *Backbencher*, p. 413.
26. Grigg, *The People's Champion*, p. 65 note.
27. Jenkins, *Winston Churchill*, p. 81.
28. Ibid.
29. Churchill, Randolph, S. and Martin Gilbert, *Winston S. Churchill*, Vol. II, p. 80.
30. Hansard, Vol. XXXIX, col. 407.
31. George, W. R. P., *Backbencher*, p. 397.
32. Grigg, *The People's Champion*, p. 65.
33. Daniel.
34. Jenkins, *Winston Churchill*, p. 144.
35. Rowland, *David Lloyd George*, p. 176.
36. Grigg, *The People's Champion*, p. 70.
37. Morgan (ed.), *Family Letters*, p. 140.
38. Rowland, *David Lloyd George*, p. 177.
39. Grigg, *The People's Champion*, p. 71.
40. Rowland, *David Lloyd George*, p. 178.
41. Grigg, *The People's Champion*, p. 77.

42. Ibid.
43. Wilson, *Sir Henry Campbell-Bannerman*, p. 639.
44. Jenkins, *Asquith*, pp. 145–7.
45. Morgan (ed.), *Family Letters*, p. 149.
46. Grigg, *The People's Champion*, p. 83.
47. Ibid., p. 82.
48. *Sunday Sun*, 11 January 1904.
49. NLW 20464C.
50. Ibid.
51. Wilson, *Sir Henry Campbell-Bannerman*, p. 426.
52. Rowland, *David Lloyd George*, p. 179.
53. Jenkins, *Asquith*, p. 148.
54. Gilbert, *David Lloyd George*, p. 287.
55. Wilson, *Sir Henry Campbell-Bannerman*, p. 447.

CHAPTER 11: THE POODLE BARKS

1. George, William, *My Brother and I*, p. 205.
2. Ibid.
3. Ibid.
4. Ibid., p. 206.
5. Ibid.
6. Ibid.
7. Ibid., p. 207.
8. Ibid.
9. Ibid.
10. Ibid., p. 206.
11. Fitzroy, Almeric, *Memoirs*, 14 December 1909, Vol. II, p. 390.
12. Amery, Julian, *The Life of Joseph Chamberlain*, Vol. VI, p. 876.
13. Hudson, Kearley, *The Travelled Road*, unpublished memoir, quoted in Grigg, *The People's Champion*, p. 101.
14. Pelling, H., *The History of British Trade Unionism*, p. 129.
15. Rowland, *David Lloyd George*, p. 184.
16. *Caernarvon Herald*, 18 January 1906.
17. Hansard, Vol. CLII, cols. 1307–8, 1 March 1906.
18. Rowland, *David Lloyd George*, p. 184.
19. Grigg, *The People's Champion*, p. 104.
20. Ibid., p. 105.
21. George, William, *My Brother and I*, p. 205.
22. Hansard, Vol. CLIV, col. 28, 20 March 1906.
23. *The Times*, 21 March 1906.
24. Hansard, Vol. CLIV, cols. 237–53, 20 October 1906.
25. *The Times*, 30 October 1906.
26. Rowland, *David Lloyd George*, p. 189.
27. Speech at Rhyl, 30 October 1906, in Rowland, *David Lloyd George*, p. 190.

28. Speech at free trade demonstration, Rochester, 7 November 1906, in Grigg, *The People's Champion*, p. 109.
29. Oxford and Asquith, Earl of, *Fifty Years of Parliament*, Vol. II, p. 43.
30. George, William, *My Brother and I*, p. 208.
31. Hansard, Vol. CLXII, col. 545.
32. Lord Newton, *Lord Lansdowne: A Biography*, p. 357, quoted in Jenkins, R., *Mr Balfour's Poodle*, p. 37.
33. Ibid.
34. Gilbert, *David Lloyd George*, p. 298.
35. Lee, Sydney, *King Edward VII: A Biography*, Vol. II, pp. 456–7.
36. Campbell-Bannerman Papers, British Library, 41.239.EV14851.
37. Du Parcq, *The Life*, Vol. II, p. 459.
38. Campbell-Bannerman Papers, British Library, MS52513.
39. *Oxford Chronicle*, 7 December 1906.
40. Gilbert, *David Lloyd George*, p. 299.
41. NLW 10/231, 29 December 1906.
42. Hansard, Vol. CLXVII, col. 1739.
43. *Sheffield Independent*, 30 August 1907.
44. Rowland, *David Lloyd George*, p. 190.
45. Ibid.
46. *Western Mail*, 12 October 1907.

CHAPTER 12: THE TWO IMPOSTORS

1. Gilbert, *David Lloyd George*, p. 5.
2. Bell, G., *Randall Davidson, Archbishop of Canterbury*, p. 504.
3. Cmd 5432.
4. *The Times*, 18 January 1907.
5. *British Weekly*, 6 May 1907.
6. Campbell-Bannerman Papers, British Library, MS41240, Vol. XXXV, 6 October 1907, quoted in Gilbert, *David Lloyd George*, p. 311.
7. Gilbert, *David Lloyd George*, p. 311.
8. *The Times*, 11 October 1907.
9. *British Weekly*, 17 October 1907.
10. Daniel.
11. Campbell-Bannerman Papers, British Library, MS41240, Vol. XXXV, 17 October 1907, quoted in Gilbert, *David Lloyd George*, p. 313.
12. PRO 37/90/116.
13. Ibid.
14. Kearney, *The Travelled Road*, quoted in Grigg, *The People's Champion*, p. 113.
15. Campbell-Bannerman Papers, British Library.
16. George, William, *My Brother and I*, p. 212.
17. Grigg, *The People's Champion*, p. 114.
18. George, William, *My Brother and I*, p. 212.
19. Grigg, *The People's Champion*, p. 115.

20. Gilbert, *David Lloyd George*, p. 16.
21. *The Times*, 8 November 1907.
22. Gilbert, *David Lloyd George*, p. 320.
23. Spender, J. A., *The Life of the Right Honourable Sir Henry Campbell-Bannerman*, Vol. II, p. 370.
24. George, William, *My Brother and I*, p. 213.
25. Ibid.
26. Ibid.
27. Daniel.
28. Spender, J. A., *The Public Life*, Vol. I, pp. 157–8.
29. The annual dinner of the *Shipping Gazette*, Trocadero Restaurant, London, 21 November 1906, in Grigg, *The People's Champion*, p. 119.
30. Grigg, *The People's Champion*, p. 124.
31. Lloyd George, Frances, *The Years That Are Past*, p. 31.
32. NLW 2912.
33. George, William, *My Brother and I*, p. 215.
34. Hague, *The Pain and the Privilege*, p. 179.
35. Ibid.
36. NLW 20462C.
37. NLW 20429C.
38. NLW 206180D.
39. Lloyd George, Frances, *The Years That Are Past*, p. 49.
40. DLG Papers, British Library, I/1/1/14.
41. NLW 207843E.
42. Morgan (ed.), *Family Letters*, p. 151.

CHAPTER 13: THE GREAT WORK BEGINS

1. NLW 10/230, Herbert Lewis diary, 23 February 1908.
2. Jenkins, *Asquith*, p. 183.
3. NLW 204626 2285i.
4. George, William, *My Brother and I*, p. 220.
5. Ibid.
6. Grigg, *The People's Champion*, p. 135.
7. Ibid., p. 136.
8. NLW 204626 2286ii.
9. Daniel, NLW.
10. NLW 204626 2286i.
11. Hansard, Vol. CLXXXVII, col. 1679.
12. George, William, *My Brother and I*, p. 224.
13. Daniel.
14. Hansard, Vol. CXC, col. 585, 15 June 1908.
15. Ibid., col. 564.
16. Ibid.
17. Rowland, *David Lloyd George*, p. 233.

18. Ibid.
19. Daniel.
20. George, William, *My Brother and I*, p. 221, 12 May 1908.
21. Hansard, Vol. CXCL, cols. 395–6, 29 June 1908.
22. Asquith Papers, Bodleian Library, Vol. XI, 9 September 1908.
23. David, Edward (ed.), *Inside Asquith's Cabinet: From the Diaries of Charles Hobhouse*, p. 73.
24. Gilbert, *David Lloyd George*, p. 323.
25. Lloyd George, David, *War Memoirs*, Vol. I, pp. 19–20.
26. *The Times*, 29 July 1908.
27. Ibid.
28. Gilbert, *David Lloyd George*, p. 351.
29. Spender, Harold, *Fire of Life*, p. 162.
30. *Daily News*, 27 August 1908.
31. Ibid., 7 March 1908.
32. 'Liberalism without Ideas', *Westminster Gazette*, vol. CLXIX, February 1908.
33. NLW 10/230, diary, 8 August 1908.
34. Swansea, 1 October 1908, quoted in Du Parcq, *The Life*, Vol. IV, p. 638.
35. Bowley, A. L. and A. R. Burnett-Hurst, *Livelihood and Poverty: A Study in the Economic Conditions of Working-Class Households in Northampton, Warrington, Stanley and Reading*, p. 4, quoted in Ian Gazeley, *Poverty in Britain 1900–1965*, p. 35.
36. Gazeley, *Poverty in Britain 1900–1965*, p. 40.
37. Jenkins, *Winston Churchill*, p. 144.

CHAPTER 14: WOMEN TROUBLE

1. Gilbert, *David Lloyd George*, p. 352.
2. HofL 22522E, 70.
3. Grigg, *The People's Champion*, p. 162.
4. *People*, 5 January 1909.
5. Lloyd George, Richard, *My Father, Lloyd George*, p. 112.
6. Grigg, *The People's Champion*, pp. 186–7.
7. NLW 22522E.
8. Grigg, *The People's Champion*, pp. 183–5.
9. Ibid.
10. Pugh, M., *The Pankhursts*, p. 180.
11. Rowland, *David Lloyd George*, p. 209.

CHAPTER 15: THE PEOPLE'S DAVID

1. Rowland, *David Lloyd George*, p. 215.
2. Jenkins, *Winston Churchill*, p. 150.

3. Ibid., p. 145.
4. Ibid., p. 144.
5. PRO Cas 46/3/1172, Asquith to Edward VII, 9 December 1908.
6. George, William, *My Brother and I*, p. 222, 9 December 1908.
7. *The Times*, 12 December 1908.
8. Masterman, Lucy, *C. F. G. Masterman*, p. 114.
9. *Liverpool Post*, 21 December 1908.
10. H. W. Massingham, 'The Position of Mr Lloyd George', *The Nation*, 6 January 1912.
11. Dangerfield, G., *The Strange Death of Liberal England*, p. 20.
12. Riddell, Lord, *More Pages from My Diary*, p. 10, 24 November 1908.
13. Ibid.
14. George, William, *My Brother and I*, p. 226.
15. Gilbert, *David Lloyd George*, p. 213.
16. Rowland, *David Lloyd George*, p. 215.
17. Spender, J. A. and Cyril Asquith, *The Life of Herbert Henry Asquith, Lord Oxford and Asquith*, Vol. I, p. 254.
18. Churchill, Randolph, *Churchill*, Companion Vol. II, p. 860, quoted in Gilbert, *David Lloyd George*, p. 363.
19. NLW, Herbert Lewis diary, 28 December 1909.
20. Riddell, *More Pages from My Diary*, 21 May 1912, p. 65.
21. Taylor, A. J. P. (ed.), *Lloyd George*, 30 May 1936, p. 322.
22. Grigg, *The People's Champion*, p. 177.
23. Ibid.
24. Ibid., p. 178.
25. Ibid.
26. Speaight, R., *Lite of Belloc*, quoted in Rowland, *David Lloyd George*, p. 219.
27. Hansard, Vol. IV, p. 492.
28. Chamberlain, Austen, *Politics from Inside*, p. 177, 30 April 1909.
29. Hansard, Vol. IV, cols. 549–50, 29 April 1909.
30. *The Times*, 3 May 1909.
31. Ibid., 15 May 1909 and 22 May 1909.
32. Ibid., 16 June 1909, quoted in Grigg, *The People's Champion*, p. 198.
33. *The Times*, 17 July 1909.
34. To J. A. Spender, 16 July 1909, quoted in Rowland, *David Lloyd George*, p. 219.
35. Harold Spender Papers, British Library, Part 3, MS 46388, 16 July 1909.
36. George, William, *My Brother and I*, p. 228.
37. Grigg, *The People's Champion*, p. 209.
38. Gilbert, *David Lloyd George*, p. 384.
39. Grigg, *The People's Champion*, p. 208.
40. Ibid.
41. Owen, *Tempestuous Journey*, pp. 180–2.
42. Ibid., p. 210.
43. Jenkins, *Asquith*, p. 200.
44. Ibid.

45. Ibid.
46. Grigg, *The People's Champion*, p. 221.
47. Du Parcq, *The Life*, Vol. IV, p.78.
48. Ibid.

CHAPTER 16: AFTER A STORM

1. Gilbert, *David Lloyd George*, p. 399.
2. Masterman, Lucy, *C. F. G. Masterman*, p. 139.
3. Lloyd George, Frances, *The Years That Are Past*, pp. 48–9.
4. Ibid.
5. Riddell, *War Diaries*, p. 248.
6. George, William, *My Brother and I*, p. 230.
7. Gollin, Alfred, *The Observer & J. L. Garvin 1908–1914*, p. 109.
8. George, William, *My Brother and I*, p. 230.
9. Ibid.
10. David (ed.), *Inside Asquith's Cabinet*.
11. Du Parcq, *The Life*, Vol. IV, p. 697.
12. Grigg, *The People's Champion*, p. 229 note 2.
13. *The Times*, 11 October 1909.
14. *Daily Mail*, 12 October 1909.
15. *Telegraph*, 11 October 1909.
16. Grigg, *The People's Champion*, p. 227.
17. *The Times*, 17 December 1909.
18. Ibid., 31 December 1909.
19. Gilbert, *David Lloyd George*, p. 401.
20. Du Parcq, *The Life*, Vol. III, p. 551.
21. Grigg, *The People's Champion*, p. 232.
22. Jenkins, *Asquith*, p. 202.
23. Spender and Asquith, *The Life of Herbert Henry Asquith*, Vol. I, p. 254.
24. Jenkins, *Asquith*, p. 132.
25. Du Parcq, *The Life*, Vol. III, p. 554.
26. Grigg, *The People's Champion*, p. 238.
27. Ibid.
28. Ibid.
29. Jenkins, *Asquith*, p. 242.
30. Masterman, Lucy, *C. F. G. Masterman*, p. 205.

CHAPTER 17: A REASONABLE WAY OUT

1. Grigg, *The People's Champion*, p. 244.
2. Gilbert, *David Lloyd George*, p. 403.
3. Ibid.
4. Marquand, David, *Ramsay MacDonald*, p. 122.

5. Lyons, F. S. L., *John Dillon: A Biography*, p. 314.
6. Rowland, *David Lloyd George*, p. 231.
7. NLW, Herbert Lewis diary, 19 February 1910.
8. Gilbert, *David Lloyd George*, p. 231.
9. Hansard, Vol. XIV, col. 55, 21 February 1910.
10. Jenkins, *Asquith*, p. 207.
11. Masterman, Lucy, *C. F. G. Masterman*, p. 116.
12. Ellis Davies journal, quoted in Grigg, *The People's Champion*, p. 250.
13. Jenkins, *Asquith*, p. 208.
14. Grigg, *The People's Champion*, p. 250 note.
15. NLW 10/231, diary, 25 February 1910.
16. Masterman, Lucy, *C. F. G. Masterman*, p. 162.
17. Wilfred Scawen Blunt, *My Diaries*, Vol. II, 13 May 1910, quoted in Grigg, *The People's Champion*, p. 257.
18. Asquith Papers, Bodleian Library, Vol. V, 13 April 1910, quoted in Gilbert, *David Lloyd George*, p. 409.
19. Magnus, P., *King Edward VII*, p. 453.
20. Morgan (ed.), *Family Letters*, p. 153.
21. Ibid., p. 152.
22. *Observer*, 8 May 1910.
23. Garvin to Sandars (Balfour's aide), 24 May 1910, quoted in Gollin, *The Observer and J. L. Garvin 1908–1914*.
24. Ibid.
25. Blake, Robert, *The Unknown Prime Minister: The Life and Times of Andrew Bonar Law 1858–1923*, p. 64.
26. Daniel, NLW.
27. Ibid.
28. Ibid.
29. Du Parcq, *The Life*, Vol. III, p. 562.
30. Ibid., p. 565.
31. Ibid.
32. Ibid.
33. Ibid.
34. Gilbert, *David Lloyd George*, p. 426.
35. Masterman, Lucy, *C. F. G. Masterman*, p. 169.
36. Morgan (ed.), *Family Letters*, p. 153.
37. Churchill, Randolph and Martin Gilbert, *Churchill*, Companion Volume II, 25 September 1910, pp. 1023–4.
38. Quoted in Jenkins, *Asquith*, p. 216.
39. Jenkins, *Asquith*, p. 217.
40. Balfour Papers, Add MSS 4862 (f216–17), quoted in Rowland, *David Lloyd George*, p. 240.
41. Chamberlain, *Politics from Inside*, p. 288.
42. Rowland, *David Lloyd George*, p. 240.
43. Masterman, Lucy, *C. F. G. Masterman*, p. 172.
44. Lloyd George, *War Memoirs*, Vol. I, p. 37.

45. Ibid.
46. Dugdale, B. E. C., *Arthur James Balfour: First Earl of Balfour*, p. 77, quoted in Gilbert, *David Lloyd George*, p. 426.
47. Grigg, *The People's Champion*, p. 283.
48. NLW 22522E.
49. Masterman, Lucy, *C. F. G. Masterman*, p. 200.
50. Ibid.
51. Ibid.
52. Blake, *The Unknown Prime Minister*, p. 69.
53. Masterman, Lucy, *C. F. G. Masterman*, p. 199.

CHAPTER 18: NINEPENCE FOR FOURPENCE

1. Masterman, Lucy, *C. F. G. Masterman*, p. 169.
2. Murray, A., *Master and Brother*, p. 88.
3. NLW 20462C/2294.
4. Churchill, Randolph and Martin Gilbert, *Churchill*, Companion Volume II, 22 April 1911, p. 1069.
5. Braithwaite, W. J., *Lloyd George's Ambulance Wagon*, H. N. Bunbury (ed.), p. 121.
6. Ibid. (note on malingering to Beveridge).
7. Fraser, D., *The Evolution of the British Welfare State*, p. 177.
8. Gilbert, *David Lloyd George*, p. 430.
9. Gazeley, *Poverty in Britain*, p. 39.
10. NLW 23664.
11. Braithwaite, *Lloyd George's Ambulance Wagon*, quoted in Grigg, *The People's Champion*, p. 172.
12. Ibid.
13. Ibid.
14. Gilbert, *David Lloyd George*, p. 438.
15. Hansard, Vol. XXV, col. 609.
16. Ibid.
17. Petrie, C., *Life and Letters of A. Chamberlain*, Vol. II, p. 277.
18. Masterman, Lucy, *C. F. G. Masterman*, p. 192.
19. *British Medical Journal*, 3 June 1911, p. 354, quoted in Gilbert, *David Lloyd George*, p. 439.
20. Hughes, E., *Keir Hardie*, p. 200.
21. Hansard, Vol. XXVIII, col. 1237.
22. Morgan (ed.), *Family Letters*, 11 October 1911, p. 160.
23. Grigg, *The People's Champion*, p. 338.
24. Hansard, Vol. XXVIII, col. 1287.
25. *Insurance Mail*, 28 October 1911.
26. Masterman, Lucy, *C. F. G. Masterman*, p. 221.
27. Gilbert, *David Lloyd George*, p. 445.
28. Masterman, Lucy, *C. F. G. Masterman*, p. 221.

29. Gilbert, *David Lloyd George*, p. 445.
30. Ibid., p. 258.
31. HofL 24/5/166, Bonar Law Papers, 31 December 1911.
32. *Contemporary Review*, January 1909.

CHAPTER 19: THE DOVE BECOMES A HAWK

1. Lloyd George, David, *War Memoirs*, Vol. I, p. 44 note.
2. Du Parcq, *The Life*, Vol. III, p. 559.
3. Ibid.
4. Ibid.
5. Masterman, Lucy, *C. F. G. Masterman*, p. 199.
6. Morgan (ed.), *Family Letters*, p. 156.
7. HofL C131516, 25 August 1911.
8. Morgan (ed.), *Family Letters*, p. 156.
9. Masterman, Lucy, *C. F. G. Masterman*, p. 203.
10. Ibid.
11. Gilbert, *David Lloyd George*, p. 457.
12. Ibid.
13. Morgan (ed.), *Family Letters*, p. 158.
14. Beaverbrook, *The Decline and Fall of Lloyd George*, p. 58.
15. Ibid.
16. Masterman, Lucy, *C. F. G. Masterman*, p. 234.
17. Wilson, T. (ed.), *The Political Diaries of C. P. Scott, 1911–1928*, p. 46.
18. Ibid., p. 284.
19. Jenkins, *Asquith* p. 234.
20. Gilbert, *David Lloyd George*, p. 461.
21. Ibid.
22. Jenkins, *Winston Churchill*, p. 201.
23. Masterman, Lucy, *C. F. G. Masterman*, p. 208.
24. Ibid., p. 209.
25. Rowland, *David Lloyd George*, p. 252.
26. Chamberlain, *Politics from Inside*, p. 437.
27. Gilbert, *David Lloyd George*, p. 463.
28. HofL C/6/11/9, 20 August 1911.
29. Gilbert, *David Lloyd George*, p. 465.
30. Rowland, *David Lloyd George*, p. 257.
31. Ibid.

CHAPTER 20: ENTER MISS STEVENSON

1. Lloyd George, Frances, *The Years That Are Past,* p. 49.
2. Rowland, *David Lloyd George*, p. 255.
3. Ibid.

4. Lloyd George, Frances, *The Years That Are Past*, p. 42.
5. Masterman, Lucy, *C. F. G. Masterman*, p. 212.
6. Rowland, *David Lloyd George*, p. 255.
7. Masterman, Lucy, *C. F. G. Masterman*, p. 212.
8. Lloyd George, Frances, *The Years That Are Past*, p. 51.
9. NLW 22521E.
10. Hague, *The Pain and the Privilege*, p. 174.
11. Lloyd George, Frances, *The Years That Are Past*, p. 51.
12. Ibid., p. 30.
13. Ibid., p. 20.
14. Ibid., p. 56.
15. Grigg, John, *Lloyd George: From Peace to War 1912–1916*, p. 82.
16. Pedersen, Susan, 'The Story of Frances Stevenson and David Lloyd George', in Wm. Roger Lewis (ed.) *Penultimate Adventures with Britannia: Personalities, Politics and Culture in Britain*, p. 38.
17. NLW 204636/21.
18. Ibid.
19. Lloyd George, Frances, *The Years That Are Past*, p. 52.
20. Ibid. p. 53.
21. Ibid.
22. Ibid.
23. Ibid., p. 55.

CHAPTER 21: RULES OF PRUDENCE

1. *Eye Witness*, 8 August 1912.
2. Grigg, *From Peace to War*, p. 46.
3. Morgan (ed.), *Family Letters*, p. 161.
4. Samuel, Herbert, *Memoirs*, p. 25.
5. Lloyd George, Frances, *The Years That Are Past*, p. 54.
6. Ibid.
7. Riddell, *More Pages from My Diary*, p. 121.
8. Rowland, *David Lloyd George*, p. 263.
9. Owen, *Tempestuous Journey*, p. 228.
10. Hansard, Vol. XLII, col. 592.
11. Ibid., col. 718.
12. Grigg, *From Peace to War*, p. 53 note.
13. Riddell, *More Pages from My Diary*, p. 146.
14. NLW 2253A 52.
15. Riddell, *More Pages from My Diary*, p. 158.
16. Percy Illingworth Papers (private collection).
17. Owen, *Tempestuous Journey*, p. 236.
18. Ibid., p. 237.
19. Hansard, Vol. LIV, col. 448, 18 June 1913.
20. Owen, *Tempestuous Journey*, p. 237.

21. Jenkins, *Asquith*, p. 253.
22. Churchill, Randolph, *Churchill*, Companion Volume II, Part 3, p. 1740.
23. Ibid.
24. Grigg, *From Peace to War*, p. 59.
25. Ibid.

CHAPTER 22: BACK TO THE LAND

1. Grigg, *From Peace to War*, p. 18.
2. Blake, Robert, *The Unknown Prime Minister*, p. 96.
3. Riddell, *More Pages from My Diary*, p. 63.
4. Hansard, Vol. XXXVII, cols. 995 and 1280.
5. Grigg, *From Peace to War*, p. 30.
6. Hansard, Vol. XXXVIII, col.1325.
7. Grigg, *From Peace to War*, p. 33.
8. Masterman, Lucy, *C. F. G. Masterman*, p. 235.
9. Riddell, *More Pages from My Diary*, p. 64.
10. Masterman, Lucy, *C. F. G. Masterman*, p. 235.
11. Riddell, *More Pages from My Diary*, p. 64.
12. Ibid.
13. Masterman, Lucy, *C. F. G. Masterman*, p. 235.
14. Riddell, *More Pages from My Diary*, p. 69.
15. Ibid., p. 70.
16. Grigg, *From Peace to War*, p. 40.
17. Masterman, Lucy, *C. F. G. Masterman*, p. 267.
18. Grigg, *From Peace to War*, p. 41.
19. Rowland, *David Lloyd George*, p. 269.
20. Percy Illingworth Papers (private collection).
21. Masterman, Lucy, *C. F. G. Masterman*, p. 259.
22. *The Times*, 13 October 1913.
23. Grigg, *From Peace to War*, pp. 99–100.
24. Ibid., p. 68.

CHAPTER 23: FULL OF FIGHT

1. NLW 20462/2349.
2. Masterman, Lucy, *C. F. G. Masterman*, p. 242.
3. Morgan (ed.), *Family Letters*, 11 April 1912, p. 161.
4. Hattersley, Roy, *The Edwardians*, p. 190.
5. Blake, *The Unknown Prime Minister*, p. 130.
6. Hattersley, *The Edwardians*, p. 192.
7. Kee, Robert, *The Green Flag*, p. 483.
8. Grigg, *From Peace to War*, p. 119.
9. Ibid., p. 120.

10. Ibid., pp. 122–3.
11. *The Times*, 11 September 1913.
12. Grigg, *From Peace to War*, p. 124.
13. Ibid., 6 October 1913.
14. Riddell, *More Pages from My Diary*, p. 146.
15. Lloyd George, Frances, *The Years That Are Past*, p. 67.
16. Morgan (ed.), *Family Letters*, p. 166.
17. NLW 22515C.
18. Grigg, *From Peace to War*, p. 90.
19. Ibid., p. 91.
20. Ibid.
21. Riddell, *More Pages from My Diary*, p. 185.
22. Ibid.
23. Rowland, *David Lloyd George*, p. 273.
24. Riddell, *More Pages from My Diary*, p. 215.
25. Percy Illingworth Papers (private collection).
26. Riddell, *More Pages from My Diary*, p. 218.
27. Ibid.

CHAPTER 24: THE PATRIOT

1. Rowland, *David Lloyd George*, p. 280.
2. Wilson (ed.), *The Political Diaries of C. P. Scott*, pp. 91–2.
3. Jenkins, *Asquith*, p. 324.
4. Ibid., p. 325.
5. Grigg, *From Peace to War*, p. 139.
6. Asquith, H. H., *Memoirs and Reflections*, Vol. II, p. 7.
7. Riddell, Lord, *Lord Riddell's War Diaries*, p. 5.
8. Ibid., p. 4.
9. Ibid., p. 6.
10. NLW 20463C (telegram, 15 August 1914).
11. Morgan (ed.), *Family Letters*, p. 167.
12. Grigg, *From Peace to War*, p. 145.
13. Lloyd George, Frances, *The Years That Are Past*, p. 73.
14. Murray, *Master and Brother*, p. 147.
15. Gilbert, *David Lloyd George*, p. 282.
16. Beaverbrook, Lord, *Politicians and the War*, p. 172.
17. Morgan, E. V., *Studies in British Financial Policy 1914–15*, p. 10, quoted in Grigg, *From Peace to War*, p. 151.
18. Lloyd George, David, *War Memoirs*, Vol. I, p. 74.
19. David (ed.), *Inside Asquith's Cabinet*, 21 August 1914, quoted in Grigg, *From Peace to War*, p. 153.
20. George, William, *My Brother and I*, p. 248.
21. Riddell, *War Diaries*, p. 14.
22. Ibid.

23. NLW 203433C/1551.
24. Riddell, *War Diaries*, p. 32.
25. Grigg, *From Peace to War*, p. 164.
26. Rowland, *David Lloyd George*, p. 286.
27. Taylor, A. J. P. (ed.), *Lloyd George*, p. 2.
28. Ibid.
29. Ibid.
30. Morgan (ed.), *Family Letters*, 11 August 1914, p. 169.
31. Grigg, *From Peace to War*, p. 169.
32. Morgan (ed.), *Family Letters*, 30 October 1914, p. 174.
33. George, William, *My Brother and I*, p. 248.
34. Grigg, *From Peace to War*, p. 175.
35. Rowland, *David Lloyd George*, p. 289 note.
36. Morgan (ed.), *Family Letters*, 28 October 1914, p. 174.
37. Ibid., 30 October 1914.
38. Ibid.
39. Rowland, *David Lloyd George*, p. 286.
40. Lloyd George, David, *War Memoirs*, Vol. I, pp. 74–6.
41. Ibid., pp. 84–5.
42. Morgan (ed.), *Family Letters*, 10 September 1914, p. 174.
43. Keegan, John, *The First World War*, p. 146.
44. Gilbert, *David Lloyd George*, p. 293.
45. Lloyd George, David, *War Memoirs*, Vol. I, p. 219.
46. Churchill, Randolph, S., and Martin Gilbert, *Winston Churchill*, Vol. III, p. 311.
47. Lloyd George, David, *War Memoirs*, Vol. I, p. 248.
48. Jenkins, *Asquith*, p. 371.
49. Ibid., p. 338.
50. Nicolson, Harold, *King George V*, p. 262.
51. Ibid., p. 269.
52. Oxford and Asquith, *Fifty Years of Parliament*, p. 72.
53. Jenkins, *Asquith*, p. 336.
54. NLW FCF2/1, 23 February 1915.
55. *Daily Citizen*, 22 March 1915.
56. Taylor, A. J. P. (ed.), *Lloyd George*, p. 235.
57. Ibid.
58. DLG Papers, British Library, C/5/7/18.
59. Beaverbrook, *Politicians and the War*, p. 162.
60. Oxford and Asquith, *Fifty Years of Parliament*, p. 68.
61. Riddell, *War Diaries*, p. 65.
62. *Letters to Venetia Stanley*, p. 517, quoted in Grigg, *From Peace to War*, p. 247.
63. *Letters to Venetia Stanley*, p. 519, quoted in ibid.
64. Keegan, *The First World War*, p. 212.
65. Taylor, A. J. P. (ed.), *Lloyd George*, 4 May 1915, p. 40.
66. Beaverbrook, *Politicians and the War*, p. 85.
67. *The Times*, 14 May 1915.

68. Riddell, *War Diaries*, p. 93.
69. Lloyd George, David, *War Memoirs*, Vol. I, p. 135.
70. Riddell, *War Diaries*, p. 93.
71. Blake, *The Unknown Prime Minister*, p. 24.
72. Lloyd George, David, *War Memoirs*, Vol. I, p. 135.
73. Ibid., p. 136.
74. Ibid.

CHAPTER 25: ARMS AND THE MAN

1. Taylor, A. J. P. (ed.), *Lloyd George*, p. 52.
2. Ibid., p. 51.
3. Ibid., p. 52.
4. Oxford and Asquith, *Fifty Years of Parliament*, 25 May 1915, quoted in Grigg, *From Peace to War*, p. 255.
5. NLW 22515P.
6. HofL F/41/5/2, 28 December 1916.
7. Judith Loades (ed.), *The Life and Times of David Lloyd George*, p. 88.
8. Ibid., p. 91.
9. Ibid., p. 73.
10. Ibid.
11. Grigg, *From Peace to War*, p. 264.
12. Ibid., p. 265.
13. Ibid.
14. Hansard, Vol. LXXXI, cols. 118–76.
15. Grigg, *From Peace to War*, p. 266.
16. Ibid., p. 266.
17. Kirkwood, David, *My Life in Revolt*, p. 107.
18. Ibid., p. 111.
19. Grigg, *From Peace to War*, p. 300.
20. Hansard, Vol. LXXXVII, col. 121, 20 December 1915.
21. Taylor, A. J. P. (ed.), *Lloyd George*, 29 December 1915, p. 87.
22. Lloyd George, David, *War Memoirs*, Vol. I, p. 432.
23. Roskill, S. W., *Hankey: Man of Secrets*, Vol. I, p. 227.
24. Ibid.
25. Lloyd George, David, *Through Terror to Triumph: Speeches and Pronouncements of the Right Honourable David Lloyd George.*
26. Morgan (ed.), *Family Letters*, 27 December 1915, p. 180.
27. Ibid., 28 December 1915, p. 181.
28. Taylor, A. J. P. (ed.), *Lloyd George*, 17 February 1916, p. 100.
29. Ibid., 23 February 1916, p. 102.
30. Ibid.
31. Ibid., 17 April 1916, p. 105.
32. Jenkins, *Asquith*, p. 374.
33. Grigg, *From Peace to War*, p. 337.

34. Ibid., p. 338.
35. Ibid.
36. Churchill, Randolph, S., and Martin Gilbert, *Winston Churchill*, Vol. III, p. 685.
37. Ibid., p. 623.
38. Grigg, *From Peace to War*, p. 321.
39. Briggs, Asa, *Seebohm Rowntree*, p. 177.
40. Ibid.
41. Taylor, A. J. J. (ed.), *Lloyd George*, 11 March 1915, p. 33.
42. Ibid., 13 March 1915, p. 42.
43. Ibid., 24 April 1915, p. 54.
44. Ibid., 19 October 1915, p. 11.
45. Ibid., p. 12.
46. Taylor, A. J. P. (ed.), *My Darling Pussy*, p. 12.
47. Ibid.
48. Ibid.
49. Taylor A. J. P. (ed.), *My Darling Pussy*, p. 14.
50. Ibid.
51. Ibid.
52. Ibid.
53. Taylor, A. J. P. (ed.), *Lloyd George*, p. 36.
54. Grigg, *From Peace to War*, p. 294.
55. Churchill, Winston, *The World Crisis*, quoted in Grigg, *From Peace to War*, p. 307.
56. Ibid.
57. Grigg, *From Peace to War*, p. 311.
58. Ibid.
59. German source quoted in Keegan, *The First World War*, p. 218.
60. Keegan, *The First World War*, p. 310.
61. Blake, *The Unknown Prime Minister*, p. 264.
62. Taylor, A. J. P. (ed.), *Lloyd George*, p. 39.
63. Riddell, *War Diaries*, 19 March 1916, p. 166.
64. Taylor, A. J. P. (ed.), *Lloyd George*, 23 August 1916.
65. Riddell, *War Diaries*, 19 March 1916, p. 166.
66. Jenkins, *Asquith*, p. 399.
67. Riddell, *War Diaries*, 27 May 1916, p. 184.
68. Clarke, Ed, *A Good Innings*, p. 152.
69. Riddell, *War Diaries*, 27 May 1916, p. 184.
70. Taylor, A. J. P. (ed.), *Lloyd George*, 26 July 1916, p. 109.
71. Riddell, *War Diaries*, 27 May 1916, p. 185.
72. Taylor, A. J. P. (ed.), *Lloyd George*, 26 July 1916, p. 109.
73. Ibid., 28 July 1916, p. 110.
74. Jenkins, *Asquith*, p. 399.
75. Rowland, *David Lloyd George*, p. 340.
76. Ibid.
77. Jenkins, *Asquith*, p. 410.

78. Frances Stevenson, *Lloyd George: A Diary*, 28 June 1916, p. 110.
79. Grigg, *From War to Peace*, p. 377.
80. Ibid.
81. Haig, Douglas, *War Diaries and Letters*, 17 September 1916, p. 232.
82. Grigg, *From Peace to War*, p. 381.
83. Ibid., p. 382.
84. Grigg, *From Peace to War*, p. 390.
85. Ibid.
86. *The Times*, 29 November 1916.
87. Rowland, *David Lloyd George*, p. 346.
88. Ibid.
89. *The Times*, 29 September 1916.

CHAPTER 26: THE FALL OF THE ROMAN EMPEROR

1. Jenkins, *Asquith*, p. 417.
2. Hansard, Vol. LXXV, col. 533, 2 November 1915.
3. Lloyd George, David, *War Memoirs*, Vol. I, p. 574.
4. Ibid., p. 575.
5. Ibid.
6. Blake, *The Unknown Prime Minister*, p. 292.
7. Riddell, *War Diaries*, 26 November 1916, p. 222.
8. Ibid.
9. Beaverbrook, *Politicians and the War*, p. 340.
10. Ibid.
11. Ibid., p. 336.
12. Jenkins, *Asquith*, p. 418.
13. Beaverbrook, *Politicians and the War*, p. 343.
14. Ibid., p. 357.
15. Ibid.
16. Asquith, *Memories and Reflections*, Vol. II, p. 158.
17. Cassar, George, *Asquith as War Leader*, p. 99.
18. Taylor, A. J. P. (ed.), *Lloyd George*, 8 August 16, p. 113.
19. Morgan (ed.), *Family Letters*, p. 183.
20. Beaverbrook, *Politicians and the War*, p. 360.
21. Jenkins, *Asquith*, p. 427.
22. Blake, *The Unknown Prime Minister*, p. 369.
23. Beaverbrook, *Politicians and the War*, p. 389.
24. Ibid., p. 398.
25. Ibid., p. 406.
26. Ibid., p. 420.
27. Ibid., p. 411.
28. Ibid., p. 413.
29. Blake, *The Unknown Prime Minister*, p. 316.
30. Gilmour, David, *Curzon*, p. 455.

31. Blake, *The Unknown Prime Minister*, p. 315.
32. Ibid., p. 320.
33. Ibid.
34. Beaverbrook, *Politicians and the War*, p. 430.
35. Jenkins, *Asquith*, p. 442.
36. Ibid.
37. Jenkins, *Asquith*, p. 442.
38. Beaverbrook, *Politicians and the War*, p. 435.
39. Gilmour, David, *Curzon*, p. 455.
40. Ibid.
41. Beaverbrook, *Politicians and the War*, p. 454.
42. Ibid., p. 456.
43. Ibid., p. 461.
44. Ibid., p. 466.
45. Ibid.
46. Jenkins, *Asquith*, p. 453.
47. Chamberlain, A., *Down the Years*, p. 124.
48. Beaverbrook, *Politicians and the War*, p. 476.
49. Ibid., p. 481.
50. Jenkins, *Asquith*, p. 456.
51. Ibid., p. 457.
52. Dugdale, *Arthur James Balfour*, p. 125.
53. Taylor, A. J. P. (ed.), *Lloyd George*, p. 133.
54. Addison, Christopher, *Politics from Within*, quoted in Morgan, Kenneth O., *The Age of Lloyd George*, p. 178.
55. Adams, R. J. Q., *Balfour: The Last Grandee*, p. 321.
56. Beaverbrook, *Politicians and the War*, p. 502.
57. Adams, *Balfour*, p. 327.
58. Mead, Gary, *The Good Soldier*, p. 234.
59. Riddell, *War Diaries*, p. 228.

CHAPTER 27: FRONTAL ASSAULTS

1. Rowland, *David Lloyd George*, p. 457.
2. Mead, *The Good Soldier*, p. 120.
3. Ibid., p. 159.
4. Ibid., p. 263.
5. Lloyd George, David, *War Memoirs*, Vol. I, p. 609.
6. Ibid., p. 610.
7. Blake, *The Unknown Prime Minister*, p. 343.
8. Lloyd George, David, *War Memoirs*, Vol. I, p. 613.
9. Grigg, John, *Lloyd George: War Leader*, p. 14.
10. Gilbert, *David Lloyd George*, p. 384.
11. Rowland, *David Lloyd George*, p. 383.
12. Ibid., p. 387.

13. George, William, *My Brother and I*, p. 257.
14. Cassar, *Lloyd George at War*, p. 87.
15. Taylor, A. J. P. (ed.), *Lloyd George*, 10 January 1917, p. 137.
16. Ibid.
17. Ibid.,12 January 1917.
18. Hankey Diaries, Churchill Archive Centre, 17 January 1917.
19. Spears, E. L., *Prelude to Victory*, p. 31.
20. Keegan, *The First World War*, p. 350.
21. Taylor, A. J. P. (ed.), *Lloyd George*, 15 January 1917, p. 139.
22. Ibid.
23. Haig, *War Diaries and Letters*, p. 267.
24. *Blackwoods' Magazine*, July 1945, quoted in Mead, *The Good Soldier*, p. 277.
25. Sauvigny despatch of 16 February 1917, quoted in Mead, *The Good Soldier*, p. 278.
26. Cassar, *Lloyd George at War*, p. 93.
27. Taylor, A. J. P. (ed.), *Lloyd George*, 28 February 1917, p. 146.
28. Cassar, *Lloyd George at War*, p. 94.
29. Ibid.
30. Frances Stevenson, *Lloyd George: A Diary*, p. 146.
31. Mead, *The Good Soldier*, p. 280.
32. Haig, *War Diaries and Letters*, 27 February 1917, p. 272.
33. Ibid.
34. Mead, *The Good Soldier*, p. 281.
35. Haig, *War Diaries and Letters*, 7 February 1917, p. 269.
36. Cassar, *Lloyd George at War*, p. 95.
37. Keegan, *The First World War*, p. 352.
38. Lloyd George, David, *War Memoirs*, Vol. II, pp. 688–92.
39. PRO Cab, 42/23/11.
40. Cassar, George, *Lloyd George at War*, p. 163.
41. Hankey, Maurice, *Supreme Command*, Vol. II, p. 648.
42. Cassar, *Lloyd George at War*, p. 107.
43. Hankey Diaries, Churchill Archive Centre, 30 April 1917.
44. Lloyd George, David, *War Memoirs*, Vol. II, p. 682.
45. Ibid., p. 690.
46. George, William, *My Brother and I*, p. 241.
47. Riddell, *War Diaries*, p. 245.
48. Rose, Kenneth, *King George V*, p. 209.
49. Ibid., p. 211.
50. *The Times*, 5 March 1917.
51. George, William, *My Brother and I*, p. 258.
52. Stevenson, *Lloyd George: A Diary*, 1 March 1917, p. 147.
53. Jones, Thomas, *Whitehall Diary*, Vol. I, p. 40.
54. Stevenson, *Lloyd George: A Diary*, 23 April 1917, p. 153.
55. Ibid.

CHAPTER 28: A WAY ROUND

1. Blake, *The Unknown Prime Minister*, p. 343.
2. MacLeod, I., *Neville Chamberlain*, p. 57.
3. Lloyd George, David, *The Truth about the Peace Treaties*, p. 261.
4. George, William, *My Brother and I*, 30 March 1917, p. 258.
5. Rowland, *David Lloyd George*, p. 408.
6. Lloyd George, David, *War Memoirs*, Vol. II, p. 1367.
7. Sylvester, A. J., *Life with Lloyd George*, p. 80.
8. Taylor, A. J. P. (ed.), *Lloyd George*, 12 May 1917, p. 157.
9. Grigg, *War Leader*, p. 96.
10. Haig, *War Diaries and Letters*, 5 May 1917, p. 292.
11. Grigg, *War Leader*, p. 97.
12. Haig, *War Diaries and Letters*, p. 292.
13. Grigg, *War Leader*, p. 158.
14. Ibid., p. 160.
15. Churchill, Randolph, *Lord Derby*, p. 273.
16. Lloyd George, David, *War Memoirs*, Vol. II, p. 1272.
17. Ibid.
18. Ibid., p. 1287.
19. Taylor, A. J. P. (ed.), *Lloyd George*, 19 May 1917, p. 158.
20. Blake, *The Unknown Prime Minister*, p. 361.
21. Ibid.
22. Lloyd George, David, *War Memoirs*, Vol. II, p. 1370.
23. Ibid., p. 1414.
24. Blake, *The Private Papers of Douglas Haig, 1914–1919*, p. 251.
25. Keegan, *The First World War*, p. 388.
26. Lloyd George, David, *War Memoirs*, Vol. II, p. 1382.
27. Taylor, A. J. P. (ed.), *My Darling Pussy*, p. 21.
28. Keegan, *The First World War*, p. 394.
29. Grigg, *War Leader*, p. 274.

CHAPTER 29: THE MAN WHO WON THE WAR

1. Haig, *War Diaries and Letters*, 4 November 1917, p. 338.
2. Ibid.
3. *The Times*, 19 November 1917.
4. Hansard, Vol. VCX, col. 893.
5. Grigg, *War Leader*, p. 311.
6. George, William, *My Brother and I*, p. 258.
7. Adams, *Balfour*, p. 332.
8. Grigg, *War Leader*, p. 348.
9. HofL F/4/2/14, 20 October 1917.
10. *Daily Telegraph*, 29 November 1917.

11. Rowland, *David Lloyd George*, pp. 405, 425.
12. Taylor, A. J. P., *English History 1914–45*, p. 97.
13. Grigg, *War Leader*, p. 414.
14. Haig, *War Diaries and Letters*, 9 February 1918, p. 380.
15. Grigg, *War Leader*, p. 418.
16. Grigg, *War Leader*, p. 414.
17. Haig, *War Diaries and Letters*, 14 March 1918, p. 387.
18. Ibid., 3 March 1918, p. 385.
19. Keegan, *The First World War*, p. 427.
20. Haig, *War Diaries and Letters*, 21 March 1918, p. 390.
21. Grigg, *War Leader*, p. 445.
22. Morgan (ed.), *Family Letters*, 28 June 1918, p. 186.
23. Riddell, *War Diaries*, p. 318.
24. Ibid.
25. Hansard, Vol. CIV, col. 1364, 9 April 1918.
26. Ibid.
27. Grigg, *War Leader*, p. 493.
28. Hansard, Vol. CV, col. 2341, 9 May 1918.
29. Adams, R. J. Q., *Bonar Law*, p. 268.
30. Riddell, *War Diaries*, 12 May 1918, p. 330.
31. Mead, Gary, *The Doughboys*, p. 221, quoted in Grigg, *War Leader*, p. 526.
32. *The Times*, 1 June 1918.
33. Haig, *War Diaries and Letters*, p. 415.
34. Grigg, *War Leader*, p. 542.
35. Ibid., p. 553.
36. Haig, *War Diaries and Letters*, 23 July 1918, p. 433.
37. Keegan, *The First World War*, p. 439.
38. Ludendorff, *War Memoirs*, p. 677, quoted in Lloyd George, David, *War Memoirs*, Vol. II, p. 1851.
39. Ibid.
40. Owen, *Tempestuous Journey*, p. 500.
41. Grigg, *War Leader*, p. 567.
42. Rose, *King George V*, p. 211.
43. Ibid., p. 212.
44. Taylor, A. J. P. (ed.), *My Darling Pussy*, p. 25.
45. Roskill, *Hankey*, p. 585.
46. Hankey Diaries, Churchill Archive Centre, 26 August 1918.
47. Lloyd George, David, *War Memoirs*, Vol. II, p. 1958.
48. HofL, Bonar Law Papers, Box 70, War Cab 491B, 24 October 1918, quoted in Grigg, *War Leader*, p. 624.
49. Hattersley, Roy, *Borrowed Time*, p. 2.
50. Haig, *War Diaries and Letters*, 30 November 1918, p. 489.

CHAPTER 30: A LAND FIT FOR HEROES

1. Riddell, *War Diaries*, p. 309.
2. Ibid., p. 509.
3. Taylor, A. J. P., *English History 1914–45*, p. 109.
4. Ibid.
5. Ibid.
6. Morgan, Kenneth O., *Consensus and Disunity*, p. 24.
7. McKenzie, N. (ed.), *The Diary of Beatrice Webb*, Vol. III, p. 299.
8. Grigg, *War Leader*, p. 511.
9. Morgan, *Consensus and Disunity*, p. 2.
10. Fisher, H. A. L., *Unfinished Autobiography*, p. 135.
11. Reynolds and Judge, *The Night the Police Went on Strike*, p. 70.
12. Ibid.
13. Riddell, *War Diaries*, p. 349.
14. Blake, *The Unknown Prime Minister*, p. 385.
15. Ibid.
16. Ibid.
17. Morgan, *Consensus and Disunity*, p. 21.
18. Ibid., p. 9.
19. Ibid., p. 27.
20. Rowland, *David Lloyd George*, p. 473.
21. HofL F/1/4/8/a.
22. Ibid.
23. NLW 20473C.
24. Jenkins, *Asquith*, p. 474.
25. Churchill, Randolph S. and Martin Gilbert, *Winston Churchill*, Vol. IV, p. 159.
26. Ibid.
27. Jenkins, *Winston Churchill*, p. 335.
28. Ibid., p. 336.
29. Blake, *The Unknown Prime Minister*, p. 382.
30. Ibid., p. 387.
31. *The Times,* 13 November 1918.
32. Rowland, *David Lloyd George*, p. 460.
33. Ibid.
34. Ibid., p. 474.
35. *The Times,* 25 November 1918.
36. Morgan, *Consensus and Disunity*, p. 40.
37. Rowland, *David Lloyd George*, p. 461.

CHAPTER 31: SPOILS TO THE VICTORS

1. Skidelsky, Robert, *John Maynard Keynes*, p. 234.
2. Sharp, Alan, *The Versailles Settlement*, p. 37.
3. Keynes, J. M., *Essay in Biography*, p. 36.
4. Skidelsky, *John Maynard Keynes*, p. 239.
5. Ibid., p. 240.
6. Sharp, *The Versailles Settlement*, p. 11.
7. Lloyd George, David, *War Memoirs*. Vol. II, p. 1980.
8. Ibid.
9. Owen, *Tempestuous Journey*, p. 535.
10. Lloyd George, David, *War Memoirs*, Vol. II, p. 536.
11. Taylor, A. J. P. (ed.), *Lloyd George*, p. 175.
12. Lloyd George, Frances, *The Years That Are Past*, p. 165.
13. Macmillan, Margaret, *Peacemakers*, p. 42.
14. Ibid.
15. Sharp, *The Versailles Settlement*, p. 11.
16. Skidelsky, *John Maynard Keynes*, p. 240.
17. Ibid., p. 244.
18. Macmillan, *Peacemakers*, p. 193.
19. Rowland, *David Lloyd George*, p. 470.
20. Lloyd George, David, *War Memoirs*.
21. Macmillan, *Peacemakers*, p. 195.
22. Rowland, *David Lloyd George*, p. 488.
23. Macmillan, *Peacemakers*, p. 200.
24. House Diary, Yale Library, quoted in ibid.
25. Skidelsky, *John Maynard Keynes*, p. 227.
26. Ibid.
27. HofL E/3/4/2, 8 January 1919.
28. Owen, *Tempestuous Journey*, p. 524.
29. Riddell, Lord, *Lord Riddell's Intimate Diary of the Peace Conference and after 1918–1923*, p. 83.
30. Lloyd George, *The Truth about the Peace Treaties*, Vol. I, p. 403.
31. Taylor, A. J. P. (ed.), *Lloyd George*, 24 March 1919, p. 175.
32. Skidelsky, *John Maynard Keynes*, p. 227.
33. Macmillan, *Peacemakers*, p. 208.
34. Ibid.
35. Hattersley, *Borrowed Time*, p. 22.
36. Ibid.
37. Owen, *Tempestuous Journey*, p. 500.
38. Macmillan, *Peacemakers*, p. 80.
39. Ibid., p. 81.
40. Hattersley, *Borrowed Time*, p. 19.
41. Macmillan, *Peacemakers*, p. 83.
42. HofL F/3/5.4, 10 January 1919.

43. Macmillan, *Peacemakers*, p. 84.
44. Ibid., p. 86.
45. Rowland, *David Lloyd George*, p. 511.
46. HofL F/21/2/47.
47. Riddell, *Intimate Diaries*, p. 21.
48. Churchill, *Aftermath*, p. 176.
49. Riddell, *Intimate Diaries*, p. 42.
50. Lloyd George, David, *The Truth about the Peace Treaties*, Vol. I, p. 536.
51. Hansard, Vol. CXIV, col. 1338, 2 April 1919.
52. Blake, *The Unknown Prime Minister*, p. 407.
53. Rowland, *David Lloyd George*, p. 489.
54. Hansard, Vol. CXIV, col. 2952, 16 April 1919.
55. Rowland, *David Lloyd George*, p. 490.
56. Hansard, Vol. CXIV, col. 3052, 16 April 1919.
57. Ibid.
58. Taylor, A. J. P. (ed.), *Lloyd George*, 16 April 1919, p. 180.
59. Macmillan, *Peacemakers*, p. 469.
60. Taylor, A. J. P. (ed.), *Lloyd George*, 8 June 1919, p. 163.
61. Lloyd George, *The Truth about the Peace Treaties,* Vol. I, p. 481.
62. Macmillan, *Peacemakers*, p. 478.
63. Ibid.
64. NLW F/36/4/17, Joseph Ward (Deputy Prime Minister of New Zealand), Paris, 2 May 1919.
65. Macmillan, *Peacemakers*, p. 480.
66. Skidelsky, *John Maynard Keynes*, p. 241.
67. Nicolson, Harold, *Peacemaking*, p. 350.
68. Ibid., p. 187.

CHAPTER 32: THE PERILS OF PEACE

1. Riddell, *Intimate Diaries*, p. 179.
2. Ibid.
3. Rowland, *David Lloyd George*, p. 512.
4. Ibid., p. 532.
5. Adams, *Balfour*, p. 341.
6. Tawney, R. H., 'Abolition of Economic Controls', *Economic History Review*, Vol. XIII.
7. Taylor, A. J. P. (ed.), *Lloyd George*, 18 March 1919, p. 173.
8. Masterman, Lucy, *C. F. G. Masterman*, p. 211.
9. Morgan, *Consensus and Disunity*, p. 49.
10. Jones, Thomas, *Whitehall Diary*, Vol. I, p. 94.
11. Morgan, *Consensus and Disunity*, p. 49.
12. Riddell, *Intimate Diaries*, p. 242.
13. Ibid., p. 35.
14. Ibid., p. 33.

15. Ibid., p. 49.
16. Hansard Vol. CXXXIII, col. 893.
17. Frances Stevenson, *Lloyd George: A Diary*, p. 191.
18. Skidelsky, *John Maynard Keynes*, p. 219.
19. *The Times*, 29 September 1919.
20. Morgan (ed.), *Family Letters*, p. 191.
21. Riddell, *Intimate Diaries*, p. 69.
22. Ibid.
23. Roskill, *Hankey*, Vol. II, p. 145.
24. Ibid., p. 148.
25. Morgan, *Consensus and Disunity*, p. 70.
26. Ibid., p. 71.
27. Ibid.
28. Hattersley, *Borrowed Time*, p. 118.
29. Jones, *Whitehall Diary*, Vol. I, 13 April 1921, p. 146.
30. Morgan, *Consensus and Disunity*, p. 73.
31. PRO CAB/63/29.
32. Rowland, *David Lloyd George*, p. 578.
33. HofL F/1/8/33.
34. Riddell, *Intimate Diaries*, p. 49.
35. Ibid., pp. 164–5.
36. Ibid., p. 165.
37. Taylor, A. J. P. (ed.), *Lloyd George*, p. 200.
38. Ibid.
39. Rowland, *David Lloyd George*, p. 510.
40. Hattersley, *Borrowed Time*, p. 208.
41. Beaverbrook, *The Decline and Fall of Lloyd George*, Appendix 30, p. 272.
42. Rowland, *David Lloyd George*, p. 538.
43. Beaverbrook, Lord, *Men and Power*, p. 400.
44. Donoughue and Jones, *Herbert Morrison*, p. 49.
45. Ibid., p. 543.
46. HofL FLS/6/1.
47. Hansard, Vol. CXLVII, col. 96, 19 October 1921.
48. Morgan, *Consensus and Disunity*, p. 272.
49. Rowland, *David Lloyd George*, p. 563.

CHAPTER 33: GOD HELP POOR IRELAND

1. Kee, *The Green Flag*, p. 611.
2. Morgan, *Consensus and Disunity*, p. 126.
3. Kee, *The Green Flag*, p. 615.
4. HofL F/45/6/13, 10 November 1918.
5. *Irish Times*, 23 December 1918.
6. Coogan, Tim Pat, *Michael Collins*, p. 123.

7. Kee, *The Green Flag*, p. 668.
8. *The Irish Times*, 22 December 1918.
9. Ibid., 22 January 1919.
10. Ibid., 1 May 1920.
11. Rose, *King George V*, p. 238.
12. PRO CAB/23/23.
13. *The Irish Times*, 11 October 1920.
14. Owen, *Tempestuous Journey*, p. 562.
15. *The Irish Times*, 18 October 1920.
16. Kee, *The Green Flag*, p. 693.
17. Coogan, *Michael Collins*, p. 186.
18. HofL F/36/2/14 and F/30/2/8.
19. HofL F/36/2/14.
20. PRO CAB/23/23.
21. Hammond, J. L., *Scott of the Manchester Guardian*, pp. 271ff.
22. Morgan, *Consensus and Disunity*, p. 128.
23. Kee, *The Green Flag*, p. 719.
24. Rose, *King George V*, p. 239.
25. Ibid., p. 240.
26. Coogan, *Michael Collins*, p. 235.
27. Taylor, A. J. P. (ed.), *Lloyd George*, p. 221.
28. Ibid.
29. Ibid., p. 223.
30. Ibid., 22 June 1921, p. 224.
31. Ibid.
32. Ibid., 24 June 1921, p. 224.
33. Longford, Frank and O'Neill, T. P., *De Valera*, p. 326.
34. Owen, *Tempestuous Journey*, p. 578.
35. Coogan, Tim Pat, *Michael Collins*, p. 234.
36. Williamson, Philip and Edward Baldwin (eds), *Baldwin Papers 1908–1947*, 8 September 1921, p. 55.
37. Ibid., p. 56.
38. Taylor, A. J. P. (ed.), *Lloyd George*, 28 October 1922, p. 234.
39. Beaverbrook, *The Decline and Fall of Lloyd George*, p. 84.
40. Hattersley, *Borrowed Time*, p. 58.
41. NLW 20462C.
42. Blake, *The Unknown Prime Minister*, p. 432.
43. Ibid.
44. Jones, *Whitehall Diary*, Vol. I, p. 168.
45. Beaverbrook, *The Decline and Fall of Lloyd George*, p. 97.
46. Jones, *Whitehall Diary*, Vol. I, p. 169.
47. Kee, *The Green Flag*, p. 727.
48. Ibid.
49. Hattersley, *Borrowed Time*, p. 60.
50. Longford and O'Neill, *De Valera*, p. 165.
51. Ibid., p. 166.

52. Sylvester, A. J., *The Real Lloyd George*, p. 271.
53. Blake, *The Unknown Prime Minister*, p. 435.

CHAPTER 34: THROWN TO THE WOLVES

1. Hardinge of Penshurst, *Old Diplomacy*, p. 240.
2. Morgan, *Consensus and Disunity*, p. 122.
3. Rowland, *David Lloyd George*, p. 568.
4. Owen, *Tempestuous Journey*, p. 600.
5. Beaverbrook, *The Decline and Fall of Lloyd George*, p. 49.
6. Cabinet minutes quoted in Morgan, *Consensus and Disunity*, p. 306.
7. Riddell, *Intimate Diaries*, p. 368.
8. Frances Stevenson, *Lloyd George: A Diary*, 3 February 1922, p. 241.
9. Rowland, *David Lloyd George*, p. 570.
10. *The Times*, 18 March 1922.
11. Owen, *Tempestuous Journey*, p. 610.
12. Morgan, *Consensus and Disunity*, p. 310.
13. Ibid., p. 322.
14. Gilmour, *Curzon*, p. 543.
15. Ibid., p. 546.
16. Riddell, *Intimate Diaries*, p. 388.
17. Rowland, *David Lloyd George*, p. 581.
18. Ibid., p. 582.
19. Ibid., p. 568.
20. Blake, *The Unknown Prime Minister*, p. 447.
21. NLW 20437C.

CHAPTER 35: NEMESIS

1. HofL F/3/5/4.
2. Hague, *The Pain and the Privilege*, p. 384.
3. Beaverbrook, *The Decline and Fall of Lloyd George*, p. 69.
4. Jones, *Whitehall Diary*, Vol. I, p. 197.
5. Rowland, *David Lloyd George*, p. 557.
6. Blake, *The Unknown Prime Minister*, p. 407.
7. Rowland, *David Lloyd George*, p. 557.
8. NLW, Herbert Lewis Papers.
9. Riddell, *Intimate Diaries*, p. 352.
10. Campbell, John, *Lloyd George: The Goat in the Wilderness*, p. 189.
11. Chamberlain, *Down the Years*, p. 181.
12. Williamson and Edwin (eds), *Baldwin Papers*, 17 January 1922, p. 61.
13. Ibid., p. 62.
14. Blake, *The Unknown Prime Minister*, p. 438.
15. HofLF/7/5/6.

16. Blake, *The Unknown Prime Minister*, p. 439.
17. Ibid., p. 440.
18. Rowland, *David Lloyd George*, p. 575.
19. Ibid.
20. Morgan, *Consensus and Disunity*, p. 539.
21. Blake, *The Unknown Prime Minister*, p. 442.
22. Riddell, *Intimate Diaries*, p. 244.
23. Jones, *Whitehall Diary*, Vol. I, p. 197.
24. Taylor, A. J. P. (ed.), *Lloyd George*, 22 June 1922, p. 242.
25. Ibid., 26 June 1922, p. 243.
26. *Evening Standard*, 12 August 1922.
27. Rowland, *David Lloyd George*, p. 572.
28. Jones, *Whitehall Diary*, Vol. I, p. 207.
29. Beaverbrook, *The Decline and Fall of Lloyd George*, p. 178.
30. Blake, *The Unknown Prime Minister*, p. 451.
31. Beaverbrook, *The Decline and Fall of Lloyd George*, p. 175.
32. Ibid.
33. Ibid., p. 182.
34. Ibid.
35. Middlemass, Keith and Barnes, John, *Baldwin*, p. 119.
36. *Observer*, 8 October 1922.
37. Middlemass and Barnes, *Baldwin*, p. 121.
38. Blake, *The Unknown Prime Minister*, p. 455.
39. Ibid.
40. Gilmour, *Curzon*, p. 552.
41. Blake, *The Unknown Prime Minister*, p. 455.
42. Beaverbrook, *The Decline and Fall of Lloyd George*, p. 198.
43. Middlemass and Barnes, *Baldwin*, p. 121.
44. Ibid., p. 123.
45. Blake, *The Unknown Prime Minister*, p. 457.
46. Morgan (ed.), *Family Letters*, 25 October 1922, p. 197.
47. Jones, *Whitehall Diary*, Vol. I, p. 192.
48. Ibid.
49. Rowland, *David Lloyd George*, p. 587.

CHAPTER 36: THE RADICAL'S RETURN

1. Rowland, *David Lloyd George*, p. 612.
2. Snow, C. P., *Variety of Men*, p. 111, quoted in Campbell, *The Goat in the Wilderness*.
3. Campbell, *The Goat in the Wilderness*, p. 40.
4. Morgan (ed.), *Family Letters*, late November, p. 200.
5. Ibid.
6. *The Times*, 21 October 1922.
7. Jones, *Whitehall Diary*, Vol. I, p. 219.

8. Morgan (ed.), *Family Letters*, p. 197.
9. Jones, *Whitehall Diary*, Vol. I, p. 240.
10. Ibid.
11. Griffiths, D., *Fleet Street: Five Hundred Years of the Press*, p. 221.
12. Hattersley, *Borrowed Time*, p. 366.
13. Middlemass and Barnes, *Baldwin*, p. 227.
14. Campbell, *The Goat in the Wilderness*, p. 47.
15. Taylor, A. J. P., *Beaverbrook*, p. 218.
16. Owen, *Tempestuous Journey*, p. 674.
17. Blake, *The Unknown Prime Minister*, p. 465.
18. *Liberal Magazine*, December 1922.
19. Campbell, *The Goat in the Wilderness*, p. 61.
20. *Daily Chronicle*, 20 January 1923.
21. Hansard, Vol. CLIX, col. 1598, 5 December 1922.
22. *Letters of the Earl of Oxford and Asquith*, 1922–27, pp. 39–40.
23. *Observer*, 25 November 1923.
24. *The Times*, 19 November 1923.
25. *Morning Post*, 19 November 1923.
26. *Daily Chronicle*, 15 December 1923.
27. Campbell, *The Goat in the Wilderness*, p. 78.
28. C. P. Scott's diary, quoted in Rowland, *David Lloyd George*, p. 605.
29. Ibid.
30. Morgan (ed.), *Family Letters*, 4 February 1924, p. 202.
31. Rowland, p. 608.
32. *Daily Chronicle*, 22 March 1924.
33. Hansard, Vol. CLXXI, col. 1607, 27 March 1924.
34. Hansard, Vol. CLXXVI, col. 3064, 6 August 1924.
35. PRO 30/69/1763, MacDonald Papers, quoted in C. J. Wrigley, *David Lloyd George and the British Labour Movement*, p. 52.
36. *Daily Herald*, 5 August 1924.
37. Cormick, Donald, *The Mask of Merlin*, p. 248.
38. HofL G/30/3/33.
39. Jenkins, *Asquith*, p. 505.
40. Owen, *Tempestuous Journey*, p. 685.
41. Taylor, A. J. P., *My Darling Pussy*, 12 August 1925, p. 86.
42. Ibid.
43. Ibid., p. 81.
44. Rowland, *David Lloyd George*, p. 613.
45. Hansard, Vol. CLXXVII, col. 1605.
46. Wrigley, *David Lloyd George and the British Labour Movement*, p. 58.
47. Hansard, Vol. CXXXIX, col. 233.
48. Bullock, Alan, *Ernest Bevin*, p. 78.
49. NLW 22528G.
50. Campbell, *The Goat in the Wilderness*, p. 141.
51. Ibid.
52. Hattersley, *Borrowed Time*, p. 132.

53. Rowland, *David Lloyd George*, p. 622.
54. Ibid.
55. HofL G/5/1/9.
56. Jenkins, *Asquith*, p. 515.
57. Taylor, A. J. P. (ed.), *Lloyd George*, 21 May 1926, p. 246.
58. HofL G/16/1/11.
59. Rowland, *David Lloyd George*, p. 627.
60. Lloyd George, Frances, *The Years That Are Past*, p. 218.
61. British Library G/8/13/7.

CHAPTER 37: NEW DEALS

1. Jenkins, *Asquith*, p. 516.
2. Ibid.
3. Campbell, *The Goat in the Wilderness*, p. 159.
4. Ibid.
5. Ibid., p. 160.
6. Lloyd George, Frances, *The Years That Are Past*, 15 May 1926, p. 246.
7. Wrigley, *David Lloyd George and the British Labour Movement*, p. 50.
8. HofL G/31/1/62, 8 December 1926.
9. Marquand, *Ramsay MacDonald*, p. 484.
10. Campbell, *The Goat in the Wilderness*, p. 83.
11. Skidelsky, *John Maynard Keynes*, Vol. II, p. 259.
12. Ibid.
13. Ibid., p. 258.
14. Campbell, *The Goat in the Wilderness*, p. 197.
15. Ibid., p. 200.
16. Hansard, Vol. CCXX, col. 1697, 22 July 1928.
17. Masterman, Lucy, *C. F. G. Masterman*, p. 345.
18. Taylor, A. J. P. (ed.), *My Darling Pussy*, 25 September 1928, p. 108.
19. Rowland, *David Lloyd George*, p. 637.
20. Hague, *The Pain and the Privilege*, p. 432.
21. Ibid., p. 433.
22. HofL G/15/7/5.
23. HofL G/18/3/6.
24. HofL G/18/7/6.
25. *The Times*, 2 March 1929.
26. Campbell, *The Goat in the Wilderness*, p. 221.
27. Ibid., p. 226.
28. Ibid.
29. Ibid.
30. Ibid.
31. HofL G/17/11/34.
32. Taylor, A. J. P. (ed.), *My Darling Pussy*, 22 January 1929, p. 114.
33. Ibid.

34. HofL FLS/4/1.
35. Taylor, A. J. P. (ed.), *My Darling Pussy*, 25 March 1929, p. 126.
36. Campbell, *The Goat in the Wilderness*, p. 235.
37. Ibid.
38. *The Times*, 29 May 1929.
39. Campbell, *The Goat in the Wilderness*, p. 239.
40. Jones, *Whitehall Diary*, Vol. II, p. 190.
41. Campbell, *The Goat in the Wilderness*, p. 247.
42. Ibid., p. 241.
43. Rowland, *David Lloyd George*, p. 666.
44. Marquand, *Ramsay MacDonald*, p. 527.
45. Middlemass and Barnes, *Baldwin*, p. 540.
46. Hansard, Vol. CCXXXV, col. 2469, 27 February 1930.
47. *Sunday Times*, 29 December 1929.
48. Jones, *Whitehall Diary*, Vol. II, p. 274.
49. Mosley, Oswald, *My Life*, p. 271.
50. Hansard, Vol. CCXXXVII, cols. 2937–45, 14 January 1930.
51. Marquand, *Ramsay MacDonald*, p. 529.
52. Ibid.
53. Campbell, *The Goat in the Wilderness*, p. 262.
54. Rowland, *David Lloyd George*, p. 693, Tenby, 25 October 1930.
55. *Daily Herald*, 16 May 1930.
56. Skidelsky, Robert, *Politicians and the Slump*, p. 363.
57. Rowland, *David Lloyd George*, p. 675.
58. Ibid., p. 676.
59. Hansard, Vol. CCLXXVIII, col. 725, 13 February 1931.
60. *Morning Post*, 14 February 1931.
61. Campbell, *The Goat in the Wilderness*, p. 283.
62. *The Times*, 16 April 1931.
63. Taylor, A. J. P. (ed.), *My Darling Pussy*, p. 130.
64. Campbell, *The Goat in the Wilderness*, p. 278.
65. Owen, *Tempestuous Journey*, p. 717.

CHAPTER 38: WANDERING IN THE WILDERNESS

1. Hague, *The Pain and the Privilege*, p. 465.
2. HofL G/28/2/2.
3. Sylvester, *Life with Lloyd George*, p. 40.
4. Campbell, *The Goat in the Wilderness*, p. 300.
5. Sylvester, *Life with Lloyd George*, 6 October 1931, p. 40.
6. Ibid., p. 86.
7. Ibid.
8. Ibid.
9. Riddell, *Intimate Diaries*.
10. NLWFLS/6/5.

11. Williamson and Baldwin (eds), *Baldwin Papers 1908–1947*, 12 June 1934, p. 321.
12. Ibid., 17 November 1934, p. 327.
13. Owen, *Tempestuous Journey*, p. 727.
14. Ibid., p. 728.
15. Ibid., p. 729.
16. Rowland, *David Lloyd George*, p. 738.
17. Ibid., p. 730.
18. Nicolson, Harold, *Diaries 1907–1963*, pp. 265–9.
19. *The Times*, 3 January 1939.
20. Thorpe, D. R., *The Life and Times of Anthony Eden*, p. 176.
21. Sylvester, *Diaries*, p. 269.
22. Sylvester, *Life with Lloyd George*, p. 148.
23. Hitler, Adolf, *Mein Kampf*, p. 396.
24. Rowland, *David Lloyd George*, p. 801.
25. *Daily Express*, 3 December 1935.
26. Owen, *Tempestuous Journey*, p. 737.
27. Ibid., p. 738.
28. Ibid.
29. Hansard, Vol. CCCXXV, col. 1589, 25 June 1937.
30. Owen, *Tempestuous Journey*, p. 742.
31. Hansard, Vol. CCCLI, col. 1870, 5 September 1939.
32. Owen, *Tempestuous Journey*, p. 744.
33. Sylvester, *Life with Lloyd George*, p. 239.
34. Ibid., p. 256.
35. Ibid., p. 259.
36. Ibid.
37. Ibid., p. 281.
38. Hague, *The Pain and the Privilege*, p. 469.
39. *Evening Standard*, 9 May 1940.
40. *Observer*, 29 October 1967.
41. Hansard, Vol. CCCLX, col. 1283, 9 May 1940.
42. Owen, *Tempestuous Journey*, p. 748.
43. Sylvester, *Life with Lloyd George*, p. 261.
44. Ibid., p. 262.
45. Owen, *Tempestuous Journey*, p. 748.
46. King, C., *With Malice towards None: A War Diary*, p. 27.
47. Sylvester, *Life with Lloyd George*, p. 267.
48. Jones, Thomas, *A Diary with Letters, 1931–1950*, p. 464.
49. Jennifer Stevenson, private collection.
50. Sylvester, *Life with Lloyd George*, p. 275.
51. Ibid., p. 277.
52. Rowland, *David Lloyd George*, p. 777.
53. Taylor, A. J. P. (ed.), *My Darling Pussy*, p. 238.
54. Hansard, Vol. CCCLXXI, col. 329, 7 May 1941.
55. Nicolson, Nigel (ed.), *The Harold Nicolson Diaries*, p. 273.

CHAPTER 39: PEACE AT LAST

1. Sylvester, *Life with Lloyd George*, p. 279.
2. Churchill, Winston, *The Second World War: Their Finest Hour*, p. 503.
3. Sylvester, *Life with Lloyd George*, p. 286.
4. Ibid., p. 287.
5. Ibid., p. 297.
6. Ibid., p. 305.
7. Ibid., p. 302.
8. Ibid., p. 306.
9. Ibid., p. 307.
10. Ibid., p. 314.
11. Lloyd George, Frances, *The Years That Are Past*, p. 275.
12. George, William, *My Brother and I*, p. 297.
13. Lloyd George, Frances, *The Years That Are Past*, p. 277.
14. Ibid.
15. Ibid.
16. Jones, *Whitehall Diary*, Vol. I, p. 206.

SELECT BIBLIOGRAPHY

(Asterisks denote several volumes. Date is of first volume.)

Adams, R. J. Q., *Balfour: The Last Grandee*, John Murray 2007
*Amery, Julian, *The Life of Joseph Chamberlain*, Macmillan 1951
Beaverbrook, Lord, *Politicians and the War*, Oldbourne Books 1960
— *The Decline and Fall of Lloyd George*, Collins 1963
Bell, G., *Randall Davidson, Archbishop of Canterbury*, Oxford University Press 1935
Blake, Robert *The Private Papers of Douglas Haig, 1914–1919*, Eyre and
    Spottiswoode 1952
— *The Unknown Prime Minister: The Life and Times of Andrew Bonar Law
    1858–1923*, Eyre and Spottiswoode 1955
Braithwaite, W. J., *Lloyd George's Ambulance Wagon*, H. N. Bunbury (ed.),
    Methuen 1957
Campbell, John, *If Love Were All*, Jonathan Cape 2006
— *Lloyd George: The Goat in the Wilderness 1922–1931*, Cape 1977
Cassar, George, *Asquith as War Leader*, Hambledon 1994
— *Lloyd George at War 1916–1918*, Anthem Press 2009
Chamberlain, Austen, *Politics from Inside*, Cassell 1936
*Churchill, Randolph S. and Martin Gilbert, *Winston S. Churchill*, Minerva
    1989
Churchill, Winston, *Great Contemporaries*, Odhams Press 1947
— *My Early Life*, Odhams Press 1949
*— *Life of Lord Randolph Churchill*, Heinemann 1966
Coogan, Tim Pat, *Michael Collins*, Hutchinson 1990
— *Eamon De Valera: The Man Who Was Ireland*, Hutchinson 1993
Dangerfield, G., *The Strange Death of Liberal England*, Harrison Smith 1935
David, Edward (ed.), *Inside Asquith's Cabinet: From the Diaries of Charles
    Hobhouse*, John Murray 1977
Davis, Walker W., *Lloyd George 1863–1914*, Constable 1939
*Du Parcq, Hubert, *The Life of David Lloyd George*, Caxton Publishing
    Company 1912
*Edwards, J. Hugh, *David Lloyd George: The Man and the Statesman*, Waverley 1929
Ensor, Robert, *England 1870–1914*, Oxford University Press 1936
*Fitzroy, Almeric, *Memoirs*, Hutchinson 1925
Fraser, D., *The Evolution of the British Welfare State*, Palgrave 1973

Gazeley, Ian, *Poverty in Britain 1900–1965*, Palgrave Macmillan 2003

George, W. R. P., *The Making of Lloyd George*, Faber and Faber 1970

— *Lloyd George Backbencher*, Gomer 1983

George, William, *My Brother and I*, Eyre and Spottiswood 1958

Gilbert, B. B., *David Lloyd George: A Political Life*, Batsford 1987

— *David Lloyd George: Architect of Change*, Batsford 1987

Gilmour, David, *Curzon*, John Murray 1994

Gollin, Alfred, *The Observer and J. L. Garvin 1908–1914*, Oxford University Press 1960

— *Balfour's Burden*, Blond 1965

Graham Jones, J., *David Lloyd George and Welsh Liberalism*, National Library of Wales 2010

Grigg, John, *The Young Lloyd George*, Eyre Methuen 1973

— *Lloyd George: The People's Champion 1902–1911*, Eyre Methuen 1978

— *Lloyd George: From Peace to War 1912–1916*, Eyre Methuen 1985

— *Lloyd George: War Leader*, Allen Lane 2002

Hague, Ffion, *The Pain and the Privilege*, HarperCollins 2008

Haig, Douglas, *Douglas Haig – War Diaries and Letters*, Gary Sheffield and John Bourne (eds), Weidenfeld and Nicolson 2005

Harrod, Roy, *The Life of John Maynard Keynes*, Macmillan 1951

Hattersley, Roy, *The Edwardians*, Little, Brown 2006

Hyde, H. Montgomery, *Baldwin*, Hart Davis 1973

Jenkins, R., *Mr Balfour's Poodle*, Collins 1954

— *Asquith*, Collins 1964

— *Winston Churchill*, Macmillan 2001

Jones, Thomas, *A Diary with Letters, 1931–1950*, Oxford University Press 1954

★— *Whitehall Diary*, Oxford University Press 1969

Kee, Robert, *The Green Flag*, Weidenfeld and Nicolson 1972

Keegan, John, *The First World War*, Random House 1998

★Lee, Sydney, *King Edward VII: A Biography*, Macmillan 1925

Lloyd George, David, *Through Terror to Triumph: Speeches and Pronouncements of the Right Honourable David Lloyd George*, Hodder and Stoughton 1915

★— *The Truth about the Peace Treaties*, Gollancz 1938

★— *War Memoirs*, Odhams 1938

Lloyd George (née Stevenson), Frances, *The Years That Are Past*, Hutchinson 1967

Lloyd George, Richard, *Dame Margaret Lloyd George*, Allen and Unwin 1947

— *My Father, Lloyd George*, Frederic Muller 1961

Macmillan, Margaret, *Peacemakers*, John Murray 2002

Mackay, Ruddock F., *Balfour: The Intellectual Statesman*, Oxford University Press 1985

MacLeod, I., *Neville Chamberlain*, Frederick Muller 1961

Marquand, David, *Ramsay MacDonald*, Jonathan Cape 1977

Marsh, Peter T., *Joseph Chamberlain*, Yale University Press 1994

Masterman, Charles, *The Condition of England*, Methuen 1960

Masterman, Lucy, *C. F. G. Masterman: A Biography*, Frank Cass and Co. 1968

Mead, Gary, *The Good Soldier*, Atlantic Books 2007
Middlemass, Keith and John Barnes, *Baldwin*, Weidenfeld and Nicolson 1968
Morgan, Kenneth O., *The Age of Lloyd George*, George Allen and Unwin 1961
— *Wales in British Politics 1868–1922*, University of Wales Press 1970
— *The Liberal Party and British Politics, 1890–1928*, George Allen and Unwin 1971
— *Consensus and Disunity*, Clarendon Press 1979
— (ed.), *Lloyd George Family Letters 1885–1936*, Oxford University Press 1973
*Morley, John, *Life of Gladstone*, Macmillan 1903
Nicolson, Harold, *Diaries 1907–1963*, Weidenfeld and Nicolson 2004
Owen, Frank, *Tempestuous Journey: Lloyd George, His Life and Times*, Hutchinson 1954
*Oxford and Asquith, Earl of, *Fifty Years of Parliament*, Cassell 1926
Pakenham, Thomas, *The Boer War*, Weidenfeld and Nicolson 1979
Pelling, H., *The History of British Trade Unionism*, Macmillan 1976
Pugh, M., *The Pankhursts*, Allen Lane 2001
Rhodes James, Robert, *The British Revolution 1880–1939*, Hamish Hamilton 1976
Riddell, Lord, *Lord Riddell's War Diaries*, Ivor Nicholson and Watson 1933
— *More Pages from My Diary*, Country Life 1934
Rose, Kenneth, *King George V*, Weidenfeld and Nicolson 1983
*Roskill, S. W., *Hankey: Man of Secrets*, Collins 1970
Rowland, Peter, *David Lloyd George*, Macmillan 1976
*Skidelsky, Robert, *John Maynard Keynes*, Macmillan 1983
Spender, Harold, *The Fire of Life*, Hodder and Stoughton 1926
— *The Prime Minister*, Doran 1920
Spender, J. A., *The Life of the Right Honourable Sir Henry Campbell-Bannerman*, Hodder and Stoughton 1923
*— *The Public Life*, Cassell 1925
*Spender, J. A. and Cyril Asquith, *The Life of Herbert Henry Asquith, Lord Oxford and Asquith*, Hutchinson 1932
Sylvester, A. J., *The Real Lloyd George*, Cassell 1947
— *Life with Lloyd George*, Macmillan 1975
Taylor, A. J. P. (ed.), *Lloyd George: A Diary by Frances Stevenson*, Harper and Row 1971
— (ed.) *My Darling Pussy*, Weidenfeld and Nicolson 1975
Taylor, S. J., *The Great Outsiders*, Weidenfeld and Nicolson 1996
Williamson, Philip and Edward Baldwin (eds), *Baldwin Papers 1908–1947*, Cambridge University Press 2004
Wilson, John, *Sir Henry Campbell-Bannerman*, Constable 1973

INDEX

abdication crisis, 625–6
Aberystwyth, 80, 99
Abraham, William, 66, 83
Abyssinia, 622, 626
Acland, Arthur, 51, 54, 336
Acton, 57, 70–1, 104
Addison, Christopher, 378, 383, 418, 446, 454, 478, 480, 483–4, 577, 581; and housing programme, 509, 524–7, 600; and Ireland, 531, 537
adult suffrage, 22, 64, 112, 237, 441, 481; see also women's suffrage
Afium Karahissar, battle of, 555
Agadir crisis, 301–5, 308–9
agricultural rating, 85–8, 122
agricultural wages, 521, 529
Aitken, Max, see Lord Beaverbrook
alcohol consumption, 366–7, 438
Alexander, King, of Greece, 554
Allenby, General Sir Edmund, 443, 455
Alsace-Lorraine, 426, 497
American Civil War, 65, 67
Amery, Leopold, 328, 440, 480, 572
Amiens, defence of, 459, 471, 479
Amritsar massacre, 548
Andes Exploring Company, 93–4
Anglo-Irish Treaty, 550, 564–6
Angora, battle of, 555
Anti-Martyrdom League, 157
Anti-Tithe League, 26, 28
Anti-Waste League, 523, 525
ANZACs, 370–1, 450
Archangel, 472, 500
Armenians, massacre of, 557
armistice and Paris peace conference, 473–5, 486–507
army chaplains, 361
army expenditure, 227, 233, 246, 525
Arras, battle of, 429, 433, 443, 469
Asquith, Herbert Henry, 67–8, 75, 79, 83, 116, 160, 176, 201, 306; and Agadir crisis, 302–3; and Boer War, 121, 135, 138–9, 143; and budget (1909), 243–6,

248, 251–2, 255–8; and conscription, 383–5; his death, 598; and DLG expulsion, 595–6; and DLG German visit, 229–30; and DLG government, 446, 455, 458, 461; and Easter Rising, 394–5; and education bills, 152, 155, 162–3, 195–6; and Irish Home Rule, 342–5, 530; and land reform, 335, 338; and Liberal government, 218–20, 222–3, 226, 228, 240, 269–75, 282, 284–5, 290, 300, 309, 327, 330, 348; and Lords reform, 264–6, 270, 272–6, 287, 347; and Marconi Scandal, 321, 325–7; and Maurice conspiracy, 466–8, 484; political downfall, 400–20, 426, 565; and post-war politics, 484–5, 520–1, 538, 581–4, 587–9, 593, 595–8; and rail strike, 307–8; and Relugas compact, 179–84; and wartime politics, 356, 360, 362, 364–7, 369–71, 373–5, 377, 383–5, 390–6, 398, 400–20, 446, 455, 458, 461, 466–8, 475, 477; and women's suffrage, 345
Asquith, Margot, 184, 221–2, 285, 326, 396, 485, 581, 584, 593
Asquith, Raymond, 234, 406–7
Associated Society of Railway Servants (ASRS), 208–9, 211–12
Astor, Lady, 515, 637
Astor, Lord, 515, 568–9, 611
Atatürk, Kemal, 553–6
Attlee, Clement, 400, 478, 525
Aubers Ridge, battle of, 372
Austria, 278, 281, 352–3, 356, 365, 425, 442, 445, 491
Austrian Credit Bank, 615

Bagehot, Walter, 550
Baghdad, 394, 425
Baldwin, Stanley, 400, 423, 540, 563–4, 571–4, 579–81, 583–4, 589, 592, 594, 605, 608–9, 611–12, 615–16; and abdication crisis, 625–6; premiership, 621–3